'Once in a while a big book comes along that compels you to drop everything, clear your schedule and focus intently. *Lucky Valley* is a publication event, a magnificent counterhistory of racial capitalism and an urgent call by one of the pre-eminent historians of our time to dismantle and redress the enduring injustices of Edward Long's world.'

Vincent Brown, author of *Tacky's Revolt: the Story of an Atlantic Slave War*

'Catherine Hall has brilliantly unearthed the crucial context of Edward Long's entanglement in the business of slavery, one in a long line of planters in England's colonial establishment in Jamaica. Hall's penetrating, extremely well-researched work is a major contribution to our ongoing struggle to dismantle the devastating, and intellectually dishonest, attempts to justify slavery by debasing those most brutally entrapped by it. *Lucky Valley* is an original and delightfully readable contribution to understanding the troubling discourse of intellectual racism.'

Henry Louis Gates Jnr, author of *The Black Box: Writing the Race*

'In *Lucky Valley* perhaps the most important historian of our age explains how the "father of English racism" described an entire socio-economic and ecological system constructed around racial oppression and provided generations of Britons with a justification for it. Edward Long's advocacy has reverberated perniciously through the past two and a half centuries, adapted to support new and proliferating forms of racism. In this magisterial and moving analysis, Hall locates the greed, privilege, hubris and anxiety that underpinned it.'

Alan Lester, author of *Ruling the World* and *Deny and Disavow: the British Empire in the Culture War*, 2e

'Catherine Hall's study of Edward Long's life and influence is indispensable. While the work is a careful, detailed examination of Long and his family, it is much more than a biography. Hall situates Long as a crucial architect of racial capitalism and clarifies the importance of his role in crafting a worldview in which slavery and slave ownership were at the very centre of modernity and empire. Hall's brilliance as a scholar of history, race and gender is well established. In *Lucky Valley* it is deployed in a work that will stand as the definitive study of slavery – its victims and its champions – during the long eighteenth century.'

Jennifer L. Morgan, author of *Reckoning with Slavery: Gender, Kinship, and Capitalism in the Early Black Atlantic*

'Reading through the lens of one exemplary figure and text of the eighteenth-century British slave empire, Catherine Hall's *Lucky Valley: Edward Long and the History of Racial Capitalism* is a critical inquiry into both the exploitative structure of racial capitalism and the perversity of the racial imagination that aimed to rationalize its unjust enrichment and disavow its inhumanity. Hall's subtle and incisive intervention is grist for the mill of a contemporary reparatory project.'

David Scott, author of *Omens of Adversity: Tragedy, Time, Memory, Justice*

LUCKY VALLEY

Why does Edward Long's *History of Jamaica* matter? Written in 1774, Long's *History*, that most 'civilized' of documents, attempted to define White and Black as essentially different and unequal. Long deployed natural history and social theory, carefully mapping the island, and drawing on poetry and engravings, in his efforts to establish a clear and fixed racialized hierarchy. His White family sat at the heart of Jamaican planter society and the West India trade in sugar, which provided the economic bedrock of this eighteenth-century system of racial capitalism. Catherine Hall tells the story behind the *History* of a slave-owning family that prospered across generations together with the destruction of such possibilities for enslaved people. She unpicks the many contradictions in Long's thinking, exposing the insidious myths and stereotypes that have poisoned social relations over generations and allowed reconfigured forms of racial difference and racial capitalism to live on in contemporary societies.

CATHERINE HALL is Emerita Professor of History at University College London and a prize-winning author. Her work focuses on Britain and empire, and includes *Civilising Subjects: Metropole and Colony in the English Imagination, 1830–1867* (2002), *Macaulay and Son: Architects of Imperial Britain* (2012), and *Legacies of British Slave-Ownership: Colonial Slavery and the Formation of Victorian Britain* (co-authored with Nicholas Draper et al.; Cambridge, 2014). Between 2009 and 2015 she was the principal investigator on the ESRC/AHRC project 'Legacies of British Slave-ownership'.

Critical Perspectives on Empire

Editors

Professor Catherine Hall
University College London

Professor Mrinalini Sinha
University of Michigan

Professor Kathleen Wilson
State University of New York, Stony Brook

Critical Perspectives on Empire is a major series of ambitious, cross-disciplinary works in the emerging field of critical imperial studies. Books in the series explore the connections, exchanges and mediations at the heart of national and global histories, the contributions of local as well as metropolitan knowledge, and the flows of people, ideas and identities facilitated by colonial contact. To that end, the series not only offers a space for outstanding scholars working at the intersection of several disciplines to bring to wider attention the impact of their work; it also takes a leading role in reconfiguring contemporary historical and critical knowledge, of the past and of ourselves.

A full list of titles published in the series can be found at:
www.cambridge.org/cpempire

LUCKY VALLEY

Edward Long and the History of Racial Capitalism

CATHERINE HALL
University College London

CAMBRIDGE
UNIVERSITY PRESS

Shaftesbury Road, Cambridge CB2 8EA, United Kingdom

One Liberty Plaza, 20th Floor, New York, NY 10006, USA

477 Williamstown Road, Port Melbourne, VIC 3207, Australia

314–321, 3rd Floor, Plot 3, Splendor Forum, Jasola District Centre, New Delhi – 110025, India

103 Penang Road, #05–06/07, Visioncrest Commercial, Singapore 238467

Cambridge University Press is part of Cambridge University Press & Assessment, a department of the University of Cambridge.

We share the University's mission to contribute to society through the pursuit of education, learning and research at the highest international levels of excellence.

www.cambridge.org
Information on this title: www.cambridge.org/9781009098854

DOI: 10.1017/9781009106399

© Catherine Hall 2024

This publication is in copyright. Subject to statutory exception and to the provisions of relevant collective licensing agreements, no reproduction of any part may take place without the written permission of Cambridge University Press & Assessment.

First published 2024 (version 2, January 2025)

Printed in Great Britain by CPI Group (UK) Ltd, Croydon CR0 4YY, January 2025

A catalogue record for this publication is available from the British Library

Library of Congress Cataloging-in-Publication Data
Names: Hall, Catherine, 1946– author.
Title: Lucky Valley : Edward Long and the history of racial capitalism / Catherine Hall, University College London.
Description: Cambridge, United Kingdom ; New York, NY : Cambridge University Press, 2024. | Series: Critical perspectives on empire | Includes bibliographical references and index.
Identifiers: LCCN 2023027904 (print) | LCCN 2023027905 (ebook) | ISBN 9781009098854 (hardback) | ISBN 9781009102766 (paperback) | ISBN 9781009106399 (ebook)
Subjects: LCSH: Long, Edward, 1734–1813. | Slaveholders – Jamaica. | Slavery – Jamaica. | Racism – Jamaica. | Capitalism – Jamaica.
Classification: LCC HT1096 .H34 2024 (print) | LCC HT1096 (ebook) | DDC 306.3/62097292–dc23/eng/20230727
LC record available at https://lccn.loc.gov/2023027904
LC ebook record available at https://lccn.loc.gov/2023027905

ISBN 978-1-009-09885-4 Hardback

Cambridge University Press & Assessment has no responsibility for the persistence or accuracy of URLs for external or third-party internet websites referred to in this publication and does not guarantee that any content on such websites is, or will remain, accurate or appropriate.

For Stuart

CONTENTS

List of Colour Plates   *page* x
List of Figures   xi
List of Maps   xiii
Acknowledgements   xiv
A Note on Language   xviii
Prologue   xix

Introduction   1

PART I: Growing up English   39

1   A Gentleman's Son   41
2   The Young Englishman   65

PART II: The Lineaments of Racial Capitalism   85

3   The Plantation   87
4   The Merchant House   156
5   Reproducing Capital: the Long Family   202

PART III: Making a Slave Society   263

6   Colonizing Geographies   265
7   Colonizing the State   313
8   Theorizing Racial Difference   372

Epilogue   416

Bibliography   446
Index   477

The plates can be found between pages 254 and 255.

COLOUR PLATES

1. Edward Long by William Sharp, after John Opie
2. 'Lucky Valley Estate' by William Berryman
3. Tredudwel Manor
4. Tredudwel coastline
5. Cartouche detail from Craskell and Simpson's map of Surrey, Jamaica
6. 'Driver, Cold Morning' by William Berryman
7. 'View of the Roaring River Cascade' from Long's *History*
8. 'A View of the White River Cascade' from Long's *History*
9. 'View of Montego Bay' from Long's *History*
10. 'View of Port Royal & Kingston Harbours' from Long's *History*
11. Francis Williams by an unrecorded artist

FIGURES

0.1	Stuart Hall, 1970s *page* xx	
1	The three main branches of the Long family tree	xxxiv
I.1	Title page of *The History of Jamaica*	2
I.2	South Street, Chichester, *c.* 1900–4	3
2.1	Title page of Edward Long's *The Anti-Gallican*	80
3.1	'Longville, Jamaica' by William Berryman	96
3.2	'Longville Ford' by William Berryman	96
3.3	Longville and Lucky Valley plantations on Robertson's 1804 map of Jamaica	101
3.4	Cartouche detail from Craskell and Simpson's map of Cornwall, Jamaica	107
3.5	Dawkins' Salt River Wharf, *c.* 1760	114
3.6	Blair's plan of Lucky Valley, 1769	117
3.7	Aerial image of present-day Lucky Valley	118
3.8	'View of a Negro village' by William Berryman	133
3.9	'Nurses and Child' by William Berryman	149
3.10	'Negro Hut with Figures in Plantain Walk' by William Berryman	152
4.1	The West India trade schematic	167
4.2	Bill of Exchange, 1778	172
4.3	Front façade of a Bishopsgate Street house, 1807	180
5.1	The Jamaican branch of the Long family tree	205
5.2	The Long family's compensation awards	207
5.3	Hurt's Hall, Suffolk, 1857	224
5.4	The mercantile branch of the Long family tree	226
5.5	Bromley Hill, Kent, 1815	241
5.6	Mary Ballard Long (née Beckford) by Henry Bone, after John Opie	246
5.7	Dower House, Arundel Park	255
5.8	St Michael and All Angels church, Tunstall, Suffolk	260
6.1	Table from Long's *History* quantifying enslaved people in St John	271
6.2	Table from Long's *History* quantifying enslaved people in Clarendon	272
6.3	The King's House from Long's *History*	276
6.4	Bath Hot Spring from Long's *History*	302
7.1	Royal and Kingston harbours from Long's *History*	342

E.1 Pottery fragments found at Lucky Valley estate   417
E.2 Catherine Hall walking towards New Longville   417
E.3 Edward Long's funerary monument, St Mary's church, Slindon   435

MAPS

1 Jamaica *page* xxxii
2 The Atlantic Basin   xxxiii

ACKNOWLEDGEMENTS

The research and writing for *Lucky Valley* has taken me many years and numerous friends and colleagues have helped me. I thank them all for their generosity. The work would not have happened without the 'Legacies of British Slave-ownership' (LBS) team and our collective commitment to thinking about British slave-owners and the part they have played in the making of modern Britain. Nick Draper, Keith McClelland and Rachel Lang were there from the beginning, alongside the postgraduates and postdoctoral researchers we were fortunate to have as part of our group. Funding from the Economic and Social Research Council and the Arts and Humanities Research Council, together with support from University College London (UCL) and the Hutchins Center at Harvard University, enabled our work. Katie Donington was with us from 2011 to 2016, participating in both the first phase of the research, on compensation, and the second phase, on British slave-owners in the Caribbean from 1763 to 1833. Kristy Warren, Hannah Young and James Dawkins all joined us for the second phase. It was Nick Draper who first alerted me to the importance of compensation and who has kept me attentive to the economy. Keith McClelland is a most constant friend, an excellent interlocutor with an eye on the 'bigger picture' and an unrivalled adviser on all matters to do with the computer. He has effected many rescues! I owe him particular thanks for the bibliography which he designed for this volume. Rachel Lang kindly produced the Long family tree for me and clarified the relationships between the three branches of the family. She also did much of the work for the maps that were curated for the LBS database (www.ucl.ac.uk/lbs), showing the locations of the estates. Katie Donington's work on the Hibbert family, *The Bonds of Family*, was our first detailed case study, while Hannah Young's research on female slave-owners and James Dawkins's on the Dawkins family have made substantial contributions to our understanding of the significance of these slave-holders. James provided research assistance for me on the Accounts Produce of the Long properties and we had two memorable visits to Lucky Valley and Suttons plantations in 2015 and 2023. Our team also benefited from other researchers and supporters. Chris Jeppesen's analysis of the wills of West Indian families has been invaluable. Mark Harvey has been a friend of LBS over the years and a vital member of our reading group.

ACKNOWLEDGEMENTS

I am most grateful to all those who have read parts or all of my manuscript as it has developed. Sally Alexander, Antoinette Burton, Nick Draper, Margot Finn, Mark Harvey, Cora Kaplan, Diana Paton, Bill Schwarz, Barbara Taylor and James Vernon have all been most generous with their time and thoughts. As far back as 2016 I had the happy idea of asking Miles Ogborn if he would be interested in talking with me about Edward Long. We instituted the Edward Long Reading Group which has met regularly ever since. We were joined by Markman Ellis and Silvia Sebastiani. Drawing on the combined skills of a historical geographer, an eighteenth-century literary scholar and an intellectual historian of the Enlightenment has been enlightening to say the least. I cannot thank them enough. We initially read Edward Long's works together. Once I started writing, they read and discussed all my drafts. I feel truly fortunate.

Conversations with other friends and colleagues have helped me with my thinking. David Scott's words always stay with me. I value our talks and his writing. Mark Nash proposed *Lucky Valley* for the title, though he doesn't remember. Erica Carter and Samia Khatun have walked and talked with me. Fabrice Bensimon, Gail Lewis, Alison Light, Jennifer Morgan and Susan Pennybacker have shared work and friendship. Anita Rupprecht, Mark Knight, Devin Leigh, April Shelford and Sarah Thomas have all been most helpful. Writing about denial with Daniel Pick was rewarding. Clare Taylor has been generous with her research and papers. Brenna Bhandar reminded me that I might find answers to questions about property laws, marriage and inheritance in court papers and contested wills. Carla Pestana, Andrew Apter and Robin Derby have been great hosts at UCLA and have heard about the project as it has grown and changed since my first visit in 2015. I always find listening to Wayne Modest instructive and was delighted to join the international Racial Capitalism Workshop initiated by Tony Bogues and Pepijn Brandon. Esther Chadwick talked with me about Long's engravings, and this connection grew into the project with David Bindman, Fara Dabhoiwala and the Victoria and Albert Museum to develop work on the portrait of Francis Williams. Teresa and Tony Davies were the first friends to search with me for Tredudwel, the house in Cornwall in which Edward Long spent years in his youth. Since then, good friends have assisted me in expeditions to Cornwall and various sites associated with Long in London, Sussex and Hampshire.

In Jamaica Emma Ranston-Young provided much needed assistance on wills, land deeds and inventories. James Robertson at the University of the West Indies (UWI) Mona has been generous with his knowledge of eighteenth-century Jamaica. Zachary Beier, then at UWI Mona, travelled with me to Lucky Valley on a field trip in 2019. Librarians at Mona, the Institute of Jamaica and the Jamaica National Library have all been very helpful, as were Audene Brooks at the Jamaica National Heritage Trust and the staff at the National Gallery. I have been most fortunate in having a Jamaican home with my husband Stuart's dear cousin, Sister Maureen Clare, at Immaculate

Conception Convent in Kingston. The Sisters have welcomed me over the years, taken me on trips to Old Harbour and other places connected with both the Long and the Hall families, and shared with me something of their multiple educational, social and economic initiatives. Caribbean fiction has provided a vital counter to living for so long with eighteenth-century colonists. As Paula Marshall's protagonist Merle puts it in her wonderful novel *The Chosen Place, the Timeless People* (1969): 'Those Englishmen were the biggest obeah men out when you considered what they did to our minds.' Erna Brodber's *Nothing's Mat* (2014) argues that fractal families, a key legacy of slavery and colonialism, offer possibilities for trauma to be lived with, that healing is possible.

The staff at the British Library, the site for most of my research, were most helpful. I owe innumerable debts to audiences who have engaged with me in seminars, conferences and meetings. Edward Long has made appearances across the UK and beyond at different stages of the work. Academics and conference and workshop organizers in Amsterdam, Belfast, Berkeley, Birmingham, Bologna, Brighton, Cambridge, Canterbury, Cologne, Columbia, Lancaster, Leiden, Lisbon, Liverpool, London, Melbourne, Miami, Oxford, Paris, Pittsburgh, Southampton, Sussex, Sydney, UCLA, Warwick, Washington and York have all kindly hosted me and given me opportunities for discussion with others. A fellowship of a month at the EHESS-Ecole des hautes études en sciences sociales in Paris in 2019 was a wonderful chance for long talks with Silvia Sebastiani and Cécile Vidal. The LBS workshop that we organized in September 2019 was a good moment for reflection on the second phase of our project with friends and colleagues from the USA, Jamaica and the UK.

It has been a pleasure to work with Michael Watson, my editor at Cambridge University Press. Rosa Martin, Natasha Whelan and Carol Fellingham Webb have all provided critical support with the production of the manuscript. Margaret Puskar-Pasewicz has done a wonderful job on the index. Two anonymous readers gave me food for thought, while Trevor Burnard's detailed comments in relation to both the proposal and an almost final draft of the manuscript have been invaluable. The questions he pressed me on turned out to be very productive – after my initial conviction that I had nothing more to say! Kathleen Wilson understood what I was doing.

I started working on Edward Long in 2014, after the death of my husband, Stuart Hall. At that time I was still full-time in the History Department at UCL. Since then many changes have happened, dear friends have died, others are not well. The political world is deeply troubling. Work as a trustee of the Stuart Hall Foundation, established in 2015 by family, friends and colleagues, has been a source of interest, debate and friendship, while working with Bill Schwarz on the series of edited collections of Stuart's work for Duke University Press has been another productive preoccupation. When I retired from my post in UCL in 2016, we established a Centre for the Study of the Legacies of British Slave-ownership under the directorship of Dr Nick Draper.

It is now the Centre for the Study of the Legacies of British Slavery, led by Professor Matthew J. Smith, and is developing work on the enslaved in the Caribbean. At the start of the first lockdown in March 2020, I decided to evacuate West Hampstead and settled in the cottage in Wivenhoe which we have had since the 1990s, when I taught at the University of Essex. I took all my files and started writing. While the lockdown was so hard for many people, it was a creative time for me. I walked most days on the estuary or in the woods with my friends and neighbours Miriam Glucksmann and Mark Harvey. We talked about what each of us was writing – the good times and the bad. It was an enormous help. The regular zoom calls during lockdown with my dear friends Sally and Bill circled around history, fiction, politics and personal life. I was thrilled when Joy Gregory, whose beautiful embroidery *The Sweetest Thing*, commissioned by Exeter's Royal Albert Memorial Museum and Art Gallery, was inspired in part by the work of LBS, agreed to design the cover for *Lucky Valley*. What a gift! When I reached the final stages with the book and worried about the material still unread and the illustrations and permissions to be thought about, I was lucky enough to find Liberty Paterson, an art historian who works on connections with the slavery business and will soon be completing her PhD. She has been a marvellous research assistant: calm, very well organized, a good reader, and full of ideas about the visual material. She has made all the difference to these last months.

Finally, our daughter, Becky Hall, and my sister, Margaret Rustin, sustain me day by day; our son, Jess, is far away in California but never far from my thoughts. The circle of family and friends are a blessing. As Freud said, it's love and work that make life worth living.

A NOTE ON LANGUAGE

Edward Long represented himself as an owner of enslaved Africans and claimed the identity of slave-owner as his legal right. His aim in *The History of Jamaica* was to support processes of enslavement and claims of ownership by fixing racialized categories in a hierarchy and presenting them as *natural*. Terminology was crucial to him. He used 'Negro' with a capital N for enslaved Africans, and White with a capital W for colonists such as himself. In my discussion of Long and his *History* I have used his terminology to show how he constructed his categories, and to denaturalize them. When writing about the politics of race in the present, I capitalize Black.

PROLOGUE

The word is the medium in which power works.   Stuart Hall

I started working on Edward Long shortly before my Jamaican husband, Stuart Hall, died in 2014. The manuscript that he left documenting his own dislocation and displacement, how he became diasporic, was published as *Familiar Stranger. A Tale of Two Islands*.[1] It tells the story of his colonial family, his coming to Oxford, his discovery of himself as a 'West Indian', his commitment to anti-colonial and left politics, and his decision to stay in Britain. His journey was the reverse of Edward Long's, the subject of this book. Two centuries earlier Long, a colonizer, left England for Jamaica, returned to England eleven years later with his ill-gotten gains and pro-slavery politics, and wrote his *History of Jamaica*. In going through Stuart's papers after his death, I found notes on his reading of Long in the 1970s. Stuart has accompanied me through these years, living as he does in my mind and my dreams, my favourite photograph of him watching over me at my desk (Figure 0.1), his books all around me. I'm in dialogue with the dead, writing through the feelings. When he arrived in Oxford in 1951 as a young Rhodes scholar, he acquired and wrote his name in many hardback copies of texts that he must have imagined as important for a Jamaican, educated in the colonial system, trying to make sense of his place in England. These included Eric Williams's *Capitalism and Slavery* and Swift's *Gulliver's Travels*. Both are extensively marked, and replete with underlinings, exclamation marks and much evidence of thought. I decided to re-read his copy of *Gulliver's Travels*, knowing that this Irish Tory satirist and polemicist was a powerful critic of colonialism and knowing that Long was familiar with it. It was an uncanny experience: there was Swift in 1720, Long in 1774, Stuart in 1951 and me in 2022, all thinking about here/there, race/skin and what makes people human.

On his final voyage Gulliver travelled to the land of the Houyhnhnms, horses who live a life of wisdom, peaceful calm and friendship. Gulliver greatly admired them and accepted them as his masters. They were deeply shocked by his accounts of the cruelty, corruption and greed of human society. The

---

[1] Stuart Hall with Bill Schwarz, *Familiar Stranger. A Life between Two Islands* (London, 2017) describes the colonial mentality of Stuart's family and his own sense of internal exile.

Figure 0.1 Stuart Hall in Birmingham in the 1970s. © Mahāsiddhi/Roy Peters.

Houyhnhnms were serviced by 'Yahoos', creatures that Gulliver found disgusting, hateful and contemptible. 'I never beheld in all my travels', he recorded, 'so disagreeable an animal, nor one against which I naturally conceived so strong an antipathy.'[2] They were ugly, brutish, hairy creatures with brown skin and sharp claws, communicating in howls and groans, and with a powerfully offensive smell. Yet this 'abominable animal' had 'a perfect human figure', albeit with a 'flat face', 'depressed nose' and 'large lips'.[3] Gulliver's 'horror and astonishment' were beyond description when the Houyhnhnms, having examined him next to some Yahoos, assured him that he was indeed of the same species, though differing 'in the softness and whiteness and smoothness of my skin' and lack of bodily hair.[4] A terrifying incident in which a young female Yahoo, 'inflamed by desire' at the sight of him naked in a pool, tried to seize him to satisfy her lust was frightful evidence of the truth of his Yahooness: 'I could no longer deny that I was a real *Yahoo* in every limb and feature.'[5] Fortunately, a gentle Houyhnhnm saved him from a terrible fate.

---

[2] Jonathan Swift, *Gulliver's Travels, The Tale of Tub, Battle of the Books, etc.* [1726, 1704] (Oxford, 1949), 266.
[3] Ibid., 273.
[4] Ibid., 282.
[5] Ibid., 317.

Reading these passages, with all the underlinings, I imagined Stuart, recently arrived in England, finding Oxford on a wintry day very cold and difficult, pondering over Swift's satire. The depictions of the Yahoos evoke racist caricatures of African barbarity: disgusting habits, guttural sounds, hairy bodies, brown skins and that smell. Did he read it like that, I wondered? What kind of place might *he* have in this white world that he now occupied? On his return to his 'beloved country', Gulliver longed for the Houyhnhnms. He longed to be different, could not tolerate the smell of his wife and children, only permitting them to sit near him at dinner once time had passed and he found their smell less offensive. He was horrified by the treatment of horses in England, and proud that his friends remarked that he had learned to trot just like one. Yet he was not a Houyhnhnm: the terrible truth was that he was a Yahoo, as were his wife and children, though fortunately of a whiter colour, less hairy and with shorter claws than those brutes he had encountered. Were all Yahoos human, all brutes? What distinguished one from another? Did whiteness matter? The Houyhnhnms had told him that two of 'the brutes', the first of their herd, had come from their own country across the seas and, 'degenerating by degrees', became 'more savage' than their ancestors.[6] Did Swift think that blackness was a sign of degeneration, as many believed in the eighteenth century? And what did he think of white mastery? A grand assembly was held by the Houyhnhnms and 'the question to be debated was whether the Yahoos should be exterminated from the face of the earth' since they were the 'most filthy, noisome, and deformed animal[s] which nature ever produced'. The responses were varied since the creatures were useful, but Gulliver was not spared by his masters and was to be expelled from the island. In his role of servant to the Houyhnhnms, Gulliver was keen to separate himself from the herd of Yahoos and suggested that the English practice of castrating young horses might be followed. Over time this would result in an ending: meanwhile, 'more valuable brutes ... asses' could be bred.[7] Did Swift know of the gelding of the enslaved? Or of the beginnings of efforts to 'breed' people? His biting account of new colonial practices, of the 'distributive justice of princes', described the seizure of land, the re-namings, the murder of natives, the establishment of a '*new dominion*' with a title by '*divine right*'. Ships were sent, natives driven out, 'a free licence given to all acts of inhumanity and lust', an 'execrable crew of butchers' employed to establish 'a *modern colony* ... convert and civilize an idolatrous and barbarous people'.[8] They could kill and enslave with impunity. Yet Swift invested (and lost money) in the South Sea

---

[6] Ibid., 323.
[7] Ibid., 322–4.
[8] Ibid.; Swift's *A Modest Proposal* (1729), recommending that poor Irish children could be sold by their parents as food for the rich, was a satire on William Petty's proposals for the Irish poor.

Company, formed to make fortunes from the slave trade. What to make of such contradictions? I can never know what Stuart thought about Gulliver, but questions about the meanings of race and difference haunted Swift's imagination as well as his and have echoed across generations into our present.[9]

Lucky Valley has its origins in one family history and tells the story of another. In 1965, the year after my marriage to Stuart, I had my first visit to Jamaica. I was nineteen and had grown up in Leeds, a manufacturing city in Yorkshire. By the time I left Leeds in 1963 there was a small but significant Caribbean and South Asian presence in the city, including students, marking the beginnings of that transformation in British society and culture that has unfolded since. I recognized difference – but not the politics of empire. Stuart had lived in London since the late 1950s. We moved in 1964 to Birmingham, a city dominated by the car industry and conservatism. Enoch Powell was building on fertile soil when he chose it as the location for his infamous 'Rivers of Blood' speech in 1968. It was a difficult place for a mixed-race couple to establish a life together. Our visit to Kingston in 1965 was to stay with Stuart's family, just three years after the island finally established its independence. I had never been to the Caribbean before, never been in a majority Black society, never experienced the destructive effects of colonialism on a people and a family, never really understood myself as white, 'the oppressor'. That first experience of dislocation, of being 'othered', of being pointed at and named on the streets as 'Whitey' was disturbing. No less disturbing was the experience of being in a society which had been colonized by the British for so long. I was seeing Jamaica's 'plural society', its established hierarchies of White, Brown and Black, living in a Brown (not a term in use at that time) middle-class household with Black domestic workers, watching the Independence Day beauty contest with its namings of every variety of skin colour, dancing to the new ska beat at Papine, and sitting on the edge of intense political discussions as to the future of the Caribbean with members of what was to become the 'New World' collective; all these were formative encounters.[10]

It has taken me years to grasp something of the complex and violent histories that have linked Britain and Jamaica and shaped my own and others' familial lives. *Lucky Valley* is the book that has grown out of those experiences. Lucky Valley, named without irony, was the plantation in Clarendon owned by an English colonist, Edward Long (Plate 1). It was the unhomely setting for the

---

[9] Stuart Hall, *Selected Writings on Race and Difference*, ed. Paul Gilroy and Ruth Wilson Gilmore (London, 2021).
[10] Hall, *Familiar Stranger*. The debate as to the character of Jamaica as a 'plural society' in the terms of M. G. Smith was a key area of discussion in the late 1950s and early 1960s, to be displaced by the debate over the nature of 'the plantation society' amongst the New World group including Lloyd Best and George Beckford. See David Scott, 'The Permanence of Pluralism', in Paul Gilroy, Lawrence Grossberg and Angela McRobbie (eds.), *Without Guarantees. In Honour of Stuart Hall* (London, 2000), 282–301.

lives and deaths of generations of enslaved men, women and children. Long was the author of the three-volume *History of Jamaica*, published in 1774. It is a text that defended slavery as necessary for Britain's wealth and argued that racial difference was *natural* and essential, that black people were born to serve. Its racialized thinking has cast a long shadow into the present. Long's family lived between England and Jamaica in the seventeenth and eighteenth centuries; their wealth derived from the slavery business. Edward Long, his family and his writing are my subject. What was and is the significance of the *History*? What was his narrative of domination and disavowal, of White power and Black subjection? Why does it matter now?

I have visited Jamaica since the 1960s but have never lived there. I gradually came to know not just Kingston and the gorgeous beaches of the north coast, but many other parts of this beautiful island. Between Kingston and Spanish Town is Old Harbour, the main port for the Spanish, now a quiet country town off the main road where Stuart's beloved grandmother and aunts lived. Old Harbour Bay, now a fishing village, was the site of the wharf utilized by the English planters and slavers, including Edward Long. The Georgian splendour of Spanish Town, the eighteenth-century colonial capital where Long and his wife, Mary, lived in the 1760s, now stands largely ruinate. Constant Spring, once the site of Norbrook plantation owned by the wealthiest branch of the Long family, is now the setting for Immaculate Conception Convent and School, the home of Stuart's much cherished cousin, Sister Maureen Clare. Together with Clarendon's cane fields and hills, these are all sites that have figured vividly in both my real Jamaica and my imagined geography of its slavery days. The emotional meaning of place, how nerves and skin can tingle in confronting a lost history, was all too apparent in my two visits to Lucky Valley.[11] The landscape was in one sense unchanged from William Berryman's early nineteenth-century watercolour (Plate 2): the hills, cane pieces, pastures and river all still there. But there are now no sugar works, no mill, no overseer's house or 'Negro village', no burial ground, no people. Acres of cane fields remain, but only remnants of the water wheel and the guttering, while fragments of pottery evoke those who lived and died there, leaving ghostly traces of plantation life. Orlando Patterson grew up near Lucky Valley. All the big estates were around there, he remembers. '*That's slavery breathing on you* ... you're just walking through cane. It's like walking through history, walking through a strange time zone to the past. The atmosphere is still very strongly reminiscent of something oppressive, as if some tragedy had happened there ... I had a strong sense that

---

[11] On both occasions, in 2015 and 2019, Audene Brooks of the Jamaica Heritage Society gave us invaluable help in finding the location, which is not on any contemporary map; we relied on local informants to direct us, Audene explaining we were 'history people'. In 2019 Zachary Beier of the UWI History and Archaeology Department facilitated the visit.

slavery was *there* ...'[12] What a contrast with my visits to Tredudwel (Plates 3 and 4), the Queen Anne manor house on the beautiful Cornish coast which Long's father, Samuel, bought in the 1740s. Edward, as a boy, enjoyed 'cold collations' with his family on the beach. Then there is the substantial house in Chichester where he wrote much of his *History* (see Figure I.2), and the house on Wimpole Street, cheek by jowl with his slave-owning West Indian friends and neighbours, who feasted on pepper-pot and schemed to defend slavery. There were even the glimpses through the trees that I managed to get of Hampton Lodge, the large country estate bought by his son in the 1780s. And then St Mary's church in Slindon, the picturesque West Sussex village where Long was buried, his marble memorial in pride of place celebrating his genealogy, his reputation and his *History*. These locales, the fruits of slave wealth, left a different kind of shiver down my spine.

It took me a long time to become a historian of the interlinked histories of the two islands. When our two children were young, we had family holidays in Jamaica. Eventually, in 1987, at a time when questions as to what it meant to be white and English or Black and British became pressing political issues, I shifted from working as a feminist historian on questions of gender and class in eighteenth- and nineteenth-century England, to working on questions of Englishness, empire and white identities. The significance of empire, I was convinced, had been ignored for too long in the domestic history of England. Jamaica and Birmingham (where we lived for seventeen years) were at the heart of my investigation. My focus was on white Baptist missionaries and the varied forms of racial thinking that they developed in the time of slavery and emancipation. The years of 1807, the ending of the slave trade, and 1833, emancipation, were to be celebrated, but being an abolitionist did not necessarily mean a belief in racial equality. Many thought that was something to be imagined for the future. My project was to understand how racial difference was knitted into white liberal thought.[13] That preoccupation continued in a different vein as I became interested in the role that historians have had in the creation of racialized national histories. I turned to researching Thomas Babington Macaulay, 'the great historian of England', and the Whig/liberal narrative that he produced. Macaulay's father, Zachary, was a dedicated abolitionist and devoted his life to the ending of the slave trade and slavery. His early experience in the 1780s as a bookkeeper and young Scottish migrant on a Jamaican plantation had left him powerfully affected by the insidious effects of the cruelties and brutalities of everyday life in a slave society. 'The air of this Island has some peculiar quality in it,' he wrote, 'for no sooner does a

---

[12] David Scott, 'The Paradox of Freedom: an Interview with Orlando Patterson', *Small Axe* 40 (2013), 224.

[13] Catherine Hall, *Civilising Subjects. Metropole and Colony in the English Imagination, 1830–1867* (Cambridge, 2002).

person set foot on it than his former ways of thinking are entirely changed.' He fled, terrified of becoming a 'vexatious' and 'pitilous' person without feelings for the enslaved, experienced an evangelical conversion, and later reflected on the 'terrible caprice and tyranny of one who, unawed by the fear of God, exercises an absolute dominion over his fellow-men'.[14] Africans were 'fellow-men' in his imagination, but they needed extensive guidance if they were to become 'civilized'. His son Thomas, brought up on a relentless diet of anti-slavery, preferred not to think about it. His vivid and dramatic *History of England* captured the national imagination with its story of white people's progress. It marginalized slavery and the Caribbean, disavowing that history, erasing the slave trade and the plantations while remembering abolition.

In 2009, in the wake of the bi-centenary of the abolition of the slave trade, Nick Draper, Keith McClelland and I launched the Legacies of British Slave-ownership project (LBS) at UCL researching British slave-owners and the compensation they received at the time of abolition for the loss of their human property.[15] Eric Williams's *Capitalism and Slavery* (1944) was one of our inspirations. Might the transmission of wealth from the slavery business to the metropole which he had explored be illuminated by systematic work on the compensation records? Williams was determined to undo the legacy of imperial historians who narrated abolition as the work of a band of humanitarians. His book, he argued in his Preface, 'is strictly an economic study of the role of Negro slavery and the slave trade in providing the capital which financed the Industrial Revolution in England and of mature industrial capitalism in destroying the slave system'.[16] His economic focus meant that he interpreted racial inequalities as a product of slavery. 'Slavery was not born of racism,' he famously wrote, 'rather, racism was the consequence of slavery', determined by the need for labour. The focus on skin was a rationalization after the event.[17] As an anti-colonialist, his political demand was for independence and sovereignty. His hope was that anti-colonialism and the creation of new nations would make it possible to build a multiracial society that would end racial hierarchies: a dream that did not materialize.[18] By the early twenty-first century, the unfinished postcolonial relationship between Britain and the Caribbean was increasingly questioned, given the persistence of racisms and structural inequalities. The presence of a growing population of the descendants of those once enslaved in the Caribbean, no longer content to

---

[14] Catherine Hall, *Macaulay and Son. Architects of Imperial Britain* (London, 2012), 4–5.
[15] See www.ucl.ac.uk/lbs. The project was building on Draper's book, *The Price of Emancipation. Slave-ownership, Compensation and British Society at the End of Slavery* (Cambridge, 2010).
[16] Eric Williams, *Capitalism and Slavery* (Chapel Hill, NC, 1944), vii.
[17] Ibid., 7.
[18] Catherine Hall, 'Writing Forward, Writing Back: Eric Williams and Edward Long', forthcoming.

accommodate to white society in the way that many of their parents had advocated and angrily demanding rights, was shifting the ground. What responsibility might metropolitan peoples owe to those once colonized?[19] What did it mean to remember abolition? What about remembering slavery? Should there be a government apology? What might the £20 million paid in compensation to individuals across Britain and the Caribbean mean to the developing debates over reparation?[20]

Our aim at LBS was to disrupt a proud story of abolition and change understandings of Britain's involvement with slavery. We documented the wealth transmitted to the metropole by planters and merchants whose profits derived from the enslaved, and the extensive political, cultural and material legacies of the slave-owners. In focusing on these multiple legacies, from the country houses to the holdings of the national galleries and museums, we opened up a Pandora's Box of questions about traces, inheritances, obligations, responsibilities, entitlements, debts and hauntings. The experience of Black and Brown people in the contemporary metropole provided ample evidence of new configurations of racisms. What impact had the racialized assumptions of the West Indians, as the white colonists were called, had on British common sense? Having a continuing interest in the significance of history writing to the making of racial inequalities and nation, my efforts centred on the stories which slave-owners and their descendants told in the wake of abolition. I found a rich archive of fiction, poetry and history, from the seafaring tales of Captain Marryat and the travel writing of Charles Kingsley to the history of Macaulay's Tory rival, Archibald Alison, almost all devoted to the defence of a recalibration of racial hierarchies. If Africans were no longer subject because they were enslaved, then what justified such subjection? Was it the body? Was it climate? Was it culture? Was it history? Slavery had ended; new legitimations of racial inequality were being crafted.[21]

In 2013 a second phase of the LBS project began investigating the Britons who owned enslaved people in the Caribbean from the mid-eighteenth century to the time of abolition, documenting the long history of the transmission of wealth from the colonies to the metropole, following the people and the plantations. Edward Long's three-volume *History of Jamaica*, first published in 1774 and never out of print since, was bound to be a major source. Named as the 'father of English racism', with his belief in the superiority of white people

---

[19] For a recent discussion of Williams and the question of debt, see David Scott, *Irreparable Evil. An Essay in Moral and Reparatory History* (New York, 2024).

[20] Compensation was also paid to slave-owners in the Cape and Mauritius.

[21] Catherine Hall, 'Reconfiguring Race: the Stories the Slave-owners Told', in Hall, Nicholas Draper, Keith McClelland, Katie Donington and Rachel Lang, *Legacies of British Slave-ownership. Colonial Slavery and the Formation of Victorian Britain* (Cambridge, 2014), 163–202.

and assumption that Black people were born to serve, Long's *History* documented every aspect of the society he knew as a slave-owner.[22] An Englishman who came from a dynasty of enslavers, his great-grandfather, Samuel Long, was one of the original settlers on the newly captured island of Jamaica in 1655 and the family owned plantations in Jamaica over generations. Edward Long was born in England in 1734 but went to Jamaica as a young man to make his fortune. A planter for eleven years, he returned to England in 1768 with his young family. He had decided to devote himself to writing an account of Jamaica, a work that would persuade his readers that the island was a colony of exceptional value to Britain and that slavery was necessary to its prosperity. He would give Jamaica its proper place on the Enlightenment map. The *History* was immediately recognized as authoritative, a rich description of this 'jewel' in the colonial crown. It provided an invaluable mine of material for those in support of slavery at a time when both the trade and the slave-owners were being publicly critiqued. Paradoxically, it was utilized by abolitionists too, since, in documenting the workings of the plantation, it unwittingly revealed evidence that confirmed the condemnation of slavery in the eyes of those hostile to it. Its influence spread to the USA and beyond. Long remains the best-known historian of Jamaica, a man who attempted on the basis of his experience on the island to theorize what he saw as essential, *natural* racial difference. White and Black were like oil and vinegar – they should never mix.

The *History* aimed to tell a story of Jamaica's development from an 'infant colony' in the 1650s to a settled and increasingly 'civilized' society by the early 1770s. Every 'document of culture', as Walter Benjamin taught us, is 'at the same time a document of barbarism'.[23] Long's *History* is no exception. What has impelled me to write about it, to keep thinking about this racist slaver? Why, when the scholarship on the enslaved is so vibrant and so politically necessary, do I choose to write about a white slave-owner? Why does he matter? What was he doing in his time, and what is his relevance for ours? Long was a key architect in the mid-eighteenth century of the practices and the theoretical justifications for racialization. He named himself and his family White, with a capital W, owners of property and freedom. Enslaved men and women, in his parlance, were 'Negroes', with a capital N. The 'White man' and the 'Negro' were both, as Fanon taught us, figments of a racist imagination: Black and White exist in relation to each other. 'Not only must the black man be black, he must be black in relation to the white man.'[24] That racist

---

[22] Peter Fryer, *Staying Power: the History of Black People in Britain* (London, 1984), 70. Fryer argues that 'Long's doctrine of innate black inferiority, may be termed the classic exposition of English racism'; 158.

[23] Walter Benjamin 'On the Concept of History', in *Selected Writings, volume IV: 1938–1940*, ed. Howard Eiland and Michael W. Jennings (Cambridge, MA, 2003), 392.

[24] Frantz Fanon, *Black Skin, White Masks* [1952] (London, 1986), 110.

imagination has lived on: I need to understand how its reverberations and reconfigurations work. Might it be better to understand the complexities and ambivalences of a man like Long rather than dismiss him as a monster? As a white English historian committed to the collaborative efforts to decolonize the discipline, I have my own issues to confront, my own debt to pay, both as one of those who has benefited from the ill-gotten wealth of Britain and as one connected with my familial link to Jamaica, my knowledge of the psychic havoc and intergenerational trauma wreaked by colonialism. Granville Sharp in the 1770s was weighed down with the 'enormous guilt' of England and expected God's retribution for the sin of slavery: he devoted his efforts to challenging the claims of slave-owners over the human property they claimed. This was a 'PRIVATE PROPERTY *which is unnatural in itself and … contrary to the laws and constitutions of this kingdom*', a private property in '*contraband goods*'.[25] He hoped for atonement. I hope for repair. In the twenty-first century, it is clear that the harm that has been done by two hundred years of slavery has not been put right by emancipation and independence. It cannot be put right. We live in the aftermath, must recognize responsibilities and focus on the possibilities of repair which cannot begin without a recognition of the realities of the past. This is difficult work, experienced very differently by the descendants of the colonized and of the colonizers. The hope is that re-writing histories can be a part of this process.[26]

Long's belief in racial difference as natural and essential was written on the figures of his imagined Africans, 'brutes' who must be tamed and might be partially civilized. In constructing that African as his 'other', he was constructing himself. The body, his white body and that of 'Black others', was the groundwork of his thought. 'The fabrication of an Africanist persona is reflexive,' wrote Toni Morrison, 'an extraordinary meditation on the self'. It is, she continued, 'a powerful exploration of the fears and desires that reside in the writerly conscious … an astonishing revelation of longing, of terror, of perplexity, of shame, of magnanimity … Savagery was "out there" – not in the violence of the slave-owner's coercive powers.'[27] White identity was sycophantic: 'in that construction of blackness *and* enslavement could be found not only the not-free but the not-me'.[28] She was reflecting on American fiction writers, but her insight captures Long, the terrors breaking through his polished surfaces. In Jamaica he experienced an authority and autonomy he had not

---

[25] Granville Sharp, *A Representation of the Injustice and Dangerous Tendency of Tolerating Slavery in England. Or of admitting the least claim of private property in the persons of man in England* [1769] (Cambridge, 2014), 73, 75.

[26] Catherine Hall, 'Doing Reparatory History: Bringing "Race" and Slavery Back Home', *Race and Class* 60.1 (2018), 3–21.

[27] Toni Morrison, *Playing in the Dark. Whiteness and the Literary Imagination* (New York, 1992), 17.

[28] Ibid., 44, 38.

known before, the absolute control he could exert over both the productive and reproductive lives of others; this new self was 'the planter', the 'West Indian', no longer just an Englishman. He aimed to provide an authoritative account to persuade his readership that Jamaica's contribution to British wealth required slavery. But he had no control over how his work would be read, either then or now. There were plenty of contemporaries who challenged him and published alternative narrations. Reading him now in Britain's current conjuncture, with ever increasing racialized and class inequalities, with threats to democratic systems, and fundamental questions about the survival of human/animal species and the planet, can focus the mind on whiteness as a metaphor for power and the part it has played in building Britain and its empire. Black historians and artists have brought those ghostly traces of the enslaved which people the interstices of the slavery archive alive and into the frame.[29] My task is to reinterpret Long's volumes through his account of White mastery and 'Negro' subjection. As a planter, he built his wealth on the plantation and the slavery business. What were the effects of being masters on the slave-owners? What damage did they do to themselves in their denial of the full humanity of others? Long's picture of Jamaica depended on silence, the disavowal, the knowing and not knowing, of the experiences of those he had enslaved. But how he practised that disavowal, how his racism was legitimated and the story he told of a benevolent colonialism have all lived on. Colonial archives need to be read with and against the grain; they can provide a route into 'imperial dispositions', those habits of ignoring, turning away, refusing to witness, that produced the 'well-tended conditions of disregard' that enabled colonizers to live with their contradictions.[30] What narrative does Long provide? How can we make sense of it now? What work can it do for us in decolonial times, when the urgent demand is to 'dismantle the colonial imperative' and address the debt owed to those whose histories were taken from them and whose bodies and minds were conscripted?[31] How were the racialized fictions constructed upon which white power rested? *The History of Jamaica* aimed to be a story of progress, but it is a text that produced unintended meanings. Like many family histories – for it was that too, the island story mirroring the family story – it was devised to close down differences, tell of success. But the slavery archive 'is both the home of those who commanded and the place from which that command might be subverted'.[32] The body of Long's writing, from his novel to his polemics and his *History*, together with family correspondence, wills,

---

[29] Stephanie E. Smallwood, 'The Politics of the Archive and History's Accountability to the Enslaved', *History of the Present* 6.2 (2016), 117–32.
[30] Ann Laura Stoler, *Along the Archival Grain. Epistemic Anxieties and Colonial Common-Sense* (Princeton, 2009), 256.
[31] Thanks to Bill Schwarz for this phrase.
[32] Jennifer E. Morgan, 'Archives and Histories of Racial Capitalism: an Afterword', *Social Text* 33.4 (2015), 153–61.

deeds and indentures, can be interrogated alongside colonial records. This archive can bear witness to the fictive nature of the binaries that were constructed. Long named men and women '*choses*' and '*chattels*', he bought and sold them. '*The human project*', as Aimé Césaire the Martiniquan poet and anti-colonialist wrote, is to refuse that 'thingification', remain human and block 'the dehumanization and estrangement of others'.[33]

I lie on my back on the floor, in the Alexander position, with my knees up and my head resting on two volumes of Long's *History* to offset the lower back pain that I am subject to as a result of too many hours at the computer. This way I hope that his words, rather than overwhelming me, can be undone, his version of history dismantled, some reparative work be done.

---

[33] Aimé Césaire, *Discourse on Colonialism* [1955] (New York, 1972), 21; Toni Morrison, *The Origin of Others* (Cambridge, MA, 2017), 37.

MAPS AND FAMILY TREE

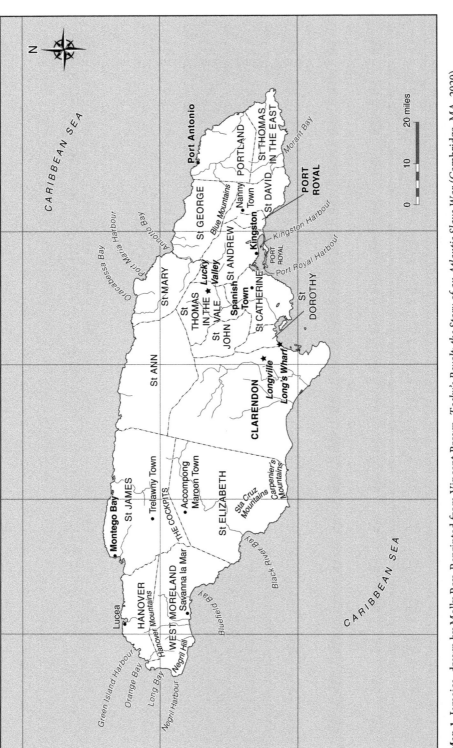

Map 1 Jamaica, drawn by Molly Roy. Reprinted from Vincent Brown, *Tacky's Revolt: the Story of an Atlantic Slave War* (Cambridge, MA, 2020).

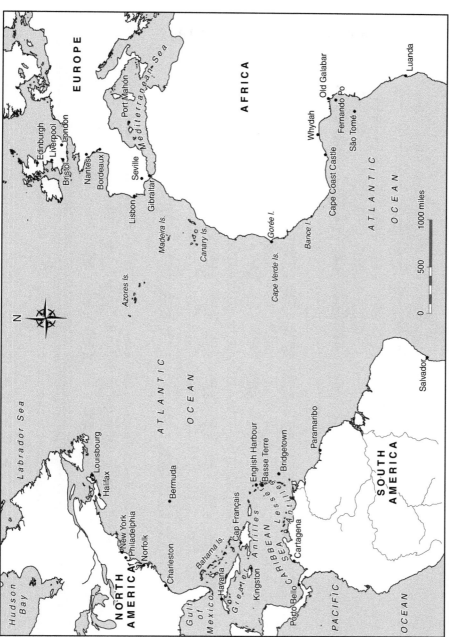

Map 2 The Atlantic Basin, drawn by Molly Roy. Reprinted from Vincent Brown, *Tacky's Revolt: the Story of an Atlantic Slave War* (Cambridge, MA, 2020).

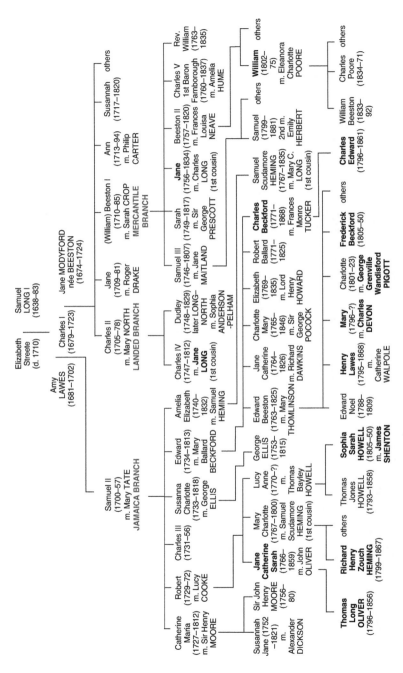

People who feature in the slave compensation records are given in **bold**.

Figure 1 The Long family tree, illustrating the three main branches. Designed by and courtesy of Rachel Lang.

Introduction

Writing a History of the Present

The History of Jamaica was published anonymously in London in three volumes in 1774 (Figure I.1).[1] It made an immediate impact. Edward Long was quickly identified as the author and was soon being called upon to speak with authority on matters connected with slavery. Long's ownership of Lucky Valley, a sugar plantation in the parish of Clarendon, with a labour force of more than three hundred enslaved men, women and children, was the major source of his wealth. After a residence of eleven years in Jamaica, during which time the labour of the enslaved steadily increased the value of his holdings, he could afford to return to England, the place of his birth and his young manhood. Some of the work had been written before leaving the island, but much of it was completed in his house in South Street in Chichester, a town within relatively easy reach of the capital, where he had settled with his wife, Mary, and their young family (Figure I.2). Long arrived in England at a time of significant change. The end of the Seven Years War in 1763 had brought a signal increase in Britain's global power. New territories meant substantial new populations of mixed ethnicities and religious beliefs, provoking questions about the meaning and extent of British subjecthood.[2] When he had left England in 1757, few voices had been raised against colonial slavery, which was commonly accepted as contributing to Britain's wealth. By the time he returned, the question as to whether slavery was legal in England, the land of liberty, had become a matter of public concern.

---

[1] [Edward Long], *The History of Jamaica Or, General Survey of the Ancient and Modern State of that Island, with Reflections on its Situation, Settlements. Inhabitants, Climate, Products, Commerce, Laws and Government* (3 vols., London, 1774). All subsequent references are to the Cambridge facsimile edition (Cambridge, 2010); 'Notice of Publication', *General Evening Post*, 14 July 1774. Thanks to Markman Ellis for this reference.

[2] Jack P. Greene, *Evaluating Empire and Confronting Colonialism in Eighteenth-Century Britain* (Cambridge, 2013).

INTRODUCTION

THE
HISTORY
OF
JAMAICA.
OR,

GENERAL SURVEY OF THE ANTIENT
AND MODERN STATE

OF

THAT ISLAND:

WITH

Reflections on its Situation, Settlements, Inhabitants, Climate,
Products, Commerce, Laws, and Government.

IN THREE VOLUMES.

ILLUSTRATED WITH COPPER PLATES.

VOL. II.

—— mea fuit femper hâc in re voluntas et fententia, quemvis ut hoc vellem de iis, qui effent idonei fufcipere, quàm me;—me, ut mallem, quàm neminem.
Cic. Orat. in Cæcilium.

LONDON:
PRINTED FOR T. LOWNDES, IN FLEET-STREET.
MDCCLXXIV.

Figure I.1 Title page of *The History of Jamaica*. Reproduced from Edward Long, *The History of Jamaica Or, General Survey of the Antient and Modern State of that Island, with Reflections on its Situation, Settlements, Inhabitants, Climate, Products, Commerce, Laws, and Government*, 3 vols. (London: T. Lowndes, 1774). Digitally printed version © Cambridge University Press 2010.

A variety of legal opinions and cases had not settled this point. The slave trade had clearly been legislated for in parliament, but what about slavery? There was no clear legal judgment on this. The Yorke–Talbot opinion of 1729 was that a slave was his master's property whether in England or in the colonies. Yorke (now Hardwicke) had opined in 1749 that a slave 'is as much

Figure I.2 A photograph from the early 1900s of Long's home in South Street, Chichester, where much of the *History* was written. © Gravelroots Archives.

property as any other thing'.[3] In 1767 Granville Sharp had taken up the case of Jonathan Strong, raising the issue of a slave-owner's rights over 'his property' once in England. Other cases were brought to law concerning the kidnapping of enslaved or formerly enslaved persons in the metropole, and the outcomes had been varied.[4] Sharp spent two years studying the law and in 1769 published *A Representation of the Injustice and Dangerous Tendency of Tolerating Slavery in England. Or of admitting the least claim of private property in the persons of man in England, etc.*, the first major work of anti-slavery by a British author. The book amassed a considerable volume of legal arguments against slavery. Both pro-slavers and anti-slavers were ready to test the issue in the courts. The case of James Somerset provided the opportunity. Somerset had been brought to England by the man who claimed ownership of him, James Stewart; he had managed to escape, but was subsequently kidnapped on to a ship for passage to the Caribbean and re-enslavement. This became the occasion to test the notion of the 'free air' of England before Lord Mansfield, the Lord Chief Justice. Mansfield's judgment in 1772 discharged Somerset and declared slavery to be repugnant in England. He demarcated between England, a place that did not permit the kidnapping of Africans in order to re-enslave them, and the colonies, places where slavery was

[3] Cited in Dana Y. Rabin, '"In a Country of Liberty?": Slavery, Villeinage and the Making of Whiteness in the Somerset Case', *HWJ* 72 (2011), 11.
[4] Katherine Paugh, 'The Curious Case of Mary Hylas: Wives, Slaves and the Limits of British Abolitionism', *S&A* 35.4 (2014), 629–51.

legitimate.[5] Abolitionists claimed this as a great victory, though the judgment only freed the individual man. Pro-slavers reacted with horror.

Long found himself in a very different atmosphere from the England he had left in 1757. His right to his human property was being challenged. His first act was to pen a furious polemic against Mansfield who had attempted, as he put it, 'to wash the blackamoor white'.[6] But his history, if it were to be authoritative, needed something much more than polemic. In the wake of the Somerset decision, it was a matter of urgency to persuade his metropolitan audience that colonial slavery was essential to British wealth and power. The necessary corollary was that black people were not equal and were born to serve those who were white. He was writing for a colonial as well as a metropolitan public, and he hoped to persuade white colonists of the need for change. If the island were to have a secure and settled future, their conduct must be modified. The Somerset trial had marked an iconic moment, a moment of rupture in metropolitan understandings of racial difference, when thinking about the slave trade and slavery as in some respects un-English broke through a common sense of its acceptability. This marked a new conjuncture, a time of intensifying struggle, when anti-slavery voices were no longer marginalized but moving into the centre ground of politics and culture. The protracted struggle that gradually ensued only concluded more than half a century later with the abolition of slavery in 1834. This was a moment that ushered in a new conjuncture, new articulations of racial hierarchy and new struggles over the meanings of race and freedom.

Long had three priorities: the first to defend slavery and the colonial system, the second to put Jamaica on the Enlightenment map, the third to identify the success of the colony with that of his family. What kind of writer was he and what kind of text did he produce? As a boy he had been schooled in the classics and he knew much of Homer by heart. The adolescent Long was a passionate reader of *Mr Spectator* and was greatly influenced by Addison's notions of 'taste' and 'politeness'. He had tried his hand at writing as a young man in England in the 1750s and had published several issues of a periodical, as well as a novel. Over his lifetime he wrote in many different forms – satires, polemics, novels, books of manners, political pamphlets, petitions and press reports – as well as the *History*. Writers could use the power of print to spread their knowledge and understanding. As a man of letters, following in the footsteps of others he had read, not least Hume and Smollett, he was convinced that

---

[5] There are many accounts of the Somerset case and its context. See particularly Christopher Leslie Brown, *Moral Capital. Foundations of British Abolitionism* (Chapel Hill, NC, 2006); Dana Y. Rabin, *Britain and its Internal Others, 1750–1800. Under Rule of Law* (Manchester, 2017).

[6] [Edward Long], *Candid Reflections upon the Judgement Lately Awarded by the Court of King's Bench in Westminster Hall on what is Commonly Called the Negroe Cause by a Planter* (London, 1772).

writers should aim at a comprehensive knowledge of society.[7] His training as a lawyer in London had meant honing the skills associated with presenting arguments and clarifying legal points. His years serving in the assembly, Jamaica's legislative body, had given him extensive political experience of debate and argument, both in the colony and in its troubled relations with the mother country. He had an intimate knowledge of the workings of the colonial state. The best historians, as Addison and Hume agreed, were those with experience of public business, possessing a familiarity with men and things.[8] His membership of the white creole elite, assured because of both his ancestry, his marriage and his property, meant that he was a part of the colony's ruling class; he could expect an audience, both in the metropole and beyond. His experience as a planter, together with his family connections to one of London's leading West India merchant houses, meant that he could write knowledgably, from a slave-owner's perspective, on sugar and commerce. The influence of Davenant and the political arithmeticians had fed his capacities as an 'actuarial historian', with interests in trade, populations and demography, the workings of economic life.[9] Living on the fringes of the Enlightenment, since Jamaica did not figure in Enlightenment thinking, he engaged with its writers and was enthusiastic as to the importance of natural history and the history of humankind.[10] His voracious curiosity, belief in the importance of education, instruction and improvement, interest in comparison, conviction that he had abandoned superstitious fears and desire to make his readers familiar with distant things all marked him as an Enlightenment man. Tristram Shandy's satire on Enlightenment learning, with its focus on 'knowledge physical, metaphysical, physiological, polemical, nautical, mathematical, enigmatical, technical, biographical, romantical, chemical and obstetrical', might have been penned with Long in mind.[11] His property and education ensured him the status of a gentleman, a man who could write and expect to publish and be noticed from a secure landed position.[12] He was both a 'planter historian', representing, he hoped, a 'planter ideal', a man of public spirit and benevolence, and a 'planter philosopher', as

---

[7] John Barrell, *English Literature in History, 1730–1780. An Equal, Wide Survey* (London, 1983).

[8] Nicholas Phillipson, *Hume* (London, 1989).

[9] The term is utilized by Ian Baucom, *Specters of the Atlantic. Finance Capital, Slavery and the Philosophy of History* (Durham, NC, 2005).

[10] Unlike the family of the Johnstones, based in Scotland, he did not personally know any of these writers, but they were central to his thinking. Emma Rothschild, *The Inner Life of Empires. An Eighteenth-Century History* (Princeton, 2011).

[11] Lawrence Sterne, *The Life and Opinions of Tristram Shandy, Gentleman* [1759] (Oxford, 2020), 50.

[12] Elizabeth Bohls stresses the importance of his position as a 'colonial gentleman' to his rhetorical strategies, but he was also an English gentleman. *Slavery and the Politics of Place. Representing the Colonial Caribbean, 1770–1833* (Cambridge, 2014).

demonstrated by his engagement with the Enlightenment thinkers on the nature of human beings. Despite his insistence on his identity as a free-born Englishman, he was also a Jamaican patriot.[13] We might now think of him as a diasporic figure, living across the two islands and attempting to negotiate that space. After years of active involvement in colonial politics, he had no interest in a seat in the House of Commons, as other West Indians did, hoping for influence 'at home'. Rather, he chose to write: that would be his political intervention.

History by the mid-eighteenth century was widely understood to be an important vehicle of national understanding.[14] Long's title, *The History of Jamaica*, was somewhat misleading, since only a small part of volume I comprised a historical narrative.[15] The subtitle clarified the scope of the three volumes: it was a *General Survey of the Ancient and Modern State of that Island, with Reflections on its Situation, Settlements. Inhabitants, Climate, Products, Commerce, Laws and Government.* This was hardly a conventional history, given the modest amount of material dealing with the past in narrative form. But centring the relation between past and present was at the heart of Long's project. His story was of the development of the 'infant colony' to what he hoped to depict as a settled and stable society. His *History* is perhaps best described as *a history of the present*, a political, economic, social and cultural representation of Jamaica in the 1760s. It tells us of the workings of racial capitalism in this particular mid-eighteenth-century Atlantic form, framed by a mercantilist system which structured the relation between metropole and colony. This was a system rooted in the 'Guinea Trade', the capture of Africans and the utilization of their lives and labour on Caribbean cane fields to produce sugar for export to Britain. Its mercantile base, the source of credit, was in London; its plantation regime was shored up by a colonial state designed to fix racial hierarchies. Long describes the workings of government and the law, the organization of capital, the production and reproduction of an economy and

---

[13] Denis Benn describes Long and Bryan Edwards as 'planter historians' in *The Caribbean. An Intellectual History, 1774–2003* (Kingston, Jamaica, 2004); Tim Watson describes the form as 'creole realism' in *Caribbean Culture and British Fiction in the Atlantic World, 1780–1870* (Cambridge, 2008); David Lambert depicts the 'planter ideal' in *White Creole Culture, Politics and Identity during the Age of Abolition* (Cambridge, 2005); Silvia Sebastiani describes Long as a 'planter philosopher' in 'Global Integration, Social Disintegration: Edward Long's History of Jamaica 1774', in Jeremy Adelman and Andreas Eckert (eds.), *Nations, Empires and Other World Products: Making Narratives across Borders* (forthcoming); Edward (later Kamau) Brathwaite, first opened my eyes to the importance of creole patriotism; *The Development of Creole Society in Jamaica, 1770–1820* (Oxford, 1971).

[14] Kathleen Wilson, *The Island Race. Englishness, Empire and Gender in the Eighteenth Century* (London, 2003).

[15] He was writing on the eve of a historiographical transformation: his work, a 'compilation', was of the mid-eighteenth century.

society built on cane, the plants that could be harnessed to commerce, the islands' inhabitants designated as free and unfree, white and black, the landscape transformed in the interests of the production of wealth and the protection of white power. Black rebellion and white fears haunt the text. Long worked hard in his writing to suppress his own anxieties and persuade himself and others that nature had ordained racial difference and inequality. He would attempt to control the world through his text.

A 'sheer variety of narrative forms' were employed by eighteenth-century writers such as Hume, Goldsmith and Robertson. Long followed this practice.[16] In the new world of print and expanding audiences, authors needed to find forms of historical narrative that met the demands of a commercial society, recognizing the values of the merchants, traders and professionals who constituted sections of this new reading public. Some of these writers were increasingly aware of the growing audience of women: Long addressed them in his more sentimental writing.[17] Conjectural history, with its combination of history and social theory and emphasis on social relations, forms of property, production and stadial thinking, the history of manners, accounts of travel and natural history, biography and novels were all defining themselves in relation to more traditional concepts of history. There was space for many different genres.[18] As Long instructed his eldest son, Edward Beeston, who was then studying at Trinity Hall in Cambridge, on the distinction between history and literature,

> I am thinking that in reading History, our attention is chiefly applied to Facts: and to the manners, vices and virtues of Mankind. But that we must look for the beautiful and exact in stile or composition in writers of a different Class, whose subject is not embarrassed with historical narrative or technical Description, Therefore, that one should not hope to study the elegance of language in Historical Tracts. There may possibly be some exceptions to this opinion among the Antients, as well as the moderns ... I am partial to Cicero for I cannot but esteem his the most complete model of elegant writing among the Romans: His language so easy yet so polished, and his periods so harmoniously turned.[19]

---

[16] Mark Salber Phillips, 'Reconsiderations on History and Antiquarianism: Arnaldo Momigliano and the Historiography of Eighteenth-Century Britain', *Journal of the History of Ideas* 57.2 (1996), 297–316.

[17] See, for example, [Long], *The Sentimental Exhibition; or, Portraits and Sketches of the Times* (London, 1774). In his novel and periodical writing, Long was attentive to the inward dimensions of private life, an arena that did not figure in his *History*.

[18] Joanna De Groot, *Empire and History Writing in Britain, c. 1750-2012* (Manchester, 2013); Rosemary Sweet, *The Writing of Urban Histories in Eighteenth Century England* (Oxford, 1997).

[19] Long to Edward Beeston Long, 17 October 1780, in R. Mowbray Howard, *Records and Letters of the Family of the Longs of Longville, Jamaica, and Hampton Lodge, Surrey* (2 vols., London, 1925), I. 146–7.

In a moment of perhaps *faux* modesty, Long drew the epigraph for his *History* from Cicero: 'This was always my wish and my judgement in this case, that I would rather any suitable person undertake the case rather than me, but rather myself than nobody at all.'[20] He clearly hoped to be an elegant writer himself, in the manner of the ancients. His 'compilation', as he diffidently named it, would combine a narrative of the 'Facts' of history, with a depiction of the 'manners, vices and virtues of Mankind', plus the 'technical Description' of estate management, sugar production and trade.[21] All this would sit alongside other forms: maps, engravings, poetry, georgic and picturesque renditions of the beauties of the island with their detour to the imaginary, even an occasional satirical piece.[22] The use of these different genres with their shifts in tone and vocabulary enabled contradictions and tensions in his writing and thinking. His optimistic vision of the economic benefits of commerce, or the civilizing effects of conditions of capture and enslavement on Africans, both aligned with progress, was juxtaposed with medicalized discourses, languages of infection, pollution and disorder associated with miscegenation, rebellion and the ever-present threat of illness and death. Long's voluminous writings bore witness to the discordant elements of his thinking and his strenuous efforts to keep his psychic balance.

His deliberate intent in writing the *History* was laid out for his readers in his opening pages. There was no adequate account of Jamaica, he wrote; several histories had been published but they only gave general outlines. This was very unsatisfactory for those who intended to settle there. He was hoping, he might have added, for many new settlers and these volumes were to encourage them. 'Having spent some years of my life there, I thought I could not devote my leisure to better purpose, than endeavouring to give an idea of its products and importance to Great-Britain.'[23] His expertise as an eyewitness was thus established: his residence had equipped him to write from experience, record with authority. Critics of slavery often wrote from hearsay; his account would be different. The naval and military history of the island was already well covered, nor would he record the speeches of governors, for they were neither entertaining nor instructive. Indeed, he produced a heavy critique of the character of the governors and their many abuses of power. He would deal with 'civil and military establishments', products, commerce, climate, soil, agriculture, counties, towns and 'natural curiosities'.[24] He would display, he promised, 'an

---

[20] Thanks to Tom Harrison for his translation from the Latin.
[21] Long, *History*, I. 2.
[22] Beth Fowkes Tobin discusses the centrality of the use of different genres to developing eighteenth-century ideas about land, labour and natural resources in the tropics; *Colonizing Nature. The Tropics in British Arts and Letters, 1760–1820* (Philadelphia, 2005).
[23] Long, *History*, I. 1.
[24] Ibid., I. 2.

impartial character of its inhabitants of all complexions' (a claim he did not meet), 'with some strictures on Negro slaves in particular, and freed persons, and laws affecting them'. His aim, he stressed, was to be accurate about commerce, for Jamaica was a commercial colony, its sugar the source of British wealth (Plate 5). It had been difficult to find adequate statistics on trade and he had been obliged to make use of many authors, hence the sense of a compilation. Since there was no adequate account of the early history of conquest and what followed, he would narrate those years, having consulted the best authorities he could find. That was the time (1655) when his great-grandfather, Samuel Long, had arrived in Jamaica, with the English military, and had settled on the island, establishing the plantations which were the source of family wealth. Though never explicitly stated, the *History* would be a record of the success of his family as well as of the island: the development from an 'infant colony' to a settled state; the uneven passage, from Samuel's early years as a colonial pioneer, to the disaster that befell Edward's grandfather Charles; the problems faced as a consequence by his own father, Samuel, and the rescue that he had effected, resulting in the possibility of the longed-for return to England.

Maintaining the liberties of the colonists, free-born Englishmen, was a primary concern. Long was writing from an *entailed inheritance*, as Burke was to imagine it, 'derived to us from our forefathers, and to be transmitted to our posterity', the special nature of English liberties, 'an estate especially belonging to the people of this kingdom'.[25] He and his fellow colonists owned this inheritance. They would pass it to their sons and grandsons. Their English liberties were their birth-right and their security. Regrettably, those liberties had been threatened, and he would have to detail many abuses of power. Those living in 'remote parts' of the British empire were subject to 'consummate tyranny' and 'injustice' meted out to them by crown-appointed officials. 'The subjects here', he wrote, 'May be compared to the helpless offspring of a planter, sent to the distance of many thousand miles from his parent, exposed to the imperious domination of strangers, and exiled beyond the reach of fatherly protection.'[26] Here was a key metaphor: the helpless colony, gendered as masculine, was neglected by the mother country, characterized as both maternal and paternal, which was failing to exercise proper fatherly protection. Rather, 'imperious strangers' were exercising unwarranted 'domination' and misuse of power. The best remedy for this, he argued, drawing on his knowledge of the improper prorogations and dissolutions of the assembly that he had witnessed, was frequent meetings of that elected body. Then the representatives of the 'commons', as he described them, the white freeholders, could bring offenders to justice. While the Romans had dealt

---

[25] Edmund Burke, *Reflections on the Revolution in France* (London, 1790), 47.
[26] Long, *History*, I. 3.

properly with the officials of their distant colonies, the same could not be said of the 'Mother-state', which had allowed provincial governors, 'so horrid a group', to exercise unlimited '*insolence of office*'.[27] Mindful of the voices of those critics of the planters who were beginning to have weight, Long reported that when the colonists

> complained of violations done to their liberty, the enemies of the West-India islands have often retorted upon them the impropriety of their clamouring with so much vehemence for what they deny to so many thousand negroes, whom they hold in bondage. 'Give freedom' (say they) 'to others, before you claim it for your selves.'[28]

Yet, he reminded his readers, the Romans and Athenians had also held others in servitude, and it was noteworthy that the more they valued their independence, the more indulgent they were to their slaves. For who doubts, he asked rhetorically, that the servant of a freeman would be better treated than 'the servant of an enslaved person'?[29] He was not suggesting, he hastened to add – thinking no doubt of the Somerset case and Mansfield's verdict that slavery was repugnant in England – that slavery should be introduced into a *free* country, but, 'where it happens to be *inevitably* necessary' and where it was 'under proper limitations' and in no way threatened the liberties of the parent state, then it should be recognized.[30] It was the liberties of the colonists, their 'birthright', their 'possession of British freedom' and 'spirit of independence', that would secure the safety of the 'mother-state'.[31] Slavery must not enslave the parent state. For Britons to be free, colonists must be free to enslave. There were two kinds of freedom: freedom from tyranny and freedom to impose it on others. Colonists' freedoms, his argument ran, would ensure the good treatment of their human property. Like Roman patriarchs they would administer justly. In a plantation economy slavery was '*inevitably* necessary', for white men could not labour in the tropics. The liberties of the colonists, and indeed of the empire, depended on the enslavement of others.

In concluding his introduction, he apologized for the confusions and repetitions that had resulted from his attempt to write 'a complete history', noted that those who came to Jamaica 'do not emigrate for the purpose of compiling histories, but avowedly that of accumulating money', and submitted his 'unpolished *survey of Jamaica*' to his readers.[32] His story aimed to be one of progress in civil society, from days of disorder to well-established forms of governance, settled towns and well-run plantations, and in the natural world,

---

[27] Ibid., I. 4.
[28] Ibid., I. 5.
[29] Ibid.
[30] Ibid.
[31] Ibid., I. 6.
[32] Ibid., I. 6, 8.

from an island with only small pockets of cultivation (he had no concept of indigenous Taino culture) to land cleared and planted, agriculture established. He would tell of improvement at every level, a society he depicted as increasingly civilized. There was much still to be done and he hoped his work would contribute to this. The tensions, however, surfaced continuously. The runaways haunting the caves, the Maroons, situated between colonists and the enslaved, in their recognized communities, the persistent rebellions of the enslaved, the need for fortifications and military and naval support, the scale of deaths, the small numbers of 'proper' white families, the ever-increasing numbers of 'mulattos', all bore witness to the fragility of the hierarchical order he hoped to celebrate. At the same time a commitment to civil history as one of progress, the forging of a new colony, was juxtaposed and jostled with a natural history of fixed categories and forms of belonging: whiteness and blackness as certified by the body.

The *History* was divided into books as well as volumes. Book I opened with an account of civil government. Long was following Hume in giving pre-eminence to the political.[33] Earlier writings on Jamaica, such as Hans Sloane's, had given much greater attention to natural history, rather than civil.[34] But Long's claim was that interest in Jamaica should no longer be focused on nature: it was a settled colony and civilized polities were governed by law. Pride of place was given to the proclamation of Charles II at the time of the Restoration,

> that all children of natural-born subjects of England, to be born in Jamaica, shall, from their respective births, be reputed to be, and shall be, *free denisons of England*; and shall have the same privileges, to all intents and purposes, as the free-born subjects of England.[35]

For the colonists this was regarded as their charter of rights and was to be fought over in the face of subsequent efforts by the crown to insist on royal prerogative. A critical discussion of the role of the council, the house of assembly, and the governor and other crown officials followed, together with a brief history of the major struggle over colonial rights in the 1680s, featuring Long's two ancestors, Samuel Long and William Beeston. The role and significance of the colonial agent and a lengthy section on the militia concluded the first part of the volume. 'I shall' now, he wrote, 'emerge from the gloomy thicket of politics, and take an excursion into the region of history'.[36] This

---

[33] The first two volumes of David Hume's history had been published in the previous decade to great acclaim: *The History of England, from the Invasion of Julius Caesar to the Revolution in 1688* (2 vols., London, 1754).

[34] Miles Ogborn, 'Discriminating Evidence: Closeness and Distance in Natural and Civil Histories of the Caribbean', *Modern Intellectual History* 11.3 (2014), 631–53.

[35] Long, *History*, I. 9.

[36] Ibid., I. 220.

concerned the conflicts over the original constitution, documents on Cromwell's instructions, the time of the Restoration and the settlement that was eventually reached with the crown. The expedition of Penn and Venables, the conquest of Jamaica, the important role of another of Long's ancestors, Colonel D'Oyley, the development of landownership and planting, the subsequent period of the dominance of the buccaneers, and the peace made with Spain in 1670 concluded the narrative history. Long was anxious to insist on the legitimacy of England's dispossession of the Spanish, taking Hume to task on this matter and arguing that he had not properly studied the relevant documents. Cromwell's war in the West Indies was just and honourable: 'far from being repugnant to the principles of national equity (as maintained by Hume) it seems manifestly consistent with the laws of nature and nations, and the rules of sound policy'. England's possession of Jamaica was 'lawful acquisition in war'.[37]

Book 2 opened with a general description of the island, the state of its population, the significance of credit, the need to extend settlement and the development of agriculture, which included a lengthy discussion of the production of sugar with details on the costings of plantations, the profits that could be made and the need for improvements. Much emphasis was given to the importance of road building as a civilizing force. An enthusiastic account of the 'Negro Trade, which is the ground-work of all', focused on the huge benefits it brought to Great Britain, while a lengthy discourse on imports and exports attempted to deliver the detailed material on commerce that he had promised. Proposals on how to deal with the scarcity of money and advice to planters on the advantages of dealing with established West India merchant houses in London concluded both the book and the volume.

The first part of volume II dealt with the topography of the island, with details on all the parishes, their ports, towns, notable estates, natural beauties and curiosities, together with estimates as to their economic improvement or decline, and is perhaps better described as a chorography rather than a topography.[38] Brief discussions of the clergy, mines and schools followed, leading to the account of the island's white and free inhabitants, from creoles to servants, Jews, Quakers and Moravians. The state of the regular troops, their conditions and their barracks was followed by sections on free blacks, 'mulattos' and 'Marons'. Book 3 concerned the enslaved, the 'Negroes of Africa', 'Guinea Slaves' and 'Creole Blacks'. It was in this context that Long engaged in his debates with a range of Enlightenment thinkers on humankind and proposed his theory of essential racial difference. Reflections on the reasons for the scale of mortality on the island led him to give an account of

---

[37] Ibid., I. 290.
[38] Darrell J. Rohl, 'The Chorographic Tradition and Seventeenth and Eighteenth Century Scottish Antiquaries', *Journal of Art Historiography* 5 (2011), 1–18.

the history of 'Negro' insurrections including the major rebellion of 1760. A short chapter on the free black figure of Francis Williams attempted to justify inequality as natural. Finally, ever conscious of critical metropolitan voices, he used a section on the Jamaican Negro Code to make proposals for improvements as to the condition of the enslaved. The volume ended with thoughts on maintaining the health of the white population and a satire on the dreadful doings of a medical quack.

The third volume and the third book dealt with the non-human aspects of natural history. After some discussion of meteorology, wind, weather, earthquakes, hurricanes, barometers and tides, maintaining nature's designs for dealing with hot climates, he provided extensive catalogues of the vegetables, fruits, fauna and flora to be found on the island and their uses. Little of this material was original and he relied heavily on the prior studies of Sloane, Barham, Browne and others. His intention was to be useful: what crops might be developed for export, what potential new enterprises could he identify? He gave advice as to the transplantation of plants and for the establishment of a botanic garden, subjects which were dear to the hearts of natural historians. A final appendix turned to the importance of what could be learned from French colonial practices and offered a few words on the 'ancient Indian inhabitants', those Taino peoples he had almost entirely ignored.

Long was keen to demonstrate the range of his sources. His historical narrative, he told his readers, had drawn on contemporary historians such as Thurloe, Clarendon and Burnet, together with official papers and documents. He castigated Hume, 'the learned historian', for failing to fully examine an important source and committing 'so capital a mistake'.[39] Many detailed tracts on commerce were cited, along with Davenant, Childe and equivalent authorities. He referenced the earlier writers on Jamaica: Sloane, who 'had first laid open a new scene of American productions', had 'possessed all that discernment and knowledge requisite for a cultivation of natural history', but had lacked opportunities 'to ground his descriptions on the result of his own personal experience'.[40] Browne was on one occasion described as an 'audacious slanderer', on another praised for a 'just remark'.[41] Anthony Robinson, a good friend of his brother Robert, had corrected many errors, in both Sloane and Browne. Long was a member, on a minor scale, of Sloane's 'informal empire of gentlemanly knowledge', with an acute sense of the class hierarchy of

---

[39] Long, *History*, I. 223.
[40] Ibid., II. 135–7; I. 134. Hans Sloane, *A Voyage to the Islands Madera, Barbados, Nieves, S. Christophers and Jamaica with the Natural History of the Herbs and Trees, Four-footed Beasts, Fishes, Birds, Insects, Reptiles, &c. Of the last of those Islands* (2 vols., London, 1707).
[41] Long, *History*, II. 284, 220. Patrick Browne, MD, *The Civil and Natural History of Jamaica (in 3 parts)* (London, 1756).

such genteel associations.[42] He passed no opinion on Leslie's history of Jamaica, but this may have been one of the texts he had in mind in commenting on the need to correct misapprehensions: he would not have appreciated his lack of sources and sense that history was 'something obscure'.[43] He made heavy use of travel accounts of West Africa such as Bosman's, while tour guides to England, such as that of Defoe, provided models for writing about place.[44] 'The inimitable Montesquieu' was cited with cautious approval, though Long would certainly have welcomed his insistence on the importance of local laws.[45] Voltaire's judgement that every Englishman was a savage was cited and explicitly taken issue with four years later.[46] Buffon was his major antagonist when it came to questions of the human, but he referenced many others, most significantly Monboddo.[47] He had read Ligon's history of Barbados and works on Antigua and North American colonies so that he could make comparisons.[48]

At the time of the publication of his volumes, he had not read the manuscript of James Knight's history of the island, written in the 1740s. This came into his hands in time for him to reflect on it in the extensive notes that he made with the intention of revising the published manuscript, something he never completed. Knight's manuscript now sits in the Long Papers in the British Library and has recently been edited by Jack Greene.[49] The similarities between the two histories are striking. Knight was writing in Stoke Newington. He had lived in Jamaica for more than twenty years, initially holding a crown appointment, and had established himself as a merchant and landowner, before returning to England in around 1737. He believed that, despite the amount of material printed about Jamaica in the period since settlement, it had

[42] The term is Richard Drayton's, in *Nature's Government. Science, Imperial Britain and the 'Improvement' of the World* (London, 2000), 37.
[43] Charles Leslie, *A New History of Jamaica. In Thirteen Letters from a Gentleman to his Friend* (Dublin, 1741), 38.
[44] Willem Bosman, *A New and Accurate Description of the Coast of Guinea, Divided into the Gold, the Slave, and the Ivory Coasts* (London, 1705); Daniel Defoe, *A Tour thro' the Whole Island of Great Britain, divided into circuits or journies* (3 vols., London, 1724–7).
[45] Long, *History*, II. 330, fn. Malick W. Ghachem, 'Montesquieu in the Caribbean: the Colonial Enlightenment between *Code Noir* and *Code Civil*', *Historical Reflections/Réflexions historiques* 25.2 (1999), 183–210.
[46] Long, *History*, II. 270. [Long], *English Humanity no Paradox: or, an attempt to prove, that the English are not a Nation of Savages* (London, 1778).
[47] Georges-Louis Leclerc, comte de Buffon, *Histoire naturelle, générale et particulière, avec la description du Cabinet du Roi* (36 vols., Paris, 1749–1804); James Burnett, Lord Monboddo, *Of the Origin and Progress of Language* (6 vols., Edinburgh, 1773–94).
[48] Richard Ligon, *A True and Exact History of the Island of Barbadoes* (London, 1657).
[49] BL Add MSS 12418-19, published as James Knight, *The Natural, Moral and Political History of Jamaica and the Territories Thereon Depending, from the first discovery of the island by Christopher Columbus to the year 1746*, edited and with an introduction by Jack P. Greene (2 vols., Charlottesville, VA, 2021).

been inaccurately and negatively represented, with bad consequences in terms of both government interest and colonial confidence in what were real achievements. Knight aimed to provide better information, promote British interest and demonstrate the improvements that were needed in the imperial system. He was writing what Greene describes as a new genre of 'provincial histories'.[50] These were being produced across the American colonies, written by creoles or long-term residents, combining documents, narrative and chorography (the systematic mapping and description of a particular region), and aiming to enhance provincial patriotism and metropolitan consciousness. The cosmopolitan histories of Voltaire, Hume and others were detached from nationalist sentiment and invested in the idea of a common European civilization. Long's history, by contrast, was of a colony and its relation to Britain.[51] Knight's themes were remarkably similar to those taken up by Long a quarter of a century later. He focused on the centrality of the metropolitan and colonial relation and the contribution that the island made to Britain, the richness of the resources – equal to the gold and silver mines of the Americas – and the need for security, from both internal and external enemies. He also stressed the need for further settlement, the belief in English rights and Whiggism, the anxious life of the planter, the importance of the merchants and the problems of dealing with the enslaved: all echoed by Long. Knight was writing at a time when there was no significant challenge to slavery 'at home': therefore, he did not need to justify it.

Long envisaged the Atlantic as a place of white power, made productive by enslaved black labour. His politics of place, rooted in the geography of the West India trade, fixed England, Jamaica and Africa in a fateful triangle, secured by Manichean racial binaries of 'White' and 'Negro'. He wrote his *History* in England, he *knew* Jamaica and he *imagined* Africa – these were the worldly spaces in which the wars of representation over the slave trade and slavery were to be fought out, and his writings were crucial to those struggles.[52] His double consciousness – as a man whose primary identification was as an Englishman, but one who became a West Indian – informed his writing. He wanted to make Jamaica legible to his metropolitan audience, recognized as an asset, a source of British wealth and power. It was a place to settle: no longer an infant colony, the pirates and privateers had gone, but fortunes could still be made.[53] Recognizing slavery as essential to its prosperity, however, was vital to

---

[50] The term is Greene's: Knight, *History*, 'Introduction', I. xvi.
[51] Karen O'Brien, *Narratives of Enlightenment. Cosmopolitan History from Voltaire to Gibbon* (Cambridge, 1997).
[52] David Lambert, *Mastering the Niger. James MacQueen's African Geography and the Struggle over Atlantic Slavery* (Chicago, 2013).
[53] Jefferson Dillman, *Colonizing Paradise. Landscape and Empire in the British West Indies* (Tuscaloosa, 2018) notes that seventeenth-century narratives of the West Indies as an abyss of immorality in need of redemption were being replaced in the eighteenth century

this colonial project. Englishmen who left the mother country to establish colonies in far distant places must be able to enjoy the freedom of their birthright to its fullest extent: they must be free to enslave others. The liberty of the Englishman was held in place by the different liberty of the colonist. Jamaica was described in great detail, based on Long's experience: readers could travel the island with him, just as Defoe had suggested in his *Compleat English Gentleman*, for a tour of the world could now be made in books and maps. Long was the 'seeing man' who looked out and possessed and would guide those who travelled with him.[54] His brief account of the continent of Africa was, in contrast, entirely derivative. England was interpellated as the absent centre, the *prospect* from which to judge, representing the norms of civilizational whiteness. England was imagined as a place of safety; his own family was now securely cordoned off from the polluting tints of black bodies. Jamaica was a place to live off, its juices extracted to be refined 'at home', and Africa a continent where its peoples were its key commodity, suited by nature to capture and enslavement.

England was 'home' and Long's reference point: his aim for Jamaica was to make it more like England. The 'mother country' was distinguished from all other European nations by its distinctive freedoms: the rights which 'the people' claimed to share in the legislatures, the right of trial by jury and the right of Habeas Corpus.[55] Since he was writing primarily for an English audience, there was no need for him to provide a description, but his imagined England underpinned his writing. It was a White homogeneous country, with uncertain places for Jacobites, Catholics and Jews. It was an old country, had a History with a capital H, kings and queens, a constitution built up over centuries, a House of Lords and a House of Commons, a legal system with courts and justices, a navy to be proud of. It had a developed agriculture, country houses, an aristocracy and gentry, cathedrals and churches, towns and villages, roads, harbours and ships, societies of concerned gentlemen devoted to 'improvement'. It was an expanding commercial empire with coffee houses, writers and artists, newspapers and bookshops, theatres and exhibitions, shops and consumer goods. It was properly hierarchical: property owners had their well-established patterns of marriage and domesticity, were maintained by servants, skilled artisans and unskilled labourers. England was a polite cosmopolitan and civilized society: it had all that Africa lacked and that Jamaica needed to develop.

---

with new narratives informed by Enlightenment ideas as to humans' control of the natural environment.

[54] The term is Mary Louise Pratt's, *Imperial Eyes. Travel Writing and Transculturation* (London, 1992), 7.

[55] Long papers. BL Add MSS 12438, f. 13.

Africa was a blank continent for Long: he focused on its rudeness and savagery, its amoral character, as the essential counterpoints to Jamaica's progress and England's refinement. The point of Africa, as far as he was concerned, was the captives it delivered to the Caribbean. Africa made Jamaica's wealth, which in turn produced British prosperity. He had been compelled to recognize that slavery was 'repugnant' to the spirit of English law.[56] But Jamaica needed its trade with Africa. In the 1770s many parts of the continent were still unknown to Europeans, but slave traders and voyagers had been bringing back accounts from the seventeenth century. Their tales found a ready audience in the eighteenth century as the natural world and its peoples were opened up as objects of enquiry. Time and space, manners and peoples, insides and outsides, the world of things: all these preoccupied Enlightenment men and women. Africa's strangeness was both alarming and enticing. Long's account of the 'vast continent' was exclusively focused on its diverse peoples, all, however, to his mind, sharing similar characteristics. Since he had no first-hand knowledge, Africa was a place that existed for him purely in his imagination: it was a blank screen on to which he could project his fantasies of otherness. His description of the landscape was minimal: 'barren desert' or 'fertile soil', varied trees or 'destitute of verdure', near the coast or far from it.[57] There were 'societies', but no 'civility, of arts or sciences', kingdoms and 'petty states', towns, 'as they are called', and villages, but he had no maps and no details.[58] For Long, Africa was its peoples: those captives some of whom ended up on his plantations and who, he liked to report, preferred Jamaica to their home country. Fear of difference haunted his imagination and he moved from the language of straight description to the language of fantasy, relying on selective readings of printed works, plagiarizing in and out of context. Snelgrave's *A New Account of Some Parts of Guinea, and the Slave Trade*, Bosman's account of Whidah and the *Universal Modern History* all provided him with material.[59] Africa was barbaric, its peoples in need of the Atlantic as a rescue from a fate worse than death. Africans, Long wanted to persuade himself and his readers, were much better off in Jamaica than in this benighted place.

The Jamaica he represented in his topographical tour of the island was not the landscape of terror associated with the rebellion of 1760 that his metropolitan audience would have encountered in the press. What was more, it was not the plantations, which along with the pens and provision grounds covered the majority of the cultivated land. As sites of labour and production they were

---

[56] Long, *History*, II. 323.
[57] Ibid., II. 373.
[58] Ibid., II. 377.
[59] For a discussion of the sources on which Long drew, see Anthony J. Barker, *The African Link. British Attitudes to the Negro in the Era of the Atlantic Slave Trade, 1550–1807* (London, 1978).

cordoned off, discussed in the sections on agriculture. Writing in England, he could partially veil the fears that were ever present on the island, and one representation of it was as a paradise, only needing English intervention to secure its prosperity. He found the island extraordinarily beautiful, and its beauty enhanced its appeal as a source of wealth and power. 'Before the discovery of America', he wrote, 'The romantic genius of a poet alone could expatiate on some Utopian island, blessed with perennial verdure and unfading spring. In Jamaica we find the idea realized.'[60]

Long employed a number of key concepts in his writing, though the definitions were often far from clear. Jamaica was a colony, a place with 'a body of people drawn from the mother-country to inhabit some distant place', as Johnson defined it.[61] It had a form of government 'almost as near as the condition of a dependent colony can be brought to resemble that of its mother country, which is a great and independent empire'.[62] It was a 'dependent colony', dependent on its mother country for military and naval protection and locked into a mercantile system which bound it to produce a key export for that mother. In the early days it had been an 'infant and unsettled colony' but was now established as a 'commercial colony', with 'colony laws', 'colony legislature' and 'colony government'.[63] It was also a 'sugar colony' and an 'industrious colony'.[64] Once established in regular form with duties and taxes, 'no colony within the British dominion', Long insisted, 'has cost the nation less for maintenance and protection, on a fair balance of account'.[65] Despite its dependent status, however, its 'colony-subjects' were 'patriots' with a true attachment to their country. Long described his ancestors, Samuel Long and William Beeston, as 'virtuous patriots' with their interest in public welfare and determination to challenge wrongful claims for the royal prerogative.[66] He made many appeals for true patriots to tackle governmental abuses, encourage 'patriotic societies' and recognize the space which the colony opened up for 'the exercise of patriotism'.[67] 'A spirit of patriotism' could bring great benefits and contribute to the spread of civilization.[68] He was even prepared to admit colonial patriotism was not exclusively white: African creoles, those born on the island, could have a 'patriotic affection' for the place of their birth.[69]

---

[60] Long, *History*, I. 363.
[61] Samuel Johnson, *A Dictionary of the English Language* (4th edn, London, 1773).
[62] Long, *History*, I. 9.
[63] Ibid., I. 19, 20, 116, 178.
[64] Ibid., II. 297, 289.
[65] Ibid., I. 305.
[66] Ibid., I. 202.
[67] Ibid., I. 436, 437, 508.
[68] Ibid., II. 265.
[69] Ibid., II. 411.

Colonial patriotism for white men was closely linked with notions of liberty. 'In our islands', wrote Long, 'the word *liberty* is in every one's mouth; the assemblies abound with the clamour of "liberty and property"; and it is echoed back by all ranks and degrees, in full chorus.'[70] Whites, he added, were nearly on a level; black people of course were not. Liberty referred to the privileges and rights enjoyed by colonists in virtue of their status as free-born Englishmen. These liberties were secured by a system of government based on consent: men agreed to 'putting themselves under government' in the interests of 'the preservation of their property ... the mutual *preservation* of their lives, liberties and estates'.[71] These were the words of the 'judicious Locke', Long's mentor in these matters.[72] In the 1670s the king and his ministers had attempted a 'total innovation' which aimed, as Long put it, 'at taking away from the common people [he meant white freeholders] their deliberative share in the framing of those laws by which their lives, liberties, and properties, were to be bound'. In 1729 'the grand charter of our liberties', the solemn compact concluded between sovereign and people, had included the confirmation of 'the liberty and property of the subject', in return for a commitment to the payment of annual revenues to the crown.[73] Liberty, he believed, was a characteristic of civilized societies, and the result of English liberty was the 'spirit of nation freedom' and of industry which marked them as such a particular people. While 'common labourers' in England 'remain content with a very limited portion of liberty', Africans in Africa had no notion of it.[74]

Liberty also carried another meaning: the relaxation of restraints, as in taking the liberty; thus Long's accounts of the many official abuses of power, such as 'the liberty to plunder'. He himself would take the liberty of exposing those abuses.[75] Sunday, he opined, 'is a day of liberty and pleasure for the Negroes'.[76] But there were dangers in any lack of surveillance, for it could lead to 'Negroes' being at liberty to form cabals.[77] Liberty meaning freedom was something that, in exceptional circumstances, such as a demonstration of loyalty during a rebellion, could be granted to the enslaved. The white colonist, in contrast, carried liberty in his very body, his capacity to be 'master of all'.[78] Liberty was a characteristic of civilized societies, those which had laws and government, valued knowledge, science and the arts, enjoyed consumer goods

---

[70] Ibid., II. 431.
[71] John Locke, *Two Treatises of Government* [1689] (London, 1821), 295.
[72] Long, *History*, I. 186–7.
[73] Ibid., I. 220.
[74] Ibid., II. 393.
[75] Ibid., I. 93.
[76] Ibid., I. 141.
[77] Ibid., I. 389.
[78] Ibid., II. 365.

and understood marriage as the basis of a good society. These were the values to be contrasted with those of 'barbarous' and 'savage' peoples. Long's model was England, a society that had once been barbarous. Europeans were civilized. Every other people that he recorded were judged in terms of their position *en route* from savagery to civilization. Mexicans had been 'tolerably civilized' when Vespucci encountered them; the Indians on the Mosquito shore would find that their wants would increase 'as they grow more civilized'; even North American Indians had something to be said in their favour.[79] The new African captives, brought into Jamaica between 1765 and 1766, he wrote, were 'all of them as savage and uncivilized as the beasts of prey that roam through the African forests'.[80] It was only plantation life, he believed, that had the potential to partially civilize those born on the island.

Long's system of social classification was imprecise and inconsistent. There were 'classes', groupings of people with similar characteristics – 'A rank or order of persons', as Johnson defined class – free or unfree, black or white: 'classes of freed persons', of 'Negroes', 'subordinate classes', gradations of species with some 'classes widely differing from each other'.[81] Classes could also be animal, vegetable or mineral: 'classes' of vegetables and 'classes' in the militia, roads were divided into three 'classes', and tradesmen occupied different 'classes'.[82] Class might also be associated with race, as in 'the different classes and races of human creatures'.[83] His use of 'race' was similarly imprecise and erratically inclusive, of both animal and vegetable. Linnaeus and Buffon had both placed humans in the animal kingdom, outside the biblical framework. This represented a major break in thinking: humankind was now located in the same system of knowledge as the rest of nature. Humans could now be understood as a particular kind of animal, could be divided into 'varieties' or 'races' or 'species', all terms commonly utilized and frequently interchangeable. What then were the boundaries between humans, or between humans and animals?[84] For Long there were 'species' of vermin, of bamboo, of marble, of striped fish, crickets and spiders, of quadrupeds and orangutans, of Whites and of Negroes.[85] Then there was 'the human race' and the 'race of mankind', 'the race of white men', 'the first race of settlers', the 'hardy race of seamen', the lower-class 'Mulattoes' characterized as 'a hardy race', the 'race of Albinoes', even quacks, whose activities in Jamaica he loathed and whom he described as 'a lethiferous race of savage animals in human shape'.

---

[79] Ibid., II. 351; I. 319.
[80] Ibid., II. 442.
[81] Johnson, *A Dictionary*.
[82] Long, *History*, I. 139, 477, 572; II. 320, 351, 356, 372.
[83] Ibid., II. 371.
[84] Jean-Frédéric Schaub and Silvia Sebastiani, *Race et histoire dans les sociétés occidentales (XVe–XVIIIe siècle)* (Paris, 2021), especially chaps. 5 and 6.
[85] Long used the term 'species' eighty times in vol. II.

Then came 'the race of oran-outangs', the 'race of swine' and a 'race' of trees.[86] What then defined a 'race'? He was unclear. The English race featured, for it had been accused of being 'most bloody, inhuman and unfeeling', an accusation which he vigorously denied.[87] His most common usage for 'race' was 'the Negroe race', as he wrote '(consisting of varieties)' including Giagas, 'a barbarous race', Hottentots, 'a lazy stupid race', and Coromantins, a 'detestable race'.[88] This was the shift in meaning which has been identified as becoming characteristic of Enlightenment discourse – race as inherited and linked to blood – a discourse to which Long's own text contributed.[89] 'Race' was crystallizing as the dominant term through which to talk about human difference.

As many commentators have noted, 'race' and 'nation' had intertwined as well as competing meanings in this period, the poles of 'an essentialised Nature and a capricious Environment' overlapping with one another.[90] The terms became separated, Nicholas Hudson suggests, during the later eighteenth century. The 'nations' of the non-European world that were described in seventeenth-century travel literature came to be associated with 'tribes', while 'nation' came to signify the distinctive social and political systems of European countries and 'race' to be utilized by ethnographers.[91] Long slipped between these meanings in his usage. He had read Hume's account 'Of National Characters' and had been sharply critical of French influence in England in the 1750s and appreciative of English virtues. By the 1770s he was more circumspect about the French since he envied their colonists for the support they received from their government. 'Men of sense', Hume had argued in his essay, 'allow that each nation has a peculiar set of manners, and that some particular qualities are more frequently to be met with among one people than among their neighbours.' He distinguished between moral and physical causes for these differences: moral included governments, public affairs, manners and customs; physical were associated with air and climate.[92] Long was well aware of the footnote that Hume had added in 1753, by which time he had begun to be convinced that there were some deeper, more fixed attributes of particular peoples. He suspected 'the negroes, and in general all

---

[86] Long, *History*, I. 221, 299, 424, 575; II. 168, 352, 363, 379, 475, 591.
[87] Ibid., II. 442.
[88] Ibid., II. 371, 373, 374, 471.
[89] Nicholas Hudson, 'From "Nation" to "Race": the Origins of Racial Classification in Eighteenth-Century Thought', *Eighteenth Century Studies* 29.3 (1996), 247–64. From my first reading of Roxann Wheeler's *The Complexion of Race. Categories of Difference in Eighteenth Century British Culture* (Philadelphia, 2000), I have found her chapter on Long and Johnson extremely illuminating; Schaub and Sebastiani, *Race et histoire*.
[90] Wilson, *The Island Race*, 6–8.
[91] Hudson, 'From "Nation" to "Race"'.
[92] David Hume, 'Of National Characters' [1753], in *The Philosophical Works of David Hume*, ed. T. H. Green and T. H. Grose (4 vols., London, 1882), III. 244.

the other species of men (for there are four or five different kinds) to be naturally inferior to the whites. There never was a civilized nation of any other complexion than white, nor even any individual eminent either in action or speculation,'[93] words which certainly resonated for Long.

Long sometimes used 'nation', meaning peoples distinguished by language or government as Dr Johnson had defined it.[94] His references to 'European nations' increasingly indicated political entities. Europe was a continent, with its separate nations and races, terms which were once again used interchangeably. Europeans were bound together by their common characteristics, yet divided by their national specificities. Voltaire valued Europe as the centre of the civilized world, to be contrasted with Asia and Africa.[95] Linnaeus had developed a classification based on four continents, four temperaments associated with them, and again Europeans had the most desirable characteristics.[96] Long shared this general understanding: Europe was an identifiable geographically known place, its peoples civilized and white. European adventurers had been some of the first to reach the Caribbean. They had served as recruits in the early military struggles against the Spanish and were needed now as migrants to increase the white population. They shared bodily constitutions and suffered from the same patterns of ill health. There were European fruits and vegetables, European languages, European ships and harbours, European imports and European trade. But Europeans were also divided by nationality, and British rivalries with both France and Spain were endemic. Europeans, he thought, should have Latin, Greek and French, 'some knowledge of the world, of men, and manners': these were the prerequisites of civilized men.[97] 'The whole British nation', the 'German nation', 'civilized nations', 'trading and manufacturing nations', and 'nations of antiquity' were clearly associated in his mind with Europe.[98] But nation could also carry the older connotations of breed, stock or race. Hottentots were at one moment described by Long as 'one of the meanest nations on the face of the earth', and a few pages later they were characterized as a 'race'.[99] Tacky, identified as the leader of the great rebellion of 1760, was associated with the Coromantin nation in Africa; Coromantins were a 'savage race'.[100] Long was

---

[93] Hume, 'Of National Characters', 252.
[94] Long, *History*, II. 390; Johnson, *A Dictionary*.
[95] Silvia Sebastiani, 'National Characters and Race: a Scottish Enlightenment Debate', in Thomas Ahnert and Susan Manning (eds.), *Character, Self, and Sociability in the Scottish Enlightenment* (London, 2011), 187–206.
[96] Paul Stock, '"Almost a Separate Race": Racial Thought and the Idea of Europe in British Encyclopaedias and Histories, 1771–1830', *Modern Intellectual History* 8.1 (2011), 3–29.
[97] Long, *History*, II. 593.
[98] Ibid., II. 87, 198, 329, 355, 386, 504.
[99] Ibid., II. 365, 374.
[100] Ibid., II. 457, 471.

certainly unclear as to the distinctions and his slippages were symptomatic of this. Could difference be explained by climate and environment? Was it fixed in the body and blood? Two registers of racism, physical and cultural, and two terms, 'race' and 'nation', were constantly juggling in his thinking.[101]

Long was successful in his claim for the authority of his writing. Hume had taught that government was founded on opinion. Long hoped to shape that opinion on the subject of slavery and to make a successful argument as to how economics and politics could reshape the natural world: Jamaica had needed intervention from elsewhere, and this was the work of the colonists. Long was writing the island into the map of the Enlightenment, orchestrating a rhetorical performance of white mastery to persuade his readers.[102] His imagined Jamaica was to carry great weight. Those he maligned and condemned could have no hope of responding in a similar way: their refusal of his categories and contempt would necessarily take other forms. His effort to keep differences in place, however, neither could nor did succeed. And once the volumes had left his authorial hands, he could not control the meanings they produced.

Reading *The History of Jamaica* Now

Many scholars have worked on Long.[103] Historians, whether literary, intellectual, geographical or medical, critical race theorists, and Caribbean writers have all discussed, critiqued and made use of his volumes. The *History* is a standard reference point for anyone working on eighteenth-century Jamaica. *Lucky Valley* places him and his writing in his political, intellectual and familial context and argues for its contemporary relevance. When I began to work on Long, I assumed that my focus would be on his theory of racial difference and inequality. The more I read of the *History*, however, the more I came to realize that he was giving an account, from a slave-owner's perspective, of the mid-eighteenth-century economy, politics and culture of Jamaica

---

[101] On the two registers of racism, see Stuart Hall, 'The Multicultural Question', in Barnor Hesse (ed.), *Un/settled Multiculturalisms. Diasporas, Entanglements, Transruptions* (London, 2000), 209–41.

[102] O'Brien, *Narratives of Enlightenment*.

[103] Just prior to submitting this manuscript for production, I learned of Folarin Shyllon's *Edward Long's Libel of Africa: the Foundation of British Racism* (Newcastle upon Tyne, 2021). Professor Shyllon's focus is on Long's racist account of Africa and its peoples. He 'built on existing denigrations', crystallized 'and put into a coherent whole, in vivid imagery, fraudulent misrepresentations and racist ideology', and attempted 'to detach the African from the human race' (44). Shyllon discusses contemporary responses, particularly that of Ramsay, and places the book in relation to some of the historiography on slavery and abolition. As he observes, 'What Long, Edwards and other planter historians wrote about Africa and Africans tells us more about themselves than about blacks' (137).

and its relation to the metropole. He describes the organization of the plantation and the centrality of the London merchants and the system of credit and debt to the whole slavery business, from the financing of the slave traders and ships' captains to the buying of captives, crossing of the Atlantic and the purchase of enslaved people once in Jamaica. This was a business in which the key commodity was people, not sugar. The constitution and governance of the colony together with its complex dependent relation to the metropole are laid out, alongside the making of distinctions between the free and the unfree, the penal codes, and the rebellions of the enslaved, including the major uprising of 1760. The beauties of the parishes, the demarcation of those places suited to white settlers, details of the wonders of the island's natural history and the multiple commodities that could be put to use, all these are categorized. And then there is Long's account of the inhabitants, classified according to their racialized characteristics. He engaged with Enlightenment writers' cosmopolitan thinking on human difference and attempted to develop a theorization of race on the basis of his experience. He demonstrated the constitutive power of racism in shaping economic, political, social and spatial relations. Grasped as a whole, he was providing a remarkable picture of the racialization of a mid-eighteenth-century mercantile capitalist system. He aimed to represent a prosperous safe island. For Orlando Patterson, whose *Sociology of Slavery* can be read as a devastating riposte to Long, this was 'the classic period of unrestrained wealth-generation based on the merciless exploitation of the enslaved and the protracted genocide of their recruitment, replacement and growth made possible by the slave trade'. Jamaican society at this time, he continues, was 'possibly the most pitilessly cruel and exploitative in modern history'. 'One can think of few more heinous cases of a crime against humanity.'[104]

A number of concepts have been critical to my reading of the *History*, including racialization, reproduction, racial capitalism and disavowal. Long's writing shows how racialization was institutionalized in Jamaica in the mid-eighteenth century and a set of ideas about race transmitted to England. Meanings of being African and being English/European were elaborated in the everyday encounters of the plantation, where masters both coerced and depended on the enslaved. Since there is nothing natural and a-historical about racial inequalities, they have to be constantly re-made and reconfigured, as do the other great classificatory systems, of gender, class and ethnicity. Studying

---

[104] Orlando Patterson, 'Life and Scholarship in the Shadow of Slavery', introduction to the second edition of his *The Sociology of Slavery. Black Society in Jamaica, 1655–1838* [1967] (Cambridge, 2022), xiv–xxv, lx. Patterson's recent discussions of eighteenth-century slavery draw heavily on the work of Trevor Burnard; see particularly Burnard's *Mastery, Tyranny, and Desire. Thomas Thistlewood and his Slaves in the Anglo-Jamaican World* (Chapel Hill, NC, 2004); Burnard, *Jamaica in the Age of Revolution* (Philadelphia, 2020).

racialization and racisms historically illuminates the continuities and discontinuities, the new practices and new legitimations that emerge in new circumstances, the new ways of naturalizing what is not natural but historical. The cultural work of recodifying, reconfiguring and *attempting* to fix gendered, classed and racialized boundaries for new colonial times was what Long did in his *History*. He learned the difference between black and white in Jamaica. Growing up in England he knew he was English, he learned his class and gendered identity, but his whiteness did not matter in the way that it did once he reached Jamaica and learned the extent to which white skin carried power. He only learned the scale of that power when he became a colonizer. Cultural identity is always a matter of becoming as well as of being and Long's sense of himself changed as he became a planter, a West Indian. His establishment of property rights over land and people, his everyday violent management of the plantation, his witnessing of the spectacular punishments for those who threatened the status quo, his activities as a colonial botanist, his domestic organization of his family and household, his activities as a legislator in the assembly, all these depended on his white skin. His body and skin, 'the grosser physical differences of color, hair and bone' as Du Bois named them, underpinned race, not because they correlated with genetic differentiation but because they were clearly defined to the eye: they were in the field of vision and seeing was believing.[105] Colour mattered: it had become a determining criterion for classifying humanity by the mid-eighteenth century. Linnaeus had divided humanity into four colours: red, white, yellow and black. It was at the heart of the development of the textile industry; chemists worked on the nature and formation of colours; questions as to pigmentation and the making of colour interested natural historians and anatomists.[106] In eighteenth-century Jamaica, white skin meant power over black people, black skin meant servitude. The habits of whiteness were learned on a daily basis across multiple sites. Whether serving in the militia, sitting in the assembly as a member of the propertied elite with a right to legislate, or assuming the sexual ownership of enslaved women, slave-owners enacted daily their racialized identities in relation to subjected others. Long was well placed to illuminate the ways in which this particular capitalist regime at this particular time across the fateful triangle of England, West Africa and Jamaica functioned, not through sameness, but through difference and differentiation, wage labour and enslaved labour, men, women and children.

---

[105] W. E. B. Du Bois, 'The Conservation of Races', in *W. E. B. Du Bois Speaks: Speeches and Addresses, 1890–1919* [1897], ed. Philip S. Foner (New York, 1970), 75. For Stuart Hall's discussion of Du Bois, see 'Race: the Sliding Signifier', in Hall, *The Fateful Triangle. Race, Ethnicity, Nation*, ed. Kobena Mercer (Cambridge, MA, 2017), 31–79.

[106] Schaub and Sebastiani, *Race et histoire*.

As well as describing the workings of the economy and the state, he also explained something of how the system was reproduced. Power lay in control of both the bodily and social reproductive practices of the enslaved. Their familial and social ties had no legitimacy. They could be separated, and sold to settle a debt; marriages had no formal recognition; women had to submit sexually and children could be taken away. Enslaved women bore the cruel double burden of labouring in the cane fields or the great house and reproducing the next generation of the enslaved from their own bodies.[107] At the same time, the marital and inheritance practices of white families were vital to capital accumulation and to the survival of white patriarchal domination. Blood ties, of both the enslaved and the colonists, were critical to the forging of slavery and to the formation of planter capital. Given the dearth of commercial, professional and financial infrastructures and the vulnerability to disease and early death, familial relations were a touchstone of commercial as well as professional trustworthiness, limiting risks in times of huge risk. For the Longs, family was business and business was family. The three branches of the family established by the early eighteenth century, mercantile, landowning and slave-holding, supported each other across generations. The Long family were ever conscious of their genealogy, knew where their family members were buried and memorialized, and were able to document their own histories. The stark contrast with those enslaved men and women who were buried in Lucky Valley, together with their dead infants – their burial grounds unmarked and unknown, their names only recorded, if at all, in surviving indentures and deeds of sale – must be remembered.

Long, I came to understand, was giving an account of what we now call *racial capitalism*. This has become a much-used term in our time, a way of describing the interconnected systems of racialized and capitalist processes and formations. I use the term as a provocation, to explore the relations between the forms of racism and the forms of capitalism that were articulated across eighteenth-century Britain, West Africa and the Caribbean that enabled sugar to become an article of mass consumption and mercantile and planter capital to accumulate.[108] Long's choice was to represent Jamaica as settled both internally and in its relation to the metropole: politics, law, governance, commerce, all at one with each other. But such a totality could never be seamless. The articulations between one level or site and another were fractious. The political could be in tension with the economic, the legal with the commercial; each had its racialized practices embedded in a wider cultural

---

[107] The scholarship of Black feminist writers has been critical to a better understanding of the centrality of reproduction to the plantation economy. See particularly Jennifer L. Morgan, *Laboring Women. Reproduction and Gender in New World Slavery* (Philadelphia, 2004) and *Reckoning with Slavery. Gender, Kinship and Capitalism in the Early Black Atlantic* (Durham, NC, 2021).

[108] Catherine Hall, 'Racial Capitalism: What's in a Name?', *HWJ* 95 (2022), 5–21.

common sense, the meanings of which depended on reinforcing racial difference. Each component or level, the colonial state or the plantation economy, had its relative autonomy but derived its rationale from its relation to the whole, the slave society.[109] Tensions and fractures could be both systemic and experienced individually. Planters and merchants, for instance, needed each other, but their interests frequently diverged. Long's attempt to theorize racial difference was embedded in his experience as a slave-owner, but his insistence on *essential* difference and his disgust at miscegenation were in tension with the need he recognized for a population of free people of colour, 'mulattos', to act as a middle rank, willing to demarcate themselves from enslaved black people. His belief in the necessity for a clear binary was in contradiction with the political and economic needs of the colony. British laws, such as the Navigation Acts, were constitutive of economic relations that facilitated Atlantic commerce. But the absence of a positive law on slavery, legalizing it in the metropole, triggered the crisis over the status of an enslaved man who escaped his master in London and led to the recognition by the slave-owners that the law would not protect their enslaved property. Metropolitan and colonial interests were not always the same: colonists who were 'free-born Englishmen' wanted parity, but failed to get it. Absentees and residents shared an economic interest but were differently situated politically. Enslaved people refused their captivity in multiple different ways, from rebelling and running away to pleading sickness, despite the systemic violence and coercion they inhabited. In the end the centre could not hold. But the picture that Long tried to construct in the *History* was that it did and it could: the cracks were papered over, anxieties sidelined, rebellions crushed. 'Racial capitalism', he wanted his readers to believe, was working.

A new interest in the history of capitalism was sparked by the international financial crisis triggered by the collapse of Lehman Brothers in 2008. The fragility of the western capitalist system was apparent, and triumphalist visions of its global dominance, facilitated by the fall of the communist system of the Soviet Union, seemed less secure. Political theorists, sociologists, historians and others began to consider once again the past, present and future of free market capitalism. Those influenced by Marxism built on earlier work and focused on the interconnections between capitalist exploitation and racial oppression. Marx's analysis of capitalism was based on nineteenth-century industrial production and assumed that 'free' labour – waged labour – was essential. Colonialism and Atlantic slavery fuelled a form of 'primitive accumulation', characteristic of a system which he saw as a prelude to industrial capitalism. 'The discovery of gold and silver in America, the extirpation,

---

[109] The notion of articulation draws on Stuart Hall's use of the term. See particularly Hall, *Selected Writings on Marxism*, ed. and with commentary by Gregor McLennan (London, 2021), esp. 165–7 for McLennan's discussion.

enslavement and entombment in mines of the aboriginal population, the beginning of the conquest and looting of the East Indies, the turning of Africa into a warren for the commercial hunting of black-skins', he famously wrote, 'signalised the rosy dawn of the era of capitalist production. These idyllic proceedings are the chief momenta of primitive accumulation.'[110] There has been much debate, and no agreement, as to the extent to which Marx grasped the significance of slavery and the slave economies to the development of capitalism.[111] Some still maintain a distinction between the 'primitive accumulation' associated with enslaved labour on the plantation and the 'free' labour of the factory system. The Marxist historical sociologist Robin Blackburn defines the mercantile capitalism associated with Atlantic slavery as 'extended primitive accumulation'. The plantations, he writes, were 'dependent and hybrid socioeconomic enterprises … an artificial extension of mercantile and manufacturing capital in the age of capitalist transition, extending their reach at a time when fully capitalist social relations were still struggling into existence'.[112] Since the labour was coerced it was not a fully capitalist system. Others disagree. The Caribbean economist Lloyd Best and his co-author Kari Levitt understand the plantation economy as a fully capitalist system. 'The Caribbean was the place where metropolitan capital established production of commodities for sale in world markets with slave labour, which was itself a traded commodity … they were the creation of metropolitan adventurer investors and the unfree labour of slaves.'[113] Eric Williams, they continue, convincingly demonstrated that the slavery of the plantation economy was a mechanism for the transfer of capital to the metropole, a process of capital accumulation: 'In no meaningful sense was plantation slavery a "pre-capitalist" mode of production.'[114]

The term 'racial capitalism' was first employed in 1976 by two South African opponents of apartheid. Martin Legassick and David Hemson challenged the view on the left that since apartheid was in direct conflict with economic

---

[110] Karl Marx, *Capital* (3 vols., Moscow, 1961), I. 761.
[111] This is a debate that is unlikely ever to be resolved. See, for example, Robbie Shilliam, 'Decolonizing the *Manifesto*: Communism and the Slave Analogy', in Terrell Carver and James Farr (eds.), *The Cambridge Companion to The Communist Manifesto* (Cambridge, 2015), 195–213; Nikhil Pal Singh, 'On Race, Violence and So-Called Primitive Accumulation', *Social Text* 128 34.3 (2016), 27–50; Stephanie Smallwood, 'What Slavery Tells us about Marx', *Boston Review*, 21 February 2018.
[112] Robin Blackburn, *The Making of New World Slavery. From the Baroque to the Modern, 1492–1800* (London, 1997), 376.
[113] Lloyd Best and Kari Polanyi Levitt, *The Theory of Plantation Economy. A Historical and Institutional Approach to Caribbean Economic Development* (Kingston, Jamaica, 2009), 10–11.
[114] Ibid., 116.

growth, this would eventually bring its destruction.[115] A racialized labour force, they argued, was essential to capitalist accumulation: racism and capitalism must be fought together. The term was taken up by Cedric Robinson, who was critical of the limits of Marxism and argued for the importance of what he named the Black Radical Tradition and the insistence those writers placed on the agency of Black people in challenging their own exploitation and oppression. 'The racial order developed in feudal Europe' and the tendency to differentiate, not homogenize, defining differences as racial, meant that 'racialism would inevitably permeate the social structures emergent from capitalism'.[116] A capitalist system required inequality for accumulation to be possible; racialized, ethnicized, gendered and class differences could all be utilized. Neither C. L. R. James nor Eric Williams ever used the term 'racial capitalism', but they understood Saint-Domingue and the British West Indies as capitalist formations organized on the basis of racial difference. In the wake of 2008 and new forms of Black activism, concrete case studies are now beginning to elaborate our understanding of how the connections between forms of racism and forms of capitalism operate in specific historical contexts. Walter Johnson's study of the Mississippi cotton economy, based on a re-reading and reinterpretation of Marx, emphasizes the intertwining of free labour and slave labour as parts of one integrated but differentiated system. The metrics of the Liverpool exchange, he argues, penetrated the labour practices of Louisiana, and the labour practices of Louisiana shaped the global market. 'Rather than a pure form – "capitalism" or "slavery" – they united, formatted, and measured the actually existing capitalism and slavery of the nineteenth century.'[117] In his study of St Louis, he extends the analysis to the history of Native American genocide and the expropriation of land. Building on W. E. B. Du Bois's understanding of the conquest of the Americas and the slave trade as something new, something unprecedented, something world-making, rooted in White entitlement and Black subjection, he argues that racism and capitalism were organically connected but not identical. 'At bottom', he writes, 'the history of racial capitalism has been one in which white supremacy justified the terms of imperial dispossession and capitalist exploitation.'[118]

But claims and enactments of white dominance and power were, and are, fuelled by dread. Elsa Goveia, the Guyanese historian of the Caribbean,

---

[115] Martin Legassick and David Hemson, *Foreign Investment and the Reproduction of Racial Capitalism* (Cape Town, 1976).
[116] Cedric J. Robinson, *Black Marxism. The Making of the Black Radical Tradition* (London, 1983), 2–3.
[117] Walter Johnson, *River of Dark Dreams. Slavery and Empire in the Cotton Kingdom* (Cambridge, MA, 2013), 10.
[118] Walter Johnson, *The Broken Heart of America. St Louis and the Violent History of the United States* (New York, 2020), 6.

understood Long's assertion of superiority as driven by his own feelings of uncertainty about slavery which he wanted to deny, and his hope that he could absolve himself from his anxieties. What if the critics were right and the slave-owners horribly cruel? But did he protest his innocence too much? Such thoughts could be put aside, displaced, by blaming ignorant overseers, 'bad apples', not men such as himself. His assumptions about African inferiority, she suggests, eased these concerns. If they were so different, they deserved servitude. His image of the African was distorted by fear. His *History* shed 'a glaring light upon the influence of slavery as it affected both slave-holder and slave'.[119] One 'glaring light' foregrounded by Long concerned the states of anxiety suffered by slave-owners. 'Anxiety affects men in this country in proportion to their sensibility, and to its duration,' he wrote.

> When once it has taken a firm hold, it is generally productive of mortal consequences. Multitudes have expired here under the pressure of this fatal cause. Hurried by levity of disposition or want of thought, into an expensive way of living, or imprudent schemes and pursuits; distress has poured in upon them at once like a deluge. Fretted, and wearied out at length with the conflict, and closely beset on all sides with implacable creditors, they have yielded passively to their fate, and sunk down into the grave, under a load that was too grievous for their mind to support ...[120]

Men dying of anxiety in their multitudes is a striking notion: what state of mind was he describing? His conscious focus was on debt, with the 'implacable creditors' as the instrument of destruction. But money was not the only source of anxiety. Planters faced a variety of natural disasters from rats to rain, drought and hurricanes. But when listing these, the spectre of fire slipped into his mind, which could be caused by 'revenge, or the drunken rage of the Negroes'.[121] In slave societies, after all, as he recognized, 'a constant virtual hostility exists', enough to cause any slave-owner anxiety.[122] Long's representation of a benevolent form of slavery, similar, he liked to think, to Grotius's description of a 'legitimate, equitable species of servitude ... founded on the principles of reason', was haunted by other spectres he repressed: the hungry, the superfluous, the sick, the disposable, the ghosts.[123] They had to be split off, not thought about, disposed of in the recesses of his mind, or, in the case of those Coromantins, the most dangerous of the Africans, kept off the island.

White power and mastery rested on the refusal to recognize the full humanity of those they enslaved. The new world of slavery, of unlimited authority

---

[119] Elsa V. Goveia, *A Study on the Historiography of the British West Indies to the End of the Nineteenth Century* (Mexico City, 1956), 62.
[120] Long, *History*, II. 543.
[121] BL Add MS 12404, f. 352.
[122] Ibid., f. 113.
[123] Long, *History*, II. 402.

over others, was lived externally with all the panoply of the whips, guns and gallows, but it was lived internally too. Long's ability to see and not see, to deny realities, was fundamental to who he was, what he wrote in his *History*, how he constructed his white selfhood. The concept of *disavowal*, first articulated by Freud and subsequently developed by a range of other psychoanalytic thinkers, can help us to think about how racism works. It has helped me to grasp the effects of racialization on those who practised it on others through systems of violence and coercion, as well as in different ways upon themselves. Remember Zachary Macaulay fleeing Jamaica in fear of becoming 'pitiless'. He feared losing his sense of the reality of the violence of slavery and becoming a different kind of man, lacking in empathy for others. Colonists, on their first arrival in Jamaica, would be shocked by the brutalities they witnessed, but would learn not to see them. Freud asked, how do we remember, forget, and reconfigure the past? How can we make a thing appear never to have happened? We can 'know', according to this account, something unconsciously even as we are consciously 'innocent' of the knowledge. Freud's thinking was based on the insight that the mind is always conflicted, and that we actively rid ourselves (sometimes unbeknownst to ourselves) of certain mental contents. The body may speak another 'unconscious' story, with uncontrolled coughing, sleep problems or migraines. By splitting off aspects of our feelings, we may misrecognize ourselves, avoid pain, bury our guilt and disclaim our desires. Freud's emphasis is on an unconscious process, the rejection of a reality that is potentially traumatic. Forgetting is understood as actively produced, not just a matter of failed remembering; rather it is willed, unconsciously. Forgetting is deliberate: the knowledge or event is denied and refused, then repressed. Disavowal is connected with a denial of external realities, a refusal to think what is unthinkable, a wish to put aside what cannot be integrated. It operates as a defence mechanism, protecting the self. Statements of denial are assertions that something did not happen, does not exist, is not true, or is not known about.[124] Disavowal is often linked to the notion of a 'blind eye', or to important clues as to what is hidden in 'plain sight', colloquial expressions acknowledging disavowal in everyday life. Acts of disavowal always exist, argued Freud, alongside recognition. 'Whenever we are in a position to study them, they turn out to be half-measures, incomplete attempts at detachment from reality. The disavowal is always supplemented by an acknowledgement.'[125] Disavowal, I suggest, was and is a crucial aspect of racist thinking, allowing racists to see and not see at the very same time. Long's writing provides an important example of how this works. He could be a loving family man and

---

[124] Catherine Hall and Daniel Pick, 'Thinking about Denial', *HWJ* 84 (2017), 1–23.
[125] Sigmund Freud, *An Outline of Psycho-analysis* [1940], in *The Standard Edition of the Complete Psychological Works of Sigmund Freud*, ed. James Strachey in collaboration with Anna Freud (24 vols., London, 1964), XXIII. 203–4.

a buyer and seller of human beings, valuing others only as 'hands' and relying on everyday humiliations and the use of physical force to extract their labour. Disavowal was necessary to his functioning in the plantation world. It was a way of dealing with anxiety and fear, a fear that was rooted not only in the sense of a terror of Black retribution but also in an inkling, refused and repressed, that the entitlement that was claimed was illegitimate.

Disavowal requires splitting, an unconscious process developed by Melanie Klein with its roots in infancy. Faced with terrifying feelings of anxiety brought on by hunger, frustration and helplessness, the tiny infant uses psychic mechanisms such as splitting and projection to cope with the dangerously contradictory and intense feelings of love and hate stirred up by the state of dependency. Splitting is a mental function which separates, hoping to keep apart the good aspects and experience of a mother (her life-affirming and loving capacities) from the bad (her hated capacity to frustrate and deprive). It is only through a process of maturation that the infant is gradually able to internalize, integrate and reconcile these experiences and feelings with the same person: the mother that I love, admire and depend on is the same mother that I hate, envy and wish to destroy. Projection is one way in which the infant expels or gets rid of states of discomfort and anxiety. Intense impulses, thoughts and feelings associated with good and bad experiences are projected out or split off in efforts to rid the infant of anxiety and protect the immature self from feeling overwhelmed. In this way, feelings, qualities and states of mind (as, for example, aggression, envy, vulnerability) can be attributed to and identified with others – no longer recognized as belonging to the self, who now feels masterful. This process, Klein argued, in which unwanted parts of the self were forcefully pushed into others, would inevitably give rise to the feeling that the person or world projected into would in turn become hostile and retaliatory, threatening to return in cruel and vengeful ways. 'If the projection is predominantly hostile', she wrote, 'real empathy and understanding of the other is impaired.' In such a state, the mind is invaded by paranoid anxieties of persecution, and the risk of such defences hardening becomes more likely.[126]

The projection saved the self from any confrontation with the contradictions and ambivalences, a confrontation that would be necessary for a more integrated sense of self. These psychic mechanisms are in play throughout life. Individual psychic fears could be solidified in the external world. Since the self is only known through its difference from the 'other', being White and being Black only gained meaning through co-constitution.[127] Long only fully

---

[126] Melanie Klein, 'Our Adult World and its Roots in Infancy' (1959), in *Envy and Gratitude and other Work* (London, 1988), 253. See also 'Notes on Some Schizoid Mechanisms' (1946). Thanks to Becky Hall for help with these formulations.

[127] A very striking example of this is the practice by some slave-owners of including in their portraits their family crests, including the heads of black men, usually labelled as 'Moors'.

understood himself as White, with the omnipotence this carried with it, when in Jamaica. Much racial stereotyping and violence arose, as Fanon argued, from the refusal of the White man to give recognition to the Black person; rather he projected on to that 'other' the 'bad' aspects of himself: his voracious sexuality, greed, envy, violence and cruelty. Colonizers practised 'a systematic negation of the other person and a furious determination to deny the other person all attributes of humanity'.[128] But disavowal, that knowing and not knowing, allowed for the possibility of embracing contradictory beliefs. Africans were ugly, savage and primitive, 'brutes' to be tamed, yet, at the very same time, they were different, strange, and had to be thought about, had their uses. Hopefully they could be placed and contained, but there was always the fear that they could not, that the hatred and anger would come back to get you. Hence the reiterated fear of colonists that the colonized planned 'white extirpation'.

As an adolescent Long had been left behind, alone, by his family, when they returned to Jamaica. He experienced depression, a state of mind that in adulthood he worked to dispel. Dangers must be contained, strict boundaries were needed, matter should not be out of place. Pollution and degeneration were always threatening: swamps encroaching on pasture, mosquitoes on domestic life, sexual desire on 'proper' reproductive practices. Black and White were different and should remain so. He was skilled at avoidance and repression, mobilizing his writing to steer clear of dangerous areas and focus on safer territories.[129] Constitutional issues could distract from a bloody history; numbers could deaden the horrors of the slave trade; planters could be the mainspring of the plantation; landscape and the picturesque could keep him safely away from the whip and the cane fields; colonial botany and systems of classification could detract attention from enslaved informants; African oath taking and obeah could provide an explanation for rebellion. He could reflect on 'the prodigious enigma' of blackness but must keep his safe distance.[130] The psychic energy involved in trying to keep boundaries intact that were in reality persistently breached must have been significant: containment involved much work. After the return to the 'mother country' in 1769, Long spent much of his time, at least until the early 1790s, pouring out volumes of words, published and unpublished, puzzling over what it meant to be human and in justification of who he was and what he had done.

---

[128] Frantz Fanon, *The Wretched of the Earth* (New York, 1966), 203.
[129] Thanks to Markman Ellis for this thought.
[130] A term used by the French anatomist Barrère. Henry Louis Gates Jr and Andrew S. Curran (eds.), *Who's Black and Why? A Hidden Chapter from the Eighteenth-Century Invention of Race* (Cambridge, MA, 2022), 190; Curran, *The Anatomy of Blackness. Science and Slavery in an Age of Enlightenment* (Baltimore, 2011).

Summary of Chapters

Part I: *Growing up English*

1   A Gentleman's Son

Chapter 1 provides a brief account of the Long family from the time of conquest in 1655 to the mid-eighteenth century, their marriages and children, their acquisition of property in land and enslaved people, their politics. It introduces the main cast of characters in the Long/Beeston family and what became the three distinct branches: the slave-owners in Jamaica, the merchant family in London and the landed gentry in Suffolk. Edward's two great-grandfathers, Samuel Long and William Beeston, were founding figures of Jamaica as a slave society. Samuel Long's acquisition of what was to become Longville and his purchase of Lucky Valley set the seal on the Jamaican family's ownership of property and enslaved people, the source of their wealth for generations to come. What did it mean to be a colonist? How did they manage their lives across the two islands? Samuel's great-grandson Edward, born in 1734, grew up in England. What was his political and familial inheritance? How was he educated?

2   The Young Englishman

Edward, aged nineteen, arrived in London destined for the law. Living as a student on a meagre allowance, he observed London society from its fringes and began to write a periodical and fiction for publication. What were his themes and preoccupations? How did he imagine genteel masculinity? What did it mean to be a young Englishman in the middle of the Seven Years War? Faced with the untimely death of his father in 1757 and the news of his modest inheritance, the advice was to head for Jamaica where he might hope to secure a fortune.

Part II: *The Lineaments of Racial Capitalism*

3   The Plantation

Long arrived in Jamaica in 1758 hoping to make money and be able to return to England soon. The plantation would be the source of his wealth, and a settlement with his older brother Robert secured him in the ownership of Lucky Valley. Having speedily made a propitious marriage into the white elite, he devoted himself for the next eleven years to every aspect of the management of a sugar plantation, all of which he subsequently described in his *History*. What picture does he give us of the planter's life, constantly 'smoothed by the allurements of profit'? What work did he do? How did he see himself? How did he acquire enslaved labour and on what gendered and racialized practices did he organize it? What did he think about the failure of enslaved women to reproduce themselves, thus threatening future prosperity?

4   The Merchant House

Making money from plantations meant engaging in the circuit of West India trade regulated through a mercantilist system that protected the interests of the 'mother country'. Long needed to demonstrate to his metropolitan readership that Jamaica brought great wealth to Britain and that the production of sugar depended on slavery. His Uncle Beeston headed the merchant house of Drake and Long in the heart of the City of London, and Long was well aware of the centrality of merchants and the use of bills of exchange to facilitate the sugar and slavery business. Given the increasing criticism of the conditions of the slave trade by the early 1770s, what picture did he provide of it? How did he describe the circuit of the West India trade? How did the merchants negotiate their relationship to slavery? What was the significance of the system of credit and debt upon which this mercantile capitalist formation depended?

5   Reproducing Capital: the Long Family

The productive and reproductive labour of the enslaved produced one form of capital; the gendered organization of marriage and inheritance amongst the planters and merchants produced another. If families such as the Longs were to survive, secure their land and increase their wealth, they had to reproduce themselves and ensure the continuity of their line: their hope was to establish a dynasty. Could colonists simply reproduce the patterns of the landed English gentry? Did the mercantile branch of the family operate differently? How was property gendered in such a way as to assure the creation and accumulation of wealth? How was inheritance organized and what part did marriage play? What does it mean to name White women 'reproducers of freedom'? And how were these racialized structures lived? What conceptions of marriage and family life were seen as necessary to an ordered colonial society? How did Long reconcile his belief in monogamous marriage and an ordered family for people such as himself with the scale of irregular relations that characterized Jamaica? He loved his wife and children, did much to support his mother and siblings. At the very same time he refused those relationships to the enslaved: they were different.

Part III: Making a Slave Society

6   Colonizing Geographies

Long was committed to a depiction of Jamaica as a successful 'commercial society' where white people could live comfortably on the labour of the enslaved. How did he map the island for his readers in such a way as to reassure them that the boundaries between the free and the unfree were secure? What picture did he provide of its defences, against both external and internal enemies? What and who inspired his poetic renditions of the beauties of this tropical paradise in which art and nature combined their glories? How could the island's fecundity be harnessed to profit? His racialized cartography utilized maps, engravings, tables and listings of commodities to illustrate boundless potential. Nature could be improved, tamed and catalogued, as people were. How could the island become more self-sufficient; what seeds might be transplanted, what crops flourish? Alarming tales of colonists' mortality could be challenged, mosquitoes kept at bay. White settlers could live a healthy life if only they would embrace moderation in all things. As an Enlightenment man, an enthusiastic reader of natural histories, Long was keen to represent the island as *en route* to a more civilized and ordered state, with more roads, more maps, more barracks, more settlements. But, he had to admit, it was a society sorely in need of more public virtue.

7 Colonizing the State

A slave society needed different laws from those of the 'mother country', and from the earliest days legal systems demarcated between the free and the enslaved. The Whig hegemony based on consent that Long had grown up with could not be practised in Jamaica: only dominance and coercion were possible. This entailed an almost absolute authority for the slave-owner over 'his property', but with the additional support, when necessary, of the colonial state. Two years after Long had settled on the island, a major rebellion broke out, named by the colonists after one of its leaders, Tacky. It could only be defeated with the aid of the British army and navy and the Maroons. The events of 1760 were critical to Long's understanding of racial difference and the security needs of a slave society. As an active member of the House of Assembly and intimately involved in dealing with the aftermath of the rebellion, his representation of it in the *History* was designed to clear the slave-owners of all blame. He named a particular group of Africans, 'Coromantees', as the villains. While fully recognizing the need for metropolitan military, naval and economic support, he also carried the mantle of great-grandfather Samuel, a profound believer in the rights of 'free-born Englishmen' in their struggles with an overmighty crown. What did the struggles over prerogative in the 1760s signify? How did Long understand the relationship between the 'mother country' and the island? What autonomy could be secured for the colonial state in its mission to defend white planter power? What judgements did he make of metropolitan authority?

8 Theorizing Racial Difference

During his eleven years in Jamaica, Long was, like other planters, *practising* racialization – enacting racial difference in every public and private space, living his whiteness as power. But he was also clearly reflecting on it, observing it, thinking about it. He was horrified by the Somerset trial: slave-owners could no longer rely on the law to secure their rights over enslaved property.

Mansfield had discovered, he wrote in his vitriolic polemic, 'the art of *washing the black-a-moor white*'. But this could not be; Black people could not become White. When it came to the *History*, his task, as he saw it, was to persuade his audience, and himself, that Blacks were essentially, *naturally*, different from Whites. What tools did he utilize? What was the basis of his claim? How did the body figure? How could he combine his insistence on natural difference with his conviction that plantation life civilized Africans, that creoles could become good servants to their masters? How did his horror of miscegenation sit with his hope that mulattoes might provide a necessary bridge between Whites and Negroes?

Epilogue

Long lived in England for more than forty years until his death in 1813. How did the American War affect his understanding? How successful were the West Indians in delaying the abolition of the slave trade? Why did he never complete the second edition of his *History*?

He endeavoured to clinch his argument as to the essential inequality of White and Black with an attempted demolition of the free black Jamaican Francis Williams. Williams had been educated in England, was a poet and mathematician, and had established a school for black boys in Spanish Town. He had been cited by Hume in 1753 as providing an example of how 'Negroes' could never do more than mimic white Europeans. For Long, Williams represented the terrifying spectre of African claims for equality: he claimed legal rights, could write Latin poetry, possessed a library of Enlightenment scholarship, taught his pupils Newtonian principles, dressed like a gentleman. It was essential to undermine him, to pour scorn on all his pretensions. But in so doing, Long demonstrated how his own privileged whiteness rested on sand. Only by denigrating blackness could he maintain his own sense of an entitled self. He needed that 'otherness' to know himself.

PART I

Growing up English

Chapters 1 and 2 describe the Long family's history as slave-owners in Jamaica and landowners in England from the time of the English invasion of the island in 1655. They follow Edward Long from his birth in England in 1734 to his boyhood in Cornwall and his young manhood in London. What kind of preparation did the young Englishman have for his departure for Jamaica in 1757 and a future as a planter and a historian?

1

A Gentleman's Son

Edward Long had a powerful identification with his great-grandfather. A 'virtuous patriot', in his description, capable of 'cool forbearance ... good sense and manly fortitude'. A man who had successfully resisted the tyrannical machinations of the crown and defended the rights of free-born Englishmen.[1] Proud of the identity of Jamaican patriot, Colonel Samuel Long was at the very same time an *Englishman* committed to the colony which he helped to create. He was a vivid figure in the imagination of his great-grandson: a worthy founder of a colonial dynasty, with a strong sense of belonging, both to the mother country and to the island colony. What was more, a second great-grandfather, Sir William Beeston, was also a key figure in the formation of the colony. Samuel's son Charles had married Beeston's daughter Jane, creating the Long/Beeston dynasty. In writing the *History*, the narrative of a colony from its birth and infancy to what he hoped was its maturity, Edward's great-grandfathers' joint commitment to the twin foundations of a plantation society – African slavery and white freedom – were his guiding principles. Slavery and freedom were inextricably connected, a racialized regime of bondage with enslaved black labour the basis for white fortune making. 'Servitude was *inevitably* necessary' in a plantation society, he wrote, since white men could not work in the tropics. 'Planters, or owners of slaves' must be 'steddily supported in the possession of British freedom'.[2] Long's own family history provided the framework for his history of the colony. His great-grandfathers, however, were the only members of that family to appear directly in its pages. The Long family story with its cycles of success and failure was the backdrop to the story he chose to tell. There was nothing secure about either the family or the colony, no simple story of progress. Long was doing his best to secure both.

Samuel Long left England in 1655 as a lad of seventeen, serving as a lieutenant on the Western Design, the expedition that Oliver Cromwell had sent to challenge the Spanish empire. A military disaster in Hispaniola was offset by the capture of Jamaica, an island that was not well defended by the Spanish. Long had acted as secretary to the commissioners appointed by

---

[1] Long, *History*, I. 199–201.
[2] Ibid., I. 5–6.

Cromwell and was related to Colonel Doyley, who became the key figure in the efforts to expel the Spanish and establish a settlement. Samuel Long was to be his closest aide. The Western Design was a significant new venture for the Protectorate, inspired by Cromwell's ambitions to disrupt Spanish power in the Caribbean and his godly hopes for a Protestant empire. 'Wee thinke,' wrote Cromwell, 'and it is much designed amongst us, to strive with the Spanyarde for the mastery of all those seas.'[3] It was gold and silver, trade and imperial competition that drove this first attempt by the English state to conquer the colony of another power in the Americas: such ventures had previously been left to individuals and companies.[4] The men who ruled England in the 1650s, argues Carla Pestana, welcomed the opportunity to implement their enthusiasm for trade and for imperial expansion through territorial acquisition, policies which they had been advocating for some time. The Navigation Act of 1651 had opened the Atlantic trade to all English merchants, hoping to build markets, national wealth and a centralized commercial empire. Colonists would have a shared English identity, belonging to the Protectorate, no longer subjects of the crown, committed to the suppression of tyranny and the protection of liberty.[5]

The Spanish had been expected to capitulate, given the size of the invading military forces. But they fought a five-year guerrilla war supported by the enslaved Africans they had brought to the island: African slavery was a well-established part of Spanish and Portuguese practice. Very few of the island's original Taino inhabitants had survived the combination of disease and the oppressive labour regimes of the Spanish.[6] The Africans effectively disappeared into independent enclaves.[7] For the majority of the English soldiers, this would have been their first direct encounter with African otherness. Some would have fought in Ireland, as the leaders of the Western Design had, and could draw on well-established tropes of barbarism and savagery. But the Irish were white, a different kind of enemy from 'the Blacks', as Major-General Sedgwick described them to Secretary Thurloe in 1656. There were many who were likely to prove thorns and pricks in our sides, he wrote, living as they did in the mountains and woods, a natural life for them. They were growing increasingly bold and bloody, had 'no *moral sense* nor understanding what

---

[3] Cited in Carla Gardina Pestana, *The English Conquest of Jamaica. Oliver Cromwell's Bid for Empire* (Cambridge, MA, 2017), 7.
[4] S. A. G. Taylor, *The Western Design. An Account of Cromwell's Expedition to the Caribbean* (Kingston, Jamaica, 1965).
[5] Carla Gardina Pestana, *The English Atlantic in an Age of Revolution, 1640–1661* (Cambridge, MA, 2004).
[6] Lesley-Gail Atkinson (ed.), *The Earliest Inhabitants: the Dynamics of the Jamaican Taino* (Kingston, Jamaica, 2006).
[7] Long saw 'These Blacks' as the ancestors of later Maroon communities. Long, *History*, II. 339–40.

the laws and customs of civil nations mean'. They would either have to be destroyed or the English would have to come to terms with them, 'else they will prove a great discouragement to the settling of people here'.[8] Already there was that sense of difference, named in terms of both skin colour and culture, of people who were outside the pale and deserved little in terms of treatment.

In the early years of occupation, the English army had limited control on the island. The naval commander had left, wages were not paid and food was extremely scarce. This was garrison government under martial law. The military campaign was badly conducted, and the colonial venture had not been thought through. Cromwell's expectation was that Jamaica would become a profitable settled colony with a diverse economy: some wives and children had accompanied the Western Design. Edward Doyley, who was soon the only surviving senior officer but had no official authorization for much of the period, sent constant requests to the metropole for money and supplies. He faced a range of problems, culminating in two mutinies in 1656 and 1660 over army pay and the impossibility of return. 'I have had a very hard taske,' he recorded in 1661, 'to command Sould^{r}s without pay Seamen without provision and the vulgar without Lawe.'[9] Food shortages made some planting a priority, but transforming soldiers into farmers was no easy task. Many officers were opposed to the idea of granting land to the rank and file, the landless, and would have preferred them to be forced 'to dig the earth as their slaves'.[10] The mortality rate was extremely high, exacerbated by disease and hunger. England's domestic political turbulence, however, meant that Jamaica was never at the top of the government's concerns.[11] When Edward Long came to record the early history of Jamaica, he gave much credit to Doyley, a family relative, for his military abilities, his wise government and his opposition to those officers who were hostile to the idea of soldiers becoming settlers. Doyley was a man whose support was likely to have been crucial to Samuel Long's place in this frontier society, peopled in 1654 by an estimated 4,500 pioneers far away from the metropole and from the immediacy of imperial power, depending already on 1,400 'Negroes'.[12]

Following the Restoration of Charles II in 1660, colonists were once again subjects of the crown. Doyley was instructed to establish a council, set up a civil government, survey the island and record land grants. Charles II and his brother the Duke of York had colonial ambitions, hoping for new arenas of royal power and wealth. The Navigation Act was confirmed in 1660 and

---

[8] Ibid., II. 339. Thurloe was the secretary to the Council of State for the Protectorate.
[9] [To Commissioners of the Admiralty and Navy] 22 January 1660[/I], HCA 1/9, pt 1, no. 2, 3. Cited in Carla Gardina Pestana, 'State Formation from the Vantage Point of Early English Jamaica: the Neglect of Edward Doyley', *Journal of British Studies*, 56 (2017), 498.
[10] Long, *History*, I. 259, 281.
[11] Pestana, 'State Formation'.
[12] Long, *History*, I. 375.

imperial protection was named as a policy.[13] The Protectorate's emphasis on the commercial utility of the colonies was reaffirmed, but now alongside an insistence on crown control. 'The monarchy was testing its strength in a field far removed from the scrutiny of a factious, turbulent Parliament.'[14] This meant testing its strength with the colonists too. What kind of colony was it to be? What rights would the colonists have? As the first English colony to be taken by conquest, the terms of government were different from those elsewhere. Martial law had ended and Charles II was interested in new sources of revenue, 'our Island of Jamaica being a most pleasant and fertile Soil, and situated commodiously for Trade and Commerce'.[15] Wanting to encourage emigration, he had proclaimed 'that all children of natural-born subjects of England, to be born in Jamaica, shall, from their respective births, be reputed to be, and shall be, *free denisons of England*'. They were 'to have the same privileges, to all intents and purposes, as the free-born subjects of England'.[16] This was a confirmation that English law would be upheld in Jamaica, vital to the settlers who needed to know that their liberties and property were secure. But a distinction was made between those born in England, 'natural-born subjects', and those born in Jamaica, 'denisons', reliant on the grace of the king.[17] From the monarch's point of view, he was granting a privilege to those in a conquered country, for the crown held ultimate authority: colonies would be economically and politically subordinate. For the colonists, it was a right not a privilege: as free-born Englishmen, many of whom had had republican sympathies, they would not be subject to arbitrary power. Conflicts over this erupted in the late 1670s, the 1720s and the mid-1760s.

In 1662 a new governor, Lord Windsor, arrived, appointed by the crown. There was to be a nominated Council of Twelve and an assembly composed of 'the representatives of the people, elected by the freeholders'.[18] 'The people' were the men of property. The 'foundation myth' of the colony, as Michael Craton describes it, was that it was a transplanted fragment of English people and their institutions.[19] Land grants and tenure were held on English terms and guaranteed by law, the assembly was patterned on the House of Commons,

---

[13] Abigail L. Swingen, *Competing Visions of Empire. Labor, Slavery and the Origins of the British Atlantic Empire* (New Haven, CT, 2015). Swingen argues for the importance of the imperial nature of the Stuarts' project, suggesting that mercantilism has been over-emphasized.

[14] A. P. Thornton, *West-India Policy under the Restoration* (Oxford, 1956), 19.

[15] Knight, *History*, II. 514.

[16] Long, *History*, I. 9.

[17] Brooke N. Newman, *A Dark Inheritance. Blood, Race, and Sex in Colonial Jamaica* (London, 2019), 53.

[18] Long, *History*, I. 10.

[19] Michael Craton, 'Property and Propriety: Land Tenure and Slave Property in the Creation of a British West Indian Plantocracy, 1612–1740', in John Brewer and Susan Staves (eds.), *Early Modern Conceptions of Property* (London, 1996), 498.

and local government was on the English model with unpaid gentlemen magistrates and juries of male freeholders. Land was to be granted to regiments, officers, then soldiers and settlers. Annual quit rents were charged on lands patented by the crown, a recognition of crown authority. Windsor had stopped en route in Barbados and issued a proclamation, 'that in all things, justice shall be duly administered, and that agreeable to the known laws of England, or such other laws not repugnant thereunto as shall be enacted by the consent of the free persons of the said island'.[20] This was an affirmation of the rights of the assembly to legislate, so long as their laws were not 'repugnant' to English law. Proclamations were the expression of the royal prerogative; the monarch was speaking across his empire. The assembly, of representative men of property, legitimated by the crown, would govern by deliberation, that is debate between equals.[21]

Windsor was replaced within weeks by a lieutenant-governor. In 1664 the new governor, Sir Thomas Modyford, who had advised on the Western Design and was already a successful planter, arrived from Barbados together with his household, including enslaved Africans. He was accompanied by more than nine hundred colonists, for it was urgent to increase the population with both settlers and labour, all necessarily from elsewhere, if the infant colony was to survive. He issued approximately eighteen hundred land patents, including to himself and his son, and encouraged the new planters, army officers, to develop their properties and buy enslaved people.[22] As the agent for the Royal African Company (RAC), he was in an excellent position to profit from this.[23] Samuel Long was amongst the colonists; he followed an old Spanish trail that crossed the Clarendon Plain and established a settlement near the Rio Minho where the Spanish had found a little gold.[24] His great-grandson recorded in 1791 that he had found patents of land obtained by Samuel in 1661 and his name appeared in a survey of landholders in 1670. Patents had been granted during the Protectorate, but they were re-patented after the Restoration in

---

[20] Cited in Agnes M. Whitson, *The Constitutional Development of Jamaica, 1660 to 1729* (Manchester, 1929), 21.
[21] Miles Ogborn, *The Freedom of Speech. Talk and Slavery in the Anglo-Caribbean World* (Chicago, 2019), 77–85.
[22] Richard S. Dunn, *Sugar and Slaves. The Rise of the Planter Class in the English West Indies* (London, 1973).
[23] Nuala Zahedieh, 'Modyford, Sir Thomas, First Baronet (*c.* 1620–1679), Planter and Colonial Governor', *Oxford Dictionary of National Biography*, 2004, https://doi.org/10.1093/ref:odnb/18871.
[24] S. A. G. Taylor, *A Short History of Clarendon* (Kingston, Jamaica, 1976); patterns of Barbadian and Irish settlement provided available models as to how to establish a plantation. Simon P. Newman, *A New World of Labor. The Development of Plantation Slavery in the British Atlantic* (Philadelphia, 2013); John Patrick Montano, *The Roots of English Colonialism in Ireland* (Cambridge, 2011).

order to make tenure more legally secure. 'In the progress of his life', wrote Long, his great-grandfather had

> patented and purchased a very great tract of land lying in various parts of the island, and not less in the whole than 16 or 18,000 acres. But his principal settlement and plantation was formed at what was then called the 7 plantations, situated on the border of the Rio Minho, in the parish of Clarendon. These 7 plantations had formerly been settled by the Spaniards and consisted chiefly of provisions, indigo and sugar.[25]

The seven plantations were to become Longville, the major seat of the family for subsequent generations. Between 1675 and 1686, Long purchased fifty-six slaves from the RAC in three 'parcels': twenty from the Gold Coast, twenty-two from the Bight of Biafra and fourteen from west central Africa.[26] Shortly before his death in 1683, he purchased Lucky Valley for £600.[27]

Thomas Trapham's vivid description of a sugar works in 1679 gives an indication of the extent to which such estates were beginning to dominate the island landscape. This one was set

> on the margin of the rising hills which still terminate our dextrous aspects; the most remarkable sugar-works allure us thither: the stranger is apt to ask what village it is (for every completed sugar work is no less) ... for besides the more large mansion house with its offices, the works, such as the well contrived Mill, the spacious boiling house, the large receptive curing houses, still house, commodious stables for the grinding cattle, lodging for the over-seer, and white servants, working shops for the necessary smiths, others for the framing carpenters, and coopers: to all which when we add the streets of the negro houses, no one will question to call such completed sugar-work a small town or village.[28]

Clarendon was one of the earliest areas to be settled, situated as it was not too far from the capital Spanish Town, with fertile land and with access to the sea. By 1664 it already had an organized militia and was producing some agricultural products.

In the early days of settlement, however, it was by no means clear that Jamaica would become a sugar colony. The first settlers were attracted by

---

[25] Howard, *Records and Letters*, I. 38. There are many records of Samuel Long's land deeds in the 1670s and early 1680s, but these have almost all been withdrawn.

[26] Trevor Burnard, 'The Atlantic Slave Trade and African Ethnicities in Seventeenth-Century Jamaica', in D. Richardson, S. Schwarz and A. Tibbles (eds.), *Liverpool and Transatlantic Slavery* (Liverpool, 2007), 146.

[27] IRO, Index to Grantees, Old Series, vol. 15, f. 12.

[28] Thomas Trapham, *Discourse of the State of Health in the Island of Jamaica* (London, 1679), 29. Cited in Lucille Mathurin Mair, *A Historical Study of Women in Jamaica, 1655–1844*, edited and with an introduction by Hilary M. Beckles and Verene A. Shepherd (Kingston, Jamaica, 2006).

Spanish gold and silver, prospects of privateering and plunder, rather than the hard work of agriculture. The island was well situated for this, close to the Spanish empire, with good access to its principal ports and major trade routes. Such activities required little capital outlay and could bring quick returns.[29] The Spanish tried to prohibit foreigners having access to their markets, but it was impossible to effectively police the seas. 'Mercantile men flocked' to Port Royal, wrote Long, 'in quest of new resources of trade in the neighbourhood of the rich Spanish settlements.'[30] The successes of these merchants, including William Beeston, meant that they could then invest in land themselves and provide credit for others. Plantations, argues Nuala Zahedieh, 'were largely financed by Spanish silver earned in lucrative illicit trade based on plunder and contraband'.[31] Those sugar estates, however, which required significant capital to establish – for land had to be cleared, roads laid, houses built, mills and boiling houses set up, labour bought – were soon to emerge as the key to fortunes. By 1673 the black population outnumbered the white, though the white had doubled in the previous decade.[32]

Charles II and his brother, James, Duke of York (later James II), implemented an expansionist imperial policy to increase revenue and power. The Company of Royal Adventurers trading into Africa was originally chartered in 1660 with James in a key position. It received a new charter in 1663, explicitly mentioning slave trading. It soon became known as the Royal African Company (RAC). Charles II's notion of lordship and absolute power, his legal concept of dominion, played a part in the colonial development of slavery. Both he and his brother extended state power significantly, aiming for an absolutist state with control over the granting of land and trading monopolies.[33] For the Stuarts, Holly Brewer argues, 'race was subsumed within a larger rationale celebrating hereditary status. One was born a slave, just as one was born a prince. Legally and ideologically, slavery was anchored in hierarchical and feudal principles that connected property in land to property in people, principles that were bent to new forms in England and its empire by Stuart kings'.[34] The purpose of the RAC was to sell enslaved Africans to English planters and to Spanish merchants, thus diverting trade from the

---

[29] Nuala Zahedieh, '"A Frugal Prudential and Hopeful Trade": Privateering in Jamaica, 1655–89', *JICH* 18.2 (1990), 145–68.
[30] Long, *History*, I. 299.
[31] Nuala Zahedieh, 'Trade, Plunder and Economic Development in Early English Jamaica, 1655–89', *EconHR*, 2nd ser., 39.2 (1986), 221.
[32] Trevor Burnard, 'European Migration to Jamaica, 1655–1780', *WMQ* 53.4 (1996), 772–3.
[33] Steven C. A. Pincus, *1688. The First Modern Revolution* (London, 2009).
[34] Holly Brewer, 'Slavery, Sovereignty, and "Inheritable Blood": Reconsidering John Locke and the Origins of American Slavery', *AHR* 122.4 (2017), 1042–3. Brewer challenges the connection between liberalism and slavery and argues that neither slavery nor capitalism is a unitary concept but should be seen as multifaceted.

Dutch, another aspect of crown policy. James had seen the potential for selling enslaved people on to Spain. The companies held monopolies on all trade to and from West Africa. Only subscribers could participate in the African trade and planters could only purchase enslaved people from the company agents in the colonies. This was a source of complaint from the colonists who resented the monopoly and would have liked the trade to be free. Relatively few captives were being landed in Jamaica in the 1660s. The demand for servants and labourers was only partially met by the convicts, the poor and the enemies of the Restoration transported to the Caribbean. 'The want of Negroes', wrote Sir Thomas Lynch in 1665, was 'the grand obstruction' to progress; 'without them the Plantation will decline, and people [be] discouraged'.[35] Under James II's twenty-eight years of governorship of the RAC, 'more than 100,000 souls' were sent to the New World.[36] Encouraging hereditary servitude was part of crown policy, as was extending colonial settlement. Dependence on slavery and convict labour went alongside rights to landownership and political participation in the post-1660 settlement.

An established legal and political system was necessary for settlement. A first assembly had been called in 1663; electors had to be freeholders with lands valued at £10 per annum. Samuel Long was elected to represent Port Royal, the key settlement of the new colony with its harbour. He was joined as an assembly man by William Beeston, who had arrived on the island in April 1660, and was to become the other founding father of the Long/Beeston dynasty. Those assembling had to take oaths before they could take office, swearing that they were possessed of an income well in excess of their debts. The speaking of oaths, as Miles Ogborn argues, turned the social attributes of freedom, masculinity, whiteness and property-holding into an active set of legal and political relations, both legitimating and consolidating the privileges associated with gender, class and race.[37] Their initial legislation, including an assembly control over taxes, was repealed when a second assembly was summoned by Modyford in 1664. The need for and control of labour was already a pressing issue. Before slave laws could be made, as Elsa Goveia argues, 'it was necessary for the opinion to be accepted that persons could be made slaves and held as slaves'.[38] Law was not the original basis of slavery, but slave laws were essential for the continued existence of slavery as an institution. They systematized and codified what was already common practice, adding the

---

[35] Calender of State Papers, cols. 1661–8, 12 February 1665, 207. Cited in Mair, *A Historical Study*, 54.
[36] Brewer, 'Slavery, Sovereignty, and "Inheritable Blood"', 1047.
[37] Ogborn, *The Freedom of Speech*, chap. 1.
[38] Elsa V. Goveia, 'The West Indian Slave Laws of the 18th Century', in D. G. Hall, E. V. Goveia and F. R. Augier (eds.), *Chapters in Caribbean History*, volume II (Eagle Hall, Barbados, 1970), 10.

powers of the colonial state and its legal apparatus to the institution.[39] Human bondage was widely accepted across the early modern world: merchants bought and sold captives, writers and theorists pondered over who could be enslaved. English prisoners were enslaved by Catholic and Muslim powers in the Mediterranean and beyond. But this was different from the racialized forms of plantation slavery which emerged in the Caribbean.[40] Slavery was seen as antithetical to Englishness, despite the fact that large numbers of English sailors had been captured and enslaved in the late sixteenth century. A much-publicized case in England in 1659 had concerned two Englishmen who had been transported to Barbados following an attempted royalist uprising in 1655. They had been sold as indentured servants for fixed periods. They petitioned parliament, insisting that they were not chattel slaves. This was 'a matter that concerns the liberty of the free-born people of England', argued one MP, while another declared that if such practices continued, 'our lives will be as cheap as those [of] negroes'.[41] Englishmen were not 'Negroes'.

The Jamaican men of property categorized the distinctions between propertied man, servant and slave as one of their first political acts, establishing what Brenna Bhandar describes as a 'racial regime of ownership' which articulated property rights and racialized subjectivities.[42] 'Law-making through deliberation and debate among white men in the assembly', argues Ogborn, 'was central both to the practicalities of colonial legislative practice and to the forms of identity that bound the English empire of liberty in the Atlantic world together and differentiated it from others.'[43] The assembly men in the early 1660s knew all about the dangers of 'masterless men', having witnessed the defeat of the Levellers and the Diggers. The slave trade was legitimated in parliamentary legislation, but there was no provision in English law for chattel slavery. The assembly followed the model of the Barbados Code

---

[39] Jerome S. Handler, 'Custom and Law: the Status of Enslaved Africans in Seventeenth-Century Barbados', S&A 37.2 (2016), 233–55; Bradley J. Nicholson, 'Legal Borrowing and the Origins of Slave Law in the British Colonies', *American Journal of Legal History* 38.1 (1994), 38–54.

[40] Michael Guasco, *Slaves and Englishmen. Human Bondage in the Early Modern Atlantic World* (Philadelphia, 2014); Linda Colley, *Captives. Britain, Empire and the World, 1600–1750* (London, 2002).

[41] Pestana, *The English Atlantic*, 212; Peter Linebaugh, and Marcus Rediker, *The Many-Headed Hydra. Sailors, Slaves, Commoners and the Hidden History of the Revolutionary Atlantic* (London, 2000), 132.

[42] Brenna Bhandar, *Colonial Lives of Property. Law, Land and Racial Regimes of Ownership* (London, 2018), 2. Bhandar's work is based on the late nineteenth century, but her argument that modern property laws emerged along with colonial modes of appropriation can be applied to a much earlier period. It is important to note, however, that free people of colour could hold property though they did not have the same legal rights as white men.

[43] Ogborn, *The Freedom of Speech*, 39.

which had been passed in 1661. Barbados, already established as a sugar economy, was by the mid-1650s producing great wealth, with its new labour regime based on bonded white labour but increasingly relying on enslaved Africans.[44] In Jamaica, sugar production had scarcely begun and the black population was only about 15 per cent, but the assembly made clear the intentions of the colonists: sugar and slavery were the future.[45] They passed a Slave Act and a Servant Act which barely altered the Barbados codes on Servants and 'Negroes'. Since English law provided 'no track to guide us where to walk not any rule set us how to govern such Slaves', they must create a new body of law, essential for their social order.[46] This was the principle of *lex loci*, that every country had its specific needs, which the independent legislature could implement. The Act 'For the Better Ordering and Governing of Negro Slaves' was signed by Modyford in 1664. '*Their* slaves, *their* Negroes' (my italics) were identified in explicitly racialized ways. 'An heathenish brutish and uncertain dangerous pride of people', they were heathen, associated with brutes, and animalized.[47]

The term 'Negro' drew attention to their blackness. It was, as Susan Amussen argues, 'a Spanish word that both acknowledged the Spanish history of enslaving Africans and distanced the English from the people they enslaved'. Slavery, she argues, was initially understood as 'inherent in bodies, not a product of law and a system of labor'.[48] But the system of law was needed, and English law had 'protean potential' that could be mobilized in support of the fragile colonial order.[49] Writing codes, putting practices into the written word, contributed to the making of new forms of common sense. Enslaved men and women could not be subject to the law of the colonists, designed for free men who possessed liberties. Captive Africans must be made kinless, rootless, cut off from their countries and cultural traditions, and subject to the power and physical and psychological authority of their masters. Yet colonists believed that given 'the right rule of reason and order, we are not

---

[44] Newman, *A New World of Labor*.

[45] Edward B. Rugemer, 'The Development of Mastery and Race in the Comprehensive Slave Codes of the Greater Caribbean during the Seventeenth Century', *WMQ* 70.3 (2013), 429–58.

[46] Barbados Slave Code: Act of 1661. Extracts in Stanley Engerman, Seymour Drescher and Robert Paquette (eds.), *Slavery* (Oxford, 2001), 105–13. In fact, they were drawing on English precedents. See Nicholson, 'Legal Borrowing'. Whipping was deeply entrenched in English employment law; Douglas Hay and Paul Craven (eds.), *Masters, Servants and Magistrates in Britain and the Empire, 1562–1955* (London, 2004); Lee B. Wilson, *The Bonds of Empire. The English Origins of Slave Law in South Carolina and British Plantation America, 1660–1783* (Cambridge, 2021).

[47] Barbados Slave Code: Act of 1661.

[48] Susan Dwyer Amussen, *Caribbean Exchange. Slavery and the Transformation of English Society* (Chapel Hill, NC, 2007), 12, 134.

[49] Wilson, *The Bonds of Empire*, 5.

to leave them to the Arbitrary, cruel, and outrageous wills of every evil disposed person, but so far to protect them as we do many other goods and Chattels, and also somewhat further as being created Men though without the knowledge of God in the world'. Given the nature of these people, named as 'goods and chattels ... yet created Men', 'we may extend the legislative power given to us of punishionary Laws for the benefit and good of this plantation'. Harsh punishment, including mutilation and dismemberment, would be necessary, alongside special courts. 'Being brutish Slaves deserve not for the baseness of their Conditions to be tried by the legal trial of twelve Men.'[50] Masters were assumed to have absolute power over their human property. But the colonial state, representing the collective interests of the planters, was there to deal with endemic unrest, disturbance and rebellion. Slaves were to be strictly controlled in their movements, and any gatherings that crossed estate boundaries were to be prevented. Negroes in possession of weapons could be put to death; runaways could be transported or sold. If any Negro were to be executed for criminal acts, it was determined, his owner would be compensated by the public purse. This was a recognition, a disavowal, a knowing and not knowing at one and the same time, that enslaved people were human beings with agency, and an assertion that they were property. Jamaican judicial practice, as Diana Paton clarifies it, 'emphasized the difference between slave and free, and valorized the slaveholder's private penal power'.[51] Law provided both the cornerstone of the protection of property and a site for the codification of racialization.

Servants, meanwhile, might be exploited and abused, but they had some rights, though significantly fewer than in England.[52] Demarcating the distinctions between indentured servants, who were living and working in appalling conditions, and the enslaved came to be seen as essential. Servants were subject to the law, while the law encouraged brutal treatment of slaves and named penalties for those who failed to act accordingly. Physical violence was at the heart of enslavement, while the scale of physical punishments for servants was somewhat restricted. In 1676 the Lords of Trade and Plantations, the body by then responsible to the crown for imperial governance, objected to the word 'servitude' in relation to servants, as 'being a mark of bondage and slavery' inappropriate for apprentices.[53] In 1681 a revision was made to the servant code, replacing *Christian*, as a way of differentiating between servants and slaves, with *white*, clarifying the centrality of skin to the distinction between freedom and slavery. A deficiency clause was also introduced, in an attempt to

---

[50] Barbados Slave Code: Act of 1661.
[51] Diana Paton, 'Punishment, Crime, and the Bodies of Slaves in Eighteenth Century Jamaica', *Journal of Social History* 34.4 (2001), 923–54.
[52] It is impossible to establish demographic details at this time. Unlike Barbados, Jamaica did not have significant numbers of convicts and white indentured servants.
[53] Rugemer, 'The Development of Mastery and Race', 445.

improve the balance of population between black and white. Slave-owners were required to employ a specific number of white servants in relation to the numbers of enslaved.[54] New regulations, additions and modifications, reflecting new dangers, were regularly made to these codes by the Jamaican assembly.

Samuel Long was as concerned to assert the rights of the colonists as freeborn Englishmen as he was to codify the position of the enslaved. The first purpose of government was the protection of property; the colonists' property was distinctive for it included people. What degree of local autonomy could they claim? What were the relative rights of the colonists and the crown? What exactly did *free denisons of England* mean in practice? 'Long was the leader', argues Agnes Whitson, 'who crystallised and directed the half expressed, unformed opinions of his fellows, and put them into practical form.'[55] His speeches in the assembly were critical, summoning the rhetoric of English liberties to defend the colonists' security of tenure while at the same time asserting the freedom to enslave. The assembly wanted control of island revenue: it provided the crucial means of asserting some autonomy and limiting the powers of the crown. Long was said to have refused to grant the governor £20 until it was authorized by the assembly. Modyford was enraged at this threat to the prerogative and threatened his arrest. After another brief session of the assembly in 1665, when the laws of England were once again declared to be in force on the island, Modyford chose to rule without calling it for the subsequent years. Before he was replaced in 1670, he warned the secretary of state that the colonists were afraid they would be 'under an arbitrary government', something which 'Englishmen abhor'.[56] Meanwhile, the governance of the colonies and the need for more effective central administration was being addressed by the crown. A new committee, the Lords of Trade and Plantations, was set up: its aim was to ensure obedience to metropolitan authority and to give much greater attention to colonial and commercial affairs.[57] Lord Vaughan arrived on the island in 1675 with a commission to establish it as a plantation economy rather than depending on privateering, which had been a mainstay of colonial prosperity.[58] The assembly men of 1675 were determined to defend their rights and Samuel Long, as Speaker, removed the king's name from the revenue bill as a way of ensuring that those rights could not be dispensed with. In response the English government launched an inquiry into the island's laws. The Lords Committee was convinced that the

---

[54] Edward B. Rugemer, *Slave Law and the Politics of Resistance in the Early Atlantic World* (Cambridge, MA, 2018), 45–6.
[55] Whitson, *Constitutional Development*, 28.
[56] Cited in Swingen, *Competing Visions*, 82.
[57] Winifred T. Root, 'The Lords of Trade and Plantations, 1675–1696', *AHR* 23.1 (1917), 20–41.
[58] Stephen Saunders-Wedd, *The Governors-General. The English Army and the Definition of Empire, 1569–1681* (Chapel Hill, NC, 1979).

Jamaica assembly, led by men such as Long, was claiming too much power. Vaughan noted that Long was 'skilled in the Law', something that would have appealed greatly to his great-grandson.[59] By this time Long had extensive property in Clarendon and was acting as a justice in the parish. He had been appointed to the council and to the post of chief justice in 1674. His politics was strongly inflected with the traditions of the parliament men of 1641, defenders of the Commons against the autocratic practices of the crown and drawing on the language of tyranny. 'He asked nor desired nothing but his rights and privileges as an Englishman', he declared, 'and would not be contented with less.'[60]

In 1677 the assembly once again insisted on their right to control revenue and to limit crown authority. The king was determined to introduce 'a new frame of legislation', they believed, removing from the assembly 'all power of defending themselves against any future act of tyranny'.[61] A new governor, the Earl of Carlisle, was appointed, who was to carry out this task. He arrived in Jamaica in July 1678, bringing with him a bundle of laws including an Act for settling perpetual revenue and instructions which would have meant that no assembly could examine or object to any new legislation. The colonial assembly's right to deliberate and propose new legislation, their relative autonomy, was under direct attack. All laws would in future be framed by the governor and his council, and sent to the king for approval, after which the assembly would approve them. This was the system, named Poyning's, which had been imposed on Ireland. Carlisle summoned the assembly. This time William Beeston was the Speaker and led the refusal, declaring that 'the mode proposed was repugnant to the laws of England' and they would live under no other laws.[62] The assembly was dissolved, having passed a revenue bill for one year which meant that the colony could function. The Lords of Trade, however, were adamant that the new laws must be presented again. The assembly was recalled, with Beeston once again elected as Speaker. They needed an assurance, they told the governor, 'of being Governed in the same manner ... as long as they were within the dominions of the Kingdome of England'.[63] In promoting the new legislation Carlisle was attempting to persuade them, Long recorded, 'to wear the badge of slavery manufactured for them by the Lords of Trade'.[64]

---

[59] Cited in Miles Ogborn, 'Deliberative Power: Speech, Politics and Empire in Jamaica's Late Seventeenth-Century Constitutional Crisis' (forthcoming).
[60] Calender of State Papers, cols. 1677–8, no. 1512. Cited in Whitson, *Constitutional Development*, 49.
[61] Long, *History*, I. 197.
[62] Ibid., I. 198.
[63] Assembly of Jamaica to Carlisle, n.d. Cited in Swingen, *Competing Visions*, 114.
[64] Long, *History*, I. 199.

Carlisle had hoped for Long's support but found him unmoveable. He was particularly incensed by the most unbecoming way in which Long had insisted in the council on his rights. Using his authority as governor, Carlisle suspended Long both from the council and from his post as chief justice. Faced with the assembly's intransigence, he decided to return to England with Long and Beeston as state prisoners. They were to appear before the king and his Privy Council and present their case. Carlisle had become convinced that the assembly would never consent 'to make chains for their posterity'.[65] In September 1680 Long appeared before the Lords of Trade. According to James Knight's account, 'He pleaded his own Cause with Such Decency, Strength of Reason and Argument, that He was not only honourably Acquitted, but His Majesty was pleased to declare that *He did not think that He had such a Subject in that part of the World*.'[66] The assembly's control of revenue, Long told the hearing, was the only way they had of mediating their relation to the crown. 'Englishmen', he insisted, 'ought not to be bound by any laws to which they had not given their consent.'[67] The hearings coincided with an ongoing political crisis in England over attempts to exclude the Duke of York from the throne on account of his Catholicism. This meant that the government had less enthusiasm than might otherwise have been the case for a constitutional crisis over Jamaica. It was eventually agreed that the new constitution would be dropped if the assembly would pass a revenue bill for seven years. This would assure the crown of its income and colonial acceptance of the imperial/mercantilist code.

Another concern of the colonists was the insufficient supply, as they saw it, of African labour and the monopoly of the RAC. Between 1674 and 1680 the RAC had delivered on average a thousand captives each year so that the African population was growing rapidly. A revised slave code in 1674 constructed chattel slavery as permanent. 'All negroes Lawfully bought or borne slaves shall here continue to bee soe,' it decreed, 'and further be held adjudged to bee goods and chattels.'[68] But the colonists' demand for labour was not satisfied. Led by Long and Beeston, they petitioned the Duke of York in 1679, asking him to persuade the company 'to furnish this island annually with a plentiful supply of Negroes at moderate rates', pointing out that this would benefit the crown since it would increase the customs.[69] Following the constitutional settlement, a further petition on the question of the RAC's monopoly

---

[65] Carlisle to Coventry, 15 September 1679. Cited in Thornton, *West-India Policy*, 194. Ogborn argues that the assembly's right to deliberate was at the heart of this constitutional crisis; 'Deliberative Power'.

[66] Knight, *History*, I. 139.

[67] Blathwayt to North, reporting Long's words, 20 October 1680. Cited in Thornton, *West-India Policy*, 198.

[68] Cited in Newman, *A Dark Inheritance*, 55.

[69] Cited in Swingen, *Competing Visions*, 116.

was presented, arguing for an opening of the Guinea trade and pointing out the benefits which the slave trade produced for the crown. In response, as Abigail Swingen has documented, the Lords ordered the company to 'take care to send 3000 merchantable Negroes yearly to Jamaica, provided they have good payments of their debts collected there, and that they do afford merchantable Negroes to the inhabitants of that island at £18 p head'.[70] This was a major recognition by the crown of the significance of slavery for a plantation economy. Jamaica would be a colony of extraction, providing sugar for the home market.

John Taylor, an Englishman who had arrived in Jamaica in 1686 with a stock of cloth and three indentured servants, hoping to make a fortune, had ended up in Clarendon as a bookkeeper but then left the island because of illness. He had returned to England and compiled a manuscript, an account of his life and travels together with his impressions of Jamaica. The agreement with the RAC who 'brought Negro slaves', he reported, meant 'the plantations improved appase, and their commodities of sugar, indigo, cotton etc began to be plenty'. This 'drawed merchants and shipping thither daylie, both from England and Ireland, loaden with bread, flour, brandy, wine, cloath, and all other necessaries and vendable merchandizes'. The ships returned 'home with sugar, indigo, ginger, logwood, fustick, and other American commodities'. The island 'began to grow exceedingly rich' and 'the industrious planter lived in great peace, ease and plenty'.[71] While expressing pity for the poor Africans who laboured in the hot sun with minimal clothing, he was also convinced that 'they deserve no better, since they differ only from bruite beast by their shape and speech'.[72]

Beeston and Long had stood together in this conflict with the crown. Edward Long concluded his account of the struggle with a 'grateful tribute of encomium' to them and their allies. 'The discreet conduct, and undaunted spirit, of those virtuous patriots,' he wrote,

> who had stood forth and successfully opposed this execrable machination, under so many disadvantages, and with so much loss to their private fortunes, are highly to be respected. Their memory deserves ... to be transmitted with honour through every succeeding generation; for it is to them we owe, in a great measure, the present flourishing state of the island, which could not have resulted from a despotic state of government.[73]

He would do his best to preserve this memory.

---

[70] Swingen, *Competing Visions*, 120.
[71] John Taylor, *Jamaica in 1687. The Taylor Manuscript at the National Library of Jamaica*, ed. David Buisseret (Kingston, Jamaica, 2008), 89.
[72] Ibid., 268.
[73] Long, *History*, I. 202.

By the time he wrote this, the descendants of Samuel Long and William Beeston had been intimately connected over three generations, their fortunes tied together. William Beeston had arrived in Jamaica in 1660 as we have seen. Based in Port Royal at a time when the smuggling trade with the Spanish colonies was flourishing, he established himself as a successful entrepreneur, purchasing shares in prize vessels and trading in prize goods and island commodities. He was elected to the first assemblies and stood alongside Samuel Long in conflict with Modyford. From 1662 he was patenting land, and by 1670 had accumulated sufficient resources to begin sugar planting. He returned to England in 1672 and married Anne Hopegood, a merchant's daughter. They settled in Jamaica a year later and he was active as both a merchant and a planter, engaging also in the factional politics of the island. His leadership of the assembly in the conflict with Carlisle led to his return to England and his re-settlement there. By 1686 he was one of London's leading West India traders. Beeston and Long had seen the importance of doing business personally with the Lords of Trade rather than through the governor. Beeston was to serve as the first agent for Jamaica in London, representing the interests of the colonists to the metropolitan government.[74] He returned once more to Jamaica, in 1692, following his appointment as lieutenant-governor and then governor. In his later years he was actively involved in the Spanish slave trade and benefited during wartime from the provisioning of troops. He died in England in 1702, having used his official position 'to gain a competitive edge in the ferocious pursuit of profit which characterized life in the high-mortality and high-risk environment of the Caribbean'.[75] James Knight's judgement, written in the 1740s, was more forgiving: 'a Gentleman of great Temperance and Moderation; for He was Contented with His Sallary and the legal Perquisites of His Government' and was never accused of any acts of power or oppression.[76] Beeston's only daughter, Jane, married the grandson of Thomas Modyford in 1699, but she was widowed in 1702 and a year later married Charles Long, Samuel Long's son. The two lines had become one.

Samuel had returned to Jamaica after the success in London to face further issues over the control of revenue. Sir Thomas Lynch was reappointed as governor in 1681 and managed to get a twenty-one-year Revenue Act passed in 1683, but the planters had a significant victory in ensuring that money collected for quit rents, fines and customs would stay on the island to cover official costs, rather than going to the crown. Samuel died that same year, aged

---

[74] Lilian M. Penson, *The Colonial Agents of the British West Indies. A Study in Colonial Administration Mainly in the Eighteenth Century* (London, 1924).

[75] This paragraph draws heavily on the *ODNB* account, initially written by P. B. Austin and revised by Nuala Zahedieh, 'Beeston, Sir William (1636–1702), Merchant and Colonial Governor', *Oxford Dictionary of National Biography*, [2004] 2008, https://doi.org/10.1093/ref:odnb/1955.

[76] Knight, *History*, I. 205.

forty-five, having accumulated significant wealth. He had married Elizabeth Streete in 1666 and she survived him.[77] Four of their children, Samuel, Vere, John and Mary, died in Jamaica and were buried in St Catherine's, the Spanish Town church. Edward's great-grandfather Samuel's tomb, covered with a black marble slab, can still be seen in pride of place in the chancel, its Latin inscription much eroded. 'We are to infer from the tenor of the epitaph', wrote Edward admiringly, 'that he had a handsome, manly person; showed early marks of genius and good sense, and that his conduct through life had been distinguished by his love of justice, his piety, and the celebrity of his actions.'[78] His inventory recorded the source of his wealth in people: the ownership of 140 enslaved men, 148 women, 50 boys and 49 girls. Their total value was £3,729.26.[79] He had clearly become one of the 'red-hot planters' that his great-grandson was to describe.[80] His total estate value was £7,273.83 with more than 11,000 acres, while his debts totalled £1,405.99. Sixty chairs and seven tables graced the hall of his splendid house in Spanish Town, complemented with £54.85 worth of plate. The bulk of his estate was left to his only surviving son, Charles (who was only four years old at the time). His bequest to his loving wife, Elizabeth, included the use of the town house and all his 'household Stuffe' for her lifetime, an annual income of £250, and '10 Cowes and calves such as she shall choose and 10 Negroes and 40 Ewes and 6 mares all such as she shall choose with pasturage for the said Cattle and their Increase during her life', providing she accepted this in satisfaction of her dower. His daughter Elizabeth was to receive £2,000 at her marriage or when she reached eighteen and '2 negroe girls and 20 Cowes' and their increase.[81] This was a typical well-to-do planter's will with its gendered patterns of inheritance: the bulk of the property was left to the son, ensuring the continuity of the line, the widow was given money and a lifetime's interest in the house, and the daughter money at her marriage. Aged twelve, she was to become the owner of two girls, probably of a similar age to herself. The widow and daughter were also granted the 'Increase' of their female human property, along with that of their cattle. Samuel Long was appropriating the reproductive lives of the enslaved women he owned by claiming their children as property. Jamaican

---

[77] Edward Long recorded the marriage as taking place in 1666; Howard, *Records and Letters*, I. 37. The account in the *ODNB* says 1661. Andrew O' Shaughnessy, 'Long, Samuel (1638–1683), Planter and Politician in the West Indies', *Oxford Dictionary of National Biography*, 2004, https://doi.org/10.1093/ref:odnb/16976. Given that their first child was born in 1667, the later date seems plausible.

[78] Howard, *Records and Letters*, I. 39.

[79] See www.ucl.ac.uk/lbs/inventory/view/5629. Inventory values are in pounds sterling. Thanks to Trevor Burnard.

[80] Long, *History*, I. 268.

[81] Will of Colonel Samuel Long, entered 18th of August, 1683. Book of Wills, vols. 3–5 (combined), f. 50. Island Record Office (IRO), Twickenham Park, St Catherine, Jamaica.

slave-owners were defining and establishing in custom a biologically driven perpetual racial slavery, through the female line. In the 1650s, slave-owners in Barbados started to use the term 'increaser' to identify female slaves of child-bearing years. And they linked the reproductive lives of women to those of their agricultural commodities: increase was used for both animals and women, as Samuel Long did. Owners could leave their own children prospects of future wealth. 'Childbirth, then,' Jennifer Morgan insists, 'needs to stand beside the more ubiquitously evoked scene of violence and brutality at the end of a slaveowner's lash or branding iron.'[82]

The year after Samuel's death, a new Act was passed for the 'Better Ordering of Slaves'. This decreed that slaves could be treated as goods and chattels in payment of debts. This enhanced the liquidity of slave property, as Edward Rugemer argues, thus strengthening the credit position of Jamaican slave-owners. While in Barbados slaves were declared real estate, to be handed down with land to descendants, in Jamaica they could be sold as personal property. Jamaica, Rugemer suggests, was looking to the 'new world of commerce' rather than imagining a stable island with landed gentry. The law not only worked to 'classify and dehumanize'. It also 'sought to reduce African people to animate capital ... Slaves were long-term capital investments that retained useful liquidity.'[83] Furthermore, 'the enslaved offspring of black women', as Hilary Beckles has noted, 'constituted first and foremost a capital addition to the inventory of assets ... In this way an enslaved woman could easily replace several times the capital outlay involved in her purchase.'[84]

Samuel's son, Charles, grew up with inherited wealth. In 1699, aged twenty, he married Amy Lawes in St Catherine's Spanish Town. She was the daughter of Sir Nicholas Lawes, who had served as governor of Jamaica. She died three years later. Their son, Samuel, born in 1700, and a daughter, Elizabeth, survived. Charles married again in 1703. His second wife, Jane, also came from the white elite. She was the daughter and heir of Sir William Beeston and the widow of Sir James Modyford, the heir of Sir Thomas Modyford. She inherited both from her father and from her first husband. Charles, as a young property owner, stepped straight into the governing class, representing Clarendon and later Vere in the assembly. By 1704 he was on the council.[85] Soon after that, his wealth enabled him to move permanently to England and,

---

[82] Morgan, *Laboring Women*, 105. Morgan's analysis of the centrality of the experience of enslaved women to the development of racial capitalism is further developed in *Reckoning with Slavery*.

[83] Rugemer, *Slave Law*, 36, 50.

[84] Hilary M. Beckles, 'Perfect Property: Enslaved Black Women in the Caribbean', in Eudine Barriteau (ed.), *Confronting Power, Theorizing Gender. Interdisciplinary Perspectives in the Caribbean* (Kingston, Jamaica, 2003), 142–58.

[85] W. A. Feurtado, *Official and Other Personages of Jamaica, from 1655–1790* (Kingston, Jamaica, 1896).

once family property disputes were sorted out, he became extraordinarily wealthy, including the ownership of shares in the RAC.[86] He left his Jamaican property under the care of his friend Peter Heywood, then chief justice of Jamaica. In 1707 Heywood visited both Longville and Lucky Valley and sent an account to England of all that was wrong. At Longville the mill, boiling house, curing house and stillhouse, the coppers and cisterns, all the accoutrements needed for the production of sugar and rum, were 'all ... in disorder ... the whole works a Pott of nastiness'. A 'stayd sober man' was urgently needed, to tell the overseer of the 'eregularetyes he sees in the plantation that matters may be timely regulated'. The cane pieces were horribly overrun with weeds and 'the Slaves' for the most part 'rejoiced to see us', for 'their great cry' was against their overseer; 'they had not had a grain of salt since you went off' and 'your poor old nurs that you gave freedom to' had not been well treated. Even 'your poor dogg dick finds mighty alteracons'. Heywood rode to Lucky Valley the next day and found the building of the new mill going well, but he was concerned that there would not be sufficient water for it in the dry season. Other parts of the works, however, were 'extremely nasty', while the cane was overgrown and the fowl in bad condition. The house was in a terrible state, leaks everywhere, and likely to fall apart. He addressed himself to the overseer, Mr Hunt, and 'told him that he had acted in your Imployment like a very ill man that he had in a great measure ruin'd your estates, abused your servants and slaves and affronted your beloved Sister'. He then discharged him. Hunt had stolen sugar, sold horses and worked the enslaved for himself. In short, Heywood told Charles, 'you have bin horribly abus'd'.[87] Mr Stafford was given charge of the estate and on the next visit Heywood found that it was in good hands. It was clear, however, that absenteeism could result in serious financial losses.

Having moved to England, Charles Long and his wife Jane established themselves in great style, with a splendid house on the south side of Queen's Square in London and a country property, Hurt's Hall, in Suffolk. Charles's political loyalties lay with the Whigs; their belief in 'the elevation of property above all other values' suited him well and there was Whig enthusiasm for plantations and debates about empire.[88] The breaking of the RAC's monopoly provided an incentive for sugar planters.[89] Charles echoed his father, Samuel's, conviction that an Englishman's reliance on law was the only bulwark against the threat of absolutism, a very present concern given France, the Stuarts and

---

[86] Personal communication, Will Pettigrew.
[87] Peter Heywood to Charles Long, in Howard, *Records and Letters*, I. 46–53.
[88] E. P. Thompson, *Whigs and Hunters. The Origins of the Black Act* (London, 1975), 197; Steve Pincus, 'Addison's Empire: Whig Conceptions of Empire in the Early Eighteenth Century', *Parliamentary History* 3.1 (2012), 99–117.
[89] William A. Pettigrew, *Freedom's Debt. The Royal African Company and the Politics of the Atlantic Slave Trade, 1672–1752* (Chapel Hill, NC, 2013).

the colonial experience. He had little in the way of familial connections in England to help him secure a position in the gentry. Gaining a seat in the House of Commons was a recognized mark of status and from 1715 he represented Dunwich (already disappearing into the sea), close to his Suffolk property. Robert Walpole was at this time struggling to establish his position at the heart of English politics and needed solid support in the Commons. He was well aware of the importance of local ties and was building his powerbase in East Anglia, the site of his family property, Houghton. William Wood, a connection of Walpole's, offered Long Walpole's help in a parliamentary election.[90] This was the beginning of the family's connection with Walpole.

Charles Long's association with Wood proved disastrous. Not content with his existing properties in land and people, Long dreamed of gold and silver waiting to be mined in Jamaica. Caught up in the excitement of making quick money in the febrile atmosphere of the 1720s, Wood and Long launched the Royal Mines Company of Jamaica, with a patent for all the gold and silver that might be found on the island.[91] They were to pay a rent to the king of one-fifth of the value of any gold or silver that was discovered. Investors flocked to the dream of bullion that would match the fabled riches of the Spanish. Miners were hired, together with a doctor, and they were despatched to Jamaica with instructions to Long's agents about the buying and hiring of enslaved labourers. When business was underway, Wood reported to Long that 'nothing is to be expected of Gold or Silver mines or copper worth working ... but this to your self and let us to do all to get rid of the Affair.'[92] Meanwhile, however, seduced by the excitement over what was represented as the unlimited potential of the South Sea Company, Long had invested not only his own money in it but also that of his shareholders. Wood warned him that the shares were dropping and advised him to sell, but the bubble burst. Long was left with huge debts and legal claims. The angry shareholders claimed that the 'Project was a mere Imposture' and 'Great Frauds' had been raised.[93] Legal claims on behalf of the shareholders were still being considered in the Court of the Exchequer in the 1740s. Charles died in 1723 a deeply disappointed man. His will made provision for his widow, Jane, and the eight children from his second marriage. 'All the net residue and remainder of his real and personal Estates whatsoever and wheresoever' was bequeathed to his first son, Samuel,

---

[90] Wm Wood to Charles Long, 3 March 1721. BL Add MSS 22639, f. 129; Yaroslav Prykhodko, 'Mind, Body and the Moral Imagination in the Eighteenth-Century British Atlantic World', PhD, University of Pennsylvania, 2011, http://repository.upenn.edu/edissertations/561.

[91] Edward Long provided an account of this episode. Howard, *Records and Letters*, I. 68–74. On the 1720s, see Thomas Levenson, *Money for Nothing. The South Sea Bubble and the Invention of Modern Capitalism* (London, 2020).

[92] Wm Wood to Charles Long, 10 January 1721. BL Add MSS 22639, f. 121.

[93] Howard, *Records and Letters*, I. 74.

after debts, funeral charges and legacies were paid. 'His own Estates descended to my father', wrote his grandson Edward, 'not only loaded with debts but with all these legacies, and the large annuity to the widow.' Furthermore, a 'violent dispute' between Samuel and his half-brother Charles was only resolved with the loss of Hurt's Hall and the Saxmundham property to Charles.[94] This was a harsh reality for Samuel, having grown up with great expectations of wealth.

The younger Samuel had been born in Jamaica in 1700 and lived there until his parents moved to England. Educated at Eton, he then entered the army, serving as a captain of a troop of Horse Guards whose responsibility was to attend on Caroline, the wife of the Prince of Wales. Caroline was a supporter of Walpole and Samuel maintained a connection with him. In 1723 he married Mary Tate, who came from a mercantile background but was without riches. Samuel's financial situation was precarious given the scale of debts he had inherited. He left the army and returned to Jamaica with Mary, no doubt hoping to improve the revenue from better exploitation of the plantations. Their first child, Samuel, was born there in 1724 but died in infancy. By 1727 they were back in England, where daughter Catherine was born in 1727, but they then returned to Jamaica, where Robert was born at Longville in 1729. He was named after Walpole's eldest son, his godfather. Charles, named after his grandfather, was born in England in 1731. Samuel was in London in 1734 when Edward was born and named after Walpole's second son, who was also his godfather. Samuel had been 'soliciting some post of profit from Lord Walpole ... to whom my Grandfather and he were very strongly attached in gratitude, for the protection they had both received from him when Chancellor of the Exchequer, against the Exchequer suits instituted by the mine adventurers'.[95] Walpole eventually appointed Samuel to be the Keeper of the King's House at Newmarket together with a place in the Customs. These two posts were worth £400 per annum. Samuel was a modest recipient in the vast system of clientage and dependency that Walpole created, in this phase of capital accumulation when many great fortunes rested on access to public money, to the perks of office and sinecures. As Walpole's biographer Plumb put it, he 'set out to engross the entire field of patronage', believing in patronage as the surest foundation of political loyalty.[96]

Newmarket, however, involved heavy expenses, with large parties gathering for the races and expecting hospitality. His growing family, and the cost of educating his first two sons at Eton, persuaded Samuel that he needed a different lifestyle, away from the expensive sociability of Newmarket. The two older boys, together with their young brother, were sent to school in Bury St Edmunds, and Samuel bought a property at Tredudwel in Cornwall, aiming

---

[94] Ibid., I. 70.
[95] Ibid., I. 78.
[96] J. H. Plumb, *Sir Robert Walpole. The Making of a Statesman* (London, 1956), 92.

for a quieter life. He would establish himself as a gentleman farmer. He adopted a modest version of improvement, unable to compete with his patron Walpole's extensive work at Houghton, but determined to create a property suited to a gentleman. There was a tension, as Raymond Williams argued, between agricultural improvement, related to soil and stock, and the improvement of houses, parks and gardens, which absorbed so much of the wealth that the new organization of land and labour was producing in eighteenth-century England. The verb *to improve*, Williams reminds us, in earliest uses referred to opportunities for monetary profit, equivalent in meaning to *invest*. In early modern England it was frequently associated with land, and enclosure. In the eighteenth century, it was a key word in the development of agrarian capitalism. Its wider meaning of 'making something better' developed from the seventeenth century, in the eighteenth often overlapping with economic opportunities.[97] Samuel Long's 'improvement' of Tredudwel was designed to increase income as well as to enhance gentility. 'The Farm house not being capacious or elegant enough to suit my Father's ideas', recorded Edward, 'he immediately engaged an Architect of eminence in the Country and with his assistance so altered and improved it with additional buildings, offices and gardens, that it struck me when I first saw it as a very pretty place.' (Plate 3.)[98]

Beautifully situated three miles from Fowey, Tredudwel enjoyed a view of the sea and Samuel hoped for a 'sweet retirement ... employed in rural or useful occupations'. An enthusiast for building, gardening and husbandry, he farmed about a hundred acres himself, his coachman doubling up as bailiff. He had stocked his garden with the best fruit trees from Hampton Court, kept sheep and cattle, bred pigeons, poultry, rabbits and hogs, shot snipe and woodcocks in the winter and brought hares into the neighbourhood. An active Justice of the Peace and close friend of the local parson, he endowed a new pew in the local church at Llanteglos. He delighted in family amusements and had a partiality for 'cold collations' by the beach in the summer. (Plate 4.) Tredudwel was 'the darling creation of his own hand'.[99] He collected his three sons from school in 1745 and they travelled from Suffolk to London. The city was in tumult because of the 1745 Jacobite rebellion, guards posted at all the gates and citizens 'training themselves to the exercise of the firelock'.[100] They stayed with Uncle Beeston, Samuel's half-brother, who was developing the merchant house and had married Sarah Crop, the daughter of a city merchant with a large fortune. The boys were taken to dine with Walpole, and then on to Tredudwel.

---

[97] Raymond Williams, *Keywords. A Vocabulary of Culture and Society* (London, 1976), 132–3.
[98] Howard, *Records and Letters*, I. 80.
[99] Ibid., I. 84.
[100] Ibid., I. 82.

A crisis in Samuel's financial affairs, however, precipitated by a sharp decline in sugar production at Lucky Valley and Longville, meant that he decided to return to Jamaica once more, in an attempt to recover his fortune. This was the pattern amongst these West Indian transatlantic families. When times were good, they could retreat to the mother country and live off the labour of the enslaved, hoping to establish themselves as landed gentry. When times were bad, with successive failures in sugar production or attorneys squandering their profits, rebellions of the enslaved or hurricanes, they returned to the island to supervise the estates themselves. Samuel's two older sons joined him there, and his wife and daughters were to follow. Edward, now aged twelve, was to be left alone in England. He was 'too young to be of any use either to my Father or myself in Jamaica', he recalled later, and 'the state of our affairs did not admit of sending me to any school in England of the higher and expensive order'.[101] He was to go to the grammar school in nearby Liskeard. His forthcoming abandonment by his family, the prospect of being alone and with strangers, was almost too much for him and he experienced a 'serious and extreme depression of spirits'.[102] This was worsened by anxieties about his mother, whose previous sojourn on the island had resulted in an illness with lasting consequences.

In Liskeard Edward boarded with Dr Star, the local physician. The family were welcoming, and though there was little money or gentility, there was a good supply of food, a great improvement on his previous school in Bury St Edmunds. An illness in the family, however, resulted in Edward being sent back to Tredudwel, where the only servants left were the old coachman and the dairy maid. She 'was an admirable Drudge, and did the offices of Cook, Butler, housemaid and valet very much to my satisfaction'.[103] After his return to Liskeard, the lonely boy found his solace in books. Homer, Livy and Sallust entranced him, while 'a gift of a set of the Spectators and Tatlers' together with Tacitus and Virgil's Georgics filled him with joy. He 'feasted upon the elegant pages of Addison with the utmost and unceasing delight'.[104] He was learning to be an educated Englishman, imbibing the lessons of the classics and of men of taste, absorbing the pleasures of the imagination. His father's 'improvement' of Tredudwel had taught him something of the meanings of land and property ownership. His Latin improved, thanks to regular exercises, and he was able to translate a whole book of *The Iliad* into Latin hexameter. Holidays were spent with the families of other pupils, and he particularly enjoyed those with John Parker, at Saltram. In Liskeard his grasp of Whiggery, the familial ideology,

---

[101] Ibid., I. 86.
[102] Ibid., I. 87.
[103] Ibid., I. 93.
[104] Ibid., I. 96.

was strengthened by his rapt attention to the lively disputations of his landlord, Dr Star, with the local postmaster.

> They were both staunch Whiggs, and the only difference I could discover between them was, that the Doctor worshipped the memory of the great Deliverer William the 3rd and the Postmaster adored the reigning Sovereign of the Brunswic race, whose officer he was proud to consider himself. Under these two preceptors I could not fail to imbibe the purest principles of Whiggism and a furious abhorrence of the Pretender and his coadjutor, the Pope.[105]

After six years at the school, Uncle Beeston approved of Edward moving to London. A new stage of his life was to begin.

---

[105] Ibid., I. 102.

2

The Young Englishman

Edward's uncle had approved of his move to London, but the young man was left to find his own way there, a source of some anxiety. Many years later he recalled the adventure of his journey. After paying a farewell visit to 'poor Tredudwel', abandoned by the family, he rode on horseback to Plymouth where he took a passage in a government transport boat belonging to the dockyard. Some of the other passengers had brought a supply of provisions with them and he was invited to partake of a very substantial 'Cornish pye, which contained a farrago of Flesh, Apples, onions, allspice and many more ingredients' for which he was grateful.[1] A terrifying night followed, in a minute cabin, more like a cupboard, with a storm that threatened to smash the boat against the Needles, the well-known rocks on the western extremity of the Isle of Wight. The voyage ended with an ebb tide that grounded them outside Portsmouth harbour. Not knowing how to proceed from there, Edward followed the advice of a young Wesleyan cabinet maker he encountered, who had served his apprenticeship in Cornwall and was hoping to hone his skills in the capital. They travelled together in a wagon, often walking ahead of the vehicle, enjoying the delightful summer weather. The Wesleyan quoted entire passages from most parts of the New Testament: 'his language was pure and energetic, and he discoursed with uncommon elocution'.[2] Their fellow travellers were an officer from the Plymouth dockyard who was *en route* to London in search of a surgeon to remove a 'monstrous wen' from his throat, a poor curate from the West Country and, hidden in the straw at the back of the wagon, a young couple, a clergyman's daughter and her papa's footman, who were eloping. After a pleasant journey with this selection of companions, all of whom were headed for the great metropolis and its many exciting yet dangerous possibilities, Edward was set down in Gracechurch Street in the heart of the City, very close to his uncle's merchant house in Bishopsgate Street.

This was Long's first visit to London since the break in the journey from Bury St Edmunds to Tredudwel with his father and two brothers in 1745. A boy then, he was now a young man embarking on the next stage of his life. Arriving

---

[1] Howard, *Records and Letters*, I. 103.
[2] Ibid., I. 105.

in the City he would have seen the magnificent St Paul's cathedral, the Palladian splendours of the Lord Mayor's Mansion House, just completed the year of his arrival, and the Bank of England on Threadneedle Street – all impressive sights for a lad from Cornwall. The City of London had been growing apace, its population now 87,000. But the City was just a small part of the growing metropolis. Its never-ending expansion into the surrounding villages had inspired Defoe to wonder in the 1720s where it might end. Matt Bramble, Smollett's grumpy country squire, noted decades later that 'London is literally new to me, new in its streets, houses, and even in its situation . . . What I left open fields, producing hay and corn, I now find covered with streets and squares, and palaces, and churches . . .'[3] London had become an overgrown monster, with its West End and East End, the river, the court, even the suburbs. The City, however, was a more finite space and this was where Long was situated, in the heart of the financial and commercial district. Perhaps he had in his mind his hero Joseph Addison's description of the marvels of London: 'It gives me a secret Satisfaction and in some measure gratifies my Vanity, as I am an Englishman, to see so rich an Assembly of Countrymen and Foreigners consulting together upon the private Business of Mankind, and making this Metropolis a kind of Emporium for the whole Earth.'[4] There will have been plenty of dirt and smoke and a hotchpotch of streets and buildings to be seen, but it was an urban adventure, full of shops and coffee houses purveying the new world of goods and information. As a child Edward had lived in Newmarket, Bury St Edmunds and Liskeard, all country towns. London was a quite different phenomenon. It was the place for a young man to be and it was the young in particular who were flocking to it, some of them in search of its new quality of urban anonymity.[5]

The family plan, approved by Uncle Beeston, was for Long to improve his penmanship and arithmetic, skills which the classical syllabus of the grammar school had neglected. After some weeks in his uncle's home, he was placed as a boarder at Christ's Hospital, following in his brother Robert's footsteps. This was an old established charity school, founded by King Henry VIII for poor children in the wake of the dissolution of the monasteries. Employing Christopher Wren and Nicholas Hawksmoor, King Charles II had extended it, creating the Royal Mathematical School in 1673, designed to train mathematicians and navigators, skills necessary for political arithmetic, commerce and the oceans. Long's master was a Mr Smith, who occupied a mansion house next to the Hospital. The accommodation he was assigned was an 'execrable garret'.[6] There were three or four hundred Bluecoat boys, so-called because of

---

[3] Tobias Smollett, *Humphry Clinker* [1771] (Harmondsworth, 2008), 99.
[4] Joseph Addison, *The Spectator*, no. 69, 19 May 1711.
[5] Miles Ogborn, *Spaces of Modernity. London's Geographies, 1680–1780* (New York, 1998).
[6] Howard, *Records and Letters*, I. 105.

the blue coats they wore, ranged in classes, and Long was placed in one of the front rows, close to Mr Smith's desk. There were several day scholars as well as the boarders, 'a son of Lord Vane and a son of Sir Edward Walpole: so that these honourable associates kept us in tolerable countenance', but his 'pride revolted not a little', he remembered, 'at mixing in a sort of school with such a profusion of Charity Boys'.[7] His sense of his own class position was not entirely secure. He had passed his adolescence far from his parents and the older siblings who would have helped him to navigate the world of the gentry. He was a country boy, albeit well read and well versed in Latin and Greek: a gentleman's son, albeit in a somewhat precarious position. But how to be a genteel young man?

Boarding with Dr Star was a far cry from the King's House at Newmarket, his first childhood home, or the comforts of Tredudwel. The allowance made for him was very tight: 'only one suit of German serge in a year', his 'hack coat for every day was patched and darned in a thousand places ... which wounded my pride very much'.[8] The doctor was 'a sweet humoured soul', but his spouse, a Devonshire lady, was known to give her forbearing husband 'a violent box on the ear' and scold her 'Squawling brats' and her servants 'outrageously' in her 'shrill accents' – worlds away from his mother's gentility.[9] One vacation was spent at the home of his father's attorney, Mr Kimber of Fowey, but he had reduced his wife 'to the state of an humble drudge, and seemed to govern every thing so despotically' that the boy was determined never to return.[10] Others were spent with the families of schoolfellows. His best memories were of those with John Parker, at Saltram, a Devonshire country house that was in the process of the kinds of 'improvement' that were increasingly popular with the gentry. John's mother, Lady Catherine Poulet, was 'a remarkable woman ... of a vigorous intellect' and 'governed everybody and everything ... except her husband's temper'. A woman of taste, a 'distinguished Connoisseur and Amasser of fine China ... her collection was of the first order in point of Beauty, variety and value'.[11] She was having extensive alterations made to the house, with masons and carpenters constantly at work, as well as an Italian artist who was engaged to stucco the new ceilings. The parkland was being embellished as well, the woods cut through with walks and adorned with a hermitage. These were all signs of a superior sensibility. There 'I rambled every morning', recorded Long, 'or solaced myself in the shade with a favourite author'.[12] This made for a more comfortable setting for a gentleman's son,

---

[7] Ibid., I. 106.
[8] Ibid., I. 90.
[9] Ibid., I. 89.
[10] Ibid., I. 97.
[11] Ibid., I. 100.
[12] Ibid.

albeit one with limited prospects but aspirations as a younger son to secure a prosperous professional livelihood and a position of gentility.

Lady Catherine was clearly someone Long admired. He was appalled, however, by Mrs Smith, the wife of his new master at Christ's Hospital. He had 'no great objection to Mr Smith himself' and found him a good instructor, 'but very many to his wife and his style of living. She had been his Housemaid, a pert and ignorant little Hussey', a veritable 'vixen'.[13] His garret was small and inconvenient and his bed swarming with bugs. He was delighted to leave when, two years later, he was placed with Mr Henry Wilmot of Grey's Inn. His family had paid £300 for him to learn the skills of the solicitor and conveyancer over the next three years. He would then, he hoped, be called to the Bar a year after that. This would raise him to the condition of barrister, increasingly demarcated from that of solicitors and attorneys. The Bar was the pre-eminent profession of early modern England, the 'upper branch' of the legal profession, a sign of which was the right barristers had established to use the title of 'Esquire'.[14] Those entering the profession would have a liberal education and a training in common law. This was a profession suited to the younger son of a family with Jamaican property who were proud of their position as free-born Englishmen. Samuel Long's extensive problems with the law in the wake of his father's losses may have inclined him to see this as a good trajectory for his third son.

Years later, writing from a home in the English countryside rented on the basis of plantation wealth, Edward recorded his different encounters during his London sojourn. They confirmed him in his class prejudices. In Mr Wilmot's establishment, it was fortunate that his fellow students were both of a similar class: William Henry Ricketts, from an established Jamaican family, who was to remain a friend over the years, and William Gee, the son of a Yorkshire squire. Their financial situations, however, were very different from his. William Ricketts had an allowance from his father of £400 p.a., which allowed him to live in a princely fashion. Gee had inherited a fortune from his father and his major interest was in fox hunting. Long, in contrast, had an allowance of £60 p.a., 'out of which I was to provide myself with Cloathes, Food, Fire, Candles, Books, Physic and amusement ... My receipts were quarterly at the house of Drake and Long, £15 p. quarter, and it frequently hapned that I was reduced to the necessity of subsisting the last week, and sometimes the last fortnight before pay-day on nothing else than Tea and Bread and Butter.'[15] But gentility, after all, resided in the self, not in riches. His sister Charlotte, who returned to England briefly in 1755, intervened on his

---

[13] Ibid., I. 106.
[14] David Lemmings, *Gentlemen and Barristers. The Inns of Court and the English Bar, 1680–1730* (Oxford, 1990), 150.
[15] Howard, *Records and Letters*, I. 107.

behalf with their father and his allowance was increased to £80 p.a. By 1756 he had decided to leave the drudgery of Mr Wilmot's office, where he was mainly occupied in copying, in order to seriously study Coke on Littleton and other approved authors, attend the Courts of Law, Equity and Exchequer, and aim to go on circuit in the following year in a 'mix company with select young Students . . . intently bent on making their fortunes by this profession'.[16]

London life also confirmed him in his dislike of female transgression. The regulation of female conduct was a common concern of the 1740s and 1750s, with novels and manuals preoccupied with questions of manners and sexuality. It is possible that Edward knew of Teresia Constantia Phillips, whose trials, tribulations and scandalous doings were to be the talk of both London and Kingston from the late 1740s. With her numerous lovers and husbands, her beauty, her public display of herself together with her Jamaican servants, she was an object of much gossip. Her denunciations of the treachery of men and her insistence on her right to defend herself in print ensured that she remained a celebrated and contested figure, courtesan and memoirist, over decades. In Jamaica between 1738 and 1741, she was living not far from Spanish Town with her wealthy lover, Henry Needham, her 'Mr Worthy' in her later account of their passionate love affair.[17] She was in London in the 1740s but returned to Jamaica in 1751, remaining until her death in 1765. She was to enjoy the patronage of Henry Moore, Edward's future brother-in-law, as his 'Mistress of the Revels' responsible for theatrical presentations and public entertainments in Spanish Town and Kingston. Questions of female agency, sexual desire and immorality were being explored in fiction ranging from Defoe's *Moll Flanders* to Richardson's *Pamela* and *Clarissa*, while social commentators and moralists such as Jonas Hanway worried about prostitutes and proposed the establishment of Magdalen houses.[18] Long's own experience of the loss of his mother combined with the varied wives he had encountered, from the elegant Lady Catherine to the 'shrill accents' of Mrs Star, the 'pert hussy' Mrs Smith. and the 'humble drudge' Mrs Kimber, may have influenced his longing for domestic tranquillity.

His intense pleasure in reading expanded to writing in the 1750s. It is striking that he did not mention this in his retrospective autobiographical fragment, perhaps because he was not proud of his early effusions or because what he was writing was predominantly intended as a family chronicle. In 1756 he published his first literary venture, *The Prater*, a periodical in thirty-five instalments, intended to be, as he put it, entertaining and agreeable reading matter for the frequenters of London coffee houses, those sites of sociability.

---

[16] Ibid., I. 110.
[17] Wilson, *The Island Race*, 136. See Wilson's account of 'The Black Widow'.
[18] Jonas Hanway, *Thoughts on the Plan of a Magdalen House for Repentant Prostitutes* (London, 1758).

Places of 'coffee, companionship, commerce and communication', they were also associated with reading, writing and forms of 'civic urbanism'.[19] Some had extensive collections of newspapers, periodicals, books and pamphlets. Tom's Coffee House, just off the Strand near Temple Bar, was a favoured spot for law students, lawyers and writers, men engaged in commerce and the professions, enjoying, according to the poetry they favoured, a polite, moderate demeanour, an interest in the arts and sciences, and a hostility to excess. Given his extremely modest income, Long's forays into urban society must have been limited, though his stay in Uncle Beeston's house in Bishopsgate Street would have given him some access to the mercantile world. But his reading had prepared him for a world which valued 'taste'. *Taste* was one of the attributes of the 'sociable man' depicted by Addison and Steele, and London was the place for him. Liberty and prosperity had created a new public world, peopled with merchants and traders as well as the old, landed classes, but the dangers of commerce must be tempered with politeness. The category of taste, argues John Brewer, emerged as part of an attempt to stabilize potentially disruptive and excessive aspects of commerce. It would overcome the traditional association between culture and commodities, in a time of massive commercial expansion.[20] Luxury carried dangers: moralists linked consumption with social dislocation and moral corruption.[21] The wrong people might damage the social fabric with their garish choices. Taste was elevated into a political discourse through which these concerns about commerce could be mediated and regulated. Persons of taste would be familiar with the theatres, picture galleries, exhibitions, pleasure gardens and masquerades that were part of the itinerary of cultural pleasures in the city. These encounters would temper their wants and moderate their desires. The profusion of new goods, the wonderful, imported luxuries and the silks, printed calicoes and porcelains, the clocks and watches, the tea, the coffee, the chocolate, the sugar, were all so tempting. Did they encourage the wrong kinds of behaviour? Was all this too luxurious, too feminine, too effeminate, too foreign? Did the mixing of the propertied with the tradespeople and newly rich undermine proper hierarchies? Taste was gendered and linked to improvement in this time of manners.[22] Possessing taste meant possessing refinement and culture, enjoying the pleasures of the imagination rather than the pleasures of the body. It was intimately connected

---

[19] Markman Ellis, 'Poetry and Civic Urbanism in the Coffee-House Library in the mid-Eighteenth Century' in Mark Towsey and Kyle B. Roberts (eds.), *Before the Public Library. Reading, Community and Identity in the Atlantic World, 1650–1850* (Leiden, 2017), 52–72.

[20] John Brewer, *The Pleasures of the Imagination. English Culture in the Eighteenth Century* (London, 1997).

[21] Maxine Berg, *Luxury and Pleasure in Eighteenth-Century Britain* (Oxford, 2005).

[22] Lawrence E. Klein, 'Politeness and the Interpretation of the British Eighteenth Century', *HJ* 45.4 (2002), 869–98.

with politeness, the art of pleasing in conversation and sociability, the capacity for moderation and mutual toleration, not enthusiasm. Politeness, in turn, was built on decorum. Refined masculinity, associated primarily with the middling sorts rather than the aristocracy and gentry, meant the capacity to balance sociability with self-command and self-government.[23] The dangers associated with commercial activity could be tempered by conversation, a key aspect of the new sociability between the sexes. There were concerns about the gentlemen who neglected public duties, the 'fops' who thought only of appearance, the softer forms of masculinity that could put the country in peril. Women were a recognized part of the reading public and would attend theatres and galleries. But much of the anxiety about the new social world was focused on women: the tea parties, the theatre audiences, the masquerades, which allowed all too much space for concealment. Then there was the alarming taste for all things French, for that meant Catholic and autocratic. These were the lessons that Long imbibed from his favourite reading, alongside the conviction that gentility resided in the self.

But the culture of taste had a further dimension. Britain had become the major slave-trading nation and the consumption of sugar was increasing as it shifted from luxury to everyday commodity: new rules and standards were required to reconcile the opposing demands of the production of goods with notions of freedom. An enthusiasm for trade and empire had been articulated in essays, pamphlets and articles from the 1700s. Empire was imagined in terms of flourishing colonies with white populations, and commercial outposts which would act as bases for trade and naval strength. It was connected with hostility to Catholic Europe. 'The imperial project existed to maximize trade and national power,' as Kathleen Wilson argues; 'colonials were considered crucial to the "empire of the sea" that contemporaries believed Britain had, or should have, dominion over.'[24] James Thomson, a Scot and a Patriot Whig (those who looked for a more aggressive foreign policy), was an enthusiastic believer in the future of a nation-state greatly enhanced by its empire. His *Rule Britannia*, with its choral celebration that Britons never will be slaves, counterposed national power to the condition of slaves. The words, as Suvir Kaul argues, both repressed and disavowed knowledge of the slavery business.[25] No organized anti-slavery voice existed at this time, but there was a growing awareness of the African presence and the African trade, particularly in the ports of London, Bristol, Liverpool and Glasgow. There were discomforts around plantation slavery and the wealth of the West Indians, as they were

---

[23] Karen Harvey, 'The History of Masculinity, circa 1650–1800', *JBS* 44.2 (2005), 296–311.
[24] Kathleen Wilson, *The Sense of the People. Politics, Culture and Imperialism in England, 1715–1785* (Cambridge, 1998), 155–6.
[25] For an excellent analysis of *Rule Britannia*, see Suvir Kaul, *Poems of Nation, Anthems of Empire. English Verse in the Long Eighteenth Century* (London, 2008), 1–8.

called, those men who returned from the colonies with habits, including the proprietorship of enslaved servants, that suggested they were not quite English.[26] What was more, they wanted to be able to exercise influence, not least on questions of sugar duties. In the 1745 election, thirteen West Indians had been elected to the House of Commons, nearly doubling their strength, and this began to provoke unfriendly comment.[27]

Despite his slave-owning family in Jamaica, Edward Long would have found the everyday sighting of black people on the streets of London a new experience. On the docks, where the sugar and rum were unloaded along with the spices and luxury goods from the east, there would have been African mariners and cabin boys alongside Indian laskars. The London press carried regular advertisements from owners attempting to locate runaways: John Smart, 'A Negro (very black) wears his wool, and not a wig'; Cato, 'A Negro Boy', had run away from his master, a captain; James Williams, 'A Negro Slave', had run away from the ship *Pleasant*.[28] Their masters were asserting their legitimate ownership and hoping to re-enslave these 'fortune seekers', as Simon Newman re-names them. Their existence was a mark of the ways in which racial slavery was being 'created simultaneously in London and in the colonies'.[29] These were vivid reminders of the presence of slavery and black servitude in England. Black boys and men were on the streets of London collecting and delivering correspondence, attending to goods and horses, acting as footmen, dressing turtle and serving soup in the homes of the *ton*, the best society. The figure of the African was familiar from a plethora of visual images adorning shops and taverns. Coffee houses such as Garraway's in Exchange Alley were the sites of plantation sales, including their enslaved populations.[30] Metropolitan society was deeply entangled in the contact zones of Atlantic slavery, as Catherine Molineux demonstrates.[31] William Beckford, London alderman, Jamaican slave-owner and ally of William Pitt in the Seven Years War, was widely caricatured as 'Alderman Sugarcane'. Smollett, a political opponent and himself married to a West Indian heiress, satirized Beckford's pretensions: 'that eminent patriot of the plantations, so much admired for his eloquence, so warmly beloved for his liberality'.[32] There was 'a need and desire to quarantine

---

[26] Perry Gauci, *William Beckford. First Prime Minister of the London Empire* (London, 2013), 100–1.
[27] Perry Gauci, 'The Attack of the Creolian Powers: West Indians at the Parliamentary Elections of mid-Georgian Britain, 1754–74', *Parliamentary History* 33.1 (2014), 201–22.
[28] See www.runaways.gla.ac.uk/: *London Evening Post*, 5 July 1753; *Public Advertiser*, 30 May 1753; *London Evening Post*, 17 February 1756.
[29] Simon P. Newman, *Fortune Seekers. Escaping from Slavery in Restoration London* (London, 2022), xxvii.
[30] Markman Ellis, *The Coffee-House. A Cultural History* (London, 2004), 285.
[31] Catherine Molineux, *Faces of Perfect Ebony. Encountering Atlantic Slavery in Imperial Britain* (Cambridge, MA, 2012).
[32] Gauci, *William Beckford*, 111.

one aspect of social life', as Simon Gikandi argues, 'that which was tasteful, beautiful and civilised – from a public domain saturated by diverse forms of commerce including the sale of black bodies'. The category of taste marked an 'attempt to use culture to conceal the intimate connection between modern subjectivity and the political economy of slavery'.[33] The discourse of taste had a racialized as well as imperial dimension: at some unconscious level, Long may have been aware of what it meant to be a white man.

West Indians and Africans were not the only 'others' about whom questions of difference and belonging circulated in the 1750s. The Jacobite rebellion of 1745 had left a deep scar and there were periodic outcries against the Scots while the figure of 'The Pretender' remained a potent force. Imperial expansion had meant migration both out and in: more foreigners were present in Britain. The years after the War of Austrian Succession were a time of deep malaise, with economic and social dislocation, unemployment, fears about crime and violence, and xenophobia.[34] There were debates in the press about 'internal others', foreigners and the question of naturalization for those born abroad.[35] Many Tories saw the naturalization of foreign-born others as a threat to English property rights and economic opportunities. Whigs tended to favour immigration as a way of building commerce and wealth. Hogarth's picture of London highlights its chaos, inequalities, disorder and volatilities, the violence and corruption of the city. Boswell was struck by the noise and the crowd when he first arrived. Visiting Indigenous royals, war chiefs and diplomats could bring an exoticism to the streets of the city.[36]

There were about eight thousand Jews in Britain, but their most significant presence was in the City where they were involved in every aspect of commercial and financial activity and their global commercial networks gave them considerable leverage. In April 1753 a Jewish Naturalization Bill had been introduced in the House of Lords and passed both houses of parliament with ease. This allowed for the possibility of a private Act permitting the naturalization of an individual Jewish man born outside England without him receiving the sacrament. He could then legally own land, own a share in a British sailing vessel and engage in colonial trade. This legislation was supported by commercial enthusiasts such as Horace Walpole and Josiah Tucker who saw it as encouraging prosperity. A popular furore, however, erupted against the legislation, with pamphlets, prints, sermons and petitions stressing the dangers to British Protestantism, the nation's laws and liberties. Voices were raised against a potential Jewish conspiracy which would emasculate British men and

---

[33] Simon Gikandi, *Slavery and the Culture of Taste* (Princeton, 2011), 6–7, 17.
[34] Nicholas Rogers, *Mayhem. Post-War Crime and Violence in Britain, 1748–1753* (London, 2012); Wilson, *The Sense of the People*.
[35] Rabin, *Britain and its Internal Others*.
[36] Coll Thrush, *Indigenous London. Native Travellers at the Heart of Empire* (London, 2016).

rob them of their property; antisemitic prints played on well-established tropes of Jewish greed, cunning and dishonesty. So great was the popular outcry that the legislation was repealed in November 1753. Sir John Barnard, an MP for London, summarized the legal heart of the matter: Jews could not be Englishmen. 'I am strictly speaking neither a friend to the Jews nor their Enemy,' he maintained, 'excepting when they aim at having equal Rights and Privilages [sic] with my Fellow Citizens and Country Men.'[37] 'The agitation sparked by the Jew Bill of 1753', argued Todd Endelman, 'functioned as a lightning rod for the articulation of nationalist sentiments at the time.'[38] Dana Rabin's analysis, with its emphasis on the centrality of law to the constructions of otherness within Britain, shows how 'the legal category of whiteness, which implied a white, male, English, Anglican subject, emerged as a site through which to identify, define and arbitrate the implications of empire at home'.[39]

In the early to mid-eighteenth century, despite war, cultivated Englishmen and Frenchmen, argues Gerald Newman, had disparaged local attachments and shared intellectual ideals embracing the whole of Europe.[40] Voltaire was the chief mediator of this French–British accord. An Anglophile, his *Letters on England*, published in English in 1733, had celebrated the 'harmony between King, Lords, and commons', the liberty and the religious toleration which had resulted from civil war, the trade which 'enriched the citizens in England, so it contributed to their freedom'.[41] The mercantile world and the commercial success that flowed from it were inseparable, to his mind, from the intellectual triumphs of Francis Bacon, John Locke and Isaac Newton. Voltaire was an enthusiast for a cosmopolitan Europe and argued in *Le siècle de Louis XIV* that European strength lay in its political diversity, based on common principles and the manifest cultural superiority of its scientific and artistic community. In *Essai sur les Moeurs et l'esprit des Nations*, he represented Europe as richer and more civilized than any other continent.[42] At the same time he was aware of the distinctive characteristics of the different European nations. For the English landed classes, their European consciousness went alongside a conviction of French superiority in manners and customs and constant efforts at mimicry; they were the *ton*, the *beau monde*. London high society was characterized by a passion for all that was French – French manners,

---

[37] Cited in Rabin, *Britain and its Internal Others*, 62. Rabin also discusses the 1753 case of Mary Squires, a 'gypsy' accused of abducting a young servant girl and attempting to lure her into prostitution.
[38] Todd M. Endelman, *The Jews of Britain, 1656 to 2000* (Berkeley, 2002), 6.
[39] Rabin, *Britain and its Internal Others*, 29.
[40] Gerald Newman, *The Rise of English Nationalism. A Cultural History, 1740–1830* (London, 1987).
[41] Voltaire, *Letters on England* (London, 1733), 29, 33.
[42] On Voltaire, see Peter Gay, *Voltaire's Politics. The Poet as Realist* [1959] (London, 1988).

literature, architecture, cookery, fashion, costume, dancing and jewellery. Amongst English writers and painters, however, from the artist William Hogarth to the authors Henry Fielding, Tobias Smollett, Oliver Goldsmith and James Thomson, men with a different class background from the landed and often struggling to survive financially, there was a deep resentment about the preference shown by the *beau monde* for everything French. They celebrated plain English virtues, those of Fielding's Tom Jones or Goldsmith's Vicar of Wakefield, attacked national corruption and decay, luxury, conspicuous consumption and moral dissolution. Addison and Steele had represented English language and literature as part of an Englishman's birthright. David Garrick popularized Shakespeare from the 1750s, claiming him as a 'hallowed national figure', celebrating English drama for its expression of English values.[43]

Anti-French feeling had a long history in England, for France was Britain's major enemy and the two countries were at war on and off between 1689 and 1815. As Linda Colley famously argued, Britons came to define themselves against the French, their Catholicism and autocracy.[44] The periodic Jacobite invasion scares and the events of 1745 encouraged a range of patriotic initiatives and discussions of national identity. The Laudable Association of Anti-Gallicans, for example, their badge a formidable St George defeating a terrible dragon, mobilized middling tradespeople and artisans in 1745. It aimed to keep out French commodities and encourage British manufactures. The Society for the Encouragement of the Arts, Manufacture and Commerce was less xenophobic but also saw the French as a major threat. A patriotic consciousness, linked particularly to issues of competition and rivalry, was becoming more explicitly nationalist, at a time when differences between nations were an object of commentary and protests were being mounted against alien influences. This economic and cultural nationalism became more strident with the onset of war in 1756. Pitt and his West Indian ally, William Beckford, successfully articulated these nationalist sentiments. The Seven Years War began disastrously for Britain with the fall of Minorca, a place seen as strategically important for British commercial interests. The defeat was viewed as a national humiliation. The invasion scare of 1757 was a source of huge anxiety, particularly given the absence of a strong military presence: the inadequacies of the militia had been all too evident in 1745. Pitt's Militia Act was passed in 1757 in response to the threat of invasion and secured the mobilization of a force for the defence of the kingdom. This war was understood differently from earlier conflicts with France in that it was fought between two nations rather than two royal houses as in the past. In this atmosphere anti-Gallicanism became rife. The French responded in kind:

---

[43] Brewer, *The Pleasures of the Imagination*, 328.
[44] Linda Colley, *Britons. Forging the Nation, 1707–1837* (London, 1992).

they constructed the British as barbarians, the opposite of civilized people, *la nation sauvage*.[45] Nationalism, and the 'idea of essential, unalterable difference between two nations', was an increasingly potent force on both sides of the Channel and a driving force, alongside imperial rivalries, of the inter-European conflicts across the Northwest, the Pacific, the Atlantic and the Indian Ocean.[46]

Taste and politeness, with their gendered connotations, underpinned by ideas of Englishness, were the defining issues for Long in his first literary venture. *The Prater* was published by T. Lowndes, a London publisher who was to deal with almost all Long's subsequent writing. Periodicals such as this were circulating widely in the 1750s, hoping to benefit from the earlier success of *The Spectator* and *The Tatler*. There were two or three every year in London in the 1750s. *The Prater* shared their typical features: regular and frequent appearance, engagement with the public sphere of private individuals rather than with party politics, letters from imagined correspondents, touches of scandal, reference to dreams and oriental allegorical tales. Long's choice of this medium for his first foray into print made sense, for it was a well-established genre and each issue was a modest venture. He perhaps imagined himself at this time as being a literary man as well as a lawyer, one of those who might be able to augment his income by writing in the range of forms, from periodicals to travel writing to novels and histories, that were finding audiences amongst the growing reading public of both men and women. *The Prater* aimed to be witty and amusing, demonstrate a knowledge of fashion and urban life, and point to the dangers of tradesmen and their wives aping their betters. He may have hoped to capture what Addison named as the 'talent of affecting the imagination that gives an embellishment to good sense, and makes one man's compositions more agreeable than another's'.[47] The caricatures who peopled *The Prater* were the product of a lively imagination. Perhaps the work might serve as a calling card, gaining Long access to literary circles.[48] Replete with epigraphs from a range of classical and contemporary authors, from Pope, Virgil and Horace, to Milton, Swift and Thomson, it critiqued the *beau monde*, especially young women of fashion, and celebrated the countryside and 'the man of sense'.

The idea of a *Prater* summoned up a pompous, foolish, ranting preacher, full of idle talk. Long's *Prater* was Nicholas Babble, an unfashionable man in his fifties who preferred the country to the city, could comment extensively on the foibles of those he met, and was scandalized by the giddy and immoral ways of

---

[45] Robert-Martin Lesuire, *Les sauvages de l'Europe* (Paris, 1762).
[46] David Bell, *The Cult of the Nation in France: Inventing Nationalism, 1680–1800* (Cambridge, MA, 2009), 94. Bell's quote is about France.
[47] *The Spectator*, no. 421, 3 July 1712.
[48] Thanks to Markman Ellis for this thought.

the Quality. The cast of characters he encountered were many and varied. There was Sir Harry Squander and the berouged woman he had married for money; Rose Plump, the picture-frame maker's daughter who agreed to model in the nude; Miss Giddy and Miss Bright who flirted and prattled; the bookseller Pinch accused of plagiarism (always a concern for writers); Jack Tattle who spent his time in the City and the coffee houses, collecting gossip; and Roger Smokey, country bumpkin. Then there was the virtuous Mr Manley, the 'man of sense', who spent his time 'rationally, usefully, and becomingly', unlike those who gratified their appetites in whatever way they chose, ruining themselves and others.[49] Marrying for money was castigated along with drunkenness and sexual immorality. Mr Worthy and his family, living in the country fifteen miles from London, represented the domestic ideal, a rather different figure from that of Teresia Phillips's 'Mr Worthy'. A charming scene was depicted: Mr Worthy reading improving matter to his family, his wife and daughters with their needlework, his son painting a landscape in watercolours. Long was already an enthusiast for James Thomson and he quoted his lines on the joys of domestic and familial life in a country setting:

> An elegant Sufficiency, Content,
> Retirement, rural Quiet, Friendship, Books,
> Ease and alternate Labor, useful Life,
> Progressive Virtue, and approving Heaven,
> These are the matchless Joys of virtuous Love,
> And thus their Moments fly.[50]

The Worthy family lived a worthy life: politeness encompassed the pursuit of harmony in propertied society.[51] Each day the men spent time in the library, the women drew flowers and did embroidery; they enjoyed visits from selected guests and performed musically for each other, including selections from Handel's *Messiah*, a great English favourite. There was conversation, a source for 'many sweet Civilities of Life'.[52] A family walk up a neighbouring hill revealed 'a joy inspiring Prospect ... Hills and Dales sweetly interchanged, the former covered with innumerable Trees, adorned with the most vivid Colors, the latter diversified with Cows and Sheep, Hay-cocks, Corn-fields, and verdant Meadows, through which our justly-celebrated River meander'd, and heighten'd the richness of the View ... the Beauties of Nature ... '[53] This was a style of writing with its emphasis on 'Prospects', on those who had the capacity to *really* see, on the picturesque and the wonders of nature, that Long was to develop later in his account of the beauties of Jamaica. His idealization of quiet domesticity

---

[49] [Edward Long], *The Prater by Nicholas Babble* (London, 1756).
[50] *The Prater*, 112.
[51] Paul Langford, *A Polite and Commercial People, 1727–1783* [1989] (Oxford, 1998).
[52] *The Prater*, 175.
[53] Ibid., 112.

may have been fuelled by the absence of his own family, his knowledge of the unhappy ending of his parents' marriage, and his observations of domestic strife in the varied households in which he had lived.

Proper relations between the sexes were a preoccupation of *The Prater*. The sphere of women, Long maintained, was the household. It was the 'valuable branches of domestic knowledge' that they should be acquainted with.[54] Households should be well regulated, and servants know their place, treating their masters with 'the most submissive respect and a kind of reverential awe'.[55] Children too should be obedient to their parents. A proper order within the household was essential. A dream sequence fantasized a new branch of government led by women who debated men's aversion to matrimony and offered remedies ranging from castration (a suggestion of the more aged) to banishment. A matron terminated the discussion with her declaration that 'Masculine women and effeminate men are in my opinion equally disagreeable.'[56] Each should occupy their proper place. Effeminacy might be associated with 'an injudicious pursuit of sensual gratifications', a lack of self-control.[57] The 'peculiar Charm' of women he defined as 'DECENCY'.[58] Yet that decency and modesty was constantly undermined by the demands of fashion, not least amongst the pretentious daughters of well-to-do tradespeople who aped the *beau monde*, rejected the sons of mercers and butchers, and sighed over young gallants. The absurdities of 'the present ridiculous mode of dress' was a favourite topic for Nicholas Babble, echoing many contemporary discourses against the propensity to adopt foreign fashions, not just amongst women but amongst those men too concerned with appearance, 'effeminate creatures', who might be thought 'Beaus of Passage', touring through Egypt, Africa and Jamaica in their outlandish costumes before returning to England for the summer.[59] The mention of Jamaica is striking with its connection to effeminacy, heat, tropicality and Africa, one of the very few traces in this work of the Long family's connections to that island. The preoccupation with dress marked the fashion for all things French, provoking Nicholas Babble's anti-Gallicanism: 'I am an Englishman, and a true lover of my native land.'[60] Patriotism had been lauded as a noble sentiment since the 1720s, but in the context of this war it had a new relevance.[61] Why French stay-makers, barbers and valets? How could it be that French artists were preferred to English ones

---

[54] Ibid., 171.
[55] Ibid., 99.
[56] Ibid., 42.
[57] Ibid., 164.
[58] Ibid., 174.
[59] Ibid., 170.
[60] Ibid., 61.
[61] Christine Gerrard, *The Patriot Opposition to Walpole. Politics, Poetry and National Myth, 1725–1742* (Oxford, 1994).

whose families were starving in garrets? But his anti-Gallican sentiments were limited, for moderation was the key. He invited his readers to laugh at the ladies' tea party he attended where he found the young women declaring their 'noble anti-gallican spirit', insisting that they would donate their jewellery and their Indian porcelain for the fight against their mortal enemy, the French. One of their number even vowed that she would give 'Pompey's silver collar' for the war effort.[62] Was Pompey a dog, or one of the black pages, so valued by ladies of fashion? A 'Pompey', with a brass collar about his neck, figured in one of the London advertisements for a 'fortune seeker'.[63] Did Long know that Pompey was a favourite name for enslaved Africans on Jamaican plantations?

One year later, Long's novel *The Anti-Gallican, or, the History and Adventures of Harry Cobham, Esquire* was published, a picaresque production combining a loose narrative of the dangers of excessive hostility to the French with a range of adventures, a defence of marriage, some chamberpot humour, bawdiness enjoyed and descried, and a panegyric to British liberty.

The epigraph on the title page of the novel read,

> *No* Smuggled, Pilfer'd *Scenes from* France *we show,*
> *He's* English, English, *Sirs, from Top to Toe.*

The Preface welcomed the 'tribe of Novellists' who had started into business in recent years and established a very lucrative trade for themselves. Fielding was celebrated as 'the Cervantes of England', a giant amongst the host of other authors of 'fabulous Adventures', some bad and some indifferent. Then there were the 'vicious Books' which fed immorality and carnality.[64] This author would, of course, do no such thing. 'My Page', he wrote, 'like the hero it treats of, is plain, rough, and unpolished', but with a good moral purpose, an intent to 'animate the generous *Briton* to a laudable defence of those invaluable Blessings he enjoys under so excellent a constitution'.[65] His form of address suggests the importance for Long of emphasizing the masculinity of his writing; there was no danger of effeminacy here. Aiming for wit and entertainment, the Preface concluded:

> No books so perfect but with Faults abound,
> The best are those wherein the least are found.[66]

Long had probably read *The Adventures of Roderick Random*, an earthy, bawdy picaresque novel full of a man's adventures including war in the West Indies. Smollett's Preface had recommended the kinds of satire introduced in

---

[62] *The Prater*, 37–8.
[63] Newman, *Fortune Seekers*, 122.
[64] [Edward Long], *The Anti-Gallican; or, the History and Adventures of Harry Cobham, Esquire. Inscribed to Louis the XVth by the Author* (London, 1757).
[65] Ibid., xiv.
[66] Ibid., xvi.

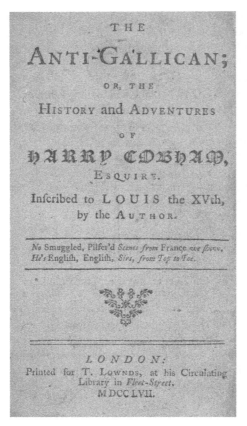

Figure 2.1 Title page of Edward Long's *The Anti-Gallican; or, the History and Adventures of Harry Cobham, Esquire. Inscribed to Louis the XVth, by the author*. Published anonymously under the pseudonym Frank Cobham, 1757. British Library, London, UK © British Library Board. All Rights Reserved/Bridgeman Images.

the course of a story, 'which brings every incident home to life; and by representing familiar scenes in an uncommon and amusing point of view, invests them with all the graces of novelty, while nature is appealed to in every particular'. This would be agreeably diverting and open 'an ample field for wit and humour'.[67] Roderick Random encountered mean grandfathers, highwaymen, sailors, prostitutes and French valets, among many other characters of the new social world of the eighteenth century. The varied cast of characters that Long created was rather similar.

[67] Tobias Smollett, *The Adventures of Roderick Random* [1748] (London, n.d.), 1.

Harry Cobham, the eponymous hero of Long's novel, was a simple country squire, 'a most-rigid *anti-Gallican*', whose excessive hatred for the French and dismay at the current degeneration of Britons almost led to disaster. 'Honest Cobham' would never forfeit his character as a true Englishman or vote for 'the Introduction of Slavery, Popery, and *Frenchmen* among us'.[68] His garden sported British trees, most notably a venerable oak, visited each morning, and statues of Britannia and the British lion. His wife, however, loved to speak French and admired French fashion. His daughter Sophia, sent to a Quaker school simply dressed by Mrs Homespun, returned home in Frenchified costume, to her father's horror. The Quaker teacher, Mrs Slyboots, had, it transpired, married her French stay-maker, who subsequently misbehaved with one of the schoolgirls. Cobham warned his wife and daughter against French habits, telling them the story of a young lawyer, Will Dupe. Teased by his friends for his devotion to his legal studies, Dupe took to drink and bad habits rather than Westminster Hall and Coke on Littleton (the texts that Long had vowed to devote himself to). Having rescued a beautiful damsel in distress – the orphaned daughter of a country clergyman who had been debauched and abandoned by a Justice of the Quorum – Dupe set her up in an establishment with an annuity of £200 p.a. However, he made the mistake of introducing to the household a promiscuous French valet, who seduced the lady with 'all the tricks of *French* gallantry'.[69]

Cobham was himself led astray, however, by the excesses of his anti-Gallicanism. A complicated plot centred on his conviction, fostered by a society of which he was the president, of an imminent French attack in support of the Pretender. The society's meetings, held in the Ship Inn in London, were devoted to drinking and smoking as much as they could prior to conducting their business. Their support of country and colonies required that they must 'consume their Product and Manufactures as fast as we can'. In the same spirit, 'a Tea-Drinker, who, for the same publick-spirited Reason, uses an immoderate Quantity of Sugar, may vaunting cry, whilst he drops the mighty Lump of Sweetness into his Bason of Tea, this I do for the Benefit of the Plantations!'[70] (Here was another trace of Jamaica.) Tobacco was the other essential ingredient of their convivial gatherings. Once armed with their porter and pipes, the serious matter of considering the necessary fortification to repel the French could be considered. Cobham's fellow members, who in truth were plotting to gain his fortune, persuaded him of the urgent need to prepare for an attack, to 'exert our native spirit' and 'chase these *Frenchmen* to their boats again with Slaughter and Confusion'.[71] Cobham must rise to the challenge,

---

[68] *The Anti-Gallican*, 8, 12.
[69] Ibid., 28.
[70] Ibid., 118.
[71] Ibid., 127.

pledging his money and his life. A series of unlikely adventures saw him tricked by his fellows, taken prisoner, mistaken for the Pretender, tried at the assizes, and escape one terrible fate only to be press-ganged and eventually rescued by French Protestants, on their way to England to escape from Catholicism. There could, it turned out, be good French people.

Meanwhile, Sophia, an avid reader of *The Spectator*, tempered her mother's enthusiasm for all things French with a proper sense of moderation. Tea could, indeed, carry a danger, for it was 'a most extravagant consumer of Time and Reputation'; tea parties were well known to be sites of malicious gossip. Sophia proposed 'Tea-Table Laws': no lies, no scandal, no ill-speaking of other women would be permitted.[72] Their own adventures, not least rescue from a highwayman, provided opportunities for discourses on 'the Oeconomy of female apparel' and the horrors of marriage for money.[73] A set-piece between the local clergyman, Mr Trueman, and his wife, in which Mr Trueman argued that women should not concern themselves with politics and that it was woman's role to submit to man, was met with an angry riposte concerning Boadicea and Queen Elizabeth I. Mrs Cobham in turn was provoked to declare, 'There can be no Sex in Souls, I see no reason why Women may not have competent Abilities for State, as well as domestic Affairs.' But God did not intend 'to assign our Sex the Superiority', she continued: 'Men hold the Prerogative of Dominion over us, by virtue of Nature's Charter; not a tyrannic Authority to treat us like menial Slaves, but as Friends and Companions in the State of Wedlock.' You men, she continued, are inclined to be arrogant. 'If you would carry yourselves with less Arrogance, we should behave with more Subordination.'[74] Her husband's excessive interest in politics had courted disaster. Fortunately, his adventures had tempered his hatred of the French. Enthusiasm was dangerous; what was needed was moderation in all things. 'Patriotism', the wise narrator concluded, 'like other Virtues, lies between two equi-distant Points.'[75]

The novel ended with a dream. A violent hubbub was exploding in the Temple of Novelty, with a crowd of men and women disputing the relative merits of their writing. A genie appeared and divided them into two groups: *Romance*, represented as Spanish, and the *Novel*, a giant figure, looking like Fielding and representing England. Our modest author, unable to come close to his hero, had to retreat into a distant corner, proud of his efforts but hoping for more success in the future. Opening a scroll he found a poem to liberty:

> Whilst George, the great support of Freedom's cause
> Defends our Faith, and rules with wholesome Laws;

[72] Ibid., 43.
[73] Ibid., 62.
[74] Ibid., 113–15.
[75] Ibid., 229.

> At once our King, our Father, and our Friend,
> Here Britons, here, with grateful Rev'rence see
> The mighty Guardian of your Liberty ...

Look from 'this blest Isle' to France, the poet continued, home of 'Tyrannic Sway', where 'Rapine rules', 'poor Industry droops' and 'pining Commerce sits neglected by'. And he concluded with these stirring lines:

> And should Invasion's horrid Tumults roar,
> Threatening with Gallic arms our Albion's Shore,
> Swift to the field your glad Auxiliance bring,
> True to your GOD, your COUNTRY, and your KING.

A new nationalist consciousness, Gerald Newman argues, was first articulated in literature. *The Englishman in Paris* (1753) and *The Englishman Returned from Paris* (1756), productions by Sam Foote, the comic actor and dramatist, had played on the bad influence of French minions, sapping the national spirit and corrupting innocent Englishwomen. John Brown's *Estimate of the Manners and Principles of the Times* (1757–8) maintained that the nation would perish if there was no revival and no rejection of effeminacy and the Gallic influence. His dedication was to William Pitt, and his hope that some great minister might emerge and that war might purge the nation of its weaknesses. A link was being made between the individual behaviour of men and the corporate body of the nation and empire.[76] Long's poem evoked a patriotic nationalism, rooted in a belief in 'Laws . . . Liberty' and the blessings of a Protestant king, counterposed to the 'Tyrannic Sway' of France, where 'Industry droops' and 'Commerce sits neglected'. These were some of the themes of his literary effusions in the 1750s, written in the shadow of war, a war which greatly strengthened a consciousness of the bonds of belonging. He had learned his lessons from Addison, was well acquainted with the demands of taste and politeness, tempered excess in favour of moderation. He had a sense of the fragility of his class identity but hoped that his gentility was secure in himself. He strongly disapproved of women out of place but could intersperse this with some bawdy humour. His Englishness was at the heart of his identity as a young man. Colonies and plantations, Africans and sugar, were not as yet central to his imagination. As Nicholas Babble had put it, 'I am an *Englishman* and a true lover of my native land.'[77]

In 1758, however, with his legal studies not yet completed, bad news came from Jamaica – first of the death of his beloved brother Charles, then of his father's untimely passing. When the will was opened, the relative paucity of his

---

[76] Lisa Forman Cody, *Birthing the Nation. Sex, Science and the Conception of Eighteenth-Century Britons* (Oxford, 2005); Carol Watts, *The Cultural Work of Empire. The Seven Years War and the Imagining of the Shandean State* (Edinburgh, 2007).
[77] *The Prater*, 61.

inheritance was revealed.[78] As yet he had earned little or no money; writing for the marketplace would threaten his status as a gentleman.[79] Uncle Beeston recommended he go to Jamaica, the place for a young man to make a fortune. The colony offered new opportunities, new times with few restrictions. Long's English birthright could be combined with a providential imperial future. He could live his nation's destiny in colonizing and civilizing others.

---

[78] Long received £1,000. The value of this today can be calculated in various ways. The UK Inflation Calendar values it as £258,348. But inflation is difficult to assess and the figure may be significantly higher. On the problem of estimating the value of the compensation money in today's terms, see Draper, *The Price*, 106–7.

[79] Norma Clarke, *Brothers of the Quill. Oliver Goldsmith in Grub Street* (Cambridge, MA, 2016).

PART II

The Lineaments of Racial Capitalism

Edward Long arrived in Jamaica in 1758. Chapters 3, 4 and 5 trace the distinctive features and characteristics of the mid-eighteenth-century form of racial capitalism rooted in the sugar and slavery business. The heart of the economic infrastructure lay in the plantation, the merchant house and the slave trade, which, together with the gendered marriage, inheritance and property relations of the families of white slave-owners and merchants, enabled capital accumulation.

3

The Plantation

Edward Long arrived in Jamaica in 1758. The island was seen in England as a place where white colonists could make a fortune. It was not only its 'fertility and beauty' that attracted settlers, but 'the profits'.[1] Once supplied with credit a planter could hope to make a tidy sum from the production of King Sugar, extracted from the labour of the enslaved. By the time Long returned to the 'mother country' in 1768, his aim as he wrote the *History* was to explain the workings of the plantation, from the purchase of land and labour to the production of the cane and the reproduction of the labour force. Profit depended on the daily practices of racialization of both black people and white: from claiming rights of property and freedom for whites (albeit on classed and gendered terms) to buying, naming and branding captives, disciplining the enslaved into labour gangs, regulating their tasks and their lives in multiple ways, claiming rights over their bodies and those of their children, and demarcating politically, legally, economically and culturally between those with power and authority and those without. The enslaved massively outnumbered the whites. Long estimated in 1768 that the white population of Jamaica, including seamen and soldiers, was approximately 20,500, while there were 166,914 'Negroes'.[2]

In the minds of the planters, enslaved men and women were *capital* of a very particular kind, human capital. Their aim was to accumulate money capital through their production and sale of sugar. Eighteenth-century planters were capitalist farmers and manufacturers operating in a mercantilist frame which secured the economic and political interests of the mother country and within a colonial system organized on the basis of racialization. They were dependent on merchants to provide the credit which enabled them to establish plantations. They paid for that credit with consignments of sugar. The merchants also financed the West India trade: the ships to be sent to West Africa, captives to be delivered to Jamaica, supplies delivered from Britain, Ireland and the North American colonies, sugar to be returned to England. Planters owned

---

[1] William Burke and Edmund Burke, *An Account of the European Settlements in America. In six parts* [1759], 5th edition with improvements (London, 1770), 63.
[2] Long, *History*, I. 377.

land, enslaved people and the works to process the cane, but they carried heavy debts: their profit depended on the successful delivery of sugar and rum to the metropole. They supervised the production and processing of the cane, consigned the goods to overseas merchants, arranged for supplies and for credit and loans. Growing sugar was an extremely risky business and many failed. The planter's capacity to accumulate capital depended on the successful extraction of life and labour from enslaved men and women, held captive in a racialized hierarchy with clear divisions of labour. *Human capital* and cattle, both mobile, were held alongside another form of capital, fixed capital, in the form of the land and the works. The slave-owner bought the enslaved man's capacity to labour, the enslaved woman's capacity both to labour and to reproduce.[3] He bought their persons, their bodies, their selves, their time.[4] Once claimed as property, these labourers did not have to be paid: there was no contract, and the only further expense for the slave-owner was to provide some subsistence. Some of the enslaved might become more valuable over time, their market price increase, as men acquired skills, women bore children. As those women aged, however, their value would be reduced. Others would die. On the plantations it was essential to preserve them as captive and prevent escape through a variety of strategies: force, terror, and a system of mastery including the exercise of sexual power and the creation of hierarchies through the granting of racialized and gendered privileges. The almost absolute authority of the slave-owner was backed by the colonial state, the militia, the military and, when it came to runaways or rebels, the Maroons. The plantation economy relied on the provision grounds cultivated by the enslaved in time outside working hours. The enslaved provided much of the food for themselves and their families and in addition were able to establish a domestic marketing system.[5] The pens which produced livestock were a further essential element of the system, supplying manure and the means of driving the mills and transporting the crops. The revolution in sugar consumption in the metropole had fuelled the transformation of the plantations into what Sidney Mintz memorably described as 'factories in the field'.[6] The large scale of landholdings, a dependence on enslaved and coerced labour, the high ratios of Africans to

---

[3] Thanks to Mark Harvey for his clarification on this point. The market value of an enslaved person depended on their continuing capacity to perform labour, either productive or reproductive. 'Picketty, Property, Slavery', unpublished paper 2021.

[4] On temporality, see Walter Johnson, 'Time and Revolution in African America: Temporality and the History of Atlantic Slavery', in Kathleen Wilson (ed.), *A New Imperial History. Culture, Identity and Modernity in Britain and the Empire, 1660–1840* (Cambridge, 2004), 197–215.

[5] Sidney W. Mintz, 'The Jamaica Internal Marketing Pattern: Some Notes and Hypotheses', *Social and Economic Studies* 4.1 (March 1955), 95–103.

[6] Sidney W. Mintz, *Sweetness and Power. The Place of Sugar in Modern History* (New York, 1985), xxiii.

Europeans, hierarchical management, an exclusive focus on sugar for export with prices protected in the British market, and high value per capita output were the common features of this system. These were the 'large integrated plantations' of Trevor Burnard's analysis, which had come to dominate the landscape between the 1690s and 1740s. They relied on a highly disciplined form of gang labour and, when times were good and the price of sugar high, functioned as an 'extraordinary mechanism for generating wealth and prosperity'.[7] 'The planters of Jamaica', concludes Barry Higman, 'built a highly productive system in which per capita output was greater than almost anywhere else yet took to themselves the lion's share of the profits. The great wealth of the few depended on the poverty of the productive many ... [they] were capitalists operating within the context of a capitalist colonial economy, always on the look-out for ways to increase private property.'[8]

In this chapter, Edward Long's arrival in Jamaica, his acquisition of the family plantation, 'Lucky Valley', and his account of what it meant to be a slave-owner, a planter, to manage such an estate with the labour of enslaved men and women and how to secure the reproduction of that labour system, are described. The *History* was written at a time when the plantation economy was flourishing but the slave trade and slavery were subject to increasing criticism in the metropole. The picture he provided was designed to persuade readers, and himself, of the benign nature of colonial slavery, whilst encouraging the new white settlers who were essential for political and social stability. Unwittingly, he provided a picture of the workings of what we might now define as racial capitalism.

Jamaica in the 1750s

Long arrived in Jamaica in 1758 in the wake of the unexpected death of his father and his favourite brother, Charles. He was twenty-three years old, had long known of the importance of the plantations to his family, but had never been out of England. His father, as we know, had gone to Jamaica in 1745, hoping that he could recover his fortune, taking his oldest son, Robert, with him. The second son, Charles, had been intended for a writership in the East India Company but heartily disliked the work and was packed off to Jamaica, where he had a successful career in the military, becoming engineer-general for the island. He died suddenly, however, in 1757. Edward's mother, Mary Tate, had been sent back from Jamaica in the late 1740s, out of favour with her husband, and had been living in England ever since. His oldest sister,

---

[7] Trevor Burnard, *Planters, Merchants and Slaves. Plantation Societies in British America, 1650–1820* (Chicago, 2015), 3.
[8] B. W. Higman, *Plantation Jamaica, 1750–1850. Capital and Control in a Colonial Economy* (Kingston, Jamaica, 2005), 5, 11.

Catherine Maria, had married Sir Henry Moore, who came from an elite white family and had recently been appointed as lieutenant-governor of the island. The second sister, Susanna Charlotte (usually known as Charlotte), had also married into the white elite. Her husband, George Ellis, came from one of the oldest families on the island who were connected into the Beckfords, the Fullers and the Palmers. On arrival on the island, therefore, Edward found some immediate family, his brother Robert and sister Catherine. Edward himself also made a 'good' marriage months after arriving. So, despite his lack of experience of plantership and relatively small inheritance, he was possessed of multiple advantages.

A letter written to his friend William Henry Ricketts soon after his arrival in Jamaica makes it clear that he was less than enthusiastic about his new life. It had been a serious shock for a young gentleman with apparently good prospects and a legal future to find himself with such a modest inheritance. 'I impute to my Father leaving me almost totally unprovided for, to be owing more to indolence, than disaffection for me,' he told Ricketts, while reporting that 'my Doom is fixed, to all intents and purposes, and without hope of recovery'.[9] Jamaica, given all he knew about it, was not an appealing prospect. His father and his favourite brother had just died there. He will have landed in Port Royal, a place which may have been associated in his mind with the tales of the great earthquake of 1692 and the smugglers, pirates, luxury and debauchery which characterized the town. Smollett's picaresque hero, Roderick Random, had spent time there, purchased 'a lace waistcoat, with some other clothes, at a sale, made a swaggering figure for some days among the taverns, where I ventured to play a little at hazard, and came off with fifty pistoles in my pocket'.[10] From Port Royal, Edward will have been rowed into Kingston, getting a good view of the magnificent harbour and the backdrop of the Blue Mountains. There is no record of his reactions on first arrival, but an account by a Dubliner who landed in the late 1740s provides a vivid glimpse of the cacophony of sounds and colours that he would have encountered:

> [i]nstead of the Morning London Cries, of Old Clothes, Sweep, etc. my Ears were saluted with Maha-a, Maha-a, the Cries of Goats, kept in Most Houses for their Milk. And presently I heard called the Names of Pompey, Scipio, Casar etc. and again those of Yabba, Juba, Quasheba (negro Boys and Girls, Slaves in the Family) which first raised an Idea of being in old Rome; and then again of my being transported suddenly to Africa ... the Inhabitants very open, courteous, lively & very ready to serve and assist a stranger. – But how different did everything appear to me ... People of

---

[9] Edward Long to William Ricketts, 26 May, Ricketts Family Papers, Staffordshire Record Office, William Salt Library, 49.90.44.
[10] Smollett, *Roderick Random*, 251.

almost all colours! – White, black, yellow in abundance. Many pale white, and great Variety in the Shades of Black and Yellow.[11]

A far cry from London, never mind Cornwall. Long's familiarity with Uncle Beeston's establishment on Bishopsgate Street meant that he was well acquainted with the commercial world and probably with the docks. But Kingston was the tropics and slavery was everywhere, the visual impact of the varied shades of white, black and yellow (what is now called brown in the Caribbean) a striking reminder of the significance of skin colour. He would certainly have seen black people in London: a collared page adding status to a fashionable lady's entourage, sailors gathered at the docks or in ale houses, and the representations of Africans on trade cards and shop signs. But the shock of seeing a society built on slavery was something else, as many travellers testified. Charles Leslie described his first impressive vision of Jamaica from the ship as they gently sailed along the shore: the mountains, woods and plantations looked delightful. But then the harsh realization: they had left England, 'with native freedom blest, the seat of Arts, the nurse of Learning, and Friend of every Virtue', and 'I was now to settle in a place not half inhabited, cursed with intestine broils, where Slavery was established, and the poor toiling Wretches worked in the sultry Heat, and never knew the Sweets of Liberty, or reap'd the Advantage of their painful Industry.'[12] Perhaps Edward remembered his mother's avoidance of 'the disgusting parts of the subject' when she had described to him her experience of Jamaica.[13]

Kingston was a busy and flourishing commercial town in the 1750s, the largest on the island, with a fast-growing population of five to seven thousand, despite horrific mortality rates. The major entrepot for the African and British trades and the only port of entry until 1758 for ships carrying African captives, it was key to the extensive commerce with both North and South America and the metropole. Its wharves bustled with people, storehouses were stocked with commodities, and two to three hundred ships could be seen in the bay. A survey of the town made in 1753 shows that white people owned practically all the properties and that they headed more than 95 per cent of the households. The significant numbers of female household heads, operating particularly in the retail and service sectors, marked one of the striking aspects of urban life, and a markedly different pattern of ownership from the rural parishes. Of the total population, 60 per cent were enslaved, a much lower percentage than in the countryside.[14]

---

[11] Unpublished private journal, cited in Trevor Burnard and Emma Hart, 'Kingston, Jamaica and Charleston, South Carolina: a New Look at Comparative Urbanization in Plantation Colonial British America', *Journal of Urban History* 39.2 (2012), 220.
[12] Leslie, *A New History*, 10–11.
[13] Howard, *Records and Letters*, I. 88.
[14] Jack P. Greene, *Settler Jamaica in the 1750s* (Charlottesville, 2016), 175–6; Trevor Burnard, '"The Grand Mart of the Island": the Economic Function of Kingston, Jamaica in the mid-Eighteenth Century', in K. E. A Monteith and Glen Richards (eds.),

Long's Atlantic crossing was during the Seven Years War, at a time when the Caribbean was a key theatre and naval conflicts were critical: he moved from one beleaguered society to another. From arrival he would have been aware that Jamaica was a militarized island, its white colonists always alert to both internal and external threats, with a visible army and navy presence. Men of war were moored in Kingston harbour, soldiers were on the streets. Ships were being seized by enemies on the high seas. The war brought money into Kingston: prize loot selling cheap, contractors serving the fleet, labourers building defences, military and naval officers enjoying time on shore.[15] As Vincent Brown argues, there was a tense symbiosis between war and business. 'Military force kept the turbulent violence of Atlantic warfare at bay while militant order allowed profit to accumulate without war's disruptions.'[16] Commerce was periodically badly affected, however, with fears of invasion as in 1756. 'There is no business to be done here with any pleasure as the Planters in general are greatly distressed for money ... The Guinea trade is in a very languid situation,' wrote the absentee planter Rose Fuller's one-time mistress to him in September 1758; the merchants could not collect their debts and 'I am afraid the long credit, and bad pay, will be the ruin of this country.'[17] Henry Bright similarly complained of 'this damned wicked French war ... the ruin of many, both planters and merchants'.[18] Garrison government had been established in Jamaica from first settlement. The colony resembled a military base, with its barracks and fortified houses ready to repel attack from the Spanish, the French or the enslaved. The governors, almost always military or naval veterans, were ready to declare martial law at times of danger, as in 1756–7, and the militia, in which all white men were expected to enlist, was regularly summoned to drill.

That level of militarization fed into the brutality of the regimes under which the enslaved lived, both on the plantations and pens (those landholdings designed for the breeding of cattle and operated with a similar system of enslavement) and in the towns. Published accounts of Jamaica in the 1740s stressed the scale of violence and cruelty exercised by the slave-owners. 'The Island of *Jamaica* being of the greatest Importance to its Mother Country, and

---

Jamaica in Slavery and Freedom. History, Heritage and Culture (Mona, Jamaica, 2002), 225–41.

[15] Thomas Truxes, 'Doing Business in the Wartime Caribbean: John Byrn, Irish Merchant of Kingston, Jamaica (September–October 1756)' in Finola O'Kane and Ciaran O'Neill (eds.), *Ireland, Slavery and the Caribbean. Interdisciplinary Perspectives* (Manchester, 2023), 87–100.

[16] Vincent Brown, *Tacky's Revolt. The Story of an Atlantic Slave War* (Cambridge, MA, 2020), 44.

[17] Cited in ibid., 75.

[18] Kenneth Morgan (ed.), *The Bright-Meyler Papers. A Bristol-West India Connection, 1732–1837* [2007] (Oxford, 2016), 329.

at the same Time so insecure', wrote an anonymous pamphleteer, 'that the Inhabitants are not only alarm'd by every trifling Armament of the Enemy, but under the greatest Apprehensions frequently from their own Slaves, it becomes a Matter of publick Concern to consider how to render so valuable a Possession safe and sure, and free from the Dangers with which it is so manifestly threatened.' The greatest danger was that posed by the extraordinary imbalance in the population, 'being at least as ten to one'.[19] The island's population was around 142,000, 9 per cent of whom were white, 90 per cent of African origin. The 90 per cent were the 'intestine' enemy, as it was named by the colonists. 'A Country that is Cultivated with Negroes or Slaves & a Small Number of White People may indeed become Rich,' wrote James Knight, 'but it cannot be deemed safe or secure.'[20] It was essential to have enough white inhabitants to bear arms. The fears associated with this imbalance drove the cruelty: 'No country excels [Jamaica] in a barbarous treatment of slaves, or in the cruel methods they put them to death,' opined Leslie. The 'too great Numbers of Negroes in Proportion to white Persons' was an ever-present threat of potential destruction.[21]

The 9 per cent who were white were united by their status as colonists, but there was a clear hierarchy between the small settlers, the urban traders and the great planters and merchants. The power of the planters was a matter of concern to the crown in the mid-eighteenth century. The revenues from Jamaica were disappointing and there was a suspicion that the crown was not receiving the quit rents that were owed, that landowners were under-recording their holdings. Admiral Knowles was despatched as the new governor in 1752 with instructions to conduct a survey. He had been on the island for fifteen years and knew it well. The material he compiled highlighted the extent to which landownership was concentrated. As Jack Greene's analysis has demonstrated, sixteen individuals composed the top 1 per cent, owning about 12 per cent of the entire acreage. William Beckford, for example, the London alderman and ally of Pitt in the Seven Years War, owned more than 20,000 acres. Fifty-two owners, some absentee and some resident, held between 5,000 and 10,000 acres.[22] At the same time, half of all personal

---

[19] Anon., *An Essay concerning Slavery and the danger Jamaica is expos'd to from the too great number of Slaves and the too little Care that is taken to manage them. And a proposal to prevent the further importation of Negroes into that Island* (London, n.d.), no pagination on introduction. This pamphlet may have been written by Edward Trelawny who had served as governor, but as James Robertson argues, there is no certainty: 'An Essay Concerning Slavery: a mid-Eighteenth-Century Analysis from Jamaica', *S&A* 33.1 (2012), 65–85.
[20] Knight, *History*, II. 633–4.
[21] Leslie, *A New History*, 39.
[22] Greene, *Settler Jamaica in the 1750s*, 41.

property in Jamaica consisted of enslaved men, women and children. Between 50 and 75 per cent of these people worked on the sugar plantations.[23]

White people were united by their determination to exercise their power over others and enjoy the economic, social and political privileges they possessed. But there were serious tensions within the white population too and the dominance of the planter elite was not always secure. Factional rivalries were frequent and on occasion erupted violently, as in the bitter dispute between planters and merchants in 1754. Governor Knowles supported the petition of a group of Kingston merchants to move the capital from Spanish Town to Kingston. He hoped to establish a counterweight to the power of the group of planters led by William Beckford and Rose Fuller. In response, the planters mobilized support in the metropole, declaring their determination to defend the independence and liberties of the assembly against the threat of despotic authority. The conflict continued for three years, with numerous petitions from both sides and hearings at the Board of Trade. James Knight, writing in the 1740s, was extremely critical of the Board, which to his mind did not have enough knowledge of commerce, with a membership drawn from the nobility and gentry. The defenders of Spanish Town argued that its relative quiet, away from the bustle of commercial life, made it an ideal site for government. It would be an economic disaster for the town if the move took place for it was entirely dependent on the presence of the administration, the assembly and the courts for its wellbeing. The Kingston group argued that a rapidly growing busy port and trading centre was far more appropriate as the capital of a commercial island. Knowles managed to secure a majority in the assembly and moved the government to Kingston, but in January 1756 the rival factions provoked a riot. Knowles imprisoned twenty assembly men, but he had overreached his powers and the Board of Trade recommended that he be removed. A ruling from the Earl of Halifax determined that the courts and records of Jamaica should stay in Spanish Town and the governor could decide on the site of the assembly. The planters had won.

Edward's father, Samuel Long, was by then well established on the island. He had served in the assembly and was a member of the council, the body appointed by the crown to balance the influence of the elected assembly. A strong supporter of Knowles, he expected his son Charles to support him. 'My Father forced him to take a Seat in the Assembly,' Edward recorded, 'and charged him on his duty to vote for the Governor's measures.' But Charles's sympathies were with the opposition and when the votes were counted it was clear that he had gone against the parental command. 'My Father renounced him for ever. Charles sickened with a fever: My Father passed his door in his way to Kingston without one kind inquiry after his health. My Brother died,

[23] Michael Craton estimates 75 per cent; *Empire, Enslavement and Freedom in the Caribbean* (London, 1997), 164. Others have lower figures, e.g. Justin Roberts estimates 60 per cent; *Slavery and the Enlightenment in the British Atlantic, 1750–1807* (Cambridge, 2013), 11.

and forgiveness came too late.'[24] Samuel Long was an unforgiving man. A lavish funeral may have assuaged some paternal guilt, but elite funerals were occasions to demonstrate status in colonial Jamaica.[25] Samuel himself was dead three months later.

After leaving Kingston, Edward Long would probably have headed on horseback for Longville, some forty miles distant, where brother Robert was living. Arriving at the estate may have been his first encounter with a plantation, although given the planters' reputation for hospitality, he may have been entertained *en route*. Nothing remains of the original settlement. Longville is now a village, just off the busy road from Maypen leading to the north of Clarendon. Old Longville House was in total decay by the time that Robert Mowbray Howard – a direct descendant and the author of the *Records and Letters of the Family of the Longs of Longville, Jamaica, and Hampton Lodge, Surrey* – visited the island, probably in the early 1920s, and a modern house had replaced it. Longville had beautiful pastures, sketched in a picturesque style by the artist William Berryman. A jobbing artist, Berryman spent several days on the plantation in the early 1800s, drawing the park, details of trees and leaves, and an elegant ruinate building in the Palladian style, possibly an orangery, which must once have been imposing. (See Figures 3.1–3.2.)

Long will have seen the great house, the pastureland, woods and cane fields, the mill, the works and some of the 311 enslaved men and women who were identified as belonging to the property in 1757, branded with either SL or RL to mark ownership.[26] Plantations such as Longville looked prosperous by the mid-eighteenth century. The scale of Samuel Long's debts, including the £700 for Charles's lavish funeral and still some inherited from his father, suggests that he had invested in people and land.[27] The 1740s and 1750s were good years for the planters, despite the disruptions of the war. The ending of the Maroon War in 1739 had been critical in facilitating a move into the west and north of the island and a steady expansion of sugar production. 'The sugar colonies', wrote Knight, 'and more particularly this Island, may very justly be deemed equal to as many Gold or Silver Mines.'[28] Jamaica was indeed 'a Constant Mine', wrote Leslie, 'whence *Britain* draws prodigious Riches', while Patrick Browne, composing his *History* in the 1750s, was keen to draw

---

[24] Howard, *Records and Letters*, I. 111. The most detailed account of the Knowles controversy is in Gauci, *William Beckford*.
[25] On the rituals of white death, see Vincent Brown, *The Reaper's Garden. Death and Power in the World of Atlantic Slavery* (Cambridge, MA, 2008), 81–91.
[26] Inventory of Samuel Long, Jamaica Archives (JA), Inventories, Liber 37, 10/11/3/37, f. 132; https://ufdcimages.uflib.ufl.edu/AA/00/02/11/44/00001/JamaicaRunawaySlaves-18thCentury.pdf, 180.
[27] Howard, *Records and Letters*, I. 111.
[28] Knight, *History*, II. 552.

Figure 3.1 Berryman's view of Longville that shows the plantation buildings alongside a grander structure that has the appearance of a classical folly; it was possibly an orangery. 'Longville, Jamaica' by William Berryman. Ink over graphite underdrawing, 1808–15. Courtesy of the Library of Congress, Prints and Photographs Division.

Figure 3.2 An enslaved woman crosses the river to join those working the fields of Longville plantation in another view by Berryman. 'Longville Ford, the First from Longs Wharf to Chapelton, Clarendon Mountn' by William Berryman. Ink over graphite underdrawing, 1808–15. Courtesy of the Library of Congress, Prints and Photographs Division.

attention to the potential of the island.[29] It is estimated that the rate of profit in the West Indies between 1756 and 1762 reached the extraordinary level of 14.8 per cent.[30] Almost all the arable land that could produce cane had been taken up, yet the economy was also relatively diversified, with numbers of

---

[29] Leslie, *A New History*, 247; Browne, *The Civil and Natural History of Jamaica*.
[30] J. R. Ward, 'The Profitability of Sugar Planting in the British West Indies, 1650–1834', *EconHR* 2nd ser. 31 (1978), 197–213.

provision settlements, cattle pens, and cocoa, coffee, cotton, indigo and pimento plantations. Underpinning the dramatic growth in the export of sugar in the 1750s, there was an extensive network of other agricultural enterprises. For the planters, however, King Sugar was the key to their fortunes and they were approaching the peak of their prosperity.

The Longville estate was in the parish of Clarendon, roughly twelve miles from Spanish Town and the sea at Old Harbour Bay. Clarendon was a predominantly inland parish but with good access for shipping. Its fifteen rivers, including the Minho, were crucial for sugar production. About six miles of savannah land stretched across the lower part of the parish and the hills gradually rose from there, gaining height farther inland, but they were neither steep nor barren. There were wide valleys between the hills, suited to cane cultivation. The strategic location of the parish allowed for the early development of sugar cultivation. In 1737 Clarendon already had sixty-six sugar works, the largest number of any parish.[31] By the late 1750s the Craskell and Simpson maps (the surveys for which were conducted between 1756 and 1761) identify 238 settlements in Clarendon, 72 of which were sugar estates with 85 sugar mills.[32] The others will have been rearing livestock and growing provisions, possibly also some coffee or cocoa. Samuel Long, Edward's father, owned 6,755 acres in Clarendon, making him one of the fifty-two second-rank landowners, those who held between 5,000 and 10,000 acres.[33] The inventory compiled after his death records that he owned 222 enslaved men and 221 enslaved women. The total value of the enslaved in sterling was £11,970 and of the estate £14,545.[34] In addition to the plantations at Longville and Lucky Valley, he had three pens, Bower's Pen, Palmeto Pen and Longville Park, for the livestock that would service the plantations as draft animals, for manure, for food and for sale. He also owned a small estate at Crawle, and Cockpit, a cattle pen.[35]

Samuel's will had been made in 1745 before he left England for Jamaica. Robert, as the eldest son, was to inherit the bulk of the property. After his death it was to go to the 'heirs of his body lawfully begotten'. Charles, the second son, had died intestate and so his property also passed to Robert. He owned 3,087 acres in the parish of St Catherine, where Spanish Town was situated. The estate was valued at £2,337.86: the twenty-six enslaved men, forty enslaved women, one boy and three girls were estimated to be worth £2,010.71. The boy was valued at £25, the three girls at £40 in total, a clear indicator of who, in the eyes of the slave-owners, was expected to deliver the most productive labour.[36]

---

[31] Knight, *History*, II. 618.
[32] Greene, *Settler Jamaica*, 52.
[33] Ibid., 41, 223–5.
[34] The inventory figures are in pounds sterling; all subsequent figures are in Jamaican currency.
[35] Inventory of Samuel Long, f. 132.
[36] Inventory of Charles Long, 1757, JA, Inventories, Liber 37, 1B/11/3/37, f. 131.

Robert shared his inheritance with Edward. On 12 August 1758, Edward married Mary Ballard Beckford in St Catherine's church in Spanish Town. She was the widow of John Palmer and daughter and heir of Thomas Beckford, so he aligned himself with key elite families on the island. The previous day the brothers had signed an agreement. This was probably one part of a wider negotiation over a marriage settlement. It documented the sale, for five shillings, a peppercorn price, of half the plantation of Longville Park (approx. 650 acres) and half the forty named enslaved people on that property.[37] This estate had originally been Samuel's property which he had given to Charles in July 1754, 'in consideration of [his] natural love and affection for him'.[38] Now it was split between Robert and Edward. It was a pen on Bower's River which ran into Old Harbour Bay. Charles had also owned a share of the pen in the Cockpit and in the stock at Longville Park, including mares, fillies, colts and a 'large Spanish stallion', presumably for his use as he rode round the island inspecting military installations.[39]

There were further property transactions in the wake of the marriage. Mary seems to have inherited Friendship Plantation in St Mary from her father, Thomas Beckford, along with enslaved people and £1,000. She had bought a house in White Church Street in Spanish Town in 1754, and she and Edward were living there in 1759.[40] The town was judged by William and Edmund Burke in the mid-1750s to have 'more gaiety' than Kingston:

> Here reside many persons of large fortunes, and who make a figure proportionable; the number of coaches kept here is very great; here is a regular assembly; and the residence of the governor and the principal officers of the government, who have all very profitable places, conspire with the genius of the inhabitants ostentatious and expensive, to make it a very splendid and agreeable place.[41]

This was a good place to live for a young white couple with prospects. On 20 June 1759 both Mary and Edward were named on the indenture selling both Friendship and the Spanish Town house to Matthew Gregory for five shillings. This included the sale of 109 enslaved men and women, all of whom were named. A second indenture bought the estate, house and people back a day later at the same price.[42] Edward was establishing himself as a property owner, thanks to his brother and his wife. Jamaica had turned out already to be a place rich in opportunities and a sense of freedom, a place for him to establish a new

---

[37] Island Record Office (IRO), vol. 173, f. 114.
[38] IRO, Index to Grantees, Old Series, vol. 156, f. 140.
[39] Inventory of Charles Long, f. 131.
[40] Mary Beckford from Jane Bonner, Indenture Records, IRO, vol. 158, f. 156.
[41] Burke and Burke, *An Account of the European Settlements*, 82.
[42] It is unclear why they sold and bought in this way. IRO, vol. 179, f. 48; IRO, vol. 179, f. 49. Friendship was sold sometime later, but it has been impossible to trace this sale.

identity, that of a white colonist, slave-owner and planter. 'The slave plantation might be characterised as establishing the relations and the material and epistemic apparatus through which new subjects were constituted': those new subjects were the planters and the enslaved.[43]

Lucky Valley: the Planter

Lucky Valley, however, did not come at a peppercorn price. As Samuel Long's personal estate together with the rents and profits of his real estate were not sufficient to cover his debts, it was necessary to sell some of the land. At the time of his death he had owned one undivided moiety of a plantation called Lucky Valley in Clarendon, held in mateship between Samuel Long and Charles Long, his brother. It was only producing a small annual income. Edward bought the property, knowing that it needed serious investment. On 15 November 1761 Edward and his brother Robert came to an agreement that Edward would purchase the estate for £9,946 14s. 3d. At the same time he bought eight enslaved people from Robert's half of Longville Park for £160 and a further eighteen persons for £810. Lucky Valley was now held 'in mateship' between Edward and his uncle, Charles Long.[44] This meant that Edward managed the cultivation and paid his uncle £400 sterling per annum in rent. It is impossible to know how Edward acquired this large sum to buy his share of the estate. The likely source, given what we know of the scale of his debts in the years to come, would have been a loan on credit from Uncle Beeston who headed the mercantile branch of the family, Drake and Long.

Long was in occupation of Lucky Valley from 1760. By the end of 1761 he was its legal possessor. It was his major property, not only for the eleven years he was on the island, but for the rest of his life. Robert had warned him that it was not a profitable enterprise; indeed, he had been running it at a loss. The supply of labour was inadequate and there were difficulties with transporting the crop. By deploying enslaved people from Longville, four miles distant on the River Minho, he had managed to raise eighty hogsheads a year, but this was far from satisfactory.

Many years later, when renegotiating his agreement with Charles Long, Edward documented the state of the plantation in 1760. Many of 'the gang of negroes' were 'superannuated, or disabled by inveterate distempers', he recorded, and there was no hospital. 'The works were truly wretched.' There was only an old and ineffective cattle mill, with 'patched up, ruinous and leaky' buildings. The boiling house roof was rotten, the sugars in the curing house damaged by water coming in from the roof. The pasture land was insufficient

---

[43] David Scott, *Conscripts of Modernity. The Tragedy of Colonial Enlightenment* (London, 2004), 127.
[44] IRO, Index to Grantees, Old Series, vol. 252, f. 13.

for the stock; there was no pen, and no woodland to supply the necessary timber, not even enough for a gate-post.[45] Furthermore, the journey from Lucky Valley to the wharf in Old Harbour Bay was sixteen miles, and the roads for the first eight miles were so bad that only mules and horses could pass. An estate at such a distance inland required not only a large number of mules and cattle for the road but also a resting place. Edward listed the essential improvements. A water mill and the management of a stream to provide water for the distilling house were vital. The works had to be rebuilt and new buildings, including a hospital, constructed. The provision grounds would have to be enlarged so that there would be a better supply of food for the enslaved. New land must be acquired, bordering the estate, so that woodland and pasture could be extended, and the cane lands increased. It was urgent to improve the road to Old Harbour Bay, hopefully by subscription with other planters, and establish an intermediate stage 'for resting and relieving the road stock; and making it a repository for the goods passing to, or from the plantation'.[46] It was clear that a great deal of money had to be spent and there would need to be effective management of the entire enterprise: the land, the works, the labour force with their provision grounds, the transport system. Improvements were vital if Lucky Valley was to be profitable. (See Figure 3.3.)

Clarendon offered good prospects to a planter who hoped to make his fortune. Brother Robert's property was in close proximity and was well established. Between Longville and Lucky Valley, on Pindar's River, was Low Ground, Nicholas Bourke's estate, so he was probably Long's closest neighbour. Bourke owned 871 acres in Clarendon in 1754 and represented the parish in the assembly in 1757, 1766 and 1768. The two men were in close political agreement and led the sustained attack on Governor Lyttelton in 1766–8, for what they saw as his assault on the liberties of free-born Englishmen.[47] Close by was Edward Morant: his income from estates reportedly averaged £20,000 sterling per annum from 1733 to 1791.[48] The parish boasted some of the wealthiest slave-owners, several of whom were living in England on the rich proceeds of their estates. Alderman William Beckford, the greatest of them all, had eight sugar estates in Clarendon, including Moore, which was very close to Longville and Lucky Valley. He was joined by the Pennants and the Dawkins. These were all families, like the Longs, who dated from first settlement. The abundant water, good soil and plentiful excellent timber made Clarendon a choice region for sugar, 'one of the largest,

---

[45] Long knew that cattle were central to the production of sugar. BL Add MSS 12404, f. 220. On the importance of the pens, see Verene A. Shepherd, *Livestock, Sugar and Slavery. Contested Terrain in Colonial Jamaica* (Kingston, Jamaica, 2009).
[46] Mr Long's Proposals for his Property at L. Valley, November 1777. Suffolk Record Office, HA/18/GD/1.
[47] See https://www.ucl.ac.uk/lbs/person/view/2146649451.
[48] See https://www.ucl.ac.uk/lbs/person/view/2146649397.

THE PLANTATION

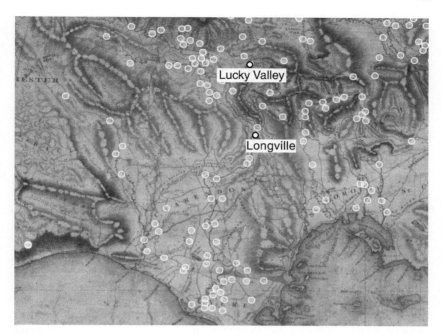

Figure 3.3 James Robertson's 1804 map of Jamaica with Longville and Lucky Valley plantations marked, from the Legacies of British Slave-ownership database. Clarendon was a fertile parish, as demonstrated by the number of plantations shown in the area. Data mapping courtesy of the Centre for the Legacies of British Slavery. James Robertson's 1804 map of Jamaica reproduced with the permission of the National Library of Scotland.

healthiest, and best-settled parishes in the whole island'.[49] It was not too far from Spanish Town, important for those planters who were elected to the assembly or had business with the administration or in the courts. The parish barracks, situated at the hamlet of the Chapel, housed a company of regulars ready to assist in case of 'intestine' trouble. The sugar and rum could be despatched from Old Harbour Bay. The climate was varied: warm and dry in the lowlands, cool and healthy in the mountains. Ginger, cocoa and coffee were grown as well as sugar and corn, and cattle flourished. The estate of Thomas Fearon, chief justice in the mid-1760s, was particularly noteworthy. 'The beauties of nature that are displayed here are innumerable,' as Long put it. 'On one place is seen a long, wavy surface, adorned with the lively verdure of canes, interspersed with wind-mills and other buildings. In another are beheld several charming lawns of pasture-land, dotted with cattle and sheep, and

---

[49] Long, *History*, II. 60.

watered with rivulets. In a third are Negro villages, where (far from poverty and discontent) peace and plenty hold their reign . . .'[50] This was Long in his retrospective and picturesque mode. The landscape, which had been transformed by enslaved labourers – the ground cleared, the cane planted, the works and village built – is represented, in this account, as resembling the English countryside.

Faced with the dilapidated state of Lucky Valley, the project for Long was to make the estate profitable: this would require new ways of seeing and commanding, new forms of oversight, new directions for all life and labour.[51] Those eighty hogsheads would scarcely sustain a household, never mind meeting his creditors. The estate was reasonably well situated. Lying at the confluence of Pindar's River and Back River there was a plentiful water supply. The wide valley between the hills was already producing cane, and there was access, albeit inadequate, to the wharf at Old Harbour Bay. Long also owned a share of Longville Park Pen, close to Old Harbour, where cattle were reared for the plantation. The urgent task was to learn the 'art of planting'.[52] Long knew something of English farming and notions of 'improvement', as we have seen. His father had shown an interest in husbandry at Tredudwel. But the modest gentleman's farm in Cornwall that he knew from his childhood and adolescence was a very different proposition from a sugar plantation. There were no planting manuals available to him: he must learn through practice and experience. Young male migrants from Scotland would have started as bookkeepers, hoping to become overseers and then possibly, having built up experience, move into plantership. Long had no such apprenticeship. He would have heard talk at his uncle's house in Bishopsgate Street of sugar and shipping. He knew that sugar had long been 'the staple of the island' and that it required 'large tracts for its cultivation'.[53] He also knew of his father's disappointment at the dwindling income he was receiving from his estate, which had driven him back to Jamaica in 1746. 'Sugar planting is a sort of adventure', as his friend Bryan Edwards later wrote, 'in which the man that engages, must engage deeply.'[54] 'There is very little difficulty in getting possession of an estate', as another erstwhile planter, who remembered the 'severe toils' of that life, noted, 'but a great deal to keep it.'[55] Long now had the land but it required large capital; the costs would be extensive, the risks many. Sugar

---

[50] Ibid., II. 65.
[51] Nicholas Mirzoeff, *The Right to Look. A Counter-History of Visuality* (Durham, NC, 2011).
[52] Long, *History*, I. 438.
[53] Ibid., I. 283.
[54] Bryan Edwards, *The History, Civil and Commercial, of the British Colonies in the West Indies* (2 vols., London, 1794), II. 244.
[55] J. B. Moreton, *West India Customs and Manners: containing strictures on the soil, cultivation, produce, trade, officers, and inhabitants: with the method of establishing*

estates, with all their 'boasted advantages', sometimes proved millstones round the necks of their unfortunate proprietors, dragging them to destruction.[56] Long's father and brother had both just died prematurely; Jamaica was a graveyard, as everyone knew. It would be a struggle and he engaged deeply in it.

By the time Long came to write his *History*, he was aiming to persuade his readers of the benefits of settling in Jamaica. 'There is scarcely any study', he assured them, 'more amusing than that of agriculture, the ruggedness of which is constantly soothed by the allurement of profit.'[57] Profit was, of course, at the heart of it, the profits which the enslaved had no access to. Long had gone to Jamaica to make his fortune: like his father and his grandfather, he would return to England as soon as he had accumulated enough capital. He looked forward to the time when he would have paid his debts. His first son, born in 1763 and named Edward Beeston, thus honouring his uncle, must be educated, as he himself had been, as an English gentleman, at an English school. But first the 'ruggedness' of the work must be tackled.

Long was not starting from scratch, but Lucky Valley was in very bad repair. The necessary works for a moderately sized plantation were a mill (cattle or water), a boiling house with coppers, a curing house with platforms and a cistern, a distilling house with stills, tanks and cisterns. Other buildings might include a dwelling-house for the overseer, a rum store, a dry goods store, offices, a corn house, stables, hogsties, a pigeon house, and workshops for the smith, the cooper and the carpenter. Many utensils were necessary, from sugar pots, cattle chains, coolers, skimmers, ladles and strainers, to hoes, bills and axes, along with tools for tradesmen, copper lamps and iron bars, waggons, and clothes and salt herring for the enslaved. Land was needed not just for the cane but for pasture, wood for timber, provision grounds so that the enslaved could grow their own food. Then the stock: mules, steers, pigs and sheep for Longville Park as well as Lucky Valley. Finally, the labouring people.

Without the enslaved the land had no value. It was their labour that created the value. Long, however, understood himself as the 'head': it was he who made it all happen, he who created the value, oiled the wheels of 'the commercial machine', he who *improved*.[58] The agency of the enslaved men, women and children who did the work on the ground was disavowed. Those who hoed, weeded, cut and carried, boiled and distilled were 'the sinews' through whose bodies the labour process flowed. They were represented as disembodied labour, *choses*, chattels, to be 'bought and sold like every other commodity in

---

a sugar plantation. To which is added the practice of training new slaves (London, 1793), 23.
[56] Ibid., 58.
[57] Long, *History*, I. 438.
[58] Ibid., I. 482.

the country'.⁵⁹ Enslaved people and stock were listed side by side in his accounts, a standard practice for slave-owners. It was the planter who did the buying and selling, planned, directed, surveyed, instructed, supervised, judged and punished. He was 'the absolute authority', as Knight put it, the *mind* and *master* of the enterprise.⁶⁰ 'As the mind must govern the hands,' in Dr Johnson's words, 'so in every society the man of intelligence must direct the man of labour.'⁶¹ The simple rules about planting that Long documented were described in the passive voice, as tasks to be performed, as if by unnamed hands. It was 'I' who thought, who determined that the ground must be properly prepared, hoed three or four times, to make sure that it was well turned. 'When the canes are young', as Knight wrote in similar style, 'the care of the Planter is then to keep them clear of Weeds,' as if he himself did the weeding. 'The Planter must also be mindful to destroy the Rats,' he continued, though admitting in this instance that 'the Mundinga Negroes' were particularly skilled at this.⁶² The choice of the manure, how to judge the best kinds for particular soils, was another anxiety for Long. Furrows or drains must be cut to make sure that any superfluous water ran away. Cuttings should be carefully chosen, planted at the right distance below ground and at the right distance apart. When it came to the 'manufacturing', both of the cane and of the rum, cleanliness was crucial. The boilers should be regularly scoured, the cisterns 'in a due state of fermentation', the fire well regulated.⁶³ These planting instructions were devised in the spirit of improvement. 'Improvement' had been a key word for James Knight thirty years earlier: indeed, his aim was 'the Improvement, Security and Welfare of Jamaica'. Hoped-for improvements in agriculture, in road building, in administration, were all designed to encourage a more settled, cultivated and civilized society.⁶⁴ But most of the planters, he remarked regretfully, while 'intent on the improvement of their Plantations ... seem to have no other View than to raise Estates in order to live in England', where 'improvement' was the watchword for the landed.⁶⁵

'Planter', carolled the planter poet James Grainger, 'improvement is the child of time'.⁶⁶ His lengthy work *The Sugar Cane* was written in the georgic mode, celebrating agriculture as part of a commercial system central to the prosperity and power of nation and empire, and insisting that the cultivation of

---

[59] Browne, *The Civil and Natural History of Jamaica*, 25.
[60] Knight, *History*, II. 474.
[61] Samuel Johnson, *Journey to the Western Islands of Scotland* [1775] (Edinburgh, 1792), 123.
[62] Knight, *History*, II. 549.
[63] Long, *History*, I. 443–6.
[64] Knight, *History*, II. 641–2.
[65] Ibid., II. 569.
[66] James Grainger, *The Sugar Cane*, in John Gilmore, *The Poetics of Empire. A Study of James Grainger's The Sugar Cane (1764)* (London, 2000), Bk 1. 280.

sugar-cane was worthy of poetry. Grainger, a Scot who trained in medicine in Edinburgh but had hopes of a London literary career, travelled to St Kitts as companion to John Bourryau, whose father had property there. He married into a planting family and worked as a medical man, composing his long poem, inspired by Virgil and with ample references to Italy and the classics, on his travels around the island to see his patients. His subject, 'the spiry Cane, Supreme of Plants, rich subject of my song', was the 'imperial cane', a source of commerce and hoped-for 'opulence'.[67] Grainger was interested in the details of agricultural production, but like Long, his narrative voice, the 'I' in the poem, worked to separate a knowledge of nature and the skills associated with farming from actual work. Labourers were represented as a 'hoe-armed gang' who must be managed; impersonal words such as 'some', 'others', were used to diminish their active agency which instead was attributed to the cane itself, together with the master.[68]

Grainger was a great admirer of Samuel Martin, author of the very successful *Essay upon Plantership*, who argued that 'A liberal education' was undoubtedly 'the principal ingredient necessary to form a good planter'.[69] He should know the rudiments of the sciences, understand governance, expect to serve in the legislature and the military, be a magistrate, ensure good laws for credit and commerce, understand figures and mechanics, know about husbandry, sugar boiling and distilling. Long would have agreed with all this and was convinced of the importance of gentility to the spirit of improvement. The philistinism of so many of the planters was a distressing matter. 'To read, write, and cast Accounts, is all the Education they desire,' Leslie had written.[70] This would not do. 'The attention of gentlemen to agriculture is of great national importance,' wrote Arthur Young; they must know about soil, manure and grasses.[71] Young's powerful case for changes in land use, from new crops, especially roots, to a focus on drainage and reclamation, planned soil fertility and stock breeding, was immensely influential. His emphasis on the connections between the agricultural interest, mercantile capital, early industrial techniques and the significance of the physical sciences in relation, for example, to the chemical qualities of the soil, had application to the sugar colonies.[72]

---

[67] Ibid., Bk 1. 22–3, 89; Bk 2. 100.
[68] Tobin, *Colonizing Nature*.
[69] Samuel Martin Senior, *An Essay upon Plantership inscribed to Governor George Thomas* (4th edn, London and Antigua, 1765), viii.
[70] Leslie, *A New History*, 21.
[71] Arthur Young, *Political Essays Concerning the Present State of the British Empire: particularly respecting 1. Natural Advantages and Disadvantages* (London, 1772), 109, 157. Young had published numerous treatises for agriculturalists from the late 1760s.
[72] On the significance of Young to the expansion of enclosure, see Raymond Williams, *The Country and the City* (London, 1973), 66.

Long particularly admired Joseph Priestley's analyses.[73] 'Planter', asked Grainger, thinking not only of the nation's commerce but also of his individual advancement and that of others, 'wouldst thou double thine estate?'

> Never, ah, never, be asham'd to tread
> Thy dung-heaps, where the refuse of thy mills,
> With all the ashes, all thy coppers yield,
> With weeds, mould, dung, and stale, a compost form,
> Of force to fertilize the poorest soil.[74]

All future (as well as past) improvements will come from gentlemen, Martin opined, and Grainger and Long assented. Long had hoped that an agricultural society would be successfully established in Jamaica, for it was a patriotic duty, he believed, for 'those gentlemen who are lovers of their country (or, to say the truth, rather lovers of their own interest)', to share their knowledge and expertise. He welcomed the new 'spirit of experiment ... which by quitting the old beaten track, promises to strike out continual improvements'. The 'shackles of antiquated prejudices' must be thrown off, along with 'those restraints which our ancestors imposed'.[75] Mr Jethro Tull's excellent treatise on agriculture 'shewed the propriety of grounding this science upon actual experiment'.[76] Long's own Baconian emphasis on science, observation and experience was part of his 'liberal education', along with his reading of Jethro Tull, who had invented the horse-drawn seed drill, and Arthur Young. He gave no formal recognition to the knowledge and experience of those who laboured: their practical skills could never be transformed into mastery. Practical experience was valued as long as it was associated with white men. This attitude to labour mirrored that of the eighteenth-century English landowners who were concerned with improving their estates, becoming capitalist agriculturalists, squeezing tenants and enclosing land, and regarded their property as providing opportunities for investment and further returns, rather than as an inheritance to be safeguarded for future generations. As Raymond Williams observed, the evacuation of labour, of the men and women who manured and pruned and harvested, who reared and killed animals, fed chickens and collected eggs, trapped pheasants and caught fish, characterized the structure of feeling that set the imagined calm of rural society with its natural order against the exchanges and counting houses of the metropolitan world.[77] Long had absorbed a part of this mindset, the blind eye of the landowner in relation to his rack-rented tenants and waged labourers, as in his idealization of the rural idyll of the Worthy family of *The Prater*. (See Figure 3.4.)

[73] Long, *History*, III. v.
[74] Grainger, *Sugar Cane*, Bk 1. 223–7.
[75] Long, *History*, I. 435–6.
[76] Ibid., I. 436.
[77] Williams, *The Country and the City*.

Figure 3.4 Colonial maps also contributed to idealized visions of plantation life in Jamaica, as seen in this cartouche. Detail from the map of Cornwall as part of the Twelve-Sheet Map of the Three Counties of Jamaica by Henry Moore, Thomas Craskell and James Simpson, 1756–61. Engraving by Daniel Fournier, 1763. Private Collection. Photo © Christie's Images/Bridgeman Images.

In Long's understanding it was the planters who were responsible for the levels of productivity, not the field workers who planted, tended and cut the cane, or the boilers, 'prime of slaves' who knew exactly when the temperature was right, or the waggoners who could judge precisely the right number of oxen to draw the sugar and rum.[78] Planters, especially those like Long who came new to sugar production, were heavily dependent on the skills of their established labour force. But those skills were disavowed in the planter's mind; the enslaved were disembodied, became 'the sinews', hands, to be valued for the varied capacities they brought to the process of production, but not as persons, with names and lives. Yet, at the very same time, Long knew the workers were not *choses*; they were human beings, flesh and blood, with strengths and weaknesses, who suffered because of the work they did and whose work was essential to the success of the plantation. Hoeing, he was well aware, was particularly heavy labour, 'and has injured multitudes of Negroes . . . no other work on a plantation is so severe and so detrimental to

---

[78] Grainger, *Sugar Cane*, Bk 3. 335.

them as that of holing or turning up the ground in trenches with their hoe'.[79] Those injuries were a problem, given 'the high price and value of Negroes', he wrote. The planters should try 'every expedient by machines ... for performing that labour that is usually performed by Negroes'.[80] It was the high price and value that mattered, how to ensure profits; it was not in the planter's interests to see his labour force decimated. 'Planter, let humanity prevail,' Grainger had recommended.[81] Long's favourite poet, James Thomson, had called on patriotic Britons to 'venerate the plough', linking the land, the husbandman, the rich granary, commerce and the oceans to nation and empire.[82] Long himself had experimented with the plough and found it very successful.

> Might not the plough, that rolls on rapid wheels,
> Save no small labour to the hoe-arm'd gang?

asked the planter poet.[83] Long agreed with him that it must be operated by a 'white person' who would have learned its ways in England. 'Negroe children' could follow, planting in the furrow, thus saving adult labour. After the planting was finished, 'able Negroes' could cover the ridges and cut drains, 'all of which will be rather an amusement than a task to them'. The plants came up stronger in ploughed land, he had observed, and 'it is morally certain', he concluded,

> that the plough in one week, at six hours in the day, is capable of what would require the labour of six hundred Negroes, employed during the same space, eight hours in the day. This machine therefore not only saves the labour of a great many Negroes, but enables the planter to cultivate more ground every year ...[84]

Being 'morally certain' about this way of increasing productivity is a striking formulation. This morality was embedded in colonial legislation, governing the conduct of planters, albeit in extremely limited ways, towards their human labour. Was it morally good to make more profit? Such a formulation speaks to Long's enlightenment faith in the practical and moral utility of progress and his assumption as to the morality of a hierarchical order. Work was a morally reforming activity.[85] It could play its part in the 'civilizing' of the creole 'Negroes' that became such an important issue for him. But perhaps it also

---

[79] Long, *History*, I. 448–9. See Austin Clarke's powerful novel, *The Polished Hoe* (Toronto, 2003).
[80] Long, *History*, I. 448–9.
[81] Grainger, *Sugar Cane*, Bk 4. 211.
[82] Kaul, *Poems of Nation*, 147.
[83] Grainger, *Sugar Cane*, Bk 1. 267–8.
[84] Long, *History*, I. 451.
[85] Roberts, *Slavery and the Enlightenment*.

points to his uncomfortable sense, something to be repressed, of the *immorality* of the forms of labour he chose to employ. Such a sense could for the most part be portioned off in his mind, but he *knew* that the enslaved people he bought, sold and worked to death were human beings with human skills and human needs. He had to deny this in order to treat them as units of production. This 'paradox', that slaves were legally defined as property but were called upon to act in 'sentient, articulate and human ways', was the knowing and not knowing, the disavowal, that was at the heart of this particular form of racial slavery.[86] Long implicitly recognized the humanity of the men and women on his plantation and understood that it was in his interest that they should survive and remain productive. Yet in his writing about them as workers he reduced them. Racialization was the necessary condition for their exploitation. As Walter Johnson argues, slave-owners 'continually attempted to conscript – simplify, channel, limit, and control – the forms that humanity could take in slavery'. Racial ideology was 'the intellectual conjugation of the daily practice of the plantations' – human beings, animals, plants were forcibly reduced to limited aspects of themselves and 'deployed to further slave-holding dominion'.[87] In practice, planters relied on a complex division of labour, both racialized, gendered and age specific, with gangs organized to perform different tasks, all in order to increase productivity.

In 1745, the year before Samuel Long returned to the island, Clarendon had 12,775 enslaved people and 11,969 head of cattle. When Edward Long left in 1768 he estimated that there were 15,517 enslaved men and women and 14,276 head of cattle, seventy sugar works were established and there were fifty water mills.[88] These were significant increases, and the 'improvement' of Lucky Valley was part of this bigger picture.[89] Scholars have recognized that there was a period of accelerated profitability in the Jamaican sugar economy from the 1760s to the mid-1770s. This was facilitated by new methods, better cane, a stronger infrastructure and possibly lower rates of mortality.[90] In the case of Lucky Valley, the combination of closer management of human capital and improvements in land, works and methods was vital. An output of 80 hogsheads of sugar when Long took over the property was increased to 220 hogsheads and 123 puncheons of

---

[86] Mintz and Price insisted on the centrality of this paradox to the system of slavery. Sidney W. Mintz and Richard Price, *An Anthropological Approach to the Afro-American Past. A Caribbean Perspective* (Philadelphia, 1976), 13.
[87] Johnson, *River of Dark Dreams*, 208.
[88] These figures on sugar works and water mills were slightly lower than those on the Craskell and Simpson maps.
[89] Long, *History*, II. 66.
[90] Burnard, *Planters*, 188. He is citing a study by David Eltis, Frank D. Lewis and David Richardson ('Slave Prices, the African Slave Trade, and Productivity in the Caribbean, 1674-1807', *EconHR*, new ser., 58.4 [2005], 673–700) and drawing on his own statistics.

rum by the time he returned to England in 1769.[91] Increasing crop sizes and productivity were taken as measures of progress.[92] Simon Taylor's calculated risk-taking, long-term financial planning and powerful work ethic had similar results with similar costs for the enslaved.[93]

Sugar was a notoriously difficult and risky crop. Faced with the problems on the estate in 1760, one of Long's first priorities was to increase the labour force. 'Investment in slaves', Trevor Burnard calculates, 'increased from 45% of slave-holder wealth in the early 1730s to 57% in the 1770s.'[94] Knight notes that planters usually bought captives 'Eight or Ten at a time', according to need, and that they came from up to 'twenty different Countries or Nations'.[95] It is impossible to know what Long thought about his purchase of people: what did he know about capture, transportation and sale before he arrived on the island? What allowed him to think that to buy and sell Africans was an acceptable practice? Had he already absorbed some of the ideas of difference between white people and black that circulated in early modern England? How much might he have seen in London that prepared him for the condition of chattel slavery? Did he go through some state of shock and horror, as some did, before accustoming himself to all that was involved? John Pinney, a planter in Nevis, was 'shock'd at the first appearance of human flesh exposed to sale'. God, he concluded, must have ordained it, 'for the use and benefit of us', otherwise there would have been some 'particular sign'.[96] Whatever the process for Long, he soon began to buy. His first purchase of human capital was from his brother Robert, as we have seen, and at several points over the following years it is possible to track further purchases of people. The names, some of which would have been imposed by the slave-owners, and the gender of these captives are all that can be traced. In February 1761, together with Robert, Long bought '3 negroe slaves named Barbadoes, Cuffee and Bob' for ten shillings from their brother-in-law, Henry Moore. Once again this was a peppercorn price, indicating an agreement between the three men.[97] A few months later Edward paid his uncle Charles Long £400 sterling for the lease of his half of Lucky Valley, estimated at 500 acres, together with the dwelling-house, works and his 'equal half-part undivided of the 139 negroe mulatto and other slaves' and of the stock and utensils. The total value of all the plantation assets was £10,964 4s. 9d.,[98] very

---

[91] Accounts Produce, Liber 5, f. 164, Liber 6, f. 69. B. W. Higman's account of Lucky Valley in *Jamaica Surveyed. Plantation Maps and Plans of the Eighteenth and Nineteenth Centuries* (Kingston, Jamaica, 2001), 84–91, is extremely valuable. Thanks to James Dawkins for the work he did in the Lucky Valley and Longville Park Accounts Produce.
[92] Roberts, *Slavery and the Enlightenment*, 4.
[93] Christer Petley, *White Fury. A Jamaican Slaveholder and the Age of Revolution* (Oxford, 2018); Higman, *Plantation Jamaica*.
[94] Burnard, *Jamaica in the Age of Revolution*, 89.
[95] Knight, *History*, II. 484.
[96] Richard Pares, *A West India Fortune* (London, 1950), 121.
[97] IRO, vol. 193, f. 90.
[98] All further figures in this section are in Jamaican currency.

close to the sum which Long had originally paid Robert. The lease was for twenty-one years and the money was to be paid twice yearly at the Royal Exchange. Long's responsibility was to pay the rent and to maintain the land and buildings.[99] The 139 enslaved people were valued at £5,969. There were seventy-two men, only one of whom was named as a craftsman, 'Jacob – bricklayer'. Barbadoes was there, but neither Cuffee nor Bob. Some of the names suggest close African connections – Coromante Warwick, Congo Warwick, Jubao Quashie. Others were named for connections with their owners – two Roberts, two Charles and a Sam – or for England – Kent, York, London, Hampshire, Suffolk and Dunwick. (Dunwich in Suffolk had been Charles Long's parliamentary seat.) Then there were Trinculo, Sambo, Cupid and Cato, as well as Sugar. The eleven boys included Mulatto James and Mulatto Ned – impossible to know the identities of their fathers – while the fifty-six women and girls included Creole Celia and Black Betty, whose children may have been Betty's Mimba and Betty's Kate. Lydia's Sarah and Nanny's Daphne were perhaps born on the plantation, while Old Bess and Old Prue may have been amongst those Long described as being 'superannuated, or disabled by inveterate distempers' in 1760.[100] Long purchased a further nine women, two with their child, and three men from William Wood, a gentleman of St Catherine, in 1764 for £778 5s.[101] These men and women will have been compelled to move away from their homes, families, friends and provision grounds. The men were probably slightly more expensive than the women. Long clearly wanted to increase the numbers of women, perhaps particularly those of childbearing age. Six months later he bought nine men and ten women from John Burke esq. in St Dorothy for £1,192 10s.[102] These were sales that once again took the enslaved from their established settlements, a practice which Long claimed to abhor in other contexts.

When contemplating debt, Long noted that it was the purchase of 'new Negroes' that was the greatest expense for the planter, 'the true source of the distress under which their owners suffer'.[103] The issue of buying new captives was a constant source of disagreement for Simon Taylor, when acting as attorney for Chaloner Arcedeckne. Taylor was in due course to establish himself as the wealthiest planter on the island. He was convinced of the need for purchases, assuring his employer that 'unless there is a very large addition of Negroes the Estate will fall back every year'.[104] Arcedeckne, enjoying his travels on the continent and his building schemes, was hard to persuade.

---

[99] IRO, vol. 199, f. 84.
[100] IRO, vol. 199, f. 84; Mr Long's Proposals for his Property. On naming patterns, see Margaret Williamson, 'Africa or Old Rome? Jamaican Slave Naming Revisited', S&A 38.1 (2017), 117–34.
[101] IRO, vol. 209, f. 126.
[102] Ibid.
[103] Long, *History*, II. 437.
[104] Betty Wood (ed.) with assistance of T. R. Clayton and W. A. Speck, *The Letters of Simon Taylor of Jamaica to Chaloner Arcedekne, 1765–1775* (Cambridge, 2002), 64.

He would have known that as a result of this expenditure planters could be in debt and find no adequate returns. Many 'saltwater slaves', as Long well knew, would be 'lost ... by disease, or other means in the seasoning'. Planters, meanwhile, 'unable to make good their engagements, are plunged in lawsuits and anxiety'.[105] In July 1767 Long was telling his friend Ricketts that he lived in hope that he would be able to crawl out of his debts and return to England. The following month he bought sixteen enslaved men and women, a major expenditure but an investment for the future.

This was his final recorded sale and it took place in August when he was beginning preparations for leaving the island. On this occasion he was not buying locally. The purchase was from Thomas and John Hibbert and Samuel Jackson, the leading Kingston factors. Grainger strongly recommended that if buying from Africa,

> Buy not the old: they ever sullen prove:
> With heart-felt anguish they lament their home:
> They will not, cannot work ...

Rather it was vital to choose those with 'health and youth, their every sinew firm'.[106] Above all, he advised, do not buy Coromantees who were widely associated with rebellion. Knight also warned against buying too many Coromantees, and this was a judgement, as we shall see, that Long probably already shared. On this occasion Long paid £755 for seven men and nine women. The *Judith* had docked in Kingston in April. Captained by Samuel Murdoch, the ship had set sail from Liverpool in May 1756 and spent time on the West African coast and in St Helena before crossing the Atlantic. Of the 429 African captives who had embarked, 333 had landed in Kingston, 71 per cent of whom were men. The recorded price in sterling was £30 3s. for each person.[107] The captives that Long purchased may have been on this ship and if the Hibberts had bought them, which was the usual arrangement, then they will have 'seasoned' the men and women for three months, preparing them for the climate and labour. They will then have been sold on to Long, probably at Hibbert House, the palatial establishment which Thomas Hibbert had begun to build two years earlier and which still stands. Behind the house was the slave yard where the 'saltwater slaves' who had been bought from the ships were seasoned, ready for sale on to the planters. Countering the levels of mortality and the low birth rate at Lucky Valley meant new labour had to be acquired. The 139 men, women and children who had comprised the

---

[105] Long, *History*, II. 437.
[106] Grainger, *Sugar Cane*, Bk 4. 67–9, 73.
[107] ID 90639, www.slavevoyages.org, accessed 27 April 2020. No figures are given for the mortality of the captives on this ship. The crew was originally thirty-five, twenty-nine of whom landed in Kingston; 350 captives landed, but 333 disembarked, with 71 per cent being male.

work force in 1760 had now become 300.[108] Simon Taylor also purchased people from the Hibberts, while on occasion he bought directly from the ships, waiting for a 'Guinea Man' to come in. One landed in Kingston in May 1771, but he judged its human cargo unsuitable as 'the Slaves rose on the coast of Guinea and murdered the Capt. Many were drove over board and drowned I did not think it prudent to buy any for you out of her they might be troublesome and think it better to wait a little till we can get some not quite so mutinous.' When a 'good cargo' came in, he reported, he would buy.[109] He normally bought twelve or thirteen persons at a time, he recorded, and told Arcedeckne that they must be easily worked until seasoned. 'To work them immediately hard only breaks their hearts,' he judged, so he allowed them three days clearing pastures and four days on provision grounds and building their houses. In 1765–6 he bought twenty-seven men and twenty-nine women, being very concerned about the numbers of 'old superannuated Negroes & Young Children' who were a burden on the plantation.[110]

The works at Lucky Valley needed attention too. Long replaced the dam head for the water mill in 1767, after the river had swept away the original.[111] This time the rock was cut through higher up the river, no doubt by the enslaved, in order to secure a better fall. In later years he recorded in his notes the increase in the fall, the new gutters that had to be built and the exact dimensions of the wheel with calculations as to the conditions for its best performance.[112] Other buildings had been improved, as had the road to the wharf, now well supplied with stores, offices and warehouses. (See Figure 3.5.)

Long was also buying land. His first priority was to extend the Spanish Town property. A deal was done with Henry Moore in 1761, again at a peppercorn price of five shillings, for 'a parcel of land with the vault thereon sunk and erected', probably a cellar or store.[113] Then in 1762 he paid £400 for a parcel of land described as next to his (his wife's property which came to him through marriage) with its 'houses and outhouses'.[114] Two years later he started buying

[108] Mr Long's Proposals for his Property.
[109] Wood, *The Letters of Simon Taylor*, 105, 135.
[110] Betty Wood and T. R. Clayton, 'Slave Birth, Death and Disease on Golden Grove Plantation, Jamaica, 1765–1810', *S&A* 6.2 (1985), 99, 104–5.
[111] It is interesting that Long never discussed in any detail the machinery required for the mill, nor did he choose to use one of the many engravings of sugar mills available.
[112] BL Add MSS 18961, f. 79.
[113] IRO, vol. 192, f. 13.
[114] IRO, vol. 193, f. 127. Long registered to vote in St Catherine in right of his wife's house, and St Catherine's register survives, JA 2/2/27, St Catharine [sic] Parish, List of Freeholders, 1757–1840, f. 34, 27 October 1763. It is described as 'a house in the Parish of St Cath <in right of his wife> which lands fronting a street Leading from the Church parade to the Jews Burial Ground.' JA. 2/2/22, St Catharine's [sic] Vestry Book, 1771–1774. The Town Precinct Deficiency Roll from 20 March 1772 to 20 June following shows 'Long, Edward 64 slaves, no cattle, no White People, no shops, liability £6.11.8'.

Figure 3.5 East view of Dawkins' Salt River Wharf in Clarendon, where stock was stored, weighed and accounted for ahead of export, *c.* 1760. British Library, London. © British Library Board. All Rights Reserved/Bridgeman Images.

land contiguous to Lucky Valley so that it could supply the pasture, woodland and provision grounds that were needed, thus facilitating an expansion of the cane pieces. First he bought 100 acres to the south of the estate and a road from William Shields for £150.[115] Then 46 acres, again bordering his land, from George Summers, 'a free mulatto man', again for £150. Further deeds have unfortunately been destroyed, but we know that before 1769 he had purchased the 400-acre Rules plantation, which extended the estate to the banks of the Juan de Bolas River to the north. By the time Long commissioned James Blair to survey the property in 1769, the estate totalled 1,462 acres, well beyond the size of an average plantation. Surveys were a way of viewing a plantation as a grid, measuring, rationalizing and exerting control over what was in reality a complex mixture of cane lands, pasture, woods and settlement. The estate had 'a rather ragged shape, the product of accretion by purchase'.[116] The plans produced by surveyors gave a legal account of the ownership of land.[117] The survey was undertaken in preparation for the family's departure for England, since in the future Long would need to employ an attorney to manage the estate for him. He was well aware of the problems associated with absentee owners and regretted they meant a 'certain' financial loss to Great Britain, but he was determined to become one.[118] 'No man's estate is so well taken care of in his absence, as to render it unnecessary for him to have an eye to it himself,' he had told Mary Ricketts in 1764, at a time when she was facing separation from her husband who had returned to the island to deal with major business

> This was after Long had moved to England, but the numbers of enslaved clarifies that it was a very substantial property. Thanks to James Robertson for this information.

[115] IRO, vol. 204, f. 56.
[116] Higman, *Jamaica Surveyed*, 84–5.
[117] On the 'plantation complex of visuality', see Mirzoeff, *The Right to Look*.
[118] Long, *History*, I. 387.

problems.[119] And a few years later, he had written to William Ricketts welcoming the fact that he was returning once again to the island and emphasizing how important a man's presence was: 'It is a debt which every proprietor of an Estate here would find it in his interest to pay, once in every 3 or 4 years, and a Man's presence here even tho' it were but for a month, is often attended with more benefits to his Concerns than a Volume of Letters.'[120]

Long was doing what he could to protect his income, and a survey was part of that process. He needed to be sure of the accurate dimensions and potential of the property. The question of boundaries was a very significant one for the plantocracy, since the heavy investment in buildings, from sugar mills to aqueducts, and other fixed capital assets meant that their security of tenure was vital. 'It is of the utmost importance to landed property', insisted Long, to pay attention to 'the true fixing of boundaries'. Uncertainty over them was a 'constant source of dispute and litigation' and the colonists were notorious for their litigious temperaments. It would be a very good idea, he thought, if proprietors were obliged to 'perambulate' their boundaries annually, thus marking them out.[121] Surveyors had been practising on the island for decades, but the mid-century prosperity of the planters saw a significant increase in their numbers.[122] There had been complaints as to the malpractices of surveyors from very early on, and Long was acid about 'the ignorance and knavery' of some who bred 'numberless disputes'. Nevertheless, he regarded their work as an important aspect of improvement and was complimentary about some of the Scots who practised the 'geometric art'.[123]

James Blair's plan shows both the old works' location and the site of the new works. This was the third part of Long's heavy investment. The old mill had used both cattle and water, but the water supply was inadequate. Long had moved the new mill closer to the centre of the cane fields, which were in the narrow valleys of Pindar's River and Back River. This meant that there was a shorter distance to transport the cane. The mill was now closer to the water supply and was powered by a water wheel, the remains of which can still be seen. This facilitated the expansion of the area under cane, while the pasture, provision grounds, plantain walks and woodland were situated on the foothills. Blair's plan named two buildings, the mill and the sheepfold. The boiling, curing and still houses were immediately south of the mill and a mill gutter ran from Pindar's River, the remains of which can also still be seen, as well as a gutter from a dam built on the Back River. There were two trash houses to the west of the mill and a complex of offices and workshops to the east. The 'Negro

---

[119] Edward Long to Mary Ricketts, 6 April 1764, Ricketts Family Papers.
[120] Edward Long to William Ricketts, 5 October 1768, Ricketts Family Papers.
[121] Long, *History*, III. 673 fn.
[122] Higman, *Jamaica Surveyed*, 28.
[123] Long, *History*, II. 292–3.

houses' were represented as four barrack-like buildings, but it is more likely that the enslaved lived in wattle and daub huts on the side of the hill, clearly visible in a later survey of 1816. The 'Negro ground', the provision grounds where the enslaved grew the majority of their own food, were on the edge of the property, at a considerable distance from the works.[124] They would never be situated on prime land that could be used for cane. (See Figures 3.6–3.7.)

Eight years later, when Long was negotiating a new partnership with his Uncle Charles, he documented the improvements he had made. There were the new water mill and the stream to supply the distilling house. He had rebuilt all the works, including adding a hospital. He had increased the provision grounds 'in order to throw a greater strength on the negroes'.[125] Woodland for timber had been purchased and pasture for cattle; previous pastureland had been converted to cane culture. He had also created a resting place on the road to Old Harbour, together with a large warehouse at Longville Park. Long regarded the development of roads across the island as absolutely central to commercial development. 'Good roads add a lustre to any country, and enrich it,' he was convinced. 'Whatever cheapens and quickens the transportation of goods, and makes their migration more easy from place to place, must of course render a country more opulent.' The great improvement in roads in England had brought civilization to places where 'the most shocking barbarism prevailed'. Here was his conception of progress: England had once been barbaric, was now civilized. The same progress must be possible in Jamaica; the whole island could be made productive. This was work that any 'patriotic legislature' should address, while landowners should cooperate to improve the roads most necessary to their own properties. Unfortunately some were 'detestably selfish'. Good roads would not only facilitate 'the constant interchange and circulation' of all products, but also be vital to the quelling of sedition and the prevention of insurrection.[126] The net result of all this was higher levels of productivity than ever before.[127]

The one watercolour of Lucky Valley that has survived is William Berryman's (Plate 2). He must have spent several days at Longville and Lucky Valley, probably in around 1810. On his return to England he was hoping to sell his five watercolours of Lucky Valley to Edward Beeston Long, Edward's oldest son, by then in possession of the property after his father's

---

[124] Jill Casid argues that, 'A close-up detail of the "Negro Ground" on the Lucky Valley estate reveals the means used to at once contain the land cultivated by slaves as their own property and yet distinguish these areas as substantially distinct in form ... the areas worked by slaves as their own property are set off spatially at a considerable distance from the plantation machinery and in name not just "ground" but "Negro ground".' *Sowing Empire, Landscape and Colonization* (Minneapolis, 2005), 201.

[125] Mr Long's Proposals for his Property.

[126] Long, *History*, I. 464–70.

[127] Mr Long's Proposals for his Property.

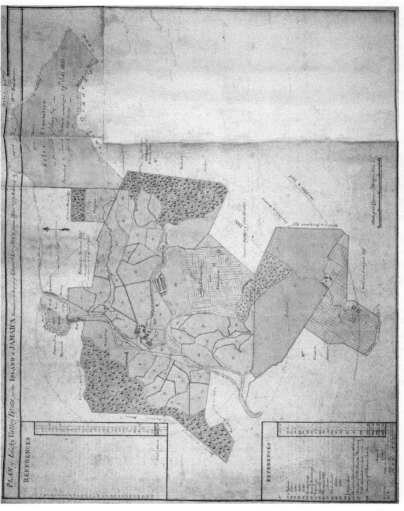

Figure 3.6 Long commissioned Blair's plan of Lucky Valley in 1769, the year he left Jamaica. Plan of the Lucky Valley Estate by James Blair, 1769, reduced and copied by William Gardner, n.d. Scale: 14 chains to an inch. British Library, London. © British Library Board. All Rights Reserved/Bridgeman Images.

Figure 3.7 An aerial image looking north over the present-day landscape of Lucky Valley, with the Rio Minho and adjacent agricultural plots. Historically, the river would have supplied water to the Lucky Valley estate through an aqueduct west of the river and dirt track. Image courtesy of Zachary J. M. Beier.

death in 1813. Berryman, however, died before he could effect the sale. His widow wrote a melancholy letter to Edward Beeston, telling of her husband's untimely death and enclosing the five drawings. Sadly only one has survived, offering a picturesque vision of the estate, something that a gentry family would be happy to display in their home.[128]

The drawing was described in the following terms:

> *Lucky Valley Estate from the westward – the hills in canes – Pinder's River – tops of plantain trees in the foreground – Buildings from the left – old overseer's house where the doctor resides – new overseer's house concealed by trees – trash house – corn store – shed and cattle pen – cooper's shop – hospital – Mr Miller's house – works – mill house boiling – and still house – rum store – piggery etc. – poultry house with sheep pen – waggon with twelve steers and sugar going down.*

In the *History*, Long used the example of Lucky Valley to provide an estimate of the capital value of a plantation of this size, producing roughly 300 hogsheads of sugar and 150 puncheons of rum annually. He made the whole process sound

---

[128] Sketches Relating to Mr Long's Properties in Jamaica, BL Add MS 43379.

simple and straightforward: the figures added up, and all the difficulties and complexities of the actual running of a plantation were erased. Writing in this way helped him to have a sense of control over the process, a control which he could only hope to have partially, given that it was the merchants who determined the price of the sugar and the enslaved who provided the labour. This was Jamaica as he wanted it to be, designed to encourage new settlers by explaining the establishment of an estate and the making of a good profit. It was *figures* that could demonstrate concretely the 'large interest' which a planter could hope for. Nevertheless, it is clear from the extensive use of figures in the *History* that his debits and credits were in the forefront of his mind.[129] His neighbour Henry Dawkins, overseeing his properties from England, could rely on detailed information about his estates from his attorney in Jamaica, as well as from Drake and Long. In later years John Shickle managed fourteen properties for Dawkins, including Suttons and Parnassus, both close to Lucky Valley. He used a multifaceted system of accounts, including detailed inventories and double-entry bookkeeping. These plantation account books provided a basis for detailed planning about the allocation of tasks and resources, how many captives needed to be bought and which cane lands should be planted when. As Caitlin Rosenthal argues, a strictly hierarchical 'rationalized web of control' was being created: violence was always at its centre. 'In many ways, account books were reflections of power as much as they were instruments of it,' she writes, 'but they also augmented planters' power by weaving multiple sources of authority together into a complex and comprehensive system.'[130] Slavery, she suggests, became a laboratory for modern accounting practices which place control at the heart of any business enterprise. The bookkeepers on the plantation would report to the overseer, who would report to the attorney, who would submit the accounts to the slave-owner. He could eventually consult the two sets of accounts, from Drake and Long and from the plantations, to ascertain his position.

Long's aim in the *History* was to make Jamaica an appealing proposition for further settlement. He provided examples of the necessary capital required for different sized plantations, pointing to the high level of profit that could be achieved. He estimated that 900 acres plus plants would be valued at £12,650, while 300 'Negroes' at £50 each plus 50 mules and 80 steers would be £17,620. The value of two cattle mills, a boiling house, distilling house, curing house, rum store, dwelling-house, offices, etc., together with all the necessary utensils plus sheep and hogs, would be £9,000. The total value was therefore £39,270, and it was the human capital which was the major asset. The income from the sugar and rum he estimated at £6,000, with the other charges on the estate

---

[129] Unfortunately no account books have survived.
[130] Caitlin Rosenthal, *Accounting for Slavery. Masters and Management* (Cambridge, MA, 2018), 139.

(taxes, duties, supplies, etc.) at £2,000. 'Such an estate', he concluded, 'appears to be worth 40,000l; for which the purchaser gains an interest of exactly 10*l.per cent per annum* ... This, although a large interest, yet will not be thought too exorbitant by those who candidly consider, that the proprietor is subject to a great variety of risques, and accidental losses.' Long was keen to point to the 'large interest', but he could only estimate this because he was writing in England. In Jamaica, as Douglas Hall argued, although planters 'were involved in a large-scale capitalistic enterprise, they could indulge in little rational accounting' since they lacked the crucial information as to the price of their sugar and rum.[131] They could document all the expenses before shipping: salaries to white workers, taxes to local government, payments to ships' captains for the enslaved, lumber, livestock and provisions, payments to local merchants for goods and credit. They could also calculate all they had received from the estate: any rent for land or enslaved labour, the sale of estate produce such as grass, livestock, molasses or rum. But once the sugar was on board, the merchant house took over accounting, and from their sales deducted the costs of shipping, marketing, commissions, interest. They decided what balance should be paid or held in account.

After his return to England, Long was able as an absentee to keep notes clarifying the highs and lows of the returns on the crops and levels of profit. The year he left the island, Lucky Valley produced 371 hogsheads of sugar and 70 puncheons of rum, but 1771 was a bad year, with only 126 hogsheads of sugar and 84 puncheons of rum. Meanwhile, 1773 delivered a bumper crop, with 442 hogsheads of sugar and 177 puncheons of rum. These latter figures, however, were never repeated. Long's average net proceeds calculated between 1770 and 1780 were £3,885, a very satisfactory income. By 1787, however, the last year for which he made an entry, only 183 hogsheads were produced, with no figure for rum.[132] He admitted in the *History* that the figures he had produced were 'unquestionably vague', but they were close to his own estate calculations. The value of a sugar crop could vary dramatically from year to year, and he listed the difficulties faced by the planter: 'dry years, hurricanes, inundations, fire, mortality of Negroes and cattle, the sudden rise of those necessary articles which he is obliged to buy every year, or the sudden fall at market in the price of sugars and rum'. And the planter had to face 'all these casualties and vicissitudes' alone; 'he stands his own insurer, undergoes infinite fatigues of body and mind'. Surely he deserved, 'after surmounting all difficulties', to sit 'down to the peaceable enjoyment of the fortune he has raised under such a crowd of disadvantages'. He 'should be esteemed', he concluded in

---

[131] Long, *History*, I, 463. Douglas Hall, 'Incalculability as a Feature of Sugar Production during the Eighteenth Century', *Social and Economic Studies* 10.3 (1961), 340–52.
[132] BL Add MSS 18961, ff. 80–2.

self-justification, 'as one well entitled to reap, without envy, the hard earned fruits of his industry'.[133]

Long's account, he emphasized, was based on 'my own single experience'.[134] The work of an industrious planter 'is one continued scene of activity', he reiterated, 'both of body and mind. He has many public duties as well as private. His slumbers are often disturbed with corroding cares, the failure of seasons, the casualties to which his property may be liable, and the importunity of creditors.' What a multiplicity of business, for which the day was often 'insufficient'.[135] How wearisome to be a planter! Knight concurred: the life of a planter was indeed an 'anxious' one.[136]

Lucky Valley: the Labour Force

Long's sense of the burdens of plantership and *his* 'suffering' has to be placed next to the suffering that he caused those labouring on the plantation – the people who were the 'sinews' of the enterprise and the source of profit. Since his intention in writing the *History* was to give a benevolent picture of slavery, there is very little material in the three volumes on the realities of the lives of the enslaved. His passive formulations as to the work to be done avoided any direct descriptions of who was doing the work and with what effects for them. The labour was depersonalized. Any account of the *workings* of the plantation can only be derived from odd comments in the hundreds of pages he wrote, together with the indentures and agreements which were designed to audit sales and profits rather than explicate labouring lives. 'Not for nothing', writes Simon Smith, have the enslaved been described as 'invisible' in plantation records.[137] The same could be said of Long's history writing. His representation of the enslaved was just that, a representation: a way of looking and describing framed by his racialized imagination. He liked to think of himself as appreciated by the enslaved, with this affirming his white selfhood.[138] There is no equivalent in the Long papers to the detailed reports sent by the overseers and attorneys on the Barham estates which have enabled Richard Dunn to

---

[133] Long, *History*, I. 461–3.
[134] Ibid., I. 464.
[135] Ibid., II. 543.
[136] Knight, *History*, I. 11.
[137] S. D. Smith, *Slavery, Family, and Gentry Capitalism in the British Atlantic. The World of the Lascelles, 1648-1834* (Cambridge, 2006), 261; see also Michael Craton and Garry Greenland, *Searching for the Invisible Man. Slavery and Plantation Life in Jamaica* (Cambridge, MA, 1978); B. W. Higman, *Montpelier, Jamaica. A Plantation Community in Slavery and Freedom, 1739-1912* (Kingston, Jamaica, 1998), for discussion of the limitations and difficulties of working with estate journals and ledgers.
[138] 'One of the ways nations could accommodate slavery's degradation was by brute force; another was to romance it'; Morrison, *The Origin*, 6.

compile extensive material on the lives of the enslaved.[139] Despite those hundreds of letters sent and received, both work and methods of punishment were rarely described in detail. These subjects were better avoided – the 'disgusting' aspects of Jamaica, as Long's mother had told him years ago.[140] Nor is there a diary such as that of Thomas Thistlewood, with his horrible factual accounts of the rapes and tortures he practised.[141] Long had to avoid writing about working lives in order to maintain the fiction that slavery was a perfectly acceptable system. He hoped to satisfy himself and his readers with formulations such as that 'Negroes ... on every well-governed plantation ... eye and respect their master as a father', and blaming low-born overseers for unfortunate examples of cruelty and excess.[142] Once he had returned to England, he could not avoid the growing critique of slave-owners and the accusation that they treated 'their Negroes with barbarity'. 'These slave-holders, (as they are pleased to call them, in contempt)', he wrote,

> are lawless bashaws, West-India tyrants, inhuman oppressors, bloody inquisitors, and a long, etc. of such pretty names. The planter, in reply to these bitter invectives, will think it sufficient to urge, in the first place, that *he* did not make them slaves, but succeeded to the inheritance of their services in the same manner as an English squire succeeds to the estate of his ancestors; and that, as to his Africans, he buys their services from those who have all along pretended a very good right to sell.[143]

He was quoting from Granville Sharp's characterization of the planter as an 'arbitrary monarch ... a lawless Basha' and his depiction of slavery as a 'many headed monster of tyranny'.[144] His ripostes were to become key arguments of the pro-slavers in the subsequent debates on the abolition of the slave trade. He had never seen and 'rarely heard' of any instances of cruelty by creole gentlemen, Long insisted, but some 'barbarian' overseers had given proof of a 'savage disposition'.[145] He positively refused the notion that Jamaican slaves were the 'most ill-treated and miserable of mankind'.[146] Men of sense should understand, he concluded, that given the high price of 'Negroes', it was wise to be humane. Yet there was accumulating evidence of the cruelty of Jamaican slave-owners. It was impossible to live among 'such Numbers of Slaves', Leslie had

---

[139] Richard Dunn, *A Tale of Two Plantations. Slave Life and Labor in Jamaica and Virginia* (Cambridge, MA, 2014).
[140] Similarly, see Alex Renton's account of the plantation correspondence over sixty-eight years that never mentions violence or punishments. *Blood Legacy. Reckoning with a Family's Story of Slavery* (Edinburgh, 2021), 175.
[141] Burnard, *Mastery, Tyranny, and Desire*.
[142] Long, *History*, II. 410.
[143] Ibid., II. 267–70.
[144] Sharp, *A Representation*, 82.
[145] Long, *History*, II. 270.
[146] Ibid., II. 441.

written, 'without observing their Conduct with the greatest Niceness and punishing their Faults with the utmost Severity'.[147] The slave codes ensured that enslaved men and women were at the mercy of their owners, always backed by the colonial state.

We know that the production of sugar and rum more than doubled in the period of Long's management of Lucky Valley and that this was facilitated by the new mill, the new land and the increased labour force. Driving through new forms of labour discipline was also crucial. Simon Taylor was able to double the production of sugar on the Golden Grove estate between 1765 and 1775 thanks to his purchase of new labour, the practice of hiring extra hands when needed, and what Higman describes as 'physical oppression' of the enslaved.[148] He also practised a system of divide and rule, providing perquisites for the skilled workers and ensuring a mix of ethnicities on each property in the expectation that some would remain loyal.[149] A routinized system of violence, from branding and the whip to dishonouring and humiliation, underpinned plantation regimes. Evidence from witnesses to the House of Commons inquiry in 1791 demonstrates that mistreatment was systemic on Jamaican plantations, and that maximal attention was given to crop production and minimal attention to the self-sufficiency of the enslaved. Long's denial of misery and cruelty was specious. The rise in the price of the enslaved during this period was not equalled by a rise in the price of sugar, which meant a steep rise in labour costs. Yet the average productivity of slaves working in sugar production as measured by pounds of sugar doubled between 1750 and 1810, especially in the period 1763–83.[150] The enslaved were working longer hours, and were subject to tighter discipline in the organization of their labour. As Justin Roberts concludes, 'improvement' was primarily about enforcing longer hours of work.[151]

Long approached Lucky Valley with an 'eye of business'.[152] His task while in Jamaica was to make money so that he could clear his debts and return to England. 'A plantation', Samuel Martin maintained, 'ought to be considered as

---

[147] Charles Leslie, *A New and Exact Account of Jamaica ... With a particular account of the sacrifices, libations, etc. at this day, in use among the Negroes. The third edition. To which is added an appendix, containing an account of Admiral Vernon's success at Porto Bello and Charge* (Edinburgh, 1740), 42.
[148] Higman, *Plantation Jamaica*, 223.
[149] Petley, *White Fury*, 60.
[150] Burnard, *Jamaica in the Age of Revolution*, 73.
[151] Roberts, *Slavery and the Enlightenment*.
[152] The term is William Beckford Jr's, in *A Descriptive Account of the Island of Jamaica: with remarks upon the cultivation of the sugar-cane, throughout the different seasons of the year, and chiefly considered in a picturesque point of view; also observations and reflections upon what would probably be the consequences of an abolition of the slave trade, and of the emancipation of the slaves* (2 vols., London, 1790), I. 268. He was very aware that he did not have such an eye himself.

a well-constructed machine, compounded of various wheels, turning different ways, and yet all contributing to the great end proposed: but if any one part runs too fast or too slow in proportion to the rest, the main purpose is defeated.' This meant that a planter must know his property intimately and 'as negroes, cattle, mules, and horses are the *nerves* of a sugar-plantation, it is expedient to treat that subject with some accuracy; for the success of the whole consists chiefly in this, as in a well constructed machine, upon the energy and right disposition of the main springs, or primary parts'.[153] Close supervision was essential, and it is clear that Long knew his property well. It was this that facilitated the imposition of labour discipline, the organization of skilled and unskilled labour in terms of overall goals, the treatment of the labour force as disposable units and the careful management of time that made the system so innovative and so effective.

The 'well constructed machine' that Long created at Lucky Valley relied on a clear division of labour rooted in classed, racialized and gendered practices. All those at the top of the hierarchy were white and male. Long himself had to be away in Spanish Town for periods of time, particularly when in attendance at the assembly.[154] An overseer, based in Lucky Valley, would be his second-in-command, managing both white employees and the enslaved, assigning tasks on a daily basis. His house would be relatively simple with three rooms and a kitchen at the back. Long's judgement of overseers was cautious. Many had had chequered careers, moving from one part of the island to another, encountering quite different soils and conditions of production and unable to build up expertise. Those who had gained experience and were sensible and thrifty could do well, live comfortably, and even establish their own properties. His advice to them was that they were bound to encounter 'factions' amongst the enslaved, ready to oppose them, and they should study the men and women under their command, 'learn somewhat of their private history', and 'show no signs of heat or passion in [their] admonitions'.[155] This recognition of 'private history' is striking, a disjunctive moment of admission when 'Negroes' become people. Long's insistence on the importance of white men conquering their passions and exercising self-control echoed his earlier literary writings on a key characteristic of white masculinity. Without self-control they would be 'totally unfit' to be managers of other men[156] – advice which, from the evidence we have, seems most unlikely to have been heeded.

The white craftsmen, stock-keepers and storemen sat beneath the overseer. Long estimated that a plantation producing 100 hogsheads would need

[153] Martin, *An Essay*, 1–2, 37.
[154] Long kept a meteorological diary which provides evidence of his travel between Spanish Town and Lucky Valley. BL Add MS 18963.
[155] Long, *History*, II. 405, 412.
[156] Ibid., II. 412.

a number of white servants costed at £140 p.a.[157] Lucky Valley was larger so may have needed more. He may, however, have been paying the Deficiency penalty tax. A series of Deficiency laws had been passed from 1681, requiring a certain number of white servants to be kept in proportion to the numbers of enslaved on a property: by the early 1770s, this was one white man to every thirty 'Negroes'.[158] This was an attempt to prevent the ratio of white to black declining further. Many slave-owners preferred to pay the penalty tax rather than maintain the white servants, and by the 1760s, despite trouble, were satisfied with employing only an overseer and perhaps a skilled craftsman. An African could be purchased for £60; the wages for a white servant would be £40–50 per annum. The Deficiency tax was used to support the presence of the regular army and Long was aware that it was dangerous to let those numbers drop. The regiments might be withdrawn when needed elsewhere, as they had been in the past, and this was a potential disaster. It was the wealthy and the absentees who were reluctant to pay, he noted, but they should understand that 'the more secure their property is rendered in the island, the more will the value of that property increase'.[159]

The main family house was in Spanish Town, so some white servants may have been employed there, but Long had little respect for white domestics. Even in Britain, he maintained, house servants were unmanageable and insolent.

> Their wages are enormous; the charge of maintaining them, their wilful waste, idleness, profligacy, ingratitude of disposition, and ill behaviour in general, are so universally, and (I believe) with good reason, complained of, that most families consider them as necessary evils, and would gladly have nothing to do with such plagues, if their rank or station in life, or their own imbecillities, could possibly admit of their keeping none.

So, if they behaved like that in England, imagine how they would be in Jamaica. They would leave all the hard work to the enslaved and play at being ladies and gentlemen. 'The Negroes are certainly much better servants here,' he opined, 'because they are more orderly and obedient, and conceive an attachment for the families they serve, far stronger than may be expected from the ordinary white domestics.'[160] The pretensions of white servants were an unfortunate effect of the distinctions made between white and black. All white people, whatever their social status, assumed their superiority and their power over others of colour, for they lived in 'a country where the complexion, generally speaking, distinguishes freedom from slavery'.[161] Long certainly wanted a clear

---

[157] Ibid., I. 460.
[158] Ibid., I. 381.
[159] Ibid., I. 384.
[160] Ibid., II. 282.
[161] Bryan Edwards, *The History, Civil and Commercial, of the British Colonies in the West Indies* (3 vols., Dublin, 1793), II. 7.

binary between black and white, but he also wanted class distinctions to be maintained, and all to know their place.

His class prejudice meant he had little time for any of 'the lower sorts of white people'.[162] He was willing to make an exception for some of the Scottish artisans, the stonemasons and millwrights who were 'in general sober, frugal and civil; the good education which the poorest of them receive, having great influence on their morals and behaviour'. But many bookkeepers, warehouse and storehouse keepers, and tradespeople were ill-qualified. There were 'carpenters who have never handled a tool; bricklayers who scarcely know a brick from a stone; and bookkeepers who can neither write nor read'. Indeed, some of 'these menial servants, who are retained for the sake of saving a deficiency, are the very dregs of the three kingdoms', more suited to Newgate Gaol than to a plantation. Even 'the better sort of Creole Blacks' were contemptuous of them.[163]

Some of the craftspeople in Lucky Valley may have been white, tasked with training the enslaved so that their wages could then be saved.[164] Long advised employing an English ploughman as we have seen, so ensuring that he would be familiar with the workings of this newfangled technology. There would be boilers, distillers, carpenters, coopers, blacksmiths, sawyers, masons, wheelwrights, farriers and carters, but most would have been enslaved. Stock-keepers would have dominated on Longville Park Pen, while wharfmen would have been busy at Long's Wharf on Old Harbour Bay. By 1777, when Long was renegotiating his lease with Charles Long, he recorded twenty-two enslaved tradespeople in Lucky Valley. There was a coppersmith/plumber for whom he had been offered £300, a clear indication of his value; one head carpenter, joiner and millwright with five other carpenters, millwrights and sawyers under him; four wheelwrights/wainwrights; and four bricklayers/masons.[165] The absence of boilers and distillers in this listing may suggest that this work was still done by white men, but if enslaved, they would have worked in the fields outside of crop time. The coopers would be responsible for the care and maintenance of the coppers sent from England, the blacksmiths for all the metal work needed, the masons for building, the stock-keepers for the cattle, and the carters for the carriage of the ripe cane and the sugar and rum. All would have had others working under them. They were the elite of the enslaved. But they were no more free of brutality than anyone else; all were subject to violence.[166]

---

[162] Long, *History*, II. 287.
[163] Ibid., II. 287–8
[164] It is interesting that the plantation records for the Barham estate at Mesopotamia have very little to say about white supervision; Dunn, *A Tale of Two Plantations*.
[165] Mr Long's Proposals for his Property.
[166] See, for example, the account of Thistlewood's interactions with Lincoln; Burnard, *Mastery, Tyranny, and Desire*, 194–8.

The adoption of the gang system, devised to make workers into units of production, was at the heart of these integrated plantations. Tasks were devised to fill the days and to ensure that no time was wasted, and that all necessary work was done. Enslaved people represented capital; any time in which they were not working for the master was money lost. 'The plantation establishment', wrote Lucille Mathurin Mair, 'saw the slave as a special kind of multi-purpose work equipment, a flexible capital asset which, unlike animals or machinery, could be deployed for any use at any time.'[167] Sugar production was a seasonal business and there were tasks specific to the months. Gangs of field workers were disciplined to work at the same rhythm and pace, orchestrated by a driver with a whip. The drivers were leading figures in the enslaved community. Their job was to keep the field gangs to time, working in unison, hoeing and planting along lines. 'As art transforms the savage face of things', carolled Grainger,

> And order captivates the harmonious mind;
> Let not thy Blacks irregularly hoe:
> But, aided by the line, consult the site
> Of thy demesnes; and beautify the whole.[168]

Grainger hoped to sanitize this labour and render it 'harmonious'. But the drivers would rely on the whip to maintain the pace. Drivers occupied an ambiguous position, crucial intermediaries between the overseer and the enslaved. It was their job to extract as much labour as was physically possible from the gangs, and their rewards, if they were lucky, were longer lives, better food and clothing, and avoidance of the heaviest work.[169] Yet they were the men most likely to punish their friends and neighbours. Their 'instrument of correction in Jamaica', wrote William Beckford Jr, the Jamaican planter whose account was written while he languished in the Fleet debtors' prison, 'whether it be in the hands of the cart-man, the mule-boy, or the negro-driver, is heard, in either case, to resound among the hills, and upon the plains, and to awaken the echoes wherever the reverberations of the lash shall pass'.[170] (Plate 6.) Long, for his part, claimed that the whip was unnecessary on a well-governed estate and that ridicule should be used to maintain discipline rather than harsh physical punishment. This was part of his picture of benevolent slavery.

The cane calendar ruled the plantation. 'In the rainy season', recorded Long, 'namely most part of the month of May, the Negroes are employed in cleaning & supplying the Canes which perished in the preceding dry months.' In August, September and October, which are also rainy months, they 'are

---

[167] Lucille Mathurin Mair, *Women Field Workers in Jamaica during Slavery*. Elsa Goveia Memorial Lecture, 1986 (Mona, Jamaica, 1986), 7.
[168] Grainger, *Sugar Cane*, Bk 1. 266–9.
[169] Randy Browne, *Surviving Slavery in the British Caribbean* (Philadelphia, 2017).
[170] Beckford, *A Descriptive Account*, 51.

employed in hoeing, dunging and planting of canes and corn'.[171] On the south side of the island, the canes fell off after the first cutting, so it was necessary to plant anew each year. The land was often divided into three parts: one part in plants, a second in first ratoons (from a bud on the canes rather than a new plant), a third in second ratoons. This work would have been done by the first gang, composed of the ablest of those men who were not required for more skilled work, and the majority of the adult women. The first gang, ruled by a driver, was the largest, probably about one-third of the total numbers of enslaved, and on a large plantation there might be more than one.

This hoeing and holing, as we have seen, was the heaviest work, digging the spine of the plantation. 'The slaves, of both sexes,' James Stephen wrote in his graphic account of a gang at work, 'from twenty, perhaps, to fourscore in number, are drawn out in a line, like troops on a parade, each with a hoe in his hand, and close to them in the rear is stationed, a driver, or several drivers, in number duly proportioned to that of the gang.' The driver held a 'long thick and strongly plaited whip, called a *cart whip*'. This was to ensure that the line worked together. '[N]o breathing time, no resting on the hoe, no pause of languor, to be repaid by brisker exertion on return to work, can be allowed to individuals: All must work, or pause together.'[172] Long had introduced the plough to try to reduce both the hours of work needed for hoeing and digging and the toll it took. His plan was for the grass gang – the children from age six – to follow the plough, planting in the furrow. They could also do other light tasks, such as weeding, collecting grass or dung from the pasture, sometimes supervised by an older woman, no longer fit for field work. Young girls might do domestic work, young boys help the stock-keepers. Between October and December, 'when it is commonly dry only now and then small showers, the Negroes are employed in mending of fences, cutting of copper wood against the crop and gathering in corn and other plantation provisions'. Some of this less heavy work would have been done by the second gang, which would include both boys and girls aged sixteen or so, who were now seen as young adults, plus pregnant women and those men and women defined as 'weak' or 'sickly'. They would also weed the cane pieces, clean the pastures and help at crop time. One summary of the labour of field hands described the shell blowing at either 4 or 5 a.m., work until 10 a.m., fifteen minutes for breakfast, 1 p.m. dinner, one and a half hour break to go to the provision grounds and tend their own crops, then work until dusk, around 6 p.m. After working in the fields, the enslaved had to tend cattle pens or pick grass, returning home at 8 p.m. Long's account was that 'They generally begin work at six in the morning, and leave off at six in the evening, having half an hour at breakfast, and on most

---

[171] BL Add MS 12404, f. 352.
[172] James Stephen, *The Crisis of the Sugar Colonies* (London, 1802), 10–11.

estates two hours at noon.'[173] Many had to do tasks other than sugar cultivation, such as helping tradespeople or carrying moulds to cattle pens.

'In January', after the holidays at Christmas, 'the canes are commonly ripe sooner or later,' wrote Long,

> according to the situation or weather when they are employed in cutting, grinding them at the mill, boiling up the liquor and making muscovado sugar until the crop is finished which it is in April or May, according to the quantity of canes that are to be cut or the strength of Negroes and Cattle, all which must necessarily go hand in hand together and not be neglected, for the Cane must be cut and pressed as soon as ripe, or the juice drys in it; the liquor must not remain in the receiver above two or three hours, but be boiled up to its proper consistency, for graining, or it will turn sour and perish.[174]

Crop time was the peak of the plantation year, when work could go on all the hours of the day and night, because of the necessity of getting the cane cut by the first gang and to the mill before the juice dried. The slave-owners represented this as a time of plenty. 'How blithe, how jocund, the plantation smiles,' wrote Grainger, waxing lyrical:

> The Negroe-train, with placid looks, survey
> Thy fields, which full perfection have atttain'd,
> And pant to wield the bill: (no surly watch
> Dare now deprive them of the luscious Cane)
> Nor thou, my friend, their willing ardour check;
> Encourage rather, cheerful toil is light.[175]

'The time of crop in the sugar islands', wrote Edwards,

> is the season of gladness and festivity to man and beast. So palatable, salutary, and nourishing is the juice of the cane, that every individual of the animal creation, drinking freely of it, derives health and vigour from its use. The meagre and sickly among the negroes exhibit a surprising alteration in a few weeks after the mill is set in action. The labouring horses, oxen, and mules, though almost constantly at work during this season, yet, being indulged with plenty of the green tops of this noble plant, and some of the scummings from the boiling-house, improve more than at any other period of the year. Even the pigs and poultry fatten on the refuse.

'On a well-regulated plantation', he concluded, 'under a humane and benevolent director, there is such an appearance during crop-time of health, plenty

---

[173] Long, *History*, II. 491.
[174] BL Add MS 12404, f. 352.
[175] Grainger, *Sugar Cane*, Bk 3. 414, 96–100.

and busy cheerfulness, as to soften, in a great measure, the hardships of slavery.'[176]

Beckford rejoiced in a similar manner. There was the 'picturesque and striking' picture of 'a gang of negroes, when employed in cutting canes upon the swelling projections of a hill; when they take a long sweep, and observe a regular discipline in their work'. This was the rhythm of the gang. Then there was the 'lively and pleasing scene' when 'every living creature seems to be in spirits and in expectation', the negroes 'alert and cheerful', even the cattle and mules 'fresh and vigorous', ready for their labour.[177] Simon Taylor presented a more honest picture to his employer, in a letter that was not for publication and was not part of the slave-owners' determination to make their representations of slavery acceptable. 'The Mill has been about ever since the beginning of December', he reported,

> & will not stop until the middle of next month which is near nine months, at which time the poor wretches of negroes have not had above six hours of rest out of 24, & what with getting their little provisions etc. what time have they had to Sleep; the Estate is to be cleaned, Pastures bill'd, Negro houses to be repair, Plant putt in, Copperwood cut, & to be again about in Decr. I have laid all these matters before your Mother & Aunt and they both see the necessity of hiring Negroes to put in the whole plant. I assure you it is an utter impossibility without murdering the Negroes to keep it up without.[178]

Once the cane was cut and milled, the juice then went to the boiling house. The head boiler was a key figure, a man of great skill. His skill was built on trial, error and danger, for his task was to use his thumb to test the boiling liquids and judge the correct moment to 'strike' – to temper the cane juice with the right amount of lime when the liquid was at the point of crystallization and ready to granulate. This passed to the curing house where the sugar, still full of molasses, was packed into hogsheads which had to drain and dry out. The distillers, also highly skilled, had to mix the right amounts of water, yeast and sugar skim with molasses and then leave it in cisterns to ferment. Outside of crop time, however, even these head craftsmen would be directed to other work.

The hope would be that enough rum had been produced to pay for the white servants, the services of a doctor, the public taxes and repairs, possibly even supplies. It never was enough for this, Long noted, but one could always hope that with good husbandry it might be.[179] The sugar was the profit.

The labour force was gendered as well as hierarchically organized. The majority of the adult women were field labourers. On the twelve estates of

---

[176] Edwards, *History*, II. 221–2.
[177] Beckford, *Descriptive Account*, 48.
[178] Wood, *The Letters of Simon Taylor*, 93.
[179] Edward Long to Mrs Mary Ricketts, 17 July 1772, Ricketts Family Papers.

the absentee Alderman Beckford in Clarendon, Westmoreland and St Ann in 1780, there were 2,204 enslaved people, including children: 802 were men, 778 were women. Of these women, 57 per cent were field workers; of the men, only 36 per cent.[180] On Moore, Beckford's estate close to Longville and Lucky Valley, there were fifty-five adult women, twenty-seven of whom were field workers, while on Bodel's Pen, 88 per cent of the field workers were female while the men worked with the cattle.[181] On Edward Manning's Clarendon estate, St Toolies, in 1766 there were 242 slaves, including 85 men and 56 women, all of whom were field workers.[182] Their ancillary tasks may have included cutting grass, working in the estate's provision garden, carrying water, watching the gates or working on roads. None of the women on these estates was a tradesperson, nor did they work with transport or stock; they were seen as incapable of handling machines, so did not benefit from any new technologies. On some plantations they looked after the poultry and pigs. A number of women worked as domestics, the major form of employment after field work, both in Long's house when he was on the plantation and serving the overseer. Domestic work may have been less physically exhausting, but there was the proximity of abuse. On Beckford's estates, 13 per cent of the women were in domestic work, as washerwomen, housewomen and cooks. Nine of the eighteen houseslaves were mulattoes. Eight per cent had skills as midwives, field nurses and seamstresses, and eleven of those fourteen were mulattoes.[183] There are occasional glimpses of girls being apprenticed as washerwomen and cooks. Both midwife and nurse were often euphemisms for superannuated field workers. A few men may have done domestic work, but since there was no Great House at Lucky Valley this seems unlikely. Sometimes older women acted as supervisors for the grass gang: Phillis, for example, was working as the driver of the grass gang on Rozells estate in 1770. She was responsible for between seven and thirty-one children and adolescents aged four to eighteen.[184] Some of the older women will have cared for the young children. The exclusion of women from the possession of recognized skills – for childcare did not count – meant that the opportunities that men had to look for profitable employment outside the estates were denied to women. Their market activities may have provided the best openings, but it is impossible to track this in mid-eighteenth-century records.

Blair's survey of Lucky Valley marks the area of 'Negro ground', the provision grounds which saved the slave-owners from having to provide basic subsistence. Their contribution was limited to an allowance of salt fish or

---

[180] Mair, *Women Field Workers*, 4.
[181] Mair, *A Historical Study*, 202.
[182] Ibid., 75–6.
[183] Mair, *Women Field Workers*, 3–4.
[184] Diana Paton, 'The Driveress and the Nurse: Childcare, Working Children and Other Work under Caribbean Slavery', *P & P* 246, supplement 15 (2020), 27–53.

herring and some maize or pease. But the provision grounds allowed enslaved men and women some possibility of control over one aspect of their lives when they had no such possibility for the vast majority of their time. 'A Negro has a kind of property, and looks upon His little Plantation as such,' wrote Knight.[185] Sylvia Wynter came to understand the plot as laying a basis for a distinctive African culture. 'Around the growing of yam, of food for survival', the African created a folk culture.[186] Land and the nourishment it provided could sustain an alternative worldview. The violence of slavery and the plantation, as Katherine McKittrick elaborates, 'produces black rootedness in place' because the land became the key provision through which the enslaved could both survive and 'be forced to fuel the plantation machine'.[187] Provision grounds offered the possibility of a 'rival geography', in Stephanie Camp's words, free from the fixtures and mapping of the masters, a site on which black lives could be lived.[188] While the overseer's house was situated to facilitate surveillance of the works, the provision grounds were at a distance from the centre of the plantation. Men, women and children could work there, sometimes in their dinner hour, at the end of their labouring day and on Sundays. The 'Negroe markets' which took place on Sunday mornings were an established feature of island life by the 1760s and there was one at the Chapel not far from Lucky Valley. Here it was possible for those who were so fortunate as to have a surplus to sell 'hogs, poultry, fish, corn, fruit, and other commodities'. It is likely that it was already market women who dominated these spaces, as it is into the present. The 'Negroes' had the majority of small silver that circulated on the island, noted Long, because of their market activities.[189]

Long wanted to represent the enslaved as having a generous diet: 'pulse, herbs, plantains, maize, yams, or other roots, prepared with pork, and fish, fresh or salt; salted beef, herrings, jerked hog, or fowls. Salt fish they are extremely fond of, and the more it stinks, the more dainty', puddings made with maize or sweet potato, 'well seasoned with the country peppers', and plenty of '*ochra*'.[190] Such a description sits grossly at odds with the evidence of hunger and malnutrition that was so prevalent on the Barham plantation at Mesopotamia.[191] Beckford's romanticized description of a group of enslaved people arriving at a beautiful retired spot on their provision grounds and throwing themselves 'into picturesque and various attitudes', with the light

---

[185] Knight, *History*, II. 494.
[186] Sylvia Wynter, 'Novel and History, Plot and Plantation', *Savacou* 5 (1971), 95–102.
[187] Katherine McKittrick, 'Plantation Futures', *Small Axe* 42 (2013), 1–15.
[188] Stephanie M. H. Camp, *Closer to Freedom. Enslaved Women and Everyday Resistance in the Plantation South* (Chapel Hill, NC, 2004), 7.
[189] Long, *History*, II. 411; See Sidney Mintz and Douglas Hall, *The Origins of the Jamaican Internal Marketing System* (New Haven, CT, 1960).
[190] Long, *History*, II. 413.
[191] Dunn, *A Tale of Two Plantations*.

Figure 3.8 William Berryman's 'View of a Negro Village' hints at the interior lives of enslaved people. Ink and pencil drawing, 1808–16. Courtesy of the Library of Congress, Prints and Photographs Division, LC-DIG-ppmsca-13412.

shining 'in playful reflections upon their naked bodies and their clothes, and which oppositions of black and white make a very singular, and very far from an unpleasing, appearance', undoubtedly had more to do with his desire to produce a visually provocative picture than any reality. When the grounds were well cultivated, he maintained, they make 'a very husbandlike and beautiful appearance', but he had the grace to admit that some areas gave a poor yield.[192] His picture of 'a negro village' was similarly unrealistic. In his imagination it was 'full of those picturesque beauties in which the Dutch painters have so much excelled', a scene of 'rural dance and merriment' with a variety of houses, hogs, poultry, cats and the charms of the plantain and coconut trees.[193] William Berryman's drawing of provision grounds and a 'negro hut' may be closer to some aspects of reality (Figure 3.8).

'Their houses are built low and snug covered with Thatch after their Country manner', wrote Knight,

> the principal Posts being fixed in the ground three feet or more, the sides, ends, partitions lined with Watles, a kind of laths neatly plaistered with Mud, and a little lime mixed, some without. They are commonly about

[192] Beckford, *Descriptive Account*, 254–6.
[193] Ibid., 227.

> twenty-four feet in length eight or nine feet in breadth and five and a half or six feet in height. They have no Windows, only small loop Holes on each side to distinguish the day from the Night, and to look out when They apprehend any danger, and Their doors are made so low that a middle sized man must stoop to go in. This Building is divided into Three apartments, at one end is His Chamber, the middle part is His Hall or dineing [sic] Room at the other end He keeps His Poultry, and it is likewise a kind of Store Room. They have all of Them a Door in the Front, and another in the back part, in order to escape any danger [;] many of Them are kept very neat and clean, but They all smell very strong of smoak by reason of the Constant fires They keep in the day as well as in the Night and not having chimneys to carry it off.[194]

The houses in the 'Negro' village at Lucky Valley would have been similar: of their own construction, wattle and daub with a thatched roof and a dirt floor. The largest ones might have a hall in the middle for cooking, eating and talking, a sleeping area, and sometimes a hut behind for pigs.[195] 'In their houses', wrote Long, once again representing a scene of comfort and respectability, 'they are many of them very neat and clean, piquing themselves on having tolerably good furniture, and other conveniences.'[196] Thirty years later John Stewart also took pains to provide a benevolent picture, one which probably applied only to drivers and the most established of the tradespeople. 'The houses of the negroes are in general comfortable,' he wrote.

> They are built with hard wood posts, wattled and plaistered, and either roofed with shingles (wood split and dressed into the shape of slates, and used as a substitute for them), or thatched with the tops of sugar-cane; or, if a short distance from the woods, with the mountain thatch. This latter, when neatly plaited, forms a very handsome roof... The furniture of this dwelling, which usually consists of three apartments, is a small table, two or three chairs or stools, a small cupboard, some wooden bowls and calabashes, furnished with a few articles of crockery-ware, a wooden mortar for pounding their Indian corn ... The beds are seldom more than wooden frames spread with a mat and blankets.[197]

When he turned to clothing, Long's account was minimal. 'Labouring Negroes' were allowed a 'frock and trowsers' for the men, while the women had a 'jacket and petticoat of osnabrig, besides woollen stuff'; 'tradesmen, and the better sort', were supplied with 'checks, handkerchiefs, hats and caps'.[198] They could

---

[194] Knight, *History*, II. 486.
[195] Higman, *Montpelier, Jamaica*; Louis P. Nelson, *Architecture and Empire in Jamaica* (New Haven, CT, 2016).
[196] Long, *History*, II. 414.
[197] [John Stewart], *An Account of Jamaica and its Inhabitants by a Gentleman Long Resident in the West Indies* (London, 1808), 231.
[198] Long, *History*, II. 426.

supplement these with their own holiday clothes. Poverty, punishment, violence, hunger and want were erased from Long's account of plantation life.

The Reproduction of the Enslaved

Labour was central to the operation of the plantation, and how that labour was to be maintained was recognized as a problem. 'Plantations depend upon keeping up the Number,' James Knight had written in the 1740s, but 'this is not so easy as some imagine'. He blamed 'Polygamy' which he saw as hindering rather than promoting 'Their Multiplying'. Planters had to rely on buying new 'saltwater slaves' when faced with the 'Death or Disability of a Negro', but prices were high and they might not have the necessary credit.[199] Knight was drawing on a reservoir of ideas about African women that had been circulating for decades, propagated in travellers' tales and early texts from the Caribbean.[200] Polygamous practices and other forms of sexuality, judged as deviant from a European perspective, were part of the range of negative associations that formed a container of racist tropes employed against Africans. Long drew on and elaborated these derogatory ideas in his *History*. The questions that were being posed in the metropole as to why 'the Negroes in our colonies do not increase in that natural proportion which is observed among mankind in other countries, and to a remarkable degree among the Blacks of Afric' would have to be answered.[201] 'As to population in our insular colonies or those of the West Indies,' Arthur Young had observed in one of his influential tracts, 'increase is there quite another thing; they consume people instead of increasing them; a contrast very striking in respect of negroes. The sugar islands require a vast annual supply.'[202] The accusation of consuming people was alarming, however well founded. Long was well aware, as we have seen, of the growing threat of abolitionist voices, of the criticisms of cruel slave-owners and a brutal trade. He recognized that the trade might be at risk. His defence was rooted in his account of African barbarism and his representation of the crossing of the Atlantic as a journey towards civilization. Some writers, he noted, seeing the numbers of 'Negroes' imported to Jamaica each year, attributed mortality levels 'to the too severe labour and oppression they are forced to undergo'. This, declared Long, was 'an erroneous conjecture'. 'We are so fond of depreciating our own colonies', he remarked, aligning himself at this point with his fellow Englishmen, 'that we paint our planters in the most bloody colours, and represent their slaves as the most ill-treated and miserable of mankind.'[203] These commentators failed

---

[199] Knight, *History*, II. 493.
[200] Morgan, *Laboring Women*.
[201] Long, *History*, II. 431.
[202] Young, *Political Essays*, 237.
[203] Long, *History*, II. 441.

to understand 'other causes, which prove more destructive than the severest toil', and missed the 'impediments in the way of a regular propagation'.[204] His task in the *History* was to explain birth and death rates on the island to his readers and demonstrate that slave-owners were in no way to blame. It was the Africans themselves who refused 'to propagate', carried diseases which killed them and were capable of being brutal to their own kind. His unresolved and contradictory understandings of racialized difference – was it *natural* or *cultural* – characterized his account of questions of birth and death. Africans were to blame for their own high death and low birth rates. But creoles, those born enslaved on the island, were, he hoped, different. They might offer a hope for a more settled society of the future: it was, therefore, imperative to improve the birth rate, both reducing the dependence on new captives from Africa and planning for a more docile and industrious labour force.[205]

In addressing the question of the importation of 'Guinea slaves', Long turned first to figures, responding to the contemporary demand for quantification while hoping to flatten the shocking realities of the slave trade and the plantations. Engaging in what Justin Roberts describes as 'statistical fantasies' was a way of attempting to manage the harsh realities of enslavement.[206] Violence could be normalized, both for himself and for his readers, by embedding the cruelty of captivity, the crossing and the plantations in figures. 'Six new Negroes it was computed formerly . . . . were required to every hundred, to keep up the stock in Barbadoes,' he wrote. The language of 'stock' immediately made the connection with cattle, summoning up the degraded status of these men and women.[207] He estimated that the figures were better in Jamaica: 'the present import' was on average six thousand per annum, 'which is about the rate of four to one hundred'. The loss, he believed, from the 'whole stock' on the island was approximately three thousand per annum. At £35 sterling per head, this made an annual loss in value of £105,000, 'a most astonishing sum',

---

[204] Ibid., II. 432.
[205] The importance of social and biological reproduction to the plantation economy has long been recognized. See, e.g., Immanuel Wallerstein, 'American Slavery and the Capitalist World Economy', *American Journal of Sociology* 81.5 (1976), 1199–1213; Blackburn, *The Making of New World Slavery*, 416–24; for a recent discussion, see Katharine Paugh, blog post 'The New History of Capitalism and the Political Economy of Reproduction', available at http://pastandpresent.org.uk/the-new-history-of-capitalism-and-the-political-economy-of-reproduction, accessed 29 June 2023.
[206] Roberts, *Slavery and the Enlightenment*, 281.
[207] The connection that was frequently made between Africans and livestock, as Kirsten Fischer argues, does not mean that slave-owners believed enslaved people were animals; rather they were evoking a degraded form of humanity. Fischer, *Suspect Relations. Sex, Race and Resistance in Colonial North Carolina* (Ithaca, 2002). Lee B. Wilson argues that the analogy between slaves and livestock was because they were believed to be the same at law; *The Bonds of Empire*.

he concluded.[208] The sum was what astonished, not the lives lost, and he noted that it might be an underestimate. In 1768 he thought an average sugar estate required about seven new 'Negroes' a year.[209] 'For all its economic success as an outpost of empire,' as Vincent Brown writes, 'Jamaica routinely destroyed its black people.'[210] Death haunted the island, a constant presence for all. Slave deaths, it is estimated, exceeded births by as much as 3 per cent throughout the eighteenth century.[211] It was the 50–75 per cent of the enslaved who worked on the sugar plantations who suffered the worst conditions, something that Long knew from his own computations. There are incomplete figures on the Barham plantation of Mesopotamia between 1732 and 1833, but there were more deaths than births: 415 new slaves were bought, 137 directly from African ships, 278 from other estates in Jamaica.[212] Amongst the field labourers between 1762 and 1831, the men were 'sickly' for 48 per cent of their working years and died aged just over forty-two, while the women were sick or disabled for nearly 60 per cent of their working lives.[213] The death rate was consistently higher than the birth rate on account of malnutrition, overwork and disease. 'Jamaica imported as many as 750,000 Africans between the late seventeenth and early nineteenth century, but on the eve of emancipation in 1838, just over 300,000 enslaved people remained. From the mid-eighteenth century through the end of chattel slavery, in one of history's greatest episodes of creative destruction, Jamaica's dynamic and profitable economy consumed its inhabitants.'[214] These were disposable lives.

The recognition of the scale of these costs – this loss of value – together with the rising price of captives spurred Long to reflect on the need for improvement. On well-settled estates, he claimed to believe, the numbers of births and deaths each year were pretty equal (though this was not so on the family estates).[215] Africans constituted the majority of those who died, despite

[208] Long, *History*, II. 432.
[209] Ibid., I. 400.
[210] Brown, *The Reaper's Garden*, 49.
[211] Patterson, *Sociology of Slavery*, 94–8.
[212] Dunn, *A Tale of Two Plantations*, 25.
[213] Richard S. Dunn, 'Dreadful Idlers in the Cane Field: the Slave Labor Pattern on a Jamaican Sugar Estate, 1762–1831', in Barbara L. Solow and Stanley L. Engerman (eds.), *British Capitalism and Caribbean Slavery. The Legacy of Eric Williams* (Cambridge, 1985), 163–90.
[214] Brown, *The Reaper's Garden*, 57. By 1750 the British Caribbean had imported about 800,000 Africans, but deaths so far exceeded births that the enslaved population was fewer than 300,000. Philip D. Morgan, 'The Black Experience in the British Empire, 1680–1810', in P. J. Marshall (ed.), *Oxford History of the British Empire. The Eighteenth Century* (Oxford, 1998), 465–86; Morgan, 'Slavery in the British Caribbean', in David Eltis and Stanley L. Engerman (eds.), *The Cambridge World History of Slavery* (Cambridge, 2011), 378–406.
[215] In 1788 when Long was actively campaigning against the abolition of the slave trade, he wrote to Pitt citing the fortunate estates where natural increase occurred. He estimated

'these new Negroes' being much indulged, being put to 'the gentlest work ... that they may be gradually seasoned to the change of climate, and trained by a slow and easy progress to undergo the same degree of labour as the rest'.[216] 'To easy labour first inure thy slaves,' agreed Grainger, 'Extremes are dangerous.'[217] Yet so many 'new Negroes' died. Long blamed this on their existing illnesses; few were 'exempt from a venereal taint' and many had the terrible yaws 'lurking in their blood'. They had been wrongly treated with mercury, which caused further problems. 'I have had occasion in the course of several years', he wrote, 'to mark the fate of many hundred new Negroes.' He was positive that 'a third part of them have perished, within three years of their arrival', as a result of yaws, which he thought was closely connected to smallpox, another major cause of death. Inoculation had recently been introduced and should much reduce this figure.[218] 'Removal ... from dry to a damp' situation, perhaps from the south to the north of the island, also had terrible consequences, especially when it was a result of 'Negroes' being sold because of debt, leaving them 'labouring under discontent, which co-operates with change of place and circumstances to shorten their lives'.[219] Here was a moment of recognition from Long, both of human responses to dislocation and of the fact that 'discontent' might be a condition of life for some of the enslaved. Planters sometimes mistakenly thought, he noted, that it was good policy to put new 'Negroes' in with 'the old settled ones'. This too could be disastrous, since they would be badly treated, forced to be their 'hewers of wood and drawers of water', gradually sinking 'under the oppression', not of the slave-owner, but of their fellows.[220] Long recommended that planters should not buy too many recruits at once. It was more politic to buy only eight or ten and then there would be a better chance of settling them and losing fewer by early death. Simon Taylor, who bought both from the ships and from the factors, rarely bought more than twelve or thirteen persons on any occasion. Despite the death rate, he assured Arcedeckne that every 'Negro' would pay for himself in three years given the work done.[221] The dead were simply part of the bigger picture of profit and loss, and profit was still winning.

---

that these amounted to 1 in 70 of a total 1,000 estates. He calculated Longville's annual decrease to have been 1.75 per cent, which meant purchasing five new slaves per annum to keep the numbers up. Michael Craton, 'Jamaican Slave Mortality: Fresh Light from Worthy Park, Longville and the Tharp Estates', *Journal of Caribbean History* 3 (1971), 1–27; Sasha Turner, *Contested Bodies. Pregnancy, Childrearing, and Slavery in Jamaica* (Philadelphia, 2017).

[216] Long, *History*, II. 433.
[217] Grainger, *Sugar Cane*, Bk 4. 158–9.
[218] Long, *History*, II. 434.
[219] Ibid., II. 435.
[220] Ibid., II. 435.
[221] Brown, *The Reaper's Garden*, 56.

Having explained the levels of mortality by illnesses brought from Africa, depression and discontent caused by the unfortunate laws on debt, and the harsh treatment of 'saltwater slaves' by 'the old settled ones', Long hoped to avoid any accusations as to the responsibility of the slave-owners.[222] He then turned to the question of the birth rate. The impact of the slave trade on African populations was a subject of contemporary debate. Some claimed it was causing depopulation, others that there was no 'apparent diminution of numbers'.[223] In his account of Africa Long had dwelt, as many did, on the extraordinary levels of population increase. In Long's mind this legitimated the slave trade's removal of 'superfluous people'.[224] Fecundity and excess were associated with sexual depravity and a never-ending supply of captives for sale.[225] The levels of increase were explained by polygamy, the softness of the air, the stimulus of the food and the 'unrestrained passions' in play. The excess of females in the population meant that, despite powerful men claiming numerous women for their harems, 'an unpaired man or woman is seldom or never seen'.[226] What was more, 'Child-birth is attended with little or no danger or difficulty' and the 'fruitfulness of the soil' meant that there was no danger of children being a burden: 'Nature does the rest' and 'nature' was different in Africa.[227] Women were 'delivered with little or no labour', and therefore had no need of midwives, any more 'than the female orang-outan, or any other wild animal'.[228] This linking of the African woman to wild beasts and orangutans was a reminder to his readers of the tales of sexual intimacy between Hottentots and apes. Women bore their children in a quarter of an hour, he maintained, and then went to the sea and washed themselves.[229] Some had twins without even screaming. This disavowal of pain in childbirth, a white man's fantasy of a black woman's painless and almost instantaneous labour, was part and parcel of Long's notion of African 'stoicism' in the face of the most appalling tortures.[230] Africans did not experience pain in the way that white people did,

---

[222] Ibid., 184: 'By distancing themselves and their business from the deaths they caused, slaveholders and their allies sought to remove as many of the dead as possible from the growing debate over slavery, and thus reduce the legions of dead slaves arrayed against them by abolitionists to a small band of spectral aberrations. Slaveholders hoped to kill symbolically those whom slavery had already killed physically.'

[223] Robert Wallace argued that the population had decreased over time; Henry Lord Kames counterclaimed. See Alison Bashford and Joyce C. Chaplin, *The New Worlds of Thomas Robert Malthus. Rereading the Principle of Population* (Princeton, 2016), 36–40.

[224] Long, *History*, II. 387.

[225] Morgan, *Reckoning with Slavery*, 111.

[226] Long, *History*, II. 385–6.

[227] Ibid., II. 385.

[228] Ibid., II. 380.

[229] It was a well-established view that birth was easy in foreign climes. Suman Seth, *Difference and Disease. Medicine, Race and the Eighteenth Century British Empire* (Cambridge, 2018).

[230] Thanks to Anita Rupprecht for discussions of the so-called 'stoicism' of 'savages', an aspect of Enlightenment thinking on difference.

a clear sign of their more primitive natures. All of which confirmed Long in his assertion of essential differences between black and white. The women, he continued, were rarely confined for more than two or three days. Immediately before she went into labour, a woman would be conducted to a river or the sea, accompanied by little children who would throw 'all manner of ordure or excrement at her, after which she is washed with great care'. Without this ritual, the community believed that she or the child would die in the lying-in. These absurd superstitions, as he depicted them, provided yet another example for Long of African barbarism. 'Thus they seem exempted', he concluded, 'from the curse inflicted upon Eve and her daughters, "I will greatly multiply thy sorrow; in sorrow shalt thou bring forth children."'[231] African women were excluded from the Christian family. The absence of pain in childbirth was another mark of difference, legitimating enslavement.

Yet it was certainly an inconvenience for planters that 'the women do not breed here as in Africa'.[232] The success of this form of mercantile capitalism, as Samuel Long had understood, rested in particular ways on the bodies of enslaved women, ensuring hereditary racial slavery. While enslaved men were both capital and labour, for a woman 'to be enslaved', as Jennifer Morgan puts it 'meant to be locked in to a productive relationship whereby all that your body could do was harnessed to the capital accumulation of another'.[233] Women's value as a capital asset was about both their labouring body and their reproductive body, their capacity to augment the property of their owner by bearing children. Those children might be the fruit of a chosen union with an enslaved mate, or of rape and enforced coupling with a white master or one of his friends. If the latter, then the 'mulatto' children (to use the contemporary term) might simply be absorbed into the enslaved population as it is estimated 80 per cent in Jamaica were, or they might be granted certain privileges.[234] The failure of enslaved women to reproduce was understood by Long as a problem. He explained it, not by the harsh and violent nature of the plantation, but by the character of the women themselves. Edward Long loved his own children: their well-being was a crucial issue for him. Yet as a slaveholder he claimed ownership of the children of enslaved mothers. This disavowal, this insistence on the

---

[231] Long, *History*, II. 380.

[232] Given the paucity of figures before the late eighteenth century, it is impossible to gather statistics on live births and infant mortality for the mid-eighteenth century. Kenneth Morgan estimates that 1 in every 4.6 children born to enslaved women were live births, and that there was 80 per cent mortality amongst newborns during the first two weeks of life; 'Slave Women and Reproduction in Jamaica, 1776–1834', *History* 91 (2006), 231–53. Craton and Greenland concur; *Searching for the Invisible Man*, 87. B. W. Higman calculates that as many as 50 per cent of children died in the first nine days of life; *Slave Population and Economy in Jamaica* (Cambridge, 1976), 49.

[233] Morgan, *Reckoning with Slavery*, 11.

[234] Daniel Livesay, *Children of Uncertain Fortune. Mixed-Race Jamaicans in Britain and the Atlantic Family, 1733–1833* (Chapel Hill, NC, 2018).

difference that underpinned the naming of one child as 'chattel' and another as 'precious', required a form of splitting between himself and the enslaved that necessitated constant work. His children were free. Children who were born to enslaved women inherited the status of unfree; they were the property of their master, they could be taken away, sold, subjected to a life of impossible labour and malnutrition. Mothers might be separated from their children and siblings from each other. While physical cruelty, from branding to whipping, left its visible scars on the body, the emotional cruelty of denying parents the right to make a life for their children was one of the most pernicious aspects of slavery. 'Natal alienation', for Orlando Patterson, goes to the heart of the forced separation, the deracination, the loss of ties of birth in both ascending and descending generations that characterized plantation slavery. For him the mother/daughter was the most important relationship on the plantation and the destruction of familial ties the longest lasting legacy of slavery.[235] The violation and violence of slavery are best understood, argues Saidiya Hartman, not in what we see but in what we don't see.[236] These ties of birth across generations were precisely what Edward Long valued so much in his own family. How did he live with his denial of this belonging to others? In the *History* he managed it by disavowal: erasing the separations, writing in some parts of his text as though family life was part of the lives of the enslaved, while simultaneously accepting the mother/child bond and refusing it.

Hereditary racial slavery had been legalized in Virginia in 1662 when the status of children born to enslaved women was clarified and perpetual bondage decreed for their children:

> Whereas some doubts have arisen whether children got by any Englishman upon a negro woman should be slave or free, *Be it therefore enacted and declared by this present grand assembly*, that all children borne in this country shal be held bond or free only according to the condition of the mother ...[237]

In making such judgements, colonists were drawing on established ideas about the difference between black and white that circulated in early modern

---

[235] Orlando Patterson, *Slavery and Social Death. A Comparative Study* (Cambridge, MA, 1982). On familial relations, see Scott, 'The Paradox of Freedom', 183–6. See also Orlando Patterson, *Die the Long Day* (London, 1972). Andrew Apter discusses the impact of West African notions of motherhood in plantation societies in 'The Blood of Mothers: Women, Money and Markets in Yoruba–Atlantic Perspective', *Journal of African-American History* 98.1 (2013), 72–98.

[236] Saidiya Hartman, *Scenes of Subjection. Terror, Slavery and Self-Making in Nineteenth-Century America* (New York, 1997), 42.

[237] Kathleen M. Brown, *Good Wives, Nasty Wenches, and Anxious Patriarchs. Gender, Race and Power in Colonial Virginia* (Chapel Hill, NC, 1996), 132.

England.[238] Richard Ligon, for example, a royalist who fled the civil war in 1649 for Barbados, described in his *True and Exact History of the Island* what he saw as the distinctive characteristics of African women, their monstrous bodies and hanging breasts. He represented women as 'weeders' and 'breeders', able to produce crops and children, different from European women.[239] Their labour was both productive and reproductive. A series of legislative landmarks in Virginia, including that of 1662, 'signified a continuing process of evaluation through which racial difference was expressed legally, incorporated into a new social order, and endowed with legal, economic, and social meaning ... They effectively naturalized the condition of slavery by connecting it to a concept of race.'[240] The Jamaican slave code of 1674 constructed chattel slavery as permanent, but it was not made legally explicit that it was hereditary.[241] 'All negroes Lawfully bought or borne slaves shall here continue to bee soe, and further be held adjudged to bee goods and chattels ... their Christianity or any law Custome or usage in England notwithstanding'.[242]

The Roman principle of *partus sequitur ventrem* (the condition of the child follows the condition of the mother's womb) was reconfigured for the colonial context. A child fathered by a white man with an enslaved African woman was transformed from kin into property. 'Maternity', argues Hilary Beckles, 'constituted the soil in which slavery grew and gave life to capitalist accumulation on a grand scale.'[243] 'Slave-women's reproductive abilities', Sasha Turner reminds us, 'were foundational to slavery's profit-making motives.'[244] The wombs of African women were critical to the constitution of racial difference, marking the boundaries between black and white: 'women's wombs were racialized', as Françoise Vergès puts it.[245] By the time Edward Long was

---

[238] Kim F. Hall, *Things of Darkness. Economies of Race and Gender in Early Modern England* (Ithaca, 1995), 2, argues that the binary of black and white 'might be called the originary language of racial difference in English culture'. In the early modern period it became increasingly infused with concerns over skin colour, economics and gender politics. See also Peter Erickson, *Rewriting Shakespeare, Rewriting Ourselves* (Berkeley, 1991).

[239] Amussen, *Caribbean Exchange*, 63.

[240] Brown, *Good Wives*, 108, 136.

[241] The account of the laws in *Jamaica in 1687* included the clause that all African and Indian slaves brought to the island and sold 'shall never have the benefit of freedom all their days, but be slaves to their masters or his assignees, they and their children, and soe to succeeding ages for ever'. But the editor of Taylor's manuscript comments that it was very difficult to know which of the laws were actually in place; Taylor, *Jamaica in 1687*, 287.

[242] Newman, *A Dark Inheritance*, 55.

[243] Beckles, 'Sex and Gender in the Historiography of Caribbean Slavery' in Verene Shepherd, Bridget Brereton and Barbara Bailey (eds.), *Engendering History. Caribbean Women in Historical Perspective* (Kingston, Jamaica, 1995), 131.

[244] Sasha Turner, 'Home-Grown Slaves: Women, Reproduction and the Abolition of the Slave Trade, Jamaica 1788–1807', *Journal of Women's History* 23.3 (2011), 39–62.

[245] Françoise Vergès, *The Wombs of Women. Race, Capital, Feminism* (London, 2020), 2.

writing in the early 1770s, the ownership of enslaved women's reproductive capacities was an established practice and did not have to be explicated for his readers; it was simply assumed as a part of the property relations of slavery. In claiming that this was the practice in Africa, that 'the children uniformly follow the condition of their mother', he may have hoped to give it some historical legitimacy.[246]

Atlantic slavery, as Diana Paton explicates, was also drawing on European patriarchal principles: assumptions of women's subordination and associations between sexual freedom and dishonour.[247] In Anglo-America marriage was a civil contract, and since enslaved people could not make contracts, they could not legally marry. By definition their children were illegitimate and in Roman law illegitimate children followed the status of their mother.[248] This was also the practice in England. Furthermore, 'chattel property law required that the increase [of domestic animals] go to the owner of the mother'.[249] These understandings informed Jamaican slave-owners' claim to the 'encrease' of their human property. There was no positive law, rather it was customary practice.[250] Statute law mattered, but it was one source of racialized practice among many: wills, indentures, bills of sale and plantation inventories all contributed to constructions of difference. There was no clear legal agreement as to the status of the children of the enslaved, and Blackstone sustained the ambiguity in the 1760s. He claimed English law and civil law agreed on the application of *partus sequitur ventrem* in regard to property, noting that in the case of 'all tame and domestic animals, the brood belongs to the owner of the dam or mother', and yet he stated '*for the most part the human species disallows the maxim*'.[251] This ambiguity suited Long well.

In early colonial Jamaica, Mair argues, the sexes were relatively evenly balanced, but 'the development of highly capitalized export monoculture ... pushed labour and population patterns in the directions charted by its needs'.[252] The figures from slave traders suggest a high proportion of men were being sent to the island in the mid-eighteenth century, but this may have

---

[246] Long, *History*, II. 389.
[247] Diana Paton, 'Gender History, Global History, and Atlantic Slavery: On Racial Capitalism and Social Reproduction', *AHR* 127.2 (2022), 726–54.
[248] Patterson, *Slavery and Social Death*, 189, notes that slave children were collectively illegitimate in Roman law.
[249] Melanie Newton, 'Returns to a Native Land: Indigeneity and Creolization in the Anglophone Caribbean', *Small Axe* 41 (2013), 108–22.
[250] Ibid. Thanks to Edward Rugemer for confirming in a personal communication that he has found no traces of the codification of maternal hereditary slavery or challenges to it in legal documents. Handler, 'Custom and Law'.
[251] Newton citing Blackstone, *Commentaries on the Laws of England* (4 vols., Oxford, 1768), II. 390 – her emphasis.
[252] Mair, *A Historical Study*, 72.

underestimated the numbers of women.[253] 'A negro man is purchased either for a trade,' wrote Beckford, 'or the cultivation and different processes of the cane – the occupations of the woman are only two, the house, with its several departments and supposed indulgences, or the field with its exaggerated labours.'[254] 'The common practice of purchasing a greater number of males than females', reported one planter, was 'on account of the superior strength and labour of the men, and their being much less liable to disease and confinement.'[255] 'It has never been the planter's care to proportion the number of females to males,' Long noted regretfully.[256] On some estates there were as many as five men to one woman.[257] On Mesopotamia, for example, there were more men than women between the 1750s and 1790s.[258] On James Reid's estate in Hanover in the 1770s, there were 90 adult men and 66 women, while on William Beckford's Clarendon estates in 1780 there were 649 adult men and boys, 604 women and girls.[259] 'You want Men infinitely more than Women,' as Simon Taylor had reminded his employer, 'for there are many things which Women cannot do, as cutting Copperwood, Wainmen, Boilers, Distillers, Stokers, Mulemen.' His plan, he told Chaloner Arcedeckne, was 'buying of the best Negro Men of Coromantee Country out of each ship' so as to build up 'a Gang of Fine People for the Estate'.[260] What was more, children too young to work were a financial burden on the plantations. He was pleased, however, to be able to report in January 1767 that 'you have been lucky in Reguard to your Negroes having a Decrease of only 4. It is true 14 have died but then you have saved ten children.'[261]

The gender balance on Lucky Valley is not known since Long failed to specify the ratio of men to women in surviving accounts. In his first major purchase in 1761, when he was buying the existing labour force of Lucky Valley from his uncle, Charles Long, the enslaved were listed as seventy-two men, eleven boys, and fifty-six women and girls: a clear majority of men. It is impossible to know whether the boys and girls were the children of those named women, or whether they had been bought from the ships. Buying boys and girls in their teens externalized the costs of raising children, avoiding losing women's labour time on the plantations in those first years when

---

[253] Morgan, *Reckoning with Slavery*, chap. 2, discusses the difficulty in establishing the sex ratio on the slave ships in the early period.
[254] William Beckford, *Remarks upon the Situation of Negroes in Jamaica, impartially made from a local experience of nearly thirteen years in that Island* (2 vols., London, 1788), I. 14.
[255] Cited in Mair, *A Historical Study*, 195.
[256] Long, *History*, II. 435.
[257] Ibid., II. 435.
[258] Dunn, *A Tale of Two Plantations*, 26.
[259] Mair, *A Historical Study*, 199–201.
[260] Wood, *The Letters of Simon Taylor*, 93–9.
[261] Ibid., 36.

children were too young to work.[262] Women were worth less than men because of their absences associated with childbearing and rearing. 'So unless she was producing children and providing additional work units in numbers sufficient to compensate for her absences from the field gangs', wrote Mair, 'the female slave offered relatively minimal returns on capital outlay.'[263] The expense of rearing children on the plantation could discourage planters from considering infant mortality as a problem. 'I am aware that there are many planters who do not wish their women to breed as there by so much work is lost in their attendance on their infants,' one witness reported to the House of Commons committee in 1788.[264] Long's purchase of slaves from William Wood in 1764 seems to have included, judging by the names, ten women, two with children, and only two men.[265] His final large purchase in 1767, before leaving for England, was of seven men and nine women, and specified 'with the future issue and increase of the said female slaves'.[266] Enslaved offspring were 'a capital addition to the inventory of assets', as Hilary Beckles puts it, utilizing plantation account books to document the way in which 'the child's human identity was subordinate to the financial statement of the capitalization process. The financial value of the child was listed in the inventory of assets in a column that included "animals, stocks, and machinery".' It was expected that the child's value would substantially increase after weaning and would exceed its mother's value by the time it was thirteen or fourteen.[267] For a slave-owner to rape 'his' female property could be a part of the process of both capital accumulation and speculation.

Long was silent on the question of rape and sexual violence on the plantation. Accounts of such brutal practices as those of Thomas Thistlewood, with his relentless and sadistic claims for rights over the bodies of enslaved women, found no place in Long's writings.[268] Sexual power as a key dimension of planter control was something he did not wish to think about. He was appalled and disgusted by the scale of cross-racial sexual activity and bemoaned the liking that unprincipled white men had for their brown concubines. With one eye on his metropolitan readers and buttressed by his own hatred of the

---

[262] Diana Paton emphasizes the importance of the spatial division that was made. The costs of birthing and rearing children were externalized to Africa, saving slave-owners' money; 'Gender History, Global History'.
[263] Mair, *Women Field Workers*, 6.
[264] Colleen A. Vasconcellos, *Slavery, Childhood, and Abolition in Jamaica, 1788–1838* (London, 2015), 16.
[265] Indenture 15 September 1764, IRO, vol. 209, f. 126.
[266] Indenture 20 June 1769, IRO, vol. 231, f. 31.
[267] Beckles, 'Perfect Property'.
[268] Douglas Hall, *In Miserable Slavery. Thomas Thistlewood in Jamaica, 1750–1786* (Kingston, Jamaica, 1989); Burnard, *Mastery, Tyranny, and Desire*; Heather V. Vermeulen, 'Thomas Thistlewood's Libidinal Linnean Project: Slavery, Ecology, and Knowledge Production', *Small Axe* 55 (2018), 18–38.

'infatuated attachments' of colonists and the resulting presence of far too many 'yellow offspring', he chose to remain silent on the sexual exploitation of the plantation economy, or of urban Jamaica with its brothels and sex-workers.[269] William Beckford, Thistlewood's neighbour, was similarly reticent.[270] These were issues that were best ignored by pro-slavery writers. We cannot know whether Long followed the conventions of planter hospitality in offering visitors access to enslaved women, or whether his overseers or bookkeepers on Lucky Valley were violating women in the ways in which contemporary documentation has established. What we do know is that he evaded and denied sexual exploitation.

The absence of 'future issue and increase', however, had to be addressed. One explanation, first mooted by Sloane, was abortion. He had noted two abortifacients: *Bromalia pinguin* grew in profusion and caused abortion in women with child, a fact which those he defined as whores were well aware of and made good use of.[271] The author of *An Essay concerning Slavery* went farther and emphasized infanticide. He imagined a dialogue between a planter and an officer which noted the absence of children amongst the enslaved. The women 'lie with both Colours', he opined, 'and do not know which the Child may prove of, to disoblige neither, they stifle it in the Birth'.[272] Long joined in the denunciations of the character of enslaved women, their lustful promiscuity and absence of shame. Their 'promiscuous embraces' would certainly hinder or destroy conception, and their venereal disease, alongside the poisonous medicines taken to repel it, might kill the foetus or sterilize both men and women. 'The women here are in general common prostitutes', he asserted, 'and many of them take specifics to cause abortion, in order that they may continue their trade without loss of time, or hindrance of business.'[273] He named three plants that could be utilized as abortifacients, marking one of the moments that revealed the extent to which he relied on enslaved informants. The pinguin, which he recorded as a tough plant used for fencing, could be found all over the island; it had a fruit with a sharp acid juice which had a number of medicinal functions, and a large dose of it was said to effect abortion. The pulp of the green fruit of the calibash tree provided another option, as did the quassi tree or Surinam bitter wood. 'Vulgarly called, by the Negroes, the *bitter ash*,' Long reported, its root, 'in decoction', may also occasion abortion, and may have been used for this 'inhuman purpose by many of the female Negroes'.[274] Abortion was registered here as a sign of

[269] Long, *History*, II. 327.
[270] Beckford, *A Descriptive Account*.
[271] Londa Schiebinger, *Plants and Empire. Colonial Bioprospecting in the Atlantic World* (Cambridge, MA, 2004), 139.
[272] Anon. [Edward Trelawny?], *An Essay concerning Slavery*, 34–5.
[273] Long, *History*, II. 436.
[274] Ibid., III. 738, 752, 821–2.

inhumanity; the scale of sickness, disease and malnutrition amongst the enslaved said nothing about the character of the planters. They could also blame bad doctors: Thistlewood knew of one who gave 'the Wild Negroe Women who frequently applied to him, something which makes them Barren'.[275]

If abortion was one cause of a low birth rate, infant mortality was represented as another. Grainger was eloquent on the horrors of worms, which Long agreed were fatal to children in the tropics, while 'others frequently perish within nine or ten days of their birth' by various sicknesses, not being kept warm and by being given rum.[276] 'Child-birth', he opined, is not so easy here as in Africa. Many women suffered from 'obstructions', many babies were killed, along with their mothers, 'by the unskilfulness and absurd management of the Negroe midwives'.[277] The midwife on the Beckford estate at Moore, Suzanna, was aged seventy-one in 1780, while Bridget at Bodles Pen was seventy-two and described as 'very weak'. It was the so-called 'superannuated' women who could no longer do field work who were allocated to midwifery, and then blamed for their lack of skill and 'absurd management'.[278] Up to the 1780s slave-owners were able to rely on the availability of new captives, and paid little attention to 'breeding'. They were more bothered by the loss of labour due to ill health than by mortality rates.[279] As long as the price of sugar enabled them to buy more 'Guiney slaves', they could keep up the levels of productivity.[280] On Golden Grove, Simon Taylor's concern was with ill health and age. Were the enslaved able to labour? Despite his preoccupation with the need to buy 'new Negroes', regularly urged upon Arcedeckne, he did not begin to concern himself with 'breeding' until the American War disrupted supplies of captives.[281] In 1765 he was exulting that a recent sale had gone very well, 'as it was in our power to give you a Choice & to let you have all Men'.[282]

Long, however, perceived that there was a problem. His attention to these matters prefigured the issues which were to become significant in England in the debates over the slave trade. Having identified the causes of enslaved women's failure to bear children, at least to his own apparent satisfaction, he turned to possible cures. His reading of Enlightenment natural histories was

[275] Cited in Vasconcellos, *Slavery, Childhood and Abolition*, 20.
[276] Long, *History*, II. 436.
[277] Ibid.
[278] Mair, *A Historical Study*, 212.
[279] See, e.g., Hilary M. Beckles, *Natural Rebels. A Social History of Black Women in Barbados* (New Brunswick, 1989). Beckles argues that slave-owners were more worried about deaths of women in childbirth than about infant mortality. Up to 70 per cent of babies born in the eighteenth century died before their third birthday; Beckles, 'Perfect Property'.
[280] Dunn, *Sugar and Slaves*, 320.
[281] Wood and Clayton, 'Slave Birth, Death and Disease'.
[282] Wood, *The Letters of Simon Taylor*, 27–8.

feeding his thinking on human difference, both of sexuality and of race. Long was very committed to proper relations between the sexes in his own class. Africans were another matter. The culture of politeness that he had learned in his young manhood valued feminine modesty and grace, abhorred vulgarity, gossip and transgression of any kind. His picture of the Worthy family in *The Prater* celebrated the domestic ideal: a masterly head of household, a virtuous wife and mother, and children occupying their proper manly and feminine roles. All this was 'Nature's Charter', as he described it in *The Anti-Gallican*.[283] The *Portraits and Sketches of the Times*, published after his return to England in the same year as the *History*, celebrated marriage as a meeting of minds and advised husbands that 'A discreet Wife is a Blessing sent from heaven'.[284] All this was for white people of his own class. But his assumptions as to the gendered character of 'nature' inflected his thinking on the enslaved. Woman's *natural* role was to bear children; it was *unnatural* to refuse it, to use abortifacients or neglect infants. He had read Linnaeus who emphasized how natural it was for women to breastfeed their children. Long heartily agreed and he deplored the white women who employed 'Negro' women as wetnurses, both because they were abandoning their responsibilities as mothers and because he feared that the nurse's 'corrupted' blood might enter the child along with her milk.[285] (See Figure 3.9.) Linnaeus's focus on *Mammalia*, Londa Schiebinger suggests, was a response to eighteenth-century contestations over women's proper role, and the politics of wetnursing and maternal breastfeeding influenced his preoccupation with the breast as a link between humans and other vertebrates. His stress on the *natural* and sexed qualities of plants, animals and humans fostered the notion of a 'continuous natural order'. 'A creature's "nature"', Schiebinger argues, 'was seen as defining its rightful place in that order.'[286] Men-midwives were playing their part in this shift in increasing numbers, claiming what had traditionally been a female occupation on the basis of their scientific authority. In their struggle for legitimation, these practitioners aimed to make sex and birth proper sites for masculine and public debate, giving a new emphasis to the natural, rather than God-given, aspects of childbirth.[287] Anatomical studies and scrutiny of the human body were giving credence to the notion of biological divergence and the sexual complementarity of male and female. The 'reproducing woman' had distinctive physical characteristics, different from the male. Human nature, with its links to the animal kingdom, rather than being always the same, was increasingly understood as marked by sex and race.

---

[283] Long, *The Anti-Gallican*, 113–15.
[284] [Long], *The Sentimental Exhibition*, 72.
[285] Long, *History*, II. 276.
[286] Londa Schiebinger, *Nature's Body. Gender in the Making of Modern Science* [1993] (New Brunswick, 2004), xii.
[287] Cody, *Birthing the Nation*.

Figure 3.9 Berryman illustrates how enslaved women were responsible for the care of white children, as well as serving their mothers. The only person named in this drawing is the baby boy – William or T. J. Sell. 'Nurses and Child Supposed to be William or T. J. Sell. 4 Paths' by William Berryman. Drawing, 1808–16. Courtesy of the Library of Congress, Prints and Photographs Division, LC-USZ62-110701.

The potential of 'breeding' as a site of experimentation with cattle was taken up by agricultural improvers and proved commercially valuable. This thinking could be applied to people. Granville Sharp was horrified by the prospect of perpetuating slavery, creating 'a breed'.[288] The comte de Buffon, a major figure for Long, in his widely read volumes on natural history, defined reproduction in relation to biological species and conceptualized it as a possible domain of human intervention.[289] But this would have its specific racial characteristics: he reiterated the idea that African women had no trouble in labour.[290] While never abandoning the idea of a universal human, Buffon emphasized the significance of *variety*. The concept of reproduction, argues Susanne Lettow, emerged from the mid-eighteenth century and marked an 'epistemic shift' from the notion of 'generation' with its biblical associations.[291] The orthodox

---

[288] Sharp, *A Representation*, 97–8.
[289] Nick Hopwood, 'The Keywords "Generation" and "Reproduction"', in Hopwood, Rebecca Fleming and Lauren Kassell (eds.), *Reproduction. Antiquity to the Present Day* (Cambridge, 2018), 287–304.
[290] Schiebinger, *Nature's Body*, 156.
[291] Thanks to Silvia Sebastiani for directing me to Susanne Lettow, 'Population, Race and Gender: on the Genealogy of the Modern Politics of Reproduction', *Distincktion: Scandinavian Journal of Social Theory* 16.3 (2015), 267–82; Lettow (ed.), *Reproduction, Race and Gender in Philosophy and the Early Life Sciences* (New York, 2014); see particularly the introduction and Lettow's chapter.

Christian notion that all individuals had existed since creation, the concept of preformation, was the belief that God had formed the 'germs' of all living beings which then unfolded. The emerging science of biology, concerned as it was with life, encouraged a new emphasis on processes of propagation and the long-term succession of individuals. Buffon used the verb 'to reproduce' and the term reproduction, and these were gradually more widely adopted. Population came to be seen as something that could be expanded and reproduction a process that could be managed and operate at multiple levels, in relation to family, species, populations or races.[292] Long never utilized the term 'reproduction', but he understood that there were improvements that could be made which would, he hoped, secure an increase in the birth rate.

The idea of hereditary transmission came to carry increased weight. This was an idea that was understood by slave-owners as of great significance, long before the discoveries of Enlightenment science, for it was the 'stain' of 'corrupted blood', carried from enslaved mother to child, that legitimated the customary descent of social/civil death. The idea of the 'corruption of blood' had a long history. It emerged as a concept after the Norman Conquest. An attainted felon was defined as civilly dead, their blood corrupted. Felony resulted in a severing of bloodlines: the felon could neither inherit property nor transmit property to their heirs. Their sin or taint was visited upon their children, and the only redemption was through royal pardon. Bad blood blocked inheritance. Corruption became the authorizing metaphor for the loss of civil status. In the colonies, the medieval fiction of the blood tainted by felony was reconfigured and became blood tainted by natural inferiority, one of the props for the legitimation of slavery. 'The racialized fiction of blood', Colin Dayan explains, 'also supplemented the metaphoric taint, not only defining slaves as property but fixing them, their progeny, and their descendants in that status.'[293] In Jamaica legal recognition depended on the amounts of black and white blood flowing into the body. Metaphorical blood became biological, social and political destiny: what he understood as the purity of English blood was a matter of great importance to Long. It must be protected from pollution.

Nevertheless, 'to augment our Negroes ... by procreation' was a matter of urgency. 'We must endeavour to remedy those evils', he encouraged his fellow planters, which 'impede or frustrate its natural effect'.[294] This would result in

---

[292] There were works calling for the selective breeding of slaves in the French colonies in the 1770s. William Max Nelson, 'Making Men: Enlightenment Ideas of Racial Engineering', AHR 115.5 (2010), 1364–94.

[293] Colin Dayan, *The Law is a White Dog, How Legal Rituals Make and Unmake Persons* (Princeton, 2011), 45–6.

[294] Long, *History*, II. 436; Long would certainly have read (and not wanted to think about) Swift's *A Modest Proposal* which viciously satirized Petty's proposals on 'breeding'.

plantations being 'well-stocked' and 'more flourishing', while significantly reducing the costs for the planters of buying 'new Negroes'. 'Prudent regulations in the right handling of their stock' could only be beneficial. He had to recognize, however, that 'those Negroes breed the best, whose labour is least, or easiest'.[295] Domestic Negroes had more children than did those on pens, and those on pens had more than those on sugar plantations. This led him to devote attention to statistics once again, distancing himself from any moral concerns about the heavy field labour of women on his own properties by turning to figures, calculating the ideal balance between aggregate numbers of 'Negroes' on an estate and the annual production of hogsheads. Three 'Negroes' to every two hogsheads was, in his judgement, a good ratio. If the numbers of hogsheads exceeded the numbers of 'Negroes', he concluded, few children would survive,

> for the mothers will not have sufficient time to take due care of them; and, if they are put under charge of some elderly woman, or nurse, as the custom is in many places, it cannot be supposed that they meet with the same tenderness as might be expected from their parent.[296]

The necessary ratio of 'Negroes' to hogsheads would, however, vary according to the soil. One estimate conducted for Jamaican parishes showed that Clarendon had 127 Negroes to each 100 hogsheads, rather than the 150 which would be preferable. The hope was that 'a just proportion of hands to the average quantity of its produce, may require no purchased recruits'.[297] If babies survived, capital would be augmented. (See Figure 3.10.)

In his attempts to justify the slave trade by insisting that captives escaped a much worse fate by their transfer to white masters, Long had repeated a story from the sea captain and slave trader William Snelgrave who had encountered the king of Old Calabar in 1730. The king had fallen ill and ordered that a child of ten months should be sacrificed. After the child was killed, it was hung up on the bough of a tree with a live cock attached to it to strengthen the spell. On a later voyage Snelgrave saw the same king sitting on a stool and 'near him a little boy tied by a leg to a stake driven into the ground, covered with flies and other vermin'. He discovered that the child was to be sacrificed that night and redeemed him at the price named by the king. 'He carried his bargain on board ship' and found that 'the infant's mother had been sold to him the very day before'. He 'pathetically described' her joy on being reunited with her child. 'The story coming to be known among all the Blacks on board, it dispelled their fears, and impressed them with so favourable an opinion of the white men, that although he had three hundred in all, they gave him not the least disturbance

---

[295] Long, *History*, II. 437.
[296] Ibid., II. 437.
[297] Ibid., II. 439.

Figure 3.10 An enslaved woman nurses a child within a small group sheltered by plantain, under the watchful eye of an overseer. 'Negro Hut with Figures in Plantain Walk' by William Berryman. Ink, pencil and watercolour drawing, 1808–16. Courtesy of the Library of Congress, Prints and Photographs Division, LC-DIG-ppmsca-13422.

during the journey.' Their horror and dismay disappeared in the face of 'so striking an example of humanity shewn to a Negro'. They found 'that a white master was likely to be more merciful towards them than a black one'.[298]

This tall tale of black cruelty and white humanity was part of Long's effort to represent plantation slavery as in no way inimical to the bond of mother and child. He hoped for an improvement in the birth rate and recommended that mothers should be encouraged 'by little helps, to take good care of their children'. A premium might be offered for each newborn. Marks of distinction, or rewards, should be given to those who were most assiduous about cleanliness and health. An annuity might even be paid for the first years. 'These politic gratuities' would 'endear the owner to the parents' and 'prove a constant incitement' to the care of the child.[299] This would be politic indeed: a way to offset the harsh reality of the slave-owner's rights to the persons and labour of these children.

Long's ideas about maternity and childcare were elaborated after he returned to England. Abolitionists were raising concerns about the levels of

---

[298] Ibid., II. 397–8.
[299] Ibid., II. 439–40.

mortality on the plantations.[300] When Long was revising the three volumes of the *History* with the intention of producing a new edition (something which never happened), he added notes on the 'Management of Negro Children'. They were clearly devised for absentees, to pass on to the managers of their estates, and dealt with care from ages one to five. James Grainger's *Essay on the More Common West-India Diseases* had advised that all Negro women should feed their own babies and that they should be weaned not later than twelve to fourteen months, since 'long nursing diminishes a woman's fecundity'.[301] As soon as a child was weaned, recommended Long, s/he should go to 'a good careful old Woman'.[302] The old woman's job would be to get them 'perfectly clean & free from Chigers', the insects which burrowed into the skin and caused great damage if they were not removed.[303] 'Negroes often lose many a joint of their toes etc., and so become less useful upon a plantation,' Grainger had reported with brutal directness.[304] The child should be carried to the river in the morning and washed unless it was too cold. Their frocks should be clean and tidy and they should have three new ones each year (significantly more generous than the allowances for adults), made by the women in the manager's house. Once a month, when the weather was good, they should be given cabbage bark (this was administered to expel worms), for 'Worms lurk in all/ How many fathers/fathers now no more/how many orphans ... '[305] This should be taken three mornings successively, then a dose of nut oil and plenty of gruel made for them. Masters should never refuse a little flour and sugar to the old woman for her young family, Long advised, 'or indeed any other little matter that can contribute in the least to comfort the poor little helpless creatures'.[306] The notion of the 'poor little helpless creatures' marked a significant shift in his language, a recognition both of the vulnerability of these little ones, whose ownership he and his fellow planters claimed in the interests of future profitability and capital accumulation, and of the critiques of the abolitionists.

---

[300] For the debates from the 1780s, see particularly Vasconcellos, *Slavery, Childhood, and Abolition*. She cites Anna Eliza Elletson, the absentee owner of the Hope Estate, who was concerned about the 'care of the breeding women, and their Children' in 1777, knowing that 'on the number, and health of the Negroes, depends the Success of a Plantation', 18; Paton, 'The Driveress and the Nurse'.

[301] James Grainger, *Essay on the More Common West-India Diseases* [1764] (Edinburgh, 1802), 18–20.

[302] BL Add MSS 12405, insert f. 355.

[303] Ibid.

[304] Grainger, *Essay on the More Common West-India Diseases*, 22. Grainger's *Essay*, a first on this subject, was written for owners and managers. It gave information and advice on common diseases and medicines.

[305] Grainger, *Sugar Cane*, Bk 4. 103; Bk 2. 120–2.

[306] BL Add MSS 12405, insert f. 355.

A 'tolerable good house must be prepared for the Old Woman and the children'. Planks should be raised above the ground for them to lie on and the watchmen in the mountain walks instructed to make mats for them. The parents should supply them regularly with food, and this should be monitored. The children should be taken to the manager's house each Sunday morning to be examined, one by one, for chigoes, with the doctor present. Each child should get a herring when discharged. The old woman should never be harsh, and periodically be treated to a dinner at the manager's house. 'This method takes a great deal of trouble from the mother's hands', wrote Long,

> who when she comes home from labouring very hard in the field, finds enough to do in the very short time that is allowed her, before she is again called out. And now, in her absence, she knows her child is in safe hands, & prevented from supping in the Ashes of Dirt, wch [sic] very often the means of their getting into a habit of Dirt eating, that has proved fatal to many estates in Jamaica. It rejoices and gladdens the hearts of grown Negroes, even those that are not parents, to see so much care and attention paid to the young Children.

'You will certainly have a much greater Increase of Children,' he concluded, returning in his mind to the question of profit, 'when the Mother knows that so much trouble is to be taken off her hands.'[307]

At no point, however, did Long engage with the grief of enslaved women over the fate of their babies and their children.[308] While with one stroke of his pen he recognized the care of 'grown Negroes, even those that are not parents' as to the fate of children, with another he wrote about the purchase of boys and girls.

The tone of these notes is very different from his earlier vituperative and misogynistic denunciations of enslaved women. But they echo the ambiguity of the tone in which he writes in the *History* about creoles, those enslaved Africans born on the plantations whose characters he both does and doesn't represent as quite different from the 'Guiney slaves'. They are his hope for the future, his demonstration that slavery could be a civilizing force and that Jamaica could become a settled society. Given his belief, spelt out in the *History*, as to the essential difference between black and white, this was a clear paradox in his thinking, one that he never confronted. The text was indeed, as Suman Seth suggests, 'in tension with itself'.[309]

---

[307] BL Add MSS 12405, insert f. 355r.
[308] On maternal grief, see Sasha Turner, 'The Nameless and the Forgotten: Maternal Grief, Sacred Protection and the Archive of Slavery', *S&A* 38.2 (2017), 232–50. Jennifer Morgan defines enslaved women's childbirth as 'rooted in loss'; *Laboring Women*, 108.
[309] Wheeler, in her illuminating account of Long, recognized this paradox; *The Complexion of Race*; Seth, *Difference and Disease*, 266.

Long's task in the *History* was to give a picture of Jamaica as a successful commercial society built on a form of slavery that was benevolent and paternalistic, and that had a future. He liked to focus on the practices of 'well-regulated' plantations, ones that were 'well-governed'. Perhaps he was thinking of the 'sickly' and 'distempered' who were despatched to Longville Park Pen for sea-bathing, in the hope that they would recover sufficiently to labour. Any evidence of cruelty was banished, the responsibility of low-born overseers who cared nothing for the longer term well-being of the property and were simply anxious to milk as much profit as they could in their own short-term interests. These were the proverbial 'bad apples' who spoilt the reputation of responsible planters such as himself. His text, however, alongside other documents, gives plenty of evidence of another reality. The absence of concrete details as to the lives of the enslaved speaks volumes in itself: he could not give them since that would negate his fiction. It would have forced him to recognize what he disavowed: the harshness and brutality of captives' lives on a sugar plantation. At the same time, other fractures in his picture crept into the text. 'Anxiety affects men in this country in proportion to their sensibility, and to its duration,' he had written, and many had 'sunk down into the grave', destroyed by the scale of their worries.[310] The 'constant virtual hostility' that he understood was characteristic of a slave society was undoubtedly a source of fear to the colonists.[311] Long's representation of a benevolent form of slavery, similar, he liked to think, to what Grotius had described as a 'legitimate, equitable species of servitude . . . founded on the principles of reason', was haunted by those he repressed – the hungry, the superfluous, the sick, the disposable, the ghosts.[312] He had made himself, a polite young Englishman, into a planter, that new colonial subject who lived in terror of those other new subjects of the plantation economy, the enslaved. Being a planter meant a troubled life, no matter how much the difficulties were denied or the profits made up for it. 'I can no more be happy here than Gulliver was with G[lumdalclitch],' he wrote to his friend William Ricketts. His brother's estate in Clarendon was 'undoubtedly the Golgotha of Jamaica'.[313]

---

[310] Long, *History*, II. 543.
[311] BL Add MS 12404, f. 113.
[312] Long, *History*, II. 402.
[313] Edward Long to William Ricketts, 12 December 1764, 5 October 1768, Ricketts Family Papers.

4

The Merchant House

If brother Robert's plantation figured as Golgotha in his private thoughts, and deaths from 'anxiety' were all too prevalent amongst the planters, how did Long think about the wider economic, political and social system within which the production of sugar was embedded? And how did this relate to the needs of his *History*? There was much to explain, and the terms he used, familiar to his contemporaries, were 'wealth', 'trade' and 'commerce', for as yet there was no concept of an economy or of economic life itself.[1] His first priority was to demonstrate to his metropolitan readers the great wealth that Jamaica brought to Britain and how this depended on slavery, for challenges were beginning to be mounted on both moral and economic grounds. Anthony Benezet's attack on the iniquity of the slave trade had been published in 1762.[2] John Wesley's *Thoughts upon Slavery* had asked how such wealth could legitimate the sin of slavery.[3] Two years after the publication of Long's *History*, Adam Smith articulated a damning critique of the costs of monopolies and of the colonies.[4] Long needed to defend the imperial system which protected colonial interests and emphasize the significance of British merchants within the whole process; after all, his family's firm was Drake and Long, pre-eminent amongst the West India traders. Knowing that critical voices were questioning the slave trade, he needed to minimize talk of cruel conditions and present an account of a benevolent slavery. Finally, he hoped to alleviate the problem of debt for the planters by some legislative changes that could be made. Debt was too often ruinous in an economy dependent on credit and with a culture of conspicuous consumption amongst the white population. This was combined with the notorious volatility of the sugar crop and, for many planters, the weight of

---

[1] Rothschild, *The Inner Life of Empires*.
[2] Anthony Benezet, *A Short Account of the Part of Africa Inhabited by the Negroes* (2nd edn, Philadelphia, 1762).
[3] John Wesley, *Thoughts upon Slavery* (3rd edn, London, 1774).
[4] Adam Smith, *The Wealth of Nations* [1776] (2 vols., London, 1910), II. Bk 4, chap. 7, 'Of Colonies', 112: 'Great Britain derives nothing but loss from the dominion which she assumes over her colonies.' Smith also stressed the damage to colonies tied into export crops. There had been hostility to monopoly and enthusiasm for laissez-faire since the seventeenth century.

payments, especially annuities, tied to estates over generations. Debt was a major source of those multiple deaths from 'anxiety' which Long deplored. His narrative had to erase the ghosts of captives on the Atlantic and enslaved persons on the plantations, focusing the minds of his readers on merchants and planters, the creators, to his mind, of national wealth. This was the work of disavowal which structured his *History*.

By the time that Long was writing in the early 1770s, what is sometimes described as the 'sugar revolution' had happened in Jamaica decades before. The diversified agriculture of early colonial Jamaica had become dominated by sugar; small-scale production with a mixed labour force of indentured servants and captives had been transformed by large plantations dependent on enslaved labour and on metropolitan capital.[5] The colony had abundant land but needed labour: slavery facilitated the capitalist exploitation of the land colonized. Settlement had spread and the majority population was black. Per capita output had greatly increased. These changes went alongside a massive boost to the Atlantic slave trade, a more complex pattern of triangular trade incorporating the North American colonies and Spanish America, a growth in European sugar consumption, an increased interest from Europeans in the colonies and development of the British economy including infrastructure for industrial development.[6] 'It was sugar above all', concludes Barry Higman, 'that made vast profits for its capitalists, consumed enormous numbers of enslaved people, created plantation economies and slave societies, and shaped the modern world in ways other crops and commodities could barely approach ... it made possible the great transformation, a disastrous development from so many points of view.'[7] Sugar was at the epicentre of global trade long before cotton.[8] But, Higman continued, too much attention to sugar can take away from the agency of its makers and the questions of moral responsibility: the danger is of creating 'a neutralized concept for historical analysis'.[9] Long knew that the entire slavery business depended on what he called the 'Negroe Trade', the trade in people and all that followed from it, but in his explication of the system their labour was minimized as far as was possible and their suffering ignored. His *History* played its part in the creation of 'a

---

[5] Nuala Zahedieh demonstrates that in the early period internal sources of capital were significant to Jamaica; 'Trade, Plunder, and Economic Development'. By the mid-eighteenth century, however, metropolitan capital appears to predominate. See particularly the discussion in Smith, *Slavery, Family, and Gentry Capitalism*, chap. 6.
[6] This paragraph draws heavily on B. W. Higman, 'The Sugar Revolution', *EconHR* 53.2 (2000), 213–36. For developments in infrastructure connected to eighteenth-century slave-ownership, see the LBS database: www.ucl.ac.uk/lbs.
[7] Higman, 'The Sugar Revolution', 229.
[8] Sven Beckert's *Empire of Cotton. A New History of Global Capitalism* (London, 2014) fails to consider the prior case of sugar.
[9] Higman, 'The Sugar Revolution', 229.

neutralized concept for historical analysis'. In so far as there were agents in Long's narrative, they were the white merchants and planters: the makers of capital. While sugar might be thought to be the ineradicable link between white consumption and black labour, much ideological work was done to erase that connection.

Racial capitalism in its eighteenth-century Atlantic configuration was rooted in sugar-based plantation slavery financed by metropolitan credit and organized within a mercantilist framework. It was a complex and hybrid system that developed across the Atlantic, dependent on the ocean currents which allowed ships from Europe to sail to Africa, from there to the Caribbean and back to Europe. It transformed African societies, Caribbean islands and the mercantile capitalism of early modern Britain in its wake.[10] This was a particular phase in the organization of racial capitalism, when goods were exchanged for people, cane transformed into sugar and rum. The circuit operated within racialized and spatial specificities, utilizing different regimes of exploitation, both wage labour and chattel slavery. It was a form of combined and uneven development: captives on the west coast of Africa, slavery in the Caribbean, wage labour in the metropole and on the seas, all characterized this hybrid system in which bills of exchange played a critical role, allowing debts to mushroom, credit to flow and capital to accumulate. There was no abstract economic logic, operating only according to the rules of the market.[11] Economic relations articulated with legal, political and cultural practices which institutionalized freedom as almost exclusively white and slavery as black. Each moment in the circuit of capital production and reproduction, on the African coast, in the ship and on the plantation, was racialized in specific ways.

The plantation, as we have seen, played a vital part in the generation of wealth through the labour of the enslaved. But the plantation was embedded in a much broader circuit which is explored in this chapter. The merchant house was at the centre of this system which encompassed the 'Negro Trade', as Long characterized the slavery business, the slave trade and its operation through a web of credit and debt.

---

[10] On the transformations in Africa, see Paul Lovejoy, *Transformations in Slavery. A History of Slavery in Africa* (3rd edn, Cambridge, 2012). Rather than an encounter between two pre-existing systems, the acquisition and sale of people was transformative for both West/Central Africa and Britain. Jane I. Guyer, *Marginal Gains. Monetary Transactions in Atlantic Africa* (Chicago, 2004).

[11] Mark Harvey's work has been very helpful in thinking about this circuit. 'Slavery, Indenture and the Development of British Industrial Capitalism', *HWJ* 88 (2019), 66–88; Mark Harvey and Norman Geras, *Inequality and Democratic Egalitarianism. 'Marx's Economy and Beyond' and Other Essays* (Manchester, 2018).

The Negro Trade

Long's chapter on 'Trade', which opened his account of the business of slavery, was devoted to demonstrating the wealth that Jamaica transmitted to Britain. The 'Negroe trade', he opined, was 'the ground-work of all'.[12] Yet he disavowed the knowledge, knowing while not knowing, that it was people who were captured, bought and sold, who were at the heart of the business of sugar. The 'Negroe trade' was like any other trade, he wanted to believe; it was simply about the exchange of commodities and the making of profit. People and the violence done to them could be forgotten. It was about sugar. Since his claim was that 'Negroes' were legally 'goods and chattels', they could be disposed of in the same way as other goods.[13] The term *slave* was one which pro-slavers preferred to use as little as possible. As his fellow West Indian planter Samuel Estwick put it, 'slave' was 'an odious word'; it was preferable to use the term '*Property*: from whence, perhaps, it will be seen, not only in a less offensive light, but where also it may find a foundation more solid and substantial for its support'.[14] The humanity of the enslaved could be linguistically effaced by naming them 'property' or 'cargo' with all the associations of blackness and chatteldom. Long's knowing, that enslaved men and women were *not* like other commodities, that they were people, could be disavowed.[15] But the disavowal was always followed by a recognition, the ghosts that haunted the text, 'the things behind the things', the people that erupted in other times and places, doing the washing, preparing the food, or resisting in some way the power of the master.[16] Long's account of the business of slavery paid scant attention to the peopling of the process, the men and women who were captured, sold and forced into labour on the plantations. He did not turn to the 'Guinea trade', as contemporaries designated it, until well into the second volume of the *History*. His narrative was designed to diminish the captives, to repress the realities, in both his own mind and that of his readers, of what traders, merchants, captains and planters were actually doing. He rendered it numerically and represented the buying and selling as if these were simply the practices of the market. Sugar and rum were produced, ships sailed, goods and chattels were bought and sold, cane planted, hogsheads delivered, duties paid, bills of exchange met, commissions taken, capital accumulated. It all

[12] Long, *History*, I. 491.
[13] [Long], *Candid Reflections*, 4.
[14] [Samuel Estwick] A West Indian, *Considerations on the Negroe Cause, commonly so called, addressed to the Right Honourable Lord Mansfield, Lord Chief Justice of the Court of King's Bench* (London, 1772), 10.
[15] This core contradiction of New World slavery that enslaved people were defined as property and yet were called upon to act in sentient human ways has been commented on by numerous scholars. See, for example, Sidney Mintz and Richard Price, *The Birth of African-American Culture. An Anthropological Perspective* (Boston, 1976), 7.
[16] Toni Morrison, *Beloved* (New York, 1987), 37.

happened: the merchants and planters did it. What mattered was the way in which the profits came back to Britain, creating wealth and power for the mother country. In the words of James Knight, 'the Sugar Colonies' enabled England to rival the Spanish empire, for Jamaica, in particular, 'may very justly be deemed equal to as many Gold or Silver Mines'.[17]

The process began, wrote Long, when 'The Negroe slaves are purchased in Africa, by the British merchants.' It was important to him to stress that they were already slaves; it was not the British traders who enslaved them, and the violence of captivity was forgotten.[18] It was Africans who had enslaved their own kind. They were paid for

> with a great variety of woollen goods; a cheap sort of fire-arms from Birmingham, Sheffield, and other places; powder, bullets, iron bars, brass pans, malt spirits, tallow, tobacco-pipes, Manchester goods, glass beads; some particular kinds of linens, ironmongery and cutlery ware; certain toys, some East India goods; but, in the main, with very little that is not of British growth, or manufacture.[19]

People were exchanged for guns, toys and textiles. Gun-makers and toy-makers in Birmingham, textile workers in Manchester, linen producers in Scotland and Ireland, 'artisans and mechanics', all free labourers – they were facilitating the 'Negroe trade', bringing prosperity to Britain.[20] White workers were granted some recognition. Moving his reader's line of vision swiftly from the African shore to Kingston harbour, 'the sale of the Negroes', he wrote, 'centers in the West Indies, so the profit arising upon them, and every other accession of gain, from whatever article of our African commerce it is produced, centers ultimately with, and becomes the property of, the inhabitants of Britain'.[21] Once on land, 'the Negroes', men and women, termed 'goods and chattels', 'are sold to the British planters'. All the instruments needed for their daily labour in the cane fields then had to be brought from Britain; these were the so-called 'plantation goods', another term which nicely covered everything from agricultural tools to instruments of torture, clothing for the enslaved and luxuries for the planters. Wear and tear in the tropics made it essential to regularly replace the bills, hoes and axes required for the production of the cane. The utensils necessary for the sugar works also had to be purchased: 'coppers, stills, mill-cases, and other mill-work of iron; ladles, skimmers, lamps, and almost innumerable other articles; to which may be added nails, locks, staples, hinges, bolts, bars and lead' and the kinds of iron work needed in

---

[17] Knight, *History*, II. 552.
[18] Long was partially right: they were already African slaves, but not the racialized chattel slaves of the plantation.
[19] Long, *History*, I. 491.
[20] Ibid., I. 493–4.
[21] Ibid., I. 491.

waggons and carts. No mention was made of the whips, guns, iron masks, shackles and chains. 'All these (at whatsoever price) must be had from Britain.'[22] The materials designed for the planters' houses, and the furniture to go in them, had to be imported from Britain. The luxuries that made life in the tropics supportable for colonists, 'the chaises, coaches, chariots', the clothes of fine fabrics, the provisions, 'such as cheese, ham, bacon, tongues, salmon, onions, refined sugars, confectionary, and grocery wares, spices, pickles, beer, porter, ale and cyder, in vast quantities', all had to be supplied from Britain.[23] Long neglected to mention the goods acquired from the northern colonies, since his aim was to focus all attention on the stimulus that the colony provided to British agriculture and industry. Then there were the necessary items to be bought for the 'Negroes': the check cottons, the osnaburg, the coarse hats, knives, scissors, razors, buttons and buckles, threads, needles and pins, 'all or most of them of British growth or manufacture'.[24] These were bulky commodities and 'require and employ an immense quantity of shipping, the freights of which, outward and homeward, insurance, commissions, and petit charges, are all paid of these islands, and are all received by British merchants and factors'.[25] What was more, the expanding military-fiscal state drew substantial revenues from the customs duties, supporting government and war.[26]

Let us 'revolve in our minds', Long wrote, 'what an amazing variety of trades receive their daily support, as many of them did originally their being, from the calls of the Africa and West India markets'. Let us 'reflect on the numerous families of those mechanics and artisans which are thus maintained, and contemplate that ease and plenty, which is the constant as well as just reward of their incessant labours'. Here was Long's picture of the comfortable domesticated family lives of free labourers, the gun-makers of Birmingham, the textile workers of Manchester, the cutlers of Sheffield, all able to enjoy 'ease and plenty' on account of the 'Negroe trade'. Then think, he invited his readers, of 'the several tribes of active and busy people, who are continually employed in the building, repairing, rigging, victualling and equipment, the multitudes of seamen who earn their wages by navigating, and the prodigious crowds who likewise obtain their bread by loading, unloading and other necessary attendances upon ships'. These 'active and busy people', free persons, 'usefully employed', were providing support to the trading and manufacturing interests,

---

[22] Ibid., I. 492.
[23] Ibid., I. 493.
[24] Ibid.
[25] Ibid.
[26] John Brewer, *The Sinews of Power. War, Money and the English State, 1688–1783* [1988] (Cambridge, MA, 1990); on the value of the trade, see Williams, *Capitalism and Slavery*, 53–5; Nick Draper estimates that sugar duties probably represented around 15 per cent of total government income in the 1770s; personal communication.

the industrious ranks of a liberty-loving nation. All this, he concluded, added up to 'a competent idea of the prodigious value of our sugar colonies, and a just conception of their immense importance to the grandeur and prosperity of their mother country'.[27] Drawing on the well-established mercantilist argument that Britain's wealth and strength owed much to the colonial relation, he cited Charles Davenant, the promoter of political arithmetic, who had noted that 'since our plantations first became thriving and profitable, the national opulence has every way augmented'.[28] Similarly, the much-quoted Malachy Postlethwayt's *Universal Dictionary of Trade and Commerce* had stressed the importance of overseas expansion. The establishment of colonies and plantations, he wrote, has altered our condition 'for the better, almost to a degree beyond credibility. Our manufactures are prodigiously increased, chiefly by the demand for them in the plantations, where they at least take off one half and supply us with many valuable commodities for re-exportation, which is as great an emolument to the mother-kingdom as to the plantations themselves.'[29] As one of the directors of the RAC, Postlethwayt was well aware that trade from Africa brought great profit to the nation. Oldmixon's much-cited work on *The British Empire* agreed: 'our *American* Plantations are an Advantage, and a very great one, to this Kingdom', he opined, and 'so far from being a Loss to us, that there are no Hands in the *British* Empire more usefully employed for the Profit and Glory of the Commonwealth'.[30] What was more, it was the sugar colonies that were most valuable. Similarly, William and Edmund Burke, in their book on the Americas, stressed the importance of colonial trade as a source of national wealth.[31] Commerce was at the heart of the defence of a civilized empire. Indeed, one of the characteristics of humankind in eighteenth-century thinking was the capacity to trade.[32] And it was overseas trade that was driving economic expansion in the eighteenth century.[33]

'The subject of trade', Long mused, 'is so diffuse, and includes such an intricate multiplicity of objects, that it is no easy task to state its various avenues to gain.'[34] Keen to demonstrate statistically the solidity of his case, he moved from prose to figures and conducted a numerical estimate of the annual profits of Jamaican colonization to Britain. Numbers, as William Petty

---

[27] Long, *History*, I. 493–4.
[28] Ibid., I. 509.
[29] Cited in Greene, *Evaluating Empire*, 26.
[30] Oldmixon, *The British Empire in America containing the History of the Discovery, Settlement, Progress and Present State of all the British Colonies on the Continent and Islands of America* (2 vols., London, 1708), I. xxxv, xxxvii.
[31] Burke and Burke, *An Account of the European Settlements*.
[32] Thanks to Silvia Sebastiani for this thought.
[33] Maxine Berg and Pat Hudson, *Slavery and the Industrial Revolution* (Cambridge, 2023).
[34] Long, *History*, I. 503.

had taught, could not be gainsaid.[35] Tables and balance sheets helped in 'moving to the safety of the realm of the abstract', comforting both himself and his readers 'with a sense of lawful endeavour and lawful profit'.[36] 'The quantitative archive', as Stephanie Smallwood argues, entered the merchant houses, the press and parliamentary papers through the ledgers of the slave traders and the bills of lading in which Africans were represented as objects: how many units of merchandise had been sold, how many pounds sterling earned, how much profit, how much loss.[37] How many 'Negroes' were bought, how many hogsheads of sugar were produced and sold, how much profit made? 'Dispassionate accounting', wrote Vincent Brown, 'exemplified by the ledgers of the slave traders – has been a great weapon of the powerful, an episteme that made the grossest violations of personhood acceptable, even necessary.'[38]

Consider, Long wrote, the export trade, the annual production of sugar and rum, requiring, he judged, 105,000 'Negroes', 40,000 road and mill cattle, and 25,000 mules and horses to work the 680 sugar estates, which covered 300,000 acres. Then there were the pens and other small settlements producing cotton, coffee, ginger, indigo and other commodities, some for export, some for domestic use. Once the exports to Britain and North America were calculated, alongside what was consumed in Jamaica, he computed the value to Britain as more than a quarter of a million pounds sterling. Then consider the imports, the goods coming into Jamaica from Britain. Taking all this into account, he could confidently assert that 'the whole accumulated profit, ultimately centers with the inhabitants of the mother country'.[39] Shipping and seamen also needed to be considered and the trade with many other parts of the world for which Jamaica was 'merely a middle agent, or factor, for Great Britain'. Addressing the metropolis from a mercantilist perspective, he failed to mention the riches that stayed on the island and made it possible to buy the luxury goods, the coaches and fine fabrics, the salmon and confectionary he had previously enumerated, but since these were purchased from Britain much of the wealth had returned to the mother country. What was more, it was obvious that there was 'a vast advantage to the nation having an island so situate and circumstanced, as to be able to extend the consumption of its manufactures, by

---

[35] Mary Poovey, *A History of the Modern Fact. Problems of Knowledge in the Sciences of Wealth and Society* (Chicago, 1998).
[36] Barry Unsworth, *Sacred Hunger* (London, 1992), 353.
[37] Stephanie E. Smallwood, *Saltwater Slavery. A Middle Passage from Africa to American Diaspora* (Cambridge, MA, 2007), 4.
[38] Vincent Brown, 'Social Death and Political Life in the Study of Slavery', *AHR* 114.5 (2009), 1238.
[39] Long, *History*, I. 503.

a variety of secret and difficult channels, into ... remote parts'.[40] The final annual balance to Britain, in his estimation, was £1,249,164 9s. 4d.[41] 'What a field is here opened to display the comforts and blessings of life,' he concluded, 'which this commerce distributes among so many thousands of industrious subjects in the mother country! What multitudes participate the sustenance and conveniences derived from it, who, without it, would either cease from existence, or not exist to any useful purpose!'[42] Jamaica could be even more valuable if new white settlers would come, including 'poor and industrious persons' who could produce the 'humbler commodities' with small capitals. A community of 'useful subjects' could be established, 'strangers' could be 'invited to a comfortable means of subsistence for themselves and their posterity'. And all this, he claimed, 'without making any one person miserable, or shedding one drop of human blood'.[43] Yet, it was the 'Negro Trade' which he knew was the groundwork for all of this, creating 'sustenance and conveniences for multitudes'. The violence and cruelty of entrapment and captivity, of the slave ships, of the sales of people, of the plantation itself, of the blood that had been and was being shed, all that was erased in Long's vision. 'Negro' was forgotten; what mattered was the trade in sugar. What was remembered was metropolitan prosperity.

What was more, sugar, he reminded his readers, was an essential commodity. It not only brought prosperity, it brought sweetness to the lives of all Britons. 'What immense sums have been saved to the nation', he wrote, 'by our entering so largely into cultivation of the sugar cane.' Sugar was vital to Britain. It was well known that 'the very poorest subjects in this kingdom are consumers of it, as well as the richest'.[44] Even the 'poor wretches living in alms houses' needed it for their tea. He knew there were concerns about 'the passion for sipping tea' amongst the poor, for it was thought to be 'a most enervating liquor', but it was certainly better than gin, and 'sugar', he was convinced, 'is a most salutary ingredient'. 'A plentiful crop of apples', he reflected, probably dreaming of apple pies, 'greatly increases the consumption of sugar.'[45] One of the striking aspects of sugar was that it was prized not for itself, but for what it facilitated: sweet tea, sweet pies, sweet puddings. The economic and social progress since Leslie had computed his negative account of the island in 1739,

---

[40] Ibid., I. 506. He was presumably referring here to the extensive smuggling that facilitated trade with Spanish America.
[41] Ibid., I. 508.
[42] Ibid., I. 507–8.
[43] Ibid., I. 513.
[44] In England, per capita sugar consumption increased from 1lb to 25lb between 1670 and 1770. Kenneth Morgan, 'Bristol West India Merchants in the Eighteenth Century', *TRHS* 6.3 (1993), 181–206.
[45] Long, *History*, I. 523–5. Long was very fond of apple pie. Howard, *Records and Letters*, I. 292.

whether judged in terms of quantities of sugar produced, seamen maintained, persons employed in the building and outfitting of shipping, those enriched by imports or those 'mouths fed' by the return on British manufactures, commodities and merchandise, was extraordinary. The only possible conclusion was that 'this island' is 'vastly profitable ... to the mother-country in every view'.[46]

Long's description of the 'Negro Trade' encompassed, in a very abbreviated form, the circuit of people, commodities and capital that he wrote about at greater length across the volumes of his *History*. The circuit he described began in London, moved from the docks to the shores of West Africa, across the Atlantic, to Jamaica, and then back to London: it could take up to two years. It was the West India merchant houses, such as Drake and Long, that sat at the centre. They provided the credit which drove the circuit. The commission system, developed in the Restoration period as a way of mitigating the problems of long-distance trade, worked on the basis that merchants would act as buyers and sellers of sugar and grant loans in exchange for a commission.[47] Men like William Beeston, Long's great-grandfather, established the pattern from the 1680s, sometimes trading in slaves themselves as he did, sometimes financing both the ships' captains on their voyages to West Africa and the planters who needed credit to buy the enslaved and establish their works, receiving the loads of sugar and rum in payment and utilizing bills of exchange, signed papers, as confirmation of debt and promise of payment.

In Edward Long's understanding, as in that of James Knight and of the mercantilist economists, the plantation economy was always subordinate to the metropole: that was the colonial relation. 'Under this system of policy', he wrote,

> our Plantations in the West Indies were formed, and have grown up and flourished ... it is not to peculiar excellences of soil or to extraordinary *skill* that they are indebted for their success, but to this *hereditary* preference at the British Market – It is this which has given a Confidence to the Merchant in the Loan of his capital; and to the Planter, in the application of that Loan, to Industry, and Improvement.[48]

The labour of the enslaved received no mention: it was capital which was at the heart of the system, not labour. Long wanted Jamaica to flourish and believed, as Edward [Kamau] Brathwaite observed, that it could achieve social progress through legislation.[49] But its future would always be bounded by dependence

---

[46] Long, *History*, II. 227–8.
[47] David Hancock, '"A World of Business to Do": William Freeman and the Foundations of England's Commercial Empire, 1645–1707', *WMQ* 57.1 (2000), 3–34.
[48] BL Add MSS 12407, ff. 14v–15v.
[49] Brathwaite, *The Development of Creole Society*, 74: 'What was radical about Long's thinking ... was not his political ideas *per se*, not his constitutionalism, but the

on the mother country. Writing from a quite different political perspective and with very different language and understanding, Best and Levitt described it thus:

> The Caribbean was the place where metropolitan capital established production of commodities for sale in world markets with slave labour, which was itself a traded commodity ... they were the creation of metropolitan adventurer investors and the unfree labour of slaves ... the society was constructed to serve the purposes of the economy.[50]

Long had a long-term stake in the country for it was his family's lifeline. The critique he made of absenteeism, for he could see that it damaged the colony, was not applied to himself. His hope was to make a fortune and return to the mother country like so many others. He would look after Jamaica by writing his *History*. He knew from experience that the planter would be subordinate to the merchant, who provided the supplies, extended the credit and handled the final sale. The planters were left to carry the risks. He accepted that the trade operated within an imperial system ensured by naval power, and determined by the Navigation Laws, which allowed metropolitan goods into the colonies on a preferential basis and ensured that colonial goods were carried in English ships to English ports.[51] The Navigation Laws had been passed to reassert control over English America after the chaos of the civil war had allowed colonists to establish commercial relations with the French and the Spanish. The colonists could buy nothing but British goods unless the foreign commodities were first taken to England. What was more, merchant creditors who traded with the colonies were protected. 'Caribbean colonies and transatlantic trade', by the mid-eighteenth century, 'were subject to fiscal-military control through the medium of naval power and metropolitan credit.'[52]

It is possible to describe the circuit of people, sugar and credit in diagrammatic form, as shown in Figure 4.1. [53] The particular circuit that is described

application of these (both in vision and in detail) to what Jamaican society could mean and could achieve, and his conviction that social progress could best be initiated through legislation.'

[50] Best and Levitt, *The Theory of Plantation Economy*, 10–11. 'The Vocation of a Caribbean Intellectual', David Scott's interview with Best, describes the imperative of the Caribbean economists in the period after independence to develop a new understanding of colonial dependence. *Small Axe*, 1 (1997), 119–40.

[51] The mercantilist system was never entirely hegemonic, as Julian Hoppit clarifies – 'Political Power and British Economic Life, 1650–1870', in Roderick Floud, Jane Humphries and Paul Johnson (eds.), *The Cambridge Economic History of Modern Britain, volume I: 1700–1870* (Cambridge, 2014), 344–67 – but it was certainly dominant.

[52] Smith, *Slavery, Family, and Gentry Capitalism*, 1–2. The instruments of control in Smith's study are identified as gentry capitalist networks. For Long it was the London merchants.

[53] I am very grateful to Nick Draper both for this diagram and for the discussions with him, Mark Harvey and Keith McClelland. Figure 4.1 inevitably simplifies the workings of the system.

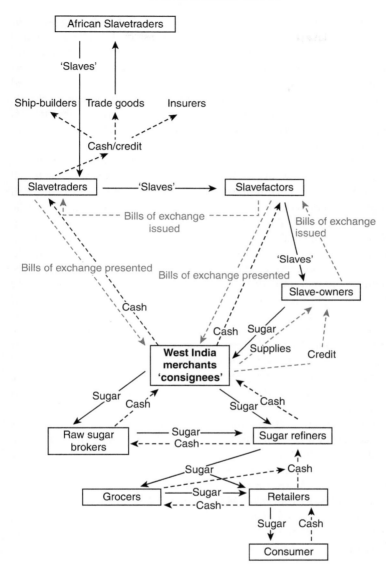

Figure 4.1 A schematic illustrating the West India trade designed by Nicholas Draper. Courtesy of Nicholas Draper.

here in diagrammatic and simplified form involved people, sugar and credit, England, West Africa and Jamaica. At the centre of the circuit, as seen in the diagram, were the merchant houses, the 'consignees', which provided the credit, *not* the enslaved who provided the labour. The credit nexus is marked in grey. The merchants provided the credit for the traders, a starting point for the traffic. The slave traders commissioned ships' captains and supplied commodities for exchange. The ships' captains, leaving from London, Bristol or Liverpool, dealt with the African slave traders and merchants on the west coast, represented as at the top of the diagram.[54] They would have acquired captives from those taken as prisoners of war or in payment of debt, or simply seized, by raiders, who had gone inland or up-river. The African slave traders exchanged men and women for a variety of commodities. The ships' captains, working for the slave traders, transported the captives, who were becoming 'slaves', across the Atlantic (figured horizontally in the diagram). On arrival in Jamaica, the captives were sold to the slave factors. Their business was to sell them on to the slave-owners, represented as another level down the diagram on the right. Traders, factors and planters were all dependent on mercantile credit, bills of exchange. The planters repaid the merchants with unrefined sugar, produced by the enslaved on the plantations, which they sent to England in a different set of ships. The merchants then sold the sugar to the brokers and refiners for further processing. They in turn sold to the grocers and retailers. The circuit of the market ended with the consumers, at the bottom of the diagram, who bought the refined sugar. Then it was the labour of women and domestic servants who turned the sugar into sweet dishes, used it as a preservative or added it to tea. The raw materials were extracted in the colony and refined in Britain; the transformation from rudeness to refinement characterized both people and goods. Across the circuit different kinds of profit were made by different agents – merchants, African traders, slave traders, ships' captains, factors, planters, sugar brokers, grocers – each with their specific sets of relations, lived either in person or at a distance.

By the mid-eighteenth century, many of the slave traders and ships' captains were financed by the merchants: they presented bills of exchange in return. The white traders used that cash and credit to buy trade goods and pay ship-builders, seamen and insurers. The captains received instructions on the prices they were to pay the African merchants and exchanged the trade goods for captives on the West African coast. Making men and women into 'chattels' was a process, rooted in terror and violence.[55] Captivity and the vicious uprooting from home and kin was the beginning, a beginning erased by Long but vividly remembered by those who suffered it. 'The enemies of our country seized us

[54] Joseph C. Miller, *Way of Death. Merchant Capitalism and the Angolan Slave Trade, 1730–1830* (London, 1988), 675: 'Merchants from very different economic systems worked out institutions and mechanisms of exchange that transformed early, unintegrated encounters, sometimes violent, into regular interactions allowing participants from both sides to engage their opposite numbers without abandoning the places that each held in their own equally vital political economies.'

[55] Patterson, *Slavery and Social Death*; Smallwood, *Saltwater Slavery*; Marcus Rediker, *The Slave Ship. A Human History* (London, 2008).

and sold us to the White people,' recorded Florence Hall, 'from the love of drink and the quarrels of their chiefs.'[56] 'Economic exchange had to transform independent beings into human commodities,' argues Stephanie Smallwood, 'whose most socially relevant feature was their exchangeability.'[57] This was facilitated by alliances between European traders and African ruling elites. Human lives were now valued, prices named, goods exchanged. A price was paid for a captive, calculated by the use that would be extracted from him/her, once they were put to productive and reproductive labour on the plantations. Their use was to produce an export commodity, sugar, which could deliver a profit. The culture of the market, of exchange, was crucial. The process had begun in the seventeenth century at the littoral, the border between landscape and sea, where gold was converted into goods in exchange for people, and people were converted into sacrifices, surrogates and pawns.[58] The RAC, at Cape Coast Castle, transformed captives into Company property: 'the slaves for sale were burned and blistered into commodity forms through the same symbolic process that transformed bullion into currency' – registered marks of gold on English guineas, the branding on the right breast of human cargo, DY for the Duke of York.[59] The branding, the shackling, the removal of clothing, the shaving, were all part of the ritual disempowerment and dishonouring of persons, as Orlando Patterson has explicated.[60] Kin were torn apart, as Olaudah Equiano described in a wrenching tale of his separation from his sister. In the early years of the slave trade Africans often held the balance of power and the development of the great slaving states gave them considerable leverage. Over time, however, this changed and African traders were increasingly disadvantaged.[61] The gold that initially brought the Portuguese to West Africa was now substituted by people, brought from increasing distances. The slave trade, as Walter Rodney wrote, 'ate into the heart of Africa'.[62] These were

---

[56] Randy M. Browne and John Wood Sweet, 'Florence Hall's "Memoirs": Finding African Women in the Transatlantic Slave Trade', S&A 37.1 (2016), 206–21.

[57] Smallwood, *Saltwater Slavery*, 35. As Guyer emphasizes, this was not about the meeting of two pre-existing sets of relations; rather it was a process of long-term European/African commercial interaction; *Marginal Gains*.

[58] Karin Barber, 'When People Cross Thresholds', *African Studies Review* 20.2 (2007), 111–23.

[59] Andrew Apter, 'History in the Dungeon: Atlantic Slavery and the Spirit of Capitalism in Cape Coast Castle, Ghana', *AHR* 122.1 (2017), 23–53.

[60] Patterson, *Slavery and Social Death*.

[61] Richard B. Sheridan, *Sugar and Slavery. An Economic History of the British West Indies, 1623–1775* (Baltimore, 1973), 250. Toby Green (in *Fistful of Shells. West Africa from the Rise of the Slave Trade to the Age of Revolution* [London, 2019]) argues that the cycles of slavery were intimately connected to the first cycles of credit and indebtedness between West Africa and western Europe and that economic inequalities arose from the inequalities of exchange in economic value.

[62] Walter Rodney, *West Africa and the Atlantic Slave Trade* (Nairobi, 1967), 4.

the unequal relations of exchange. The ending of the RAC's monopoly in 1698 meant that 'the right of a free trade in slaves was recognized as a fundamental and natural right of Englishmen' and the volume of the trade increased exponentially.[63]

English traders became skilled at collecting the goods which were in demand in West Africa, the guns and textiles that they could access from the Midlands and the north of England. Ships' captains also needed to be well informed: an experienced captain with a good sense of the African traders and the goods they wanted was critical to the success of a voyage. Once on the ships, the captives experienced new levels of cruelty, new recognitions of the meanings of enslavement. Terror was at the heart of the system: 'it is the spirit of the trade', wrote John Newton, the slave captain turned evangelical, and like a 'pestilential air, is so generally infectious' that few escape it.[64] For Equiano, 'from the time I left my own nation I always found somebody that understood me till I came to the sea coast'. It was on the slave ships that he passed from African to European control, his name was taken from him and he registered the horrors and terrors associated with 'white people'.[65] Abubakr al-Siddiq, an educated Muslim boy captured in 1805 and sold to an English slave ship, saw slavery as beginning either on board ship or when he arrived in Jamaica. He did not see his time as a captive in Africa as enslavement. Following his capture he was marched to Lago:

> There they sold me to the Christians, and I was bought by a certain captain of a ship at that time. He sent me to a boat, and delivered me over to one of his sailors. The boat immediately pushed off, and I was carried on board of the ship. We continued onboard ship, at sea, for three months, and then came on shore in the land of Jamaica. This was the beginning of my slavery until this day. I tasted the bitterness of slavery from them, and its oppressiveness.[66]

The predominantly white seamen who worked on the ships learned to demarcate themselves as free, different from their human cargo, yet subject to brutality themselves and dependent on a wage. A slave ship was a setting, argues Emma Christopher, 'in which a white man's skin came to be highly meaningful and imbued with privilege and power'.[67] The crossing of the Atlantic, a one-way passage for the captives, was a forced migration system.

---

[63] Williams, *Capitalism and Slavery*, 32. This insight of Williams into the right to trade in slaves as a fundamental right of Englishmen was elaborated by Pettigrew, *Freedom's Debt*. The trade was fully deregulated in 1712.
[64] Cited in Rediker, *The Slave Ship*, 220.
[65] Olaudah Equiano, *The Interesting Narrative and Other Writings*, ed. Vincent Caretta (London, 2003), 51, 65.
[66] Emma Christopher, *Slave Ship Sailors and their Captive Cargoes, 1730–1807* (Cambridge, 2006), 163.
[67] Ibid., 17.

In this transitional phase, captives were still merchant goods in law rather than the productive labour goods, property in persons, they became once bought by slave-owners.[68] Many captives would die on the ships and the traders would calculate on the numbers of the dead, how it would relate to price and profit. 'The language of accounting thus rationalized shipboard mortality, portraying the European agent of commodification as the passive victim of the African who died – as an investor robbed of his property *by* that property.'[69]

On landing in the Caribbean the captains would sell the surviving captives – fed, washed and oiled by the sailors, their value doubled since they left the African coast – to slave factors. 'Negroes now are and are very likely to remain in great Demand' in Kingston, wrote the Bristol merchant Henry Bright in 1753. He managed twenty-one slaving voyages between 1749 and 1766. ''Tis our opinion', he continued, 'that is the most advantageous Trade to the Adventurers, as well as the Factors, and what we chuse to employ our Money in preference to any other.'[70] Guinea factoring, wrote another British merchant, was 'the only way to enrich you and close your days in England'.[71] John Tailyour and his partners sold 17,295 captives from fifty-four ships over twelve years and he was able to return to Scotland as a rich man.[72] The factors, in competition with each other, would wait for the ships to arrive, inspect and purchase people, record the names of ships, captains and the numbers of the enslaved, inform their customers of a forthcoming sale, and check on the 'stores' where those purchased might be kept until the sales were completed.[73] 'We were conducted immediately to the merchant's yard', recorded Equiano, 'where we were all pent up together like so many sheep in a fold, without regard to sex or age.'[74] The most common way for the enslaved to be sold was on shipboard, when buyers rushed by boat to the 'scramble', an accurate name for this inhuman practice, anxious to secure healthy labourers, not the 'refuse'.[75] The factors would then sell the slaves to the slave-owners, who would pay for them with *their* bills of exchange, at long term, eighteen months or two, or even

---

[68] Goveia, 'The West Indian Slave Laws'.
[69] Smallwood, *Saltwater Slavery*, 139.
[70] Morgan, *The Bright–Meyler Papers*, 106.
[71] Cited in Nicholas Radburn, 'Guinea Factors, Slave Sales and the Profits of the Transatlantic Slave Trade in Late Eighteenth-Century Jamaica: the Case of John Tailyour', *WMQ* 72.2 (2015), 255. For more material on Tailyour, see Livesay, *Children of Uncertain Fortune*.
[72] Radburn, 'Guinea Factors'.
[73] Katie Donington, *The Bonds of Family. Slavery, Commerce and Culture in the British Atlantic World* (Manchester, 2020), 50–77. See also David Richardson, *Principles and Agents. The British Slave Trade and its Abolition* (New Haven, CT, 2022) for material on the late eighteenth century.
[74] Equiano, *Interesting Narrative*, 60.
[75] Trevor Burnard and Kenneth Morgan, 'The Dynamics of the Slave Market and Slave Purchasing Patterns in Jamaica, 1655–1788', *WMQ* 58.1 (2001), 205–28.

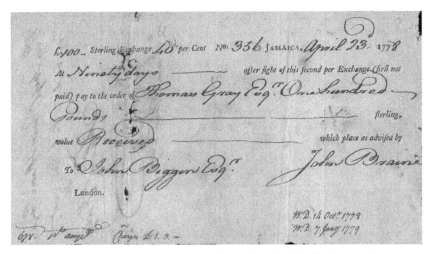

Figure 4.2 Credit underpinned the West India trade. This bill of exchange for £100 was issued in Jamaica in 1778, payable in London after ninety days. Image © Noonans Mayfair.

three, years. The bills replaced sugar as the principal means of payment. (See Figure 4.2.) They were tendered to the captains, who conveyed them to their principals. The factor would hope that the planters would pay up before *his* bills were due in London. Acting as intermediaries, heavily reliant on a network of connections and trust, they had relatively little leverage. There were rarely enough captives available to meet planter demand, but many factors also imported plantation goods and exported rum and sugar on a small scale. The factors' profit came from the commissions they secured, from both the traders and the planters, while many also engaged personally in the trade.

Two different sets of bills of exchange facilitated the circuit: one set was issued by the factors on a commission house in London to pay the slave traders, the other by the planters to the factors and returned to the commission house to clear the debt on the sugar. The bills were imaginative embodiments of commodities, designed to enable long-distance trade, and ordered a person in a distant place to pay a specified amount.[76] The system depended on the willingness of the acceptor of the bill to take responsibility for the payment. As Pat Hudson argues, 'A small number of West India Houses in London, with secure reputations, some closely tied to sugar importing and processing, came

---

[76] Higman, *Plantation Jamaica*, 107. The system is also explicated in Richard Pares, 'A London West-India Merchant House, 1740–1769', in Pares and A. J. P. Taylor (eds.), *Essays Presented to Sir Lewis Namier* (London, 1956), 75–107; S. G. Checkland, 'Finance for the West Indies, 1780–1815', *EconHR* new ser., 10.3 (1958), 461–9.

to accept final responsibility for the payment of slave-trade bills.'[77] They were receiving commissions associated both with the purchase of enslaved people and with the selling of the plantation sugar.

On the plantations, cane would be transformed by the enslaved into muscovado sugar, an unrefined sugar containing natural molasses, which was shipped to the mother country. The merchants sold the sugar on behalf of the planters, took a commission, and applied the net proceeds to the planters' bills of exchange and to other debts they might be holding. The planters aimed to cover their costs on the island by selling rum and some lower quality sugar. They could not maximize the price of their export sugar for themselves and had to rely on the merchants to do it for them: a source of tension and resentment between planters and merchants. Planters were only allowed to perform the initial processes of extraction so that metropolitan interests were protected.[78] The dockworkers and warehouse men would have been wage labourers in Britain, and indentured servants and the enslaved in Jamaica. The merchants would then sell the sugar to brokers and sugar refiners, who employed white wage labour for the further task of producing refined sugar for the domestic and export markets. By the mid-eighteenth century, there were about 120 sugar refineries in England, with some also in Scotland; the majority were in London, relatively small in scale, and usually employing fewer than ten employees.[79] They were in a weak position relative to the merchants, who had a degree of control over the wholesale market and could be price makers rather than price takers. They in turn would sell on to the grocers and retailers who would sell to the consumers. It was the consumers who paid the final price: their only power was the desire to consume, a power that was to be mobilized by female abolitionists. Profits were made from the succession of cash and credit transactions that began with the slave traders and captives, reaped commissions from factors and planters, provided revenue for the government, and ended with bags of sugar at the grocers and cups of tea at home.

The cycle of the circuit and the long delays between the sailing of the slave ships, the purchase of the captives, the landing in the Caribbean, the production of the sugar and its refining and distribution, meant that credit and the commission system that went alongside it were essential. The merchants held the bills of exchange for traders, captains, factors and slave-owners. The relations between these parties were in no way equal: the merchants as the creditors held the upper hand, and at each stage commissions were paid.

---

[77] Pat Hudson, 'Slavery, the Slave Trade and Economic Growth: a Contribution to the Debate', in Catherine Hall, Nicholas Draper and Keith McClelland (eds.), *Emancipation and the Remaking of the British Imperial World* (Manchester, 2014), 36–59.

[78] Adam Smith argued that English merchants had successfully reserved for themselves the right to refine, 'sometimes by high duties, and sometimes by absolute prohibition'; *Wealth of Nations*, 2, 78.

[79] Williams, *Capitalism and Slavery*, 73–8.

The merchants were the pivot of the system, dealing with both traders and planters. Their profit came both from the trading relation and from agricultural and industrial production, realized through the combination of the unequal relations of production with the relations of exchange.[80] The profit to the planter was the residual of the market price of the raw sugar and all the costs, including those of the consignee or commission agent. In the sugar economy the point of departure for the trade was the captive.[81] If all went well, mercantile capital accumulated. This was a distinctive form of capitalist wealth, rooted in a heterogeneous set of economic relations alongside differently racialized relations, on the African coast, in the slave ships, in the ports and on the plantations. At the centre were the merchants, who lived it all at a distance but were able to dominate on account of the credit they supplied. But none of it worked without the captives.

The Slave Trade

Long had to recognize that the 'Guinea trade' was the starting point of the circuit, but he chose to be as brief as possible. His short chapter on 'Guiney Slaves' followed the lengthy account of essential racial difference which he provided in the *History*. Africans in Guinea were thus already categorized for his readers as rude and barbarous. That barbarism would be contrasted with the civilizing conditions of the plantation, producing industrious creoles. He hoped to sanitize the trade for his readers and himself, and move swiftly on to his next chapter distinguishing between African and creole slaves. But the trade had to be protected and he relied on notions of the nature of Africans to do the work for him. His book was intended as an intervention and was followed up in later years with active lobbying.[82] The system was vital to the prosperity of the nation and was now, he asserted, properly regulated. There were, he acknowledged, 'bad apples' amongst the traders and captains but they were the exception. Well aware that trouble was brewing from abolitionists, his *History* was a sustained attempt to head off their critiques. His tone of writing on the slave trade was very different from that on the merchants and the plantations, for he had no direct experience and relied on highly selective passages from travellers' journals and universal histories for his fanciful account of conditions in West Africa. 'Pro-slavery writers constructed an almost entirely imaginary picture of a continent in the grip of the most extreme

---

[80] Harvey and Geras, *Inequality and Democratic Egalitarianism*; see particularly chap. 3.
[81] See Miller, *Way of Death*, 681, on the fact and the risks of slave mortality, this flesh and blood 'commodity that died with such ease', in the words of one colonial governor.
[82] David Beck Ryden, *West Indian Slavery and British Abolition, 1783–1807* (Cambridge, 2009); Ryden, 'Sugar, Spirits and Fodder: the London West India Interest and the Glut of 1807–15', *Atlantic Studies* 9.1 (2012), 41–64.

cruelty,' as Anthony Barker pointed out.[83] They ignored the many positive references to both the land and the peoples and focused on the negative.[84] Long aimed to demolish what he saw as a series of misconceptions: that Africa suffered from depopulation as a result of the trade, that the English were doing something illegal, and that violence was a problem. His account followed what had become a standard defence: the trade was legitimate and it was doing a kindness to Africans since their lives in Jamaica were so much better than the life, or probably death, that they would have faced in their own country. Africa and Africans, in his narrative, were represented as barbaric. The one-way journey across the Atlantic was a journey to civilization.

His attempts to sanitize, however, were undercut by the 'things behind the things', the figures in his text which marked his disavowal, the forms of recognition that disrupted the incomplete act of disavowal. He could not entirely repress the realities. The 'Guiney Slaves' chapter opened with a brief geographical description of 'whence the Negroe slaves are transported' and then 'computed' that over the past hundred years 'not less than four millions ... have been shipped'. What did this figure of four millions 'shipped' mean to him? Did the ghosts of the four millions in any way disturb him? They were no sooner mentioned than discounted: their disappearance had made no difference to Africa, they were 'superfluous'. The Atlantic slave trade had had no bad effects. Depopulation 'has not, and cannot happen'.[85] A particular form of slavery, he maintained, was well established in Africa. Since there was no conception of liberty, as there was in civilized countries, there was no shame or misery attached to being a slave. Owners calculated their 'wealth, pride and dignity' in the number of slaves they possessed, so had every interest in ensuring their multiplication. Slaves were treated in the manner of 'an European merchant in the care and improvement of his money'.[86] Polygamy was widespread, ensuring an ever-expanding birth rate, and Long cited Willem Bosman's account of Whidah and his supposed encounters with men who had fathered more than two hundred children. The combination of gold and other rich commodities alongside this ever-growing population of 'superfluous people' had made Africa, he wrote, into 'an object of much valuable commerce'.[87] The Portuguese had been the initiators of the trade, not the English, and they had found the sale of slaves already well established. In the early decades, the 'incurable ignorance and unskilfulness' of the African merchants had meant that slaves were very cheap, but European rivalries had taught 'crafty natives' of their interest and now they had been able to

---

[83] Barker, *The African Link*, 141.
[84] Richardson, *Principals and Agents*, notes that by the 1760s even writers such as Postlethwayt were having doubts about the slave trade, 106–7.
[85] Long *History*, II. 384.
[86] Ibid., II. 384.
[87] Ibid., II. 386.

drive up the price and create wealth for themselves.[88] African slave-owners, Long maintained, had absolute dominion over their slaves, could kill them or sell them, treat them as 'beasts of burthen', 'breed' them, 'like cattle, to make profit by the sale of them'.[89] Passions were 'unrestrained' and childbirth easy: women's fecundity a source of superfluity, thus facilitating the export of people.[90] Prior to the European trade, slaves and prisoners of war were sacrificed and buried alive. 'Slaves', he concluded, were considered in Africa 'actual *staple products*, as much as wool and corn are to Great Britain.'[91] Long thus represented slaves as 'products', 'things', already 'objects', *before* they were sold to the European merchants. It was fortunate for these 'superfluous people' that they were saved from death by 'Black merchants' who travelled far into the interior to find them.[92] In Africa 'the children uniformly follow the condition of their mother' – they were treated like beasts, were bred and sold like cattle: any notion of a comparison with the practices of the plantation was apparently banished from his mind.[93] Yet the reference to hereditary slavery may well have acted for him as a justification for the continuance of the practice in Jamaica.

No one in Africa, Long maintained, questioned the right to buy and sell people. Here he hoped to make it appear that there was a legitimate contract. No one doubted, he wrote, that every contract made in Africa 'for the purchase of a slave, is there understood by the three parties, the buyer, the seller, and the person sold, to be perfectly firm and valid; the one knows what he buys, the other what he sells, and the third, that his services are thus translated to his new owner'.[94] The violence of entrapment and capture were denied. There was no question of '*illegal duress*'. It was 'universally acknowledged', he insisted, 'and sanctified by publick notoriety, established usage, and the general full consent of all the inhabitants'.[95] The slaves who were bought, he claimed, were captives in war, had been sold by brutal family members, or were criminals. On the basis of a treatise he had recently read, he claimed that 99 per cent of them were felons, sold for an offence: they were not kidnapped. African states had a right to deal with their criminals, just as the English did, for every member of a community was bound by laws which they had not made themselves.[96] Those who engaged in war knew there would be consequences. He wanted

[88] Ibid., II. 388.
[89] Ibid., II. 389.
[90] Jennifer Morgan points out that women's fecundity is thus represented as undermining African society from both within and without; *Laboring Women*, 41.
[91] Long, *History*, II. 390.
[92] Ibid., II. 392.
[93] Ibid., II. 389.
[94] Ibid., II. 393.
[95] Ibid., II. 393–4.
[96] Seth, *Difference and Disease*, 224–5.

to believe that one result of this was the small number of women transported. 'Of the slaves shipped from the coast,' he wrote, 'not a sixth part are women; and this happens from there being fewer female criminals to be transported, and no female warriors to be taken prisoners'.[97] (This was a direct response to any possible abolitionist claims of the violence done to women. The figures do not tally with the figures of enslaved men and women at Lucky Valley or with the TransAtlantic Voyages Database.)[98] Africans disposed of their unwanted population just as the English did, in the Americas, and African states competed for them, knowing their value. At one time, Long acknowledged, the trade had been carried out by 'irregular rovers' of many nations.[99] But now it was properly conducted, regulated by the African Company and parliament, which deemed 'Negroes' purchased from Africa as 'a lawful commercial property'.[100] There were penalties for improper practices, and some accidents were inevitable. 'It is better surely', he asked rhetorically, 'that a few should perish by such casualties, than that all should die by the hand of an executioner.'[101] It was true that some force was necessary (here again was the acknowledgement): the enslaved had to be bound on their journey to the coast, to prevent escape, and shackled at the factories and on board. But, given their many acts of violence, their 'murdering whole crews, and destroying ships', such 'rigour' was unavoidable. Long resorted to his assumptions about essential African difference: it was an inevitable consequence of their 'bloody and malicious disposition'. They had to be confined, 'as if they were wolves or wild boars'.[102]

He knew also that they feared leaving their country. Their 'false terrors' of being eaten or having their bones ground to gunpowder, he maintained, would only be eradicated by experience. It was these 'terrors' that explained their suicides, not the brutality to which they were subjected. He told a story narrated by William Snelgrave, sea captain and slave trader, of a terrified mother whose infant child was about to be sacrificed and was saved by a white master. 'The Whites were not such bugbears as they had been led to believe.'[103] For the most part the African merchants and the captains were careful of the health of their charges, knowing that this was in their interest. There would inevitably be accidents and mishaps, but the introduction of ventilation on the ships was a marked improvement. Once on land, 'to say

---

[97] Long, *History*, II. 385.
[98] Jennifer Morgan notes that Long's observation about the lack of women 'was keyed to an interpretation of the relationship among sexuality, population, and culture that exonerated the English from wrongdoing on the African continent'; *Reckoning with Slavery*, 36.
[99] Long, *History*, II. 395.
[100] Ibid., II. 497.
[101] Ibid., II. 399.
[102] Ibid., II. 397.
[103] Ibid., II. 398.

the truth', he wrote, 'the condition of the Negroes in general in Africa, and in our colonies', was so different that there was no point of comparison. An anecdote of his own was offered as proof: 'a Negroe who had lived several years in Jamaica' when questioned was clear that he wished to live the rest of his life there, having exchanged 'abject slavery ... brutal and licentious tyranny' for shelter, food, clothing and protection in law. If there were instances of cruelty, then 'the owner is, without doubt, either a madman or a fool', for it was in their interest to be humane.[104] In Jamaica, 'Negroes' enjoyed *'perfect freedom'* when compared with their previous condition, since 'what is deemed *slavery* in one place, is far from being reputed so in another ... the servitude they live under has neither horrors nor hardship'.[105]

In these few pages Long had named captives 'staple products', 'superfluous people', of 'malicious disposition', 'naturally thieves and villains'. He had animalized them like 'wolves or wild boars'. Given the savagery of their disposition, he maintained, 'Such men must be managed at first as if they were beasts, they must be tamed, before they can be treated like men.'[106] The strangeness and seeming savagery of Africans, as Winthrop Jordan wrote, 'were major components in that sense of *difference* which provided the mental margin absolutely requisite for placing the European on the deck of the slave ship and the Negro in the hold'.[107]

Meanwhile, traders were doing lawful business, captains were as careful as they could be given their own investment and that of their employers, owners knew that it was in their self-interest to be humane, and merchants were accumulating capital.

The Merchant House

When it came to the merchants, Long was on home ground. The West India merchants sat at the centre of the circuit of the sugar economy and 'the house of Drake and Long was the oldest and most respected firm in the Jamaica trade'.[108] Beeston Long senior, as he came to be known, born in 1710, was the second son of Charles Long by his second marriage. The fortune of his mother, Jane (née Beeston), had been saved from the disaster of his father's speculation and he was able to establish himself as a merchant, probably building on the West India trade which his grandfather, William Beeston, had established. He had married Sarah Crop, the daughter of a London merchant, Abraham Crop, 'with a fortune of £30,000', a most fortunate

---

[104] Ibid., II. 399–400.
[105] Ibid., II. 400–1.
[106] Ibid., II. 401.
[107] Winthrop D. Jordan, *White over Black. American Attitudes towards the Negro, 1550–1812* (London, 1969), 97.
[108] Checkland, 'Finance for the West Indies', 463.

alliance. At that time a large family party was held at the King's House in Newmarket, when his half-brother Samuel was living there, with 'fireworks, ... Balls, and Entertainments of every kind'. It was remembered by his nephew Edward as 'a scene of jollity for some time'.[109] By 1740 Beeston Long had established a partnership with his brother-in-law, Roger Drake, who came from a family of London merchants with trading interests in the East Indies and Virginia.[110] Partnerships were a relatively novel development, usually involving two or three people, who were very often kin, either through the family of origin or the family of marriage. They set up initially on Crutched Friars, near Fenchurch Street, and Beeston Long settled in Bishopsgate Street, where Samuel visited with his three sons in 1745 and Edward arrived having left Cornwall in 1753. (See Figure 4.3.)

By the mid-eighteenth century, the West Indian merchants were a very well-established grouping in the City of London, tending to deal with larger amounts than other traders and dominating the sugar trade.[111] The need to pay sugar duties at the waterfront meant that they had to be well capitalized. The Bank of England had been founded in 1694, initially to finance the war with France, and facilitated a new system of public debt and provided funds for the next century to support the fiscal-military state. Merchants, especially the City merchants (a term mainly used for those operating in overseas trade), played an increasingly significant part in the development of a commercial empire. James Knight, however, writing in the 1740s, was convinced that they were not given sufficient weight in governing circles, their new money looked at askance by the landed. Knight cited the well-known political arithmetician Charles Davenant to emphasize the connection between liberty and commerce, erasing the spectre of chattel slavery by referring to political slavery: 'they who either are Slaves, or who believe their Freedoms precarious, can neither succeed in Trade, or Meliorate a Country'. 'Merchants', he opined, 'ought to be considered as one of the most useful Societys to the Common Wealth; and in Some Countrys are deservedly distinguished, however Neglected and Slighted in a Nation, which has a great dependence on Trade.'[112] By the early eighteenth century, London was beginning to rival Amsterdam as the commercial centre of Europe; by the 1760s it was operating

---

[109] Howard, *Records and Letters*, I. 79.
[110] Thanks to Clare Taylor for her unpublished notes on 'The Longs – Absentee Merchants and Members of Parliament'. Unfortunately no records of the firm have survived.
[111] There were also West India merchants in Bristol, Liverpool and Glasgow. See, for example, Pares, *A West India Fortune*; Morgan, *The Bright–Meyler Papers*; Morgan, 'Bristol West India Merchants'; Morgan, *Bristol and the Atlantic Trade in the Eighteenth Century* (Cambridge, 1993); T. M. Devine, 'An Eighteenth-Century Business Elite: Glasgow West India Merchants, c. 1750–1815', *Scottish Historical Review* 57.163, pt 1 (1978), 40–67.
[112] Knight, *History*, I. vii, 19.

Figure 4.3 The counting house of Drake and Long was at 17 Bishopsgate Street from at least 1758. This elevation of a Bishopsgate Street house from 1807 recalls one of the typical counting house designs with a three-window front over multiple storeys. Designs for Bishopsgate Street house, City of London: elevation of the front façade, drawing by John Baker, 1807. RIBA Collections.

across the globe. Colonial commerce had exceeded European trade for the first time as the demand for tea, tobacco and sugar rose in the domestic market and foreign markets sought British manufactured goods as well as the prized tropical re-exports that they could access. Credit had to be mobilized for overseas trade, and the West Indian trade needed merchants who had the financial capacity to extend long-term credit. London had a large and growing market for sugar, was a financial, exchange and shipping centre, and was the seat of the imperial government: it was well situated for the growth of the West India merchant houses. The bustling port of London, with its export trade dominated by wool, ensured the city's pre-eminence as a place of mobility and exchange. The Thames, that 'great artery of trade', provided links to the regions as well as to the global market.[113] Much rebuilding had taken place in the City, and the main pediment of the new Mansion House 'depicted London trampling on its rivals to usher in plenty'.[114] The majority of the merchants still lived there, sometimes in the counting house, sometimes in a separate residence. The more prosperous also had country houses, 'retiring homes', in areas around London, whilst remaining in commerce.[115] Beeston Long was building up an establishment at Carshalton in Surrey from 1755, now a public park in the London borough of Sutton.

Drake and Long acted as the merchant house or consignee, named as such since the planter had consigned their crop to them. They acted for their kin in Jamaica and many other significant families. It was important that they had roots in the colony. William Beeston, like many of the early merchants, was a planter and slave trader, as well as governor. He *knew* the island and the elite families, and could understand the problems of long-distance commercial agriculture.[116] The house would have been in close touch with Samuel Long, and then Edward, relying on them as their colonial correspondents with information about people and the doings of the assembly. London merchants worked with associates and agents overseas who, as David Hancock emphasizes, brought people and products together, facilitating commercial integration. Their outlook tended to be practical and opportunistic, yet with a belief in their own capacity to improve and civilize, 'attuned to a rational, enlightened Euro-Atlantic culture of refinement'.[117] Drake and Long were the consignees for the Dawkins family, amongst other leading members of the planter elite, between 1749 and 1812. The Dawkins, like the Longs, had been in Jamaica for generations and were also major slave-owners in Clarendon. Henry Dawkins moved to England once he had made a sufficient fortune, and in 1758 he became a partner in Drake and Long, though probably never active. He would, however, have had extensive useful knowledge about the island. It became Drake, Long and Dawkins, of 17 Bishopsgate Street.[118]

---

[113] Donington, *Bonds of Family*, 79.

[114] Perry Gauci, *Emporium of the World. The Merchants of London, 1660–1800* (London, 2007).

[115] John Pinney, the planter and merchant, writing in 1778, was anxious to be seen as a country gentleman and hoped to avoid the name of 'West Indian'. Pares, *A West India Fortune*, 141.

[116] Hancock, 'A World of Business to Do'.

[117] David Hancock, *Citizens of the World. London Merchants and the Integration of the British Atlantic Community, 1735–1785* (Cambridge, 1995), 21.

[118] On the Dawkins family, see James Dawkins, 'The Dawkins Family in England and Jamaica, 1664–1823', PhD, University College London, 2018; thanks to Clare Taylor, unpublished note, 'Drake and Long'. The firm went through various iterations as partners came and went: in 1768 it was Beeston Long and Co., and in 1770 was back

The financing of international trade depended, as we have seen, on bills of exchange, the legal instruments which facilitated the payment for goods without coin.[119] These bills stood in for the real currency, which was enslaved men and women. Trust between payer and payee was crucial: indeed, the word *credit* had a narrow financial meaning, but also a more general meaning of carrying a reputation for honesty and competence. Paper bills had many advantages over coin, of which in any case there was a serious shortage in Jamaica. Knowing that these bills would be accepted, not refused, or 'protested', was vital. Respectability and honour therefore ranked high in mercantile circles; those who reneged on bills were likely to be ostracised. Mercantile correspondents, argues John Smail, understood the risks and obligations that defined their relations and used a language of honour to try to protect themselves.[120] A common code of conduct developed, as Perry Gauci explains, associated with the concern for reputation. The dress code was one of modest refinement: gold watches, gold-topped canes and gold rings might be acceptable but nothing too extravagant. Reliability, punctuality, thrift and good faith were valued alongside a plain and modest writing style and form of address. Merchants were men, but their occupation could put their manliness in question. How comfortably did manly virtue sit with mercantile activity? The notion of a self-regulated public performance of solidity and respectability could offset the association of mercantile work with risk, the danger that they might be seen as creatures of passion and fantasy, living in a world of speculation. Sobriety of conduct was essential since their failures, which were not infrequent, might be associated with character flaws, immoral conduct and effeminacy. It was the opinion of other men that counted most in securing their reputations; attention was necessary to how others saw you.[121] The counting house provided an important site for the performance of mercantile identity and the maintenance of reputation. There are occasional traces of women who contributed to the running of a business; Frances Dickinson had an ineffective husband, John Frederick Pinney, who relied on her to deal with

---

to Drake and Long, before becoming Long, Drake and Dawkins in 1789. By the 1830s it had ceased trading.

[119] Jacob M. Price, 'Credit in the Slave Trade and Plantation Economies', in Barbara L. Solow (ed.), *Slavery and the Rise of the Atlantic System* (Cambridge, 1991), 293–339.

[120] John Smail, 'Credit, Risk and Honour in Eighteenth-Century Commerce', *JBS* 44.3 (2005), 439–56. 'Character' was an important signifier of personal credit, operating not only in relation to merchants but right across the web of consumer culture that expanded exponentially in Georgian England. See Margot Finn, *The Character of Credit. Personal Debt in English Culture, 1740–1914* (Cambridge, 2013).

[121] See, for example, amongst the merchants of Philadelphia, Toby L. Ditz, 'Shipwrecked: or Masculinity Imperiled: Mercantile Representations of Failure and the Gendered Self in Eighteenth-Century Philadelphia', *Journal of American History* 81.1 (1994), 51–80.

correspondence.[122] This was probably unusual; in the substantial merchant houses, women's labour took on many other forms: the provision of capital through marriage and inheritance, the care of the household, servants and young male employees, the reproduction of the family and the maintenance of networks of kin.

The counting house was the 'real center of London commerce'.[123] Bishopsgate Street was situated in the heart of the commercial district within easy reach of the Royal Exchange, the Bank of England, Lloyd's, the Custom House and the Jamaica Coffee House, giving the partners easy walking access to people and information, sea captains, brokers, buyers and competitors. No details of the property have survived, but David Hancock's account of John Sargeant's counting house on Mincing Lane gives a vivid picture of the likely interior. Both a business and a family house, there was no formal distinction between the two, but an emphasis on order throughout suggested the focus on the imperatives of a commercial life. The mahogany merchants' bureaus, a feature of both the partner's large and comfortable room and the office provided for the clerks, were key items of furniture. With their sixteen drawers, plus shelves, pigeon holes and compartments designed to file correspondence, they were the 'ultimate symbol of order'.[124] Maps and charts covered the walls in the clerks' room, and a counter, leather stools and single desks with quills, inkstands and candlesticks furnished the tools of the trade. The ground floor was dominated by business plus a dining room and kitchen; upstairs were bedrooms for the family, apprentices and servants. Simple mahogany furniture (the wood for which would have come from Jamaica), painted walls and porcelain dishes spoke of comfort rather than luxury.

The work of the merchant's house was extensive and varied: they were dealing both internally and externally, with domestic suppliers of many kinds, as well as with the traders and planters, all of which gave them a pivotal position and made many others dependent on them. Supplying credit and judging which planters might be a safe bet was only the beginning. Sugar was a notoriously risky business: crops were extremely variable, and failures and bankruptcies at both ends of the chain were relatively frequent. The merchants were wise to take good care in choosing their creditors. Once credit was laid out and bills of exchange signed, the merchant's chief business was to sell sugar at the right time according to the price and the state of the market. Prices were volatile and it required skill and experience to know when to sell. War, bad weather, a glutted market and trouble at sea were some of the many potential pitfalls. Collecting information was vital too: knowing when ships were arriving and leaving, when war threatened or government change was

---

[122] Pares, *A West India Fortune*.
[123] Hancock, *Citizens of the World*, 90.
[124] Ibid., 102.

coming. The Jamaica Coffee House in St Michael's Alley was one of the first meeting places along with taverns and dining clubs where contacts might be found and news exchanged. Letters had to be written and accounts copied in the counting house. By the mid-eighteenth-century, clerks would be employed to do some of this work. Grocers might be visited on a weekly basis to collect money due for the sugar they had sold. There would be negotiations at the waterside when the ships came in: sugars examined as they came ashore, invoice weights compared with landing weights, casks examined for discrepancies and for variations in quality. Duties had to be paid at the port before goods were released. The merchants would have an agent in the Custom House who would cast up taxes due on imported sugars, claim deductions for prompt payment and know when to petition commissioners for concessions.

The house would also do a range of work for the planter, buying supplies of every description for the plantation which would need to be shipped out, from tools for the production of the canes and nails for the plantation works to osnaburg to clothe the enslaved, cheese (probably from Ireland) and wax candles for the planter's house, even fine mahogany furniture, transformed by English cabinet makers from the mahogany planks which had come from Jamaica.[125] The merchant house of Lascelles and Maxwell, first analysed by Richard Pares, tended to deal on a regular basis with the same tradespeople.[126] The merchants also invested money for the planters, sometimes engaged in metropolitan land sales for them as Drake and Long did for Henry Dawkins.[127] They would hire skilled contract workers such as blacksmiths, carpenters, wheelwrights and coopers, white men who would be sent out to service the plantations and train the enslaved. The Bluecoat School was seen as a promising source of bookkeepers given the training provided there in writing and accounts. The Lascelles tried to get the interest of Mr Smith, the writing master, the very one to whom both Robert and Edward Long had been sent.[128] The merchant house would order the machinery for the plantation works made according to specification. Sourcing shipping insurance was another important activity, probably dealing after 1771 through Lloyd's of London, the major market for maritime insurance. Payments would need to be made for legal fees and to ships' captains, freight organized, warehousing provided for the sugar and rum, dockworkers hired to load and unload. They would deal with government departments, prosecute law-suits when necessary and follow dealings in Chancery. They also performed more personal services, placing the children of planters in schools, acting in loco parentis as Uncle Beeston did for

---

[125] Jennifer L. Anderson, *Mahogany. The Costs of Luxury in Early America* (Cambridge, MA, 2012).
[126] Pares, 'A London West-India Merchant House'.
[127] Dawkins, 'The Dawkins Family', 91.
[128] Pares, 'A London West-India Merchant House', 92.

Edward Long, receiving correspondence for their clients: Edward Long's letters to Mary Ricketts were sent to London on ships care of Drake and Long.[129] All these services would be paid for by commission, added to the planter's account. Drake and Long acted for Chaloner Arcedeckne, a major absentee in the 1760s and 1770s. He was charged a commission rate of 2.5 per cent in 1773.[130] Services for him included shipping five packing cases containing a marble tablet memorializing his father, Andrew Arcedeckne, to be erected in St Catherine's, Spanish Town.[131] Arcedeckne's attorney on the island, Simon Taylor, assured him that he was 'obliged to you for your orders to Mr Long to accept Bills when drawn by me on you. You may depend on it, I shall only draw as there is occasion for money on your Account.'[132] He also reported that he had drawn the usual bills on him with Drake and Long, but that unfortunately an accident had happened with five hogsheads of sugar lost on board; he 'doubted not that you and Mr Long would be able to settle together'.[133] There was never any question as to the relative power of the merchants and planters as Edward Long knew well. Writing to his friend Mary Ricketts at a difficult time for the planters, he pointed out that 'the Merchants are neither easy nor careless about the consequences; If a panic has struck them, they will naturally limit and contract their advances for some time, waiting to see the turn of public affairs, & with this view, they will drive us all into the narrows of Economy for fear of the worst.'[134] 'The 'narrows of Economy' was a telling phrase, an evocation of the power which the merchants could exercise on those in debt to them.

The merchant houses kept a range of accounts, including a journal recording the status of goods, cash, bills, stocks and ships, invoice books and waste books. The merchant's perspective, writes Vincent Brown, was 'a discourse of exchange' that sought 'equivalences between units, flattening the social world by rendering it in the abstract'.[135] In the double-entry ledgers, the opposite parts of every account directly faced each other. On one side would be the credit, all the bills of exchange drawn on planters and factors; on the debit side all the bills that had been accepted, protested or were still outstanding. As Barry Higman explains,

> the merchant's account current included, on the debit side, all the money in his hands received by sale of sugar and other commodities, as well as

---

[129] Ricketts Family Papers.
[130] M965. Vanneck-Arc/3C/1773/2, *Sales of 50 Hhds of Sugar & 25 Puncheons of Rum from Jamaica for Chaloner Arcedeckne Esqr* (London: Institute of Historical Research, Senate House), cited in Dawkins, 'The Dawkins Family', 92.
[131] Higman, *Plantation Jamaica*, 147.
[132] Wood, *The Letters of Simon Taylor*, 109.
[133] Ibid., 146.
[134] Edward Long to Mary Ricketts, 18 February 1775, BL Add MS 30001, f. 52.
[135] Brown, *The Reaper's Garden*, 28.

remittances and transfers. On the credit side were payments and remittances he had made and the debts owed him by planters and other traders. The merchant's balance depended on rates of exchange, which could earn a profit or loss. The merchant's overall profit and loss account was derived from the closing of the journal and ledger.[136]

The surviving account books for Drake and Long's dealings with Henry Dawkins were based on the two-column charge/discharge system.[137] This was used on large landed estates in Britain until the end of the eighteenth century and was designed to facilitate periodic accounts where the steward recorded what had been received and disbursed. It provided an elaborate cash account and acted as a rough check on efficiency.[138] Sidney Pollard argued that this was a system based on double-entry bookkeeping, but of a particular kind. On the debit side were all the receipts, on the credit side all the payments, which included items for the household and cash payments to the master. The system of the accounting house, Pollard believed, was the most important source of accounting practice in eighteenth-century Britain, for

> not only had it developed double-entry book-keeping, the logical basis of all widely used systems, but it also had to grapple at an early stage with the problems of large-scale enterprise, and the supervision of businesses at a distance; that is to say it had to aid in the management of firms too complex to be directly controlled by a single head.[139]

Double-entry bookkeeping has been analysed by Mary Poovey as central to the formation of modern systems of knowledge. The internally consistent forms of writing and exchange came to represent honest and virtuous practices, thus indicating creditworthiness. The double entries offsetting credits and debts meant it was possible to keep track of transactions, while the balances at the end of each page and the order it appeared to guarantee proclaimed the credibility of the merchants. Double-entry bookkeeping was, Poovey suggests, both a system of writing and a mode of government: the two columns totted up gave an appearance of balance. All had to obey the rules. The system drew on the legacies of William Petty's thinking, his 'political arithmetic', his insistence on arguments based on numbers, weights and measures. 'Petty used the trope of mathematical method to promise

---

[136] Higman, *Plantation Jamaica*, 107. My understanding of mercantile accounting systems has relied heavily on Barry Higman's work.
[137] MS 181A, Accounts Current with Drake and Long, vols. I & II, Dawkins Plantation Records, National Library of Jamaica, cited in Dawkins, 'The Dawkins Family', 91.
[138] Higman, *Plantation Jamaica*.
[139] Sidney Pollard, *The Genesis of Modern Management. A Study of the Industrial Revolution in Great Britain* (London, 1965), 212, cited in Higman, *Plantation Jamaica*, 106. Higman notes that Christopher J. Napier does not agree that the charge/discharge system was a form of double-entry bookkeeping.

impartiality in most of his economic writing.'[140] All the figures were supposed to confirm the objective, disinterested and accurate nature of the material being presented. Petty's work in Ireland, his measurements of population and wealth, the figures he produced claimed simply to reflect a reality and 'seemed to efface the personal interests of the person who made knowledge from numbers'.[141] By the mid-seventeenth century, argues Jennifer Morgan, 'demographic rationality had established a clear distinction between those who count and those who are counted'.[142] The Irish could be made white; Africans were commodities.

Petty's thinking had a further dimension directly related to the development of the slavery business and its financialization. As Paul Gilroy argues, Petty was an early theorist of racial hierarchy. His schema was 'the first English statement of what would become the fundamental principle of racialized rule. The novel relationship he proposed between observable differences, cognitive capacity, and the natural constitution of humans was part of the gradual shift from race as static taxonomy to race as a matter of historical lineage.'[143] 'That of man it selfe there seems to be several species,' argued Petty,

> to say nothing of Gyants and Pigmies or of that sort of small men who have little speech and feed chiefly upon fish ... for of these sorts of men, I venture to say nothing, but that 'tis very possible there may be Races and generations of such since we know that there are men of 7 foot high and others but 4 foot ... I say there may be races and Generations of such men whereof we know the Individualls ... there be others (differences) more considerable, that is, between the Guiny Negroes & the Middle Europeans; & of Negroes between those of Guiny and those who live about the Cape of Good Hope, which last are the most beastlike of all the Souls (Sorts?) of Men whith whom our Travellers are well acquainted. I say that the Europeans do not only differ from the aforementioned Africans in Collour ... but also in Naturall Manners, & in the internall Qualities of their Minds.[144]

Distinctions in the colour of the skin, in 'natural' manners and in the 'internal' qualities of the mind: it was these differences which were used to classify Africans as 'brutes' and to legitimate selling African peoples into slavery.

---

[140] Poovey, *A History of the Modern Fact*, 131.
[141] Ibid., 124; J. G. A. Pocock defined 'political arithmetic' as 'a quantitative means of estimating every individual's contribution to the political good by measuring what he put into and withdrew from the national stock'; *The Machiavellian Moment. Florentine Political Thought and the Atlantic Republican Tradition* (Princeton, 1975), 425.
[142] Morgan, *Reckoning with Slavery*, 106.
[143] Paul Gilroy, *The Tanner Lectures on Human Values* (New Haven, CT, 2014), 35.
[144] Rhodri Lewis (ed.), *William Petty on the Order of Nature. An Unpublished Manuscript Treatise* (Tempe, AZ, 2012), 122. Thanks to Paul Gilroy for first drawing my attention to Petty.

The practices of counting and measuring people were crucial to the process of turning them into commodities. The standard accounting text of the eighteenth century, John Mair's *Book-keeping Methodised*, included sections, as Hazel Carby has explicated, on the practices appropriate for colonial territories. In the sugar colonies 'people' meant 'Whites', he advised, and 'Negroes' should be listed like any other form of goods. 'Mair's accounting pages', writes Carby, were presented as a simple matter of transcription and calculation. 'Transcribing "negroes" as goods confirmed their dehumanization while the precision and detail of the formal design and manner of the book-keeping entry proclaimed accuracy and asserted the right to trade in flesh.'[145] 'Normative processes of violence' were 'embedded in numerical evidence, in the development of demography and other quantitative approaches to population, and in the ways men and women were reduced to monetary or commercial value'.[146]

The few ledgers of Drake and Long that have survived indicate that their major business was with the commodities produced by the enslaved, and the commodities required for their production of the sugar and rum. On occasion, however, they appear to have been trading in people. An entry on 11 April 1761, for £1,250, for example, dealt with bills paid to attorneys acting for Dawkins. Of this sum, £750 was to go to Hibberts and Jackson, the Kingston factors, almost certainly for the purchase of enslaved people.[147] The enslaved themselves were defined as chattels by the traders, captains, sailors, factors and planters. The circuit of production was documented at each stage in forms of numerical representation which facilitated a distancing between the merchant and his clerks and the human realities of the production of sugar. The hogsheads of sugar and puncheons of rum which arrived in the port of London were recorded in terms of weight and price; the dead labour embedded in them disappeared in the violent abstraction of these figures. Slavery happened somewhere else: distance excused the merchants. While the planters argued that they were not responsible for enslaving, that it was the traders who did it, the merchants could represent themselves as far from the physicality of the slave ships or the plantations. Yet enslaved boys might well be found in the merchant houses, as witnessed by the advertisements for 'runaways'.[148] 'Shielded from the everyday realities of plantation life', as Katie Donington puts it, 'polite mercantile culture provided a civilising veneer for slavery's depredations. Abstracted into the tidy rows and columns of the merchant's ledger the human cost of colonial productivity was transformed

---

[145] Hazel V. Carby, *Imperial Intimacies. A Tale of Two Islands* (London, 2019), 251.
[146] Morgan, *Reckoning with Slavery*, 55.
[147] James Dawkins, personal communication. T. S. Ashton (ed.), *Letters of a West Indian Trader. Edward Grace, 1767–70* (London, 1950), 34–5 includes letters indicating that Grace was acting directly in purchasing captives. Nick Draper, personal communication.
[148] Newman, *Fortune Seekers*.

into profit and loss in pounds, shillings, and pence.'[149] In the era of abolition, merchants could even claim to be enemies to slavery in the abstract.[150] The captives who had been dragooned into the slave ships, the enslaved men and women who worked on the plantations, appeared nowhere in these records. Their persons and their labour were erased in the recording of value, in the credit and debit accounts.

Many merchants also had interests in shipping, usually owning a part; one-sixteenth or one-eighth were common holdings. Other partners might be the ship's captain, whose reputation was vital to the success of the voyage. The major point of owning ships was to keep friends and debtors attached to the merchant house. Drake and Long became known for their transportation of military supplies to Jamaica, such as resin, turpentine and tar, and during the American war they were heavily involved in transoceanic freight.[151] Samuel Long collaborated with Richard Atkinson, notorious for his extraordinarily lucrative rum contract, in organizing shipping at a time when Jamaica was facing a serious threat in the American war, while his father, Beeston Long, had been called in to adjudicate on the price that Atkinson had negotiated for what he claimed was his top-quality Jamaican rum.[152] Fortunes were often built up from a variety of activities. The success of the Bright/Meylers based in Bristol involved dealings in land, acting as commission agents, owning shares in ships, buying and selling provisions, lending money, taking mortgages in security and, most significantly, trading in slaves.[153] Holding official positions could be another important source of contacts and business. The wealthiest merchants might become aldermen, even MPs, opening up new investment possibilities. The wealth of merchants was a constant source of comment, much of it critical and linked to anxieties about luxury and the moral dangers associated with new money: furthermore, there were the threats associated with credit and debt.

Credit and Debt

While merchants could disavow their involvement in the cruelty of slavery by geographical separation, for the planter the denial was more difficult: it required ideological work. It was Long's insistence on *difference* that allowed him both to know that 'The Negro Trade was the ground-work of all' and to disavow it. Enslaved persons were the source of value, but the transformation

---

[149] Donington, *The Bonds of Family*, 98.
[150] See, for example, William Alers Hankey in 1832; Draper, *The Price of Emancipation*, 54.
[151] David Syrett, *Shipping and the American War. A Study of British Transport Organisation* (London, 1970).
[152] Richard Atkinson, *Mr Atkinson's Rum Contract. The Story of a Tangled Inheritance* (London, 2020).
[153] Morgan, *Bright–Meyler Papers*.

of men and women into 'slaves', units of production, meant that their labour could be represented in disembodied terms and the work of the plantation be described as the planter's work. The idea of credit allowed for another kind of obfuscation. Its paper form meant that the issue of *what it was for* could be forgotten, the human cost veiled by the bills of exchange. In order to buy land and labour, planters needed credit: debt was the unfortunate corollary of credit, and in Long's mind it was debt, the repayment of the credit, that was the heaviest burden of the planter, the source of the anxiety which displaced any lurking fears as to the immorality of the plantation economy. Like all planters Long had to rely on credit and he understood its centrality to the circuit of sugar production. He was keen to give a positive picture of it in his *History*. 'Credit has been found necessary to, and is become a part of commerce,' he assured his readers; this was the new world of trade, an economy which was still not fully established.[154] Enslaved men and women bought on credit not only could pay for themselves relatively soon, but provided they lived long enough, their labour could facilitate the purchase of new captives. 'Credit', as Jacob Price puts it, 'did not so much change the fundamental character of slave cultivation as accelerate the processes of initiation and expansion of slave systems.'[155]

'Money is particularly necessary in this island, to purchase labourers,' Long explained to his readers; 'In most other countries the labourer is hired.' Purchasing people should simply be thought of as a different way of procuring labour. Labourers in Jamaica had to be bought, but the purchase money did not stay in the country; rather 'it passes to, and enriches, our mother country'.[156] This was a source of satisfaction, though he must also have known that it was the Africans' loss. 'Money is to be understood', he elaborated, 'only as the symbol of a thing, or measure of external commerce.' In this 'species of commerce', gold and silver played a minimal part: 'in place of it is *credit*'. As long as the planters could get credit in Britain, he continued, they would not need gold or silver. Planters who bought 'Negroe labourers' would draw 'bills of exchange on some merchant in Great Britain for that purpose'.[157] It was the merchants of Great Britain who should provide the credit, he insisted; they were the respectable ones, and it was they who had supported Jamaica. 'The now-flourishing condition of the most considerable estates in the island had its origin in the credit and support of the British merchants,' he maintained.[158] This had been, and must continue to be, a harmonious and mutually beneficial relationship. It was vital that the merchants should

[154] Long, *History*, I. 530.
[155] Price, 'Credit in the Slave Trade', 294.
[156] Long, *History*, I. 533–4.
[157] Ibid., I. 533–4.
[158] Ibid., I. 385.

continue to believe that 'their money and credit can be employed no where abroad with greater safety and advantage than in *their* island' (my italics); the value of the land meant that their investment was secure, as long as the mother country continued to provide security. A vast mountain of debt, he noted, was continually resolved into 'bonds and mortgages'.[159] In his mind it was clear that the more British merchants invested in 'the same common bottom', the better assured the island would be of imperial protection.[160] 'So shall thy merchant cheerful credit grant/And well earned opulence thy cares repay', carolled Grainger.[161] While Long reminded British merchants that Jamaica was *their* colony, delivering its profits to them, Grainger reminded them that they could hope for wealth. Many of the greatest mercantile fortunes 'derive their splendour from this connection, the interest, the attachment, and benefit', Long noted, and this had all been reciprocal. Resident planters and absentees should do what they could to facilitate this mutually beneficial relationship, 'conciliate a solid credit with the merchants of the mother-country' and maintain 'inviolable honour and good faith'.[162] It was the 'honest wealthy merchants in Great Britain' who ought always to have preference in the granting of credit.[163]

Long needed to explain the importance of credit to his readers in this way because the idea of credit had provoked deep ambivalence since its emergence as central to the British economy from the end of the seventeenth century. Initially associated with public finance, the creation of the Bank of England and the National Debt, it had facilitated an association between national prosperity, the activities of the government and the prosecution of war. Large and small investors could lend capital to the state, investing in a future with a guaranteed return. 'The big breakthrough for states', argues Susan Strange, 'came at the turn of the [seventeenth] century with the introduction of a new kind of money – state promises to pay. Two Scots, John Law and William Paterson, both saw that by this means money could be created with which to replenish the resources of the state by issuing pieces of paper carrying the "guarantee" of the monarch.'[164] This state borrowing had the effect of encouraging private investment. Credit was initially focused on financing the state through government stock with its promise to pay at a future date. It was known that this date would never be reached, but the tokens signified repayment. The price was determined by the state of public confidence in the government, the belief that it would pay. The investor imagined some moment

---

[159] Ibid., I. 385, 564.
[160] Ibid., I. 558.
[161] Grainger, *The Sugar Cane*, Bk 1. 490–1.
[162] Long, *History*, I. 385.
[163] Ibid., I. 395.
[164] Quoted in Marieka de Goede, *Virtue, Fortune and Faith. A Genealogy of Finance* (Minneapolis, 2017), 22.

which would never exist in reality. Credit, explains Thomas Levenson, was 'money's most dynamic incarnation[; it] makes promises expressed in numbers that connect the future to the present'.[165] This was an idea facilitated by the scientific revolution, for Newton had taught that it was possible to calculate the future, Petty had developed a quantitative science of society and Davenant had reasoned with figures on matters relevant to government. (These were all skills that Long was to put to use.) Credit soon expanded to facilitate overseas trade, providing goods and services which would be paid for in the future. 'Property', as Pocock puts it, '– the material foundation of both personality and government – has ceased to be real and has become not merely mobile but imaginary.'[166] The imagined value of stocks, bonds and bills of exchange was now at the heart of the circuits of exchange. And men must behave in ways that confirmed their belief in promises: the slave ship would get to the west coast of Africa; men, women and children would be captured, bought and sold; planters would acquire labour; cane would be planted; sugar would be produced and returned in hogsheads to the London docks. The creditors would wait in anticipation of their profit. All this could be imagined but probably was not. As Carl Wennerlind demonstrates, the public frenzy over the South Sea Company disregarded factors that were well known. There was plenty of press coverage of mutinies and rebellions, but 'a form of unwilled or built-in blindness' operated, ensuring that the humanness of enslaved people 'did not even enter the minds of the public'.[167]

Credit, together with the ways in which shares and tallies had become marketable properties, was hotly debated in the 'paper wars', which were at a height between 1698 and 1734. Major figures, from Davenant and Swift to Pope, Defoe and Addison, argued about the possibilities and dangers of trusting in imagined futures rather than in the solidity of land. Public debt, argued critics such as Swift and Pope, was a form of idolatry or fetishism, encouraging the idea that nothing could be transformed into something, paper into money, debt into wealth.[168] 'The concepts of promise and pledge underlying credit', argues Marieka de Goede, 'were seen to deliver England to the whims and fancies of its emerging financial class.'[169] These were the stockbrokers and speculators who threatened political stability. 'Of all beings that

---

[165] Levenson, *Money for Nothing*, xiv.
[166] J. G. A Pocock, 'The Mobility of Property and the Rise of Eighteenth-Century Sociology', in *Virtue, Commerce and History. Essays on Political Thought and History, Chiefly in the Eighteenth Century* (Cambridge, 1985), 112. Ian Baucom expands this insight in his investigation of marine insurance and the case of the Zong; *Specters of the Atlantic*.
[167] Carl Wennerlind, *Casualties of Credit. The English Financial Revolution, 1620–1720* (Cambridge, MA, 2011), 230.
[168] Patrick Brantlinger, *Fictions of State. Culture and Credit in Britain, 1694–1994* (Ithaca, 1996).
[169] Goede, *Virtue, Fortune and Faith*, 25.

have existence only in the minds of men', mused Davenant, 'nothing is more fantastical and nice than credit; it is never to be forced; it hangs upon opinion, it depends upon our passions of hope and fear; it comes many times unsought for, and often goes away without reason, and when once lost, is hardly to be quite recovered.'[170] His ambivalence about both trade and credit, for it brought wealth but encouraged luxury, and made way for both war and debt, was characteristic of many of the interventions in these debates. Questions about investment and speculation, the dependence on opinion, the play of hope and fear, would have been powerfully evocative for Long. His grandfather had speculated and lost in the South Sea Bubble, having relied on his favourable imaginings of the prospects of the Atlantic slave trade. His father's fortunes were blighted as a result, weighted down not only by the debts associated with the Bubble but also by the burden of annuities bequeathed to him in his father's will. Long's own life chances were shaped by that history. Paper credit, as he recognized, was 'the symbol of a thing'; it stood for gold, or enslaved people, or sugar, and was less durable than land. '[I]t symbolized and made actual', as Pocock argues, 'the power of opinion, passion and fantasy in human affairs.'[171] But it carried concrete dangers: for Long, failure and debt. His fears may have been magnified by his reading of *Gulliver's Travels* with its biting critique of colonialism and public debt, but perhaps softened by Hume's defence of the benefits of external commerce.[172]

Credit was represented as an inconstant female figure by both Defoe and Addison. Defoe defended the possibilities of wealth based on credit and commerce, provided it went along with a gentlemanly ethic, a topic dear to Long's heart. *Lady Credit*, the imaginative embodiment of paper money, money's 'younger sister', was both coy and necessary: 'If once she be dis-oblig'd,' wrote Defoe, 'she's the most difficult to be Friends again with us.'[173] Across Defoe's writing *Lady Credit* appears as both innocent lady, virtuous virgin and gentlewoman, and spoiled flirt, demanding mistress and prostitute.[174] Public discussions of the new credit structures and the South Sea Bubble centred, as Catherine Ingrassia has shown, around female 'figures of disorder'.[175] The sexualized representations of credit which circulated can be linked to the figure of the ancient goddess Fortuna, the mistress of chance and luck, a fickle and capricious mistress, a 'despotic female ruler over men's

---

[170] Cited in Pocock, *The Machiavellian Moment*, 439.
[171] Pocock, *The Machiavellian Moment*, 452.
[172] See Brantlinger, *Fictions of State*, on Swift; Hume, 'Of Commerce', in *The Philosophical Works of David Hume*, III. 287–98.
[173] Cited in Pocock, *The Machiavellian Moment*, 452–3.
[174] Goede, *Virtue, Fortune and Faith*, 31.
[175] Catherine Ingrassia, *Authorship, Commerce and Gender in Early Eighteenth Century England* (Cambridge, 1998), 24.

affairs'.[176] Yet she was essential, Defoe believed, if armies were to be raised, fleets fitted, banks established, annuities sold and, we might add, captives bought and sugar produced. *Lady Credit* had to be managed. This meant that passions of hope and fear must be moderated, restraint and self-control were essential, and excess to be deplored – just the lessons that Long had taught in *The Prater* and *The Anti-Gallican*.[177]

Long, as we have seen, had grown up with Mr Spectator. Addison's allegory of Public Credit perhaps informed his thinking. On one of his 'Rambles, or rather Speculations', Addison wrote, he had looked into the great hall of the Bank of England:

> I saw towards the upper end of the Hall, a beautiful Virgin seated on a Throne of Gold. Her Name (as they told me) was Publick Credit. The Walls, instead of being adorned with Pictures and Maps were hung with many Acts of Parliament written in Golden Letters. At the Upper end of the Hall was the Magna Charta, with the Act of Uniformity on the right Hand and the Act of Toleration on the left. At the lower end of the Hall was the Act of Settlement, which was placed full in the eye of the Virgin that sat upon the Throne. Both the sides of the Hall were covered with such Acts of Parliament as had been made for the Establishment of Publick Funds.

But the lady was very nervous, fearful of any attack, apt to collapse 'in the twinkling of an eye', despite the Acts of parliament securing liberty, the Protestant monarchy, religious toleration and the national debt. Hideous phantoms, Anarchy, Tyranny and Bigotry, appeared in the hall and the lady 'fainted and dyed away' at the sight, while the heaps of money bags that had been piled around her 'now appeared to be only Heaps of Paper'. Fortunately, this 'sudden Desolation' vanished and 'a second dance of Apparitions ... very amiable Phantoms' led by Liberty, Monarchy, Moderation in religion and 'the Genius of Great Britain' took its place. The money bags swelled and the heaps of paper changed to 'Pyramids of Guineas'.[178] *Lady Credit* was secured by the crown, parliament and British traditions of liberty. In Jamaica, as Long pointed out, private credit was also secured by land and, as he well knew but left unsaid, by the enslaved.

Addison's famous paean of praise to the Royal Exchange may also have been in the historian's mind as he discoursed on the merits of British merchants and colonial trade. 'There is no Place in the Town which I so much love to frequent as the *Royal Exchange*,' Addison had written.

---

[176] Goede, *Virtue, Fortune and Faith*, 31.
[177] See the discussion of fathers' attempts to educate sons as worthy 'men of credit' in Sarah M. S. Pearsall, *Atlantic Families. Lives and Letters in the Later Eighteenth Century* (Oxford, 2008).
[178] *The Spectator*, no. 3, 3 March 1711.

It gives me a secret Satisfaction, and in some, measure gratifies my Vanity, as I am an *Englishman*, to see such a rich an Assembly of Countrymen and Foreigners consulting together upon the private Business of Mankind, and making this Metropolis a kind of *Emporium* for the whole Earth ... I am wonderfully delighted to see such a Body of Men thriving in their own private Fortunes, and at the same time promoting the Publick Stock; or in other Words, raising Estates for their own Families, by bringing into their Country whatever is wanting, and carrying out of it whatever is superfluous.

'There are no more useful Members in a Commonwealth', he believed, 'than Merchants. They knit Mankind together in a mutual Intercourse of good Offices, distribute the Gifts of Nature, find Work for the Poor, add Wealth to the Rich, and magnificence to the Great.' Addison was celebrating the merchants, those dealing with solid commodities, West India merchants dealing in sugar and rum, 'making this Metropolis a kind of *Emporium* for the whole Earth', rather than financiers dealing in stocks and shares. His self-fashioning as a 'Citizen of the World' would not have appealed to Long, but he would have been very content with Addison's satisfaction in being 'an *Englishman*'.[179]

Lady Credit was a fickle figure: her other half was debt. Long knew full well that planters depended on credit, but it was the repayment of credit that resulted in the debt which so persecuted white West Indians, including himself. 'The cords of credit and debt', Walter Johnson writes in relation to the cotton economy, 'of advance and obligation ... cinched the Atlantic economy together.' They 'were anchored with the mutually defining values of land and slaves: without land and slaves, there was no credit, and without slaves land itself was valueless'.[180] The same was true of the sugar economy. 'Debt ... one of the most substantial evils in life', especially in a society 'where men often adventure without limits', stalked Long's *History* and haunted his imagination.[181] The problem began with the expense of establishing a plantation and the fact that 'few men ... have embarked in the planting-business with capitals sufficient and equal to the design'.[182] Long estimated JA £5,000 as the cost of setting up a modest sugar estate of 300 acres, with thirty 'Negroes' producing a hunded hogsheads of sugar a year.[183] The land had to be bought and cleared, the labour purchased – for land without labour was useless – and works built, for cane could not be processed without works. Consequently, planters carried heavy debts from the outset. It took approximately seven years for a new estate to begin to produce a profit. The credit that financed the plantations was predominantly relatively short-term, unsecured

---

[179] *The Spectator*, no. 69, 19 May 1711.
[180] Johnson, *River of Dark Dreams*, 87.
[181] Long, *History*, II. 544.
[182] Ibid., I. 391.
[183] Ibid., I. 457.

debt carried in the bills of exchange and the current accounts which the planters held with their consignees.[184] This was not speculation on the stock exchange or with public credit. But a good deal of the credit was long-term, tying planters into interest payments. Once the planter's account had reached a sum that the merchant needed to secure against the estate and enslaved people, a bond or mortgage might be agreed.[185] Two years after Long published his *History*, with his celebration of mercantile capital, Adam Smith published his *Wealth of Nations*, bemoaning the scale of the loss, as he saw it, of this capital to the colonies. In the twentieth century, Richard Pares challenged Smith, arguing that capital imports were mainly short-term credit from merchants to planters on current accounts that could run in arrears. The capital, in his view, mainly came from the planters themselves, and mortgages as security for loans were uncommon until after the 1760s, expanding post-1775.[186] Simon Smith, however, on the basis of evidence from the Lascelles, shows that mortgages were already in use from the 1740s. From the mid-eighteenth century, long-term lending on security of mortgages was increasingly important, fuelling the boom in sugar planting and suggesting that Adam Smith may well have been right about the significance of metropolitan capital.[187] This was a view that Long would have agreed with from a quite different perspective.

The Debt Recovery Act of 1732 had been a victory for creditors, allowing them to seize land and slaves, and a potential disaster for the planters. Jamaican laws, on the other hand, were on the whole sympathetic to debtors, given the understanding of the necessity for credit. In recent years, however, Long noted, the merchants had been less willing to grant long credit to colonists since they were more able to invest with equivalent returns at home. The interest rate on loans had been fixed at 5 per cent in 1752, but it was now easy for London merchants to get this interest rate domestically. In one of his many suggestions to the metropolitan government, Long proposed that the interest rate should be raised to 6 per cent so that loans to Jamaica would be more attractive.[188] He was eloquent on the bad practices of certain lawyers in Jamaica, scoundrels who took advantage of debt and managed to charge interest rates sometimes between 10 and 20 per cent, leading to the ruin of planters. Giving vent to his antisemitism (and perhaps drawing on tropes familiar from the debates in the 1750s), his example was of a loan from 'some rich Jew' who insisted on

---

[184] Price distinguishes between three different levels of credit: primary for plantation costs, secondary for mortgage payments, and tertiary for dowries and family settlements. 'Credit in the Slave Trade'.

[185] Long, *History*, I. 564.

[186] Richard Pares, *Merchants and Planters*, 4th supplement to *EconHR* (1960).

[187] S. D Smith, 'Planters and Merchants revisited', *EconHR* 55.3 (2002), 434–65; Smith, *Slavery, Family, and Gentry Capitalism*, especially chap. 6.

[188] Long, *History*, I. 555–61.

payment of interest in the courts, pretended lenity and extracted another bond, 'consolidating all the interest, and law-costs, into principal, and allowing another exorbitant premium'.[189] Creditors on the island sought speedy returns and were implacable in pressing their claims. The 'priority-act', favouring creditors and obliging moneylenders to bring actions and obtain judgments as quickly as possible, was a particular problem. It was well known that Jamaican courts were extraordinarily busy and that white colonists were exceedingly litigious. The creditors pressed as hard as they could, while the debtors practised every 'art of corruption' to avoid the attack. Meanwhile, the Provost Marshal, or High-Sheriff, the judicial representative of the crown whose office was responsible for debt seizure, comes 'like a cuttle-fish', in Long's words, a fish with eight arms and two tentacles equipped with suckers to secure its prey, 'involving every thing in confusion and obscurity, and snatches the prey from both'. This law was a disaster for the planting interest, destroying the mutual confidence which ought to combine merchant and planter, wounding the planter in his 'credit and character', as well as in his fortune, and encouraging him to engage in 'mean tricks and subterfuges', while taking the merchant away from his warehouse and books to consult lawyers and chase officials. Furthermore, Long continued, the move to the courts not only encouraged corruption amongst the officials, but fed and multiplied 'the host of pettyfoggers', the wretched lawyers, 'that generation of vermin, who are bred in knavery, and nourished by corruption; who fatten on the distresses of mankind, and, like stalking horses, delude the unwary into shipwreck, that they may strip and rifle them'. The law on real estate was seen as ineffectual,

> so the merchants were necessarily driven to secure themselves by taking bonds for their demands, which, being once fixed upon judgment, are esteemed rather more eligible than a mortgage security, because they execute equally well upon the debtor's personal estate and are not clogged with the real ... their objects therefore are the planters' slaves, cattle, implements, furniture and other goods.[190]

The creditors 'rush in a body on the planter, assault him on all sides, and every one gets a bite at him, till he is torn in pieces, or (as the common saying has it) irrevocably *gone to the dogs*'.[191]

---

[189] Ibid., I. 558.

[190] Long, *History*, I. 393. Long was pointing here to the ambiguity of the law on enslaved people as property. There was tension over their status as real property or personalty. Mortgage deeds tended to encompass the enslaved people as well as the land, often by listing those covered by the mortgage by name, because the enslaved gave the land its value rather than vice versa. Securing the land and the enslaved thus gave more protection to the creditors, and the preference among creditors for judgment debt which Long is asserting is not reflected in much of the eighteenth-century material consulted. Personal communication, Nick Draper.

[191] Long, *History*, I. 399.

The most disastrous aspect of this law, Long was convinced, was 'the seizure of Negroes for bond debts ... a measure that has brought ruin upon a great many once flourishing plantations'. It left the land bereft of value. He had seen four sugar estates dismantled and ruined in one parish in the previous few years. What was more, he opined, offering a benign picture of himself as a humane planter, it was 'the highest degree of cruelty annexed to [the] condition' of the enslaved:

> It cannot be imagined, but that they have a powerful attachment to the spot where they were born; to the place which holds the remains of their deceased friends and kindred; to the little grounds they have cultivated, and the trees they have reared with their own hands; to the peaceful cottage of their own building, where they were wont to enjoy many little domestic comforts, and participate in refreshments with their friends and families, after the toils of the day.[192]

'What severer hardships can befall these poor creatures', he asked, 'than to be suddenly dispossessed of all these comforts and enjoyments, divided from each other, sold into the power of new masters, and carried into distant parts of the country, to settle themselves anew in a situation less agreeable, and less propitious to their health.'[193] This astonishing passage – an evocation of the quiet enjoyments of plantation life, possibly to be disrupted by cruel sale forced by ravenous creditors on unwitting planters and potentially resulting in death for the 'poor creatures' as well as bankruptcy for the unfortunate debtor – is one of the very few moments in the thousands of pages of the *History* when Long appeared to reflect on the lives of the enslaved. Written in a quite different tone from his vituperative passages on the character of the African, or his abstracted calculations of numbers of 'Negroes' or 'stock', it is witness to his recognition that anti-slavery voices were mustering and would have to be answered, and to his recognition that enslaved people had emotional and domestic lives, an acknowledgement, usually disavowed, of the full humanity of 'the Negroes'. Occasionally planters and enslaved were recognized as having interests in common: both belonged to the land, each in their different ways lived on it and worked it, their lives tied, albeit totally unequally, to it. For local creditors, the debt was simply a debt that must be met, no matter how. For the metropolitan merchants, Long hoped, the more their money was tied into the island, the more they would safeguard its future: the alliance of merchants and planters in defence of the slave trade gave some credence to this view.

Rapacious local creditors – sometimes named as rich Jews, as we have seen – who drove up interest rates from 6 per cent to 16 or 20 per cent, were a problem, alongside pettifogging lawyers and corrupt officials.[194] But so too,

---

[192] Ibid., I. 398–9.
[193] Ibid., I. 399.
[194] Ibid., I. 557.

Long moralized, were self-indulgent planters. Debt was ubiquitous amongst them, but it was not seen as something shameful. Indeed, it was a 'settled maxim' on the island that 'you are not distinguished, or of any note, unless you are in debt'.[195] They were 'too much addicted to expensive living, costly entertainments, dress, and equipage'.[196] *Lady Credit* had encouraged them to indulge in luxury, always a danger. Without moderation and control of the passions, they put themselves and others at risk. They were 'fond of monopolizing large tracts of land', taking on more debt, greedy to extend their property without the wherewithal to cultivate it. They liked notions of generosity and hospitality, ending up 'harassed and unhappy', unable to pay and in danger of being reduced to being 'slaves for life', a term that Long used without reflection.[197] And debt was not confined to those with substantial property. It was a shocking sight to see the white debtors cast among the black criminals in the Spanish Town gaol, 'especially in a country where it is thought politically expedient to maintain a distinction between Whites and Negroes'. It was astonishing that 'the debtor and the criminal should be huddled together; and that White persons who have committed no other offence than that of insolvency, should be associated with the most bestial and profligate wretches of the Negroe race'.[198]

As a response to these problems, Long advocated reform of the credit law and of the laws for recovery of debt, alongside better regulation of the Provost Marshal's office. A few 'spirited regulations' could improve the credit of the colony, and since he hoped to 'merit the character of a faithful, zealous advocate for the injured, rather than that of an entertaining Historian', he would not hesitate to mention them.[199] Security of property was crucial to the availability of credit, and this meant that the defences of the island must be maintained, with regular troops stationed and necessary fortifications. New credit laws, raising the interest rate by 1 per cent, should be passed to encourage 'honest wealthy merchants in Great Britain' to choose to invest in the plantation economy. British merchants were the key, those with integrity, who would 'provide a steady support in time of need, and an humane indulgence in bad years'.[200] They would be prepared to grant long terms of credit, so that planters would not be harassed for payment: 'In *his* hands,' unlike creditors on the island who wanted payment in money, 'sugar is still deemed a good pledge of payment, and every quality of it finds vent, either by exportation to foreigners, or by the grocer, sugar baker, or distiller'. It was in the true interests of the planters 'to connect more firmly than ever with the merchants of Britain': their

---

[195] Ibid., I. 265–6.
[196] Ibid., II. 265.
[197] Ibid., II. 266.
[198] Ibid., I. 14.
[199] Ibid., I. 97.
[200] Ibid., I. 397.

attachment to the island would be strengthened in proportion to the scale of their loans and, for their own sakes, they would seek reassurance from the government of proper protection against hostilities.[201] At the same time planters should learn that a 'moderate, but disencumbered, fortune' was 'more comfortable in the enjoyment, than a vast speculative one, under the constant oppression of heavy interest, law-suits, a servile dependence, and unceasing anxiety of mind'.[202] Moderation in all things was, on occasion, one of his epithets.

Once back in England, Long sympathized with Mary Ricketts about her husband's very serious financial problems. 'Those who have never experienced,' he wrote,

> what it is to be incessantly harassed & worried by a multitude of creditors; to be driven to the wall, and forced to promise impossibilities; & then to be upbraided for breach of performance; who make no candid allowance for the million of accidents which cross the husbandry of a Jamaican planter, nor consider that the best intentioned man, may fall into mistakes, that these mistakes may lead to distress, & that men when in distress, cease to be free agents

– such people did not understand and were too apt to blame a lack of moral principles. 'For my own part,' he concluded, 'I have suffered, & I feel for him.'[203] *Lady Credit* was a necessity, but she was a mixed blessing. Debt was a curse, but it also provided some moral cover for enslavement. The responsibility really lay with the creditor, and that money would return to England.

Edward Long, I have suggested, gives us an account from a planter's perspective of how what we can now call the circuit of racial capitalism worked, and how the wealth and power of the mother country were increased. 'The Negro trade', he argued, 'was the ground-work of all', but this acknowledgement of the centrality of enslaved men, women and children went alongside his disavowal. They were essential, but disregarded. They were numbers to be counted together with other forms of stock in the computation of hogsheads of sugar produced, exports achieved and commercial activity generated. In his narrative, it was English merchants, in partnership with planters, who were the makers of wealth. His neglect of 'the things behind the things' was essential for his benign rendition of the system. Exploitation and oppression were banished, racialized relations naturalized. 'The merchants of the mother country', argued Long, were 'the true fountain-head of credit' and it was credit that drove the circuit.[204] The merchant houses like Drake and Long were at the heart of the

---

[201] Ibid., I. 537.
[202] Ibid., I. 570.
[203] Edward Long to William Ricketts, 17 September 1772, Ricketts Family Papers.
[204] Long, *History*, I. 395.

business. The slave trade was regrettable but necessary; only Africans could provide the labour for the plantations, but once they reached Jamaica there was a hope that these barbaric people could be somewhat civilized. Long dreamed of achieving a more settled form of slavery in the future. The settlement of a substantial part of his debts enabled his return to England. Like the rest of his extended family, he believed it was the place to be.

5

Reproducing Capital: the Long Family

Both the plantation and the merchant house were central to the functioning of racial capitalism, and both planters and merchants knew that maintaining the supply of enslaved labour was critical to this. But if families such as the Longs were to survive and increase their wealth, they had to reproduce themselves too and ensure the continuity of their line. When thinking about the present and future of Jamaica, Edward Long was concerned, as we have seen, with the failure of enslaved women to reproduce, for it threatened the functioning of plantation slavery. At the same time, he was anxious to increase the numbers of white settlers, seeing an improvement in the balance of the island's population as a necessary aspect of security. But what about the reproduction of his own family and of their freedom? How could wealth be accumulated? How would it be possible to avoid mortality on this island of death? What patterns of life were right for them? What were his responsibilities to his dependants? How might he ensure a prosperous future for his children?

Moving from a consideration of the workings of the plantation and the merchant house to a focus on the family property of white owners and slave-holders requires analysis of very different kinds of evidence. Long's *History* did not address directly his stewardship of his inheritance and that of his children, but it was just as important to him as his stewardship of Lucky Valley. 'Capital comes dripping from head to foot, from every pore, with blood and dirt,' wrote Marx.[1] The blood was not only the blood shed by workers, free or unfree: blood ties between white men and women were critical to the forging of colonial slavery and to the formation of planter and mercantile capital.[2] As Long might have written, we are now leaving one sphere of the economy to enter another: the family economy of a new kind of capitalist, with interests in the ownership of land, commerce and people. The plantation, the merchant house and the propertied white family constituted together the lineaments of eighteenth-century racial capitalism.

---

[1] Marx, *Capital*, I. 759–60.
[2] For an earlier formulation of some of these arguments, see Catherine Hall, 'Gendering Property, Racing Capital', in J. H. Arnold, M. Hilton and J. Ruger (eds.), *History after Hobsbawm. Writing the Past for the Twenty-First Century* (Oxford, 2018), 17–34.

Conceptions of racialized difference depended on drawing lines between those who belonged to the white, pure-blood family and were legitimate and those outside it, whether free or enslaved. The Long family was financed over generations by the labour of enslaved men, women and children on the plantations that they owned in Jamaica and by the West India trade. They derived the majority of their wealth from the slavery business, living off the labour of others. But they also constituted that wealth themselves through their practices of marriage and inheritance. Marriage was for 'the genuine English breed': children must be born within wedlock and legitimate progeny clearly distinguished from illegitimate.[3] Marrying money was highly desirable, and for the most part the men in the eighteenth century married women from the wider West Indian families whose property also came from the slavery business. Two of Edward Long's sons became English landed gentlemen on the basis of 'good' marriages of this kind. His daughters married into other slave-owning families or into the gentry or minor aristocracy of Britain. By the late eighteenth century, both men and women of the family aspired to be absorbed into the wider 'English' landed classes. White families were structured through hierarchies of gender and gentility as well as race.

Colonists travelled with established ideas about the place of men and women, of men's patriarchal power as property owners and heads of households and women's subordination.[4] Enslaved women, as we have seen, were valued both for their 'increase' and for their labour: the enslaveability of the 'increase' marked the boundary with white women, whose babies were not enslaveable.[5] White women, members of slave-owning and mercantile families, were also valued for their 'increase', though such a term would never be used for them. Without heirs, how could white freedom be perpetuated? White women were 'reproducers of freedom'.[6] They carried freedom in their white bodies and their blood; their dependent status secured their capacity to serve as the counterpart both to the productive and reproductive capacities of the enslaved woman and to the more brutal figure of the white male colonist.[7] White women also brought new property into a family, through marriage and/or inheritance. The gendered organization of property relations was crucial to the maintenance of the white family and its potential for capital accumulation and dynastic survival.[8] The counterpoint to this was the denial of family life, as

---

[3] The term is Edward Long's, *History*, II. 274.
[4] Amussen, *Caribbean Exchanges*.
[5] Morgan, *Laboring Women*.
[6] Cecily Jones, *Engendering Whiteness. White Women and Colonialism in Barbados and North Carolina, 1627–1865* (Manchester, 2007), 21.
[7] Gyatri Chakraborty Spivak, 'Three Women's Texts and a Critique of Imperialism', *Critical Inquiry* 12.1 (1985), 247–72. See Spivak's brilliant analysis of *Jane Eyre*.
[8] Paton, 'Gender History, Global History' notes that the gendered practices ensured that profits stayed with white people.

the colonists understood it, to the enslaved. The lives of the slave-owners' families were built on shattered generations of enslaved men and women: it was the violence of social death that produced in slave societies this particular iteration of the white reproductive woman.[9] 'White family legacies were produced over time', as Walter Johnson puts it, 'out of the broken pieces of slave families and communities divided by sale and estate settlement.'[10]

In this chapter I explore the propertied and marital relationships of this transatlantic family, the Longs, and the emotional economy, in so far as it is possible, of Edward Long. The gendered organization of property was rooted in beliefs and practices of what constituted 'proper' white family relations. Edward Long recorded his opinions on marriage and parenthood; unfortunately, only fragments of those of the women of his family have survived.

Gendering Property

I argue that the family's survival over six generations and beyond owed much to their strategic marriages and patterns of inheritance. (See Figure 1, the Long family tree.) Samuel Long (1638–83), Edward Long's great-grandfather, was one founding figure of the dynasty (here dubbed Samuel I; I use Roman numerals to distinguish individuals called Samuel, Charles and Beeston in subsequent generations and different branches of the family). William Beeston (1636–1702) was the other. The son of Samuel I and his wife, Elizabeth Streete (d.1710), was Charles I (1679–1723). William Beeston and his wife, Anne Hopegood, had a daughter, Jane (1674–1724), who became Charles I's second wife. Three distinct branches of the Long family grew from Charles I's two marriages: the Jamaican branch, the mercantile branch and the landed branch. Together they constituted the wider family. Charles I's first wife was Amy Lawes (1681–1702), the daughter of Sir Nicholas Lawes, a governor of Jamaica. She died in 1702 having birthed a son, Samuel II (1700–57). Charles I's second wife, Jane Beeston, was William Beeston's only child, who was widowed when her first husband, Sir Thomas Modyford, died. Charles I and Jane had two sons, Charles II (1705–78) and Beeston I (1710–85), among other children. Samuel II, the child of the first marriage, inherited the plantations of Longville and Lucky Valley. He and his descendants constituted *the Jamaican branch*. (See Figure 5.1.) Samuel II's half-brother Charles II inherited from the second marriage. His mother had brought extensive property that was protected from her husband's debts in the wake of the South Sea Bubble. Charles II and his children became part of the landed gentry, with property in Jamaica and England: they are *the landed branch*. Beeston, his

---

[9] Elizabeth Maddock Dillon, 'Zombie Biopolitics', *American Quarterly* 71.3 (2019), 625–52. Thanks to Jennifer Morgan for this reference.
[10] Johnson, 'Time and Revolution', 206.

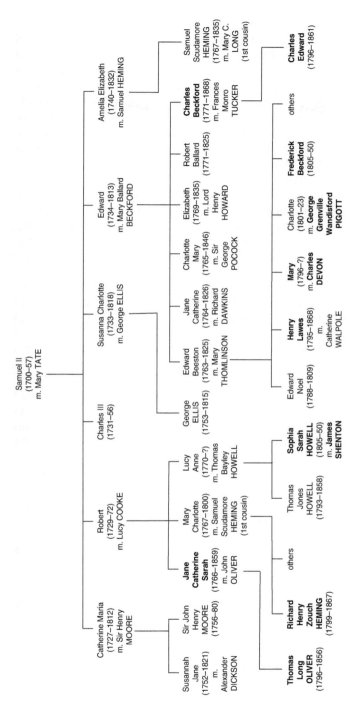

Figure 5.1 Details from the Long family tree illustrating the Jamaica branch. Designed by and courtesy of Rachel Lang.

younger brother, took up his grandfather's mercantile interests and founded the West India house of Drake and Long. His subsequent prosperity enabled his oldest son, Samuel III (1746–1807), to become a landed gentleman in England, while the second son, Beeston II (1757–1820), took on the family business. They are *the mercantile branch*. The three branches of the family remained close. The Jamaican branch and the mercantile branch were economically interdependent as we have seen. All members of this extended family, to a greater or lesser extent, relied on the slavery business in its different manifestations for their livelihoods. The Beeston Longs were mainly focused on mercantile enterprises, but there was overlap in the extended family's ownership of and dependence on slave estates. They provide a striking example of the ways in which wealth based on slavery accumulated and was transmitted to the metropole.[11] Given the prevalence of death in Jamaica, alongside the ubiquity of debt, it was relatively unusual even for elite families to survive over such a long period.[12] The Longs were also unusual in that there is no evidence of 'outside' families or 'reputed' children educated or recognized in adulthood, no evidence of relationships with enslaved women, and only one example of an illegitimate child: Robert's daughter, Henrietta Maria, born to a women of colour in 1759.[13] Nobody in this family, except possibly Samuel Long and William Beeston who died there, ever intended that they would live their lives on the island. Each generation of planters hoped that the profits generated by their enslaved workers would be sufficient to support a life in England.

Following the family across generations allows us to see how sugar and slavery were a family business. 'The empire was a family enterprise,' as Emma Rothschild writes about the extended family of the Johnstones who lived and worked across Scotland, the East Indies and colonial America in the eighteenth

---

[11] Patterson, *Sociology of Slavery*, 35–6, notes in his analysis of 'Abstract of Wills Relating to Jamaica, 1695–1792', BL Add MS 34181, the extent to which wealth made on the plantations returned to Britain.

[12] Pares quotes John Pinney warning his son that few West Indian fortunes reached beyond a third generation; *A West India Fortune*, 141. Trevor Burnard (in 'A Failed Settler Society: Marriage and Demographic Failure in Early Jamaica', *Journal of Social History* 28.1 [1994], 63–82) notes that in the early colonial period very few white marriages survived long enough to establish viable families. But there were other slave-owning families of comparable lifespan to the Longs – both the famous, like the Beckfords, the Dawkins and the Hibberts, and the more obscure, like the Vassalls, the Morants and the Fosters.

[13] Robert Long's child with 'Ann Clark, a mulatto' was baptized Henrietta Maria Long, in Clarendon on 21 June 1759. It is unclear whether Ann was free. Parish of Clarendon, Copy Register, 1667–1837, Baptisms, Burials, Marriages f. 126. I owe this reference to Shyllon, *Edward Long's Libel of Africa*, 55.

century.[14] The Long family was a business with its roots in Jamaica. For four generations key members lived on the island and directly managed plantations. But the business was to make money from the plantations and the West India trade in the hope of supporting a genteel lifestyle in the metropole. By the time of the fifth and sixth generations, they were settled in the metropole, though living off slavery, including the compensation payments. On the surface they were fully integrated into the domestic economy and culture. What had begun with the two colonists, Samuel Long and William Beeston, constituted by the time of emancipation three family lines of approximately fifty people. (See Figure 5.2.)

What did it mean to be a transatlantic family? The connections between the two islands were close and many members of the family travelled the Atlantic as documented here. The reason to go to Jamaica was always to make money; returning to the mother country meant spending it. The only spoils for West Indians were people and money; there were none of the silks and cashmere stoles, the tiger skins and elephant tusks with which East Indians could decorate their homes and their relatives.[15] Samuel Long was the first to cross

Figure 5.2 The Long family's compensation awards as detailed on the Legacies of British Slave-ownership database. Courtesy of the Centre for the Legacies of British Slavery.

---

[14] Rothschild, *The Inner Life of Empires*, 172. For the wider Atlantic context, see Pearsall, *Atlantic Families*.
[15] Margot Finn and Kate Smith (eds.), *The East India Company at Home, 1757–1857* (London, 2018).

the ocean, arriving in Jamaica in 1655 and dying there in 1683. He married Elizabeth Streete on the island and returned to England once, in 1680. William Beeston arrived in 1660, spent a year in England in 1680 and several years at the end of that decade, before returning in 1692 to Jamaica where he died in 1699. Samuel and Elizabeth's son, Charles I, and William and Anne's daughter Jane were both born on the island, but after their marriage they travelled in 1706 to England where they settled. Charles I's first child with Amy Lawes, Samuel II, was born on the island. He returned there in the wake of his father's death, together with his English wife, Mary Tate (d.1765), hoping to restore order to the family property in the face of parental debts. Their son Robert (1729–72) was born on the island, but the rest of their children were born in England where they lived in the 1730s and early 1740s. (Both Elizabeth and Mary lost their first-born in infancy.) Samuel II returned to Jamaica in 1746 with son Robert and was later joined by his two older daughters, Catherine (1727–1812) and Susanna Charlotte (1733–1818), his second son Charles III (1731–56), and briefly by his wife, Mary. The two daughters married into West Indian elite families but later returned to England. Charles III died on the island in 1756 and his father in 1757. The following year Edward, the third son arrived, married a white creole, Mary Ballard Beckford (1736–97) and they lived there together until they settled in England in 1769. Edward's older brother Robert returned to England in 1763, leaving his illegitimate daughter, Henrietta Maria – who carried his name but of whom nothing more is known – and married an English woman. Edward and Mary's son Edward Beeston (1763–1825) and two of their daughters were born in Jamaica but never returned after they moved with their parents to England. Four men of the family died in Jamaica – Samuel I, William Beeston, Samuel II and Charles II – along with two of the women, Elizabeth Streete and Amy Lawes. For Edward Long the presence of a substantial white population was central to the future and prosperity of a Jamaica built on slavery. But he never intended to settle there for life himself. His primary object, as with many colonists, was, avowedly, 'that of making money'.[16] Being transatlantic, crossing the Atlantic, taking on the identity of both West Indian and Englishman, belonging fully to neither place, was the price of being this kind of colonizer. The contemporary celebration of diasporic identities marks a very different moment in the postcolonial world.

Capitalists, whether slave-owning, mercantile or landed, hoped that they and their families could survive and flourish over time. Although the nature of their property and their methods of preserving and transmitting it differed, all elite slave-owners adopted and adapted the testatory modes and practices of English landed property owners. It was a priority for a family such as the Longs, a 'lineage-family' as Naomi Tadmor names them, to reproduce

[16] Long, *History*, I. 6.

themselves.[17] Eighteenth-century Britons were familiar with such families, with their strong sense of ancestry, pedigree and lineage descent. Their family names, reproduced over generations, their focus on property and marriage, their notions of historical time linked to their own families, the royal family and the nation, all marked their sense of themselves. Many colonists in Jamaica, much to Edward Long's dismay, had no such commitment to family. For the Longs and similar elite families, legitimate biological reproduction, an issue in itself given mortality rates, was essential if property was to stay within the bloodline. So too was the reproduction of the social relations of production: the establishment and sustenance of a household, the education of children, provision for dependants, hopes, indeed, of the accumulation of wealth. Their gendered practices, their assumptions as to the proper hierarchies of men and women, whether white or black, were as important to the merchant and planter capitalists in their own families as they were to their management of enslaved or labouring populations. The fears as to the failure of enslaved women to reproduce became an increasingly pressing issue given the rising price of captives and threats to the slave trade. The slave-owners' denial of the mother–child bond and wider kin relationships to enslaved people, together with their control of both bodily and social reproductive practices on the plantations, were key axes of slave-holding power. For a young boy or girl to inherit enslaved property was a way of learning the distinctive nature of their white identities. But for that power to be maintained, their own families had to survive over time.

Historians have long argued for the importance of gender in creating and transmitting capital in early modern England. A major route for that capital came through marriage and inheritance: women were productive and reproductive labourers, from the bearing and rearing of children to working directly in family enterprises, organizing the household, bringing contacts, and acting as status bearers, so critical to the maintenance of trust.[18] Women brought property into marriages and the most important component of wealth was inheritance.[19] 'Gender in this aspect of capitalism', as Amy Erickson writes, 'is evident not in work patterns but in property law ... the gender specific structure of English property law was at least part of the reason why England was early to develop a capitalist economy and also why the cash economy, the debt–credit markets, and public investment apparently spread so completely throughout the society'.[20] The peculiarities of English marriage law, she

---

[17] Naomi Tadmor, *Family and Friends in Eighteenth-Century England. Household, Kinship and Patronage* (Cambridge, 2001), 73–102.
[18] Leonore Davidoff and Catherine Hall, *Family Fortunes. Men and Women of the English Middle Class, 1780–1850* [1987] 3rd edn (London, 2018).
[19] Amy Louise Erickson, *Women and Property in Early Modern England* (London, 1993).
[20] Amy Louise Erickson, 'Coverture and Capitalism', *HWJ* 59 (2005), 1–16. Familial capitalism, argues Richard Grassby, was the motor of economic growth. Grassby, *Kinship and*

suggests, combined strict coverture for married women with the legal independence of single women and widows, enabling them to be economically active in the market. In English law, which the colonists adopted and adapted, coverture meant that a married woman could not make contracts in her own name, or make a will, or sue or be sued without her husband, and she forfeited control over her dowry and all personal property. The basis of coverture, as Erickson explains, 'was ostensibly an economic exchange. The bride's portion was exchanged for her maintenance during marriage, for the groom's responsibility for her contracts (since without property she could not contract) and for a guarantee of subsistence in her widowhood, in the form of dower or jointure.'[21] At her husband's death she was entitled to dower of one-third of his real property for life, one-third of the personal property outright. Families were concerned to protect their daughters and familial wealth from spendthrift or greedy husbands. They also hoped to stop husbands controlling the wife's property after her death. During the seventeenth and eighteenth centuries, marriage settlements establishing trusts for the benefit of wives after marriage or preventing the disposal of their property were utilized by elite families. Married women could not make wills, but marriage settlements could circumscribe this prohibition. Nevertheless, as Susan Staves notes, deep patriarchal structures continued to determine that 'women functioned to transmit wealth from one generation to another'.[22] The women of the Long family did indeed transmit wealth in this way.

The Longs were a transatlantic family but with strong English roots. Their inheritance practices were English but inflected through their ownership of plantations: slave-owners left human property – enslaved persons – to their descendants. Slave property was protean: enslaved people were treated as real estate in some legal contexts and as personalty, 'chattels', in others, as we have seen. They were not 'dowerable'. Since Jamaica's foundational myth, as Michael Craton describes it, was that free-born Englishmen were occupying extensions of sovereign territory, this had licensed them to implant English laws and institutions, including forms of land grant and tenure and laws of marriage and inheritance, such as the use of strict settlement. This was a 'form

---

Capitalism. Marriage, Family and Business in the English Speaking World, 1580–1740 (Cambridge, 2001).

[21] Erickson, *Women and Property*, 100. Dower was gradually replaced as marriage settlements were used to provide for the woman during coverture and her widowhood. The provision for a widow in a marriage settlement in lieu of dower was called jointure.

[22] Susan Staves, *Married Women's Property in England* (Cambridge, MA, 1990), 5. At the same time significant numbers of single women were able to engage in financial markets and it is clear that women continued to be economically active at all levels of the economy. Alexandra Shepard's research demonstrates the importance of women's initiatives to early modern growth; 'Crediting Women in the Early Modern English Economy', *HWJ* 79 (2015), 1–24.

of legal arrangement which made it possible to tie up the succession of a specific landed estate for a generation ahead', as John Habakkuk defined it, 'by ensuring that the apparent owner at any given time was only a tenant for life with very limited powers'. The landowner was seen as a temporary custodian of the family estate for his descendants, and his aim was to transmit property from one generation to another whilst ensuring provision for family members. 'Land', as Habakkuk explains, 'was the appropriate asset for the expression of dynastic ambition.' It was held as a trust, not simply another form of property, for as Dr Johnson put it, 'influence must ever be in proportion to property'.[23] Settlement was intended to ensure that each owner would never be more than a life tenant. The eldest son would be made a life tenant on the death of his father, and on his death *his* eldest son would be named as tenant in tail. The settlement would also empower the life tenants to charge the estate with a jointure (replacing a dowry), an annual income for a wife, if she survived her husband, and with provision for younger sons and daughters. These were the inheritance practices of the landed. Mercantile property was treated quite differently since it did not derive primarily from inheritance and its main form was personalty – goods, money and paper assets. Few merchants made settlements since their primary interest was not in creating a dynasty and they were more likely to practise partible inheritance, dividing their assets between all their children. They sometimes made use of trusts but personalty could not be tied up across generations. Since one division of the mercantile branch of the Long family became landed, their inheritance practices crossed these categories.

In colonial Jamaica, family law 'was pervaded by the interests of propertied men', as Lucille Mathurin Mair describes it.[24] Their positions as planters, however, made for inheritance practices that were in some respects specific to the slave society they had created. The fact that property included people and the peculiar nature of the 'property in people' that gave value to their land holdings forced adaptation of English norms. Plantations in the Long family, for example, were held at points in moieties, or half-shares, by two (male) relatives, an outcome rarely if ever seen in landed estates in England. The focus of many of what became the elite planter families of the island was on land, the dynastic ambitions that went with it and that were important to the preservation and extension of their powers. This meant that primogeniture and marital choices were of vital importance as tools. Women transmitted property, men dominated property ownership.

---

[23] John Habakkuk, *Marriage, Debt and the Estates System. English Landownership, 1650–1950* (Oxford, 1994), 1, 5. The following description draws heavily on Habakkuk's account. Dr Johnson's citation, 73.

[24] Mair, *A Historical Study*, 149.

For the elite planters the aim was to establish a dynasty, to secure the interests of kin across generations and to become landed gentry. 'Dynastic considerations', as Gauci writes in relation to the Beckford family, 'lay at the heart of the strategies of successful transatlantic figures.'[25] The gendering of property in a patriarchal order was a vital aspect of the reproduction of the relations of eighteenth-century Atlantic racial capitalism. Marital and inheritance practices facilitated the transmission of capital across white women's bodies. The economic dependence of the wives and daughters of planters and merchants enabled the persistence of male power. Race operated as a material reality. White family strategies were focused on bringing new assets in through marriage and protecting property in so far as was possible through settlements and inheritance practices. The legal documents utilized, the entails, settlements, wills and trusts, were designed to perpetuate wealth and status across generations, delineate family responsibilities and affective ties, and codify and enshrine hierarchies of power, those of gender, class and race. Family connections were vital to marriage partnerships: women brought land, capital, both human and otherwise, and networks, along with their own labour and their vital reproductive functions, particularly their capacity to bear sons who could inherit estates intact. Men's power was potentially increased by marriage. The operation of coverture limited women's independence whilst giving men unfettered control over resources. At the husband's death, the widow was reliant on provisions in his will subject to the marriage settlements and trusts used on occasion to limit damage to the wife's interest.[26] Primogeniture was practised in order to preserve estates, and land was frequently entailed across two generations, with the second generation renewing the entail, limiting the heir's freedom to sell.[27] Daughters inherited land when there was no male heir, and Caribbean heiresses were objects of great interest in the English marriage market. Widows and younger children were provided for, with charges on the estates or through funds invested. In the eighteenth century, slave-owners (in common with English landowners) increasingly sought to replace dower with annuities to their widows. Dower, or the 'custom of the City', survived longer in mercantile wills, with a further third to the eldest son and the rest divided among the younger siblings; but even merchants generally left their real estate, whether a country estate outside London or an estate in Jamaica and the enslaved people attached to it, to their eldest, or on rare occasions, most favoured son.

---

[25] Gauci, *William Beckford*, 31.
[26] R. J. Morris notes this in England; *Men, Women and Property* in *England, 1780–1870* (Cambridge, 2005), 263. Maxine Berg demonstrated trusts were primarily to ensure that property remained in the woman's family; 'Women's Property and the Industrial Revolution', *Journal of Interdisciplinary History* 24.2 (1993), 240–1, 249.
[27] Nicholas Draper notes that primogeniture was rarely free from entail; *The Price of Emancipation*, 182.

The eldest son succeeded to all real property if the parent had died intestate. Trustees were almost invariably men. A wife was occasionally made an executor or guardian during the minority of children. Sons usually gained control of their property at twenty-one, while daughters received it at the time of a marriage settlement or at twenty-one if still unmarried. The settlements were designed by fathers to protect the interests of their daughters, by husbands to ensure the inalienability of the familial inheritance. Property was to remain within the extended family: cousin marriages were a favoured tool.[28] This was a system which supported plantations and the monopolization of land in Jamaica and facilitated investment in landownership in England. There is no evidence from the Long family wills of any substantial sum ever going to anyone outside the extended kin.[29] Some absentees were quite willing to acknowledge illegitimate children, as were William Beckford and Bryan Edwards.[30] It is impossible to know whether the silence as to 'reputed' children in the case of the Longs is the result of denial.[31]

'Will making', as Trevor Burnard puts it in his study of Jamaican wills, 'was summing up, a final opportunity for an individual to come to terms with family, kin and friends, a chance to pass on accumulated assets, and an occasion to influence the conduct and fortunes of coming generations.'[32] Resident slave-holders in Jamaica, both men and women, had different preoccupations from elite families such as the Longs: they left property to wives, daughters and illegitimate children. Christine Walker found that in nearly half the 330 male wills she studied, the testators left their wives all their real and personal estate. More than 80 per cent of them named their wife as executor. 'Husbands defined property as a family resource rather than a masculine prerogative.'[33] They did not follow primogeniture and preferred island-born daughters to male kin overseas. There were significant numbers of single white

---

[28] On cousin marriage in England, see Davidoff and Hall, *Family Fortunes*; Leonore Davidoff, *Thicker than Water. Siblings and their Relations, 1780–1920* (Oxford, 2012); Adam Kuper, *Incest and Influence. The Private Life of Bourgeois England* (Cambridge, MA, 2009).

[29] The only exception is two legacies left to Charles Lee of Kingston by Charles IV and his brother Dudley. It is unclear who Charles Lee was. I am deeply grateful for the research assistance that Chris Jeppesen gave me on Jamaican wills.

[30] Gauci, *William Beckford*; Chris Jeppesen's unpublished research indicates that Edwards almost certainly fathered three children with Charlotte Fox. Edwards's legacies were used to invest in the ownership of slaves and appear in the LBS database. The case reveals the need to explore the silences and inferences in wills and supplement this research with wider archival work. It helps to show how the combination of race, legitimacy and empire knitted together to create a culture of secrecy and how these secrets could be negotiated in wills.

[31] It is possible that further research may reveal new evidence.

[32] Burnard, 'Family Continuity and Female Independence in Jamaica, 1655–1734', *Continuity and Change* 7.2 (1992), 181.

[33] Christine Walker, *Jamaica Ladies. Female Slaveholders and the Creation of Britain's Atlantic Empire* (Chapel Hill, NC, 2020), 189.

women who preferred long-term relationships out of wedlock and were able to hold substantial property, particularly in enslaved people. Their sexual virtue, Walker suggests, was not seen as significant, with no penalty for illegitimacy as in England and no conception of a domestic sphere.[34] This was a part of what disturbed Long so much: his vision of a 'proper' Jamaica had no place for these irregularities amongst those he would have seen as the 'lower order whites'.[35] There is no surviving evidence as to what he thought about Robert's child, Henrietta Maria Long, who was given family names but then, it seems, conveniently forgotten. He must have known of her since he was already in Jamaica when she was born. Resident slave-holders had few problems in recognizing their mixed-race children and 'housekeepers'. In Christer Petley's sample of twenty-four wills probated in Jamaica, almost 50 per cent left legacies to illegitimate mixed-race children or women of colour.[36] This was a very different pattern from that of elite families: property was certainly defined as a family resource, but framed by patriarchal power.

In societies organized on the basis of private property, 'arrangements for its transmission over time are of central importance in reproducing the social and economic order'.[37] Wills provide invaluable evidence but are also limited. As official legal documents they follow established patterns. They are produced at a particular moment, often close to death, and give a snapshot of a person's wealth and how the testator wishes it to be distributed. Codicils sometimes give indications of changes that have occurred in financial affairs. Wills do not necessarily cover wealth transfer that has happened prior to the will, as, for example, in a daughter's marriage settlement or sums that have been invested in purchasing a commission for a son. The re-visiting of marriage settlements in many of the wills of the Long family is very valuable, as the original documentation has not survived. We cannot know what has been excluded: the absence of 'reputed' children does not mean that they did not exist. Debts are not documented and these can only be estimated when an indenture exists which dealt with personalty. Mortgages do not get recorded. Despite these limitations, the wills of the Long family reveal much about their familial strategies in pursuit of survival and accumulation.

---

[34] Ibid., 215.
[35] Long, *History*, II. 287.
[36] Petley, '"Legitimacy" and Social Boundaries: Free People of Colour and the Social Order in Jamaican Slave Society', *Social History* 30.4 (2005), 481–98.
[37] Janet Finch, Lynn Hayes, Jennifer Mason and Lorraine Wallis, *Wills, Inheritance and Families* (Oxford, 1996), 3–4. In *Family Fortunes* Leonore Davidoff and I explored the use of wills by the Birmingham and East Anglian middle classes in the late eighteenth and early nineteenth century. On nineteenth-century England, see also Morris, *Men, Women and Property*.

Edward Long on Marriage and Family

Family strategies on property were underpinned by beliefs about the proper relations between the sexes, lived in the everyday emotional practices of husbands and wives, parents and children. The structures of ownership provided the framework for the lived relations, though there could be tensions, associated, for example, with changing attitudes to arranged marriages. The authority of the husband and father and the economic dependence of the mother, alongside her central role as the bearer of children and organizer of the household, were core values. Protecting property was a way of sustaining them across generations. We have almost no access to Mary Tate's desires or experiences. Edward Long, however, was eloquent on these matters. He was proud of his ancestral bloodline, particularly his great-grandfather's role as a founding father of the colony. The history of his family and the history of Jamaica were intimately connected in his mind, for the History of the island – History with a capital H – began, in his rendition, with the conquest. History meant England and the founding of a colony which he hoped would become a little (tropical) England. Family was for him the building block of society; family networks were vital to survival and success. Dynastic ambitions, always tied to the purity of blood, were to be tended across generations. Well-governed individuals in properly regulated families would secure the colony. The Long family must play their part.

Concerns about the declining numbers of the white population were endemic. If colonial Jamaica was to flourish, its white population must grow, and anxieties as to the imbalance between the numbers of enslaved Africans and free whites surfaced as early as 1702. This was addressed in the Deficiency laws which attempted to regulate the numbers of white residents on each plantation. But young male emigrants did not solve the problem, even if they could be encouraged to come. If the white population was to reproduce itself and grow, legitimate marriages were crucial. 'In all civilised states', Long opined, 'the ceremonies that accompany the union of a man with a woman, which fix and regulate the ties of marriage, and the state of children' were central.[38] It was the marriage alliance between the families of Long and Beeston that had set in motion the building of an intergenerational extended family. Subsequent marriages did much to consolidate their wealth and power. 'A new creole oligarchy could', wrote Mair, 'by its judicious matrimonial policies consolidate its claims to power.'[39]

Once his parents had gone to Jamaica, Uncle Beeston and his household were important to Long. As a young man in the 1750s living an extremely modest bachelor life in London, he had celebrated marriage and domesticity in

---

[38] Long, *History*, II. 491 fn.
[39] Mair, *A Historical Study*, 12; Higman, *Montpelier, Jamaica*. Marriage and inheritance were critical to the establishment of the Ellis family.

his writings.[40] The Worthy family, whose doings he described in *The Prater*, his castigation of marriage for money and stress on the importance of the right choice of partner in matrimony, and his critique of excessive patriarchal authority in domestic settings all spoke to the language of sentiment. The capacity for affection, it was believed, was a mark of civilization, one of the boundaries that separated the 'barbarians' from the 'civilized'. Long seems to have been marked by his experience of his parents' marital breakdown and the unhappiness of his mother, condemned by her husband, Samuel, not only to a lonely and relatively indigent life, but also to the brutal separation from her daughters which had been imposed on her. His enthusiasm for family and marriage, his own care and attention to his children and his close relations and support for his sisters all speak to his determination that they should not suffer the despair and depression he had undergone when left alone in Cornwall as an adolescent. Family networks must care for all – a pattern grossly at odds with the practices of the plantation.

His connections with his own father had been limited. Away at school as a young boy, the short period of family life at Tredudwel was vividly remembered. A 'trifling incident' that he recounted in his autobiographical fragment, 'to illustrate the noble disinterestedness of his [father's] nature', was remembered as an instance of paternal kindness. As young boys, he and his brother had fallen out of their boat into a pond and returned home filthy and soaked, expecting to face their father's anger, only to find him treating it as a joke.[41] Fatherly attention, however, seems to have been in short supply apart from this brief period in Cornwall: it was his mother Edward talked with. An improving letter when Edward was seventeen and about to go to London told him that, 'Your Uncle Beeston'

> gives me great hopes that you will answer my expectations in taking the advantage you now have in cultivating and improving your mind with usefull Knowledge to enable you to go through the world with credit and reputation, in whatever station of life it may be your lot to be placed ... You must be well acquainted with the arts and sciences and endeavour to gain a thorough knowledge of men and things and learn how to render yourself usefull to the Community and agreeably to all companys in which you may endeavour to attain the Character of a gentleman.

The letter concluded with hopes that Edward would deserve to be 'placed high in the esteem' of his affectionate father and his relations.[42] Long was never to

---

[40] As a trainee lawyer he may have been aware of the debates that were going on amongst attorneys in the 1750s over the sexual rights of men over their wives. Lisa Cody, 'Coverture and Consent in Eighteenth-Century English Marriage', seminar paper, Institute of Historical Research, London, 28 November 2020.
[41] Howard, *Records and Letters*, I. 85.
[42] Ibid., I. 125.

see his father again, and it was his father's untimely death and the meagre (in the terms of his family) inheritance left to him which led to his immediate decision for Jamaica. His father clearly exercised his authority even over adult sons. The story of his anger and rejection of Charles III on the grounds of his disobedience in following parental political instructions may have had an impact on Edward's own care and concern for his sons and daughters throughout his life. Care, however, was for his blood family. It was split off in his mind from his exploitation of the enslaved men, women and children on his properties. He maintained the traditions of his ancestors and was in turn followed by his descendants in exercising care in the preservation and extension of family property, making choices and utilizing strategies adopted over generations. 'Every good Citizen', he maintained, must 'prove himself worthy of the Inheritance which he was born to enjoy', and 'He and his Right of Property, are ever inseparable'.[43] The naming patterns that the family chose were a way of resurrecting the dead and asserting the connection to the living, an indication of a belonging within a family. Their family names placed them in history in a way that was impossible for those they claimed as their property. Established names – Samuel, Elizabeth, Charles, Jane – were constantly reiterated, but combined with the inclusion of new names – Ballard, Lawes, North – marking new marital alliances. These naming practices could span a century or more, a statement of the historicity of the family: Henry Lawes Long died in 1868, more than 150 years after the death of Amy Lawes and more than 200 years after the birth of her father, Sir Nicholas Lawes. The repetitions were a kind of branding, a statement of belonging of a very different kind to the branding they inflicted on the enslaved with their initials, SL, RL, EL.

Long wished that more white men in Jamaica shared his vision of the family. Their reluctance to marry and preference for unregulated relationships with women whom he saw as their racialized and class inferiors seriously troubled him. Perhaps the spectre of Henrietta Maria, Robert's child, haunted him. He quoted 'the inimitable Montesquieu' on the horrors of seeing white and mixed-race children all together. 'Slavery should be calculated for utility, not for pleasure,' he had written. 'The laws of chastity arise *from nature*, and *ought in all nations to be respected*.'[44] In England, opined Long, 'the institution of marriage is regarded as one of the main links of society, because it is found to be the best support of it.' It was understood that 'a promiscuous intercourse and an uncertain parentage, if they were universal, would soon dissolve the frame of the constitution, from the infinity of claims and contested rights of succession: for this reason, the begetting an illegitimate child is reputed a violation of the social compacts, and the transgressors are punishable with

---

[43] BL Add MS 12402, Appendix to Bk 1, chap. X, 79.
[44] Long, *History*, II. 330 fn.

corporal correction.'[45] In the colony this was regrettably not the case. It was the duty of 'every good citizen', he believed, to raise 'in honourable wedlock a race of unadulterated beings'.[46] Illegitimacy had no place in his moral schema. Unfortunately, there were no such prohibitions in Jamaica, and young white women, he opined, shared some of the blame with promiscuous women of colour. If white creoles were to become 'more desirable partners in marriage', more fit 'to be the companions of sensible men', able to convince men to commit themselves, then a better system of education was essential. Only then would the island become 'more populous', with the right kinds of people.[47] He very much hoped that the colony was entering a state of reformation: it used to be the case that 'the name of a *family man* was held in the utmost derision'. Fortunately, intemperance, duelling and gambling were in decline, and the increasing connection between the sexes, including polite conversation, had promoted, he hoped, 'temperance, urbanity, and concord'.[48]

The Sentimental Exhibition was a volume that Long published the same year as the *History*. It was intended as entertaining and polite moralizing on society, an elaboration on the discourse of sentiment that he had adopted years before. The text was marked by his sojourn in Jamaica and his recognition of the power of passion, alongside his dismay at the conduct of many white creole men. He moralized on men's fear of marriage, their concerns about the expense of a legitimate establishment, and desire for the sexual freedoms that could be enjoyed outside of it. It was English women, he was convinced, who needed to change. In order to 'render Wedlock more desirable, there is a Reformation necessary in the Conduct of Married-Women; they should assimilate it nearer to that of the Kept-Mistress'. Both desire and enjoyment were necessary for love, he believed, and a marriage of minds provided the best hope of happiness. Wives should aim to please their husbands, emulate mistresses and give their husbands as much freedom as possible. This was advice that would not have found a place in most English conduct manuals. More conventionally, he argued that wives should not treat their husband's money as their own, even if they had contributed to it. Ever mindful of the dangers of debt, he strongly recommended 'Frugality' as a 'principal Supporter of connubial Tranquillity and Happiness. A strict Observance of it, with a certain Method, Order, and Oeconomy in domestic Management', especially if observed by both husband and wife, would bring great rewards. 'Happy are the Pair', he opined, 'who can mutually resolve to adopt Common Prudence

---

[45] Ibid., II. 325.
[46] Ibid., II. 327.
[47] Ibid., II. 280.
[48] Ibid., II. 281.

for the Rule of their Conduct.'[49] 'Nothing in this World is of greater Consequence than a fortunate Choice of Partners in the Nuptial Union,' he concluded. 'A discreet Wife is a Blessing sent from heaven; well might *Solomon* say, her price is above rubies! For she herself will set no value upon the richest Brilliants, in Competition with the Interest of her Husband and Family. The Wife of a different Turn becomes a real Curse to her Husband ...'[50]

Edward Long was a 'feeling man' in relation to his own family and class, capable of sympathy. But he had no capacity for feeling 'with' those 'others' outside his psychic frame: they were expelled from his understanding. The structures of the white family, property ownership, marriage and inheritance, including that of enslaved people, were *lived* in his identifications and feelings, determining his disavowals of the full humanity of those he claimed as 'his property'.

Managing Family Property

Between them, the Long family owned slave property in Jamaica, landed property in England and substantial assets in mercantile enterprises and government and banking stock. Male power was at the heart of the family. United by blood and their whiteness, masculine authority and female dependence were assumed. The men were heads of households with political rights based on their property ownership. The women brought property into marriage and inherited it through their families. But they lived as dependants and their property was understood to be *family property*, subject to male authority. None of the women of the Long family was active economically in the market, though their economic and social contribution to the family was significant, transmitting capital, running households, bearing and rearing children. The branches of the family owning land and enslaved people practised primogeniture when possible, the standard way to organize inheritance among the landed classes of early modern England, as we have seen, and a pattern adopted by the white elite in colonial Jamaica. It made sense, both legally and economically, for those aiming to safeguard estates, provide for dependants and advance dynastic ambitions. 'Few planters chuse to parcel out their plantations among their children,' Long wrote, 'as is done in the northern colonies, because these properties are not easily severable; and therefore are transmitted whole and undivided to one child, to preserve them in the family; but they are burthened with annuities, or fortunes, payable to the other children, generally

---

[49] [Long], *The Sentimental Exhibition*, 71–3. Karen Harvey, *The Little Republic. Masculinity and Domestic Authority in Eighteenth-Century Britain* (Oxford, 2012), cites much similar material.

[50] [Long], *The Sentimental Exhibition*, 66–72.

sufficient to maintain them in England.'[51] Land was traditionally seen as the basis of power and status, and the privileging of the eldest son could be strengthened through the use of entail limiting the heir's capacity to sell or will away parts of the estate. In Jamaica, land alone was not enough: enslaved persons had to be attached to that land, since it was their work that created value. Those parts of the family which owned English land privileged primogeniture when they could. Intentions and desires were, however, frequently disrupted by contingencies: death and the lack of male heirs altered patterns of succession.

The mercantile branch of the family practised a hybrid form of inheritance, since the wealth they accumulated enabled them to buy land. The priority for these families was to keep property in the family, privilege a male heir if there was one, and provide for dependants.

Landed Property

The four Jamaican estates owned by the family were Longville, Lucky Valley, Longville Park and Norbrook. Bequeathing plantations in Jamaica always meant bequeathing the enslaved too. The wills made by the men of the Long family were designed to ensure their authority beyond the grave. The limitations on the freedom of the heir included entail (not always specified as male) and life tenancy, while trusts were utilized in an attempt to ensure that the provisions of the will would be met. Trustees were always male and were usually family members, business associates or close friends.

Samuel Long had established the plantations of Longville and Lucky Valley, the first source of family wealth, by the time of his death in 1683. He left the majority of his property to his young son, Charles. His widow and daughter were taken care of with money, cattle and 'Negroes', including their 'increase'. It could be advantageous for women to own enslaved persons, since they could be sold and function as a form of currency on the island.

Charles I, in turn, at his death in 1723, left his ancestral estates of Longville and Lucky Valley, together with human property in Jamaica and substantial debts and costs on that property, including an annuity for his wife, Jane, to his eldest son, Samuel II. It was neither a trust will nor an entail, but Charles expressed the wish that if Samuel died, the real estate would pass to Charles II, his first son by his second marriage. Charles II was able to claim a moiety (share) of Lucky Valley after his mother's death the following year, much to the anger of his half-brother. Lucky Valley was thus owned by Samuel and Charles Long. Samuel II left the real estate entailed to his eldest son, Robert, again with provisos for his dependants. He had made his will in 1745 before leaving for Jamaica. At that time his children were relatively young and his relationship

---

[51] Long, *History*, I. 511.

with his wife was untroubled. The will stipulated that the plantations were to be kept for a term of ninety-nine years if Robert should live that long. After his death they were to go to the 'heirs of his body lawfully begotten' and, if there were no issue, then they should pass to the second and then to the third son. If there was a failure to produce sons, then it should be for 'the use of all and every of my daughters and to the heirs of their bodies'.[52] The emphasis on heirs 'lawfully begotten' was to clarify that no illegitimate children should inherit. The inclusion of the daughters meant that they were prioritized over possible male nephews or cousins; wider kin were crucial, but not to the exclusion of the direct line. Samuel's trustees and executors were his brothers, Charles Long and Beeston Long, and his brother-in-law, Roger Drake. They were instructed 'to manage and take care of my said estates in Jamaica and to retrieve and take the rents issues and profits and apply these to fulfilling legacies to wife and children'. There were further instructions as to the jointures or settlements that could be made in the future by his sons to 'any wife or wives they may respectively happen to marry not exceeding in the whole one moiety of my said estates and so as not more than one moiety thereof be in jointure at any one time'. The estate must be protected. They were also appointed as guardians of the children up to age twenty-one. The guardians could use 'any part of the principal money for placing out sons as clerks apprenticeships or for their advancement and benefit'.[53] Uncle Beeston took his trusteeship seriously. He advised Edward on his father's death and took responsibility for the payment of the annuity to Samuel's widow, Mary Long (née Tate). In return for their duties, the trustees could take the 'usual commission' and charge any necessary expenses upon the estate.[54] The merchant house of Drake and Long continued to act for their kin in Jamaica: an essential link for the family, facilitating both personal affairs and the cycle of the West India trade.

Longville had been entailed by Samuel II to Robert, Edward's older brother. He had no male heir, and this resulted in the division of the Longville estate between his legitimate daughters since Samuel had not stipulated a male entail. Robert had travelled to Jamaica with his father in 1746. Edward remembered him as a somewhat persecuting elder brother: 'in his Boyish years of a most tyrannical overbearing disposition, under which I was sometimes a sufferer'. Consequently, he had relied on Charles, 'his dearly beloved protector', only three years older than himself and to whom he was intensely attached, to defend him. Robert, however, 'proved himself a very worthy man' and helped him greatly in the wake of their father's will and in their dealings over the inheritance.[55] They spent time together, shooting game on various family

---

[52] Will of Samuel Long II, 1758. The National Archives (TNA), PROB 11/835/405.
[53] Ibid.
[54] Ibid.
[55] Howard, *Record and Letters*, I. 83.

properties. Robert was an enthusiastic botanist, an interest he shared with his brother, and a good friend of Anthony Robinson, whose drawings of birds, to which the brothers had contributed, he collected.[56] Robert had been instructed to go to Jamaica, and his decision to return to England in 1763 suggests that he felt no great attachment to the island, or to Ann Clark, the 'mulatto' mother of his child. He was not active in island politics and his failure to improve productivity at Lucky Valley indicates that he had limited interest in plantation management. He left Longville under the care of an attorney. Soon after his return to England, he married Lucy Cooke and was to live the rest of his life on the proceeds of his Jamaican properties. In his will, probably written in the wake of his marriage, he referred to two monetary legacies of £2,000 and £1,000 from his father, Samuel, secured on real and personal estate in Jamaica, which he left to Lucy together with all his other unspecified property, an unusual will for a slave-holder and landowner.[57] His two executors were Lucy and his father-in-law, George Cooke, who appears to have had substantial claims on the estate.[58] The couple's three daughters, all of whom were born in England, all had children. The property stayed in the Long family, passing through the daughters to their husbands under coverture. Robert's grandson, Thomas Long Oliver, received a share of the compensation for Longville and Longville Park.[59] The husband of grand-daughter Sophia Sarah lost his claim to his share of Longville as it was mortgaged.[60] Robert had managed his property less effectively than brother Edward. The combination of the lack of a single male heir, together with absenteeism, left Longville significantly encumbered.

Edward had purchased a moiety of Lucky Valley from his brother Robert in 1760. This would have meant that they agreed to breaking the entail. He leased the other portion of the estate from his uncle at least until the early 1770s when he established sole ownership. By the time of his death in 1813, he was not a wealthy man. The original version of his will, together with a codicil, was written in residences owned by other members of the family: his cousin and his daughter's father-in-law, the Duke of Norfolk. Despite diminishing returns on sugar, however, he had been able to protect the family inheritance, his Jamaican property, subject to annuities and debts. His eldest son, Edward Beeston, inherited the plantations and passed them on in turn to his eldest surviving son, Henry Lawes Long. Edward Beeston's will opened with the

[56] Anthony Robinson's Jamaica Birds. National Library of Jamaica, MS 178.
[57] Will of Robert Long, 1772. TNA, PROB 11/979/275.
[58] Howard, *Records and Letters*, I. 131–2.
[59] 'Thomas Long Oliver', Legacies of British Slave-ownership database, http://wwwdepts-live.ucl.ac.uk/lbs/person/view/45891, accessed 1 November 2020.
[60] 'James Shenton', Legacies of British Slave-ownership database, http://wwwdepts-live.ucl.ac.uk/lbs/person/view/2146633740, accessed 6 November 2020.

bequeathing of Lucky Valley, all its plantation and sugar works in the parish of Clarendon, Jamaica and

> all that my undivided moiety or half part of all that other plantation called Longueville situated in the parish of Sant Dorothy [this was Longville Park] together with all houses and appointments thereto respectively belonging and all and said and singular the plantation utensils, slaves, cattle, dead and live stock to the said plantations respectively belonging or where maybe in or about the same or any of them at my decease and whether of a real or chattel nature unto and to the use of my eldest son Henry Lawes Long, his heirs, executors, administrators and assigns to and for his and their own use.[61]

Edward Beeston Long was born in Jamaica but had left as a child of five and never returned. Nevertheless, these were his family lands, a very different order of 'family lands' from those plots, the provision grounds, cultivated by the enslaved and claimed by freedmen after emancipation.[62] His son Henry lived his life in England, with an income drawn in part from Jamaica. Educated at Harrow and Trinity, he married Lady Catherine Walpole, the daughter of the Earl of Orford, in 1822. This reinforced the family connection with the Walpoles which dated back to his great-great-grandfather Charles I and established an alliance with the minor aristocracy. Hampton Lodge, acquired by his father, became their home and he served as a JP in Surrey. He received a share of the compensation for Longville Park and the whole of the compensation for Norbrook, having counterclaimed as heir-at-law to Charles IV, thus profiting from the failure of male heirs to his relatives on the landed branch of the family.[63] The compensation for Lucky Valley was shared between the husbands of two of Edward Beeston Long's married daughters, Mary and Charlotte (under the provisions of coverture), and his younger son, Frederick Beckford Long.[64] (He had provided for his younger children in this way.) The property first acquired by Samuel I passed through daughters to the men of the sixth generation.

Longville Park had been transferred by Samuel II to his son Charles III in 1734. Following Charles's death intestate in 1756, it went to his older brother Robert who agreed to split it with Edward. In line with Samuel II's will, Robert's share was divided between his daughters. Edward Long left his share to his son Edward Beeston who in turn divided it.

---

[61] Will of Edward Beeston Long, 1825. TNA, PROB 11/1705/415.
[62] Jean Besson, *Martha Brae's Two Histories. European Expansion and Caribbean Culture Building in Jamaica* (Chapel Hill, NC, 2002).
[63] 'Henry Lawes Long', Legacies of British Slave-ownership database, http://wwwdepts-live.ucl.ac.uk/lbs/person/view/21011, accessed 6 November 2020.
[64] 'Charles Devon', Legacies of British Slave-ownership database, https://www.ucl.ac.uk/lbs/person/view/-212072970; 'G. G. Wandisford-Pigott', https://www.ucl.ac.uk/lbs/person/view/46207; 'Frederick Beckford Long', Legacies of British Slave-ownership database, http://wwwdepts-live.ucl.ac.uk/lbs/person/view/22852, accessed 17 November 2020.

Figure 5.3 Hurt's Hall, Saxmundham, Suffolk, the seat of the landowning branch of the Long family. Designed by Samuel Wyatt, 1803; drawn and published by Henry Davy, 1857. RIBA Collections.

William Beeston's acquisition of Norbrook was the original property in Jamaica which contributed to the establishment of the landed branch of the family. It was inherited by his daughter Jane Beeston/Modyford/Long. In her will of 1724 she entailed it, together with her half of Lucky Valley, to her son Charles II and his heirs. Charles II, heir to his mother's protected inheritance, was wealthy enough to establish a seat in Suffolk, Hurt's Hall, which he passed to his eldest son, Charles IV of Saxmundham (who was tenant-in-tail under his grandmother's will). (See Figure 5.3.) His will decreed that the property should go to 'first, second and all other sons of me and my said wife and to the heirs male of the bodies of said first, second and other sons successively, and for default of such issue to the use of the daughters ...' If it were to go to daughters, it should be divided equally between them and held as tenants-in-common.[65] Charles IV inherited the estate, but since he and his wife had no children, the property went to his brother Dudley North for life in 1812, with remainder to his widow, Jane Long, who was

---

[65] Will of Charles Long of Hurt's Hall, Saxmundham, Suffolk, 1778. TNA, PROB 11/1048/205. Legacies of British Slave-ownership database, http://wwwdepts-live.ucl.ac.uk/lbs/person/view/2146633756, accessed 31 October 2020.

tenant-in-tail under her husband's will.[66] It finally passed back to the men in the person of Henry Lawes Long, Edward Long's grandson.

Inheritance, it is clear, was rarely a simple matter. The hope was for a male heir, since without them estates could not be held intact. But contingencies mattered. Edward Long's Jamaican branch of the family maintained the estate intact until the sixth generation. Brother Robert's possession of Longville, however, went to his wife and was then divided between their three daughters and their respective husbands. Robert's grandsons shared the compensation. William Beeston also had no male heir and daughter Jane's extensive property, protected by settlement, passed to her son, Charles II. But the male line of the landed branch also failed, and their Jamaican estate, Norbrook, passed to Edward Long's grandson. The male line of the family remained in command.

Mercantile Property

William Beeston was the first in the extended family to engage in mercantile business both in the City and in Port Royal, but he also became a plantation and slave-owner and died without a male heir. It was his grandson, Beeston Long, who developed the family firm of Drake and Long, going into partnership with his brother-in-law, Roger Drake. Merchants, as we have seen, had different interests from the landed and were much less preoccupied with the creation of a dynasty. At his death in 1762, Drake willed half his property to his 'dear wife', Jane Long, his partner's sister. The property was 'for her own use and benefit in full satisfaction of all alarms and demands by virtue of any writing or agreement made upon or previous to our marriage or by the custom of the City of London or otherwise'. This was in addition to 'all my jewels, plate, rings, watches, household goods, linen, china, pictures and furniture whatsoever both at my house in London and in the country', plus his liquor, provisions, coach, chariot, horses, harness and furniture, garden tools and utensils. The 'household stuff' frequently went to widows. The other half of the property was to be divided between their three sons: the oldest was not singled out. What was more, if any daughters were born, it was to be 'share and share alike'.[67] Jane was appointed guardian of the children and an executor, along with Beeston Long and a friend. The executors were empowered to invest in government stocks, land or mortgages to meet necessary costs. These kinds of investments were one of the important routes through which money from the slavery business became absorbed into the domestic economy. The executors were also enabled to place the sons in 'trades or employment' suited to their advancement. Unlike his partner, Beeston, Drake did not imagine that his eldest son would live as a landed gentleman. (See Figure 5.4.)

---

[66] 'Charles Long of Saxmundham', Legacies of British Slave-ownership database, http://wwwdepts-live.ucl.ac.uk/lbs/person/view/2146650895, accessed 31 October 2020.
[67] Will of Roger Drake, 1762. TNA, PROB 11/877/486.

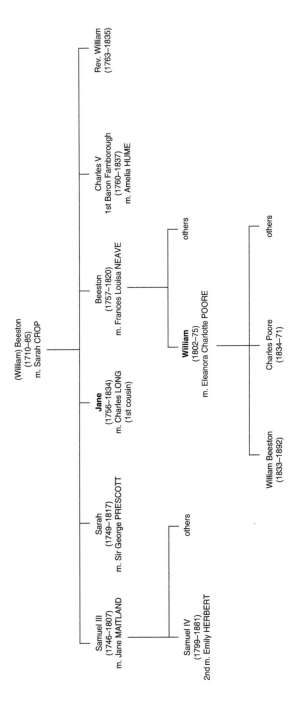

People who feature in the slave compensation records are given in **bold**.

Figure 5.4 Details from the Long family tree illustrating the mercantile branch. Designed by and courtesy of Rachel Lang.

Beeston senior's own will, proved more than two decades later in 1785, was a hybrid, mixing landed and mercantile patterns of inheritance. Beeston (Uncle Beeston), second son of Charles Long and Jane Modyford, had received £1,462 after his mother's death in 1724. By the late 1730s his business was established enough for him to marry Sarah, the daughter of a well-to-do merchant. The marriage settlement provided for Sarah through the will of her mother, Joanna Crop. Over the years Beeston's business had flourished and he had acquired a country property at Carshalton, Surrey, only ten miles outside London. All his real estate went to his oldest son, Samuel III, and this had been laid down in the terms of his marriage settlement with Sarah, who had brought significant property to the marriage.[68] Samuel III, at his death in 1807, in turn bequeathed the residue of his estate, which included land in London, Suffolk, Surrey and Cambridgeshire, to his eldest son, Samuel, subject to an £800 annuity for his widow, Jane Maitland (secured in the marriage settlement), plus £1,000, his leasehold house in Mill Street and household goods, his carriages and horses. His two younger children were to receive £6,000 each at twenty-one.[69]

Beeston senior had left very substantial cash legacies to his other children. The trustees, his brother-in-law Richard Crop, nephew George Drake and two eldest sons, Samuel and Beeston, held stock in South Sea annuities 'purchased with part of the portion or fortune of my said late wife'. This was to be invested in bank annuities which would provide support for his daughter Sarah, now married to George Prescott, a banker. Son Samuel received £2,000 plus the estate. The younger children, Jane, Beeston junior, Susannah, Charles and William, all received £16,000: rough parity between younger siblings as was usually the case. The sons, however, had more control over the money than their sisters. His grandchildren had already received legacies from their grandmother.[70] His second son, also Beeston (junior), took on the family business and married Frances Louisa Neave, the daughter of an immensely wealthy City merchant with property in England and Antigua who had settled substantial sums on his daughters. This marriage marked the place of the Beeston Longs in the highest echelons of City life.[71] The residue of his estate

---

[68] Will of Beeston Long senior, 1785. TNA, PROB 11/1125/323. Legacies of British Slave-ownership database, http://wwwdepts-live.ucl.ac.uk/lbs/person/view/2146644619, accessed 2 November 2020.
[69] Will of Samuel Long III, 1807. TNA, PROB 11/1471/11.
[70] Will of Beeston Long senior, 1785.
[71] 'Sir Richard Neave', Legacies of British Slave-ownership database, https://www.ucl.ac.uk/lbs/person/view/2146638551/#commercial-summary, accessed 2 November 2020.

went to his brothers in trust, Charles and William, subject to legacies for his wife, son and daughters. The trustees were instructed to sell real estate in order to fund the legacies. There was no question of a landed dynasty here.[72]

Beeston Long had made a fortune through Drake and Long and his oldest son became a landed gentleman. His second son not only maintained the business but married mercantile money and was able to leave substantial sums to his wife and children. His priority was to share the property between his children.

Wives, Widows and Daughters

While men exerted their control over property in their wills, women's lack of control is evidenced in the small number of female testators amongst the elite. As early as 1670 there were three women listed as substantial landowners in Jamaica in their own right, but by the mid-eighteenth century the increased monopolization of land, the decrease in the numbers of small landholders and the growth of the integrated plantation had ensured that there were very few large-scale female landowners.[73] In 1754, for example, the list of landholders with 4,000 or more acres in Jamaica included no women.[74] Long noted the small numbers of white women in St James: in 1774 he estimated there were sixty-two sugar plantations, nineteen of which had no resident white females.[75] When women were there, they were likely to be on the smaller estates. A 1750 survey, studied by Christine Walker, of all landowners, not just sugar planters, indicated that women controlled 11 per cent of the property in rural parishes, a significant figure, and a higher estimate than is usually expected, indicative of their involvement in agriculture.[76] Many of them may have been of mixed race. White women and women of mixed race owned many enslaved persons, particularly in urban Jamaica, as work on Spanish Town, Kingston and Port Royal has demonstrated, together with the LBS findings from the compensation records of the large number of female slave-owners across the Caribbean.[77] It was more difficult for women to hold real property and it was very unusual for them to be managing large estates.[78] Anna Eliza Grenville inherited Hope Estate and brought it to her marriage. She regarded it as her property, as Hannah Young has shown, and took

---

[72] Will of Beeston Long junior, 1820. TNA, PROB 11/1633/319.
[73] Mair, *A Historical Study*, 12.
[74] Greene, *Settler Jamaica*, 223–5.
[75] Cited in Mair, *A Historical Study*, 106–8. BL Add MS 12435, Long Papers, Inventory 41, table 2, 3–4.
[76] Walker, *Jamaica Ladies*, 122. Long's failure to recognize the extent of women's ownership is another mark of his skewed vision.
[77] Greene, *Settler Jamaica*; Walker, *Jamaica Ladies*; Hall et al., *Legacies of British Slave-Ownership*.
[78] Walker has the example of Mary Elldridge who managed Spring Plantation in the 1730s.

some interest in it, though never in the enslaved. Yet it was subsumed into the family portfolio, an outcome of her position as a married woman.[79] In her sample of forty Jamaican wills probated in the late eighteenth century, Mair found only one instance in which a daughter, in the absence of a surviving heir, inherited all real and personal property.[80] Very few women in the extended Long family, either in Jamaica or in the metropole, enjoyed direct access to land or capital.[81] The intention was to keep the control of property within the male line; women would be provided for in ways that safeguarded long-term familial interests.

The absence of a male heir could result in serious family conflicts. A long intra-familial dispute followed in the wake of Sir William Beeston's death in 1699. There was no son and Beeston was a very wealthy man on the basis of his slave-trading, his office-holding, and his Jamaican and English property. He left approximately £30,000 in addition to the land.[82] Both his widow, Anne, and only daughter, Jane, claimed the inheritance. Jane was the second wife of Charles I. She was a highly desirable wife, not only as the daughter of William Beeston but also as the widow of her first husband, Sir Thomas Modyford, who died in 1703 leaving her substantial property.[83] The death of her father led to a prolonged dispute over his will between his widow, Anne, and Jane, a conflict between mother and daughter.[84] Jane's claim was strongly backed by her new husband, Colonel Charles Long (Charles I), who was to become the founder of the landed branch of the family. Beeston's will, dated 1699, had left £3,000 to Jane and all the remainder of the property to Anne, with the claim that Jane had married without her parents' consent. In the will Anne was allowed to dispose of the property as she wished and, in the event of no provision, it was to go at her death to William Beeston's two nephews. Jane was effectively

---

[79] Hannah L. Young, 'Gender and Absentee Slave-Ownership in Late Eighteenth-Century and Early Nineteenth-Century Britain', PhD, UCL (2017); 'Negotiating Female Property and Slave-Ownership in the Aristocratic World', *HJ* 63.3 (2020), 581–602.

[80] Mair, *A Historical Study*, 152.

[81] Stephanie E. Jones-Rogers, in her study of southern US women (*They Were her Property. White Women as Slave Owners in the American South* [New Haven, CT, 2019]), has focused on married women who owned enslaved people in their own right. She argues that 'when it came to the nineteenth-century market in slaves, southern women were savvy and skilled indeed ... They created freedom for themselves by actively engaging and investing in the economy of slavery and keeping African Americans in captivity ... Many slave-owning women continued to view their property as theirs alone, even after they married. They did not resign themselves to every aspect of their changed legal status. They did not accept the legal subsumption of their identities into their husbands"; xvi–xvii, 55.

[82] Zahedieh, 'Sir William Beeston', *ODNB*.

[83] 'Sir Thomas Modyford', Legacies of British Slave-ownership database, https://www.ucl.ac.uk/lbs/person/view/2146652855, accessed 10 December 2020; Howard, *Records and Letters*, I. 63.

[84] Howard, *Records and Letters*, I. 63–7 gives the Long family's version of the dispute. Zahedieh, 'Sir William Beeston', *ODNB*, provides other details.

disinherited. Anne gifted to Jane an additional £1,000 after her husband's death on his instructions and Jane acknowledged that she had received this. According to Edward Long's version of the story, the will was invalid according to the Statute of Frauds in English law because the witnesses were in a different room from Beeston when signing. The widow, it was claimed,

> taking advantage of her husband Sir William Beeston's feeble state of mind and body when he lay on his death bed, caused a will to be drawn up in which she devised to her own use his whole Estate real and personal for her life, and in remainder after her death to his and her daughter. It came out afterwards in positive evidence that she held his hand and guided his subscription to this will, while the subscribing witnesses to it (who were all of them her menial servants) were in another room at the time and not present at the transaction.[85]

Anne claimed, on the contrary, that the witnesses were all in an adjoining room with the door open and everyone visible. Grandfather Charles, wrote Edward, 'on finding that by this deception his wife had been unjustly excluded from any share in her father's property during the lifetime of her mother, determined to try the validity of the will' and instituted a law-suit. (Meanwhile, in the absence of her mother in England, Jane had taken possession of the Jamaican estates.)[86] The Supreme Court of Jamaica determined in Charles's favour. Anne, however, with her new English husband, Sir Charles Orby, challenged this verdict and a series of cases ensued in the English courts. Charles moved to England in 1706 with his family to pursue the business. The final judgment from the Privy Council was in favour of the widow, on the grounds that the English statutes were not in force in Jamaica.

Charles and his allies were outraged. The security of their property and their persons depended on the recognition of English law in the colony. Charles's friend and advocate Peter Heywood, who was the chief justice on the island, wrote to him, assuring him that he did not agree that the laws of England were not in force in Jamaica and he was resolved 'to hold the Courts as my predecessors have done before me, until the Queen signifies her pleasure to the Contrary . . . If I do not, I am sure the Negroes will quickly be uppermost in this island.' If the law was not secure, he demanded, how would 'Treasons, Murder, Felonies' be tried? How would 'the merchants trading with us . . . be satisfied for their commodities and loans? and how her Majesty's peace shall be kept, that we may not be daily cutting one another's throats? Which if we do, the strongest man, will have what he thinks fit, and at last we shall be so reduced, as to become slaves to our slaves.'[87] The implications were totally unacceptable: if colonists could not rely on the rule of law, they could not

---

[85] Howard, *Records and Letters*, I. 63.
[86] Zahediah, 'Sir William Beeston', *ODNB*.
[87] Howard, *Records and Letters*, I. 64–5.

maintain the system of slavery and would indeed be reduced to a form of slavery themselves. Charles Long reiterated Heywood's analogy with slavery, evoking republican rhetoric on the tyranny of the crown, when he wrote to his friend in 1711: 'all inheritances must be tried according to ye Statute, and common Laws of England. If this is not allowed you may without anymore struggle deliver up our necks to ye yoke of slavery and call ourselves no more Englishmen.'[88]

Edward Long, who was to draw on this same rhetoric in his struggle with the crown in the 1760s, commented on the 'absurdity and inconvenience of the principles' on which the Privy Council had acted. Such a decision was wholly inconsistent with the colonists' claim that the English common law was their law, except in the exceptional circumstances of *lex loci* demanded by chattel slavery. 'My wife is the daughter and heir of Sir Wm Beeston,' his grandfather had claimed: this was the basis of his right.[89] Charles prepared to take the case before the House of Lords, but his mother-in-law and her husband decided to settle.[90] The rents and profits were to be shared during Lady Orby's lifetime. After her decease, Colonel Charles and his wife would receive the whole. The estate owned a large part of the area on which Kingston was built, which became very valuable as the town expanded, and included the sugar plantation of Norbrook, which remained in the family for generations. The sale of parts of the land had enabled Charles to move to England with £30,000, his grandson believed, which would have facilitated the lease of the splendid house in Queen's Square and the purchase of Hurt's Hall. The costs of the dispute demonstrated the difficulties caused when there was no male heir with undisputed rights.

Elite families could protect their daughters' property from coverture and the marriage settlement of Jane Long (née Beeston) provides an example of this and of the significance of women's inheritance to the transmission of wealth. Once her rights were firmly established, her estate, at her death in 1724, proved to be critical to the making of the landed branch of the family. Samuel II's half-brother, Charles II, the first child of his father's second marriage to Jane, benefited greatly from his mother's Beeston and Modyford inheritance. A marriage settlement had protected it from his father's debts. The Suffolk properties had been willed to Samuel II by his father, but he had to relinquish them, since his father had borrowed from his wife's estate. According to Edward's account, gleaned from his uncle, this caused a violent dispute with his half-brother which Uncle Beeston stepped in to mediate.[91] Samuel had lost the right to what he had understood to be a major part of his inheritance. This,

---

[88] Ibid., I. 66.
[89] Ibid., I. 65.
[90] The evidence from the court cases, argues Nuala Zahedieh, is inconclusive. Each side of the argument gave a different story, with claims and counterclaims. Personal communication, 13 September 2020.
[91] Howard, *Records and Letters*, I. 70.

together with his father's debts, necessitated the choice of Tredudwel, followed by Jamaica. The Jamaican branch of the family was now led by Samuel, the landed branch led by his younger half-brother, Charles. Jane's will, made in 1723, a year before her death, left her land to her son Charles, to be held in trust until he was twenty-one (he was in fact eighteen at the time). This included the farm and manor of Saxmundham in Suffolk, lands and tenements at Dunwich, land in Middlesex, the plantation at Norbrook 'with all negroes, stock, cattle, utensils etc' and half of Lucky Valley, 'with all negroes, stock, cattle etc', plus a pen and plots of land in Kingston. Jane was also in a position to leave her house in Queen's Square to Charles for the rest of the lease and to will £1,000 to each of her two younger sons and four daughters.[92] The will stipulated that, if necessary, the Suffolk property could be sold to fund the legacies, but Norbrook was not to be sold. This might indicate both the value of Jamaican property at this time, worth more than land in Suffolk, and possibly also Jane's attachment to the island of her birth and source of her father's wealth. Charles II was recorded as possessing a property of more than 2,000 acres in the parish of St Andrews in 1754, much of which was still undeveloped. Norbrook had some 'Indifferent Land some Part Rocky & Mountanious', and yielded 55 hogsheads of sugar, 9 puncheons rum, 2,972 pounds of coffee and had 86 cattle and 100 acres in provisions. Charles also had land in St David as well as Clarendon, held 153 enslaved persons and had five white servants.[93] He never lived in Jamaica, but kept Norbrook and leased his half of Lucky Valley to his planter cousins. His marriage to Mary, daughter and heir of Dudley North esquire of Glemham Hall, Suffolk, brought him further property worth £28,000 following the death of his wife's brother, Dudley North. The enslaved people and land that came to him through his mother and his wife enabled him to live the life of a very well-to-do country gentleman, based in Suffolk at Hurt's Hall. At his death in 1778, he left his son Charles (Charles IV, Charles Long of Saxmundham) his real estate and his second son, Dudley, £25,000. He was careful not to make claims on his wife's property since he was not a blood relative. Since their two sons were his wife's blood relatives, however, he judged that they would have the right to dispose of that property if it were sold.[94]

Men assumed a right to property and were in a position to exercise that right. When a man died without an heir, who should profit? How much influence could a widow yield? Edward Long's older sister Charlotte, under instructions from her father, Samuel, had married George Ellis, a major slave-owner, 'the eldest son and inheritor of an ample estate'.[95] He died while she

[92] Will of Jane Long, 1724. TNA, PROB 11/598/401.
[93] Greene, *Settler Jamaica*, 246, 103, 107, 239.
[94] 'Charles Long of Hurt's Hall', Legacies of British Slave-ownership database, http://wwwdepts-live.ucl.ac.uk/lbs/person/view/2146633756, accessed 10 December 2020.
[95] Howard, *Records and Letters*, I. 109.

was pregnant with their son. In his will he had stipulated dower of £1,200 p.a., but there was no provision for a child. His brother John immediately claimed the entire property, bar the annuity. The relations were very divided as to a proper outcome. Should the heir be the adult brother, or the unborn child? 'At length my sister', recorded Edward, 'by advice of my Father, consented to a Treaty of Pacification', the tenor of which was,

> that she should peaceably suffer John Ellis to go into possession, and that she should give up £500 p. annum of her Dower, pending her child's minority: and it was stipulated on the part of John Ellis, that if the child proved a Boy, it should be under his care and be educated at his charge from a certain age (I think 10) and on his coming of age should be entitled to receive £20,000 current money (as an equivalent for what my Sister had given up) and enjoy the little sugar estate called Caymanas and some pasture land adjoining (worth about £1,000 Sterling per an.) but for his life only; in case he should then assent to this Treaty, and by executing a release to his Uncle Confirm to him the quiet and absolute right for ever to the property he had thus usurped.[96]

The property had been 'usurped'; the widow and child could not rival the power of the brother. If the child had been a girl, the conditions would presumably have been even tougher. Charlotte had her rights of dower but nothing more. She brought the child to England in 1755 and Edward, as the young George Rose Ellis's uncle on the maternal side, was to become his adviser in the difficult relation with his Uncle John. While he was still a minor, there were tensions over the use of the property associated with his life interest. George was suspicious that any suggestions made were connected to his uncle's long-term plan rather than his immediate need for an income. 'You will allow that I have a difficult card to play', he wrote to Edward, 'as I must be really guided by my own Friends at the same time that I appear to pay the most implicit deference to his advice; I must therefore contrive to make him advise those very measures which I have previously determined to follow.' His uncle had bought lands contiguous to his own, but it was unclear whether this would really be of benefit to him. However, he must appear to believe in his uncle's stated 'regard for my Welfare ... I certainly have a right to guard against a Man', he concluded, 'who wishes to injure a person who never wronged him, under the deepest of all masks – that of apparent Generosity.'[97] When property was at issue, whose blood would count? In this instance a brother on the island displaced an unborn heir.

Ellis never lived in Jamaica. He was to become a literary man, a friend of Walter Scott, writing poetry and publishing *Specimens of the Early English*

---

[96] Ibid.
[97] Ibid., I. 134.

Poets (1790) which went through six editions between 1801 and 1851. These interests may have been a bond with his Uncle Edward whom he took to calling 'Brother', declaring his wish 'to strengthen every tye which can unite us in the strongest manner'.[98] He became a Member of Parliament in 1796, representing Seaford for the Tories alongside his Uncle Charles Rose Ellis. Described as a 'moderate' West Indian, one of the epithets used to neutralize pro-slavery positions, he was against immediate abolition of the slave trade but prepared to support restrictions.[99] At his death he still held property in land and enslaved people in Jamaica and was worth £30,000.[100]

The property that Jane Long, the daughter of Beeston Long senior, brought to her marriage with her cousin Charles Long of Saxmundham, was protected by settlement. At her death in 1834, her will referenced the trust – money drawn from her father's mercantile business – that had been established for her. One of the daughters of William Beeston (Uncle Beeston) and Sarah Crop, she was also able to leave property as a widow. Her marriage to her cousin Charles IV of the landowning branch was an alliance between the mercantile and the landed branches of the family. Cousin marriages were a well-established way of keeping property within families and binding together kin relations, familiar to the aristocracy, gentry and merchant classes. Jane had a substantial inheritance from her father of £16,000. The couple had no surviving children, which meant that a trust was set up: the property was to go after the death of Charles IV's widow to his brother Dudley, or failing that, to his cousins, Charles V and William, sons of Beeston Long. It would be kept in the male line if possible and in the extended family. Jane received £10,000 in her husband's will and held Norbrook for her lifetime. In her will she rehearsed her marriage settlement with Charles IV, which gave her a life interest in the Suffolk estates and the reversion of the Jamaican estates, and under which she was entitled to raise £6,000 against the estates and leave it as she saw fit. Accordingly, she left substantial sums to her siblings of the mercantile family: £1,500 to her brother Sir Charles Long and £1,000 to Lady Amelia, his wife; £1,500 to her brother Rev. William Long; together with £1,000 to the three daughters of her late brother Beeston Long senior, and £1,000 to Charlotte Spicer, wife of Henry Spicer esq. From her personalty she left a further £3,500 to each of her brothers, Sir Charles Long and Rev. William Long, plus an annuity for her aunt Susannah Long, and a further £2,000 or so in monetary legacies to godchildren, and even a brooch with her mother's hair. Her residual

---

[98] Ibid., I. 155.
[99] David R. Fisher, 'George Ellis', in R. Thorne (ed.), *The History of Parliament. The House of Commons, 1790–1820* (London, 1980).
[100] 'George Ellis', Legacies of British Slave-ownership database, https://www.ucl.ac.uk/lbs/person/view/2146632390, accessed 20 January 2021. See Humphrey Gawthrop, 'George Ellis of Ellis Caymanas: a Caribbean Link to Scott and the Bronte Sisters', *eBLJ [British Library eJournal]*(2005).

heir was her brother Rev. William Long.[101] By the time of her death in 1834, there were ninety-three enslaved persons on the Norbrook estate. The limitations on her right to Norbrook, defined as for life, meant that the compensation went to Henry Lawes Long (named for his great-grandmother), who successfully claimed as 'heir-at-law and surviving trustee' of Charles Long against his widow, Jane.[102] Families could compete for their collective resources as well as consolidating them.

Women who had brought property into a marriage were able to enjoy access to it in later life if a settlement had been made on marriage. The daughterly mercantile inheritance of Frances Long (née Neave) had been protected in this way. She died in 1842, long after her husband, Beeston Long junior, and as a wealthy widow was able to distribute £25,000, held in trust at the bank for her lifetime. Her will was characteristic of those of other women and very different from those of the men whose focus was on securing property rights over generations. She listed gifts for a number of relatives, naming them and thus emphasizing the importance of these personal contacts. Frances's beloved son William was appointed as executor and residuary legatee, but £7,000 was to be raised and divided between her sister, grandchildren, nephews and nieces, a goddaughter, a cousin by marriage (named as a sister), and a female friend. Then there were £100 for orphan children and £50 to the mistress of the asylum, plus modest sums for servants.[103]

When there were no children and property had come through the wife, she might inherit a life interest in the land. This was the case with Sophia North Long of the landed branch at the death of her husband, Dudley North Long, in 1829. Dudley had married into the Pelhams, thus entering the lesser aristocracy, and took on the name of North. He had inherited Norbrook from his brother Charles and sat for a variety of parliamentary seats between 1780 and 1821.[104] Sophia was named as one of his executors and empowered to grant leases on the lands in Suffolk. But she had no power to bequeath the estate. At her death most of the property was to go to her brother, passing back to the family of origin.[105]

Propertied men expected to provide for their widows for their lifetimes. Within the Long family they were usually supported with annuities which financed a fixed income for life, and were designed to ensure that property did not pass outside the family. It was passive rather than active property, income,

---

[101] 'Jane Long née Long', Legacies of British Slave-ownership database, https://www.ucl.ac.uk/lbs/person/view/2146650899, accessed 30 January 2020.
[102] 'Henry Lawes Long', Legacies of British Slave-ownership database, https://www.ucl.ac.uk/lbs/person/view/21011, accessed 30 January 2020.
[103] Will of Frances Louisa Long née Neave, 1842. TNA, PROB 11/1958/95.
[104] 'Dudley Long North', Legacies of British Slave-ownership database, https://www.ucl.ac.uk/lbs/person/view/2146650897, accessed 30 January 2020.
[105] Will of Dudley Long North of Glentham, Suffolk,, 2 April 1829. TNA, PROB 11/1754.

not for investment.[106] The annuity was charged against the profits of the estate or secured against government or East India Company (EIC) stock. It was normally paid quarterly and trustees or executors would be appointed to make the payments. Annuities were embedded in the slave economy as early as the 1680s. Elizabeth Long received an annuity of £250 in Samuel I's will, a hefty sum. It was secured on the estate and the enslaved people and depended on the abandonment of any claim on dower.[107] Smaller annuities were often granted to daughters, especially if they were unlikely to marry, and to spinster aunts. The money was not heritable, severely limiting the control of the annuitant. The three hundred wills that Nick Draper has examined for the period 1750–1850 demonstrate that annuities represent an under-recognized route by which wealth from slavery was transferred to Britain and entered the domestic economy. In his sample there were instances of the annuity being subject to reduction if the widow remarried, but there is no evidence of this in the Long family wills.[108] Indeed, Samuel III's will (he had joined the landed gentry) was explicit in protecting his widow's annuity of £800 from any subsequent husband.[109] All the Long widows except Elizabeth, Samuel I's widow, died in England. Jane Long, Charles I's widow, as we have seen, was able to control some of her inheritance through her marriage settlement, but in addition she had her annuity of £600 charged on the Jamaican properties. The annuity of Mary Long (née Tate, Edward's mother) was £400, charged on the Jamaican estates, but on occasion the money was withheld. Most of the annuities were substantial: that of Catherine Moore (Edward's sister) was £600 and explicitly depended on her relinquishing any claim to her jointure.[110] Sarah Prescott (née Long), Beeston senior's daughter and widow of Sir George Prescott, received an annuity of £800 through her marriage settlement, money from the West India trade.[111] Occasionally a sister-in-law received a large annuity, as in the case of Charles Long's wife, Amelia, whose brother-in-law Rev. William Long left her an annuity of £1,000.[112] The scale of these bequests indicates the confidence these testators had in the profitability of their

---

[106] Davidoff and Hall, *Family Fortunes*, 315.
[107] Will of Colonel Samuel Long, 1683, Jamaica Island Record Office, Book of Wills, vols. 3–5, f. 50.
[108] Nick Draper, 'The Role and Significance of Annuities in the British Caribbean Plantation Economy', unpublished paper (2019). He estimates that in the 1820s annuities probably represented about 10 per cent of the wealth flowing into the metropole from the slave economy.
[109] Will of Samuel Long III, 1807.
[110] Mair, *A Historical Study*, 153.
[111] Will of Sir George Prescott, 1801. TNA, PROB 11/1362/23.
[112] Will of Rev. William Long, 1835. TNA, PROB 11/1851/8.

estates.[113] Unmarried daughters and aunts were also provided for in this way but tended to receive much smaller amounts. The same Samuel Long willed his Aunt Susannah, sister of his father, Beeston senior, an annuity of £50 in 1807. Furthermore, she was allowed to live rent free for life in the house she was then occupying in South Audley Street.[114] Six years later she was bequeathed an annuity of £150 by her nephew Charles III.[115] Another seven years on and she received a further annuity of £50 from her nephew Beeston Long junior.[116] She would seem to have been a much-loved aunt.

It is impossible to know the extent to which these annuities were paid and it would have been difficult for widows to recoup arrears. In bad years for the sugar crop they may not have been paid and, if merchants were acting as trustees and were owed money, they may have withheld payments.[117] The Pinneys reduced and cancelled the annuities of their debtors, aware, as their historian rather unsympathetically writes, of 'the widows and old maids quartered upon them from every county of England'.[118] A number of widows made claims to the compensation commission on the grounds of their unpaid annuities.[119]

Occasionally men would also act to undermine coverture and benefit daughters or sisters. In that way they insured that the woman was protected and kept property within their own family. Sir Henry Moore, the former lieutenant-governor who was critical to the suppression of the 1760 revolt and had married Edward Long's sister Catherine, had a son who died without heirs. Moore wanted to leave Moore Hall in Jamaica to his sister Susannah, but was determined that her husband, Alexander Dickson, should not get control of the property. He established a trust with his brother-in-law Edward Long and another friend. Moore Hall was not to be subject to Susannah's husband's debts. Susannah later passed it on to Edward Beeston Long and he and his brother Robert Ballard Long were named the trustees. The estate of Moore Hall, together with its 'mansion house' which had been devised to him by Susannah, was to be sold to raise the £4,000 he owed to his brother Charles Beckford Long, to pay any debts to his merchants, Messrs Rutherford and Logan, and to finance an annuity for his youngest son, Frederick Beckford Long. Male kin served as trustees to protect property within the extended

---

[113] This confidence may have receded in the decades leading to emancipation, a sign of the threatened decline of the plantation economy. See Draper, 'The Role and Significance of Annuities'.
[114] Will of Samuel Long III, 1807.
[115] Will of Charles Long of Saxmundham, 1813. TNA, PROB 11/1540/466.
[116] Will of Beeston Long junior, 1820.
[117] Douglas Hall drew attention to the ways in which annuities and interests on debt were millstones around the necks of planters; Hall, 'Incalculability as a Feature of Sugar Production', 347–50.
[118] Pares, *A West India Fortune*, 247, 249.
[119] Draper, 'The Role and Significance of Annuities'.

family against the claims of a husband and subsequently to draw that property into their own family inheritance.[120] In a different scenario, Edward Long secured his daughter Catherine's annuity of £400 in his will against the debts of her husband: an indication that all was not well in that household.[121]

Women's property was important. It facilitated both the accumulation of wealth and its dispersal across families. But patriarchal power provided the framework within which women's limited control could operate. Wives were supposedly provided for, but if a husband chose to exert his authority over his wife, as Samuel II did to Mary Tate, she had no recourse and her marriage settlement, in this case agreed in 1723, did not protect her.[122] The limitations of the sources mean that we have almost no access to the experience of these women: only the bare bones of the wills and settlements detailing what their families of origin may have secured or hoped for them in the event of their outliving their husbands. The few surviving wills of widows give some indication of the intricate webs of family and friendship that defined their lives.

Providing for Siblings

The younger sons of the Long family knew that they would not inherit the land. But care was taken in providing for them. There were a range of possibilities, typical of the landowning and mercantile classes: the merchant house, the East India Company (EIC), the military, the church or the law were the most obvious. In each case this would mean an expansion of family interests, sometimes extending over parts of the empire. Many West Indian families had connections with the East Indies.[123] These interests might bring direct economic benefits, or access to political influence, military glory or cultural capital. Younger sons could not expect to live as landed gentlemen, unless they made particularly good marriages. While the hope was that the eldest son would live off the land, with enslaved or free labour, assisted by a 'good' marriage, the expectation was that younger sons would need to supplement family money. Charles III, for example, Edward Long's brother, was the second son of Samuel II. He was intended for the EIC, for the family had connections through Beeston Long's partner, Roger Drake. As Edward recounted, Charles

---

[120] Will of Edward Beeston Long, 1825. Legacies of British Slave-ownership database, https://www.ucl.ac.uk/lbs/person/view/2146633760, accessed 10 December 2020.
[121] Will of Edward Long, 1813. TNA, PROB 11/1544/130.
[122] Howard, *Records and Letters*, I. 75–6.
[123] Chris Jeppesen, 'Growing up in a Company Town: the East India Company Presence in South Hertfordshire', in Finn and Smith, *East India Company at Home*, 251–71. There is much scope for future research on the familial webs that crossed the Atlantic, Pacific and Indian oceans.

was by my Uncle Beeston's advice sent away to learn accounts, bookkeeping etc, and the Dutch and French languages at Leyden, in order to qualify himself for a writer's place in our East India Company's service, which he was to obtain by the interest of my Uncle Mr Drake, who was not only one of the E. India Directors, but had a nephew at that time Governor of Calcutta.

Charles, however, did not take to the 'the sordid manners of a Dutch Compting house', abandoned his post and escaped to London to Uncle Beeston.[124] The EIC scheme was given up and he was sent to Jamaica, 'where preferring the Military profession my father bought him a commission in the 49th Regimt of Foot then in Garrison there, and he was afterwards appointed Engineer general of the island'.[125] Samuel had himself been in the army before his father's death and no doubt had military connections: the purchase of a commission was a well-established route into a key state institution. By the time of his early death in 1757, Charles owned a significant amount of property, including 318 'Negroes', men and women, boys and girls, at two pens at Longville Park and the Cockpit.[126] This property was then divided between his surviving brothers. One of Edward Long's younger sons, Robert Ballard, also chose the military. He had served as a major in the French wars and fought in Ireland in the wake of the 1798 rebellion. His father provided him with £2,000 that year to purchase a lieutenant-colonelcy in a cavalry regiment, money that was understood to be part of his paternal inheritance.[127] At the time of his father's death, he was unmarried and was left an annuity of £400.[128] Edward Beeston's younger son, Frederick Beckford, followed in the family footsteps to Harrow and Trinity and then the law. He was to become the Inspector General of Prisons in Ireland, a new branch of officialdom and an interesting choice for the descendant of a slave-owning family. In addition to the compensation he received for a share of Lucky Valley, he unsuccessfully claimed for Moore Hall but lost his claim to the mortgagees.[129]

The men of the Long family inherited through their siblings, uncles, aunts and cousins as well as their parents: all were part of the same extended family enterprise. Beeston Long's younger sons were left large sums of £16,000 each as we have seen. Charles V, the third son of Beeston and Sarah, followed

---

[124] Howard, *Records and Letters*, I. 82.
[125] Ibid. I. 96–7.
[126] Inventory of Charles Long: Trevor Burnard, Database of Jamaican inventories, 1674–1784, https://www.ucl.ac.uk/lbs/inventory/view/5624.
[127] Howard, *Records and Letters*, II. 302.
[128] Will of Edward Long, 1813.
[129] 'Frederick Beckford Long', Legacies of British Slave-ownership database, http://wwwdepts-live.ucl.ac.uk/lbs/person/view/22852, accessed 17 November 2020.

a different trajectory from either of his two older brothers, one the gentleman landowner, the other the merchant. The substantial inheritance from his father enabled him to confirm his status as a gentleman and a 'man of taste' by going on the Grand Tour in 1786–8, exploring Rome and laying the foundation for his lifetime interest in the arts and his practice as a collector. Breaking with the family mores, he enjoyed the company of a French mistress who birthed a son.[130] The Tour honed his credentials as a man of the world, properly cognizant of ancient European civilizations.[131] On his return to England he became a political ally of his college friend, Prime Minister William Pitt, entered parliament and spent many years in government office. He was able to become a collector, buying artworks, establishing his reputation as a connoisseur and demonstrating to himself and others his capacity for aesthetic judgement. He used his position to facilitate the formation of a particular national public culture, a properly English culture, rooted in European high taste but distinctively domestic, intended to rival that of their wartime enemy, Napoleon. He engaged in the memorialization of national heroes of the war, white men including Major-General Dundas, celebrated for his activities in the West Indies. Together with his wife, Amelia Hume, herself a watercolourist who exhibited at the Royal Academy, he improved Bromley Hill, the country villa they had acquired close to Pitt's residence at Holwood, with elegant additions in Italianate style and neo-classical interiors. The villa was described as uniting beauty with utility, rooted as it was 'in well-cultivated taste'. The extensive grounds, judged to be a miracle of landscape design, were turned into an admired garden with picturesque walkways, bronzes and a Westmacott statue of Flora, 'a work of fair example, where Nature has done a little And Art much'.[132] (See Figure 5.5.)

In 1802 the government established a committee of national monuments known as 'The Committee of Taste'. It included seven leading connoisseurs and collectors and was chaired by Charles Long. The committee supervised competitions, selected designs, awarded commissions, monitored progress on the erection of monuments and inspected sculptures on site. They acted as arbiters of a national culture which was racialized.[133] Charles Long was among the Select Committee of Directors deciding the arrangement of the artworks. Their inaugural contemporary art exhibition in 1806 categorized blackness as animalized by placing a painting with a black protagonist in the animal section.

---

[130] Thanks to Clare Taylor for her extensive collection of notes and cuttings on Charles Long.

[131] Howard Colvin, 'Long, Charles, Baron Farnborough (1760–1838), Politician and Connoisseur of the Arts', *ODNB*, 2004, https://doi.org/10.1093/ref:odnb/16962.

[132] George Cumberland, *Bromley-Hill. The Seat of the Rt. Hon. Charles Long MP* (London, 1816), 12, 55.

[133] Holger Hoock, *Empires of the Imagination. Politics, War and the Arts in the British World, 1750–1850* (London, 2010).

Figure 5.5 A south-west view of Bromley Hill, Charles and Amelia Long's Italianate villa in Bromley, Kent. By John Buckler, 1815. © Heritage Image Partnership Ltd/Alamy Stock Photo.

It also portrayed indigenous peoples as ethnographic specimens. These 'spaces of display', argues Catherine Roach, served an important role in 'visualising imperial and racial ideologies'.[134]

Charles was to play a significant part in the purchase of the Elgin Marbles. He sat on the parliamentary inquiry in 1816 which investigated the circumstances of acquisition and established whether the marbles should be bought for the nation. Elgin was defended with a narrative of rescue and stewardship against the charge of spoliation which had been made. The inquiry decided the monuments were best given asylum under a free government and were bought for the nation.[135] Charles was also involved with another major cultural enterprise, this time to transform London into an imperial city. A close friend and adviser of the Prince Regent, he worked with successive governments after 1815 in the building of churches, law courts, royal palaces and parks, the National Gallery, the British Museum and Trafalgar Square. When he retired from office in 1826, he was made Baron Farnborough. This was a man who was at the heart of the cultural establishment. He served as a trustee of both the British Museum and the National Gallery. He and Amelia Hume had no children. He left paintings by Old Masters, some of which are now in the

---

[134] Catherine Roach, '"The Higher Branches": Genre and Race on Display at the British Institution, London, 1806', *Art History* 44.2 (2021), 314.

[135] William St Clair, *Lord Elgin and the Marbles* (Oxford, 1998).

National Gallery, while the money he left to the British Museum was used to purchase manuscripts by Handel, the favoured musician of the Georgian court.[136] His legacies to these national institutions signify one of the routes through which the wealth generated by slavery's violence passed into the heartlands of English culture, through symbols of European civilization.

Charles was a passionate Englishman of a different kind to his cousin Edward, who was more than twenty years older, his Englishness irrevocably mixed with his West Indian identity. Charles's family money came from the slavery business but was effectively washed through, the traces erased. In addition to his paternal legacy, he was left £4,500 by his sister Jane who had married Charles III (of the landed branch), money which again was connected with the West India trade.[137] By the time of his death he had also benefited from a government pension. Most of his estate stayed within the family, going to his nephew Samuel, the first son of his older landed brother, Samuel III. The trustees, on this occasion not family members, were to ensure that Samuel did not sell the land and that all the legacies were paid, with the paintings and manuscripts disposed of according to his directions.[138]

Charles V's younger brother, William Long, was the only member of the extended family to enter the church, becoming a canon of Windsor. He benefited significantly from the wills of his father and his siblings. He died two years before brother Charles and made him sole executor. His real estate went to his nephew William; all residual property was to go to Charles once the legacies had been paid to his sister, his nephews and nieces.[139] Family property was distributed across close kin. These younger sons extended the status of the family in a variety of ways. While Edward Long's son Charles Beckford married an heiress and was able to establish himself as a landed gentleman, his brother Robert Ballard entered the military and his cousin Charles extended the family's cultural capital, just as Edward himself did through his writing. The Long family is remembered not on account of its wealth, its plantations and country houses, and its longevity, but for the three volumes of the *History of Jamaica*.

---

[136] David Hunter, 'Handel Manuscripts and the Profits of Slavery: the "Granville" Collection at the British Library and the First Performing Score of *Messiah* Reconsidered', *Notes* 76.1 (2019), 27–37; thanks to Maxine Berg for this reference. 'Sir Charles Long 1st Baron Farnborough', Legacies of British Slave-ownership database, https://www.ucl.ac.uk/lbs/person/view/2146638829/#cultural-summary, accessed 20 April 2021.

[137] Will of Jane Long, 1834.

[138] Will of Charles Long, 1st Baron Farnborough, 1838. TNA, PROB 11/1893/320.

[139] 'Rev. William Long', Legacies of British Slave-ownership database, http://wwwdepts-live.ucl.ac.uk/lbs/person/view/2146650901/, accessed 28 October 2020.

Making Marriages, Caring for Family

The family's carefully considered property arrangements were designed to take account of the financial needs of the different members of the family. The emotional life of the family was a different but closely related dimension. Paternal authority was embedded not only in the ownership of property but in choices about schooling, profession and marriage. Edward Long had decided opinions on all of these issues.

He had learned the hard way the implications of a parental marriage which did not bring substantial benefits. Samuel II (Edward's father) was faced, as we have seen, with the loss of his father's fortune in the wake of the South Sea Bubble. This was a lesson Edward never forgot. Land was a much safer form of property than paper. For his father, one possible way of lessening the debts he had been left with would be to sell some of the less profitable land in Jamaica, so Samuel quitted his army post and sailed for the Caribbean. His marriage to Mary Tate had taken place in 1723, the year of his father's death. Retrospectively, Edward regarded this as an unsuitable marriage 'in point of fortune to a man whose own Estate was so harassed and dismantled, and liable to so many serious incumbrances'. Family marriages did not always deliver all that might be desired. Of Mary Tate's £3,000 dowry, £500 was paid outright, and the rest was to be invested in lands in the vicinity of London, yielding a yearly income of £300 which would be settled on her for life. The promised income would be charged against Lucky Valley and Longville and secured against the many costs on Samuel's property given the terms of his father's will. These included an annuity of £600 for 'Dame Jane Modyford' (widow), legacies and portions for the younger children of the second marriage amounting to £7,000, a mortgage and all the other extensive debts resulting from the debacle of the South Sea Bubble.[140]

Mary's experience of Jamaica was not a good one. A baby, Samuel, was born in 1724 but died in infancy and was buried on the island. Her daughter Catherine was born in 1727 and her son Robert in 1729. While living at Longville, as she recounted to Edward, 'in the bloom of youth', she had contracted a serious illness and had entirely lost the use of all her limbs. She was put on board ship, 'more dead than alive' and accompanied by her coffin in case she died while at sea.[141] On arrival in England she was taken to Bath but never entirely recovered, having difficulties with her hands and compelled to walk with a stick. As a result of this experience she dreaded returning to Jamaica, and this may have been one of the reasons for the delays in leaving England to join her husband after his departure with Robert in 1745. These

---

[140] Howard, *Records and Letters*, I. 75–6.
[141] Ibid., I. 87.

delays greatly annoyed Uncle Beeston and were to play a significant part in Samuel's rejection of her and insistence on their separation.

The income stipulated by the marriage settlement was not paid to Mary. After her separation from her husband and return to England, she was left with an allowance of £200 p.a. and 'on this she made shift to live within bounds', with the help of one maid.[142] Samuel was angry with her for what he saw as an unwarranted interference in the matter of her daughters' possible suitors, a matter which in his view was entirely within his authority. Mary, with daughters Catherine, Charlotte and Amelia, had spent some weeks in lodgings in Plymouth waiting to sail to Jamaica. Edward was invited to join them for his school holidays. The town was crowded, for there had been a great victory over the French fleet, the captured ships had been brought into port, and there was much celebration and gaiety. A number of officers became regular visitors, enchanted by the company of the young ladies. Captain Holwell was 'passionately attached' to Charlotte, but Edward conceived an 'instantaneous dislike to his Pride and dullness'. Lieutenant Prescot, meanwhile, seemed much taken with Catherine. Holwell was very attentive to Mrs Long and Edward concluded that there would soon be a match. Charlotte, however, took him aside and 'complained bitterly' of her mother's 'great imprudence to countenance pretentions of this nature unauthorised by my Father, and to favour their rashly entering into connections with men, whom he might entirely disapprove, and who perhaps were neither proper nor eligible matches for them'. She was also enraged by what she saw as her mother's 'extreme partiality' for her youngest daughter. She told Edward that she planned to tell her father of the whole business once in Jamaica. It later transpired that she had indeed told him and he was disgusted by what he saw as his wife's 'lingering in England in order to provide her Daughters with Husbands'.[143] He was already very annoyed with Mary since Beeston had complained that she had failed to reach Plymouth in time to take the passage that Drake and Long had procured for her. She had then refused a second arrangement on the grounds that the cabin provision was totally unsatisfactory. All this produced much tension between husband and wife and resulted in their separation. Samuel arranged the marriages of both his older daughters to members of the Jamaican elite. Mary subsequently returned to England with her youngest child, Amelia. Samuel then forbad her access to her daughter, a decision that Edward thought cruel.

Samuel's death in 1757 would have resulted in better treatment for his widow if the terms of his will had been met. Made in happier days before his departure for Jamaica in 1745, he had left Mary the use of Tredudwel and its contents for life, but she does not appear to have benefited from this.

---

[142] Ibid., I. 109.
[143] Ibid., I. 94–6.

Her annuity was to be £400.[144] Shortly before her death in 1765, she wrote to Edward, distressed that she was unable to give any financial assistance to her youngest daughter. The expenses she had had on account of her illness and 'your Uncles withholding one Fourth of my annuity this year' had left her with no resources. Clearly Uncle Beeston was once again the manager of family moneys in the metropole. If the crop delivered to the merchant house did not cover the annuities, then they might not be paid.

Edward Long learned from his father's mistake. He secured his place in the colonial elite in the year following his arrival in Jamaica with his marriage to Mary Ballard Beckford. (See Figure 5.6). A descendant of Peter Beckford and Bridget Beeston, she was connected to key families who had been on the island since the 1660s. Her father was Thomas Beckford, her mother Mary Byndloss, also a descendant of one of the original colonists, Colonel Thomas Ballard. Mary had inherited from her first husband, John Palmer, who came from another significant colonial family, as well as from her father. She brought property to the marriage. This included Friendship estate – over which there was a negotiation with her relative Matthew Gregory, probably to end an entail so that it could be sold – and the house in Spanish Town in which she and Edward lived. The kin connections that she brought would have been vital to Edward as he sought to establish himself on the island. He had relatively little capital and an urgent need to make his way in the world. This wider circle of kin placed him amongst leading families. His father and his brother Charles were both dead, but his father had served in the council and Charles in the assembly, so he was well positioned for public office. His sister Charlotte was married to Sir Henry Moore, lieutenant-governor of the island. Edward was appointed to his first public duties as early as 1759, being entrusted with the Public Dispatches.[145] In 1760 he was appointed sole judge in the Vice-Admiralty court thanks to an intervention from Uncle Beeston.[146] The following year he was elected to the assembly. While Edward was establishing himself as both a planter and a judge, Mary was fulfilling her role as a 'reproducer of freedom'. Her first child, Edward Beeston, was born in Jamaica that same year, his name a recognition of the significance of that branch of the family. Catherine was born in 1764, Charlotte in 1765 and Elizabeth in 1769: all were given Long family names, those of a great-grandmother and two aunts. Twin sons, Robert Ballard and Charles Beckford, with names marking the importance of their Jamaican kin, were born after the family returned to England, in Chichester in 1771.

These years of childbirth and childcare would have dominated Mary's life. It is impossible to gauge her attitudes, including to breastfeeding and care of her

---

[144] Will of Samuel Long II, 1758.
[145] *JAJ*, vol. 5, 132, 160.
[146] Howard, *Record and Letters*, I. 175.

Figure 5.6 Mary Ballard Long (née Beckford), whose marriage with Edward brought him significant property and heirs. Following her death in 1797, Henry Bone copied John Opie's portrait of her for the creation of a miniature. Pencil drawing squared in ink for transfer, 1797. © National Portrait Gallery, London.

children. Given Edward's hostility to wetnurses, especially in Jamaica, it seems likely that she fed the children herself. Some of the sixty-four enslaved people registered in 1772 to the house in Spanish Town will have been domestics during the family's occupation, cooking, cleaning, washing and involved in childcare. Once the move to Chichester had taken place, where the three youngest children were born, it is likely that the servants were white. Devoted white servants were named in wills, being left modest bequests, in a way that was unimaginable for the enslaved. We cannot know if any enslaved persons accompanied the family to England. Edward's horror of the polluting presence of black people in the 'mother country' would suggest not.

As a father he took a great interest in his children, especially his first-born son with whom he appears to have had a very close relationship throughout his life.[147] He took care over his education both at school and in Trinity Hall, maintaining a correspondence on his reading and his essay writing. He instructed him in what he believed were the 'natural' inequalities and hierarchies which produced 'a general harmony + order in the universe'.[148] Once the lad's studies were complete, the question of marriage loomed: there was no talk of a profession, he should live as a gentleman. The Jamaican properties were expected to support the family from now on and sugar was maintaining a good price. Edward could afford to write without having to be concerned with the literary marketplace, unlike many of his contemporaries who wrote ceaselessly in an effort to support themselves and their households.[149] Edward Beeston, however, as the heir to the property, would need to marry well if he were to be able to maintain a country estate and enter the solid ranks of the English upper class as his father hoped to do. The enslaved on Lucky Valley and Longville Park had to cultivate enough cane to support his parents and provide settlements for his siblings as well as securing his inheritance. He must make an appropriate choice of wife. His father wrote to him in 1785, when he was twenty-two and travelling in France, telling him that his sisters had just toasted the health of Miss Mary Thomlinson who had come of age. He had not been present, 'but they tell me she is handsomer than ever', he wrote:

> The object is *worth your pursuit*; but considering her fortune, I think it likely she will attract many admirers: I cannot but think that if she is not already fixed, which I imagine she is not, you would stand a fairer chance than many others. What I say to you on this subject you know is sacred, and secret between you and me: It is my duty to point out whatever occurs to me as a method of ensuring your future independence and with it, no small degree of happiness.

Having established her financial credentials, he added that, 'She has every quality of heart that is amiable.'[150]

His father's advice was taken, the secret preserved and his 'future independence' secured, an 'independence' that was entirely dependent on the labour of others. The couple were married in St Marylebone parish church the following year. Mary Thomlinson, the daughter of an MP, had a considerable fortune inherited from her grandfather, John Thomlinson of East Barnet: property in Buckinghamshire and London, mortgages, bonds and securities, an annuity, a right of dower on land in Grenada and a plantation in Antigua – the

---

[147] Pearsall, *Atlantic Families*, discusses the great weight put on the father/son relationship.
[148] Copies of Letters from Edward Long. Edward Long to his eldest son Edward Beeston Long then at Harrow, n.d., Cumbrian Archives Centre DHW/832.
[149] See, for example, Jeremy Lewis, *Tobias Smollett* (London, 2003).
[150] Howard, *Records and Letters*, I. 181.

total amounting to a substantial property of more than £5,000.[151] Her money was vital to the purchase of Hampton Lodge with its manor, land, mill, cottages and fishery in 1799. His father had requested him to establish a family vault once he had a property and this was done at Seale: their memorials would be built in stone. It may have been in the wake of this purchase, which saw the family settled on their own property rather than in rented accommodation, that Edward Long petitioned for the restoration of the ancient barony of Zouche of Haryngworth, an inheritance through his mother, but this was refused.[152] He did, however, receive a grant of alteration in the family arms so that, as he told his daughter Elizabeth, 'they are now exactly as our ancestors bore them'.[153] Edward Beeston's marriage settlement had secured £6,000 on the plantation of Lucky Valley which he then inherited at his father's death in 1813. In addition he received all other Jamaican properties, together with any debts owing, along with his father's books, manuscripts and family portraits.[154] He himself died twelve years later. His will bequeathed Lucky Valley and his half of Longville Park, together with 'the plantation utensils, slaves, cattle, dead and live stock', to his eldest son, Henry Lawes, and his heirs. Edward Beeston Long's two daughters, Mary and Charlotte, were provided for on their marriages, with settlements secured on Longville Park.[155]

Edward Long's second son, Charles Beckford, also made a very profitable marriage, with a Jamaican heiress, Frances Monro Tucker, resulting in his acquisition of the Crescent estate in St Mary. The property had previously come to her father, Lucius Tucker, through marriage. Edward Long was a friend of Tucker's. Both had spent time in Jamaica and become absentees, living in Marylebone. Long was named guardian and trustee for Frances when her father died in 1791. He was also tasked, together with his son, with providing for an illegitimate child: '£2,000 of my £10,000 in the 3 per cent annuities' was to go

> to my friends Edward Long of Wimpole Street and Edward Beeston Long of East Barnet upon trust to pay the interest and dividends to Elizabeth Grey, a mulatto girl now about the age of 4 years old during her natural life and after her death the sum to go to her children share and share alike.[156]

---

[151] Ibid., I. 181–2.
[152] Ibid., I. 118; II. 320.
[153] Ibid., II. 337.
[154] Will of Edward Long, 1813.
[155] Will of Edward Beeston Long, 1825; https://www.ucl.ac.uk/lbs/person/view/2146633760; 'Charles Devon', https://www.ucl.ac.uk/lbs/person/view/-212072970; 'G. G. Wandisford-Pigott', https://www.ucl.ac.uk/lbs/person/view/46407, Legacies of British Slave-ownership database, accessed 3 May 2021.
[156] Will of Lucius Tucker, 1792. TNA, PROB 11/1220/189; Legacies of British Slave-ownership database, https://www.ucl.ac.uk/lbs/person/view/2146641695, accessed 1 March 2021.

This is the only occasion on which father and son took responsibility for a child of mixed race. There is no record as to what Edward Long thought of this commission, given his deeply ambivalent feelings about miscegenation. What is clear, however, is that some of his friends had far fewer scruples as to 'pure blood' than he did. Robert Lee Cooper, who had gone to Jamaica in 1749 with a parcel of ribbons and become a prosperous attorney and one-time Island Solicitor with the help of the powerful Fuller family, returned to England at the same time as Long. They were close friends and Lee did legal business for Long, visiting him in Chichester in the early 1770s. Priscilla Kelly, his 'housekeeper' who became his wife, was a mixed-race creole, as were his children. Two of his sons were at Harrow, becoming absorbed into the English upper class alongside Edward Beeston Long.[157]

While Elizabeth Grey was kept safely at a distance, Frances Tucker, following the death of her father, went to live with the Long family. She married Charles four years later.[158] Edward Long had initially thought that it was unnecessary to make any provision in his will for Charles since he was so well situated, but he later felt anxious that this might be misconstrued. As a demonstration of the 'great regard and affection' he had for Charles, he willed an annuity of £200 to him, payable from his estates. His papers and manuscripts about Jamaica also went to Charles. Crescent estate brought Charles £3,979 in compensation payments for 233 enslaved persons. Colonial property, however, was less productive than it had once been. An undated codicil to the will that Charles made in 1825 left £100 to Robert Sympson then residing in Brussels (a popular location for those short of money) and regretted his inability to leave him more owing to 'the deplorable state of my affairs in Jamaica'.[159]

The marriage of Edward's daughter Catherine in 1799 was not so straightforward. She told her father that she hoped to marry Richard Dawkins. Richard's father, Henry Dawkins, a fellow West Indian living off his Jamaican and English properties, strongly opposed the marriage on the grounds that that there was not enough fortune on either side.[160] Edward had initially agreed with this, anxious not to appear to challenge parental authority. A letter to Richard explained his position: 'The severe conflict my mind has lately undergone, has arisen from a natural felicity of Temper', he explained, 'which generally makes me averse to Denial, where my inclinations would rather persuade me to Compliance.' It is hard to imagine what the enslaved persons on his plantation or the rebels of 1760 or 1765 would have made of his description of his 'natural felicity of Temper' or indeed of his

---

[157] Anne M. Powers, *A Parcel of Ribbons. The Letters of an Eighteenth-Century Family in England and Jamaica* [2012] (n.p., 2022).
[158] Howard, *Records and Letters*, I. 281.
[159] Will of Charles Beckford Long, 1836. TNA, PROB 11/1863/167. Legacies of British Slave-ownership database, https://www.ucl.ac.uk/lbs/person/view/18715, accessed 6 June 2021.
[160] On Henry Dawkins, see Dawkins, 'The Dawkins Family'.

aversion to 'Denial'. 'After a deliberate consideration to what is necessarily due to my Honour and character', he continued,

> I find it impossible for me to recede from the written declaration given under my hand to your Father; which makes *my* consent to your marriage with my daughter depend upon *his* ... I am of opinion it would not be consistent with those Principles I have endeavoured to practice in my conduct through life, if, ether my Daughter should appear to have made such an undue advantage of your Partiality for her, as to draw you into a situation, which your Father has pronounced to be *ruinous*; – or, if I sho[d] appear to have been the prompter of an open defiance of parental authority, which, in the case of my own children, I, as a Father, ought to condemn ... I am convinced it is *your* Father who ought to decide for you on this occasion, the only objection he has suggested, cannot possibly be removed but by your proving to him, that the income you are warranted to rely on, will be amply sufficient for your comfortable maintenance in the nuptial state, without any probable hazard of subjecting his fortune to future inconveniences, or yourself to distresses. My Family have no demands to make upon him; no settlement to stipulate, nothing in short to ask or expect beyond that amiable reception of my Daughter.[161]

His conviction was clear: the father's authority was paramount in questions of marriage. It is striking to note, however, that he did not expect a settlement (probably because he could not afford a dowry); all he asked was that Catherine should be welcomed into their family.

This, however, did not mark the end of the matter. The young couple would not give each other up. A few months later Edward wrote to his daughter who was staying with her sister Charlotte. 'After thoroughly discussing your business in my own mind,' he told her, he had written what he thought was the most appropriate letter to Mr Henry Dawkins and he was attaching a copy for her approval before sending it. 'What can I possibly wish for in the world but to see you happy. And I firmly trust you will be so,' he continued. He had come to the conclusion that he could no longer oppose the marriage. Unfortunately the news on the sugar crop from Jamaica was not good and he expected that it would make 'Mr D. more irritable than ever. It is a Risque however that we all share. My property is subject to the Risque & so must your dependence on it be, & there is no help for this. You know the insignificant Returns I have received these last three years, make frugality a Duty at present, from which I cannot depart.' An income for Catherine depended on the productivity of the 'Negroes' at Lucky Valley. The marriage would need to be simple, no 'parade', no 'ostentation'. It might be better to save any money for 'essential services'.[162] The letter he enclosed for Henry Dawkins assured him that

---

[161] Howard, *Records and Letters*, I. 272–3.
[162] Ibid., I. 277.

I endeavoured to dissuade my Daughter from all further thoughts of marrying Mr R.D., I advised her, by all means to wean herself from an attachment that appeared so offensive to *his* Parents, & I hoped she had pride enough to restrain her from desiring an alliance with any family not cordially disposed to receive her. These and many other arguments I have tried, but I fear to little purpose; for altho' I begin to flatter myself that the affair was at an end, yet I now find, they are determined upon it at all events. My Daughter has just assured me in the strongest language, that her whole Happiness depends upon her becoming your Son's wife; and since this is the case, I am convinced, it will be ineffectual for me to oppose Inclinations which I have not authority to control; nor is it possible for me to disapprove the object of her choice, on whom her prospect of Happiness is so immutably fixed.[163]

The reply he received from Bath was terse: 'I have this moment received your letter & am very sorry I cannot give it any other answer than by repeating what I have before said; that I can never give my consent to my sons marrying where there is not sufficient fortune on either side to enable them to live comfortably and therefore I protest against the match.'[164] Dawkins was clear that Catherine was no match for his son: the family were too straitened in their circumstances. He expected something better. Edward now cautioned his daughter that since Richard's father was convinced they would not have a sufficient income to 'Keep house & live comfortably', it would be up to her to see that they managed so as not to have to appeal to him since, 'if ever such an application should happen', he might well reject it and 'enjoy the Triumph of having seen and forewarned his son' of the likely consequences of an unsuitable match. She would need to pay close attention to housekeeping, of which she had no experience. He would himself help her whenever he could afford it, but 'I cannot in the present situation of my affairs engage for more than I first promised.' He warned her against exasperating her future father-in-law in any way; it would be terrible to be the cause of Richard's disinheritance. Mr D. has many children, he reminded her, and there might be rivalry over the money.[165] Meanwhile, she should let him know all her debts, and he and her mother would make arrangements for the ceremony. It took place in December 1791. Long's support of his daughter in face of opposition on the grounds of inadequate fortune is striking. His own father had insisted on marrying his two older daughters to men he chose on the grounds of their property and position. His parents' separation was ostensibly the result of his father's anger over his wife's conduct in claiming a right to approve of possible suitors in the absence of her husband. Edward was of a different generation, one which was beginning to have more time for questions of 'Inclination', at

[163] Ibid.
[164] Ibid., I. 277–8.
[165] Ibid., I. 279–80.

least for those who were not first-born. Catherine was a daughter; the hopes and expectations may have been less, and shifting notions as to the rights of sons and daughters may have played their part. As we have seen, he believed in the importance of companionate marriage for those of his own class. His belief in passion may have persuaded him that he had no authority to control Catherine's 'Inclinations'; her happiness was at issue and her choice should prevail.

By the early 1800s Edward Long was not a wealthy man: the profits from sugar were declining in value and there were many demands on the Jamaican property. Mary had predeceased him, to his great sorrow, and he became very close to his youngest daughter, Elizabeth, who was unmarried. He wrote frequently to her when she was away staying with her sister Charlotte, who had married Sir George Pocock, the son of a successful naval commander, and was living in London. 'It's a pity we are creatures so mortal, – so easily blotted out of the world, and yet so very susceptible of grief and solicitude,' he wrote, having heard of the recovery of a friend from a serious illness:

> The existence of the dearest friends we possess, hangs but upon the thread of a Cobweb, – It is best for us no doubt that we do not moralise too intensely upon this frail subject, nor give way to incessant fear, like the owner of a valuable piece of china, in hourly terror lest accident or heedlessness sh(d) shiver it into atoms. Yet something I believe of this sort every affectionate Parent, fond wife, and true friend, experiences more or less.[166]

The difference in language from the ways in which he addressed questions of life and death amongst the enslaved could not be more stark. Numbers distanced him from any recognition of their human pain and freed him from contemplating individual deaths and their meanings. Emotions of love, grief and empathy had no place when writing about African and creole deaths on the plantation. 'Those persons most excite our compassion', as Adam Smith had written, 'and are most apt to affect our sympathy who most resemble ourselves, and the greater the difference the less we are affected by them.'[167] Long effected a split between his feelings about those he cared for and those others who, he wanted to believe, were simply different, less human, did not experience loss in the same or a similar way to himself, his family and friends, were closer to animal life.

Long built a safe world for himself and his extended family in England. Jamaica was haunted by death and dangers; he could protect his children from

---

[166] Ibid., II. 307.
[167] Adam Smith, *Lectures on Jurisprudence* [16 February 1763], in R. L. Meek, D. D. Raphael and P. G. Stein (eds.), *The Glasgow Edition of the Works and Correspondence of Adam Smith, volume V* (Indianapolis, 1982), 109.

'Golgotha' in Chichester or Wimpole Street.[168] To bring his wife and children safely home, none buried in Jamaica, may have been a triumph for him. He perhaps shared some of his friend Mary Ricketts's feelings about the island. Island life 'was a lingering death' in her experience. 'I make it my last and most earnest request', she had written to her husband, 'that our child may never go to a country I cannot think of without the utmost horror, nothing but the most settled aversion,' peopled by 'talky wretches, the negroes'.[169] Long's mother had also had bad experiences of Jamaica – the loss of her first child, the illness which left her partially disabled, then her husband's angry rejection of her condemning her to a lonely life. Long's own experience of severe depression as an adolescent was the result of being left alone in England while the rest of the family went to Jamaica. This was not the picture he wrote of the island in his *History*, but it may have informed his need to foster a loving family circle in the metropole. Jamaica was not a place to live once a fortune was made.

It is clear that the Long family were very attached to each other and able to spend much time together, in each other's houses and on holidays. Elizabeth and her father were in Wimpole Street some of the time, but frequently visiting out of London, with family in Surrey, Hampshire or Berkshire. 'Society' seems to have had limited appeal. Elizabeth had been to a masquerade but not greatly enjoyed it: 'it is the mien or look of the people which confounds and alarms me so that I have not the power of saying one single thing that is not so stupid or foolish as to make me wish I had not spoke at all', she told him.[170] They liked to gossip about family matters – 'The strict decorums of Relationship are so many fetters on the tongue,' wrote her father – and about the doings of acquaintances.[171] 'I think he has only had 3 wives,' her father commented to her in relation to Mr M.'s new marriage, 'and why should he not have a fourth, I cannot imagine. For I am certain the more a reasonable man is habituated to married life, the better he must like it, and the less able will he be to exist happily without it. Yet it seems to me', he continued,

> that Mr M.'s love has generally mingled a small portion of avarice in his bargains. I mean by avarice, the love of money – or, in other words, an ample fortune; so that he is not only a Platonic, but a Plutonic admirer; (Pluto you know is the God of Riches.) This I take to be one of the most conspicuous features in his amiable character, making his Love point its arrows at two great Objects instead of one, or as the common saying is, killing two birds with one stone, or perhaps, three, if the Lady possesses wit: and what an excellent Sportsman must he be who can hit Beauty, Wit and Wealth all at once.[172]

[168] Mary Ricketts to Edward Long, Ricketts Family Papers.
[169] Mair, *A Historical Study*, 18.
[170] Howard, *Records and Letters*, II. 310.
[171] Ibid., II. 317.
[172] Ibid., II. 318.

These were intriguing words from the man who had strongly advised his son to pursue Mary Thomlinson.

Two years later Elizabeth herself was married, after a period during which she had nursed her father through 'a long and dangerous illness'. Her husband was Henry Howard, a younger son of the Duke of Norfolk, and it cost her father a severe pang to let go of this 'dear child of my heart', this 'dearest and best of daughters'. 'I perfectly hated Col. Howard as the cause of separating you from your Father,' he wrote to her, but had become more composed. 'I feel like a child that has lost its proper Guardian,' he reflected, 'since I have no one here to control or direct me, except my own wayward fancy. However, I promise you, that I will take no sort of liberties nor discontinue my Draughts.' He needed to believe 'that you have always your eye upon me'.[173] Thanking his new son-in-law for a splendid gift of venison, he assured him that he would always be a good friend to him, provided he could rely on his care and love for Elizabeth. He was alone, he wrote to his 'dear child', in the wake of a large family party in Bognor, now possessing 'a Solitude, which is even chilling to me', he told her, 'who, you know, am a Philosopher, and fond of retirement. I am persuaded it is impossible but we must Languish and pine in the absence of friends we love.'[174] He wrote to Mary Ricketts from Bognor, thanking her for her congratulations on the marriage and telling her that his satisfaction was mixed with sadness. He had often expressed his wish to see Elizabeth 'established in my lifetime', concerned that she should not be left 'at large in the world to be subject to the vicissitudes & inconveniences which generally attend the situation of single women', or the mortifications of dependence on relations. He had sacrificed his own comforts, he wrote, to securing her happiness and had resolved to become part of their family. (This may have been a sacrifice in some respects, but it meant that he could maintain a family life.) It was an honourable alliance and Mr Howard was a gentleman universally well thought of, particularly for the 'sweetness of his disposition'. He was, however, only moderately well provided for with what was usually seen as that most important possession, '*money*'. Fortunately, given his connections, his expectations were respectable.[175]

Long moved in with the Howards at the Dower House in Park Bottom, Arundel, for the last years of his life. (See Figure 5.7.) He continued to spend time with his other children and was impressed by the beauty of the countryside round Hampton Lodge. 'I do not know any spot', he told Elizabeth, 'which commands a more pleasing home-view, or that combines a greater variety of wild and cultivated Country, wood, water and heath all blending together in

---

[173] Ibid., II. 323–4.
[174] Ibid., II. 327.
[175] Edward Long to Mary Ricketts, 30 September 1801, Ricketts Family Papers.

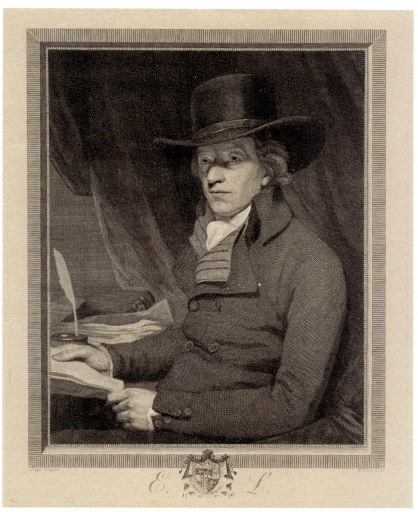

Plate 1 Quill to hand, this is one of the only surviving portraits of Edward Long. Line engraving, 1796, by William Sharp, after a painting by John Opie. © National Portrait Gallery, London.

Plate 2 William Berryman's idealized depiction of Lucky Valley plantation. 'Lucky Valley Estate', Clarendon, Jamaica, watercolour drawing, *c.* 1815. British Library, London, UK. © British Library Board. All Rights Reserved/Bridgeman Images.

Plate 3 Tredudwel Manor, the Long family's Cornish home. Photograph by Catherine Hall.

Plate 4 The coast near Tredudwel Manor where the Long family took their picnics. Photograph by Catherine Hall.

Plate 5 Racial capitalism at work, as seen in this cartouche. Detail from the map of Surrey as part of the Twelve-Sheet Map of the Three Counties of Jamaica, by Henry Moore, Thomas Craskell and James Simpson, 1756–61. Engraving by Daniel Fournier, 1763. Courtesy of the Library of Congress, Geography and Map Division.

Plate 6 William Berryman's drawing of a Driver as he sets out for the day with the whip over his shoulder. 'Driver, Cold Morning', grey ink drawing, 1808–16. Courtesy of the Library of Congress, Prints and Photographs Division, LC-DIG-ppmsca-13420.

Plate 7 'View of the Roaring River Cascade'. Reproduced from Edward Long, *The History of Jamaica Or, General Survey of the Antient and Modern State of that Island, with Reflections on its Situation, Settlements, Inhabitants, Climate, Products, Commerce, Laws, and Government*, 3 vols. (London: T. Lowndes, 1774). Digitally printed version © Cambridge University Press 2010.

Plate 8 'A View of the White River Cascade'. Reproduced from Long, *The History of Jamaica*. Digitally printed version © Cambridge University Press 2010.

Plate 9 'View of Montego Bay'. Reproduced from Long, *The History of Jamaica*. Digitally printed version © Cambridge University Press 2010.

Plate 10 'View of Port Royal & Kingston Harbours'. Reproduced from Long, *The History of Jamaica*. Digitally printed version © Cambridge University Press 2010.

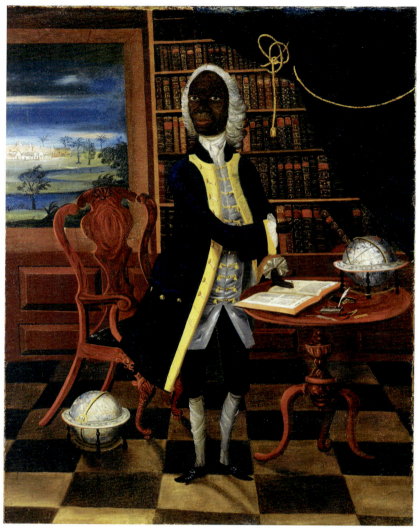

Plate 11 Francis Williams's portrait was donated to the V&A in 1928 having previously been owned by the Long family. Unrecorded artist, oil on canvas, *c.* 1745. © Victoria and Albert Museum, London.

Figure 5.7 Long died in 1813 at the Dower House in Park Bottom, Arundel, which was the seat of his son-in-law, Henry Molyneux-Howard. Courtesy of Arundel Museum and West Sussex County Council.

the Landscape.'[176] The war with France brought troubles for 'us sugar growers', he complained; 'our West India products still remain a drag upon our hands, because we cannot procure them admission into any port or place on the Continent where the influence of France prevails so as to exclude them'.[177] The raising of the tax on sugar in 1803 made things even more difficult. The reductions in Edward's income were significant and the Duke of Norfolk allowed the Howards to live rent free in the Dower House, where Long had two rooms. He became deeply attached to his grandchildren, especially Henry, telling Elizabeth with delight of Harry's companionship with a young 'labourer's boy about his own age called George. He is the Robinson Crusoe and George the man Friday.'[178] Harry had clearly understood his position as a young master. Proper relations of deference had been established, with George acting as the 'native' Friday to the young Howard's Robinson Crusoe. Long was irritated when the boy's other grandfather, the duke, wanted to send him to school aged seven without having paid any attention to the child. In his opinion, he confided to Elizabeth, most parents who sent away young children to school did it for their own convenience rather than in the interests of the child. He remembered from his own childhood being sent away

---

[176] Howard, *Records and Letters*, II. 331.
[177] Ibid., II. 334.
[178] Copies of Letters of Edward Long. To Lady Henry Howard from her father. Cumbrian Archives Centre, DHW/832.

to school and learning nothing until he was twelve. Once again, where did the plantation sit in his mind? What of the grass gang, with those children of five and six weeding and toiling?

Long's strong sense of family and blood connection included his three sisters and their children. His youngest sister, Amelia, belonged to the least prosperous branch of the family. She had returned with her disgraced mother to England in 1755 and was sent to a school by her father, who had forbidden any further contact with her mother. The schoolmistress had finally felt so sorry for Mary that she allowed her to look at her daughter through a slit in a screen. Edward had heard from Robert in 1763 that Amelia had married Mr Samuel Heming without informing anyone. She had told her mother they were going to Yorkshire; in fact they had set sail for Jamaica. Two years later Mary was very concerned about Edward's account of 'my poor Emma' and wrote to him, trusting 'you will still continue your goodness to her as I am but too well convinced she will meet with no acts of Friendship from any of her Relations except you and myself'.[179] On her death Mary left everything to Amelia since she knew the other children were all well provided for. Samuel Heming came from a colonial family, but there were difficulties with his estate. He died sometime in the late 1770s and in his will noted that his affairs were too unsettled to make provision for his wife, Elizabeth Amelia. Nor could he make an equal division among his children 'so as to fix and settle an adequate provision on each'. This was due to a trust for a term of years on his sugar works in the parish of St Ann called Saville (*sic*). He left the property in trust, counting on his executors to provide for his three sons, Richard Samuel Edward, Samuel Scudamore and George Francis.[180] Amelia was left in straitened circumstances and became very dependent on brother Edward. As her sister Charlotte (now Lady Lindsay) wrote to Edward, 'Poor Mrs Heming's Fate has been a very melancholy one, tho' even she has cause to be thankful that Providence has given her such a friend as she has met with in you: otherwise what would have become of her and her children, for where has she met with assistance, but from you, or thro' your means.'[181] Amelia herself wrote to Edward in 1787 seeking assistance with school fees: 'really taxes are so high and every necessary of Life so dear that Money melts imperceptibly ... take compassion on me therefore my Dr Brother, for without your assistance, what can I do'.[182] She was very worried about the hurricane that had seriously affected the crops that year: how might that reduce his income? All the family knew about the importance of the cane to their well-being.

---

[179] Howard, *Records and Letters*, I. 116.
[180] 'Samuel Heming of St Catherine', Legacies of British Slave-ownership database, http://wwwdepts-live.ucl.ac.uk/lbs/person/view/2146648853, accessed 28 October 2020.
[181] Howard, *Records and Letters*, I. 249.
[182] Ibid., I. 251.

Edward was himself very worried as to his Jamaican affairs. He wrote to Beeston in January 1787 expressing his concerns, and grateful that his son took an interest. His nephew George Heming was in need of financial support. It had been hoped to send him to Cambridge, but he, Edward, could not commit himself financially for more than a year since his own situation was unclear. 'When I reflect on the precariousness of my ability to contribute', he wrote, 'as well as on the uncertainty of my life, I am quite unsettled in my resolution what to do.'[183] Nearly all the canes on which the crop depended had been destroyed in the hurricane and the aqueduct swept away. Things were less bad at Lucky Valley than at Longville, but he thought he might have lost at least £2,500 income. It was a matter of serious concern to him that so many depended on him. 'My great unhappiness', he confided to his 'dear son',

> is the having so numerous a Family depending upon one, who is so little enabled to requite their expectations or to promote and establish their future comfort in life in the manner becoming their merits or corrisponding to their wants. Here you see the real source of every infelicity that I feel; for the common accidents and misfortunes of life no otherwise affect my mind, than as they touch that string.[184]

These were the years of the 'crisis of slave subsistence', in Richard Sheridan's words, when tens of thousands of the enslaved died of hunger and malnutrition, their permanent state of weakness accentuated by the effects of the American war and a sequence of natural disasters.[185]

Such scales of want were unknown in the Long family. Edward intervened on behalf of his nephew Samuel Scudamore Heming with his brother-in-law Sir David Lindsay's brother, Admiral Sir John Lindsay, and was able to secure him a place as a midshipman.[186] Amelia was supported for many years by the family, finally making a successful claim on the Seville estate in St Ann. Samuel Scudamore did inherit a share in that estate from his father. His marriage to his first cousin Mary Charlotte Long, the daughter of Robert and Lucy Long, also brought him a share in Longville.[187] Their son Richard received the compensation for 168 enslaved persons on Seville. His claim was unsuccessfully contested by Rutherford and Jegon of London, merchants who were engaged in other business for members of the Long family, notably Edward Beeston Long.[188]

---

[183] Ibid., I. 252.
[184] Ibid., I. 253.
[185] Richard B. Sheridan, 'The Crisis of Slave Subsistence in the British West Indies during and after the American Revolution', *WMQ* 33.4 (1976), 615–41.
[186] Sir John Lindsay was the father of Dido Elizabeth Belle.
[187] 'Samuel Scudamore Heming', Legacies of British Slave-ownership database, http://wwwdepts-live.ucl.ac.uk/lbs/person/view/2146635767, accessed 28 October 2020.
[188] 'Jamaica St Ann 752 (Seville)', Legacies of British Slave-ownership database, http://wwwdepts-live.ucl.ac.uk/lbs/claim/view/19927, accessed 28 October 2020.

A deeply affectionate father, a loving husband, a devoted friend: this is Long's self-representation that we can extract from his writings. What sense can we make of it in the light of his activities as a slave-owner?

Conclusion

The Longs were part of a wider West India network in both Jamaica and England. They were related to the Moores, the Ellises, the Beckfords, the Palmers, the Gregorys, amongst others – elite colonial families.[189] Edward Long, as Mair puts it, 'represented the classic creole concentration of kinship and influence'. They were intimately connected with the West Indians in the metropole and engaged in the pro-slavery struggles of the last decades of the eighteenth century. Some of them married into the landed gentry and minor aristocracy. The wills of the landed branch of the family include significant annuities and legacies to numerous servants, from cooks, maidservants, laundresses and gardeners, to coachmen and farriers. This was money left on the basis of services rendered: Edward Long was typical in leaving £20 to his 'faithful servant Jane'.[190] English servants were named, remembered and rewarded in ways that enslaved and commodified persons never were.[191] Samuel III lived in lavish country gentry style at Carshalton, Charles IV at Hurt's Hall, Charles V in his Italianate villa, Charles Beckford at Langley Hall, and Edward Beeston Long at Hampton Lodge. Charles V was the only member of the family who left significant philanthropic bequests, not only to the British Museum and the National Gallery but for hospitals, clergy widows and church building. These families had effectively disguised their slavery connections. Their lives had scant connection with the source of their wealth: they seemed to be living the pure-blooded white English life that Edward Long hoped for.

Charles Edward Long, Edward's grandson, followed in his footsteps, devoting much of his life to securing the name of the family. He was the only surviving son of Charles Beckford and his wife, Frances. They had money, thanks to Frances, and the boy was educated at Harrow and Trinity. Having inherited an ample fortune, he was able to live very comfortably, devoting himself to antiquarian and genealogical interests. Like his Uncle Charles V, he was a strong supporter of the British Museum. He seems to have shared the family view as to the rights of property owners. A pamphlet on the Game Laws published in 1824 argued that game should be considered as property and

---

[189] Mair, *A Historical Study*, 158–9.
[190] Will of Edward Long, 1813.
[191] As Kathleen Wilson argues, colonial households run by commodified persons were enacting repetition with a difference from English households with their waged servants; *Strolling Players of Empire. Theater and Performances of Power in the British Imperial Provinces, 1656–1833* (Cambridge, 2022).

could, therefore, be legally sold.[192] An anonymously published essay, *Negro Emancipation No Philanthropy* (1830), probably written by him, was a defence of the slave-owners, warning that abolition would be 'an outrageous violation of private property' and making a strong case for the payment of compensation. The example of Haiti was clear, he asserted: 'The West Indian archipelago must be governed by absolute authority.' Echoing his grandfather's fears, he threatened his readers: 'At present we are distinctly verging towards that euthanasia of West Indian Empire, a Mulatto Government.'[193] His devotion to familial honour was further marked by his published defence of his Uncle Robert Ballard Long's military conduct in 1811, which had been critiqued in an account of the Peninsula War.[194] As a trustee of the marriage settlement of his cousin Mary Long (Edward Beeston Long's daughter), he received £2,000 in compensation for 156 enslaved persons on Lucky Valley, a place to which he had never been.[195] Once again family property had passed through a woman to the sixth generation of men. Charles Edward Long donated his grandfather's papers, together with many other materials he had himself collected, to the British Museum. They are now archived in the British Library as the Long Papers and have allowed historians a particular route into eighteenth-century Jamaica, one chosen by a protagonist of his familial interests.

Try as they would, however, any hopes of forgetting the Jamaican connections or maintaining clear distinctions between black and white were disappointed: the boundaries could not be sealed. The names told their own story, for those who knew Jamaica: Beeston, Beckford, Ballard, all carried their associations with the island and with slavery. Some fathers were willing to recognize their 'reputed' children, as Alderman Beckford and Bryan Edwards, Edward's friend and fellow historian, did. Unexpected associations were never far away. Not all the extended family were wealthy as we have seen, but none were poor. Mary Long lived in straitened circumstances; Amelia Heming struggled to support her family. Periodically their intimate associations with slavery, usually denied, surfaced. One of Amelia's sons, Samuel Scudamore, was named after his godfather, Scudamore Winde, a slave-owner and merchant of St Catherine, who died in 1776. Winde left a personal estate of more than £68,000, plus enslaved persons and property in Herefordshire. A series of substantial legacies were earmarked for his illegitimate children; the mother of

---

[192] George Goodwin and Michael Erben, 'Long, Charles Edward (1796–1861), Genealogist and Antiquary', *ODNB*, [2004] 2008, https://doi.org/10.1093/ref:odnb/16963.

[193] A Jamaica Proprietor, *Negro Emancipation No Philanthropy. A letter to the Duke of Wellington* (London, 1830), 24, 53. Larry E. Tise, *Proslavery. A History of the Defense of Slavery in America, 1701–1840* (London, 1987), 93, suggests that Charles Edward Long was the author of this pamphlet and there seem to be convincing arguments for this.

[194] Goodwin and Erben, 'Long, Charles Edward', *ODNB*.

[195] 'Charles Edward Long', Legacies of British Slave-ownership database, https://www.ucl.ac.uk/lbs/person/view/42166, accessed 3 March 2021.

Figure 5.8 St Michael and All Angels church in Tunstall, Suffolk, where Ann Long's husband, Rev. Philip Carter was the vicar. Image courtesy of Keith McClelland.

one of them – Patt, a 'negro woman' – he had manumitted. 'My natural son' Robert Winde was left an annuity and a cash legacy, as was his daughter Penelope.[196] In addition there were other legacies, including one of £500 to Catherine Long, Edward's daughter, and one to a mixed-race godchild. Winde was clearly fairly intimate with the Long family. The Hemings lived in Jamaica for some years: their connection with a household such as that of Scudamore Winde demonstrates the impossibility of drawing the kind of clear boundaries between white families and others that Edward Long dreamed of.

Occasionally the connections were closer. Ann, the daughter of Charles I and Jane, died in 1794. Both her husband, Rev. Philip Carter, the Anglican vicar of the substantial church in Tunstall, Suffolk (see Figure 5.8), close to Hurt's Hall, and her daughter had predeceased her. She wished to be buried beside them in Tunstall, near to the family properties. Her own very modest property was left to her sister, bar small personal gifts to other women. She was clear that she had nothing worth the 'acceptance' of her 'dear brother', nephews and nieces. She was the poor relation. She specified, however, the

---

[196] 'Scudamore Winde', Legacies of British Slave-ownership database, http://wwwdepts-live.ucl.ac.uk/lbs/person/view/2146660205, accessed 28 October 2020.

significant sum of £100 for 'my black servant Henry Norbrook cancelling his bond'. The bond cannot be specified: had he perhaps paid for his manumission? In a codicil she added, she gave £5 to his daughter Hannah.[197] Norbrook was the family plantation inherited through Jane Modyford/Long/Beeston. Henry Norbrook was born around 1713, so it is possible that he was brought to Suffolk by one of the Longs. He married a local woman, Hannah Cooper, and their daughter Hannah was baptized in Tunstall in 1761. Her baptism record was accompanied by a note written by the parish clerk. 'The registering of Henry Norbrook as a Negro', it read, 'may assist some future person in observing how long in time the colour wears out by marrying with white men or women Hannah being his first child.'[198] Hannah and Henry had five other children born in Tunstall.[199] Why did the parish clerk record this note? What was known of the Long family's connections with Jamaica and slavery? Who were the servants in neighbouring Hurt's Hall? Were they all white? To what extent had debates about the black population in England filtered into the rural districts of Suffolk? The parish clerk was ruminating on skin colour: how long would it take for white to cancel out black? The question was one that sorely troubled Ann's cousin Edward. In 1786, in the context of growing anxieties about the numbers of the black poor on the streets of London, he had been asked to confer with the Committee of West Indian Planters and Merchants 'upon the means of preventing in future, the introduction of Blacks into this Country'.[200] He warned of 'degeneration', of the 'bronzing' of the pure-blooded white population, and hoped to keep black and brown people safely sequestered in the colony.[201]

Long believed in the importance of his family and others like them. The vast majority of references to family in the *History* were to white families: the family of Christopher Columbus, the houses in Spanish Town which were not very convenient for families, descendants of ancient English families, the royal family, a rector's family, an officer's widow with her family, every 'master of a family', the numbers of servants expected by a creole family. Yet when he came to describe creolized Africans he saw, perhaps in spite of himself, that they had families too. The creole slave in Jamaica, he wrote, 'had food and cloathing as much as he wanted, a good house, and his family about him',

---

[197] Will of Ann Carter, 1794. TNA, PROB 11/1246.
[198] Caroline Bressey, 'Invisible Presence: the Whitening of the Black Community in the Historical Imagination of British Archives', *Archivaria* 61 (2006), 50.
[199] Henry and Hannah Norbrook family tree: http://trees.ancestry.co.uk/tree/4416130/person/-1441477233. David Norbrook is a living descendant of this family, personal communication.
[200] Standing Committee of the Committee of West India Planters and Merchants Minutes, London Tavern, 10 March 1786, M915, Reel 2, West India Committee Papers, Senate House Library. Thanks to Katie Donington for this reference.
[201] [Long], *Candid Reflections*, 54.

whereas in Africa he would be 'destitute and helpless'.[202] This was his attempt to paint a benign picture of the lives of the enslaved for his readers. But he also observed that 'They are all married (*in their way*)' and that it was cruel to tear 'Negroe labourers' from 'their settlement and family' in payment of debts. After all, 'since Negroes are the sinews of West-India property, too much care cannot be taken of them'.[203] Here was his recognition of the human needs of those held by violence in servitude: the recognition of what he knew and wanted not to know, the humanity that he denied, that sat at the heart of the disavowal practised by this family as they enjoyed their ill-gotten gains, protected them in law and passed them on from one generation to another.

[202] Long, *History*, II. 400.
[203] Ibid., II. 414, 502.

PART III

Making a Slave Society

Chapters 6, 7 and 8 turn to the work of the colonists in attempting to make and secure a slave society. Long delineated in his *History* the racialized gaze which tried to map and place boundaries between White and 'Negro' on the ground as well as in the mind, the central role of the colonial state in legitimating slavery and hoping to manage rebellion, and the essential work of the philosophers and natural historians in codifying and fixing racial difference and inequality.

6

Colonizing Geographies

Edward Long was engaged in his *History* in making, marking and, he hoped, fixing racial binaries – fixing not only people, but animals and commodities in space and *place*. Jamaica was to be a *known* place with assigned identities, established boundaries, clarity as to who and what belonged where. Who should live where? Who could travel and how? How might white people protect themselves and be safe in this environment? What animals did they need? How could tropical abundance be put to use? This process of colonization involved violence, both to people and to the environment. Long's representation focused on Jamaica's natural wealth and the island's potential as a site of regeneration: Englishmen who were unable to secure a 'competent provision' at home could transplant themselves, just as sheep, horses and plants could be put to new use. The island was a part of the new world in which people, goods and ideas were cycled, recycled and consumed between Europe, Africa and the Americas.[1] It was a place with ample resources for all. Beggars, he claimed, conveniently forgetting the scale of hunger on the plantations, were unknown. A little-known island was to be transformed in the minds of his readers into familiar yet exotic terrain, a tropical place that could be a source of income and a home to Englishmen. He laid the island out as an object of inquiry and a place of promise, utilizing a variety of forms. Maps were there, to place it on the globe; lengthy descriptions of its landscape, from its sublime beauties to its cane fields, towns and harbours; engravings to fix images on the mind; statistics to record progress; useful advice on health, dress and diet; natural history listings to name the rich resources – all designed to sketch the properties of the island and demonstrate not just its present value and suitability for settlers, but its potential as an imperial possession. Long was engaged in colonizing and racializing Jamaica, making named places, privatizing the land, defining those territories which had been transformed by the settlers, marking out what more needed to be done, surveying potential sites for new 'industrious' white families, locating the areas suited to 'Negroes', noting Maroon territory, labelling the enclaves of Jewish merchants and Moravian missionaries. Different kinds of humans, he was explaining to his

---

[1] Joseph Roach, *Cities of the Dead. Circum-Atlantic Performance* (New York, 1996).

audience, could be attached to different kinds of places, just as different commodities were suited to different soils and different animals could be domesticated.[2] His *History* spelt out the fantasy that such boundaries could be fixed. He aimed to minimize the transgressions.

Such efforts to contain were inevitably fractured; bodies did not stay in place. Black domestics cared for white children, white overseers beat and entered black bodies. Insects became dangerous enemies attacking their victims. The fantasy that the ownership of property and people carried ownership of the island was fraught with contradiction. Long gave racialized meaning – colonial meaning – to place. The meanings would have been different for enslaved men and women: what might they have called 'Lucky Valley'? As Sylvia Wynter insists, the dominant cultural logic that Long and others like him were inscribing was never watertight: there was always something in excess. In creating the provision grounds, the plantations facilitated a place of rootedness for Africans, a plot of belonging, a site for a different form of life, a different kind of otherness, a different notion of humanity.[3] A strategy to save money for the planters by making the enslaved grow their own food became a 'rival geography'.[4] Long, however, was attempting to marginalize in his writing any alternatives to his project of making Jamaica a place for white colonists supported by black labour.

Long's topography of the island, his recommendations for the health of the white population, his climatic comments and 'synopsis of vegetables and other Productions of this Island, proper for Exportation, or Home Use and Consumption' were all designed to persuade a metropolitan public that Jamaica was indeed a safe and productive place for them, its racialized boundaries secured.[5] From the earliest years of the colony, black mobility had been restricted by penal codes that Long revisited. White men could move as they pleased. The enslaved could not: they must be fixed in their place, only allowed to travel in the interests of their masters, requiring tickets to leave the plantations, disciplined if they transgressed and were caught. The code of 1696, Long recorded, had decreed that 'Straggling slaves, apprehended without a ticket (or pass), are to be punished with *moderate* whipping.' Similarly, 'Hawking about' and selling goods other than those which were permitted

---

[2] McKittrick, 'Plantation Futures'.
[3] David Scott, 'The Re-enchantment of Humanism: an Interview with Sylvia Wynter', *Small Axe* 8 (2000), 119–207; Sylvia Wynter, 'Jonkonnu in Jamaica: Towards the Interpretation of the Folk Dance as a Cultural Process', *Jamaica Journal* 4. 2 (1970), 34–48; Wynter, 'Unsettling the Coloniality of Being/Power/Truth/Freedom: Towards the Human, after Man, its Overrepresentation – an Argument', *CR: the New Centenniel Review* 3.3 (2003), 257–337; Katherine McKittrick, *Demonic Grounds: Black Women and the Cartographies of Struggle* (Minneapolis, 2006).
[4] The term is Edward Said's, elaborated by Camp, *Closer to Freedom*, 7.
[5] Long, *History*, III. 674.

for the Sunday markets would be punished.[6] Punishments were enumerated for runaways. In 1749 there were restrictions on 'Slaves hunting cattle, horses, mares etc.' with 'instruments of death' unless they were in company with their masters.[7] None were to carry fire-arms about the island without a ticket. After 1760 yet further restrictions were put in place to prevent 'the evils arising from irregular assemblies of slaves', their dangerous habits of going from place to place without tickets.[8] It was vital to attempt to control passage across the plantations and prevent conspiracy. 'Free Negroes, Mulattos or Indians' were required to register in the vestry books of their parish and carry certificates with them, wearing 'the badge of their freedom'.[9] Yet there were many reasons why limits on the movement of 'others' could never be entirely fixed. Long celebrated the 'two Negroes, belonging to Mr Beckford, [who] having taken horse at the first alarm' in 1760 rode to Spanish Town to warn the lieutenant-governor, who 'immediately dispatched two parties of regulars and two troops of horse-militia' to attack the rebels.[10]

Limiting 'irregular' mobility, by the wrong people, was a priority. Improving mobility for the colonists, however, was essential. Long was preoccupied, as we have seen, with the importance of better roads to facilitate the movement of troops and goods. 'Good roads add a lustre to any country and enrich it,' he argued; 'dispatch' was the 'soul of business'.[11] 'Negroes' serving white needs must, of course, travel: drivers carrying the cane from the plantations to the quayside, footmen accompanying official carriages, grooms following the horses ridden by the planters, baggage handlers for the militia, all these were necessary. The ownership and use of horses was an important status symbol and sign of authority. Sitting astride a horse, carrying a whip, surveying those beneath, were symbols of white mastery for planters, attorneys and overseers.[12] Walking, in contrast, was a sign of subordination. Long noted how even 'the poorest free Negro', anxious to distinguish himself from the enslaved, 'will not be without a saddle-horse or two'.[13] Not content with providing instruction on the proper building of roads, Long discussed carriages and wheels at some length, all relevant to the construction of a more profitable and polite society.

Horses had multiple uses: in warfare, for status, for pleasure, for travel and as a commodity. They were there to serve humans. Long gave a vivid description of an experience on horseback: a near-hit by lightning was accompanied

---

[6] Ibid., II. 485–7.
[7] Ibid., II. 488.
[8] *JAJ*, 6 and 16 December 1760.
[9] *JAJ*, 16 December 1760.
[10] Long, *History*, II. 450.
[11] Ibid., I. 464.
[12] David Lambert, 'Master–Horse–Slave: Mobility, Race and Power in the British West Indies, c. 1780–1838', *S&A* 36.4 (2018), 618–41.
[13] Long, *History*, II. 33.

by terrifying thunder. His petrified horse required no whip or spur, those instruments of human command, to speed him on. White men's control was over beasts as well as men. Cromwell had noted in 1655 that Jamaica was well supplied with horses, an important aspect of its suitability for settlement. Those horses played their part in the long struggle to drive out the Spanish and in the campaigns against the Maroons who could not withstand 'horse platoons'.[14] The 'horse-militia' was deployed against the rebels in 1761. The failure to breed horses on the island was foolish, in Long's opinion, and their importation from North America an unnecessary expense. Horse dung was used for cane, horses drove some of the sugar mills, horses were replacing 'Negroes' in the production of indigo, horse hair was valued by saddlers and coach makers. Horses, alongside oxen and mules, were essential to the running of the plantations.

In mapping the land with his racializing gaze and turning 'space' into named 'place', Long was also hoping to moralize it, securing not only economic but 'morally certain' prospects.[15] Such a project required its legal framework alongside its discursive and material practices: poetry, prose, engravings, maps and tables were all put to work to be studied alongside the penal codes and listings of commodities. His racial cartography, however, could never be secure. The boundaries were porous and constantly transgressed: enslaved women washed and dressed colonists, runaways joined the Maroons, rebellions happened. Topographical description was augmented with advice on health in an attempt to halt the scale of white mortality, while documentations of the island's abundance emphasized the potential that was there to be enjoyed. Long's focus on improvement was always in tension with his fears of degeneration; his determination to keep 'Negroes' in subjection rested on his disavowal of dependence.

Topography/Chorography

Chorography, the systematic description of a place or region, was influential in early modern England. Dugdale, Pennant and Camden collected facts and surveys, reflected on past and present, used a recognizable authorial voice and a degree of native knowledge. Long built on these approaches. His detailed accounts of the parishes were set in a wider context of his imagined geographies, rooted both in his bodily experience and in his attempted theorizations of racial difference. Place mattered: he was a creole patriot. He invited his readers to move from parish to parish with him as he created a building block for white settlement. Long knew the island. He had traversed it many times on horseback, often riding fifty miles in a day. Sometimes he might be visiting friends

---

[14] Ibid., I. 342, 40.
[15] Ibid., II. 213.

and family, sometimes consulting with neighbours about politics or horticulture, sometimes attending the local quarter sessions or slave court; sometimes administering punishment or checking on roads and defences for the assembly, sometimes on his regular route between Spanish Town and Lucky Valley. He might be managing the plantation or paying attention to natural beauties, points of archaeological or historical interest, numbers of barracks and fortifications, levels of productivity, distinguished residences with their gentlemanly occupants and possibilities for development. Each parish was summed up in terms of its economic success or decline, with a tally of numbers of sugar estates, the 'stock' – both cattle and 'slaves' – and the hogsheads of sugar produced in recent years, showing, whenever possible, the great advances which had taken place. Sugar and commerce were the staples of the island's wealth. This was a book representing Jamaica as a prosperous place with a rosy future, a growth point in an expanding commercial empire. Part of Long's task was to de-toxify it, as Dian Kriz has argued – to shift the English imaginary with its burgeoning anti-slavery sentiments away from whips and cruel slave-owners to Jamaica as a place that could civilize, offering a territory between the darkness of Africa and the light of England, a moralizing space for brute Africans, and a middle way between rudeness and refinement.[16] Long's task was two-fold: to make Jamaica familiar to his metropolitan readers and to legitimate its colonial difference: slavery. His property ownership secured his position as an enlightened man, with the leisure to politic, to travel, to botanize, to read and to write his manuscript from a distance – hardly the position of a detached observer, a Mr Spectator, since he was a planter, yet capable, he claimed, of displaying 'an impartial character'.[17] His cartographic vision was rooted in his assumption that sugar was the key to the island's wealth; his was the eye of a planter. Although he was enthusiastic about the need for a more diverse agricultural base and looking for ways to make Jamaica more self-sufficient, the picture that he painted was selective. The pens for stockbreeding and the urban enterprises received very little attention, and the recent scholarly judgement, based on quantitative data, that 'in mid-eighteenth-century Jamaica the typical settler was not a sugar planter but a producer of provisions or livestock and certainly not the holder of a vast conglomerate of properties but the proprietor of a single settlement' would have surprised him.[18]

The maps were there to constitute knowledge for the readers, to give shape to distant lands and seas, to make visible what was new and different.[19] A series of six provided the frontispiece to the first volume of the *History*, placing

---

[16] Kay Dian Kriz, *Slavery, Sugar and the Culture of Refinement. Picturing the West Indies, 1700–1840* (London, 2008).
[17] Long, *History*, I. 2.
[18] Greene, *Settler Jamaica*, 70.
[19] Miles Ogborn and Charles W. J. Withers (eds.), *Georgian Geographies. Essays on Space, Place and Landscape in the Eighteenth Century* (Manchester, 2004).

Jamaica in its regional context, relevant to both war and commerce. The Caribbean had been a major theatre of conflict in the Seven Years War, a crucial site of European competition and military action. The dangerous proximity to those traditional enemies, France and Spain, was highlighted by Cuba to the north and Saint-Domingue and Hispaniola to the east. The island's trade routes to Honduras (for mahogany) and across the Spanish Main and to the north and east (for the very profitable re-export of the enslaved) clarified Jamaica's significance as an entrepot. When it came to Jamaica itself, the three counties, Middlesex, Surry (*sic*) and Cornwall, were mapped from an engraving of 1774. Long may have been consulted on this, since Lucky Valley was one of the very few plantations to be named, while Old Harbour Bay and Long Island were clearly visible.[20] The major towns of Spanish Town, Kingston and Montego Bay were marked along with numerous barracks, suggesting that the map was probably commissioned for military purposes. A detailed map provided of Port Royal and Kingston harbour would have served navigational purposes and was there to assure a safe and secure location, with good commercial access, while a plan of Port Antonio surveyed in 1771 was likely associated with the hopes of greatly extending its defences as a naval base against the French, which Long discussed in detail.[21]

His 'Topographical Description of the Island', the first half of volume II, opened with a listing of the counties, with their familiar English names signifying connection, reminding his audience of English settlement and securing familiarity in the face of difference, and the eight parishes, again with their English names, some, as with Clarendon, recalling important historic personages. Having embarked from the colonial capital with its impressive architecture, he gradually traversed the island, ending up in those districts waiting to be colonized. A number of conflicting imperatives informed his writing. Jamaica was a commercial colony, its 'society composed of industrious planters and merchants' as he put it, conveniently ignoring the majority population, and he must demonstrate its progress.[22] At the same time, the scope for much further development had to be clear – the available land and the opportunities for hard-working white settlers. Given the absence of any landowning aristocracy that secured gentility, he must demonstrate the civilized state of the island and the place of the white elite with their elegant residences and capacity to enhance tropical beauties and create landscapes. Then it was vital to show that the island was secure, with defences in place, 'Negroes' contained and white power in command. Long negotiated these needs, sometimes conflicting – which were his needs as well as those he projected on to his readers – by utilizing a variety of genres and voices, drawing

---

[20] Long, *History*, II. Frontispiece.
[21] Ibid., II. 102, 174.
[22] Ibid., I. 70.

on both his literary and imaginative skills alongside his familiarity with the sugar economy and political arithmetic.

His central focus was on a representation of Jamaica as a place for white colonists. But the island was built on the West India trade; he knew the plantation economy and need for enslaved labour. The majority black population comprised the underbelly for him, the sinews, as they were frequently characterized, which were essential to the prosperity of the island. 'Negroes' were present in his topographical account, but always in limited and specified ways. Most importantly, they were counted numerically at the end of the description of each parish, the increase or decrease over decades taken as an indicator as to whether the economy had improved or declined. Quantification, once again, provided a foil to any underlying anxieties as to the 'things behind the things' – the dead, the hungry, the enslaved women who failed to reproduce.

In St John, for example, he noted with regret the decrease in the numbers of 'Negroes' from 5,875 in 1740 to 5,455 in 1768 and the reduction in cattle from 2,837 to 2,726 over the same period, showing that the parish was not 'getting forwards'. (See Figure 6.1.) 'Let me here remark', he continued, 'on the great utility of comparing the present and past state of the parishes together.' This was his particular task as a historian, to reflect on past and present. St John had good air, 'a fruitful soil, and regular seasons'. It ought to be a profitable place, yet there were signs of decline. He suspected that the lack of good roads was one of the issues, alongside the depressed state of those settlers who had failed. A 'patriotic government', he insisted, should investigate the causes and remedy them.[23] Clarendon, on the other hand, showed a most healthy increase in the numbers of both 'Negroes' and cattle, from 10,769 people in 1734 to 15,517 in

State of the Parish:

	Negroes.	Cattle.	Sugar-plantations.	Hogsheads.	Other Settlements.
1734,	5242	2561			
1740,	5875	2837			
1745,	5728	2250			
1761,	5888				
1768,	5455	2726	21	2200	50

Figure 6.1 Table from Long's *History* quantifying enslaved people alongside cattle, sugar and the number of plantations in St John. Reproduced from Long, *The History of Jamaica*. Digitally printed version © Cambridge University Press 2010.

[23] Ibid., II. 52–3.

	Negroes.	Cattle.	Sugar-works.	Annual Produce. Hogſheads.	Other Settlements.
1734,	10769	11027			
1740,	11575	12299			
1745,	12775	11969			
1761,	13772				
1768,	15517	14276	70	8000	180

Figure 6.2 Table from Long's *History* quantifying enslaved people alongside cattle, sugar and the number of plantations in Clarendon. Reproduced from Long, *The History of Jamaica*. Digitally printed version © Cambridge University Press 2010.

1768 and from 11,027 cattle to 14,276, and the parish now had seventy sugar works producing 8,000 hogsheads annually. (See Figure 6.2.) It was clear that it was in a 'flourishing state', with 180 other settlements producing coffee, ginger, corn and cocoa.[24] What was more, there was still much undeveloped land and a great need for new settlers. In summarizing his figures on the levels of economic production across the three counties, he noted that Cornwall came out exceptionally well. Though it had fewer 'Negroes' and cattle than Middlesex, yet it was more productive owing to the 'freshness' of land, the quantities of rain, the quality of the cane land and the accessibility to shipping. Here was the planter speaking economic truths: it was a combination of the numbers of 'Negroes', preferably available with 'speedy importation', the cattle, the land, the levels of skill in sugar production, and the numbers of water mills and proper roads that together enabled high levels of sugar and rum production. His overall conclusion on the state of the economy, backed up by his figures, was that 'astonishingly great progress' had been made since Leslie's survey in his *History* published in 1741. 'How vastly profitable' Jamaica was to the mother country.[25] How vital enslaved 'Negroes' were.

Long noted the presence of 'Negroes' at a variety of other points in his descriptions of the parishes, usually about work. They were assigned to serve in the forts, should always be used for heavy labour such as clearing land and building roads – occupations that tended to kill Europeans – and were required to sail the small wherries ferrying from Port Royal to Passage Fort. But they must be in place. He was enraged by those 'Negroes' who escaped from St Ann on the north coast and this fuelled a long disquisition on the scandal of human 'lost property'. These escapees hoped to find their freedom in Cuba but were usually seized by the Spanish, 'a thievish race' in his estimation. 'Expostulations' had been made about these 'fugitives, or rather stolen goods'

---

[24] Ibid., II. 66–7.
[25] Ibid., II. 227–8.

over a long period, but to no effect. They were able to work for a wage and soon gain manumission. It was a disgrace, flagrant robbery and a breach of good faith between two nations: there should be reprisals. 'The sovereign of Great Britain', remonstrated Long, 'holds an interest in all the Negroes possessed by his colony-subjects.' His revenue is 'very greatly benefited and supported by the produce of their personal labour'. What was more, 'the nation at large holds an interest in them by the number of manufacturers set to work; by the shipping and mariners; by the articles necessary to cloathe, feed and employ these labourers; and by their general consumption of British merchandizes'. This was a matter of 'national concern'.[26] 'Negroes', as he had asserted in his polemic against Mansfield, were, after all, *'choses, merchandize* for *sale'*.[27] He referred angrily to the Somerset judgment that owners could not reclaim their property once they were in England: was it now acceptable for the Spanish to kidnap and keep enslaved property? His insistence on 'merchandize' and 'property' was undercut by his recognition that 'Negroes' were human; they could escape. Africans appeared at other points in the *History*, as rebels and as objects of inquiry in his discussion of the 'human', even occasionally as unnamed interlocutors, giving him information on some aspect of creole life. They might be mentioned alongside cattle, as in his recognition that 'Negroes' and horses were distressed by the coldness of the air in the Blue Mountains, or that the rain could be so heavy in the low-lying lands of Portland that it could wash away buildings, cattle and 'Negroes'. He might describe their habit of washing in the River Cobre or the capture of an alligator. There were sporadic mentions of 'Free Negroes', especially in reference to the populations of Spanish Town and Kingston. But his topography was predominantly white.

Long's major effort was to paint the island as a place for white people, with the 'Negroes' there only to service them. St Catherine took pride of place in his account, 'entitled to preference' since it was 'first inhabited by the English' and contained the 'ancient metropolis' of St Jago de la Vega, now known as Spanish Town.[28] Its latitudinal and longitudinal location relative to London was referenced, followed by its distance from Kingston and Port Royal. Since Spanish Town had no harbour of its own, the proximity to Port Royal was vital. Just as he had chosen to open his first volume with the colonial constitution, a traditional subject for historians, so he opened the second with the seat of governance, drawing attention to its impressive architecture, while regretting the conduct of the first English settlers who had neglected or destroyed the 'magnificence' of the original Spanish buildings.[29] The town, he admitted, was not well designed, but the church of St Catherine (where, he might have added,

---

[26] Ibid., II. 85–9.
[27] [Long], *Candid Reflections*, 30–2.
[28] Long, *History*, II. 1.
[29] Ibid., II. 4.

his father and great-grandfather were buried) was an 'elegant building of brick' and had been 'thoroughly repaired' in 1762.[30] The present rector was Dr Lindsay, who described himself as 'particularly intimate with Lady Moore's nearest relations' and whose strongly pro-slavery writings ended up in Long's papers.[31] The King's House, as the governor's residence was called, had been planned under Moore's administration and erected at great expense. It was a mark of the planters' renewed confidence in Spanish Town, following the defeat of the proposed move to Kingston, and sugar meant there was money to undertake it. 'It is now thought', Long wrote with pride, 'to be the noblest and best edifice of the kind, either in North-America, or any of the British colonies in the West Indies.'[32] Long had served on the assembly committee which decided what furniture was required for the public rooms. This involved extensive use of the polished mahogany for which Jamaica was famous, including for thirteen mahogany settees, twenty-four Windsor mahogany chairs and five dozen plain mahogany chairs with fan backs, alongside brass busts and other accoutrements. All this was indicative of the significance, in the minds of the members, of the council and assembly and of court deliberations: the members should be properly seated with due recognition of their status.[33] Long's detailed description of the King's House, with its lofty portico, its twelve Ionic columns of Portland stone, its white marble grandeur and its elegant saloons, was relentlessly European in tone, though the bronze busts of philosophers and poets with 'the darkness of their complexion' rather suggesting the idea of 'Negroe Caboceros, exalted to this honourable distinction for some peculiar services' introduced a discordant note, perhaps indicative of his memory of those Africans who had supported the English against the Spanish.[34] The provision of commodious apartments and offices, of private rooms and stables, coach houses and kitchens, made a truly impressive residence suited to the dignity of the commander-in-chief. The great square fronting the house was still under construction and the new buildings for the courts and the assembly rather lacked architectural skill. An idealized engraving, somewhat at variance with this description, accompanied his text (Figure. 6.3).[35]

---

[30] Ibid., II. 5.
[31] On Lindsay, see B. W. Higman, *Proslavery Priest. The Atlantic World of John Lindsay, 1729–1788* (Kingston, Jamaica, 2011), 119.
[32] Long, *History*, II. 7; James Robertson, *Gone is the Ancient Glory. Spanish Town, Jamaica, 1534–2000* (Kingston, Jamaica, 2005).
[33] *JAJ*, 5, 2 and 9 October 1762.
[34] Long, *History*, II. 7.
[35] Engravings and prints required a different production process from written text and it is impossible to know to what extent Long instructed the engravers and printers. His finished volumes were a multi-person endeavour.

The engraving offered a vision of the governing and administrative centre for the island as an impressive set of large-scale buildings set in a spacious square with an enclosure in the middle of it.[36] The official carriage, presumably with its white occupants, travelled across the foreground, with the Palladian buildings on either side. The tiny figures of a black coachman and footman, properly accoutred, and an exoticized black woman carrying fruits on her head, together with an even smaller dog running behind the coach, magnified the scale of the buildings and presented no threat to this ordered fantasy. A white soldier, stationed with his bayonet outside the House of Assembly, ensured tranquillity, while the building looming behind the square may have been the armoury with its stash of weapons and ammunition.[37] Visual representation was one of the many sites of struggle in the war of positions over slavery, and the carefully chosen engravings in Long's *History* played their part in a delineation of the island as a place of untroubled beauty, its black population disempowered, its violence disavowed. The artist had used his power to naturalize racial domination. As Geoff Quilley and Kay Dian Kriz argue, while colonial social, political and economic institutions were taking shape, 'the character of their essential underpinning by the black Atlantic was being bleached and historically suppressed'.[38] Such a picture of the empty grandeur of Spanish Town was greatly at odds, not only with the majority enslaved urban population who peopled the streets but with Long's own account of the colossal, unfinished 'pile of bricks and mortar' opposite the King's House, or, in other parts of his text, of the deep inadequacies of the colonial government, and especially of the ignorant and ill-prepared governors.[39] He was pleased, however, to be able to record great improvements in the previous twenty years in the elegance of the planters' houses, with their piazzas, copied from the Spanish, where the 'master of the house' would 'sit in an elbow-chair, with his feet resting against one of the piazza-columns; in this attitude he converses, smokes his pipe, or quaffs his tea, in all the luxury of indolence'.[40] Here were the signs of creolization which seemed to indicate a more settled way of life, an intention to stay on the island. But the 'orders of architecture' were 'confusedly jumbled together' and the general rule of building tended to be '*make-shift*'.[41] The splendour of the King's House, a properly

---

[36] For a discussion of the engraving, see Geoff Quilley, 'Questions of Loyalty: the Representation of the British West Indian Colonies during the American Revolutionary War', in John Bonehill and Geoff Quilley (eds.), *Conflicting Visions. War and Visual Culture in Britain and France, c. 1700–1830* (Aldershot, 2005), 114–35.
[37] Many thanks to Esther Chadwick for her discussion with me about Long's engravings.
[38] Geoff Quilley and Kay Dian Kriz (eds.), *An Economy of Colour. Visual Culture and the Atlantic World, 1660–1830* (Manchester, 2003), 9.
[39] Long, *History*, II. 9.
[40] Ibid., II. 21.
[41] Ibid., II. 22.

Figure 6.3 'A View of the King's House and Public Offices at St Jago de la Vega'. Reproduced from Long, *The History of Jamaica*. Digitally printed version © Cambridge University Press 2010.

white space, serviced by the enslaved and symbolizing a prosperous and well-governed colony, was juxtaposed to the disgrace of the gaol, and here his language became animated by his visceral disgust, as he wrote of the 'vile sophisticated compound' of new rum and pepper, brewed by Jewish retailers which soldiers and other poor whites gathered to drink, and the character of the common soldiers, 'the very refuse of the British army'.[42] These were the contrasts which littered his text, undermining any simple rendition of hopes for the future, for there was always the threat of decay.

Spanish Town lived off the courts and the government: when they were sitting 'universal gaiety prevail.'[43] Long's emphasis was on representing the town as a proper seat of colonial power. Kingston was quite different: a commercial town. Here the imperative was to consider its facilities, encourage its growth and prosperity, for its recent history was not encouraging: the decline of the Spanish trade had hit it badly and Montego Bay was now a serious competitor for the 'Guinea trade'. Planned from its earliest foundations in 1693, 'in propriety of design it is, perhaps, not excelled by any town in the world'. Its harbour, capable of holding a thousand ships safely at anchor, was the key to its importance, and a map demonstrated how the finger of land on which Port Royal stood protected the entry for shipping.

Much of Long's text on Kingston was concerned with health, for if trade was to grow and new white settlers were to be encouraged, mortality rates needed to be reduced. He was anxious for public buildings that would cater to the traders. The public building in Spanish Town, he averred, fostered proper respect. Designated premises dealing with customs and naval affairs, a convenient place where 'traders and men of business can regularly meet, to carry on their negociations with each other', should be a priority. These would bring great benefits, keeping 'the springs and movements of the commercial machine' in 'exact order'. It was important to avoid 'confusion and delay'. Long had many ideas as to how to improve the commercial flow across the island, often using bodily metaphors, encouraging 'a livelier current, where the clogs and impediments to its free circulation are removed'.[44] This would save time, something which merchants valued highly. 'Lively' was one of his favourite adjectives, perhaps a reflection of his own restlessness and desire for change. He paid minimal attention to the books, scientific instruments, horticultural seeds and coffee houses, a feature of the expanding cosmopolitan population.[45] He noted the large number of Jewish merchants and their dominance in the Spanish trade. Two main taverns, Ranelagh and Vauxhall,

---

[42] Ibid., II. 30.
[43] Ibid., II. 33.
[44] Ibid., II. 117.
[45] James Robertson, 'Eighteenth Century Jamaica's Ambivalent Cosmopolitanism', *History* 99.337 (2014), 607–31.

had accommodation for balls and assemblies and the 'very pretty theatre' (much patronized by Henry Moore).[46] Theatre was an important source of entertainment during wartime, but an opportunity for the kind of mixed sociability that Long disliked. 'War, so fatal to some states, has ever been the best friend of this town,' he realized, for it increased the demand for consumer goods, brought in new people and wealth, and facilitated 'profitable traffic in these seas' since they could not be so closely monitored.[47] In a time of peace, Kingston stagnated.

Montego Bay, on the north coast in the parish of St James, however, was growing. A 'most thriving district' with its rich cane lands, it was now displacing Savanna-la-Mar with its 'indifferent harbour' and weak defences at the western end of the island.[48] It had been made a free port, a move meant to discourage contraband, but unhelpful, in Long's opinion, because it encouraged foreign shipping and, therefore, competition. Montego Bay had emerged as the '*emporium*' of the west. Built on the 'Guinea branch' of the trade, it had become the 'great mart' of the Negroes, serving the new plantations.[49] It boasted four hundred substantial brick houses. One of the 'opulent merchants' had

> carried on the Guiney branch with so much success, as to remit bills in the year 1771, to Great-Britain, for near 50,000l sterling, on account of new negroes alone; and as only two of these bills (which were both under 300l) were protested, we have, in this instance, the strongest indication possible of the happy circumstances enjoyed by the planters in this part of the country.

The 'happy circumstances' were the numbers of saltwater slaves coming into the north coast and providing labour. The town's good harbour meant that it was 'commodious for foreign trade'.[50]

The picturesque engraving of Montego Bay (Plate 9) offered a prospect from the surrounding hills, looking across the new settlement, still with large numbers of trees, to the sea beyond and tiny ships bobbing on the water. There was no violence represented here: the ships were sanitized by distance, with no sign of their human cargo or of the labourers who were clearing woods and building. The cultivated fields, the road, the large house on the left, together suggested a prospect, a future. The blasted tree at the centre of the engraving, hewn down to make way for new settlement, was suggestive of the human inroads into the environment. This was a place with potential. The engraver allowed the viewer a privileged position from which to perceive

---

[46] Long, *History*, II. 117 On the theatre, see Wilson, *The Island Race* and *Strolling Players*.
[47] Long, *History*, II. 121.
[48] Ibid., II. 213, 193.
[49] Ibid., II. 215.
[50] Ibid., II. 213.

the pristine scene that was, in reality, the 'great mart of the Negroes', peopled with 'opulent' merchants, living off the fruits of the 'Guinea trade'.

Long knew that if the town was to grow it needed new roads, particularly linking it to Spanish Town.[51] He waxed lyrical on the 'multitude of conveniences' which this would bring to settlers as well as traders, for 'a commercial island, like the human body, will always enjoy the best health and active vigour, when the circulation is carried on, freely and without impediment, from the heart to the extremities, and back again from these to the heart'.[52] And if that free circulation could extend across the seas, with harbour linking harbour, then trade, secured by providence, could be the central force driving civilization around the world, linking island to island and each to the metropole. He might have cited Grainger:

> In vain hath nature pour'd vast seas between
> Far-distant kingdoms; endless storms in vain
> With double night brood o'er them; thou dost throw,
> O'er far-divided nature's realms, a chain
> To bind in sweet society mankind.[53]

It was trade, carolled Grainger, that enabled 'white Albion' to hold 'the balance of the world/Acknowledg'd now sole Empress of the main'.[54]

If commerce was central to the descriptions of the towns, Long's tone shifted when he came to the beauties of the tropics and could utilize georgic, picturesque and pastoral vocabularies. He had added new registers to his literary efforts of the 1750s; there was the language of history for the constitution, of political arithmetic, commerce and capital for trade and agriculture, and then that of poetry for describing the beauties of the island and emphasizing the civilizing presence of white colonists. As literary scholars have suggested, the mixing of genres, characteristic of some long eighteenth-century poems, provided a way of expressing contradictions in a period when they had not been resolved.[55] Long utilized different registers and genres in his text, voicing contradictions that could be neither recognized nor contained. Separating sections on the economics of the West India trade and the plantation from

---

[51] The new motorway linking Montego Bay, Spanish Town and Kingston was finally completed a few years ago, built by the Chinese and established as a toll road in order to repay their investment – and consequently very little used by local people.
[52] Long, *History*, II. 218.
[53] Grainger, *Sugar Cane*, Bk 4. 348–52; Markman Ellis, '"The Cane-land Isles": Commerce and Empire in Late Eighteenth-Century Georgic and Pastoral Poetry', in Rod Edmond, and Vanessa Smith (eds.), *Islands in History and Representation* (London, 2003), 43–62.
[54] Grainger, *Sugar Cane*, Bk 4. 353–5.
[55] This is an argument first articulated by John Barrell and Harriet Guest, 'On the Use of Contradictions: Economics and Morality in the Long Eighteenth-Century Poem' in Felicity Nussbaum and Laura Brown (eds.), *The New Eighteenth Century* (London, 1987), 121–43. The argument was developed by Kaul, *Poems of Nation*.

the topography, literally placing them in different 'books', was one strategy. Another was to employ different kinds of language. A tension between virtue and commerce was inescapable in a society rooted in slavery. In the metropole, Gikandi argues, the culture of taste was supposed to harmonize the two: Long was trying something similar in his *History*.[56] He could not avoid English 'repugnance'. Rather, he had to confront it and hope to persuade his audience that slavery could be lived with quite comfortably, provided that it was at a distance. The harmony he sought was between commerce, agriculture and slavery. He had imbibed a culture of taste as a young man. Addison's evocation of the 'man of polite imagination', with his access to the 'pleasures that the vulgar are not capable of receiving', possessing 'a kind of property in everything he sees', may have been in his mind as he travelled on horseback around the island, contemplating the 'prospects' and formulating hopes for the future.[57] Steele's definition of the gentleman could spur him on: a man of clear understanding, exercising reason, knowledge and judgement, void of 'inordinate passions', well educated, with a knowledge of the arts and sciences, principled in religion.[58] These were his values. He was supposed to be disinterested, which was an impossibility: a planter and a West Indian, he was writing to defend the inheritance of himself and his family. But he could claim a certain distance, as a writer, with the capacity to observe.[59] His contemporaries Johnson, Fielding, Goldsmith and Smollett all aimed for a comprehensive knowledge of society. He could claim this for Jamaica.

His favourite poet seems to have been James Thomson, though he was also enthusiastic about Virgil, Pope, Milton and, of course, Shakespeare. The new translation by Dryden of Virgil's *Georgics*, which celebrated agricultural life and labour, had an enormous impact on a generation of poets contemplating a changing Britain. The georgic genre that they adopted was 'both a set of conventions and a mode of social understanding'. It managed, both morally and imaginatively, to secure 'the links between the economic realms of country, city, and empire'.[60] Thomson, a Scot, in his many reworkings of *The Seasons*, so beloved by eighteenth- and nineteenth-century readers, utilized the georgic along with the pastoral. He forged connections between rural labour, commerce, patriotism and empire: an empire won from nature by industry and cultivation. In 'Spring' he urged Britons to venerate the plough, in

---

[56] Gikandi, *Slavery and the Culture of Taste*, 113.
[57] Joseph Addison, *The Works of Joseph Addison*, ed. George Washington Greene (6 vols., New York, 1854), VI. 325.
[58] Barrell, *English Literature in History*, 37.
[59] Tobin, *Colonizing Nature* argues that the georgic allowed a shift from the agricultural producer to the writer: the poet could organize and select material.
[60] Karen O'Brien, 'Imperial Georgic, 1660–1789', in Gerald Maclean, Donna Landry and Joseph P. Ward (eds.), *The Country and the City Revisited. England and the Politics of Culture, 1550–1850* (Cambridge, 1999), 160–79.

'Summer' he ventured to Africa. Guided by providence, Britons could dominate the world through their command of agriculture, of trade and of the oceans. The poem sought to justify the fruits of a new world of division, inequality and competition, whilst denying the costs.[61]

Grainger defined his *Sugar Cane* as West Indian georgic. It was consciously modelled on Virgil, celebrating cane growing as heroic, a struggle waged by man on nature and other men, with intellectual labour providing the key to prosperity.[62] The georgic, defined by Addison as 'some part of the science of husbandry put into a pleasing dress, and set off with all the Beauties and Embellishments of Poetry', allowed some place for labour.[63] It was this physical labour which transformed cane into material goods that could be bought and sold. Long mobilized the georgic, the picturesque or painterly, and the pastoral to justify the fruits of King Sugar, while denying exploitation and violence. The picturesque, Elizabeth Bohls argues, 'tended to exclude traces of agricultural labor from the represented landscape', while the georgic 'dignified and aestheticized labor'.[64] The burgeoning tradition of estate gardening and the aesthetics of wild nature informed Long's vision. His depiction of the walk taken by the Worthy family in *The Prater* demonstrated how he had learned the lessons of the English landscape gardeners of the 1740s and 1750s. The non-productive land of the estate garden, with its 'natural' look, so different from the formal gardens championed by the French, was to be celebrated, in sharp contrast to newly enclosed land, measured, assessed and boundaried, designed for the maximization of profit and the new wealth associated with agrarian capitalism.[65] The 'natural' became something to value, with variegated vistas and points of taste. Jamaican plantations were measured, assessed and surveyed as we have seen, the land carefully parcelled out in terms of the needs of sugar production. Estates, with areas properly landscaped, could provide a balance, accommodating 'the picturesque aesthetic, the topographic impulse, and the priorities for scenic travel'.[66] It was not just sugar that was consumed in writing on the Caribbean; it was also landscapes and bodies.[67] Echoes of Pope's villa at Twickenham, with its grotto and 'wild garden', the

---

[61] Kaul, *Poems of Nation*.
[62] Gilmore, *The Poetics*, 'Introduction'.
[63] Addison cited in Gilmore, *The Poetics*, 27.
[64] Elizabeth A. Bohls, 'The Gentleman Planter and the Metropole: Long's *History of Jamaica* (1774)', in Maclean et al., *The Country and the City Revisited*, 180-96.
[65] Ann Bermingham, *Landscape and Ideology. The English Rustic Tradition, 1740-1860* (London, 1987).
[66] John E. Crowley, 'Picturing the Caribbean in the Global British Landscape', *Studies in Eighteenth Century Culture* 32 (2003), 323-46. Crowley notes the increasing numbers of topographical landscapes after 1763.
[67] Mimi Sheller, *Consuming the Caribbean. From Arawaks to Zombies* (London, 2003).

symmetry of the house contrasted with the asymmetry of the garden and the mysterious grotto, can all be found in the *History*.

Landscapes guaranteed a value other than money – aesthetic and moral value. A correct viewpoint could ensure that the land would be constructed in such a way as to demonstrate its harmony. Seeing it, as Addison had said, meant possessing it, harnessing the land to generate not only capital but also culture and civilization. The scene or prospect could be recorded, ordered, made present to the reader who could command it from their armchair, another form of mastery. They oversaw, just as the enslaved were subjected to the eyes of the overseer. 'The trees and vistas frame the man-made elements – windmills, sugar mills, negro huts . . . a landscape shaped by cultivation, formed into groves and domestic enclaves set in natural splendour.'[68] This was the space naturalized: the clearing of trees, building of roads and damming of rivers, the hours of enslaved labour that had made the 'wild' into a landscape forgotten. Take the route to Lime Savannah, which Long described in his own parish of Clarendon: the 'gentle rising, which commands a distant view of the whole', the cattle and ponds, and the 'truly romantic' road with its 'deep gloom of lofty trees, ever verdant, and rising in wild gradation', opening to reveal the establishment of Mr F—n, formerly chief justice of the island. Thomas Fearon owned more than 7,000 acres in Clarendon, as well as other properties. He was, in Long's estimation, a man of extraordinary talents.[69] Here was Steele's gentleman, with his 'comprehensive, and accurate knowledge of places, persons and things . . . throughout the known world', yet he had 'never trod any other spot' than Jamaica. His studies and his well-furnished library with its 'collection of the best authors', his 'uncommonly sagacious faculties', all ensured his gentility: he was a man 'worthy of being esteemed'.[70] White men might be surrounded by the enslaved but they were inhabiting an Enlightenment milieu. Fearon's old house was delightfully positioned, with an 'extensive prospect', comprehending the finest part of Clarendon. 'The beauties of nature', enthused Long, 'are innumerable . . . with the lively verdure of canes, interspersed with wind-mills and other buildings . . . several charming lawns of pasture-land, dotted with cattle and sheep, and watered with rivulets.' Then there were the 'Negroe villages, where (far from poverty and discontent) peace and plenty hold their reign'.[71] This was a far cry from his statistics on 'Negro' mortality, a disavowal of rebellion, whips and cruelty. He was careful to add, however – keeping commerce in mind immediately after

[68] Sheller, *Consuming*, 51; Dillman, *Colonizing Paradise*.
[69] Long, *History*, II. 63; Thomas Fearon was a neighbour of Long's, served with him in the assembly and as custos of Clarendon. 'Thomas Fearon junior', Legacies of British Slave-ownership database, http://wwwdepts-live.ucl.ac.uk/lbs/person/view/2146651785, accessed 15 March 2021.
[70] Long, *History*, II. 64.
[71] Ibid., II. 65.

the glories of Mr F—n's estate – that produce was shipped from Old Harbour Bay, just as it was from Lucky Valley.

In the parish of St Mary, The Decoy, the seat of Sir Charles Price, was even more impressive. Price and his son, also Charles, were like Fearon, major figures in the governance of the colony.[72] Long will have known them well. The Price family had been on the island since 1658 and had accumulated extensive property. By his death in 1772, Sir Charles senior was probably the largest slave-owner in Jamaica.[73] Profits from sugar could fund European-style monuments and his impressive marble tomb is the most elaborate in St Catherine's cemetery in Spanish Town. Its most striking epitaph reads: 'His Life was Gentle and the Elements so mixed in him that Nature might stand up and say to all the world, THIS WAS A MAN.' Long would have agreed. Price was a perfect gentleman in his rendition. Born in Jamaica, he was 'endued with uncommon natural talents, which were improved by education, and polished by travel in the early part of his life'. Having returned to Jamaica he took a lead in public affairs and demonstrated a 'truly patriotic attachment', which included a capacity, much admired by Long, to be a critic of pernicious governors. He 'enriched and embellished' the island with his liberal use of his wealth and his 'taste for improvements'. His house was fronted by water, home to teal and wild-duck in the winter, providing pleasure for sportsmen. The elegant garden was 'shaded with the cocoa-nut, cabbage, and sand-box trees', signs of colonial difference, while his kitchen garden reassured of sameness for it was filled 'with the most beautiful and useful variety which Europe, or this climate, produces'. The 'octagonal saloon ... richly ornamented with lustres and mirrors' and a 'grand triumphal arch' might have evoked the fine grounds of Saltash or other properties which had inspired Long as a boy. 'Clumps of graceful cabbage trees are dispersed in different parts, to enliven the scene; and thousands of plantane and other fruit trees occupy a vast tract ... not many years ago a gloomy wilderness.' The transformation was astonishing. Digging in a marl pit to explore the geological structure, Long uncovered 'a vast quantity of petrifactions', probably cockles, raising intriguing questions for the amateur scientist as to how they had got there so far from the sea. Sir Charles's home he described as a veritable paradise, the abode of 'chearfulness and hospitality', a 'temple of social enjoyment', constantly welcoming to 'worthy men', gentlemen of rank.[74] Sir Charles had indeed raised

---

[72] 'Sir Charles Price 1st Bart., of Jamaica', Legacies of British Slave-ownership database, http://wwwdepts-live.ucl.ac.uk/lbs/person/view/2146636974, accessed 15 March 2021.

[73] Stuart Handley, 'Price, Sir Charles, First Baronet (1708–1772), Politician in Jamaica', *Oxford Dictionary of National Biography*, 2004, https://doi.org/10.1093/ref:odnb/22743; Michael Craton and James Walvin, *A Jamaican Plantation. The History of Worthy Park, 1670–1970* (London, 1970), 71–94.

[74] Long, *History*, II. 76–7 fn.

his establishment into a *place*, a place made for those who were white, those who were 'worthy'.

Long utilized the language of landscape aesthetics, facilitating 'imaginative intertwinement between colony and metropole, at the same time obscuring the ugliness of slavery's site-specific practices'.[75] Such a language required distance: the observer must frame, contain and compose the picture and direct the eye of the viewer. Orange Cove in Hanover, for example, was 'so various, so picturesque, and admirably fine', its combination of details so united in 'forming this landscape', that it was almost impossible for either a painter or a historian to capture. Nature and art, Long wrote, had combined all their skills. It was the tasteful combination of the two that transformed not only the landscape but also those who viewed it. 'Wherever the passing eye' wandered, there were a thousand delightful objects: 'a wide plain, richly carpeted with canes of the emerald tint, differently shaded, and striped with fringes of logwood, or penguin-fence ... rills of crystal water ... a high swelling-lawn, smooth and fertile, whose gently-sloping bosom is embellished with herds and flocks, and whose summit is crowned with Negroe-villages, or clumps of graceful trees.' On a neighbouring hill 'is a windmill in motion; boiling houses, and other plantation-buildings, at the foot: there, in the various duties which cultivation excites, are labourers, cattle, and carriages; all briskly employed', and beyond that the sea, the route to England and Africa. Labour was not erased in this account, like the cattle and the carriages; men and women were 'briskly employed' with their 'various duties'.[76] The picturesque could naturalize the injustices of plantation society, make 'Negro villages' into a delightful vista. In similar vein, 'a most luxuriant and extensive landscape' could be seen from the foothills of the Blue Mountains.

> In front are cane-fields of the liveliest verdure, pastures, and little villas intermixed; the towns and ports of Kingston and Port Royal; the shipping scattered in different groups; the forts, the hills of Healthshire, the rocky breakers, and cayes whitening with the surge; and, beyond these, a plain of ocean extending to the Southern hemisphere ... These objects form together a very pleasing combination.[77]

The combination mattered. The prospect was offered to his readers in its variety: the cane, the towns, the shipping, the forts, the sea, all enriched by nature: together they made possible the West India trade.

The landscapes created by wealthy plantation owners were something to celebrate. Then there were the wonders of Jamaica's natural beauties. In the parish of St Ann were two remarkable waterfalls. Roaring River Cascade had

---

[75] Bohls, *Slavery and the Politics of Place*, 8–9.
[76] Long, *History*, II. 208–9.
[77] Ibid., II. 126.

been created by shallow tree roots on a branch of the River Alto, which had caused water to leave deposits, forming incrustations and 'cisterns' which

> spread in beautiful ranks, gradually rising one above another, and bearing no ill resemblance to a magnificent flight of steps in rustic work, leading up to the enchanted palace of some puissant giant of romance. A sheet of water, transparent as crystal, conforming to the bend of the steps, overspreads their surface; and, as the rays of light, or sun-shine, play between the waving branches of the trees, it descends glittering with a thousand variegated tints ...

Its natural 'flight of steps' and 'enchanted palace' created the appearance of a 'Fairy region'. The water tripped and danced, collecting neighbouring rivulets, composing several lesser, but most enchanting falls. 'Description fails', Long concluded, 'to convey any competent idea of its several beauties': an engraving completed the vision, a vision to please the eye, avoiding the ugly truths of plantation life.[78]

The engraving features three tiny figures, dwarfed by the magnificence of the scene, something to delight the viewer (see Plate 7). A groom (it is impossible to tell whether he is black or white) tends to the horses while a figure, possibly the draughtsman, points out to a scenic tourist the stalactite rocks, the anchovy pear-trees, the reservoirs brim full of water, 'transparent as crystal', the 'exotic confusion and strange threatening forms' of the boughs, limbs and trunks of the trees.[79] The terraced landscape with bursts of sunlight breaking through made it a scene for spectators, a spot to behold. Roaring River Cascade, however, could not compete with the White River Cascade, its beauties 'beyond the power of painting to express'.[80] Nevertheless, an engraving, of which Long may have been the draughtsman, offered a vision of the majesty of the waterfall, 'exceeding the grandeur of Tivoli' (thereby evoking the Grand Tour), yet not matching Niagara (encompassing the globe). Here too the figures were tiny, accentuating the majesty of the falls and the grandeur of nature (Plate 8).

The richness of the surrounding woodland with the trees rising each side of the water, the 'placid surface' of the pool and the elegant palms standing like 'straight columns' constituted a tropical vision.[81] A black figure can just be

---

[78] Ibid., II. 93.
[79] Ibid., II. 93; Quilley, 'Questions of Loyalty', 123.
[80] Long, *History*, II. 94. The art historians Geoff Quilley and Tim Barringer both think that Long may have been the draughtsman for this this and other illustrations. Quilley, 'Pastoral Plantations', in Geoff Quilley and Kay Dian Kriz (eds.), *An Economy of Colour. Visual Culture and the Atlantic World, 1660–1830* (Manchester, 2003), 106–28; Barringer, 'Picturesque Prospects and the Labor of the Enslaved', in Barringer, Gillian Forrester and Barbaro Martinez-Ruiz (eds.), *Art and Emancipation in Jamaica* (New Haven, CT, 2007), 41–64.
[81] Long, *History*, II. 95.

glimpsed on the left while two small figures, one a woman, highlight the scale of the cascade, as they regard the magnificent spectacle of the 'resistless, roaring, dreadful' flow of the water. The signs of the tropics and of otherness, the irregular rocks and the falls were the differentiated elements which together produced the harmony of the picturesque. As William Gilpin argued in his influential *An Essay on Prints*, picturesque was a term 'expressive of that peculiar kind of beauty, which is agreeable in a picture': the artist could improve on nature.[82] The viewer could look at the world with an improving eye, an eye which could indeed improve not only the landscape but the viewer too. The idea of landscape, the 'pleasing prospects' beloved by Long, never included working scenes, though always promising wealth. It required an 'elevated sensibility' to be able to separate oneself and observe, to be both practical and aesthetic.[83] The separation of production (the land and the sea) and consumption (the landscape) meant the capacity to control and possess the land and its prospects.

If painting failed to fully express the beauty, poetry could do some of the necessary work, and Long quoted Thomson to capture the sublimity of this scene.

> Wide o'er the brim, with many torrent swell'd,
> And the mix'd ruin of its banks o'er-spread;
> At last, the rous'd up river pours along,
> Resistless! Roaring! Dreadful! – Down it comes
> From the rude mountain, and the mossy wild,
> Tumbling through rocks abrupt, and sounding far:–
> Then o'er the sanded valley floating spreads,
> Calm; sluggish; silent; – till again, constrain'd
> Between two meeting crags, it bursts away,
> Where rocks and woods o'er hang the turbid stream.
> There gathering triple force, rapid and deep,
> It boils! and wheels! and foams! and thunders through![84]

One might almost think, as Long noted elsewhere, that Thomson 'had made the tour of this region, so appositely has he described it'.[85] Sir Charles so loved its natural beauty that he would have no alterations made. The palms were 'placed by the hand of nature at such even distance from the banks on each side, that art could not have done the work with more attention to propriety and exactness'.[86] Nature had risen to the stature of a work of art. But Sir Charles complemented the splendour of this wonder, situated on his property,

[82] Cited in Rachel Newman, 'Conjuring Cane: the Art of William Berryman and Caribbean Sugar Plantations', PhD, Stanford University (2016), 50.
[83] Williams, *The Country and the City*, 120–1.
[84] Long, *History*, II. 94.
[85] Ibid., II. 185.
[86] Ibid., II. 95.

and marked his ownership by building some apartments fronting the cascade, to accommodate a 'club of gentlemen' who could together enjoy the natural beauties. Each year they met to shoot 'ring-tailed pidgeons', plentiful in this part of the tropics.[87] What was naturally sublime was further embellished by the tasteful gatherings arranged by this cultured man.

Jamaica also boasted 'celebrated curiosities', for the New World was a place of marvels, evoking both fears and excitement. One grotto was 'Gothic in its appearance'. A visit provided a mysterious adventure for Long and his friends. They crawled through the subterranean labyrinths, struck by the lifelike figures made by the rock formations and the dripping water, from a 'madona' to a 'venerable old hermit' whose features they were able to complete 'in the theatric mode' with a stick of charcoal. The gloom, 'the dismal echo of our voices', the 'hollow sounds of their trampling' as they made their way through the passages with their 'torch-wood', the multitude of bats – all this 'recalled to our minds' the descent of Aeneas into the 'infernal regions' of the underworld. Pitt's translation of Virgil's immortal description of the passage through the 'dismal gloom' to 'Grim Pluto's courts, the regions of the dead', was summoned up. They expected at any moment to come across Cerberus or some other 'horrid inhabitant of Pluto's dominion'.[88] Long knew his Homer and his Virgil. His writing attempted to lighten the fears of an encounter with the dead; this was a 'poetic delusion'. The 'dim light of their torch' was surely different from 'The moon scarce glimm'ring through the dusky grove,' and the 'deep, soft and yielding soil' turned out to be a *congeries* of bat's dung'.[89] But the underworld was a place of reckoning, where people were held to account. Some were perpetually tortured for their sins, others permitted to walk in pleasant groves. He knew he would not meet the monster, Cerberus, but what about the ghosts of those the colonists had expelled and expunged? The picturesque surface veiled the dead and departed beneath. What about those rebels dying on gibbets, those heads exposed at crossroads? Did this figure in some recess of his mind, haunting his imagination? Might he be called to account?

The grotto extended into a maze of passages, cloisters and apartments, with shapes and 'sparkling icicles', canopies, thrones, skulls, busts and 'beautifully-variegated foliage' striking the imagination and exciting 'the utmost curiosity'.[90] The 'turns and windings' of this 'infernal wilderness' exceeded, Long was convinced, the Cretan labyrinth, which Theseus had been compelled to unravel.[91] After the range of classical allusion and the fears summoned up, he was glad to be reminded of a more proximate problem, for 'it is supposed

---

[87] Ibid.
[88] Ibid., II. 95–7.
[89] Ibid.
[90] Ibid., II. 97–9.
[91] Ibid., II. 100.

that run-away Negroes were not unacquainted with so convenient a hiding-place'. This was a disturbing thought, but he could reassure himself. Most of the houses in this parish on the north coast were 'made defensible with loop-holes', 'guarding against the insults of foreign enemies', while also being 'fortified against internal ones'.[92] Enemies, real or imagined, were dangerously close. 'Grim Pluto's courts' were not a place to enter: he disavowed the violence of the colonists, projecting it on to their enemies.

If Thomson and Virgil were favourites, so too was Milton whose evocation of paradise reminded readers of the Garden of Eden. The 'beauties of these spicy groves' included the 'orange, limon, star-apple, avogato-pear' and other favourite trees, 'impetuous' rivers and 'babbling' rivulets. Trelawny, a new parish, a land which combined echoes of paradise with a 'savage aspect', invited transformation. It could, with 'great improvements', become 'valuable plantations'.[93] Tropical luxuriance was juxtaposed with commercial promise and a new order of things. Large parts of the island, particularly in the west and the north, awaited settlement. Mr P—k's Richmond estate on the north coast, for example, sported an elegant mansion with Ionic columns and Venetian windows, but – and here there was a marked change of tone – it was all too close to the locations from which 'Negroes' escaped to Cuba. More settlement was essential, a whitening of place. A little way inland there was 'primitive forest, full of large cedar, mahogany, and other valuable timber-trees', fertile soil and cool, temperate air. This was 'a desirable field' for introducing new colonies of industrious people.[94] Indeed, the island was 'almost as much an undiscovered country, as the regions bordering on the South pole'.[95] Long told a story of a poor white couple who had made their fortunes through hard work from 'the very meanest and smallest beginnings', accumulating enough 'to purchase a Negroe', augment their produce and eventually become proprietors of a valuable estate, now enjoyed by their heirs.[96]

Linking the tropical to the more familiar pastoral, Long evoked 'the gay scenes of nature', not least the cane pieces, 'spread through the vales', initially looking like ploughed land in England and coming to resemble European corn. The ripe cane was likened to European corn in time of harvest, a picture of rural charm with 'the busy slaves, like reapers, armed with bills instead of sickles to cut the ripened stems; and teams of oxen in the field, to bring the treasure home; whilst the labourers chear their toil with rude songs, or whistle in wild chorus their unpolished melody'.[97] The enslaved, now happy reapers, singing and whistling, were bringing the treasure, the sugar to be, safely to the

[92] Ibid.
[93] Ibid., II. 222.
[94] Ibid., II. 91.
[95] Ibid., II. 223.
[96] Ibid., II. 217.
[97] Ibid., I. 362–3.

mill. Crop time became a charming vision. Such scenes were always complemented by their commercial dimension. A 'pleasing combination' of sea, harbour and ships evoked the sugar on its journey to the metropole – the key to planter wealth and to the colony's relation to the 'mother country'.[98]

Enthusiasm for the island, its products, its potential and its beauties certainly dominated Long's account of the parishes. Questions of security and defence, however, were ever present. He may not have wanted his audience to focus on the troubled waters of which he was himself only too well aware. But he knew that it was essential to demonstrate in the wake of 1760 and the Seven Years War, and with increased tensions between the North American colonies and the 'mother country', that the island was a safe place for white colonists. Despite his desire to represent Jamaica as white, with the black presence positioned away from centre-stage – those others who could be seen but could not see themselves – his detailed topography was punctuated with anxious undercurrents, haunted by dangerous spectres. The woods offered places of refuge for 'wild Negroes', the caves might serve as hiding places for runaways, the sea was another escape route, could the Maroons really be relied on to fulfil the treaty? The lack of roads made access to many parts of the island extremely difficult. Long's account of rebellions was partitioned off in another section of the book, but as he travelled with his readers from parish to parish, he was careful to discuss the defences against both internal and external enemies. How were the regular troops situated? What was the condition of the barracks? Where were the best sites for European troops to be stationed? What improvements were needed? Having served on the assembly's committee for forts and fortification over several years, he knew the state of the defences: once again he could write as the eyewitness, the expert. This time his discourse was not framed by 'prospects' and 'scenes'; rather it was a detailed tally, a reckoning of the system of defence for an embattled colony. Internal and external enemies were always in mind. White safety was the key. Numbers of soldiers, numbers of barracks, numbers of guns were now what needed to be documented, together with his recommendations for urgent government action. He was pleased that the assembly had recently granted new money for defences, but proposed the appointment of an inspector-general whose job would be to regularly assess and report on the island's security.[99]

Spanish Town, as the capital, was not well served. The 'lofty brick building' of the barracks and its outbuildings could house three hundred men, but the accommodation for officers was inadequate. As a result they took lodgings elsewhere, and 'for want of their residence' in the barracks, the privates have 'often committed riots ... in the neighbourhood'.[100] Long was always clear

[98] Ibid., II. 126.
[99] Ibid., II. 176.
[100] Ibid., II. 17.

about the need for class hierarchies to be maintained: he had no illusions about white equality. The only sense in which whites were equal was that they were not 'Negro'. New buildings were urgently required for military discipline to be restored. Kingston did better, with a 'very well-designed and convenient' set of barracks for two hundred officers and men, with the officers' quarters properly separated from those of the men.[101] Protection for the harbour was a key issue and Long described the several forts. Rock Fort, in a horribly unhealthy spot, defended the town from an eastern attack. The assembly had recently granted money to improve the facilities. Fort Charles had 126 guns, barracks for more than three hundred, a house for the commanding officer and a hospital. Port Royal was 'deservedly valued'. Ships approaching the harbour had to pass through a narrow channel. The Twelve Apostles, a battery of twelve guns, stood on one side, a fort on the other, and the battery of Augusta in front, with eighty-six 'large guns, kept in excellent order', and a magazine. 'The ships, in passing up the channel towards Kingston, must come within point-blank shot of a whole line of guns.'[102] It was deemed impregnable. (See Plate 10.)

As a commercial island, dependent on trade, it was crucial to defend the many harbours. On the north coast privateers had been a major problem, and there was always the danger of French or Spanish attack. St Ann on the north coast had an adequate battery and barracks, but Montego Bay could do with much improvement. Long was enthusiastic about the plan which had long been discussed of making Port Antonio, with its direct access to the windward passage, into a naval base. Then there was the issue of inland defences. In 1760 it had been clear that there were not enough. Delve barracks in Westmoreland had been built after the insurrection; St Mary boasted four barracks because it had been at the centre of the revolts in both 1760 and 1765. Clarendon had its parish barracks at Chapel, not far from Lucky Valley, and a company of regulars were quartered there. Proprietors often took matters into their own hands with fortified houses, even batteries. But Long believed in the responsibilities of the colonial state, in tandem, of course, with the 'mother country'.

Finally, Long addressed a different aspect of racializing space. The island needed schools for the children of the colonists. The absence of 'a proper seminary for the young inhabitants' was 'one of the principal impediments to its effectual settlement'.[103] The custom of sending boys to England, 'like a bale of dry goods, consigned to some factor', was most unsatisfactory.[104] Boys and young men needed 'the watchful attention of a parent' to administer proper training. Left to their own devices, after a 'youth spent in foppery, licentiousness and prodigality', many finished their education quite unprepared for their

---

[101] Ibid., II. 106.
[102] Ibid., II. 151.
[103] Ibid., II. 246.
[104] Ibid.

return to Jamaica.[105] As for the girls, what they required was a preparation for 'becoming good wives and mothers', not an elaborate academic curriculum.[106] Since many parents, with numerous children, could not afford to send their daughters to England, they tended to offer little, if any, casual instruction. As a result girls adopted the bad habits of those around them, were not 'weaned from the Negro dialect' or 'improved by emulation, and gradually habituated to a modest and polite behaviour'. 'A boarding school for these girls' was what was needed. Once they had acquired the elements of grace and polish, they would become 'objects of love' to 'deserving youths' and draw them away 'from a loose attachment to Blacks and Mulattoes, into the more rational and happy commerce of nuptial union'.[107] If such a school could be established under a committee of the principal ladies in the island, it would bring great benefits.

A seminary for boys should be a priority. It could build on the one established in Clarendon, and he proposed a detailed plan for its development. The buildings, publicly funded, should be properly laid out, with a school house, a chapel, a dwelling-house for the master, land for provisions, cattle and sheep, 'Negroes' to labour and a white overseer. 'To guard against any calamity likely to happen from insurrections among the Negroes', there should be a barrack erected close by, with soldiers permanently on duty. 'A certain number of white servants' were necessary, to ensure that the boarders did not form 'a too early familiarity and intercourse with the Negroes, adopt their vices and broken English'.[108] The school should be designed for middling families, to train industrious planters, surveyors, bookkeepers and mechanics. The boys should study reading, writing and arithmetic, bookkeeping and surveying, Spanish and French (useful for trading relations), and agriculture and botany, in hopes of improvements in the island. They should also have physical training, preparing them for 'a course of life which requires agility and strength of body, and occasionally the use of arms'.[109] The sons of gentlemen, destined for the professions, would still need to go to England. (Long had been determined to return to England in time for his children to be educated there.) Britain would gain in the long term, since it was vital to wean the colonists from 'that detrimental habit of emigration, that unhappy idea of considering this place a mere temporary abode'.[110] He concluded his scheme with costings and a heartfelt plea that the assembly would consider the matter with the gravity it deserved.

---

[105] Ibid., II. 249.
[106] Ibid., II. 250.
[107] Ibid.
[108] Ibid., II. 254.
[109] Ibid.
[110] Ibid., II. 258.

Health

Lavish spending on defence was essential, but so was the matter of the health of the island's white population. Given Long's preoccupation with the importance of sustaining and increasing the white population in Jamaica, it was vital for him to persuade his readers that, despite all stories to the contrary, the island was a healthy place to live. His racialized topography represented the island as a place suited to white people, who would always be serviced by those who were black. 'Negroes' were ever present, whether explicitly mentioned or not, but in subordinate positions, frequently unseen, in the cane pieces, servicing the elegant homes and gardens of the elite, labouring in the commercial centres, the harbours and the warehouses, or held in the 'slave-pens'. Then there were the 'Mulattoes', defying all attempts to keep white properly white and black properly black. When writing on health, his focus was on white people: places were categorized in terms of their suitability for European constitutions and much advice was offered as to how to adapt to the tropics. Adaptation was necessary. Since Jamaica was widely understood to be a graveyard for Europeans, his aim was to demonstrate that moderation and care were all that were necessary for white people to survive and live good lives in the Torrid Zone. He drew on the medical practices that had developed in Jamaica from the early days of conquest, shaped by the demands of commerce, whether those of the surgeons who played a key role on the slave ships or Sir Hans Sloane who had treated both the colonists and the enslaved.[111] Long's great-grandfather, William Beeston, had been one of the first to take an interest in the curative properties of the island's water, an interest he developed. Since racial boundaries were porous, with plantation life involving bodily contact of many kinds, Long commented too on 'Negro' practices, some of which, despite himself, he realized were effective. Disavowal enabled him to deny what he knew and wanted not to know.

When turning from the picturesque landscapes that he had described across the parishes to questions of health, he was obliged to acknowledge the scale of European deaths. This was familiar to a metropolitan audience from both military and naval sources. It had become a matter of public concern in the late 1730s and early 1740s as the scale of deaths amongst the military in the Caribbean theatre of war became apparent. Almost three-quarters of the troops on the Cartagena expedition were dead by 1742, the majority killed not in war but by yellow fever.[112] Mosquitoes played as large a part in conflict as did European enemies. White men could not control the natural forces they

---

[111] Pratik Chakrabarti, *Materials and Medicine. Trade, Conquest and Therapeutics in the Eighteenth Century* (Manchester, 2010).
[112] Seth, *Difference and Disease*, 103.

had unleashed.[113] Smollett's fictional account of Roderick Random's stay in fever-ridden Jamaica had Roderick concluding that the 'unhealthiness of the climate' and the prevalence of yellow fever meant that he might make a good living there as a surgeon.[114] Long's poetic evocation of the beauties of the island shifted to a different tone when it came to *Regulations for Preserving Health in Jamaica*, with more alarming and matter-of-fact depictions of the dangers of the tropics, with their lowland swamps and 'putrid fogs'.[115] Hopes of improvement were threatened by the external world.

His anxiety about putrescence, the tendency of the body to collapse from within, had surfaced many times, albeit marginally, in his account of the parishes, as did a catalogue of places described as unhealthy. The presence of 'putrid air', 'putrid fogs', 'putrid effluvia', 'putrid slime' and 'putrid vapours', all threatening 'putrid fevers', were dotted throughout his topography, all capable of infecting and polluting.[116] His preoccupation with disgust animated his language, whether depicting the horrors of 'effluvia', 'fogs' or 'slime'. It was 'putrid fevers' which were the killers in Jamaica, particularly yellow fever. Dr William Hillary's essay on the distinctive diseases in Barbados, published in 1759, had described yellow fever as induced by the tropical climate. A 'putrid bilious fever', it was caused by infectious miasmata or great heat of the water or air: the blood dissolved and the body literally rotted from within. Hillary saw it as indigenous to the West Indies and probably all countries within the Torrid Zone, but his explanation of its presence in Barbados depended on the slave trade: it was enslaved Africans, he believed, who had brought it to the island. [117] The question of the relative weight of climate and of culture in explaining causes of disease remained a puzzle and one that Long could not resolve.

The 'putrescence paradigm', a term utilized by Mark Harrison and taken up by Suman Seth, concerned a set of ideas and practices that dominated understandings of warm climates in the later eighteenth century.[118] Putrid diseases involved the putrefaction of bodily solids or fluids, usually blood or bile. It was a process of bodily decay. It could be caused by heat or by effluvia, especially the air from swampy marshes. Citrus juices were understood to be a good antidote, something which Long enthusiastically endorsed. The idea of putrefaction was deeply disturbing to him; complete dissolution of the body was a terrifying spectacle for someone who was so anxious to preserve and control boundaries. The fluids in the body, he believed, could become 'putrescent' if

---

[113] J. R. McNeill, *Mosquito Empires. Ecology and War in the Greater Caribbean, 1620–1914* (Cambridge, 2010).
[114] Smollett, *Roderick Random*, 243.
[115] Long, *History*, II. 107.
[116] Ibid., II. 66, 108, 109, 113, 119, 201, 210.
[117] See Seth's account of Hillary, *Difference and Disease*, 57–86.
[118] Mark Harrison, *Medicine in an Age of Commerce and Empire. Britain and its Tropical Colonies, 1660–1830* (Oxford, 2010), 64–88; Seth, *Difference and Disease*, 115–17.

exercise was neglected.[119] The 'ingenious', 'judicious and benevolent' Dr James Lind was the authority for him, with his sobering account of putrescence.[120] Lind's *Essay on Diseases Incidental to Europeans in Hot Climates* (1768) told the story of a group of gentlemen, newly arrived from England, whose dramatic reaction to the change in climate provided a horrific lesson. They were closeted in 'small, close, and suffocating chambers' in Port Royal and Kingston, and 'expired with the whole mass of their body dissolved, and flowing at every pore; the stifling heat of their rooms having produced a state of universal putrefaction in the body even before death'.[121] Such an end was horrifying, particularly to someone who believed that the purity of white blood was key to white power. Long's efforts were devoted to advising on ways to avert such a fate.

The change from a temperate to a tropical climate could result in alterations to the body, requiring adaptation. From the 1750s there was a growing recognition of the significance of location. Lind's work was based on his experience as a naval surgeon in the West Indies and Guinea. Writing initially on scurvy, he then focused on Europeans in hot climates. Recognizing that every country had healthy and unhealthy places, he nevertheless argued that 'the countries beyond the limits of Europe which are chiefly frequented by Europeans, are very unhealthy, and the climate often proves fatal to them'.[122] They must regulate their activities: the heavy work of clearing the ground, for example, was fatal. Lind's examples were mainly drawn from Africa but he had noted similar phenomena in Jamaica. Disease was coming to be associated with particular places, and health and illnesses understood as geographically specific. This understanding of the relation between health and geography led to the development of discourses of both medical geography, dealing with the distribution of disease, and medical topography, detailing particular locales.[123] Long engaged in both these discourses, relying on authors ranging from Sloane and Dr Trapham, to Hillary, Lind and Benjamin Franklin for medical expertise. He drew on a well-established humoralist approach, emphasizing the importance of the natural balance of the body. Toxins must be evacuated, not by bleeding but by perspiration, vomiting and bowel movements, for which he recommended chocolate. Diet and exercise were vital and moderation was the key. He added his own medical topography to his discussion of Jamaican localities and was careful to point out that England too had its

---

[119] Long, *History*, II. 506.
[120] Ibid., II. 506, 131.
[121] Ibid., II. 114.
[122] James Lind, *An Essay on Diseases Incidental to Europeans in Hot Climates* [1768] (London, 1771), 30.
[123] Emily Senior, *The Caribbean and the Medical Imagination, 1764–1834. Slavery, Disease and Colonial Modernity* (Cambridge, 2018).

unhealthy places, such as the Essex, Kent and Lincolnshire marshes; most of Jamaica, he insisted, was perfectly healthy.

Lind defined unhealthy places, mentioning low swampy spots with many mosquitoes. This definition was adopted by Long. Unhealthy situations included those where there was a very rapid change from 'stifling heat' to 'chilling cold', those with 'thick noisome fogs' or 'innumerable swarms of large muskeetoes' and other flies, those where meat and corpses deteriorated very quickly, and the channels of dried-out rivers, emitting 'disagreeable smells'.[124] The putrid fevers were understood to be the result of 'vitiated' or 'morbid air', the air that was heated by the sun, rose from 'foul oozy shores', stagnant water, 'fetid mud' and swampy grounds. It entered the lungs and circulation and induced a disposition to 'putrescency' and 'malignant disorders'.[125] Aerial contagion meant 'morbid air' was to be avoided. Marshy and low-lying ground, areas where mosquitoes were likely to gather, were particularly obnoxious. 'It is most dangerous to pass the night in such places,' wrote Long, who had clearly suffered from mosquitoes: 'it is at such time that these insects collect in swarms, and make war on every daring intruder.'[126] It was as though 'the hand of Providence' had placed them there to 'drive away, every human being'.[127] The image of mosquito warriors, launching forth from their 'skulking holes', was less threatening than that of Coromantees, but nevertheless a real danger, one of the many fragmented and splintered projections of his 'anxiety', that state of 'anxiety' that he was convinced killed many colonists.[128] The 'muskeetos' were a preoccupation for Long; like fire, they summoned up his fear of retribution, and their buzzing, humming and biting gave him no peace. They hide during the day, he wrote:

> Their usual time of sallying forth, to attack mankind, is about sun-set ... they do not make their assaults without giving notice, with a kind of shrill hum, in the pitch-pipe tone *A*; so that, when a considerable number of them are assembled in a room, they perform a full concert; which affords but a melancholy presage of the approaching onset, and may be called their war-song. When they are ready to begin the attack, they descend gradually with a seeming caution; and, after wheeling in circles for some time, like birds of prey, dart down at once with a sudden swoop upon any naked part of the body that presents itself most favourably.

He had much advice as to how to guard against them, including covering water in storage jars, wearing 'musketoo-boots', a sort of half trouser, and using nets at night for protection.[129] His detailed account of the bite itself was based on

---

[124] Long, *History*, II. 509.
[125] Ibid., II. 505.
[126] Ibid., II. 506.
[127] Ibid..
[128] Ibid., II. 518.
[129] Ibid., III. 883–4.

very close observation: the 'diminutive cannibal' with its fine proboscis penetrated the pores of the skin. Then it 'set its little pump, or tube, at work, first, by means of a well-disposed mechanism, exhausting it of the air contained in it, after which, the blood rises according to the laws of hydrostatics, and continues its ascent in a full-tide till satiated'.[130] A little lime juice on the spot gave some relief.

Long shared the settlers' conviction that felling trees left less space for 'miasmas' but had observed the destruction of mahogany with concern. The 'creole ecology' that sugar had created, with land cleared for cane, stock and the boilers, the storage of water and semi-refined sugar, mahogany exported, all reduced the habitats for the birds that fed on insects and created ideal conditions for rats and mosquitoes.[131] Fortunately the presence of alligators, holding their jaws 'extended to admit the muskeetos, and when a sufficient number are collected, suddenly enclose and gulp them down, as a child does carraway confits', provided some relief for him, which he associated with the wondrous balance created by providence.[132]

Colonists must learn how to live safely in this new environment with its fearsome insects and heated air 'between the Tropics'.[133] Seasoning had been discussed by many authorities. Sloane, while keen to demonstrate the similarities between England and Jamaica, had noted that newcomers frequently suffered from an acute disease, after which they adapted to the new environment. Medical men had recognized the extent to which disease seemed to be associated with strangers moving to new places: 'seasoning was a distemper that plagued English bodies out of place'.[134] Grainger's experience in St Kitts led him to argue in his essay on 'West-India diseases' that it was not only Europeans whose bodies had to adapt to a new climate, it was Africans too.[135] Long challenged the received opinion that for a European a first fever after moving from a cold to a hot climate was necessary. A sickness might be caused by this change, but it did not guarantee a seasoning of the body. 'Thorough and proper seasoning', he believed, resulted from living on the island for a length of time.[136] It was habits, he wanted to believe, not climate, that were key to survival.

He recognized that many Europeans had died in the early days of settlement, but blamed this on fevers they brought from elsewhere and the initial overconcentration of population in the port towns which had been chosen for

---

[130] Ibid.
[131] McNeill, *Mosquito Empires*.
[132] Long, *History*, III. 869–70.
[133] Ibid., II. 505.
[134] Seth, *Difference and Disease*, 93.
[135] James Grainger, *On the Treatment and Management of the More Common West-India Diseases* [1764], ed. J. Edward Hutson (Kingston, 2005); *Sugar Cane*, Bk 4. 158–9.
[136] Long, *History*, II. 517.

purposes of trade, not health. They had failed to grasp the need for fresh air and did not know of the importance of inoculation against smallpox, or of the remedies such as Jesuit bark. His focus was on external causes, the 'malignant disorders' that had been imported from the Spanish territories, or fevers contracted from English gaols.[137] Sailors, he noted, a group with whom he had little sympathy, were a particular problem since they brought in 'infectious disorders' and congregated in the port towns, drinking too much and spreading disease.[138] Kingston was notorious for its mortality rates and he was compelled to recognize it as an 'unwholesome spot'. On the west of the town, the salt marshes and swamps made for 'putrid fog' and 'exhalations', while to the east there were salt ponds and lagoons, causing the people in Yallahs to live in a 'pestilential atmosphere'. The dangers of leakage were always present. What was more, the proximity of the Spanish territories brought dangers: parts of Cartagena and Porto Bello were notorious for their 'fatal consequences'.[139] Ships should be forced to quarantine if they arrived at Port Royal with fever on board. The cemetery in Kingston was quite inadequate and it was foolish not to adopt the habits of the Turks, for example, who knew how to deal with corpses in a warm climate. Insisting on British burial habits was 'unquestionably absurd'.[140] Similarly, if house builders would only recognize that the Spanish used jalousie shutters for good reasons, avoiding closed rooms and a lack of fresh air, this would be a great improvement. There were other filthy habits and 'artificial annoyances', such as repairing streets with 'offals and nastiness', which really had to change. 'Natural evils', he concluded, 'if they cannot be removed or remedied, must be acquiesced with: but for an intelligent people to take pains to poison themselves' was utterly foolish.[141] Fortunately, Kingston had hills nearby.

The hills and mountains were the places to live: rising ground allowed for 'free and salubrious air'.[142] Europeans could be healthy all year round if they occupied 'elevated situations', with dry soil suited to European plants, few trees and no stagnant waters, where sheep could even retain their 'fleecy covering'.[143] A climate as proximate as possible to the temperate north was clearly to be treasured. If people chose to 'obstinately run the hazard of their life and health' by sleeping in 'unhealthy places', then it was their responsibility.[144] There were numerous 'spots of ground' which, with 'industry and cultivation', could become 'healthy and delightful rural retirements'.

---

[137] Ibid., II. 108.
[138] Ibid., II. 513.
[139] Ibid., II. 107–10.
[140] Ibid., II. 115.
[141] Ibid.
[142] Ibid., II. 514.
[143] Ibid., II. 512.
[144] Ibid., II. 511.

Gentlemen who could afford a horse or carriage could do their business during the day and then, after sunset, retreat to 'such places of health'.[145] It was time for planters to reflect on the 'oeconomy of health', reflect on those particulars which 'reason and experience' recommended, recognize the need to live less anxious lives and protect themselves better from disease.[146] Long defined his own place of residence, Spanish Town, as 'healthy', enjoying 'a natural salubrity' of air, with 'no marshes about or near it', and the rain water draining pretty quickly into the river.[147] Lucky Valley, though partially low ground and situated by a river, had hills rising behind it. White servants should be provided with housing on dry ground, 'raised above the earth', floored, built of timber or brick but not stone which 'was not good in this climate'. The 'natural and benevolent disposition of the planters' would surely mean that they would be willing to cope with this expense.[148] By the early years of the nineteenth century, even the 'Negro huts' at Lucky Valley were situated on the hills.

Many could not avoid unhealthy places 'from the urgent nature of their employment and circumstances'. In this case it was essential to take precautions, to guard against 'local mischiefs'.[149] Sleeping in high apartments, burning fires with lignum vitae and other resinous woods when there were 'swampy exhalations' after heavy rains, avoiding morning chills and never going out with an empty stomach were all useful pieces of advice. The acid steam of burning brimstone was best of all for 'correcting putrid air and checking contagion'.[150] Long's advice was directed at colonists, but given the price of 'Negroes' it would be as well to pay attention to their survival too, and inoculation, for example, seemed to work for both white and black. He told the story of 'a Guinea merchant of Kingston whose Negroes were seized with the small-pox, then raging malignantly in the town'. The merchant lodged them all in a warehouse where a large quantity of pimento was stored ready for export, the odour of which 'was so powerful as to subdue the offensive stench of the disorder, and refreshed the patients so much, that they all got through it safely'.[151]

Those who were compelled to live in 'humid situations' could protect themselves by smoking tobacco, wearing flannel and ensuring a diet including plenty of vegetables. When recovering from sickness, a good fish soup was an excellent remedy, as were tinctures of bark and orange peel. Wearing light clothes was a priority; it was essential to allow 'free discharge from the skin' so that the humours were able to pass through.[152] It was absurd to dress with

---

[145] Ibid., II. 512.
[146] Ibid., II. 514.
[147] Ibid., II. 513.
[148] Ibid., II. 514–15.
[149] Ibid., II. 515.
[150] Ibid.
[151] Ibid.
[152] Ibid., II. 518.

heavy European fabrics or insist on the latest London fashions. Readers should learn from the Spanish and how they dressed in the tropics, with linen and fine caps rather than wigs, the ladies in very fine and loose attire. The 'improper, ridiculous, and detrimental' hair fashions adopted by English women in the West Indies outraged him: 'half a yard perpendicular height, fastened with some score of heavy iron pins, on a bundle of wool large enough to stuff a chair bottom, together with pounds of powder and pomatum' might literally be affirmed to turn all heads! 'Nothing', he concluded, 'can be more preposterous, and absurd, than for persons residing in the West-Indies, to adhere rigidly to all the European customs and manners.'[153] White hats were an essential for the climate: white servants should be provided with them, and he strongly advised against wearing black, even for funerals. It was vital, he warned, to change out of wet clothes in order to avoid catching a chill. As to diet, he was enthusiastic about vegetables: 'instinct has taught the natives ... in all hot climates, to live chiefly on vegetable diet and subacid fruits'.[154] Too much meat was a great mistake. He warned, however, that after violent rains fruit and vegetables became saturated with water, and if 'Negroes' then ate too much of them they were liable to dangerous fluxes. 'The most appropriate diet, in my opinion, for the West-Indies, is a constant mix of animal and vegetable food, (if any thing) inclining to the vegetable.'[155] He recommended the pepper-pots, much enjoyed by West Indian absentees, which constituted 'the ordinary food of the Negroes'. Made with some meat or fish, greens, roots, plantains, okra and pulses, or any mix of these, it was 'unquestionably a most wholesome kind of food for Europeans newly arrived', especially if there was not too much pepper.[156] On arrival Europeans should immediately adopt a rather different diet to the one they were accustomed to: less meat, less wine, no rancid butter or cheese, avoiding 'excesses in eating and drinking' and taking exercise in moderation could ensure a healthy life.[157] The best way to become 'seasoned' was simply to stay in the climate and adjust over time, becoming, he might have added, creolized.

It was very noticeable to Long that 'The natives, black and white, are not subject, like Europeans, to bilious, putrid, and malignant fevers: they are not only habituated to the climate, but to a difference in respect to diet and manners; which works no small changes in mens [sic] constitutions.'[158] But what did it mean to consider changes in 'men's constitutions'? When writing about health Long recognized the importance of climate: but were the effects on the body or on culture? White creoles, he believed, had distinctive physical

[153] Ibid., II. 522.
[154] Ibid., II. 524.
[155] Ibid., II. 526.
[156] Ibid., II. 527.
[157] Ibid., II. 529.
[158] Ibid., II. 534.

characteristics, with deep eye sockets protecting them from the sun and supple joints that enabled them to move and dance with ease. 'Although descended from British ancestors, they are stamped with these characteristic deviations.'[159] What part had climate played in this, he wondered? And if climate did alter white people, then what about 'Negroes'? He was anxious to persuade colonists to adapt culturally: to eat, and dress, and exercise differently. 'Negroes', he thought, had adjusted to the climate, just what he was recommending for white colonists. They understood how to deal with the effects of living in marshy areas, burned fires all night so that the chill could be corrected and mosquitoes discouraged, ate plenty of vegetables and knew the healing power of particular plants. There were differences between white and black bodies: the capacity of 'Negroes' to bear the heat of the sun was much greater than that of Europeans, as Franklin had observed. This was associated with their 'quicker evaporation of perspirable matter', something which he could also deride with repulsion.[160] When it came to considering the health of the population, he could see that 'Negroes' had knowledge from which it was possible to learn, and his habitual diminishing of their human capacities could be momentarily dislodged. There were similarities between white and black creoles: both groups changed in the tropics. Creolization had good effects for Africans: the plantations could be civilizing. It was more troubling in relation to the colonists.

The ill health of the colonists was explained by their habits, not by the climate. 'Their excessive indulgence in a promiscuous commerce on their first arrival with the black and mulatto women' enraged him. 'They are almost *morally* sure of being very speedily infected' (my italics).[161] Such behaviour doomed them in his eyes, both morally and physically. They seemed to be 'engaged in a perpetual conspiracy against their own health ... incessantly inflaming and irritating their blood and juices with an acrimony, that is productive of mortal distempers', indulging in 'fiery spirits', violently exercising in the hottest parts of the day, sitting up late at night before 'plunging headlong into venereal debauches and, a mercurial regimen' with all its dangers.[162] They were, in effect, killing themselves. His remedy was moderation. It would certainly help if there were more properly trained medical men, and he strongly recommended the establishment of a college, on the lines of Codrington College in Barbados, which was to teach 'Negroes' 'physic and surgery'.[163] He called on the assembly to regulate apothecaries and prevent the frightful activities of quacks. Contemptuous of many of the ignorant white

[159] Ibid., II. 262.
[160] Ibid., II. 533.
[161] Ibid., II. 535.
[162] Ibid., II. 537–8.
[163] Ibid., II. 594.

practitioners operating in Jamaica, he resorted to a satirical account of one such, 'Apozem'. Apprenticed to an apothecary, he had learned nothing. Employed as a surgeon on a slave ship with three hundred captives, eighty of them had died, along with nine white seamen. The captain got rid of him to a planter. He had no difficulty in finding work but meted out death with mercury, opium and laudanum, made huge profits on his poisonous remedies and claimed the skills of a man-midwife, dentist, apothecary and farrier. He spread desolation, eventually falling victim to his own drugs. And, Long noted, he did not even have Latin.[164]

While aware of the many plants that had poisonous qualities and of those which could be utilized as antidotes, Long had no apparent fear of the wide-scale use of poisons by the enslaved as a weapon against their enslavers. There was no poisoning scare in Jamaica equivalent to the events in Saint-Domingue in 1757.[165] His main concern was with the use of such plants by obeah and myal-men and the ways in which white creoles, particularly women, were poisoning themselves with laudanum. The 'science of physic' should be encouraged on the island, for colonies were places where new diseases might take hold and 'this exalted art, if duly cultivated' could have very important effects, particularly for a 'trading people'.[166]

Early rising; a balanced diet; plenty of sugar, for he was convinced of its medical benefits; gentle exercise, preferably on horseback; umbrellas, as used by the French, Spanish and Portuguese for protection against the sun; and dancing, 'for the natives of Jamaica are dancers from their infancy', and this was especially important for women – 'an excellent antidote to cares, and a happy promoter of nuptial unions':[167] all these constituted a responsible regime, he concluded, that could not only ensure survival, but also be good for the island, replenishing the white population. His readers might reasonably have noted that he had not trusted to his own advice, but like so many of his fellow well-to-do West Indians, had returned to the metropolis.

Individuals must take responsibility for their own actions, but collective action was necessary too. Bath Spa, once a delightful and fashionable resort on the island, was now horribly dilapidated. (See Figure 6.4.) Degeneration always threatened in the topics, heat causing putrescence. The contrast with the Bath that many of his readers would have known – the elegant Georgian town with its glorious crescents and Roman baths – could not have been greater. The name encouraged a sense of similarity, his depiction emphasized difference.[168] The healing capacities of the Jamaican spring, situated in St

[164] Ibid., II. 583–90.
[165] Trevor Burnard and John Garrigus, *The Plantation Machine: Wealth and Belonging in French St Domingue and British Jamaica, 1748–1788* (Oxford, 2016).
[166] Long, *History*, II. 590.
[167] Ibid., II. 538–42.
[168] Ogborn, 'Discriminating Evidence'.

Figure 6.4 'A View of the Bath Hot Spring'. Reproduced from Long, *The History of Jamaica*. Digitally printed version. © Cambridge University Press 2010.

Thomas-in-the-East, had been recognized as early as the 1690s and demonstrated to Long's ancestor, Sir William Beeston. Two men, both 'greatly reduced', one with 'bellyache' and the other with venereal disease, had been much restored by the waters. A public-spirited benefactor had left money to provide facilities for poor whites who could not afford to support themselves when taking the waters. A romantic road led to the spring, the 'inspiriting effects' of which were well known; it was even possible to get drunk on these waters. A town had been established at a short distance and 'persons of fortune' had built houses there, while a corporation bought '30 Negroes' to maintain the road and plant provisions, a town square with a hospital for the poor was constructed, plus lodging houses and a billiard room. The place became 'a scene of polite and social amusement', with 'a crowd of company' gathering to enjoy the benefits. The political divisions of the Knowles era, however, had unfortunately 'destroyed all that harmony between families' and Bath fell into decline. Houses had decayed, the lodging houses fell into disrepair, the hospital had been converted into barracks and the billiard room was in ruins. Long had himself observed the 'tattered remains of a once superfine green cloth, which covered the table, all besmeared with the ordure of goats and other animals, who took their nightly repose upon it'. Providence had granted the 'salutary stream', its virtues now 'neglected and unheeded'.[169] This was shameful:

[169] Long, *History*, II. 160–7.

a wilful abandonment of a resource which had improved the health and sociability of the white elite. White men of property must act together to preserve their own health and that of the wider population, and fend off the ever-present danger of regression and atrophy. Consistent effort was required to hold decline at bay.

Natural History

Long was well aware of the importance of a knowledge of natural history to the wealth of Jamaica.[170] Indeed, it should be a part of a 'complete history'.[171] His comments on the health of white colonists were designed both to warn of the dangers of a tropical island and to provide remedies and reassurance in the face of such fears. He opened his third volume with a shift in tone and a celebration of the fecundity of the island, extolled as its natural balance, secured by the Divine.[172] The island could be cleared and settled, colonization safely proceed. The language of pollution was displaced by the language of abundance. His observation of the natural world required reference to the Divine, though natural history was rooted in a materialist description of animals, things and people. The animals and plants were there to serve the colonists, the system of classification an imperial construction. Once he had established what he saw as the providentially secured equilibrium of Jamaica in the first sections of volume III, the rest of the book, which dealt with a catalogue of vegetables, animals, fowl and fish, was written in a strictly utilitarian mode with commerce in mind. Once again his account of the island was imagined and organized in the interests of white colonists: this was their place, settled by them, the enslaved providing the necessary labour, the horses the required mobility, the plant life the commodities. He represented Jamaica as settled, only requiring an increase in the white population for its rich potential to be exploited. There was no apparent sense of peril from 'Negroes' in this volume; rather they appeared as useful informants, though never dignified with a name. The dangers, internal and external, had been dealt with. Now he could focus on the resources.

As an Enlightenment man, Long wanted to secure his credentials in the cosmopolitan world of gentlemanly science. Jamaica was not known for this and he wanted to put it on the map. There were amateur gentlemen, but with poor internal communications and high levels of mortality it was hard to develop scientific or medical societies.[173] His frequent references to the experiments of Dr Priestley, 'the ingenious Mr Franklin' and Dr Hales, the tables of

---

[170] Ibid., II. 136.
[171] Ibid., I. 6.
[172] Even poisons could find their antidote in this divinely balanced scenario.
[173] Robertson, 'Eighteenth Century Jamaica's Ambivalent Cosmopolitanism'.

Dr Halley and the findings of Sir Isaac Newton on gravity, were all demonstrations of his range of familiarity with leading figures.[174] His interest in air, morbidity and putrefaction had been fed by Priestley's influential paper published in 1772, signalling his engagement with current debates. He did not himself directly experiment, but he observed and documented phenomena which others had theorized. 'Among the late advances towards an improved system of natural philosophy', he wrote in his *Preface*,

> there are none which reflect more honour on the human faculties, than those which have penetrated as it were into the invisible world, and (by the test of experiment, aided by rational inductions) brought forth to our perception some of those stupendous agents, whose subtility had escaped our sight, and whose activity and power confounded and perplexed our judgment.[175]

Dr Priestley had discovered how vegetables and the sea cleansed the air, theories further elaborated by Dr Hales. 'Wonderful phenomena' such as 'tempests, volcanos, lightning and earthquakes' could 'lose their horror', be understood as 'necessary and propitious', and he made an analogy with returning health 'to our distempered frames'.[176] He quoted Hales's 'good remark':

> natural philosophy is not a mere trifling amusement ... for it not only delights the mind, and gives it the most agreeable entertainment, to see in every thing the great wisdom, power, and goodness, of the Supreme Architect; but is also the most likely means of rendering the gift of kind Providence, this natural world, the more convenient and beneficial to us, by teaching us how to avoid what is hurtful, and pursue what is most useful and conducive to our welfare.

How thankful we should be that the 'Gracious being' had 'permitted our attainment of the useful parts of knowledge'![177] Scientific gentlemen were making these 'penetrations' into the 'invisible world', just as the colonists were penetrating and conquering new territories.

The marvel, Long explained, was the work of the Divine in providing remedies for the 'putrefaction' and 'corrupted atmosphere' of the hot climate. The action of the sea, the rivers, the hills and plants worked to 'guard against, or to disarm' the hostile elements. An 'exact *equilibrium*' was 'regularly maintained'.[178] This picture of a benign and balanced world was emphasized in his meteorological remarks. He made use of his observations recorded over seven years in his diary.[179] Lightning could cause much damage, but it also, as

[174] Long, *History*, III. 631.
[175] Ibid., III. iii–iv.
[176] Ibid., III. iv.
[177] Ibid., III. 632.
[178] Ibid., III. viii.
[179] BL Add MSS 18963.

Dr Hales explained, was a purifier, burning away 'foul vapours'.[180] It rained very heavily in Jamaica, 'with a violence rarely seen in England'; he had frequently been soaked to the skin. How excellent it was that the Deity 'admirably' adjusted 'his distributions', so that the heat of the tropical island was offset with rain.[181] The trade winds, the salt, the tides and the currents kept the ocean in the tropics constantly in motion: 'the Almighty' had provided 'necessary preservatives against the inclemency of the climate'. Those who act 'agreeable to the dictates of right reason', he opined, reiterating his belief in moderation, 'may enjoy every gratification of health and felicity in a reasonable extent'.[182] A quotation from Pope's *Essay on Man*, a favourite text of Long's, emphasized how the work of the Almighty always brought rewards.

> In human works, tho' labour'd on with pain,
> A thousand movements scarce one purpose gain:
> In God's, one single can its end produce;
> Yet serves to second too some other use.[183]

The most valuable scientific discoveries, Long maintained, were those which explained abstruse matters and directed 'their application to most useful purposes of human life'.[184] Scientific experiments, particularly when combined with practice and experience, could be put to useful – meaning economic – purpose. Long could act as a mediator: his direct encounters with Jamaica's natural world could yield fruit, information on prices, shipping, trade winds, sugar and salt. As an 'agent of empire', he could advise the metropole on the commodities that could be developed, and be actively involved in the expansion of imperial trade and power.[185] At the same time, this 'seeing man' possessed his contact zone as a site of intellectual labour and celebrated practical outcomes. He may well have been thinking of himself and the contribution he was making in his writing when he penned the lines: 'commerce stands so largely indebted to physic and its sister botany, not only for materials of import and export, but the abilities of men employed in collecting those materials'.[186]

Long understood that a knowledge of science would facilitate the best possible use of resources. In his proposal for a boys' seminary he had included the idea of a botanic garden. Such a garden, he wrote, should be

---

[180] Long, *History*, III. 645.
[181] Ibid., III. 651.
[182] Ibid., III. 672.
[183] Ibid., III. 674.
[184] Ibid., III. iii–iv.
[185] The term is David Mackay's cited in Schiebinger, *Plants and Empire*, 11.
[186] Long, *History*, II. 590.

stocked with those plants of the island, or of the Southern continent, most distinguished for their virtues in medicine, or value for commercial purposes. It is certain, that nature has not only furnished this island with several vegetable productions useful in trade and manufactures, but likewise an unlimited variety of medicinal balms, barks and roots, adapted to the cure of most distempers incident to the climate.[187]

The botanic garden, as Richard Drayton has explained, was imagined as a means through which 'the power of God might be understood and mustered to human purposes, an Eden in the fallen world which might guide Christians towards the Paradise to come'.[188] Long was a devotee of Milton and had quoted lines from his lyrical evocation of paradise in his description of the parish of Trelawny. The conquest of the natural world was something worth aiming for, some consolation for the fall. A nature governed by rationality, by the classificatory systems of natural history, 'allowed Europeans to see themselves as magistrates of Providence, equipped by their knowledge of its laws with responsibilities over all of Creation'.[189] The botanic garden that Long proposed for the school provided a template for how he imagined the island's potential. It was scandalous that the gentlemen of Jamaica, unlike those of St Vincent, had not understood the benefits of such a development. The assembly should take the initiative and the London Society of Arts would help with the provision of useful plants from the nurseries around London.[190] Natural history and philosophy operated for Long within a providential frame; he could indeed hope to be a 'Providential Magistrate'. The work of agricultural improvement could be guided by science and religion. 'The general system of the world', he believed, revealed a regular order and gradation, from inanimate to animated matter: 'We ascend from mere inert matter, into the animal and vegetable kingdoms.' All were connected, 'in a wonderful and beautiful harmony, the result of infinite wisdom and contrivance'.[191] 'Nothing befalls us', he believed, 'except by the permission, or the direction, of Divine Providence.'[192] Life's inevitable difficulties must be faced, not avoided with palliatives such as laudanum or spirits.

His lengthy 'synopsis of vegetables and other Productions of this Island, proper for Exportation, or Home Use and Consumption. Of Exotics, cultivable for one or other of these Purposes; and of its noxious and useful Animals, etc.' drew heavily on others. Sloane was a worthy predecessor, whose belief that 'nature was a mechanical entity designed by God to be exploited for human profit' and vision of 'providential order and cornucopian abundance for

---

[187] Ibid., II. 259.
[188] Drayton, *Nature's Government*, 12.
[189] Ibid., 45.
[190] Long, *History*, III. 913.
[191] Ibid., II. 356.
[192] Ibid., II. 545.

human benefit' suited Long well.[193] His alignment of the interests of the state, trade, colonization and himself provided a model. Barham's *Hortus Americanus* had been more focused than Sloane on enlightening a colonial audience, while Browne too had extended the identification of Jamaican species. There was little that was original in Long's listings, and his interest was not in the system of classification but rather in the use of the species. His index of 250 trees and plants was necessarily selective. Which foreign plants, for example, could be cultivated on the island 'with great propriety'?[194] How could seeds be safely transported? The scale of his observation of insects and fowl, from the 'entertaining' activities of wood-ants to the 'ravenous' cockroaches who devoured perriwigs, bed bugs and the carrion-crows, 'living sepulchres of departed beasts', provided a remarkable demonstration of his ever-inquisitive mind and eye.[195]

Gentlemanly conversations about botanical and horticultural matters were part of white sociability on the island.[196] From the mid-eighteenth century onward, as Miles Ogborn writes, 'the extension of the plantation complex with its network of great houses, the development of the island's roads, and a notion of "conscious equality" between white men of different social ranks within a racially ordered society had provided the basic social infrastructure which enabled the polite exchange of natural historical knowledge'.[197] This might involve dinners, talk, the exchange of information, the gift of plants and seeds. White colonists had a shared sensibility, of new plants, birds, fish, insects, as well as soil, manure and labour.[198] Their hunting and shooting provided them with 'exceedingly fat and delicious' duck and teal, while the ring-tailed pigeon was 'one of the principal dainties' of the island.[199] Oysters were quite as good as those in Colchester. These men's conviviality was a modest copy of the metropolitan circle of gentlemanly scientists, those members of the Royal Society who argued that science was to be applied, transforming the world for the better whilst providing genteel amusement.[200] 'Ingenious' gentlemen in Jamaica, wrote Long, had introduced new species; Mr Wallen grew oriental bamboo on his estate in St Thomas-in-the-East, Mr Beckford the American nutmeg at his plantation in Clarendon. Transplantation was essential to

---

[193] James Delbourgo, *Collecting the World. The Life and Curiosity of Hans Sloane* (London, 2017), 14, 125.
[194] Long, *History*, III. 903.
[195] Ibid., III. 887–8.
[196] April G. Shelford, 'Before Breadfruit: Natural History and Sociability in Eighteenth-Century Jamaica', unpublished paper, August 2016, with kind permission of the author.
[197] Ogborn, *The Freedom of Speech*, 127.
[198] Thomas Hallock, 'Male Pleasure and the Gender of Eighteenth-Century Botanic Exchange: a Garden Tour', *WMQ* 62.4 (2005), 697–718.
[199] Long, *History*, III. 864.
[200] John Gascoigne, *Joseph Banks and the English Enlightenment. Useful Knowledge and Polite Culture* (Cambridge, 1994).

imperial development: sugar, coffee and indigo, the vital export crops, were all transplanted. 'Europe's naturalists', as Londa Schiebinger puts it, 'not only collected the stuff of nature but laid their own peculiar grid of reason over nature so that nomenclatures and taxonomies ... often also served as "tools of empire".'[201]

Long had delighted in Mr F—n's garden, full of its colonial transplants. His travels around the island involved that hospitality for which white colonials were famous. Some of his white informants were named: Mr David Riz had produced an excellent idea about possible uses of the prickly pear as a substitute for cochineal. Unfortunately, he had been met with no interest in the metropole. Long remained hopeful that 'the endeavours of ingenious men in these remote branches of the empire may hereafter be more regarded, by the patriots of Britain, and the guardians of its commercial interests'.[202] Mr Robinson, 'practitioner in physic and surgery', had invented a method of making not only sago from mountain cabbage but also soap from aloe, for which he was granted financial support by the assembly.[203] Anthony Robinson had taught Thomas Thistlewood the Linnaean system of classification.[204] Thistlewood exchanged nuts and seeds with his neighbour William Henry Ricketts, who was a close friend of Long's from London days, drawing on that sense of 'conscious equality' which allowed a small pen keeper, once an overseer, to mix with an elite gentleman.[205] Robinson was also a close friend of Long's brother, Robert, who collected many of his drawings of birds. They went shooting together, often in the vicinity of Bowers' River close to Longville Pen. Robert provided some of the descriptions of fowl in Robinson's manuscript of 'Jamaica Birds' and Edward appears to have done one or two of the drawings. A large black bird named as a 'Dabchick of Clarendon' gives some sense of his skill as a draughtsman. It was drawn hanging by the neck by some twine from a pole and noted as 'A Whimsical but a very just Figure of Nature', probably intended to frighten off prey.[206] To the modern viewer it is evocative of the dead Africans left to hang at crossroads, as a source of terror for the living. The rector of Spanish Town, Dr Lindsay, friend of the Moores and of Long and a strong pro-slavery advocate, was another who travelled the island,

---

[201] Schiebinger, *Plants and Empire*, 11.
[202] Long, *History*, III. 733.
[203] Ibid., III. 711; *JAJ*, 5, 18 December 1767.
[204] April G. Shelford, 'Birds of a Feather: Natural History and Male Sociability in Eighteenth Century Jamaica' (unpublished paper, 2006), cited in Ogborn, *Freedom of Speech*, 123.
[205] Douglas Hall, 'Botanical and Horticultural Enterprise in Eighteenth-Century Jamaica', in Roderick A. McDonald (ed.), *West Indies Accounts. Essays on the History of the British Caribbean and the Atlantic Economy in Honour of Richard Sheridan* (Kingston, Jamaica, 1996), 101–25; Burnard, *Mastery, Tyranny, and Desire* on Thistlewood's scientific and horticultural interests, 101–36.
[206] Anthony Robinson's Jamaica Birds, National Library of Jamaica (NLJ), MS 178, Picture 26.

doing watercolours of flora and fauna, his interest lying in the wonders of nature rather than in economic botany.[207] Images, both in print and in manuscript folders, as well as plants, could be talking points for botanically minded gentlemen.

White colonists needed to be reminded of the importance of improvement, always a theme for Long, whether in relation to the plantation or the wider economic interests of the colony. He was concerned as to the scale of tree felling and its effects. Indeed, the *History* became 'a very influential text for colonial advocates of forest protection'.[208] Opening land for a plantation meant clearing the trees, but he advised that new planting should be done on waste land: trees were friendly to the atmosphere, as Dr Hales had shown: they helped to clear putrid air. The 'graceful and valuable' mahogany, 'which furnishes a constant share towards the annual exports from the island', and the value of which 'either for sale, for use, or beauty' was so great, had been almost exterminated from the coast. It was now found in woodland, mountainous areas and 'the uncultivated districts of Clarendon' and should be planted on waste lands. Men with families, Long suggested, could 'produce a future fortune for their younger children' if they took this up.[209] Unfortunately Spanish mahogany, of an inferior quality, was replacing it in the British market and he strongly recommended a strengthening of duties on the Spanish wood to protect the Jamaican. What was more, the mahogany cutters of Jamaica had to create roads through the interior to access the wood, and this promoted settlement, a very valuable asset. Similarly, wild plantain trees, which were very beautiful but bore no fruit, should be planted when land was exhausted, for their moisture was beneficial.

Long believed in the importance of science for the future of the island, but his focus was on economic botany and horticulture. His predecessors had done much to classify the range of vegetation, but there were 'a very great number of plants and minerals . . . to be described and classed' and a 'judicious analysis of their properties and use' would be very desirable.[210] But he did not himself intend 'a display of science', since his aim was to indicate 'the useful qualities of each plant, whether for manufacture, food, medicine, or commerce'.[211] His initial discussion of potentially major export crops – indigo, coffee, cotton, cocoa (sugar had been dealt with elsewhere) – advised as to their cultivation, estimated the numbers of 'Negroes' needed for this labour, and suggested what profit might be hoped for. Indigo, for example, had been extensively cultivated at one time and required considerable skills. Heavy duties imposed had ruined

[207] Higman, *Proslavery Priest*.
[208] Richard H. Grove, *Green Imperialism. Colonial Expansion, Tropical Island Edens and the Origins of Environmentalism, 1600–1860* (Cambridge, 1995), 159.
[209] Long, *History*, III. 842–3.
[210] Ibid., II. 136.
[211] Ibid., III. 712.

'several industrious families' and skills had been lost. But production could be revived. 'No part of the world', he opined, 'affords a better soil for the culture of Indigo than the interior parts of Jamaica,' places such as his own parish of Clarendon. The key ingredient for dyeing cloth 'a fine blue', it was good for export, easy to transport, high in value and required relatively little capital. Long had small settlers in mind. 'Fifteen Negroes are deemed sufficient to manage and attend twenty acres; and twenty-five Negroes are allowed to fifty. Four Negroes are therefore about equal to five acres; which proves that it may be entered upon by men of exceedingly small capitals.' With 'prudent management' a planter with five acres could make £300 per annum.[212] He was enthusiastic about coffee too, which could 'furnish subsistence to a greater number of white inhabitants', adding 'to the strength and security of the island', and cited at length a 'sensible' pamphlet by a Mr Ellis of Dominica on the subject.[213] Planters should pay more attention to quality, since 'the goodness of every commodity always claims the preference at market, commands the best price, and becomes the quickest in demand'. 'Eight Negroes', in his opinion, could 'clean and gather from fifty to sixty acres, and upwards, according to the bearing of the trees; and fifty acres will yield, at least, 500l *per annum*, if well taken care of'.[214] Heavy duties were once again an issue, and the mother country needed to pay attention to this if they hoped for successful competition with the French. Cotton production could also be extended. The tedious work of hand picking and cleaning 'is easily performed by children or invalids, who are fit for no other work', he maintained, while 'three Negroes' could perform the heavier work, leaving plenty of time to grow corn and provisions. He pointed to the numbers involved in the manufacture of 'fustians, calicoes and Manchester velvets', a proof of the value of West Indian production of raw materials, contributing to rather than competing with British manufacture.[215] The best use of nature, he was proposing, was to cultivate commodities that could be traded widely. His assumptions as to an enslaved labour force underpinned every plan for expansion.

When it came to the myriad plants unsuited to export he was much briefer, often providing only their vernacular names, different from both their African and Latin names, with common-sense descriptions and details as to their utility. Where did they grow? What soil was best? What could be done with them? How many 'Negroes' were required to cultivate them? How many hours of labour? Botanical knowledge was particularly valuable as it was clear that the island was rich in vegetables that could heal local illnesses. He regretted the lack of knowledge as to these amongst the white practitioners. He had noted

[212] Ibid., III. 679.
[213] Ibid., III. 691 fn.
[214] Ibid., III. 685.
[215] Ibid., III. 694.

that African traders brought 'valuable drugs' as well as people into the island.[216] What was more, he was compelled to recognize that 'many of the Negroes are well acquainted with the healing virtues of several herbs and plants, which a regular physician tramples under foot'.[217] American diseases were different from European, something that Sloane had not seen, and local knowledge was valuable. Lime juice, roots and herbs could be efficacious. Knight had understood this and recognized African skills. Some enslaved Africans had made 'very Surprising Cures', he had noted, particularly one belonging to Mr Dawkins of Clarendon: he was 'of Opinion, that many Secrets in the Art of Physic may be obtained from those Negro Doctors, were proper Methods taken'.[218] Long, however, undercut his own observations: 'brutes are botanists by instinct', he insisted. In Africa they had 'subdued the diseases incident to their climate which have foiled the art of European surgeons at their factories'. But these were applied randomly, 'without any regard to the particular symptoms of the disease; concerning which, or the operation of their *materia medica*, they have formed no theory'.[219] It was instinct, not theory or rationality, that was in play. He reported that Esquemeling in Costa Rica had seen monkeys utilizing instinct in similar ways. Both Africans and monkeys, he concluded, got from the Creator 'means conducive to their preservation'.[220]

Long continued to remark on 'instinct' as responsible for 'Negro' cures, while recognizing how effective they were and asking many questions of his enslaved informants as to their use and preparation. Africans were never allowed to be 'ingenious', as the white colonists were in Long's opinion, and they were never named. Cockspur could be used for gonorrhoea, trumpet tree leaves for poultices, papaw trees planted for healthy air, bitter ash for abortion, broad-leaved broom-weed leaves were used to make a bath by 'Negroe women' when their children were scabby, fit-weed for hysterics. 'Upon enquiry among the Negroes' as to the Manchineel tree which made very handsome furniture, he learnt that if drops of the juice went into their eye while they were 'felling the trunk, or hacking off the limbs ... it would give them a severe pain for several hours afterwards, occasioning an inflammation, which was relievable by applying lime-juice to the part'.[221] Then there were the local foods to be consumed as well as produced. 'Negroes' were particularly fond of avocado pears, used palm trees for oil, okra for pepper-pot ('that celebrated and desirable hotchpotch'), Guiney-corn and plantain were essential parts of

---

[216] Ibid., I. 491.
[217] Ibid., II. 127.
[218] Knight, *History*, II. 496.
[219] Long, *History*, II. 380–1.
[220] Ibid., II. 381. As scholars have recognized, there was a decline in respect for African knowledge from the mid-eighteenth century as *materia medica* became the province of professional European men.
[221] Long, *History*, III. 838.

their diet, and they enjoyed alligator and rats.[222] They made cups, saucers and bowls from calibash, baskets from wild-cane; he had even noticed that 'wild Negroes' used the inner bark of the lace-bark tree to make clothes.[223] Yet, Long remarked, 'necessity, that great spur of invention', was lacking in the colony and there was little disposition 'to improve what nature offers' – one further disavowal of all that he had observed as to how the enslaved utilized everything that they could to survive and to make a life.[224]

As he wrote, his summary was 'of those trees and plants which, I think, appear in general to be the most useful in respect to commerce, and the accommodation of settlers, not omitting those medicinal properties for which they have been chiefly distinguished'.[225] His overriding concerns were to increase the wealth and health of white colonists and bring in new migrants so that the island could be made both safer and more productive. Jamaica's future was as a white colony, built and sustained by black labour.

Long's imagined Jamaica had its racialized boundaries firmly in place, its black population confined to ticketed mobility, its gorgeous landscape unsullied by a black presence, its road system expanded to ensure the safety and commercial success of its white population who could be protected against internal and external enemies, its colonists improved in health, its natural abundance commodified; this was his imagined Jamaica. Other realities intruded: the ever-absent presence of the enslaved who were 'the sinews', the skilled 'Negro' doctors who understood American disease better than the European trained medical men, the runaways in the caves and grottos, the dissolved bodies associated with yellow fever, the swamps, mosquitoes and Coromantees. Degeneration of the white body sat alongside colonial 'improvement', ruinate plantations were saddled with debt: the effort to hold all that threatened at bay was immense. Long's *History* was his contribution to that task. So too were his efforts on behalf of the colonial state.

---

[222] Ibid., III. 775.
[223] Ibid., III. 748.
[224] Ibid.
[225] Ibid., III. 847.

7

Colonizing the State

Leaving the Mother Country

Edward Long settled down in 1769 in the substantial Georgian house at 45 South Street in Chichester to write his *History*. Following in Hume's footsteps, he opened his work with the government and constitution of the colonial state, its relation to the mother country and its distinctive practices. He may well have been remembering back to his arrival on the island in early 1758. That was a journey he had not planned, but was necessitated by the death of his father and the urgent questions he faced as to how he might secure a fortune. His journey 'home', to the mother country, eleven years later, was, on the contrary, long planned, and only possible once his financial position and his ability to support his growing family from the fruits of the labour of others was secure. He had suffered from periods of ill health in the year before their departure and this made it all the more urgent to leave the tropics and return to the temperate zone.

The England he was familiar with from the 1750s was the site of heated debates as to who belonged to the national community. What was to be done with Jacobites, with Catholics and with Jews? The idea of England was rooted in homogeneity: could it be heterogeneous?[1] By the time he left in 1758, the country was already in the throes of war with France, and English nationalism and xenophobia were in full flow. He had learned, as we have seen, to envisage France as a dangerous enemy, though also satirizing excessive Francophobia in his novel *The Anti-Gallican*. His rough, unpolished but courageous protagonist, 'Honest Cobham', was 'English, English, *Sirs, from Top to Toe*'. He would never 'vote for the Introduction of Slavery, Popery, and *Frenchmen* among us'.[2] Conflicts with France had begun in North America in 1753 and the defeat of British forces in 1755 had left the French in control of the Ohio country.

---

[1] Samuel Johnson's definition of a nation was 'a people distinguished by another people, generally by their language or government'; Mahmood Mamdani, *Neither Settler nor Native. The Making and Unmaking of Permanent Minorities* (Cambridge, MA, 2020) is thought-provoking on the problem of living with difference.

[2] Long, *The Anti-Gallican*, 16.

When news of this reached England there was a public outcry over the government's poor military preparedness, an outcry fuelled by a tradition of demands from the so-called 'Whig Patriots', utilizing a language of liberty to claim a more aggressive foreign policy.[3] Further defeats followed. It was Austria's decision to break their treaty with Britain and align with France, however, that made a European war almost inevitable. Admiral Byng was sent to Minorca to prevent its seizure by the French. His failure led to violent public demonstrations over what was interpreted as a national humiliation. Byng was scapegoated, court-martialled and executed. War with France followed, declared in May 1756.

The mid-1750s were marked by a sense of deep national malaise. Fears of emasculation and degeneracy, as Kathleen Wilson has explored, were mobilized by texts such as John Brown's *Estimate of the Manners and Principles of the Times* (1757–8), which maintained that the nation was in acute danger and urgently needed a revival of patriotic English masculinity. The earlier critique of the corruption of Walpole's administration had fostered an oppositional ideal of public good.[4] In 1757 an unlikely alliance was struck between the Duke of Newcastle and William Pitt, who had been his outspoken enemy. Pitt deemed the country to have been insulted and defeated, its national spirit in decline. He knew, as Macaulay later put it, what 'the resources of the empire, vigorously employed, could effect', and he had long supported those who demanded a more aggressive foreign policy.[5] 'Imperial aspirations', argues Wilson, 'enmeshed with the patriotic critique of corruption and a populist, libertarian vision of the polity ... accountable government, a public-spirited citizenry and imperial ascendancy all seemed to go hand-in-hand ... [E]mpire entered public political consciousness as a birth-right, as much a part of the national identity as the liberties and constitutional traditions for which Britain was celebrated the world over.'[6] French wealth and maritime and colonial power could be attacked in the West Indies and North America.[7] Empire came to be seen as a way of nurturing and consolidating national potency, and Pitt, supported by his West Indian ally William Beckford, articulated these sentiments, offering a positive picture of an energized state, representing global expansion as benevolent and patriotic. Higher taxation, the mobilization of the militia, and the presence of the army and navy would be the costs to be borne. The new government was committed to war and by November 1758 a British

---

[3] Gerrard, *The Patriot Opposition to Walpole.*
[4] Personal communication, Mark Knight, 12 November 2018.
[5] T. B. Macaulay, 'William Pitt. Earl of Chatham' [January 1834], in *Literary and Historical Essays* (Oxford, 1913), 263.
[6] Wilson, *The Sense of the People*, 201.
[7] Eliga H. Gould, *The Persistence of Empire. British Political Culture in the Age of the American Revolution* [1993] (Chapel Hill, NC, 2000).

fleet had sailed from Portsmouth. The early attacks on France were unsuccessful, but 1759 was the year of triumph.

Mercantile interests were closely aligned with the enthusiasm for war with France, England's major commercial and colonial rival. Since the seventeenth century, state intervention in economic policy and matters of foreign trade had markedly increased. These policies came to be defined by Adam Smith as the 'mercantile system' which monopolized 'colony trade'.[8] Cromwell's Western Design had rested on a notion of empire building through territorial expansion and commercial regulation. It was actively supported by colonial merchants and their political allies. The Navigation Acts of 1651 provided one cornerstone of a wider set of practices. Overseas expansion meant a strengthening of the state since foreign policy was one of the most centralized aspects of government.[9] Charles II and James, Duke of York confirmed the Navigation Acts in 1660 and viewed the creation of the RAC monopoly of the slave trade as essential to defeating international competition and increasing their colonial revenue. The colonies must be subject to royal prerogative and kept dependent. While the Dutch were the key rivals for the Stuarts, the accession of William III brought new alignments and France was increasingly identified as the major commercial rival. Mercantilist thinking promoted by figures such as Charles Davenant and Malachi Postlethwayt stressed the importance of protecting British trade against foreign rivals and was enthusiastic about the possibilities of colonial riches. 'Colonies', wrote Davenant,

> are a strength to their mother-kingdom, while they are under good discipline, while they are strictly made to observe the fundamental laws of their original country, and while they are kept dependent on it. But otherwise, they are worse than members lopped off from the body politic, being indeed like offensive arms wrested from a nation to be turned against it as occasion shall serve.[10]

Wealth in land was understood to be finite, trade a zero-sum game so that competition between rivals would be inevitable and necessary. National strength depended on a favourable balance of trade and a foreign policy that focused on promoting British naval power and colonial supremacy. The Navigation Acts restricted commerce to British shipping and sailors and were designed, alongside the use of monopolies, duties, drawbacks and bounties, to secure these policies. Imports should be limited, exports encouraged, thereby facilitating a flow of bullion into the mother country. British sugar, protected by duties against foreign competitors, could be bought cheaply and sold dearly in European markets. As James Knight maintained, the wealth

---

[8] Smith, *The Wealth of Nations*, II. 107–8.
[9] Elizabeth Mancke, 'Empire and State', in D. Armitage and M. J. Braddick (eds.), *The British Atlantic World, 1500–1800* (London, 2002), 193–213.
[10] Cited in Williams, *Capitalism and Slavery*, 55.

derived from the sugar colonies could rival the gold and silver of Spanish America.[11] Colonies were a strength to the mother country provided they were dependent and accepted that their interests were subordinate. They should not attempt to develop manufacturing interests, and indeed the sugar colonies were not allowed to fully refine the cane in order to privilege domestic manufacturers. Wars were fought to protect monopolies and mercantile interests, first against the Dutch command of trade, then against French and Spanish rival mercantilisms.

Alternative economic visions were always present: the enthusiasm for 'improvement' belied the notion that the value of land was fixed, and Hume in the 1750s defended trade and labour as the source of wealth, countering the view that all trading nations were rivals and believing that an increase in trade and industry promoted the riches of all.[12] Many Whigs agreed that labour was the source of wealth, not land, and wealth was not finite. Oldmixon, one of the pre-eminent Whig imperial ideologists, argued that 'every hand employed in the Sugar Plantations is fourty times as good as one that stays at home', a view that Edward Long would later echo.[13] Merchants favoured forms of free trade, and colonists in Jamaica, for example, were angry at the limited quality and irregular delivery from the RAC of the enslaved Africans whose labour they required in ever increasing numbers: pressure from free traders led to the erosion and eventual loss of the RAC monopoly.[14] But mercantilist practices framed the metropolitan/colonial settlement that survived into the nineteenth century.[15]

Long had left England at a moment that has been interpreted as a critical turning point for state, nation and empire. It was a moment that started with defeat but ended with Britain as the dominant global power, its empire hugely extended and fundamentally changed in character by the new populations.

---

[11] Knight, *History*, II. 552.
[12] Hume, *Philosophical Works*, 3; see particularly 'Of Commerce' and 'Of the Jealousy of Trade', 287–98, 345–8.
[13] Oldmixon, *The British Empire in America*, I. xxv. Pincus, 'Addison's Empire'; Pincus, 'Rethinking Mercantilism: Political Economy, the British Empire and the Atlantic World in the Seventeenth and Eighteenth Centuries', *WMQ* 69.1 (2012), 3–34. This stresses the importance of party politics to the shifts in economic and imperial policy.
[14] Pettigrew, *Freedom's Debt*.
[15] Williams, *Capitalism and Slavery* famously argues that the abolition of slavery marked the triumph of free trade and manufacturing interests against those of the mercantile sector. Julian Hoppit argues that mercantilism was never hegemonic and that it was always contested and contradictory, but agrees that it was probably most relevant to the imperial sector; 'Political Power and British Economic Life'; Hoppit, *Britain's Political Economies. Parliament and Economic Life, 1660–1800* (Cambridge, 2017); Philip J. Stern and Carl Wennerlind (eds.), *Mercantilism Reimagined. Political Economy in Early Modern Britain and its Empire* (Oxford, 2013) argue that mercantilism is best understood as a focus of debate which extended much beyond the party issues identified by Pincus.

The question as to how to govern this expanded empire was to be a major preoccupation of the metropolitan state in the decades to come.[16] Three texts published in 1759, Voltaire's *Candide*, Johnson's *Rasselas* and the first two volumes of Sterne's *Tristram Shandy*, all reflected on the flows of people and things characteristic of the new commercial world, and how to create communities in times of war.[17] What kind of state was needed? What kinds of people inhabited it? How were the relations between them to be ordered? Eighteenth-century thinking on the state emphasized that the art of government was to subdue conflicting interests. Disinterested men of public virtue should direct a strong central authority, blessed as the country was with a constitution which allowed for competing interests to be harnessed. But how were the new interests in this expanded imperial world to be contained?

The growth of what came to be a full-scale fiscal-military state was clear in the context of war and the colonial expansion which required a reinforced state formation: the state was indeed *stating*.[18] The more efficient systems of taxation and growing administration went alongside the allocation of resources for empire that far outstripped those for the domestic economy and exceeded those provided by the French, Spanish and Portuguese empires.[19] The expenses of settlements, of salaries for officials, of ships and ports and roads, were multiple. Britain was able to take on ever increasing military commitments thanks to a radical increase in taxation, particularly excise, the development of public deficit finance in the shape of the national debt, and an unprecedented growth of public administration devoted to the organization of the fiscal and military activities of the state. But England remained 'a society in which military might remained both subordinate to and separate from civilian government'.[20] The strength and funding of the army and navy were determined by parliament which was establishing its supremacy. Parliament, argues Paul Langford, was able to claim a monopoly of tax-levying power and use it in ways which imposed a vision of the state and its interests on the community which it represented.[21]

---

[16] Jack P. Greene, *Exclusionary Empire. English Liberty Overseas, 1600–1900* (Cambridge, 2009); P. J. Marshall, *The Making and Unmaking of Empires. Britain, India and America, c. 1750–1783* (Oxford, 2007).
[17] Watts, *The Cultural Work of Empire*, 31–57.
[18] Brewer, *The Sinews*. The reference is to Philip Corrigan and Derek Sayer, *The Great Arch. English State Formation as Cultural Revolution* (Oxford, 1985), 3: 'States, if the pun be forgiven, state ... They define, in great detail, acceptable forms and images of social activity and individual and collective identity ... Indeed, in this sense, "the State" never stops talking.'
[19] Steve Pincus, 'Thinking the British Empire Whole', seminar presentation, King's College London, October 2020.
[20] Brewer, *Sinews*, 43.
[21] Langford, *A Polite and Commercial People*.

As public affairs came to be understood as an expression of propertied interests, one of those interests, which was increasingly vocal, was that of the West Indians, represented by the absentees, whose numbers were increasing. Regular visits to Uncle Beeston's counting house to collect his allowance would have given Long a sense of the West Indian presence in London. The growth of empire and commerce alongside changes in government had led to the emergence of lobbying groups, with specific trading interests. The absentees were soon to organize themselves more formally and Beeston Long was to act as their first chair. William Beckford was the best known of the West Indians. 'Alderman Sugarcane', as he came to be called, was a man of importance in the London of the late 1750s. Coming from the major Jamaican slave-owning family, Beckford had been sent to school at Westminster, then to Oxford, followed by a period on the continent. He returned to the island in 1736 to settle his father, Peter's, estates and was soon active in the House of Assembly as his forefathers had been, facing the challenge of the Maroon War. His well-established connections with London merchants ensured his opposition to Walpole's reluctance for war with Spain. Enemies, he knew, threatened Jamaica both internally and externally. Following the settlement of family disputes over property, he returned to England, which he conceived of as 'home', while the island was his 'country'.[22] By the time Long arrived in London in 1753, Beckford had been named as an alderman and in 1754 he was elected to represent London in the House of Commons. He spearheaded efforts to gain West Indian parliamentary representation, and succeeded by dint of electoral bribery in getting members of his family and friends elected.[23] They needed to be as close as possible to the heart of government, convinced as they were of the importance of imperial power to the future of the islands. Beckford's strategy, argues Perry Gauci, was to align island interests with those of the fast-changing metropolis with its expanding commercial sector. As a planter he would always be aware of mercantile interests, for the two were closely integrated in the West India trade, though different factions would periodically be at loggerheads. The colonies, in his mind, were an indivisible part of the mother country, an idea that Long came to share. Beckford was heavily involved in the conflicts over the removal of the capital from Spanish Town to Kingston in the mid-1750s. A fierce critic of Governor Knowles and a staunch defender of the planting interests of the Jamaican elite, he was strongly opposed to the demands of the Kingston merchants. He gave evidence to the Board of Trade inquiry into the controversy which resulted in the Earl of Halifax's ruling in favour of Spanish Town. From 1756 he had Pitt's ear and hoped to be able to rely on him, given his enthusiasm for empire and commerce, to protect West Indian sugar and recognize Jamaica's vulnerability in

---

[22] Gauci, *William Beckford*, 40.
[23] Gauci, 'The Attack of the Creolian Powers'.

the Caribbean theatre of war. He urged Pitt to attack Martinique and lobbied him for more troops for the island.[24] Long left England an innocent on the specifics of planting, but not on the subject of the empire and the value of imperial power to the sugar interests.

Long had learned his Whiggism from childhood and, as we have seen, from his schoolmaster in Liskeard. In the years following the Jacobite rebellion, the thread running through this Whiggism was provided by Locke. Civil society was based on consent: 'the great and chief end therefore, of men's uniting into commonwealths, and putting themselves under government, is the preservation of their property ... the mutual preservation of their lives, liberties and estates'. And men 'could never be safe ... nor think themselves in civil society, till the legislature was placed in collective bodies of men, call them Senate, Parliament, or what you please'.[25] These were principles that were to be echoed by Long throughout his life, tempered perhaps, at least when in England, by Addison's 'Polite Whiggism', where the armed citizens would be replaced by the taxpaying citizen under parliamentary governance and taste would act as a civilizing agent.[26] Mr Spectator was always interested in the connections between commerce, empire and domestic politeness and could sit comfortably beside figures such as Defoe with their enthusiasm for wealth, enlightenment and progress. Next to consent, liberty was the key: the liberty of the subject to have his property protected, a liberty secured by the law.

Long was training as a lawyer and was studying legal texts alongside attending the Courts of Law, Equity and Exchequer prior to his departure. The decision that he should leave England precipitately prevented his completing his terms, but he was granted an *exgratia Call* and was able to assume his barristerial gown in May 1757.[27] He could have chosen to practise as a lawyer in Jamaica, but turned to planting, his family's traditional interest. His first encounter with the legal profession had not impressed him. His sojourn in the household of Mr Kimber of Fowey, the attorney with a 'tolerable business' who had been entrusted by his father with overseeing Tredudwel and was to 'discharge my Bills and Board' at Liskeard, dismayed him. Kimber treated his wife despotically and his 'hauteur, stiffness and formality ... extremely disgusted me'. Kimber's lack of politeness was an unhappy introduction to the profession and 'I resolved never to be his Guest again.'[28] Long must, however, have garnered a considerable knowledge of the law and the power of the state. Passing through London in 1745 as a boy of

---

[24] Gauci, *William Beckford*.
[25] Locke, *Two Treatises of Government*, 295, 268.
[26] J. G. A. Pocock, 'The Varieties of Whiggism from Exclusion to Reform: a History of Ideology and Discourse', in *Virtue, Commerce and History. Essays on Political Thought and History, Chiefly in the Eighteenth Century* (Cambridge, 1985), 215–310.
[27] Howard, *Records and Letters*, I. 111.
[28] Ibid., I. 97.

eleven, he had registered that guards were posted at the city gates checking for arms. The Jacobite rebellion had thrown 'all London into Tumult'.[29] It would have been too soon for him to witness the disembowellings and mutilations of prisoners, along with the heads on spikes that were soon to be displayed on Temple Bar. In Cornwall his father was an active JP, delivering the brutal physical punishments of his patron Walpole's bloody code, the Black Act, to the vagabonds, unemployed and criminals who appeared before him. 'There is hardly a criminal act', as the criminologist Leon Radzinowicz wrote, 'which did not come within the provisions of the Black Act; offences against public order, against the administration of criminal justice, against property, against the person, malicious injuries to properties of varying degrees – all came under this statute and all were punishable by death. Thus the act constituted in itself a complete and extremely severe criminal code.'[30] Henry Fielding, when discussing the increase in the numbers of robberies at mid-century, had explained it in terms of the divisions between high and low: 'So far from looking on each other as brethren in the Christian language, they seem scarce to regard each other as of the same species.'[31] 'The Black Act could only have been drawn up and enacted by men who had formed habits of mental distance and moral levity towards human life,' wrote E. P. Thompson in his analysis, 'or, more particularly, towards the lives of the "loose and disorderly" sorts of people.'[32] When Long was seeking legitimation for the violence of the Negro Codes in his *History*, he recalled the sanguinary punishments, the beatings, chainings, burnings, mutilations and brandings characteristic of early modern English discipline, before the country became more civilized. The villeinage laws, he maintained, kept the common people under 'abject slavery' and a 'savage complexion' still remained.[33]

Staying with his mother and sisters in Plymouth prior to their departure for Jamaica, Edward encountered the power of the state in its military and naval glory as success against the French was celebrated. He subsequently met his sister's would-be suitor, Lieutenant Prescot, now promoted to captain, *en route* to suppress a disturbance among Cornish tin miners. When he was a young man in London, the hangings that took place at Tyburn and Newgate eight times a year were popular public spectacles. James Boswell never missed one if he could avoid it. Sympathy, Hume had written, was associated with close proximity, the desire for approval from friends and neighbours. 'We find in common life, that men are principally concern'd about those objects, which are

---

[29] Ibid., I. 82.
[30] Radzinowicz cited in Thompson, *Whigs and Hunters*, 22.
[31] Fielding, *An Enquiry into the Causes of the Late Increase in Robbers* [1751] in *Complete Works* (1967), 13, 164, cited in E. P. Thompson, *Customs in Common* (Harmondsworth, 1993).
[32] Thompson, *Whigs and Hunters*, 197.
[33] Long, *History*, II. 493–6.

not much remov'd either in space or time,' he reflected.[34] Preoccupied with similar thoughts, Adam Smith asked in his *Theory of Moral Sentiments*, 'To what purpose should we trouble ourselves about the world in the moon?'[35] The limits of Boswell's sympathy, Vic Gattrell notes, 'were determined pretty precisely by the social distances between himself and suffering others'.[36] Long had seen the coercive state in action, perfectly able to use violence against rebels and masterless men of any kind. But Whig hegemony, that winning of consent, which maintained some political stability until the 1790s in the face of Wilkite radicalism, an anti-Catholic mob and food riots, depended on the widespread belief in the 'rule of law'. The law may have been first and foremost an instrument of class power, devoted to the protection of property. It was, after all, 'by their property eighteenth-century men were known', and Long's father had returned to Jamaica in order to consolidate the family property, held over generations.[37] Land offered stability. Commercial wealth was an increasingly important part of the British economy, but commerce had its dangerous sister, luxury, and business life was uncertain. So too was planting, intimately tied as it was to trade. The appeal of English land was that it appeared to offer security. Land was celebrated as the seedbed of patriotism, the landed, those men of disinterested public virtue. An individual's property was integral to their political persona, and though parliament was quite prepared to abolish common rights in the interests of 'improvement', it was careful to offer compensation when the rights of the propertied were infringed. The notion of property was deeply entwined with liberty: both protected by the rule of law the idea of which saturated the rhetoric of eighteenth-century England. 'The first and primary end of human laws', as William Blackstone put it, 'is to maintain and regulate these absolute rights of individuals', among them the 'three great primary rights of personal security, personal liberty, and private property'. Equality before the law was embedded in this, necessitating 'a general conformity of all orders and degrees to those equitable rules of action, by which the meanest individual is protected from the insults and oppression of the greatest'.[38] Whig hegemony was expressed, argued E.P. Thompson, 'not in military force, not in the mystifications of a priesthood or of the press, not even in economic coercion, but in the rituals of the study of the Justices of the

---

[34] David Hume, 'Of Contiguity and Distance in Space and Time' [1739–40], in *Philosophical Works*, II. 205–9, 206; Onni Gust, *Unhomely Empire. Whiteness and Belonging, c. 1760–1830* (London, 2021), 25–6.

[35] Adam Smith, *The Theory of Moral Sentiments* [1759] (London, 1767), 123; Carlo Ginzburg, 'Killing a Chinese Mandarin: the Moral Implications of Distance', *Critical Inquiry* 21.1 (1994), 46–60.

[36] V. A. C. Gattrell, *The Hanging Tree. Execution and the English People, 1770–1868* (Oxford, 1994), 285.

[37] Paul Langford, *Public Life and the Propertied Englishman, 1689–1798* (Oxford, 1991), 195.

[38] Blackstone, cited in Rabin, *Britain and its Internal Others*, 4.

Peace, in the quarter sessions, in the pomp of Assizes and in the theatre of Tyburn'. The occasional victory of the people over the greats 'went a long way to give popular legitimacy to the law and to endorse the rhetoric of constitutionalism upon which the security of landed property was founded'.[39]

Long left England a Whig, with a belief in the intimate connection between liberty and property, assumptions that consent was necessary to government and that law would protect established rights, a knowledge of the military and coercive power of the 'mother state', as he named it, and a sense of himself as an entitled Englishman. Some of these lessons would serve him well in the new world of the 'infant state of the colony'.[40] But he would soon learn that the colonial state, a slave state, operated very differently. Nothing approaching Whig hegemony was possible in Jamaica, only dominance and coercion.[41] Far from the military being subordinate to and separate from civil government, authority rested on armed force. What was more, a colonizing state needed a unified ruling bloc; factions were seriously dangerous. 'In a colony', wrote Long, 'which by the nature of things, can flourish no longer than whilst its inhabitants are at peace with each other, and employed in the avocations of industry; nothing surely can be more impolitic, and baneful to the mother country, than to introduce party feuds.' This 'contagion' could spread; 'even our very Negroes turn politician'.[42] How was liberty to sit side by side with chattel slavery? Yet it must. By the time he was addressing his metropolitan peers in the 1770s and defending slavery, he knew that the planters' defence of *their* liberties provoked claims of hypocrisy. 'When the planters have complained of violations done to their liberty', he wrote in the opening pages of the *History*, 'the enemies of the West-India islands have often retorted upon them the impropriety of their clamouring with so much vehemence for what they deny to so many thousand negroes, whom they hold in bondage. "Give freedom" (say they) "to others, before you claim it for yourselves".' Yet the Romans and Athenians had held many in servitude while prizing their own liberty: 'the higher estimation they put upon their own independence, the more indulgent masters were they to their slaves', he maintained. This was his blueprint for Jamaica. 'The planters, or owners of slaves, in our colonies,

---

[39] Thompson, *Customs in Common*, 113–14.
[40] Long, *History*; these terms appear *passim*.
[41] Notions of 'liberty' and the 'rule of law' could not survive what Ranajit Guha, in his classic text *Dominance without Hegemony. History and Power in Colonial India* (Cambridge, MA, 1997), 67–8, described as 'the inexorable urge of capital to expand and reproduce itself by means of the politics of extra-territorial, colonial dominance'; 'Colonialism', he wrote, 'stands thus not merely for the historical progeny of industrial and finance capital, but also for its historic Other.' Sudipta Sen, 'Uncertain Dominance: the Colonial State and its Contradictions (with Notes on the History of Early British India)', *Nepantla: Views from South* 3.2 (2002), 391–406.
[42] Long, *History*, I. 25.

cannot be too steddily supported in the possession of British freedom': their freedom secured not only the humane treatment of the enslaved but the stability of an island where slavery was *'inevitably* necessary'. He would not suggest for a moment that slavery should be introduced into a 'free country', but Jamaica could not be free.[43] It was a slave state, dependent on coercion to function: violence was essential, not least to constantly remind the enslaved of their subjection. Long's *History* was a sustained argument for a particular kind of state, the one that he and his great-grandfather were making.

Joining and Making a Slave State

Long must have watched the progress of the war with alarm as he sailed the Atlantic. Jamaica was in danger of a French invasion in 1756, 1757 and 1758 and was suffering from much dislocation of trade due to both martial law and enemy attacks.[44] He landed, as we have seen, in a garrison society, racialized, masculinized and militarized, subject to martial law and beset by enemies, both internal and external. 'War suffused the landscape of plantation agriculture,' as Vincent Brown has described it, 'the work routines of plantation production, and the sexual exploits of white men, whose everyday belligerence was underwritten by the legal regime, an armed population of slaveholders, and the formal British military.'[45] Long had soon acquired both land and enslaved people to work that property, and thanks to his new wife, Mary, he had a home in Spanish Town and significant kin connections. He was ready to step into his place in the island's political elite, following his forefathers. His great-grandfather Samuel had been a key figure in early assemblies, holding governors to account and challenging the prerogative. Edward would have been familiar with his imposing marble tomb in Spanish Town with its encomium on his character. His father, Samuel, had served in the assembly and the council, where he had been a strong supporter of the beleaguered Governor Knowles, as well as acting as the custos, or sheriff, of Clarendon. In January 1756 Samuel had been elected as chair of the Joint Committees of the Council and Assembly and 'appointed to view the Forts, Fortifications and Stores', no doubt in view of the threat of war and invasion.[46] He too was buried in Spanish Town.[47] His son Charles was paid £741 7s. 6d. that same year for his work as chief engineer on the forts and fortifications.[48] The Long men were

---

[43] Ibid., I. 5–6.
[44] Burnard and Garrigus, *The Plantation Machine*.
[45] Brown, *Tacky's Revolt*, 46.
[46] NLJ, MS 60, Minutes of the Council of Jamaica, vol. 32, 1755–1758, 30 January 1756.
[47] He was clearly no paragon. After his death he was investigated by the assembly for unlawful activities associated with local office. George Metcalf, *Royal Government and Political Conflict in Jamaica, 1729–1783* (London, 1965), 142.
[48] NLJ, MS 60, Minutes of the Council of Jamaica, vol. 32, 1755–1758, 24 June 1756.

embedded in the colonial establishment, which was also always a military establishment. They were doing what men of property were expected to do: they were the supposedly 'disinterested men of public virtue' who would rise above private interest and work for the good of 'the people'. But the meanings of such rhetoric were different in Jamaica. 'The people' still meant those who had consented, white men of property, but now slave-holders, owning property in people, rather than landowners employing 'free' labourers.

With father and brother both dead and Robert apparently having little interest in island politics, it was Edward who quickly established himself as ready to take his place in the echelons of power. A first step was his appointment by the assembly in November 1759 to be 'entrusted with the public dispatches ... take receipts from the several custos's, or chief magistrates' of the island's parishes for the papers that they would receive.[49] The following year, thanks to Uncle Beeston's intervention with the Admiralty, he was named as sole judge in the Vice-Admiralty Court, a position which he must have hoped, especially in a time of war, would bring him substantial fees.[50] One month later he began his career as an assembly man, elected to represent not Clarendon but the neighbouring parish of St Ann.[51] Electors had to be white, or above three removes from 'negro', aged twenty-one or more, and with a freehold of at least £10 p.a. in the parish where they were voting: such conditions ensured an extremely limited franchise. To stand for the assembly, a man had to have a freehold of minimum £300 p.a. or a personal estate of at least £3,000. Long was called in to take the oaths of allegiance, supremacy and abjuration.

Oath taking, as Miles Ogborn has explained, was critical to understandings of law and personhood in colonial Jamaica. Who could speak, where and when, and what that speech could carry were central to definitions of power, amongst both white men and Africans. The social attributes of freedom, masculinity, whiteness and property holding were transformed into active legal and political relations by oath taking. For assembly men their oaths were a performance that legitimated and consolidated racialized, class and gender privilege. Maroons and Coromantees (as they were named by the colonists) built on African practices, and used oaths to seal authority and commitment. Long was a certified member of the governing class once the rituals were performed, ready to deliberate and debate, and engage in 'the practicalities of colonial legislative practice'.[52] The governor could issue the proclamations of the crown; the assembly could *deliberate*. The word carried gravity; this was not

---

[49] *JAJ*, vol. 5, 24 June 1756.
[50] Ibid., vol. 5, 23 October 1760; Michael Craton, 'Caribbean Vice-Admiralty Courts and British Imperialism', in *Empire, Enslavement and Freedom*.
[51] *JAJ*, vol. 5, 11 November 1761.
[52] Ogborn, *Freedom of Speech*, 39.

simply talk. The assembly had established its right to make laws, provided that they were not deemed 'repugnant' to the mother country, but such legislation was subject to crown approval. This was the right they had won in the conflicts in which Edward's great-grandfather had engaged and that had finally been confirmed in 1729, the island's Magna Carta, as it was called. The assembly secured the confirmation of its legislative functions; the *quid pro quo* was their guarantee of revenue for the crown. Since the money granted was never enough to cover the costs including official salaries, public works and the militia, governors were obliged to call the assembly regularly in search of further resources. The assembly kept control of the money and limited executive authority whenever possible. While the crown saw the main purpose of the assembly as being to provide for the upkeep of the colony through taxation, the assembly saw their function as to hold the executive to account and resist attempts to limit their rights.[53] As Knight put it, though they were 'a Conquered Country, yet They are not a Conquered People' and having travelled far had created 'a Seperate and Distinct Dominion'.[54] The mercantilist framework which assumed colonial dependence was a frequent source of friction and conflict between governors and the assembly.

It would have become clear to Long that a colonial state such as Jamaica, a slave state, had both similar and different imperatives to those of the metropolitan state.[55] It must be able to make laws specific to a tropical island with a majority enslaved population. It had an interest in population management, racial codifications, laws as to who belonged and on what terms, powers to control the mobility and the cultural practices of the enslaved. But its subordination was also clear: local laws had to be agreed in the metropole and these limitations were resented. Much as he wanted the constitution of Jamaica to mirror that of Britain as much as possible, indeed he would have liked to make it more 'truly British', Long was fully aware that specific laws were needed for the colony, quite different from those of the mother country.[56] 'When a legislature is established in a commercial colony not half peopled, and where a species of slavery has been admitted,' he wrote, 'new objects, new incidents, are daily arising, to call for new legislative regulations.'[57] These included the need for 'the better order and government of slaves', preventing obeah, regulating 'Free Negroes, Mulattoes and Negroe towns', managing

---

[53] Frederick G. Spurdle, *Early West Indian Government. Showing the Progress of Government in Barbados, Jamaica and the Leeward Islands, 1660–1783* (Palmerston, New Zealand, n.d.); Metcalf, *Royal Government and Political Conflict*; Benn, *The Caribbean*.
[54] Knight, *History*, I. 221.
[55] Kathleen Wilson, 'Rethinking the Colonial State: Family, Gender, and Colonial Governmentality in Eighteenth-Century British Frontiers', *AHR* 116.5 (2011), 1294–322.
[56] Long, *History*, I. 193.
[57] Ibid., I. 20.

buildings and roads, markets and fisheries, encouraging settlers, dealing with the courts and the militia, and much more.[58] Legislation was for the 'relief or benefit' of the inhabitants (always imagined as white), 'who, it cannot be denied, are the best judges of the evils they feel, and their proper remedies'.[59] Local issues should be determined locally; the legislature must have relative autonomy which included the use of discretionary violence.[60] The problematic issue was, of course, slavery. What was to happen when colonial legislation was seen as 'repugnant' to English law? At the same time, conflicts over crown prerogatives carried many echoes of the House of Commons. Long's training as a lawyer was probably one of the reasons for the weight he was soon able to carry in the assembly.

In the wake of abolitionist critiques of the cruelty of slave-owners, he may have puzzled as to how to give an account in his *History* of the violence of the penal clauses of Jamaica's equivalent to France's *Code Noir*. Their sanguinary aspects might provoke hostility. How could he represent the code in such a way as not to undermine his efforts to persuade metropolitan readers that the island was becoming ever more enlightened? He addressed the issue at the end of his second volume of the *History*, when he had made his case for the essential difference between Black and White, thus legitimating quite different legal systems. Despite the class differences of which Long was well aware, the fact of skin meant that in law, 'the Whites are nearly on a level: and the lowest can find the way of bringing the highest to public justice for any injury or oppression'.[61] This was the English common law transposed to the colony. 'The Whites never considered themselves as the *pares* of the Blacks,' he noted.[62] It registered as a terrible shock if they ever received similar treatment. The assembly had recorded in 1761 their shame that there was no separate gaol for Whites; this should be dealt with urgently as a matter of 'common humanity'.[63] More than a decade later Long evoked horror for his readers with the spectacle of the gaol in Spanish Town, where a dozen Whites and about a hundred 'Negroes' were normally crowded together. 'In this delightful place of custody', he wrote,

> debtors and malefactors of all sorts, all sexes, and complexions, are promiscuously crowded; a circumstance highly disgraceful to the publick humanity, more especially in a country where it is thought politically expedient to maintain a distinction between Whites and Negroes. It is therefore not a little astonishing, that the debtor and the criminal should

---

[58] Ibid., I. 21.
[59] Ibid.
[60] Eliga H. Gould, 'Zones of Law, Zones of Violence: the Legal Geography of the British Atlantic, circa 1772', *WMQ* 60.3 (2003), 471–510.
[61] Long, *History*, II. 431.
[62] Ibid., II. 485 fn.
[63] *JAJ*, vol. 5, 16 October 1761.

be huddled together; and that White persons, who have committed no other offence than that of insolvency, should be associated with the most bestial and profligate wretches of the Negroe race, as if it was intended to shew that incarceration, like death, is a leveller of all distinctions.[64]

The 'political expediency' of maintaining a distinction between Whites and 'Negroes' was at the heart of the Jamaican judicial system. And 'publick humanity' demanded no less.

His documentation of the penal clauses of 1696, with all their horrible and cruel punishments for infringements of any kind, was undercut, he hoped, by extensive footnotes justifying and explaining some of the most ferocious clauses, thus minimizing English 'repugnance'. 'Inhuman penalties' were now, he could assure his readers, entirely obsolete and should be expunged from the record. Mutilations were 'barbaric' and a 'Christian legislature' should discourage any 'sanguinary disposition' and give examples of *'justice in mercy'*.[65] A slave accused of killing a white person would now be dealt with by two justices and three freeholders, 'who are indifferent and unbiased', he claimed, on oath to judge according to evidence. This was 'sufficient to answer all the needs of impartial judicature with respect to *these people*' (my italics). The practice of the slave courts, he was anxious to point out, was drawn from that of the army and navy.[66] All penal laws, he explained, are 'made *in terrorem*, and for prevention'.[67] *These people*, it was clear, were a different 'species' (his word) from colonists, who were subject to English common law and trial by jury.[68] While 'in every just war between civilised states' it should never be forgotten that the enemies were 'men', the enslaved occupied a different category.[69] 'The Negro Code of this Island', he explained, had been based on the Barbados code. He was convinced this had drawn on England's villeinage laws, with all their 'severity', laws which demonstrated the 'abject slavery' of the labouring poor in the relatively recent past.[70] (The villeinage laws were a subject of contest in the Somerset case.) 'The first emigrants to the West Indies,' he argued, 'it is natural to think, carried with them some prejudices in favour of the villeinage system, so far as it might seem to coincide with the government of Negroe-labourers.'[71] His use of 'natural' indicates what kinds of class prejudices he assumed those early emigrants fostered. The Africans 'first imported' were 'wild and savage to an extreme'. The English followed the Portuguese who 'had begun, long before, to trade in

---

[64] Long, *History*, II. 14.
[65] Ibid., II. 485 fn
[66] Ibid., II. 496.
[67] Ibid., II. 487 fn.
[68] Ibid., II. 372.
[69] Ibid., I. 297.
[70] Ibid., II. 493–4.
[71] Ibid., II. 495.

Negroes as a commodity, and to hold them as mere chattels and moveables'.[72] The Portuguese practice was adopted.[73] The African trade became 'a national concern' and parliament 'considered Negroes, purchased from that continent, as a lawful commercial property', and declared them 'to be as houses, lands ... and personal estates, transferable, and amenable to payment of debts'.[74] This definition of 'Negroes' as chattels was critical. 'English law provided colonists with a discourse and with plural modes of proceeding,' as Lee Wilson argues, 'that aligned with the commercial imperative to treat people as property in a variety of transactions.'[75] Too much emphasis on statute law, she suggests, has resulted in the neglect of the sets of rules and practices, the performative and procedural aspects of law, its 'protean potential' for the management of slavery.[76] English colonists made a conscious decision to treat enslaved people as chattel property, a form of 'personal property' which carried few restrictions on transmission as compared with land, 'real property', with the limitations that had been established on inheritance. 'From antiquity', as David Brion Davis argued, 'chattel slavery was modeled on the property rights traditionally claimed for domestic animals.'[77] In Jamaica enslaved people were treated as chattels in marriage settlements, wills and inventories, listed with other personal property, cattle and household goods. 'Classifying slaves as chattel property was a crucial first step in creating societies in which human beings could be transformed into moveable units of wealth, in which the slave became "a person with a price".'[78] This did not mean that slave-owners believed they were the same as horses or dining tables. They knew that they depended on their labour and skill in a different way from the labour of cattle, and they knew, if faced with resistance, they would treat them as criminal, capable of agency. The chatteldom of the enslaved was a legal fiction, but one with horrific consequences. The slave-owners' refusal of personhood was at the heart of their disavowal. They knew and did not know: the law encompassed this ambiguity. Once it was accepted that persons could be made slaves and held as slaves, special slave laws were established which attempted to deal with the complexity of their position. Slaves, argued Elsa Goveia, were *a special kind of property* (my italics), property in persons, or as Edward Rugemer would put it, 'animate capital'.[79] A slave was merchandise when bought and sold in the slave

---

[72] Ibid., II. 497.
[73] Goveia, 'The West Indian Slave Laws', 10, argues that it was the Spanish example of slavery that was critical in the West Indies.
[74] Long, *History*, II. 497.
[75] Wilson, *The Bonds of Empire*, 3.
[76] Ibid., 5.
[77] David Brion Davis, *The Problem of Slavery in the Age of Emancipation* (New York, 2014), 11.
[78] Walter Johnson, *Soul by Soul: Life inside the Antebellum Slave Market* (Cambridge, MA, 1999), 2.
[79] Goveia, 'West Indian Slave Laws', 21; Rugemer, *Slave Law*, 2.

trade; once acquired by a planter s/he was part chattel and part real property. As chattels they could be sold up for debts if other moveable assets were finished; in other cases they could be disposed of in accordance with the laws of inheritance of real estate. If charged with criminal offences, as in the penal code, they were men and women.

Long's perusal of his ancestors' wills and indentures made clear the treatment of people as things, but so too did his position as a judge in the Vice-Admiralty Court. These courts governed life in naval and merchant vessels, dealing with prize cases, petty crime, sailors' wage claims, contract issues and violations of the Navigations Act. Litigants in these courts made claims on the basis of property rights in human beings. 'The chattel principle', named by the American fugitive W. C. Pennington, is a term which captures the way in which, 'like other pieces of property, slaves spent most of their time outside the market, held to a standard of value but rarely priced'.[80] Once bought, enslaved men and women would only have been priced again when sold to some other owner. But if captured on a naval vessel in wartime and subject to the judgment of the court as to the ownership of the 'cargo', they would have been brought before the court as 'objects that could be condemned, appraised, and sold'.[81]

Long's attempted whitewashing of the penal clauses tallied with his silence on state or slave-owners' violence. These were not matters he wished to draw attention to. Very few archives of the slave courts have survived, but an account of the decisions of slave courts in St Andrew between 1746 and 1782 demonstrates that 'the dominant experience of legalities from the slave's point of view was of terror and violence'.[82] The most common punishments, for crimes ranging from theft, to running away, to violence against others, were flogging, mutilation, transportation and death. Slave law, as Diana Paton argues, backed up and legitimated the private power of the slave-owner: the slave courts played a key role in transforming naked violence into legitimate punishment. 'Slave courts demonstrated to the enslaved that, for most intents and purposes, their masters and the law were one and the same.'[83] The punishments focused heavily on the body and were those used for treason in England. '*These people*' were the dispossessed; they had lost all civil rights, and like felons their blood was tainted. 'In so far as the slave was allowed personalty before the law he was regarded chiefly, almost solely, as a potential criminal.'[84]

---

[80] Johnson, *Soul by Soul*, 19.
[81] Thanks to Lee Wilson for her work on these courts. Wilson, *The Bonds of Empire*, 123. Wilson notes that the Jamaican court records are in a poor state of preservation, but it is clear that cases were heard involving slaves that included claims for them as property.
[82] Paton, 'Punishment, Crime', 934.
[83] Vincent Brown, 'Spiritual Terror and Sacred Authority in Jamaican Slave Society', *S&A* 24.1 (2003), 31.
[84] Goveia, 'The West Indian Slave Laws', 25.

They had no legal personality in civil law, but were subject to criminal law, a criminal law that was draconian in its practices.

The violent act of transforming a human into a slave, Orlando Patterson recognized, was institutionalized by law. The law recognized the slave as a person who could be tried for criminal acts, but then deprived that slave of all civil rights. Patterson emphasized the centrality of both violence and coercive powers, and the symbolic aspects of the dishonouring associated with social death, the making of a 'genealogical isolate', the rituals of branding and naming.[85] An understanding of blood was also critical to this process, providing a metaphorical dimension to the process of depersonalizing. So-called 'corrupted blood' became articulated to an understanding of racial slavery, marking biological, social and political destiny.[86] Blood and descent had long been associated with both individual and national identity, determining who you are and where you belong. In civil law, *jus sanguinis*, the right of blood, assured nationality by descent. The particularities of English people were associated with the land and its climate, the places in which they and their ancestors had settled. Fears as to the safeguarding of the purity of English bloodlines had arisen in the context of the colonization of Ireland.[87] The New World presented far more alarming possibilities of degeneration, given the small minority of white people and the majority black population. The tropics were testing indeed for colonials. Would they remain satisfactorily English? This demographic imbalance, as Brooke Newman elaborates, led to a preoccupation with questions as to who might be considered white, the boundaries of which shifted over time. 'Genealogical definitions of whiteness which defined white status through the absence or gradual diminution of African ... blood, allowed for the possibility of white racial regeneration, a gradual whitening of the population through mixture over several successive generations.'[88] Long had much to say on this issue, convinced as he was of the dangers associated with 'corruption of blood', fearing the effects of African or 'mulatto' wet nurses as we have seen. The 1751 Act of the Jamaican Slave Code provided an example of the legal acceptance of the concept in the colony. 'To prevent the bloody, inhuman, and wanton killing of slaves,' the code read,

> any person, so offending, to be adjudged, for the first offence, on conviction, guilty of felony, and have benefit of clergy; and suffer the further punishment of imprisonment, as the court shall award, not exceeding the term of twelve months; and, for the second offence, such person to suffer

---

[85] Patterson, *Slavery and Social Death*, 5.
[86] Dayan, *The Law is a White Dog*.
[87] R. R. Davies, *The First English Empire. Power and Identities in the British Isles, 1093–1343* (Oxford, 2000); Montano, *The Roots of English Colonialism*.
[88] Newman, *A Dark Inheritance*, 16.

death, but not to work corruption of blood, nor forfeiture of lands, chattels, etc.[89]

White men, despite killing enslaved persons, would not suffer from its harsh implications for their blood was not 'corrupted'.

Concerns over degrees of whiteness were one aspect of the colonial assembly's attempts to manage population. How to think about a population had been a topic of concern since the seventeenth century, inspired in part by William Petty and his schemes for Irish colonization and making the Irish English. 'Political arithmetic was an ambitious art of government by demographic manipulation' as well as a methodological innovation bringing empirical evidence and quantitative techniques to bear on economy, society and politics.[90] In early colonial Jamaica interracial relations were sometimes legitimated because of the need for free persons, and parish records demonstrate that significant numbers of women did not choose to marry and their children were accepted as family members.[91] But limitations on the rights of free people of colour were periodically introduced. Attempts to increase white settlement were also regularly made. Long, influenced by political arithmetic and seriously interested in trying to understand the relation between land and labour on the island, was convinced that 'a colony without wise laws can become depopulated'.[92] He promoted varied attempts to manage the population, from encouraging an increase in both the enslaved and white populations to limiting the rights of free people to inherit substantial properties and excluding Coromantees from the island.

Once attending the assembly he discovered the range of concerns of the colonizing state. It included the preparation of bills dealing with taxation, duties and the management of 'Negroes', the establishment of standing committees, responses to parochial and individual petitions, mounting investigations and making reports. The forty-one members, the majority of whom were planters, were frequently at odds with the governor and the council (appointed by the crown and prone to act with the governor). Possessed with a powerful sense of their own importance, each man was insistent on being the absolute master of himself and his actions; buoyed up by the degree of their undisputed authority on their estates, they regarded themselves as the guardians of the liberties of 'white subjects', 'free-born Englishmen'.[93] They were renowned in the metropole for their factionalism and their turbulent and ungovernable spirit. 'Managing a Colony Assembly' was, 'of all farces ... surely the greatest,

---

[89] Long, *History*, II. 492.
[90] Ted McCormick, *William Petty and the Ambitions of Political Arithmetic* (Oxford, 2009), 10.
[91] Walker, *Jamaica Ladies*.
[92] Long, *History*, II. 402.
[93] Ibid., I. 185 fn, II. 320.

& most stupid,' Governor Trelawny had declared in 1747. Only two or three of the assembly members, he complained, could see beyond their noses, but they loved to prate on liberty, which meant the right to do as they wished.[94] The assembly was called by the governor and normally met between October and December, before crop time when planters needed to be on their estates. Spanish Town would then be filled with the notables of the island and their equipages; dinners, balls and the races were the talk of the town.

Long entered the assembly in the wake of the major revolt of 1760, that 'war within an interlinked network of other wars', when much attention was necessarily being devoted to attempts to deal with its effects and prevent any recurrence.[95] He was quickly drawn into a range of responsibilities, initially dealing with the 'autoclaps', the aftershocks of the rebellion.[96] In addition to the preparation of bills, there were major reports to be written, on the numbers of 'mulattoes' inheriting substantial estates, the rebellion in St Mary in 1765 or the extensive addresses prepared in relation to the 'privileges controversy' which occupied the assembly and paralysed much of the work of the colonial government in 1765–7. Then there were the committees: between 1761 and his departure from the island at the end of 1768, Long served on committees handling a variety of administrative and political problems. Many were centred on security, from road making, the inspection of fortifications and barracks, regimental accounts, the raising of parties for the suppression of rebellion, and rewards for those of the enslaved who had been loyal to their masters, to the state of the militia.[97] Internal security and the defence of the island were, as Burnard and Graham have shown, the major item for the colonial budget after 1760, absorbing up to 60–70 per cent of island revenue.[98] The colonists were quite prepared to pay what was necessary for their defence and taxes were relatively high. Other committees were focused on 'improvement', ranging from the inadequacy of schools for the children of the colonists to the provision of taxes for new chapels, new possibilities for settlement or the state of the spa facilities at Bath. The economy was another major preoccupation: how to stem illegal trade with the Spanish, negotiate on the rum duties, improve the mahogany trade or tackle the problems with raising credit. Others again were to do with governance, whether the poll tax, investigations into the malpractices of public office and the courts of justice, or attempts to check on absentees who were not paying their quit rents. Long was an active assembly man and in

[94] Cited in Ogborn, *Freedom of Speech*, 84.
[95] The description is Brown's, *Tacky's Revolt*, 7.
[96] The term is Kei Miller's in *Augustown* (London, 2016).
[97] Andrew Jackson O'Shaughnessy, *An Empire Divided. The American Revolution and the British Caribbean* (Philadelphia, 2000).
[98] Trevor Burnard and Aaron Graham, 'Security, Taxation and the Imperial System in Jamaica, 1721–1782', *Early American Studies: an Interdisciplinary Journal*, 18.4 (2020), 461–89.

the months before leaving Jamaica he was elected Speaker, once more following in the footsteps of both great-grandfathers, Samuel Long and William Beeston, a demonstration of the key position he had come to occupy in the assembly.

As a patriot Long had much to say about the need for improvement in colonial Jamaica. Whilst staunchly defending it against its abolitionist critics, he hoped for a more secure and prosperous society.[99] The slave state might no longer be an infant, but it was still a child with new needs. The mother country, Long was prepared to admit, simply did not care enough. What really mattered in the metropole was whether the consignments of sugar arrived on time. He wanted as much autonomy for Jamaica as possible, but at the same time to be a part of the mother state: these were inevitably contradictory desires. 'Colony government' should be seriously attended to in the imperial parliament, laws amended and problems addressed.[100] The constitution needed alterations, never mind the attempts by the metropolitan authorities to limit the rights of the assembly. The status of the council was profoundly wrong. The members were chosen by the crown and the governor: how could they possibly exercise any independence? The appointment of unsuitable governors was also a very sore point and the system of patenting appointment was open to serious abuse. Officials should be paid and should be local.

His critique of the mother state was complemented by his admiration for the French monarchy's colonial policies. Despite his hostility to the French as the natural enemies and competitors of the British, he was impressed by the scale and level of support for their Caribbean colonies.[101] There was 'a spirit in the French monarchy which pervades every part of their empire': an autocratic government with a clear sense of purpose had advantages.[102] The French took 'judicious precautions' to ensure good government, while British colonies were 'so ill regulated in many respects'.[103] Perhaps Britons were too addicted to liberty, a disturbing thought for Long. The French were 'formidable competitors' for the sugar market; indeed, it was mortifying that their production of sugar and indigo was exceeding that of the British colonies, and their territories were dangerously close, prone to change hands during war.[104] In the 1750s, as we have seen, Long had been concerned about the alien French influence in England. Then there was the war, with France the enemy. By the 1770s his attitude had shifted to one marked by envy. French colonists had clear advantages over their rivals. 'The French government considers a planter, in their

---

[99] Knight, *History*, also detailed many improvements that were needed.
[100] Long, *History*, I. 403.
[101] Trevor Burnard, 'Edward Long's Vision of Jamaica, and the Virtues of a Planned Society in the *History of Jamaica*', in his *Jamaica in the Age of Revolution*, 43–70.
[102] Long, *History*, III. 941.
[103] Ibid., I. 433, 403.
[104] Ibid., I. 403.

islands, as a Frenchman venturing his life, enduring a species of banishment, and undergoing great hardships, for the benefit of his country.'[105] The British, in contrast, simply wanted their colonies as a source of wealth. 'France, like a skilful gardener, has been careful in the choice of plants, and treated her colonies as a favourite nursery, in which none should be fixed that were not vigorous, healthy, with all the promising appearances of thriving luxuriantly and producing good fruit.' Britain, on the contrary, 'treats her plantations as a distant spot, upon which she may most conveniently discharge all her nuisances, weeds, and filth, leaving it intirely to chance, whether any valuable production shall ever spring up from it'.[106] These 'nuisances, weeds, and filth' were the 'the lowest orders of white inhabitants', 'our inferior class of people', who Long had little time for.[107] The French had managed the balance between Whites and 'Negroes' on the islands, they supported emigrants, demanded little in taxes, built good fortifications, and had a properly regulated system of management of the enslaved, the *Code Noir*. Recognizing the need for better fortifications if their trade was to be protected in wartime, they had succeeded in transforming Cape Nicola Mole from a place of 'poverty and desolation' to a 'secure and opulent *emporium*' in ten years.[108] A strongly fortified settlement and well-established town was populated with Acadians, German families had been settled in the surrounding land and delivered provisions, the harbour was filled with ships, the free port bustled with commerce; a spectacle to envy indeed. Why did the British authorities not invest in Port Antonio on this scale? In every respect French colonists could expect more from their government than the British, and far from regarding French emigrants as potential pollutants, Long hoped that they, especially if they were Protestant, would swell the ranks of white Europeans in Jamaica.

If the mother state lacked drive, so too did the assembly. Long always had two audiences in mind: the metropolitan and the colonial. In the aftermath of 1760 and of Somerset, he had to find a way to counter abolitionist critiques without abandoning slavery. What came to be identified as 'amelioration', a modified form of slavery, was his chosen route. Some changes would have to be made to the plantation regime so that it could be deemed acceptable in Britain. At the same time he had to persuade the planters that this was the only way forward. He strongly defended the rights of the assembly against the 'tyranny' of the crown. But he greatly regretted the lack of public spirit amongst the white elite and argued for a more 'patriotic legislature'.[109] True patriots were men such as his great-grandfathers, virtuous, manly and disinterested.[110] The assembly had been

[105] Ibid., I. 96.
[106] Ibid., I. 433–4.
[107] Ibid., I. 128.
[108] Ibid., III. 949.
[109] Ibid., II. 464.
[110] Ibid., I. 201.

'very remiss', for example, in neglecting the importance of collecting information on population, trade and settlement.[111] He had had to collect such material himself in order to give a proper account of the state of the island. This was the kind of information that the political arithmeticians he admired were compiling for England. He believed in the notion of 'the public good', by which he meant the pursuit of a stable and prosperous economy and society: this was his 'first and great principle'.[112] It required the pursuit of collective rather than only individual interests: sadly some planters were 'detestably selfish', unwilling to invest in projects which would bring them no direct profit.[113]

If only Jamaica were more like England: then absentees might not absent themselves. The English had effected a huge improvement in roads over recent years, making the transportation of goods cheaper and quicker, the country more opulent. Planters had been hampered by the lack of good roads and he waxed lyrical on the benefits that could accrue from better communications (not least because it facilitated quelling sedition), laying out detailed plans for road building. Colonists sent their sons to England to be educated: why didn't the assembly invest in schools? He had no desire for an Anglican establishment with an interest in the conversion of the enslaved, but the 'lewd' and 'disreputable' state of some of the clergy was most regrettable. 'Some labourers of the Lord's vineyard were much better qualified to be retailers of salt-fish, or boatswains to privateers, than ministers of the Gospel,' he recorded acidly.[114] The assembly devoted much time to the rates of duties, but better credit arrangements needed to be made and more intervention was needed on agriculture. And then there was population; despite concerns about the shrinking white minority, not enough had been done to encourage settlement.[115] The legislature had failed to suppress the monopolization of land by a few, who then hoarded it until it could be sold at a high price. An insistence on the payment of quit rents would be one way to tackle this, since it would encourage settlement and ensure profitability. Industrious white settlers were urgently needed and Long devised a settlement plan, racially structured and drawing on North American examples. Three townships were proposed, on land that was lying 'waste and useless'.[116] Each settler, assumed to have a family, would be granted land, a house built to a certain model, a plantain walk, provision ground and 'one Negro'. In order to ensure seasoned labourers, it might be desirable to choose 'Mulattos', who if they performed well for five years might be rewarded with freedom. Planters would be granted twenty acres, this modest acreage ensuring they represented

---

[111] Ibid., I. 59.
[112] Ibid., I. 122.
[113] Ibid., I. 470.
[114] Ibid., II. 238.
[115] This was one of the issues around improvement that Knight also raised; *History*, II. 632.
[116] Long, *History*, I. 420. Long's enthusiasm for some aspects of the North American colonies was tempered by their religious enthusiasm, for which he had no taste.

no competition to the big estates; tradesmen would receive five acres; a good road would be built, along with a room, properly defended with 'loop holes and flankers', for public business.[117] A surgeon and superintendent would be appointed. A classed and racialized male hierarchy would thus be ensured, with white inhabitants, professionals, then modest industrious planters, then tradesmen, then 'Mulattos' occupying the middle ranks, then 'Negroes'. The women, scarcely mentioned in his detailed plan, would presumably do domestic work and care for children, alongside some agricultural labour. He imagined that regular soldiers might be willing to quit their regiments and settle. Since they were already seasoned to the climate, they would be most suitable, particularly given their experience with both internal and external enemies. An allowance could initially be made for each man, woman and child. He very much hoped that the assembly would 'awake to a sense of their true interest' and see the importance of investing in such schemes.[118]

Long's experience in the legislature was critical to the *History* that he was to write. His extensive knowledge of the island, from its constitution and its roads, barracks and military preparedness to its towns and plantations, its commerce and its revenue, was based in large part on the committees that he had served for the assembly and the reports that he had prepared. Thucydides had maintained that to write history it was vital to have experience of the state. Long had this experience: he wrote from the perspective not only of a planter but also of a legislator who had been at the heart of government. What was more, and just as relevant in a garrison state, he had experience in the militia and came from a family with strong connections to the military. Great-grandfather Samuel had been on Cromwell's expeditions, grandfather Charles was a colonel, father Samuel had served as a young man. His wife, Mary Ballard Beckford, was descended from Colonel Ballard who was an officer with Penn and Venables, and their son Robert Ballard was destined for the military. The 'constant virtual hostility' that in Long's view characterized a society built on slavery meant that 'Every slave owner ... is by necessity soldier': in Jamaica, 'the whole body of freeholders constitute a perpetual or standing army'.[119] (Unfortunately the wretched state of the militia made this something of a dream.) This was a very different situation from that in England, where the idea of a standing army was viewed with grave suspicion. Armed colonists, in command of the courts and backed by the military, were 'the people': their freedoms must be protected by both the imperial and the colonial state. The rebellion of 1760 was a formative experience for Edward Long, shaping his notions of the past, present and future of the island. It clarified the fundamental difference between the colony and the mother

---

[117] Ibid., I. 420–2.
[118] Ibid., I. 427.
[119] BL Add MSS 12404, Annotated vol. I of *History*, f. 113.

country, one a slave state, the other a 'free country'. The constitutional crisis known as the Privileges Controversy, which erupted in the mid-1760s, focused his mind on another major issue that troubled the colonists: how to defend their rights against the power of the prerogative. In each case definitions of slavery and freedom were at the heart of the conflict and Long's writing played a crucial part in elaborating the specificities and needs of this colonial state.[120]

1760

Long knew that he was entering a war zone when he arrived in Jamaica, but since the treaty that had been made with the Maroons in 1739, the island had appeared to be quiet. From the time of conquest there had been many uprisings. 'Rebellion, or the threat of it', wrote Patterson, 'was an almost permanent feature of Jamaican slave society.' In the years between 1655 and 1740, their common element was that 'they led to the emergence of the Maroons as an independent group within the society and their final legal recognition as freemen by the whites'.[121] 'All sustained slave revolts must acquire a Maroon dimension,' he argued, involving guerrilla warfare, strategies of flight, ambush, blowing of the abeng horn and other collective practices.[122] Some of the Africans who had been enslaved by the Spanish and fought with them had formed bands in the mountains, living off what they could grow or obtain from forays into local plantations: these were the origins of the Maroon settlements. Rebels who were able to escape death or forced return to the plantations following uprisings in 1673 in St Ann, 1678 in St Catherine or 1690 in Clarendon escaped if they could to the mountains and joined these Maroon bands settled in the Cockpit country or Nanny Town. By the late 1720s there were probably thousands living in the interior. The Maroon War that was fought over more than a decade in the late 1720s and 1730s was a major conflict that the colonists could not win and was only settled by the treaties of 1739. James Knight, who was on the island for some of those years, wrote a detailed account of the 'Rebellious Negroes', as he described them, documenting the ways in which their attacks intersected with the threat of war with the Spanish. 'They began to grow formidable by continual desertions' and 'threatened the Subversion of the Island'.[123] The combined forces of the militia and British redcoats could not defeat them.

When Long came to write about the 'Marons', as he called them, he reiterated the established view of their origins on the island. Africans attached to the

---

[120] Ogborn, *Freedom of Speech*, chap. 2, 69–108.
[121] Patterson, *Sociology of Slavery*, 266–7.
[122] Orlando Patterson, 'Slavery and Slave Revolts: a Sociohistorical Analysis of the First Maroon War, 1665–1740', in Richard Price (ed.), *Maroon Societies. Rebel Slave Communities in the Americas* (2nd edn, Baltimore, 1996), 246–92.
[123] Knight's *History* gives details of the struggle and of the treaties; I. 324–86, II. 498–511, at 498–500.

Spanish, some free and others enslaved, had escaped into the mountains and ventured out from their hideouts to harass the English soldiers. He cited Major-General Sedgewick's prophecy that 'these Blacks would prove thorns in our sides; living as they did in the woods and mountains, a kind of life natural and agreeable to them'. Sedgewick had reported that they were 'enterprising and bloody' and without '*moral sense* ... they must either be destroyed or brought in upon some terms or other; or else they will prove a great discouragement to the settling of people here'.[124] It was Long's kinsman D'Oyley's success against the Spanish, he opined, that broke their spirit, and some surrendered. But others stayed in their 'inaccessible retreats within the mountainous wilds', refused 'to quit their savage way of life' and continued to attack settlers.[125] In 1693, their numbers increased and they commenced more open hostilities. By 1730 they were 'so formidable' that two regiments of regular troops were brought in to defeat them. 'When They Engaged', Knight had reported, 'They constantly kept blowing Horns, Conch Shells, and other Instruments, which make a hideous and terrible Noise among the Mountains in hopes of terrifying our Parties, by making Them imagine Their Number and Strength much greater than it really was.'[126] For Long, the enemy's 'dastardly method of conducting the war' meant that they avoided 'pitched battle', murdered under cover of darkness and concealed themselves in the many 'secret avenues' that they knew made them invincible. They would never engage in open attack but 'skulked about the skirts of remote plantations, surprising stragglers, and murdering the Whites by two or three at a time, or when they were too few to make any resistance'. They attacked at night, stealing in and setting fire to cane pieces. This foe, this 'most despicable and cowardly enemy', in his judgement, 'were not reducible by any regular plan of attack'. They had 'only life and liberty' to lose, which made them particularly dangerous.[127] The assembly had resolved to build a series of fortified barracks, with strong garrisons, near enemy strongholds, and this was a somewhat more successful strategy. In addition they brought two hundred Mosquito Indians from territory under colonial control and paid them to assist in the suppression. The Indians instructed their white guides in ways of startling the enemy, marching in the 'most profound silence' in order to surprise. They were indeed, Long recognized, 'the most proper troops to be employed in that species of action ... known as *bush-fighting*', a new and unsettling way of conducting war for British troops.[128]

---

[124] Long, *History*, II. 338.
[125] Ibid., II. 339.
[126] Knight, *History*, II. 502.
[127] Long, *History*, II. 342.
[128] Ibid., II. 344.

By 1739 both sides were weary of conflict and Governor Trelawny proposed 'overtures of peace'. A treaty was concluded: the Maroons' leaders, including Cudjoe, who Long claimed to have met in later years, secured the Maroons in possession of 'a perfect state of freedom and Liberty', able 'to enjoy and possess for Themselves and Posterity for ever' 1,500 acres of land and the right to cultivate it, to hunt and sell produce.[129] This free black population formed two separate communities in different parts of the island, 'leeward' and 'windward', and 'provided a constant reminder for all that to be black and to be enslaved were not synonymous'.[130] Their legal rights in land were unique among people of African descent on the island. But those legal rights were circumscribed. Their leaders dealt with crime within their own communities and were expected to 'wait on the governor once a year if required'. If injured by a white person they should seek redress from a magistrate and they were not permitted to purchase slaves or grow sugar. Two white men were to 'constantly reside with Cudjoe and his successors, to keep up friendly correspondence'.[131] In return for their freedoms they would assist the colonial authorities in the suppression of rebels or foreign enemies and would be paid for bringing in runaways. For Knight, the island was finally delivered 'from an intestine Enemy, who threatened no less than the extirpation of the White Inhabitants'.[132] This threat of 'extirpation' was the language that Long was to use in his account of 1760: a reflection of the fear among white colonists of their own extinction. But it was never possible to be sure of the Maroons: they could choose which side they were on depending on circumstances.

The years following the treaties were the years for westward expansion into territory now deemed safe. Confident of Maroon support over runaways and rebels, the colonists relaxed. 'The planter's way of thinking', one erstwhile resident, probably Governor Trelawny, reflected in the 1740s,

> seems to be that *Negroes* are not of the same Species with us, but that being of a different Mould and Nature as well as Colour, they were made intirely for our Use, with Instincts proper for that Purpose, having as great a propensity to Subjection, as we have to command, and loving Slavery as naturally as we do Liberty; and that there is no need of any Art or Discipline to subject ten Men or more, to one, no need of any Management, but that of themselves they will most pleasantly submit to

---

[129] Knight, *History*, II. 503–8. The land was possessed communally. Maroon status was different from that of other free blacks, who could own land individually but again had limited legal rights, enjoying what Long described as 'limited freedom'. Long, *History*, II. 321. Jean Besson argues that the treaty established a corporate Maroon identity based on treaty lands; *Transformations of Freedom in the Land of the Maroons. Creolization in the Cockpits Jamaica* (London, 2015).
[130] Ogborn, *Freedom of Speech*, 25.
[131] Long, *History*, II. 345.
[132] Knight, *History*, II. 510.

hard Labour, hard Usages of all kind, Cruelties and Injustice at the Caprice of one white Man.

Slave-owners appeared to be unaware of the dangers that he saw as so apparent given the vast disparity in numbers between the colonists and the enslaved.[133] For Patterson, their behaviour oscillated between 'extreme hysteria', when violence broke out, and 'unbelievable smugness'.[134]

Long cannot have been prepared for the major revolt which began in April 1760 in Fort Haldane in the parish of St Mary. It spread to different parts of the island and was not entirely over until October 1761. He had only recently established his proprietorship of Lucky Valley, which needed much attention if it was to become productive. Clarendon was never in the direct path of the rebels, for which he must have been profoundly thankful. But located as it was in the centre of the island, between what were the two major sites of the rebellion in the north-east and the west, it could not escape untouched. A 'conspiracy' was uncovered there in July 1760, thankfully frustrated 'by the vigilance of officers'; a later attempt by 'twelve Coromantins', as Long described them, was defeated by loyalists; while the final battle was fought at Mile Gully, just across the border from the parish of St Elizabeth.[135] Spanish Town, however, where he was living, was the seat of government, inevitably in the eye of the storm. It seethed with rumours and fear from the first news of the rebellion. The lieutenant-governor, Henry Moore, was based there and it was the meeting place for the council and assembly. The town boasted a significant military presence, situated as it was conveniently close to the centre of the island. Detachments of regulars were sent off to varied parts throughout the rebellion. Martial law was declared on 10 April, the militia summoned (and were on permanent duty while martial law was in place) and numbers immediately ordered out.[136] Numerous executions and burnings of captured rebels were to take place in the town, spectacles intended to spread terror of the retaliations which followed disorder. The unexpected death of the new governor, George Haldane, only months after his arrival in 1759, placed Lieutenant-Governor Moore, who had previously served in that position, once more in command. He was Long's brother-in-law, married to his sister Catherine, and a man whom Edward came to admire greatly.

---

[133] Anon. [Trelawny?], *Essay Concerning Slavery*, 19.
[134] Patterson, *Sociology of Slavery*, 276.
[135] Lt.-Gov. Henry Moore, 24 July 1760. Vincent Brown, *Slave Revolt in Jamaica, 1760–1761. A Cartographic Narrative*, http://revolt.axismaps.com/; Long, *History*, II. 456–7. Long always refers to the Coromantins; the usual term is Coromantees.
[136] It is likely that Long served in the militia in 1760, though there is no direct evidence for it. In 1766 he was named as a Brevet Colonel in the militia. BL Add MSS 18959, f. 94.

The revolt began with an attack by approximately a hundred Africans on Fort Haldane on the north coast of the island.[137] Rebels then gathered inland, coming from several estates, including Zachary Bayly's Trinity and Ballard Beckford's Frontier. Bayly was a leading merchant and slave-owner, uncle and benefactor of Bryan Edwards; Ballard Beckford was a member of the council and a relative of Long's through marriage. The local militia mustered, regulars were despatched from Spanish Town as soon as the authorities had heard the news, and the Maroons were summoned to fulfil their treaty obligation and assist in the suppression of the rebels. The war meant that troops and naval support were more speedily available than they might otherwise have been. British soldiers were attacked and the Maroons and the militia pursued the rebels into the woods where battle was joined on 14 April. Twenty rebels were killed and approximately two hundred captured. Those named as the leaders, Tacky and Jamaica, were both killed. In the days that followed a conspiracy was reported in Kingston. Calls for support from the navy resulted in a vessel sailing to Port Maria with arms and stores and returning to Port Royal with prisoners. (See Figure 7.1.) In May and June there were judicial executions in Spanish Town and Kingston. In May rebellion erupted in Westmoreland, at Masemure estate, and it quickly spread to other properties, involving hundreds. The militia and British army units were once again deployed, while the rebels, now numbering more than a thousand, constructed a fortified encampment and were able to repulse attacks. A Maroon force surrounded the barricade and were joined by soldiers, reinforced with new troops arriving on navy vessels. Their assault, together with the militia, resulted in the defeat of the rebels. Hundreds were killed and others escaped into the mountains and launched ambushes from there. They were hunted, with many captured, killed or transported, while some committed suicide. Judicial executions were carried out in Savanna-la-Mar, including that of Wager, aka Apongo, a leader of the Westmoreland rebellion. By July 1760 Moore thought that the danger was nearly over. Pockets of rebels, however, continued to be active in Westmoreland and St Elizabeth, and in October the assembly accepted the proposal of a Captain Hynes that he should mount a party to capture those remaining. A band, led by Simon (Long named him Damon), trekked from Masemure in the west across St Elizabeth to Mile Gully in Clarendon where a final battle took place. At least 1,500 rebels had been engaged in these

---

[137] For accounts of the rebellion, see Brown, *Tacky's Revolt*; Brown, *Slave Revolt in Jamaica, 1760–1761*; Devin Leigh, 'The Origins of a Source: Edward Long, Coromantee Slave Revolts and *The History of Jamaica*', *S&A* 40.2 (2018), 295–320; Jason T. Sharples, *The World that Fear Made. Slave Revolts and Conspiracy Scares in Early America* (Philadelphia, 2020). See also Devin Leigh and Clifton E. Sorrel III, 'How to Control the History of a Slave Rebellion: a Case Study from the Sources of Blackwall's Revolt in St Mary's Parish, Jamaica, 1765', *Journal of Caribbean History* 5.1 (2021), 19–56, on the divisions amongst the planters as to how to interpret the revolt.

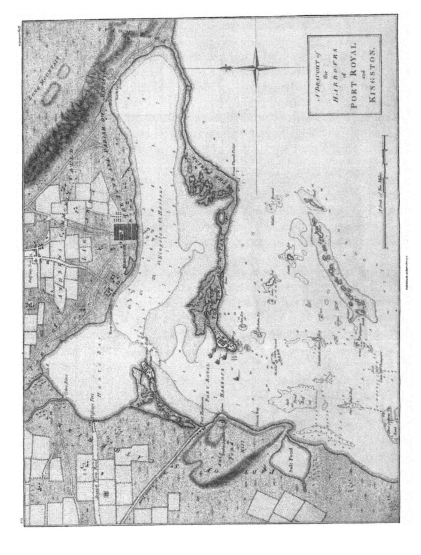

Figure 7.1 'A Draught of the Harbours of Port Royal and Kingston'. Reproduced from Long, *The History of Jamaica*. Digitally printed version. © Cambridge University Press 2010.

conflicts. Sixty white people had been killed, along with at least four hundred rebels and more than five hundred transported. Skirmishes continued into the autumn of 1761. Long estimated costs of more than £100,000 'in ruined buildings, cane-pieces, cattle, slaves and disbursements', with a similar amount for new barracks and fortifications, while trade had also been seriously disrupted.[138] The costs, in human lives and in property, were heavy. In Vincent Brown's interpretation, Tacky's Revolt, the Westmoreland Uprising and Simon's march provided the arc of this long insurrection of the enslaved, part of what he describes as a Coromantee War, rooted in the connected histories of Europe, Africa and America.

Edward Long wrote his account more than a decade after the events. He would by then have known of the rebellion in Berbice in 1763 which lasted for more than a year and involved a majority of the enslaved population.[139] His description of the events of 1760 needs to be read in both its metropolitan and colonial context. As Michel-Rolph Trouillot famously argued in his discussion of the Haitian revolution, 'planters, administrators, politicians, ideologues found explanations that forced the rebellion back within their worldview, shoving the facts into the proper order of discourse'.[140] Or as Walter Johnson put it, 'They told themselves stories about what happened that emphasized their own agency and reworked the unfathomed aspirations of their slaves ... into a part of history as they recognized it.'[141] Long's account was composed at a distance, but the fears the events had engendered were vivid in his imagination. There was no escaping the reality of black political agency: they had conspired and acted. He had experienced black rebellion in a way that shaped his horror of white 'extirpation', a terror that always lurked for the colonists. He attempted in the *History* to orchestrate events into a proper order of things, securing the worldview of the slave-owners and crushing the hopes of the enslaved. The fractures and fault-lines were covered up in the attempt to create a seamless narrative. The costs of the rebellion had been high. But the settlement with the Maroons that had been made in 1739, combined with the support of the British military and navy and the militia, had enabled them to defeat the rebels. Their energetic programme of preventive legislation, which Long had participated in, followed. This further limited the mobility of the enslaved, identified obeah as a source of trouble, provided rewards for the faithful, ensured compensation for those slave-owners whose human property had been executed or transported, and attempted to harden the lineaments of racial difference. A small-scale rebellion in St Mary in 1765 had been

---

[138] Long, *History*, II. 462, 471.
[139] Marjoleine Kars, *Blood on the River. A Chronicle of Mutiny and Freedom on the Wild Coast* (London, 2020).
[140] Michel-Rolph Trouillot, *Silencing the Past. Power and the Production of History* (Boston, 1995), 91.
[141] Johnson, 'Time and Revolution', 215.

suppressed and Long had been personally involved in the investigation that followed, including reading the interrogations of prisoners.[142] There was further trouble in 1766: once again it was repressed and stability restored at a price. The planters were optimistic about the years ahead and prepared to pay for their security; this would be money well spent.[143] The 1760s were indeed a time of great prosperity for the planters.

Long was writing the account in England, not in Jamaica. He had been able to afford to return with his growing family to the mother country. Twin boys were born in 1771: there were now six children, all of whom survived, a sharp contrast with the children of the enslaved. Life in peaceful Chichester was a far cry from Spanish Town or Lucky Valley. He was writing at a distance from the fears and anxieties associated with the plantation and a potentially hostile black majority. Yet he knew of the continued threats on the island, for the disproportion between whites and blacks was 'sufficient', as the Jamaican agent Stephen Fuller put it, 'to keep the Island in continual apprehensions'.[144] Furthermore, he had a new problem in the wake of the Somerset judgment, and a different enemy to contend with: abolitionists who threatened to challenge the slave trade and even the institution of slavery itself. Hundreds of pages in the second volume of the *History* were a sustained attempt to demonstrate that, even if slavery was repugnant to English law, British wealth depended on it, and black people were innately inferior to white and suited to subjection. Was the failure of the enslaved population to reproduce itself a result of the depredations of the plantation system? Especially provocative accusations had been made by Granville Sharp, as to the excessive cruelty of Jamaican slave-owners. 'We are so fond of depreciating our own colonies', wrote Long in response, 'that we paint our planters in the most bloody colours, and represent their slaves as the most ill-treated and miserable of mankind. It is no wonder therefore that Jamaica comes in for a large share of abuse; and even our common news papers are made the vehicle of it.' He had read, he reported 'that the cruel usage inflicted on Negro slaves in Jamaica by their masters, is the reason why insurrections there are more frequent than in the French or other sugar-islands'.[145]

His narrative was an attempt to persuade himself and others that such accusations were false. His efforts to represent himself as an enlightened

---

[142] BL Add MSS 18271, ff. 40a–40; Leigh and Sorrell, 'How to Control the History of a Slave Rebellion', demonstrate the disagreements between the planters as to their understanding of the events of 1765. These were ironed out of the story which Long told in the *History*. It is worth noting that Long believed in due process of law when dealing with what was defined as black criminality. Witnesses should be properly questioned and evidence was required.

[143] Burnard and Graham, 'Security, Taxation'.

[144] O'Shaughnessy, *An Empire Divided*, 38.

[145] Long, *History*, II. 441.

Englishman were disrupted by the claim that the West Indians were barbaric in their cruelty. 'The planters of this island', he complained, 'have been very unjustly stigmatized with an accusation of treating their Negroes with barbarity.' 'Some alledge', he continued, citing Sharp, 'that these slave-holders, (as they are pleased to call them, in contempt) are lawless bashaws, West-India tyrants, inhuman oppressors, bloody inquisitors, and a long, etc. of such pretty names.'[146] The colonists must be defended in the face of increased references to their brutality. Versions of some of the events of 1760 had provided Britons with a picture of 'white Jamaicans' as 'natural tyrants who were fundamentally un-British'.[147] The English provincial press took a more ambivalent position. Initial stress was laid on the brutality of the rebels and scant sympathy was shown for those subjected to judicial punishment. By the end, however, this was tempered with both criticism of the militia, which meant that British troops were increasingly needed, and concerns over the scale of the damage and the bad effects of martial law on trade. There was even some sympathy for the enslaved, linked with suggestions for reform.[148] What concerned Long were the criticisms of the planters. He would utilize 'the most credible and authentic testimonies in my power to procure', to demonstrate with 'how little regard to truth the insurrections, that have happened in Jamaica, are ascribed to extraordinary cruelties exercised over the slaves'. He would provide incontestable proofs 'that so impudent a calumny could have no other foundation than malevolence, complicated with ignorance'.[149]

Long's narrative was framed by his claim for authority as a West Indian. Others were under the misapprehension that the Maroons were responsible for the rebellion. This had been suggested in one of the earliest public reflections on 1760, in the *Modern Universal History*. As an eyewitness he asserted his authority over those who were 'ill-informed' or 'but little acquainted with Jamaica'.[150] It was true, he noted, that the initial behaviour of those Maroons summoned from the community at Scots Hall had been 'extremely ill'.[151] They were owed money, they declared, for runaways that they had captured, and would do nothing until they were paid. Subsequently, however, they had adhered to the treaty and were critical to the restoration of law and order. He was well aware that the security of the island depended on Maroon compliance and at pains to minimize any suggestion that they might have

---

[146] Ibid., II. 267.
[147] Burnard, *Jamaica in the Age of Revolution*, 4; Burnard and Garrigus, *The Plantation Machine*.
[148] Thomas R. Day, 'Jamaican Revolts in British Press and Politics, 1760–1865', MA thesis, Virginia Commonwealth University (2016).
[149] Long, *History*, II. 475.
[150] Ibid., II. 445.
[151] Ibid., II. 451.

conspired with rebels.[152] It was true that the existence of the Maroon communities and the freedoms they enjoyed might well have been an incentive for those on the plantations; they might have had 'a remote hope' of winning similar freedoms.[153] But the Maroons, Long wanted to believe, were allies of the colonial state, not enemies; yet it was always feared that they would side with the strongest. With their guaranteed rights and their property, they lived, as Kathleen Wilson argues, an in-betweenness that troubled any simple black/white binary, but this was something that had to be contained.[154]

It was the presence of so many imported Africans, he insisted, that was at the root of all slave rebellions, and his story opened with the 'Coromantins', both the heroes and the villains of his tale. Their 'tragedy', as he defined it, began in St Mary, 'a most proper theatre', with its woods, its plenteous provisions, its small number of Whites and numerous Coromantins.[155] It was the Coromantins, he had come to believe, who were responsible for the scale of rebellions in Jamaica.[156] Since it was unthinkable to see the fault as lying with the planters, then it made sense to scapegoat a group amongst the enslaved, rather than having to accept that the entire black population might be hostile. Long was not the first to define this group of Africans, usually named as Coromantees, as the problem. There had been accounts of their violence from the seventeenth century.[157] Knight was convinced of their responsibility for trouble. They 'are Fractious', he wrote,

> and in their Nature Deceitfull, Revengefull, and blood thirsty, and require a Stricter hand being kept over Them than those of any other Country; for which reason every prudent Planter, is cautious of having too many of them in his Plantation, and therefore the common Custom is to Mix other Countries with them; for there never was as I have heard of in this or any other Colony, any Plot or Conspiracy, but they were at the bottom of it.[158]

---

[152] Michael Sivapragasam, 'After the Treaties: A Social, Economic and Demographic History of Maroon Society in Jamaica, 1739–1842', unpublished PhD, University of Southampton (2018), 'challenges the simplistic view of the Maroons as collaborators, and argues that their story was a complex one of divisions between Maroon towns, a lack of coherence, and they were often inefficient hunters of runaways. The Maroons sometimes collaborated with the colonial authorities, and then assisted runaways to escape during the Second Maroon War'; iv.
[153] Long, *History*, II. 443.
[154] Kathleen Wilson, 'The Performance of Freedom: Maroons and the Colonial Order in Eighteenth Century Jamaica and the Atlantic Sound', *WMQ* 66.1 (2009), 45–86.
[155] Long, *History*, II. 447.
[156] Thistlewood's was the only eyewitness account of the events in the west of the island and he thought that it was Africans of different ethnicities who were responsible. Burnard and Garrigus, *The Plantation Machine*.
[157] Brown, *Tacky's Revolt*, 87–92.
[158] Knight, *History*, I. 484.

Coromantees were Africans captured on the Gold Coast, speaking more than one language and coming from different regions and kingdoms. They had found a common identity and were identified as such by others in Jamaica. Celebrated for their physical strength and distinguished 'by their aversion to husbandry', they were feared for what was seen as the 'martial ferocity of their disposition'.[159] Slave-owners were all too familiar with them and hoped to be able to rely on the 'great and natural ... Antipathy' between Africans 'of different Countries' and 'mutual apprehensions of falling into Subjection, one of the other, should They Shake off the Yoke of the English'.[160] Grainger had warned against them in *The Sugar Cane*:

> Yet, if thine own, thy childrens life, be dear;
> Buy not a Coromantee ...
>
> They, born to freedom in their native land,
> Chuse death before dishonourable bonds:
> Or, fir'd with vengeance, at the midnight hour,
> Sudden they seize thine unsuspecting watch,
> And thine own poinard bury in thy breast.[161]

'The most turbulent and desperate of any on the coast of Guiney,' Long opined, 'war and contention are their favourite amusements'; agricultural pursuits were left to their women. Their priests, or obeah men, were 'their chief oracles in all weighty affairs'. It was these *'imported Africans'*, Long believed, not creoles, who had been responsible for rebellions from the earliest days of the colony.[162] The numbers of new captives coming into the island each year explained the scale of 'mutinies and plots' in Jamaica in comparison with other sugar islands. 'No small numbers of them had been warriors in Afric, or criminals,' he maintained, a common defence against the stories that they had been seized and kidnapped. 'All of them [were] as savage and uncivilized as the beasts of prey that roam through the African forests.'[163] This 'abandoned herd' had been banished from their country on account of their vile misdeeds and vices: it was no surprise that once condemned to a 'life of labour and regularity', they resisted.[164] 'The rebellions (properly speaking)', Long insisted, 'are confined to those Negroe slaves, who have at different periods renounced obedience to their British masters, and sought to rescue themselves from a life of labour by force of arms.'[165] It was they who had engineered the diabolical plan, the 'grand enterprize, whose object was no other than the entire

---

[159] Long, *History*, II. 446.
[160] Knight, *History*, I. 482.
[161] Grainger, *The Sugar Cane*, Bk 4. 81-9.
[162] Long, *History*, II. 444.
[163] Ibid., II. 442.
[164] Ibid., II. 444.
[165] Ibid., II. 445-6.

extirpation of the white inhabitants'.[166] The threat that haunted the colonists was that they would be destroyed by those whose lives they had expropriated. Feelings of white entitlement turned to feelings of vulnerability that fuelled and legitimated white aggression.[167] It was fear which justified brutal suppression and should secure the support of those in the metropole.

But the Coromantins did not only plan to exterminate the Whites, Long continued, they also intended 'the enslaving of all such Negroes as might refuse to join them; and the partition of the island into small principalities in the African mode; to be distributed among their leaders and head men'.[168] 'Vulgar opinion' in England, he opined, 'confounds all the Blacks in one class.'[169] This was far from the truth. Africans were not all the same; there were important divisions amongst them. Ebo men were lazy, Minnahs 'timid and despondent' and prone to suicide, 'Angolas ... most stupid'.[170] Such divisions could be utilized. The crucial distinction, however, was that between 'saltwater slaves' and creoles, those who had been civilized by their life on the island. Long believed it to be central to the future stability of Jamaica. This was the splitting between 'good' and 'bad' Africans that was essential to his worldview. In his account of the rebellion he was careful to remark on the faithful and loyal 'Negroes', including the two 'belonging to Mr Beckford', who had ridden as fast as they could to Spanish Town to warn the governor.[171] Some he even named: trusty 'Jemmy' who revenged his master's murder by killing a rebel; 'Yankee', who attempted to defend the plantation house at Esher and then rushed to give warning to the neighbouring estates; 'Caffee', who pretended to support the plotters and then revealed their secrets.[172] These were the loyalists who must be publicly rewarded.

The Coromantins were the ones to blame. They were both wanted and feared by the planters, who tended to separate them. This had meant that they were 'chiefly awed into subjection, by the superior multitude of Creole Blacks'.[173] In 1760, however, they had managed to communicate with each other, to talk and plot, to plan their insurrection in 'profound secrecy'. Almost all of them were privy to it.[174] Yet the whites had no suspicions. This was an acknowledgement of how little masters knew of the talk in the slave villages

---

[166] Ibid., 447.
[167] I am drawing here on Johnson's analysis in *The Broken Heart of America*.
[168] Long, *History*, II. 447.
[169] Ibid., II. 444.
[170] Ibid., II. 403.
[171] Burnard and Garrigus in *The Plantation Machine* suggest the dominant theme in the writing about the rebellion was the horror at loyal blacks who turned against their masters. This is not a particular focus for Long and he was anxious to emphasize the loyalty of some.
[172] Long, *History*, II. 449–50, 455.
[173] Ibid., II. 444.
[174] Ibid., II. 447.

and the markets, the talk which they did not hear but imagined. Conspiracies abounded in the minds of the planters, the truth of which it is impossible to establish. But as Miles Ogborn reminds us, the evidence which the colonists were able to collect about slave conspiracies, from interrogations, from torture and from the tales of those who hoped to escape recrimination, was 'quite literally, all talk'.[175] This was the speech of the enslaved which the slave-owners rarely heard, and when they did, interpreted through their own lenses. The events of 1760 were so shocking to the colonists partly because large-scale revolts were unusual across slave societies. Everyday forms of resistance took many forms, from inefficiency, satire and deliberate evasion to damaging tools, suicide, illness and escape. The dense woodlands and mountains of Jamaica provided opportunities for runaways, but they were frequently recaptured given the incentives for Maroons to reap rewards. Many enslaved Africans chose not to rebel.[176] The loss of provision grounds was a disincentive; they were precious places, carrying possibilities of ownership and belonging. Permanent escape was hard, especially given the proximity of the Spanish, ever on the lookout for captives. Conflicts amongst the enslaved were multiple, associated with different ethnicities and plantation hierarchies as well as the African/creole divide. The militia never lacked arms and the colonists united at times of danger. Reprisals were terrible. The landscape of terror which the colonists created – with men hanging until death in wire cages, burnt alive, heads on pikes at cross roads – were all designed to create fear. Long's account of the actual uprisings, notably in St Mary and Westmoreland, was accompanied by the discovery of numerous 'conspiracies' across different parishes, leaving the planters in a state of terrified expectation. His fear of conspiracies was associated with his disavowal of the cruelty of the exploitation he himself practised. Angry arsonists and murderers might haunt his dreams and fuel those anxieties he saw as so prevalent amongst the colonists. After 1760 planters could not escape the threat of insurrection, however committed they were to security.[177] 'The conspiracy scare phenomenon', argues Jason Sharples, common across plantation societies, emerged from a combination of enslaved people's traumatic experience of terror and 'enslavers' awareness of their culpability and exposure to the people whom they exploited'.[178]

If one priority for Long was to name and blame the Coromantins, a second was to absolve the slave-owners, including, of course, himself. Far from being cruel, he insisted, it was their indulgence which had resulted in trouble. Drums were allowed on the plantations; musical instruments were thought to be

[175] Ogborn, *Freedom of Speech*, 124.
[176] Kars in *Blood on the River* provides a complex account of this, given the scale of testimonies that she was able to draw on in relation to the Berbice rebellion.
[177] Claudius Fergus, '"Dread of Insurrection": Abolitionism, Security, and Labor in Britain's West Indian Colonies, 1760–1823', *WMQ* 66.4 (2009), 757–80.
[178] Sharples, *The World that Fear Made*, 12.

inoffensive but were in fact used for dangerous conspiracies. 'Riotous assemblies', prohibited in England, were sites of unrest. If licentiousness was permitted amongst the 'most ignorant and the profligate', then trouble was inevitable. 'Games' had been converted into 'plots', liberties abused. 'The discipline of laws, and the energy of good government' was required. It was an 'Absolute necessity' to keep 'a Vigilant Eye, and strict hand over Them'.[179] The authority of the slave-owners, delegated to them by the colonial state, had to be further secured. Some planters had foolishly kept large stocks of arms on plantations where there were few whites, inviting trouble from 'mutinous savages'.[180] Wickedly avaricious shopkeepers had secretly sold gunpowder. This kind of irresponsibility must be remedied. Furthermore, good treatment of duplicitous Coromantins was met with treachery. It was shocking to note the betrayal of 'a gentleman ... remarkable for his humanity and kind treatment of his slaves'. Confident of their 'faithful attachment' to him, on hearing of the dangers he had armed twenty of them, all Coromantins, only to hear them assuring him they would not harm him but seeing them marching off to join the rebels.[181] Amongst this group were some of the most dangerous men who had been fighting for the French in Guadeloupe and were taken prisoner there, then sold into Jamaica. They had acquired military skills which they brought with them, one of the links between the local revolt and the global Seven Years War. Kindness to the enslaved reaped no rewards, Long assured his audience.

He reminded his readers of an earlier occasion, when a gentleman known for his humanity was physically assaulted in bed by a domestic, an 'ungrateful villain', whom he had treated with generosity. Having cruelly murdered him, the gang then engaged in ritual horrors, demonstrating their barbarity. Having cut off his head, 'they sawed his skull asunder, and made use of it as a punchbowl'.[182] The physical and sexual brutality of the rebels was essential to his horror story. As Mary Louise Pratt noted, European fears of being mutilated were frequently projected on to the rebellious, while Mimi Sheller argues that Europeans displaced the facts of their own domination by their bodily fears of harm from others.[183] At Esher estate, owned by William Beckford, one of the first to be attacked, the whites had barricaded the main house, but the door was soon broken down, the overseer murdered and the doctor 'dreadfully wounded', to the extent that his eventual recovery was 'next to miraculous'. The rebels then 'ravished a Mulatto woman', who had been the overseer's kept mistress. Some of the Esher 'Negroes', however, pleaded for her life on the

---

[179] Knight's formulation; *History*, II. 492.
[180] Long, *History*, II. 443.
[181] Ibid., II. 452–3.
[182] Ibid., II. 447.
[183] Pratt, *Imperial Eyes*; Sheller, *Consuming*.

grounds that she had sometimes saved them from a whipping.[184] Long was disgusted by the scale of concubinage and the sexual practices of many of the colonists. The gang rape of a concubine drew attention not only to the immorality of the overseer, but also to the promiscuity of Africans, as he saw it, and his fears of the sexual prowess of African men, with its horrid appeal to the lower class of English women.[185] In Long's mind the rebels were driven by their fantasy, 'the vainglorious desire of subduing the country'. Harsh treatment had nothing to do with it. The ringleaders of the revolt in St Mary, he maintained, 'belonged to a gentleman distinguished for his humanity, and excessive indulgence towards his slaves', and none of the prisoners had complained of ill-treatment.[186]

The hero of Long's narrative was his brother-in-law, Sir Henry Moore, the lieutenant-governor, who had saved the colony by his intrepid actions. 'He happily possessed', Long wrote admiringly, 'in addition to great abilities, uncommon presence of mind, prudence, and bravery, a most consummate knowledge of the geography of the island, and of every road and avenue in several districts.' This enabled him to act decisively as soon as news of the revolt reached him, sending troops and the militia to the right areas and summoning the Maroons. In Long's opinion, the crown frequently appointed governors who had no knowledge of the island and were entirely unsuited to the post. He was unstinting in his disapproval of this practice. Moore, however, was the exception. His paternal grandfather had been an early settler in Barbados who had moved to Jamaica. His father, Samuel, was a planter and his mother, Elizabeth, had been born in England. In a familiar pattern for elite colonial families, he was sent to school in England, to Eton, and then to Leiden University. On his return to Jamaica he married Catherine Long, a marriage chosen by her father. Moore's property comprised 774 acres in St Mary (Moore Hall) and 904 in Vere.[187] (Moore Hall was eventually to pass into the Long family.) Moore served in the militia before entering the assembly and then being appointed to the council in 1752. After a stint as the island secretary, he was appointed as lieutenant-governor following the recall of Knowles in the wake of the conflict over the site of the capital. He clashed with the council in 1759 over his insistence that martial law should be declared given the war with France. He was briefly replaced by Haldane as governor, but the latter's untimely death meant that Moore was once again appointed as lieutenant-governor. He proved to be an effective military and political leader, cooperating well with Admiral Holmes in the deployment of the navy and himself

---

[184] Long, *History*, II. 449.
[185] [Long], *Candid Reflections*.
[186] Long, *History*, II. 472.
[187] 'Sir Henry Moore 1st Bart.', Legacies of British Slave-ownership database, http://wwwdepts-live.ucl.ac.uk/lbs/person/view/2146649433, accessed 18 January 2021.

commanding two regiments of regulars, twice narrowly avoiding death. His recognition that 'the late calamities' had 'fully shewn where our laws are defective, and where new regulations will be required' galvanized the assembly.[188] A rebellion 'more formidable than any hitherto known in the West Indies' was extinguished, not least by the 'precaution and judgement', as Long described it, of the lieutenant-governor.[189]

If Moore was the hero, Tacky was the anti-hero of Long's piece. He wanted to tell his story with a structure that would be familiar and would make sense to both himself and his readers. Rebellions had leaders and were defeated by other leaders. The idea of a guerrilla war, fought by different groupings, across varied terrains, with no agreed strategy, was frightening and hard to encompass. But the Maroons now had to be relied on to fight the Coromantin rebels, utilizing some of the same tactics. By focusing his account on St Mary, the area that he knew best, by diminishing the events and the timeline in Westmoreland, and by emphasizing the 'grand plan', Long was able to present a seemingly coherent story. Naming leaders was a way of organizing the conflict so that it was recognizable. Tacky was described as the 'general', 'chief' and 'leader' of the rebellion in St Mary. Widely believed by his followers to be invulnerable thanks to the ministrations of an obeah man, he escaped early conflicts without a wound. Following a defeat by a party of militia and Maroons, however, he was shot down and killed. Long was at pains to diminish him and pour scorn on Coromantin superstitions. Yet his negative depiction was at odds with his recognition of Tacky's qualities as 'a young man of good stature, and well made ... handsome', only to be disavowed by a description of him as 'rather of an effeminate than manly cast'. 'He had flattered himself', it was said, 'with the hope of obtaining (among other fruits of victory) the lieutenant governor's lady for his concubine'. This was Long's sister Catherine and represented the ultimate horror, underpinned by the fear of black potency which he worked so hard to deny. His ambivalence was caught in these contradictory representations; his effort to impose fixed meanings on the black body could not hold. The threat was not only to exterminate the white men but to possess the white women, a visceral fear that was to be repeated time and again in relation to colonial uprisings. His description of Tacky as 'effeminate' had a particular edge. Effeminacy in his mind was associated with 'an injudicious pursuit of sensual gratification' and lack of self-control, as he had written in *The Prater*.[190] Both characteristics were now associated in his mind with blackness. 'He did not appear to be a man of any

---

[188] Joseph S. Tiedemann, 'Moore, Sir Henry, First Baronet (1713–1769), Colonial Governor', *Oxford Dictionary of National Biography*, [2004] 2005, https://doi.org/10.1093/ref:odnb/19116; *JAJ*, vol. 5, 18 September 1760.
[189] Long, *History*, II. 462.
[190] Long, *The Prater*, 164.

extraordinary genius,' he continued, and was probably only chosen on account of his looking something like a famed African leader. This reminded Long of a story of a planter who had erected a bronze statue of a gladiator on his estate. When the Coromantins saw it, 'they were almost ready to fall down, and adore it', transfixed by a striking resemblance to one of their princes.[191] African barbarism, Long was telling his readers, took different forms: physical brutality sat alongside irrationality, expressed in childish superstitions and excessive veneration of princes. Tacky's head was taken to Spanish Town and 'stuck on a pole in the highway' to deter others. But it was soon stolen, 'as was supposed by some of his countrymen, who were unwilling to let it remain exposed in so ignominious a manner'.[192] Long did not add that they would probably have buried their leader's head with proper ceremony.

He was keen to document other instances of African superstition. Cubah, an enslaved woman belonging to a Jewess, had been named queen and was placed under a canopy at their meetings, with 'a sort of robe on her shoulders, and a crown upon her head'. Ridiculing their pretensions, Long recounted that 'her majesty was seized, and ordered for transportation': she managed to persuade the captain to put her on shore again, but was discovered and executed.[193] This moment of recognition of the involvement of a woman in the rebellion was only to provoke scorn. Women carried the baggage and organized food for the rebels, he noted, but otherwise they were invisible to him.[194] The wooden sword with a red feather in it, found in Kingston and supposedly a Coromantin signal for war, marked another instance of African superstition, for feathers had a particular significance in obeah practice. The discovery of 'an old Coromantin' in St Mary, 'a famous obeiah man or priest', involved a direct encounter with their magical powers, though again Long both took note of it and attempted to ridicule it. This obeah man had been 'a chief in counseling and instigating the credulous herd', giving them powder to rub on the body, claiming that this would make them invulnerable and assuring them that Tacky could not be hurt by the white men; he would merely hurl their bullets back at them creating havoc. The 'old imposter' was caught with 'feathers, teeth, and other implements of magic'.[195] He was summarily hanged in full attire and this persuaded some of the rebels, Long hoped, to distrust such boasts.

The prohibition of the practices of obeah was one of the many clauses in the new act to remedy the ills arising from irregular assemblies of slaves. This

[191] Long, *History*, II. 457.
[192] Ibid.
[193] Ibid., II. 455.
[194] See the discussion by Leigh and Sorrell of the erasure of women from his account of the 1765 rebellion; 'How to Control the History'. Morgan discusses women's resistance and the absence of women in the reports of rebellions in *Reckoning with Slavery*, 206–44.
[195] Long, *History*, II. 451–2.

marked an important moment in the process by which it became 'the ultimate signifier' of the difference between the Caribbean and Europe.[196] The bill was already going through its necessary stages when Long joined the assembly. Slave-owners had been well aware of the potential of obeah and the spiritual beliefs and rituals associated with it to act as a source of resistance from the time of the Maroon wars in the 1730s. Spiritual protection was a part of Maroon fighting strategy, but the colonists had paid little attention to its importance at that time, their concern being with military defeat and if that could not be secured, an effective treaty. By 1760, however, obeah was recognized as associated not only with the 'wild negroes' but with Coromantees and creoles. The obsession with these African spiritual practices which they had such difficulty in understanding may have been related to the absence of any vibrant religious life amongst the colonists themselves. What Wilberforce would have defined as 'real religion', associated with the evangelical revival, the experience of conversion and a strong commitment to prayer and individual conscience, had no place in colonial Jamaica. John Lindsay, the pro-slavery priest who described himself as 'particularly intimate with Lady Moore's nearest relations' and gave his unpublished manuscript into the care of Long, delivered a sermon in Spanish Town in 1760 which expressed shock at the numbers of empty seats in the church, lack of respect for the clergy, indifference to God's providence, the need for repentance, and the vengeance of God through earthquake, hurricane, drought and the rebellion of the enslaved. 'What do we ourselves deserve, grovelling, despicable maggots, for thousands of rebellions against the Majesty of Heaven?' he demanded, having given a fearsome account of the legitimate gibbeting of rebels.[197] The rebels' 'stoicism' in the face of horrendous torture may have provoked questions as to what these beliefs were that enable people to survive. One answer – African difference – found its expression in obeah.

By the time Long wrote his *History*, he was interested in recounting creole beliefs including obeah. Creoles 'firmly believe in that apparition of spectres', he declared. 'The most sensible among them fear the supernatural powers of the African *obeah-man*, or pretended conjurors; often ascribing those mortal effects to magic, which are only the natural operation of some poisonous juice.' Some of these 'execrable men', he continued, the obeah men, recently introduced the 'myal dance' and created a society which others were invited to join. Every 'Negro' initiated, they promised, would be 'invulnerable by the white men'. They utilized a herbal infusion, from a 'branched colalue', common in the lowlands of Jamaica, which after 'the agitation of dancing' induced a deep, apparently lifeless, trance. When the person was rubbed with another infusion

---

[196] Diana Paton, *The Cultural Politics of Obeah. Religion, Colonialism and Modernity in the Caribbean World* (Cambridge, 2015), 1.
[197] Higman, *Proslavery Priest*, 115.

'(as yet unknown to the Whites)', they woke invulnerable. An experiment had, however, been tried and the man died after being shot. For some time this 'brought the priests and their art into great disrepute'.[198]

Long had conversed with some creoles, he told his readers, on their customs and habits. Bits of 'red rag, cat's teeth' and such like, they told him, were attached to the doors of their houses when they left home, in order to deter thieves. This was only to frighten 'the salt-water Negroes', they assured him.[199] Yet they, like the colonists, both laughed at and feared magical powers. The preoccupation of white observers with obeah or other occult practices, as Simon Gikandi noted, 'functioned in a fascinating dialectic of attraction and repulsion'.[200] Long took some care in depicting creole funerals, 'the very reverse of our English ceremony', claiming to describe the rituals that presumably he had observed. The mourners seemed joyous, the atmosphere was that of a festival with food and drink, music, singing and dancing. As the body was being escorted to the grave, those carrying the corpse had to struggle with the apparent attempts by the deceased to resist interment. Once in the ground, only a very small amount of earth would be deposited on the coffin. In the case of the death of a spouse, a month would pass before a song was performed, rejoicing that the deceased was now 'in the enjoyment of complete felicity'. Following this ritual 'a considerable heap of earth' would be put on the grave, denoting 'covering it', accompanied with more drinking and dancing. This signalled the end of the mourning, and the widow or widower would be 'at liberty to take another spouse immediately'. Long associated these rituals with both Highland wakes and 'ancient Irish' customs, suggesting the potential for the transformation from barbarism to civilization.[201] It might be possible to 'improve' creoles, to make them more fully human.

His observation of these funeral rituals alerted him to the importance of grave-dirt. He recorded, 'The Negroes strew grave-dirt on the highway when any thing is stolen from them,' while cursing the thief: 'May the thief be reduced to the same state and condition as the corpse which lies buried in the grave whence this dirt was taken ... may he not live to enjoy his theft.' Grave-dirt took on spiritual and transformative meanings; it was 'a material ingredient in their solemn oaths'. 'A small quantity of the earth' was mixed with water. The person rendering the oath then dipped a finger in the mixture and crossed it on various parts of the 'juror's naked body' as the oath was spoken, declaring that the bowels should rot and the head never cease to ache if the oath be broken. The remaining mixture was then drunk so that the oath had literally been swallowed.[202] The oath should be administered by an obeah

---

[198] Long, *History*, II. 416–17.
[199] Ibid., II. 420.
[200] Gikandi, *Slavery and the Culture of Taste*, 259.
[201] Long, *History*, II. 421–2.
[202] Ibid., II. 422–3.

man, though it could also be effected by an old black man or woman. It had no power if it was tendered by a white person. When Coromantins gathered to conspire, Long wrote, the obeah man, after several ritual acts, 'draws a little blood from every one present; this is mixed in a bowl with gunpowder and grave dirt'. The grave-dirt signalled the relation between the living and the dead, the past, present and future. 'The fetishe or oath is administered', he continued, 'by which they solemnly pledge themselves to inviolable secrecy, fidelity to their chiefs, and to wage perpetual war against their enemies; as a ratification of their sincerity, each person takes a sup of the mixture, and this finishes the solemn rite.'[203] 'Few or none of them', Long concluded, had ever been known to break this oath, even over years. They would dissemble 'their malice under a seemingly submissive character' until the time was ripe to pursue their ends.[204] This, of course, was a different kind of oath from the ones that he had himself sworn in the assembly, legitimating his place as a legislator. Each, however, was attempting to effect a transformation: 'obi men' called on the spirits, colonists on God and the crown. In each instance the intention was to bind men as a collective in defence of, or as an assertion of, power. Political authority nearly always has a sacred dimension, and in Jamaica the sacred spiritual authority associated with the established church resonated with demands for domination while the enslaved invoked their supernatural beliefs in their struggles.[205]

Obeah men and women used 'everyday, if liminal, materials – feathers, bones, bottles, eggshells, grave dirt, beads – to manage the power of the spirits'. The objects became something more than material 'through the performance of ritualised speech and action'.[206] Long, like his fellow colonists, both believed in and doubted black supernatural power while being convinced that it was a form of communication for rebels. His definition of it as superstition and his focus on its associations with witchcraft and 'pretended sorcerers' were designed to label it as irrational, associated with darkness, not enlightenment.[207] His description of 'the old imposter', caught with 'feathers, teeth, and other implements of magic', who they summarily hanged, was an attempt to ridicule. The claim that their powders could ensure bodily invulnerability, that men could be apparently slain, yet the power of the obeah man could 'restore the body to life', were foolish myths.[208] They exposed 'the influence which superstition holds'.[209] But he, like his fellow colonists, feared this power which they did not understand and could not control.

---

[203] Ibid., II. 473.
[204] Ibid.
[205] Brown, *The Reaper's Garden*.
[206] Ogborn, *Freedom of Speech*, 156.
[207] Long, *History*, II. 428.
[208] Ibid., II. 416.
[209] Ibid., II. 428.

It was the fear which led them to name it as a crime. The colonial state's act of 1760 added a new dimension to its forms of cultural repression, in direct response to the rebellion. It made African spiritual practice illegal. It referred to professed communication with the Devil and evil spirits and declared that '*Obeia*-men, pretended conjurors, or priests, upon conviction before two justices, and three freeholders of their practices as such, to suffer death, or transportation, at the discretion of the court.'[210] The plot had indeed been diabolical, a term that came to be utilized by the planters with reference to later rebellions.[211] It also made explicit the association with blood, feathers, grave-dirt and other materials that Long was to detail. The wish was to suppress obeah itself, as Diana Paton argues, whilst at the same time claiming not to believe in its power.[212] In later years Long was to return to the question of obeah. He and his fellow slave-owners gave it pride of place as a signifier of difference in their account to the parliamentary inquiry into the slave trade.[213]

Criminalizing obeah was only one of the new restrictions imposed after 1760. Moore's words at the assembly's first meeting stressing the need for new legislation were speedily responded to and a committee established to make recommendations and prepare bills. The mobility of the enslaved was further restricted, overseers were not to leave estates on Sundays and holidays, free 'Negroes', 'mulattos' and Indians must carry certificates denoting their subordinate status, those who had been loyal should be rewarded, and absentees, widely regarded as having particular responsibilities, should compensate for their non-residence. Fortifications must be strengthened, new barracks built, including in Clarendon, and more regulars deployed. The initial ill-discipline of the militia and the attempts by some to avoid service – especially, in Long's mind, Jews, prone as he was to antisemitism – was another of the preoccupations. To underline the dangers of Jamaica's polyglot population, he told the story of a Jew who was acting as gaoler to a prisoner in Savanna-la-Mar. The rebel tried to persuade his keeper to release him. 'You differ from the rest of the Whites,' he told him, urging the Jewish man to think of himself as allied with the rebels. Together they could drive the white colonists out and divide the land between themselves. He promised to reveal some hidden treasure if only his chains were loosened, but 'the Israelite was either too honest or too unbelieving' to go along with this plan and the next day

---

[210] Ibid., II. 489.
[211] See, for example, Clare Taylor, 'Planter Comment upon Slave Revolts in Eighteenth Century Jamaica', *S&A* 3.3 (1982), 243–53.
[212] Paton argues that the decision to name it as a crime was associated with the decriminalization of witchcraft in England, an attempt to suppress popular belief in it. The colonists could not therefore use older legislation against obeah. *Cultural Politics*, 40.
[213] Report of the Lords of Committee of Council, *PP*, 1789, vol. 69, 217–18. See Paton, *Cultural Politics*.

reported what had passed.[214] Race could in certain circumstances be trumped as the primary sign of difference.[215] Jews might be free and almost white, but they were not equal. Their forms of disaffection could be dangerous. Long wanted to simplify his story, to make it about the binary division between Coromantin and White, to cover up other fractures, but his own narrative did not fit that frame. He had documented the differences, the ethnicities, at length in the *History*. The security of the island depended on the Maroons, as well as 'the Mulatto man who was said to have slain three with his own hand', and the 'brave North Briton' who did the same.[216] Englishmen could not do it on their own. He devoted many pages in the *History* to the militia, clearly convinced that the improvements that had been made after 1760 were quite inadequate. Their lack of discipline and equipment was all too evocative of 'Falstaff's tatterdemallions'. His class prejudice ensured that he was convinced little could be expected from the 'lowest orders of white inhabitants'. He hated miscegenation, but an effective militia, including 'mulattos', would go some way to preserving stability. If 'slaves' had to be 'entrusted with arms', then they should be promised freedom in case of good behaviour. White officers must ensure discipline, for the vital ingredient of an effective militia was a proper hierarchy.[217]

The new legislation was still going through the assembly at the time Long entered it in October 1761. One of his earliest duties was to serve on a committee dealing with the state of forts and fortifications, essential in the present emergency.[218] In November an act was proposed capping the inheritance of illegitimate mixed-race and black people.[219] This too was a direct response to the rebellion amid fears that the growing population of free propertied men of colour was disturbing the sanctity of the racial divide and threatening white privilege. Their numbers were increasing and their claims might become disruptive. The events of 1760–1 had demonstrated the fragility of the status quo, and the assembly men wanted to strengthen racial demarcations and prevent a dangerous reduction of the numbers of the white population in relation to those racialized as black or yellow (brown). Limiting the amounts illegitimate mixed-race and black people could inherit might keep their numbers down and their position subordinate. 'Divers large estates, consisting of land, slaves, cattle, stock, money and securities for money, have from time to time been left by white persons to mulattoes,' the bill declared,

[214] Long, *History*, II. 460.
[215] Wilson, 'The Performance of Freedom'.
[216] Long, *History*, II. 450.
[217] Ibid., I. 128, 138.
[218] *JAJ*, vol. 5, 4 February 1762.
[219] Brooke N. Newman, 'Gender, Sexuality and the Formation of Racial Identities in the Eighteenth-Century Anglo-Caribbean World', *Gender and History* 22.3 (2010), 585–602; Newman, *A Dark Inheritance*; Livesay, *Children of Uncertain Fortune*, 66–87.

'not being their own issue born in lawful wedlock ... [S]uch bequests tend greatly to destroy the distinction requisite, and absolutely necessary, to be kept up in this island between white persons and negroes, their issue and offspring, and may in progress of time be the means of decreasing the number of white inhabitants in this island.'[220]

There were strong objections to this bill, both from three members of the council and from the Lords of Trade, on the grounds that such legislation was 'oppressive' and 'repugnant to the spirit of the English laws', tending as it did to deprive men of their right to dispose of their property as they wished.[221] To demonstrate the need for the new law, the assembly conducted an investigation into recent 'devises', and as Long reported in the *History*, 'the amount in reality [sic] and personalty was found in value between two and three hundred thousand pounds'. This was an alarming sum, including as it did four sugar estates, seven pens, houses and other lands. 'After duly weighing the ill consequences that might befall the colony, by suffering real estates to pass into such hands', the assembly persisted in arguing for the legislation. In a colony 'where slave-holding is legally established', Long argued, certain laws were required, appropriate to the locality, which would not be required in the mother country, the doctrine of *lex loci*. Given the weakness of the institution of marriage in Jamaica, a situation as we have seen that Long greatly regretted, and in a colony in which 'three fourths of the nation were slaves', it was inevitable that 'a man's right of devising his property by will ought justly ... to be more circumscribed ... than is fitting in the mother state'.[222] A lengthy debate ensued, and much antagonism between the assembly and the metropolitan authorities, but the bill was finally confirmed in 1769. The members of the assembly were quite prepared, while putting the cap on inheritance for the illegitimate, to allow a tiny number of privilege petitions, as Daniel Livesay and Brooke Newman have shown, allowing wealthy free people of colour to become legally white.[223] But this flexibility was hardened too as the definition of whiteness was strengthened. Only those with sufficient documentation to prove that they were four degrees removed from an African ancestor, rather than three degrees as previously was the case, could hope to be recognized as legally white. The cap was aimed at keeping that number as small as possible. Long, as we have seen, was in favour of a 'lower rank' of industrious 'mulattos', 'forming the centre of connexion between the two extremes, producing a regular establishment of three ranks of men, dependent on each other, and

---

[220] Jamaica House of Assembly, Laws and Statutes, etc., 2 Geo III, viii (1761), cited Livesay, *Children of Uncertain Fortune*, 70.
[221] Long, *History*, II. 323.
[222] Ibid., II. 324.
[223] See Livesay, *Children of Uncertain Fortune*, 60–89; Newman, *A Dark Inheritance*, 120–8.

rising in a proper climax of subordination, in which the Whites would hold the highest place'.[224]

By February 1762 Moore had departed and William Henry Lyttelton arrived as the new governor. 'Public tranquillity remained undisturbed' for some time, but then, in November 1765, a new disturbance, this time very short lived, broke out in St Mary.[225] Relations between the assembly and the governor were already extremely fractious, and were not improved by the planters' conviction that Lyttelton had failed to send troops to support the suppression of the uprising and had left them to deal with it alone. Long was a member of the committee which investigated 'the rise, progress, and means used to suppress, the late insurrection in the parish of St Mary', and he presented their lengthy report to the assembly.[226] On the basis of the evidence they collected from tortured prisoners, loyal 'Negroes' and planters, they concluded that the intention was 'to destroy the white people', starting with Ballard's Valley. The 'plan of the conspirators was general among the Coromantees' of several estates and had initially been instigated by a 'Coromantee negro named Blackwall', who had been involved in 1761. 'The flame', they maintained, 'has only been smothered' and 'the Coromantees, who religiously adhere to the oath which is taken upon entering into these bloody associations, will, in all likelihood, embrace the first favourable occasion to renew their attempts'. Their 'savage, and martial temper is well known', as was their responsibility for most, if not all rebellions that had taken place on the island. Their presence endangered 'effectual settlement'. As a result the committee proposed a bill for 'laying an additional duty on all Fantee, Akim and Ashantee slaves, and on all other slaves commonly called Coromantee, that shall, from and after a certain time, be imported and sold in this island'.[227]

No such bill was passed, however, much to Long's regret. Many planters were not prepared to lose Coromantee labour and were willing to attempt to contain it. Months later another disturbance erupted in Westmoreland, this time involving thirty-three Coromantees, once again confirming Long's suppositions. He reminded his readers of the words of a dying Coromantin, about to be executed for his part in the rebellion. He cautioned 'the white persons present, "never to trust any of his countrymen"'.[228] It was this which justified the brutality of the punishments inflicted upon them. And given that slavery was a state of war, as Locke had put it, violence could only be met with violence.[229] Long had strongly countered the accusation that the planters were cruel, but it was necessary in the mother country to legitimate the cruelty

[224] Long, *History*, II. 333.
[225] Ibid., II. 465.
[226] *JAJ*, vol. 5, 6 August 1766.
[227] Ibid.
[228] Long, *History*, II. 472.
[229] Locke, *Two Treatises of Government*, 200.

of their reprisals. He disavowed the pain of torture by claiming that Coromantins despised death and smiled when in agony. At the same time he knew that the enslaved could only be terrorized by sharing that pain. He told the story of two of the rebels, ringleaders in St Mary, their names Fortune and Kingston. They

> were hung up alive in irons on a gibbet, erected in the parade of the town of Kingston. Fortune lived seven days, but Kingston survived till the ninth. The morning before the latter expired, he appeared to be convulsed from head to foot; and upon being opened, after his decease, his lungs were found adhering to the back so tightly, that it required some force to disengage them. The murders and outrages they had committed, were thought to justify this cruel punishment inflicted upon them *in terrorem* to others. [230]

The terror that the colonists had experienced must now be physically inflicted on the rebels. Long knew this was cruel, the description was horrific, 'but they appeared to be very little affected by it themselves', he insisted, drawing on the notion of Africans as unfeeling brutes. His depiction of Fortune and Kingston's 'hardened insolence and brutal insensibility' allowed him to disavow their suffering. African stoicism in the face of anguish was a stereotype that was widely circulated amongst pro-slavery writers as legitimation for their own brutality.[231] It can be interpreted as a performance of refusal, the refusal to give any satisfaction to the masters, to demonstrate to them the limits of their power.[232] In later years, when Long was revising his volumes with the idea of another edition, he inserted a note: 'this unfortunate Negroe was charged with assisting in the murder of the overseer at Esher, and suffered as an accomplice tho' it afterwards but too late appeared that he was entirely innocent of the murder'.[233] He did not record his reaction to the appalling injustice that had been inflicted.

For Vincent Brown, 1760 was one episode of a much larger war; for Trevor Burnard, it was the beginning of a new phase of imperial relations, one that was to define the difference between Jamaica and the American colonies, for it confirmed Jamaican loyalism and dependence on British military and naval power.[234] For Thistlewood, enslaved Africans were the problem. For Long, the spectre of 'extirpation' could not be forgotten: any hopes for a settled society must rest on a combination of armed force and the capacity of the plantation to

---

[230] Long, *History*, II. 458.
[231] Bryan Edwards wrote poetry on this theme. Brown, *Tacky's Revolt*, 230.
[232] Kathleen Wilson argues for the importance of performance as an aspect of race politics; 'Three Theses on Performance and History', *Eighteenth-Century Studies* 48.4 (2015), 375–90.
[233] BL Add MSS 12405, f. 365r; thanks to Miles Ogborn for reminding me of this reference.
[234] Burnard, *Jamaica in the Age of Revolution*, 103–30.

'civilize' creoles, producing a docile and industrious labour force. White freedom depended on slavery.

The Rights of Free-Born Englishmen

The colonists had left the mother country to settle in a 'distant place', but they were determined to carry with them their rights and liberties as Englishmen.[235] The colony was structurally dependent on metropolitan power. Colonists sought as much autonomy as they could grasp, especially to make local laws and control island revenue. Their struggle for what they defined as freedom was as vital to them as that other struggle that defined the colony's history, between slave-owners and enslaved. As Edward's great-grandfather Samuel Long had declared, 'he asked nor desired nothing but his rights and privileges as an Englishman, and that he ought to have and would not be contented with less'.[236] Sixty years later James Knight wrote in similar vein: 'our British Colonies are, and must be considered as distinct, though subordinate Dominions and that they cannot have Laws made for them, nor Justice administered to them, from Home'.[237] And he cited the terms of Charles II's proclamation, as Long did in his *History*, confirming 'that all children of natural-born subjects of England, to be born in Jamaica, shall, from their respective births, be reputed to be, and shall be, *free denisons of England*; and shall have the same privileges, to all intents and purposes, as the free-born subjects of England'."[238] The rights of colonists against the claims of the prerogative formed one of the issues in the forefront of Long's mind as he wrote the *History*. He was determined to appeal to metropolitan readers, reassert those rights and detail the problems, as he saw them, of the existing practices of colonial government. Jamaica was still an 'infant colony', the colonists 'helpless offspring', exiled 'beyond the reach of fatherly protection' and subject to much abuse. The mother country, far from exercising maternal care, had abandoned them to mean, avaricious and dishonest governors, 'so horrid a group', who had exercised tyranny and violated their liberties.[239] These arguments were informed by his years in the assembly, particularly the struggle that he had engaged in between 1764 and 1768 over an apparently arcane issue of the privileges of the assembly. While never discussing in the *History* the details of the 'Privileges Controversy' as it came to be called, his experience of that conflict, together with the shock of the Somerset decision

---

[235] Samuel Johnson's definition of a colony: 'a body of people drawn from the mother country to inhabit some distant place'.
[236] Calender of State Papers, cols. 1677–8 no.1512, cited in Whitson, *Constitutional Development*, 49.
[237] Knight, *History*, II. 521.
[238] Ibid., II. 521; Long, *History*, I. 9.
[239] Long, *History*, I. 3–4.

and the critiques of 'the enemies of the West-India islands', framed his writing.[240]

Long's first years in the assembly, as we have seen, were dominated by the rebellion and its aftermath. Moore's departure in 1762 brought a change, with the arrival of William Henry Lyttelton as the new governor. It was no longer his brother-in-law in command, a man deeply familiar with the island and the ways of the colonists. Lyttelton was a different proposition: the son of a baronet, ten years older than Long, he had been educated at Eton and Oxford. A kinsman of Pitt, he had gone into politics and became a servant of the crown. In 1755 he was appointed governor of South Carolina, a very rich colony populated by a small number of whites and a large majority of enslaved Africans producing rice and indigo. The colony was vulnerable to both French and Native American attack. Lyttelton persuaded the rather fractious assembly to invest in defences, asserting their responsibilities against their expectation that the crown should pay. Initially he sought to conciliate the neighbouring native peoples. But a conflict with the Cherokee resulted in him leading an armed incursion into their territory to enforce harsh terms. A long and costly war followed, but Lyttelton was strongly supported both by the colonists and by the British.[241] The governorship of Jamaica was a reward. Lyttelton soon found it a somewhat poisoned chalice.

In the early months of his office he had declared martial law when faced with the ongoing conflicts in the Caribbean and the fears of a Spanish invasion. The news of a British success at Havana was welcomed by all, but by October 1762 governor and assembly were at odds. The king had refused four of the assembly's bills, including the cap on inheritance, as 'repugnant to the laws of England'. This provoked a sharp response that shocked Lyttelton. No disrespect was intended, the assembly men claimed, but the Lords of Trade, responsible for perusing legislation and making recommendations to the king, 'have endeavoured to represent the legislature of this island in a very disadvantageous light to his Majesty'.[242] Loyal submission to the monarch was thought of as a guarantee of colonial liberties and freedom. The subject owed allegiance and obedience, the monarch offered protection and privileges; the relationship between subject and sovereign was understood as a reciprocal bond.[243] The Lords of Trade, however, were another matter. The colonists insisted on their rights to frame their legislation. That was the basis of their Magna Carta: they would grant revenue, the crown would recognize their right

---

[240] Ibid., I. 5
[241] P. J. Marshall, 'Lyttelton, William Henry, First Baron Lyttelton and First Baron Westcote (1724–1808), Colonial Governor and Diplomat', *Oxford Dictionary of National Biography*, 2004, https://doi.org/10.1093/ref:odnb/17311.
[242] *JAJ*, vol. 5, 9 October 1762.
[243] Hannah Weiss Muller, *Subject and Sovereign. Bonds of Belonging in the Eighteenth-Century British Empire* (Oxford, 2017).

to legislate and would secure their property. But that legislation had to be confirmed. From the point of view of the crown, the function of the assembly was to provide revenue for the upkeep of the colony via taxation and to provide support for the parent state, whether by sugar or cotton. Colonial assemblies were dependent on the favour of the crown, rather than possessing any inherent rights as Englishmen.[244] The colonists saw it differently. In Jamaica the settlement of 1729 had confirmed their rights to 'their deliberative share in the framing of ... laws', which secured 'their lives, liberties, and properties': this was at the heart of their rights as free-born Englishmen. This birth-right, as Long later put it, was 'indelibly blended' into the very nature of Englishmen and they carried their laws with them.[245] The efforts to take these away from those Long described as the 'common people' were a present threat to their position.[246] Lyttelton, dismayed at the challenge to the sovereign's will and disappointed by 'your great misconduct', prorogued the assembly. He was already finding that the aspirations of the assembly men for the same powers and privileges as the House of Commons were so deeply rooted that it was beyond his power to shift them.[247] Prorogation and dissolution were the two weapons in his arsenal for dealing with a fractious assembly.[248] He was to use both many times in the subsequent years.

The assembly was summoned again the following week, Lyttelton hoping that they would be more obliging. The whole house, however, resolved that 'his majesty's subjects of this island are declared to be entitled to the benefit and protection of the laws of England, and to the rights and privileges of Englishmen'. For more than eighty years they had enjoyed 'that most essential privilege, the power of enacting laws for their own good government and support'. 'This colony', they continued, 'now so beneficial to its mother country, could scarcely have subsisted or made any considerable progress as a sugar-colony, without the benefit of the constitution it enjoys.' Few British subjects would have been induced 'to venture their lives and fortunes, in a climate so unhealthy, and at a distance so remote from Britain, as Jamaica is, with a less degree of protection than its constitution affords'.[249] This was the key to their security. By November hostility to Lyttelton was being openly expressed, and a proposal was made to send a resolution to the king asking for his removal on the grounds of his claims for improper fees and requesting that

---

[244] Jack P. Greene, *Peripheries and Center. Constitutional Development in the Extended Polities of the British Empire and the United States, 1607–1788* (London, 1986).
[245] BL Add MSS 12404, f. 1.
[246] Long, *History*, I. 19.
[247] Trevor Burnard, 'Harvest Years? Reconfigurations of Empire in Jamaica, 1756–1807', *JICH* 40.4 (2012), 533–55.
[248] *JAJ*, vol. 5, 12 October 1762; Metcalf, *Royal Government and Political Conflict*.
[249] *JAJ*, vol. 5, 21 October 1762.

he should be replaced by a person 'more grateful to his majesty's subjects of this island'.[250]

By the time the assembly reconvened in October 1763, relations with the governor had improved. This did not last. By December of the following year the conflict over the privileges of the house had begun.[251] The spark was somewhat arcane: it concerned the rights of the assembly to arrest and imprison any person in breach of its privileges during its sittings, a right that mirrored that of the House of Commons. That privilege had been exercised against a trader who had seized the coach horses of a member for the non-payment of a debt but had been overridden by Lyttelton from his position in the Court of Chancery. The assembly, conscious of their position as 'the true guarantees of the constitutional rights of the people', were determined to stand on the dignity of their position, however minor the issue.[252] A committee of the whole house judged that the governor had been in flagrant contempt of their privileges; they would do no further business, and they would prepare an address to the king asking him to interpose his authority 'by restraining his excellency's arbitrary exercise of power'.[253] Long was on the committee to produce the address, together with his neighbour Nicholas Bourke. Lyttelton dissolved the assembly again and did not summon it until the following March, by which time the government was in serious need of money. The Lords of Trade, acting for the king and determined in the wake of the Seven Years War to limit the rights of the representative assemblies and extend metropolitan control of the colonies, declared that no breach of privilege had occurred. This conflict in Jamaica was one of a number of similar clashes between the crown and the colonies which were to culminate in the American War of Independence.[254]

Both sides appealed to London, hoping to mobilize support. In August 1765 Nicholas Bourke's pamphlet *The Privileges of the Island of Jamaica Vindicated* was published, its three editions suggesting that it was widely read in Britain. Bourke, coming from an Anglo-Irish family but ready to identify as an Englishman, had emigrated to Jamaica around 1740. Well connected to the elite families, his uncle Andrew Arcedeckne was a prominent lawyer and his wife the daughter of the chief justice, Thomas Fearon. He represented Clarendon and owned much property there, working with Long on many of the assembly committees and sharing his political allegiances. The rhetoric of

---

[250] Ibid., vol. 5, 19 November 1762.
[251] Jack P. Greene, 'The Jamaica Privilege Controversy, 1764–66: an Episode in the Process of Constitutional Definition in the Early Modern British Empire', in *Negotiated Authorities. Essays in Colonial Political and Constitutional History* (Charlottesville, VA, 1994), 350–93.
[252] Long, *History*, I. 158.
[253] *JAJ*, vol. 5, 21 December 1764.
[254] Greene, *Peripheries and Center*.

the rights of the people against the arbitrary authority of the crown was at the heart of the pamphlet. It drew on the traditions of free-born Englishmen, celebrating 'those great men', venerable patriots', who had stood firm against the tyranny of Charles I, and hailing 1688 as a vindication of ancient rights and liberties.[255] The assembly, wrote Bourke, considered 'their privileges as derived to them from their constituents, and that they are not concessions from the crown, but the right and inheritance of the people'. The inhabitants of Jamaica, he argued (and in his understanding only white male property owners were inhabitants),

> are all British subjects, entitled to the laws of England and its constitution, as their inheritance, possessing their rights and privileges by as free and certain a tenure as that by which they hold their lands, as that by which the king holds his crown. Never was it pretended till now that a British subject became a slave, or forfeited any of the rights and privileges of an Englishman, by settling in a British colony.[256]

Were the subjects of the colony, he asked rhetorically, 'not freemen, but slaves ... not the free subjects, but the outcasts of Britain; possessing these invaluable blessings only as tenants at will, the most uncertain and wretched of all tenures, and liable to be dispossessed by the hand of power?' It was the rights of British subjects which secured property and with property went personhood, 'the personhood of whiteness', the entitlement to the earth, as Du Bois was later to term it.[257] The only distinction between freedom and slavery, Bourke maintained, was 'that a freeman has his life, his liberty, and his property, secured to him by known laws, to which he has given his consent'.[258] The crown might claim that the colonists had no rights, only concessions from the crown. The colonists insisted on the legitimacy of their rights, won by consent. Bourke recognized that the assembly of 'our little colony' could not have the scope of the House of Commons, but any form of government imposed without consent would be 'degrading us from the rank of Englishmen, and reducing us to a condition of slavery'.[259] Only slaves would suffer oppression in this way. The Irish, he warned, had been cheated out of their liberties by Poynings: that must not happen to Jamaica. 'His majesty', he concluded, 'and every honest man in Britain, will think the better of us, for shewing a manly resolution and constancy in defence of our privileges... [W]e

---

[255] Nicholas Bourke, *The Privileges of Jamaica Vindicated* [1766] (Jamaica, 1810), 8.
[256] Ibid., 19.
[257] W. E. B. Du Bois, 'The Souls of White Folk' [1920], in Du Bois, *Darkwater. Voices from within the Veil* (Oxford, 2007), 15. See also Cheryl Harris, 'Whiteness as Property', *Harvard Law Review* 106.8 (1993), 1707–91.
[258] Bourke, *The Privileges of Jamaica*, 29–30.
[259] Ibid., 32.

have received our liberties as an inheritance from our fathers, and we are bound to transmit them to our children, unimpaired.'[260]

The controversy over the Stamp Act was preoccupying the metropolitan authorities by this time and Jamaica was a minor irritant. Lyttelton was instructed to seek a reconciliation and he requested a leave of absence. He was replaced as lieutenant-governor by Roger Hope Elletson who had been born on the island, educated at Eton and Cambridge, owned two properties in St Andrew and had served in the assembly and the council: a man much more acceptable to the colonists.[261] The assembly, however, had not done with Lyttelton, and a committee, including Long and Bourke, was established to inquire into his conduct as governor. The recent insurrection in St Mary was under investigation at the same time. Long reported to the assembly on both committees, an indication of his status in the chamber. Their critique of Lyttelton was damning. He had, they maintained,

> brought with him to this island, or adopted very soon after his arrival here; a design of subverting the constitution of our government, that he considered this constitution (of which we and our ancestors have been in possession ever since the first settlement of this colony) as flowing to us, not from our being Englishmen, but from concessions of the crown, which were revocable at pleasure; and that our legislature, though it has ever enjoyed and exercised the highest and most important powers of legislation, had not better foundation for its rights and privileges, than the will and pleasure of the sovereign, nor could exercise any powers but what is derived from his majesty's commission and instruction to his governors.[262]

In addition to this major charge, they accused him of numerous transgressions: he had been motivated by the acquisition of wealth, had delayed the courts and impeded justice, strangely neglected the assembly, created 'scenes of confusion and distress', left the troops disheartened, the militia deserting, the 'Negroes' rising. 'The melancholy effects' of all this, they concluded, were that 'our properties diminished in their value', their minds were 'disturbed by continual violations of our best established rights, our free condition degraded into slavery, our credit sunk, and our distresses aggravated to desperation'. Those inhabitants who could leave would 'seek an asylum in some of our sister colonies' where liberty was valued. 'Nothing can contribute more to fill the minds of free-born subjects with discontent and inquietude, than an arbitrary and tyrannical administration of government.'[263] Three days of debate on the

[260] Ibid., 45.
[261] 'Roger Hope Elletson', Legacies of British Slave-ownership database, http://wwwdepts-live.ucl.ac.uk/lbs/person/view/2146640755, accessed 4 February 2021.
[262] *JAJ*, vol. 5, 12 August 1766.
[263] Ibid.

report left the assembly divided. In effect, however, they had already won, having successfully defied the Lords of Trade. Elletson had declared governors accountable to the laws of the country, Lyttelton had gone, and the record of his offending action in Chancery had been erased. As Jack P. Greene concludes, despite crown hopes of reducing the authority of the assemblies, the reality was that, on the ground, the process was one of negotiation and consent.[264]

Long referred to Bourke's pamphlet *The Privileges of the Island of Jamaica Vindicated* in his *History*, noting that it had cited the account by his ancestor Sir William Beeston of the original foundation of government.[265] This sense of male ancestry, associated with blood but also with a tradition of political discourse, was a powerful part of Long's and Bourke's belief in their historic rights. They in turn would pass this inheritance to their sons (both of whom in fact became absentees and whose descendants enjoyed compensation). Samuel Long and William Beeston were their admired forebears. They evoked the colonists' golden thread of liberty from the parliamentary struggles against Stuart tyranny, in 1641 and 1688, to the proclamation of Charles II, conflict over Poynings, Jamaica's Magna Carta of 1729, and the privileges controversy. They had secured their property and white personhood against the threat of 'slavery'. 'He and his Right of Property', opined Long, 'are ever inseparable.'[266] There was no apparent conflict for them in using the language of slavery in relation to themselves. A split operated in their minds between the chattel slavery they exercised over 'their' enslaved property and their conception of political slavery. Political slavery evoked the condition of subjection to the arbitrary and tyrannical conduct of the crown. 'A slave', wrote Bourke, 'holds everything at the pleasure of his master, and has no law but the will of his tyrant.'[267] Long utilized this language, disavowing any possible connection between what the white male inhabitants of Jamaica might suffer and the experience of enslaved Africans on his plantation. He knew, but refused to *know*, in the sense of understanding, what metropolitan critics meant when they pointed to the connections. Colonists, Long believed, rightly sought 'a mutual Confidence, founded rather on the Love and Gratitude of Free Subjects, confirmed in the fullest Enjoyment of their Birthrights'. They could not accept 'the Awe and Fear of mere wretched Slaves, stripped of their Rights and Franchises, and held in base Submission, by the sole Power, of unlimited Prerogative, of Military Force, or Parliamentary Tyranny'. This had nothing to

---

[264] Greene, 'The Jamaica Privilege Controversy', 392.
[265] Long, *History*, I. 18. Security of property rights was a key distinguishing feature of empire. P. J. Marshall, 'Parliament and Property Rights in the Late Eighteenth Century British Empire', in John Brewer and Susan Staves (eds.), *Early Modern Conceptions of Property* (London, 1996), 530–44.
[266] BL Add MSS 12402, f. 79.
[267] Bourke, *The Privileges of Jamaica*, 30.

do, in his mind, with those Coromantee claims for freedom from subjection to 'the sole Power' or will of their masters, or of their masters' 'Military Force'. Free subjects were racialized as white and ruled themselves; chattel slaves could be bought and sold and were black. There had been numerous attempts by the crown, Long wrote, to impose a 'badge of slavery'.[268] But free-born Englishmen would not brook subjection. He called on the 'judicious Locke'. 'The will of the people alone', Locke had written, 'can appoint the form of the commonwealth; which is by constituting the legislative, and appointing in whose hands that shall be.'[269] For 'the people' independence meant freedom 'from all Subjection to another's *Will* . . . he is absolute Master of himself and his actions'.[270] The White freeholders of Jamaica were characterized by an 'independent spirit'.[271] The 'manly resolution' which the slave-owners drew on in their conflicts over their rights, so different from Coromantin 'deceit' or Tacky's 'effeminacy', was rooted in their conviction of white entitlement.

Mary Nyquist, in her reading of what she terms 'antityranny ideology', identifies a political discourse that was mobilized over the seventeenth and eighteenth centuries in a variety of contexts, and allowed a plasticity that could include figurative enslavement. Chattel slavery, she argues, was theorized in connection with the household from Aristotle to Locke and beyond; it became part of the private realm. Those in the private realm did not have the privileges of those in the public. Locke's 'Of Slavery', she suggests, used a peculiarly abstract theoretical language 'to rationalize, at one and the same time, a radical right to resist tyranny and a right to exploit those who have been enslaved'. A narrow political radicalism was combined with an assumption of social and economic inequalities. Locke's defence of slavery was 'skilfully integrated with his theorization of the state of nature and the state of war, together with the civil subject's right to resist tyranny'.[272] Legal political resistance was implicitly racialized; it belonged to white subjects. The association of freedom with propriety in the self and with property went alongside the power of life and death over the enslaved whose service was appropriated.[273] Long followed Locke in the belief that slavery was indeed a '*State of War*', a 'State of Enmity and Destruction', for 'Men are not under the ties of the Common Law of Reason, have no other Rule, but that of Force and Violence, and so may be treated as Beasts of Prey, those dangerous and noxious Creatures, that will be

---

[268] BL Add MSS 12402. This was an insertion into his notes for the revision of vol. I, 76; manuscript insertion, no pp.
[269] Long, *History*, I. 186–7.
[270] BL Add MSS 12402, addition, 32.
[271] Long, *History*, I. 57.
[272] Mary Nyquist, *Arbitrary Rule. Slavery, Tyranny, and the Power of Life and Death* (Chicago, 2013), 328–9.
[273] There is an extensive scholarly debate on Locke's attitude to slavery. For a recent intervention, see Brewer, 'Slavery, Sovereignty'.

sure to destroy him'.²⁷⁴ The events of 1760 had fully demonstrated this truth. Slavery was, as Locke had written, nothing but *'the State of War continued between a lawful Conqueror and a Captive'*, a state of one man's absolute power over another.²⁷⁵ Slaves were 'the natural enemies of society', as Montesquieu had understood; 'their number must be dangerous': violence and coercion were inevitable, especially given the 'exaggerated passions' of the tropics.²⁷⁶ English conquerors, 'the forces of the state', Long believed, had found the island in a 'state of nature'.²⁷⁷ It had needed Jamaica's 'industrious planters and merchants' to transform Jamaica into a plantation economy.²⁷⁸ God had given the land, the judicious Locke had certified, 'to the use of the Industrious and the Rational': clearly these men were the planters.²⁷⁹ They could claim their right to their property not only from their patents from the crown, but from *their* labour, not that of the enslaved, which had improved the land and made it their own. Their hard-won freedoms must be defended. The struggle between freedom and slavery, in its very different iterations, was indeed at the heart of Jamaica's colonial history.

Long knew that 'Negroes are the sinews of West India property' and that it was in the interests of the slave-owners to be humane; indeed, 'too much care cannot be taken of them'. With his eye on the critics, he noted that, 'In the opinion of very sensible writers ... the interest of our colonies demands, that the Negroes should be better treated.'²⁸⁰ This underpinned his insistence on the difference between 'imported Blacks', with their 'savage manners', and creoles. Creoles, he was convinced, are now 'more humanized than their ancestors'.²⁸¹ A distinction might be made between the two groups. The vital distinction might no longer be so simple as between Whites and Blacks, but between creoles and imported Blacks. The contradiction with his own argument that it was a matter of 'species' was jettisoned. Creoles had been 'humanized', civilized by their plantation experience. What was more, 'Mulattos', after a period of servitude, could become the *'medium'* (his italics), his picture of a proper hierarchy once more in the forefront of his mind.²⁸² The penal laws should be tempered for the creoles; mutilation should cease, whipping be brought within limits. God had ordained Africans to labour, but their 'just

---

[274] Locke, *Two Treatises of Government*, 200.
[275] Ibid., 207. He effected an epistemological suppression by placing chattel slavery outside his purview. Thanks to Mark Harvey for this point.
[276] Long, *History*, II. 431, I. 25.
[277] Ibid., I. 161, 351.
[278] Ibid., I. 170.
[279] Locke, *Two Treatises of Government*, 214.
[280] Long, *History*, II. 502–3.
[281] Ibid., II. 497.
[282] Ibid., II. 503.

subordination' did not preclude 'our loving, and treating them humanely'.[283] Rebels, conspirators, rioters and runaways would necessarily be dealt with most severely. The 'gentlemen of Jamaica', Long opined, should 'raise their island to the same rank of superiority in the wisdom and mildness of its laws, as it already enjoys in its extent and opulence'.[284] This island could become, he dreamed, not just a slave state – the one he had helped to make, which could be inherited by his descendants – but a truly civilized place, characterized by a form of 'legitimately equitable species of servitude', as imagined by Grotius, which would be entirely acceptable to the mother country and would allow him to live comfortably as an enlightened Englishman on the fruits of racial capitalism.[285]

---

[283] Ibid.
[284] Ibid.
[285] Ibid., II. 402.

8

Theorizing Racial Difference

When Long turned to his account 'Of the Inhabitants' of the island, a form of inquiry well established by voyagers from the seventeenth century and most spectacularly fictionalized and satirized by Jonathan Swift in *Gulliver's Travels*, a text with which he was familiar, he faced his most difficult challenge. Unlike Swift he had no interest in placing his 'Dear Native Country' and its inhabitants under the microscope. It was Jamaica that was to be scrutinized and he believed himself to be in a very good position from which to do it. An Englishman and a West Indian, he *knew* the place and the people and could interpret it to Britain. He knew that, like Gulliver, he could only be happy in his 'Dear Native Land'. Longville was a veritable 'Golgotha'. When might he manage his deliverance from Egypt? he had asked his friend William Ricketts.[1] But such thoughts must not be reflected in his *History*. He was now safely ensconced in green and peaceful Chichester, a life that he had longed for. His task was to persuade his metropolitan audience that colonial slavery was both legitimate and essential to British wealth and power. White colonists would need to change, not least in their own conduct, if the island were to have a secure future and he would address this too. Then his brethren, the absentees, probably numbering around three thousand in Britain, must be mobilized in defence of their way of life. He had successfully marginalized the enslaved in his account of the history, constitution and politics, commerce and agriculture of the island, even the topography: they were the haunting presences, the absent labour. Now, however, they had to appear, and his depiction of these 'inhabitants' must naturalize and de-historicize slavery, and represent it as a timeless institution.

From the moment of his arrival in England, Long was honing his thinking about the law, slavery and blackness. His first publication was a biting satire on the law, *The Trial of Farmer Carter's Dog Porter for Murder*. This was followed by his polemical attack on Mansfield's decision, *Candid Reflections*, and then two years later by the *History*.

---

[1] Edward Long to William Ricketts, 12 January 1764, 14 September 1766, Ricketts Family Papers.

The three volumes of the *History* reflected his deep anxieties and confusions: he wanted to assume and demonstrate mastery, but he lived in fear of Africans, those 'internal' enemies who haunted the dreams of white colonists. At the same time the criticisms of the slave-owners were biting deep and he needed to show 'humane' intentions. But how could this be reconciled with the need for authority and power? His writing on 'The Inhabitants' bore witness to these difficulties and he structured it in such a way as to attempt to deal with the conflicting concerns: he celebrated the white creoles before denigrating Africans and attempting to prove their essential difference. His crucial task was to *naturalize* and *normalize* racial difference and hierarchies, to insist on them as both part of the natural world and part of a new common sense. This was hardly a simple matter, especially given his own unacknowledged confusions and contradictions and the range of contemporary thinking on the 'enigma of blackness' which he needed to acknowledge. Europeans had been preoccupied with the nature of those colonized others that they had encountered more frequently after 1492, when Columbus had arrived in the Caribbean. Were they fully human? Some of the comparative analysis of peoples built on classical traditions and focused on political relations and the distinction between civilization and barbarism. Anatomists in the seventeenth century had turned their attention to the body, while natural historians were classifying humans as part of a natural world including animals and characterizing groups in terms of skin colour and facial features.[2] Long was reading many of these accounts while drawing on old established ideas of blood and purity. Another influence was the emerging history of human societies based on comparison between different stages of development. He knew that England had once been sanguinary and uncivilized; now it was a place of culture and politeness. His *History* was intended to demonstrate the changes that Jamaica had gone through, once an infant colony, now a settled society. The natural historians who emphasized that it was climate and environment which made for 'varieties' of human beings dominated these debates, and Long's argument over this with the comte de Buffon was never far from his mind. Buffon's hierarchical picture of human species 'actually rendered necessary the slavery of certain groups'.[3] But his explanation of the 'varieties of men' ('variety' was a term commonly utilized in the eighteenth century to designate different groups) depended on climate. All these ideas jostled in Long's writing with the often-fantastical stories of African and other exotic voyages which he used to detail the doings of savages and cannibals. He struggled to maintain a spirit of 'philosophic inquiry' based on a rational mind that controlled passions and allowed him to 'extirpate old prejudices', banish 'ignorance and

---

[2] Schaub and Sebastiani, *Race et histoire*.
[3] Laurent Dubois, 'An Enslaved Enlightenment: Rethinking the Intellectual History of the French Atlantic', *Social History* 31.1 (2006), 4.

bigotry' and 'display ... the beautiful gradation, order and harmony' of the globe.[4] He held fast to a notion of divine providence but one that operated at a very abstract level, somehow assuring harmony from on high. This had little connection in his mind with the ground or with the idea that 'plantation Negroes might all be converted to the Christian faith'; he was singularly lacking in respect for many of the Anglican clergy on the island.[5] His memories of the plantation, what he was convinced he had observed and understood as to the 'nature' and 'habits' of Africans, informed all his writings. He knew that his status as an eyewitness was critical to his credibility. He *knew* in a way that Buffon and many of the other writers that he cited, who had not *known* Africans, could not. It was the combination of these knowledges that should surely prove the inexorability of difference not only to his readers, but also to himself. His task was to demonstrate that racial difference was *natural* and fixed. Such essentialism was, however, counteracted by his belief in improvement, his hopes for the mitigating and civilizing effects of plantation discipline and labour, and the distinction he both made and unmade between 'savages', those captives from Africa, and 'creoles', those born on the island. The land was being *improved*; could people, even Africans, also be *improved*? These were tensions he could not resolve: his contradictory thinking fractured his account of racial difference. The *History* unravelled its own racist logic, as Roxanne Wheeler argued, 'by bringing conflicting views of human difference together'.[6] Was race fixed? Or was it not?

The Trial of Farmer Carter's Dog: Candid Reflections

Shortly after he returned to England, Long published anonymously a biting satire on the law, *The Trial of Farmer Carter's Dog Porter for Murder*. Written before the Somerset trial, it makes clear that he was already enraged by what he saw as the follies of the English legal system. It was a play, replete with a full cast of characters and stage directions. The trial was of a dog, Porter, prosecuted for chasing a hare into a pond in which it drowned. The justices were 'just-asses'. The prisoner, being a dog, cannot speak. Torture it, says the First Council, with thumbscrews and presses; 'the law', he insists, 'can not only make *Dogs* to speak, but explain their meaning too'.[7] And when nutcrackers are applied to its

---

[4] Long, *History*, II. 337.
[5] Ibid., II. 428.
[6] Wheeler, *The Complexion of Race*, 210; Seth, *Difference and Disease*; Sebastiani, 'Global Integration, Social Disintegration'.
[7] [Edward Long], *The Trial of Farmer Carter's Dog Porter for Murder. Taken Down Verbatim and Literatim in Short-hand. And now Published by Authority, from the Corrected Manuscript of COUNSELLOR CLEAR-POINT, Barrister at Law. NB. This is the only true and authentic Copy; and all others are spurious* (London, 1771), 11. It cannot be proved that Long wrote it, but there is much substantiating evidence; Piers Beirne,

tail, the dog barks. But, claims the Second Council, how could he have a jury of peers, of twelve dogs? It is impossible to try a dog as a man. Nevertheless, the trial commences. A statement is made of the dog's violent attack and maceration of Mr Hare. Witnesses are called, each more absurd than the last. Lawrence Lurcher and Toby Tunnel are drunk. Mrs Dripping, the squire's cook, had roasted the hare for her master's dinner. Farmer Carter appears and defends his dog, Porter, his constant companion, protector of his family and home from many dangers. Indeed, he argues, Porter was ensuring that Mr Hare did not eat his master's turnips. He was trying to exercise *habeas corpus* and bring Mr Hare before the bench. 'I will have Justice,' swore Farmer Carter; 'You, all of ye, deserve hanging more than your prisoner . . . *You* pretend to be Judges.'[8] But he is dragged out of the court protesting. 'Faction and insolence are grown to such a pitch, that it is high time, for wise and virtuous magistrates, like your Worships, to interpose,' proclaims the First Council. Pass 'Sentence of Death upon the *Culprit* at the Bar,' he urges. The President of the Court, by the name of A. Bottle, declaims, '*Ill* should we execute the Trust reposed in us, if we did not seize every Opportunity, to oppress the Poor and flatter the Rich.' The poor 'are all run mad with *Politics*, resist their Rulers, despise their Magistrates, and abuse *us* every corner of the kingdom'. The prisoner must be hanged, is the verdict of the Magistrate, 'in *terrorem* to all other offenders'.[9] The dog is summarily strung up.

But there is a sequel. Farmer Carter gives the dog a handsome funeral which all principal dogs attend. On his gravestone is an epitaph:

> Here lie the remains of Honest Porter . . . *tried* for a crime he never committed, upon *laws* to which he was unamenable, before *men* who were no judges, found *guilty* without *evidence*, and *hanged* without *mercy*: to give to future Ages an Example, that the Spirit of *Turkish* Despotism, Tyranny, and Oppression, after glutting itself with the Conquest of *Liberty* in *British Men*, has stooped at length to wreak its bloody Vengeance on *British Dogs!*[10]

The moral of Long's tale was that law in the wrong hands was an ass and the hanging of the dog was memorialized with an epitaph denouncing despotism. He refused to see – although his anti-slavery opponents might well have pointed to it since it was in plain sight – that his satire on a law that could make dogs speak might be correlated with colonial laws which tortured rebels

---

'A Note on the Facticity of Animal Trials in Early Modern Britain; or, the Curious Prosecution of Farmer Carter's Dog for Murder', *Crime, Law and Social Change* 55 (2011), 359–74.

[8] Long, *Farmer Carter's Dog*, 36.

[9] Ibid., 39, 41. 'In terrorem' is the term Long used in relation to the horrifying gibbeting of rebels; *History*, II. 458.

[10] Long, *Farmer Carter's Dog*, 48.

to obtain confessions and refused the enslaved the right to speak or be tried by their peers in a regular court of law. He was certainly playing with the idea of the relation between the animal and the human, most relevant to the thoughts that were circling in his mind as to the relation between the orangutan and the African. Could dogs speak? 'We have seen *learned horses, learned* and even *talking dogs*,' he was to write in the *History*.[11] The horses in *Gulliver's Travels* had a language. Was there a clear boundary between animal and human, black and white, civilized and savage? And satire was an ambivalent form, posing dangers as well as offering security.

Long was trained in the law and acted for years as judge in Jamaica's Admiralty Court. He was contemptuous of many of the inadequate lawyers practising in Jamaica and would soon violently attack in print England's Lord Chief Justice, Lord Mansfield. The legality of slavery was emerging as a matter of debate. The Yorke–Talbot opinion of 1729 was that a slave was his master's property whether in England or in the colonies, and Hardwicke (Yorke as was) had declared in 1749 that a slave 'is as much property as any other thing'.[12] But Granville Sharp had brought a series of cases to law concerning the kidnapping of enslaved or formerly enslaved persons in the metropole and the outcomes had been varied.[13] In 1769 Sharp published *A Representation of the Injustice and Dangerous Tendency of Tolerating Slavery in England. Or of admitting the least claim of private property in the persons of man in England, etc.*, the first major work of anti-slavery by a British author. Sharp's interest was in laws and rights, not in skin. The book amassed a considerable volume of legal arguments against slavery. Long knew of these debates: the law lacked clarity. As the First Council put it, 'the Law, where it says nothing, may be meant to say, whatever your Worships will be pleased to make it'.[14] Law should be a matter of law, not opinion, and when it came to opinion, new and challenging voices could be heard. Gronniosaw's autobiographical narrative of slavery as a possible route to Calvinist freedom had been published in 1772. Maurice Morgann's *A Plan for the Abolition of Slavery in the West Indies* appeared that same year: it was critical of the slave trade and of the cruelty of slavery, and looked to the state to gradually eradicate it.[15] John Millar's *Origin of the Distinction of Ranks* had commented, in discussing slavery, on the 'curious spectacle' that 'the same people who talk in a high strain of political liberty, and who consider the privilege of imposing their own taxes as one of the unalienable rights of mankind, should make no scruple of reducing a great proportion of their fellow-creatures into circumstances by which they are not only

---

[11] Long, *History*, II. 375.
[12] Cited in Rabin, 'In a Country of Liberty?', 11.
[13] Paugh, 'The Curious Case of Mary Hylas'.
[14] Long, *Farmer Carter's Dog*, 37.
[15] Brown, *Moral Capital*; Greene, *Evaluating Empire*.

deprived of property, but almost of every species of right'.[16] Adam Smith's *Theory of Moral Sentiments* (1759) attacked those who cruelly exercised their 'empire over mankind' and called for sympathy, the capacity to use the imagination to feel for others, while Phillis Wheatley's poems were circulating, evoking just that.[17] James Beattie's *An Essay on the Nature and Immutability of Truth* (1770) insisted that all human beings were the same and called for an end to slavery.[18] This was indeed a new conjuncture, requiring a strong intervention.

The Somerset trial ended with Mansfield's verdict freeing Somerset and allowing the application of *habeas corpus* to an enslaved man, thereby vindicating his personhood. *Candid Reflections*, signed 'A Planter', was Long's enraged, vicious and ugly polemic against Lord Mansfield's decision.[19] It utilized his legal, historical and rhetorical skills, emphasizing the commercial value of the West India trade and insisting on the legal status of 'Negroes' as 'merchandise'. Opening with a biblical citation, he pointed to the significance of skin and the impossibility of changing colour. 'Can the Ethiopian change his skin, or the leopard his spots?' he asked. The law was an ass, if it could 'wash the blackamoor white'.[20] The West Indians were glad that the case had been brought, for they wanted a clear legal decision. 'The unlearned Planter', however, was 'still left in ignorance of the reasons on which his Lordship's judgement proceeded'. How could 'our Negroes' claim *habeas corpus* given the laws made by parliament which established 'Negroes' as property? Slavery was not a colonial invention; its roots lay in English villeinage, which had never died, Long claimed, challenging Granville Sharp's account of its obsolescence. A species of it 'sprang up in the remoter parts of the English dominion, the American plantations'. Parliament had subsequently declared 'Negroe labourers merely a commodity, or *chose* in merchandize', and the planters adhered to this. They

---

[16] John Millar, *The Origin of the Distinction of Ranks* [1771, rev. edn 1773], ed. Aaron Garrett (Indianapolis, 2012), 278–9.

[17] Adam Smith, 'Of the Influence of Custom', in *Theory of Moral Sentiments*, Part 5, 316. For a discussion of the limitations of Smith's capacity for sympathy, see Gust, *Unhomely Empire*; Vincent Carretta, *Phillis Wheatley. Biography of a Genius in Bondage* (Athens, GA, 2011).

[18] James Beattie, *An Essay on the Nature and Immutability of Truth* (Edinburgh, 1770); Silvia Sebastiani, *The Scottish Enlightenment. Race, Gender, and the Limits of Progress* (London, 2013), 110–15.

[19] There are many discussions of Long's pamphlet. See Jack P. Greene, 'Liberty, Slavery, and the Transformation of British Identity in the Eighteenth-Century West Indies', *S&A* 21.1 (2000), 1–31; Srividhya Swaminathan, 'Developing the West Indian Proslavery Position after the Somerset Decision', *S&A* 24.3 (2003), 40–60; Rabin, 'In a Country of Liberty?'; Seth, *Difference and Disease*.

[20] [Long], *Candid Reflections*, Advertisement.

deemed their negroes to be fit objects of purchase and sale, transferrable like any other goods and chattels: they conceived their right of property *to have and to hold*, acquired by purchase, inheritance, or grant, to be as strong, just, legal, indefeasible, and compleat, as that of any other British merchant over the goods in his warehouse.

'Negroes' were not persons in law; they were *'merchandize'*. How, then, had they become *'subjects of the realm*, and held entitled to all the rights, liberties, and privileges of natural, or free-born subjects?'[21] Their labour was essential in the tropics, a 'natural necessity'. Without them there would be no profitable American colonies. What was more, their constitutions were 'by nature and the Divine Will appropriated to these climates'.[22]

For Long, the idea that a 'Negro' was 'a subject of the realm' was horrifying. It fundamentally challenged the basis of colonial slavery on which his family depended. The success of Lucky Valley rested on enslaved labour; white freedom and white power rested on black subjection, the denial of personhood. Mansfield's naming of slavery as 'repugnant' in the English context was a threat to the West India trade and the plantation economy. Slavery, Long insisted, was an English institution. The slave trade had been initiated by the Portuguese, but it had been legitimated by parliament and the crown. Indeed, the 'whole kingdom' had both consented to it and benefited from it for more than two centuries. The Act of 1732 had declared '*Negroes* to be the same in the hands of the owner, as lands, houses, hereditaments, or other real estate, and liable to be taken in execution, and transferred by sale, in the same manner as personal things'. How then could 'Negroe slaves emigrating from our plantations into this kingdom . . . be deemed *free subjects of the realm?*'[23] It was the job of parliament to make the law: what right had judges to challenge it and turn law into opinion? Colonial laws, legitimated by the crown, should be respected: why could a planter not reclaim his property in England? 'Negroes' were not naturalized subjects by birth: they could not claim the same protection as a free-born Englishman. If English law were to decide they were no longer commodities, then compensation must be paid to the slave-owners. Even if he were to admit that the African trade was 'diabolical' in some of its practices, no guilt rested with the planters. They had legally purchased property that had already been acquired. Something more than magical English air was required to break these contracts. 'Mr *Blackstone* judiciously remarks', wrote Long, delighted to be able to cite such an eminent authority, 'so great is the regard of our law for *private property*, that it will not authorize the least violation of it; no, not even for the *general good of the whole community*'.[24]

---

[21] Ibid., 2–4.
[22] Ibid., 21.
[23] Ibid., 30–3.
[24] Ibid., 45.

If that were the case, then planters whose property was taken away should be compensated.

Having drawn on legal and historical arguments in favour of slavery, Long's tone shifted to a more hysterical evocation of the dangers posed to pure English blood by the presence of black people already in England. Mansfield's judgment would open the doors to thousands more *Quacos* and *Quashebas*, he warned, his language a vehicle for his contempt. Fugitive Africans, now confirmed in their fantastical notions of English liberty, would flock to 'our' shores. He would have known that the number of black people present in the metropole was already a subject of concern to some anti-slavery enthusiasts as well as to West Indians.[25] Given their 'spirit of mutiny' and 'impatience under servitude', once kindled, what evil might ensue?[26] 'Blacks' were already all too present, having 'eloped' from their owners with the help of 'Negroe solicitors', a juxtaposition which was alarming.[27] They were living in indolence, mixing with 'vicious servants' and 'abandoned prostitutes'. 'The lower class of women in *England*, are remarkably fond of the blacks, for reasons too brutal to mention,' he wrote, expressing his horror of miscegenation and his fear of African potency.[28] Drawing on notions of blood contamination, infection, pollution and degeneration, he warned of the risks to the higher classes. The whole nation, already beginning 'to be bronzed with the African tint', was in danger of becoming like the Portuguese or the Moors, both in skin colour and in morals. This was a 'venomous and dangerous ulcer' and every family was in danger.[29] What was more, these 'runaway gentry' and '*renegado blacks*' would bring no skills, and their offspring, 'a *linsey-woolsey* race', would bring no credit to Britain and displace white people. They might well become beggars, a burden on the poor rates, and prevent 'our own poor' from gaining employment.[30] 'Negroes' were not needed in England, they were of far more use in the colonies. His tone shifted again as he attacked the totally absurd idea of emancipation. 'Negroes' would not work if they were free. They would return to a state of nature, whereas in the colonies they were useful and industrious and gave employment to many in Britain. The loss of the colonies would be a disaster for Britain. The East India trade would decline too, for who would drink tea without sugar? Their rivalrous enemies would seize the opportunity and flourish.

In conclusion he hoped that in 'pleading the cause of the injured *planters*, I shall not be misunderstood to stand forth a champion for *slavery*'. This, he

---

[25] Brown, *Moral Capital*, 93–6.
[26] [Long], *Candid Reflections*, 62.
[27] Newman, *Fortune Seekers*.
[28] Felicity A. Nussbaum, *The Limits of the Human. Fictions of Anomaly, Race and Gender in the Long Eighteenth Century* (Cambridge, 2003).
[29] [Long], *Candid Reflections*, 46–9, 54.
[30] Ibid., 51–2.

realized, would be no way to represent himself to an English readership. But he resorted immediately to his key defence: British wealth depended on African labour. Then he returned to the question of legality: 'How far the late judicial sentence may be consistent with the spirit of *English law*?' he wondered. He was sure, 'that it cannot be made compatible with the spirit of *English commerce*'. Do not tear down, he pleaded, 'those essential pillars, of commerce, trade and navigation, upon which depended England's own freedom, both civil and religious'.[31]

Long's response to the Mansfield judgment focused on the law, but the Somerset verdict had made it clear that the West Indians could not rely on English law to defend slavery. Two previous opinions as to the legality of slavery in England had been reversed, and this threatened the status of colonial law. Mansfield had argued that no positive law had been passed to affirm planters' property rights. There was an attempt by the West Indians led by Rose Fuller to introduce a bill sanctioning slavery in England, but this failed.[32] Long wanted to insist on the uniformity of English and colonial laws against Mansfield's affirmed supremacy of English law and the writ of *habeas corpus*. But Mansfield had not nullified colonial laws: he operated with a distinction between metropole and colony. It was well established across the empire that the power of masters over servants had to be regulated according to the laws of that place, *lex loci*: this meant many variations existed.[33] Spatial distinctions were critical to Mansfield, as Dana Rabin argues: his judgment defined unfree labour in terms of race and space. Freedom and whiteness were associated with the metropole, where villeinage was dead and slavery was 'repugnant'; unfreedom and blackness could be left for the colonies.[34]

Long's stress on the commercial value of the West India trade to Britain's wealth and power, his claim that if property were to be stolen then the planters must be compensated, and his insistence that if 'Negroes' were free they would return to a state of nature, all became an established part of pro-slavery discourse. His reference to skin, and the impossibility of 'washing the blackamoor white', was to be greatly elaborated in the *History*. While his pamphlet was in the press, he read his fellow West Indian Samuel Estwick's diatribe against Mansfield. Estwick challenged Mansfield on issues of law and property. But he also focused on what he characterized as the African body and mind. 'The Ethiopian cannot change his skin, nor the Leopard his spots,' wrote Estwick. 'From this then, my Lord,' he continued, 'I infer, that the measure

---

[31] Ibid., 74.
[32] Douglas A. Lorimer, 'Black Slaves and English Liberty: a Re-examination of Racial Slavery in England', *Immigrants and Minorities: Historical Studies in Ethnicity, Migration and Diaspora* 3.2 (1984), 121–50.
[33] Lauren Benton, *A Search for Sovereignty. Law and Geography in European Empires, 1400–1900* (Cambridge, 2002).
[34] Rabin, 'In a Country of Liberty?', 21.

of these beings may be as compleat, as that of any other race of mortals; filling up that space in life beyond the bounds of which they are not capable of passing; differing from other men, not in *kind*, but in *species*.'[35] Long plagiarized Estwick's words and arguments in his *History*. New legitimations for racial difference must be established and the body was critical to this.

Of the Inhabitants

Long organized his thinking about 'The Inhabitants' through a system of classification, a way of ordering different peoples. Such classifications were a concern for cosmopolitan Europeans, and across the *History* Long referred to many peoples: Turks, Indians, Jews and Chinese. The Caribbean was a place of many crossings.[36] His priority, however, was to reduce such variations to a binary of White and Black. Moving from Whites to Blacks his chapters dealt with the governors and the governed, ending with the need for strict regulation combined with 'humane' mastery in the interests of stability. He opened with a predominantly positive representation of 'The Whites' on the island: those who he needed to believe were capable of effectively ruling the colony. This was followed by brief discussions of free Blacks and people of colour, and then his three major sections on 'Guinea Slaves', 'Creole Blacks' and 'African Negroes', an account designed to legitimate enslavement and racial difference. His intention throughout, as necessary for himself as for his readers, was to naturalize the boundaries, to make the dividing lines between these peoples – White, Brown and Black – fixed, not open to question. This meant the disavowal of all that did not fit, was not fixed, and that was all too apparent in Jamaica.

In addressing the reality of the motley population, Long had to confront all those he feared, Africans, Maroons and people of colour, who fuelled the persistent anxieties that haunted him and had made it imperative to leave Jamaica. Africans were never absent from the three volumes of the *History*, but Long worked hard to hold them in the place he designed for them. They were the object, never the subject, of his account of the governance of the island, of the plantation managed by his all-seeing eye, of the landscape magically transformed by white property owners. Occasionally an enslaved person disrupted his narration, Tacky, or a faithful and loyal unnamed 'creole'. But in describing 'the Inhabitants' he could not avoid writing directly about those whose personhood it was imperative for him to disavow. He had to theorize racial difference. Enslaved rebels, Maroons enjoying their freedom in their own lands, even free Black men working in Kingston and Spanish Town,

---

[35] [Estwick], *Considerations on the Negroe Cause*, 81–2; Ogborn, *Freedom of Speech*, 12.
[36] Julius S. Scott, *The Common Wind. Afro-American Currents in the Age of the Haitian Revolution* (London, 2018).

peopled his imagination with spectres of 'white extirpation', the nightmare scenario of the colonists. 'Mulattos' forced him to face his horror of miscegenation and its complicated effects. His text was designed to contain them all: by classifying and describing them, he aimed to lock them into his and the colonial system's authority and power. His writing, he knew, would be contested, his account of the plantation challenged. Those in favour of slavery needed him: much was at stake. He would be accountable to those friends and family members who peopled the West India lobby, increasingly finding themselves on the defensive. He must make a strong case. He minimized the dangers from the Maroons to persuade himself and others that they would not abandon the security which the treaty gave them. 'Mulattos' could, after all, be useful. His grotesque account of 'Guiney Slaves' was designed to demonstrate to his readers their savagery and difference; the 'Creole Negroes' were to provide some comfort, some hope that it would be possible to continue holding a majority population in servitude.

He wanted to construct Jamaica as an island built on a Black/White binary, a slave society in which 'Whites' were serviced by 'Negroes'. The problem with this was that there was no simple binary: there were free black people and immoral white people and growing numbers of people of colour. He drew on new theories to help him. Natural historians, scientists and law-makers, fascinated by European expansion and the 'discoveries' of 'the Americas' with their new peoples and plants, were deeply interested in classification. Bernier in 1684 had been the first to divide the world into four races. Linnaeus had included men in his initial work on plants, and in 1758 had posited that there were four categories of humans, each with their particular temperaments. Locke, a key thinker for Long, had posited the notion of humans as historical beings, and Long was a historian, writing about somewhere new, a place whose history prior to the conquest he scarcely recognized. History began with the colonists; it was about change over time: could nature be the same? Europe was different from Africa and Asia, as Voltaire had written; it was associated with civilization and progress.[37] Europe could represent 'not only civilization but harmony in diversity through the balance of power; freedom as opposed to the despotism of Asia or the slavery of Africa; and energetic activity versus passivity'.[38] Notions of a new order, a natural not biblical order, were gaining influence. 'The natural qualities of plants, animals, and humans – stripped clean of history and culture – now defined a continuous natural order that stretched seamlessly from nature to culture and back again,' writes Londa Schiebinger. 'A creature's "nature" was seen as

---

[37] Sebastiani, 'National Characters and Race'; Stock, '"Almost a separate race"'.
[38] David Bindman, *Ape to Apollo. Aesthetics and the Idea of Race in the Eighteenth Century* (London, 2002); Gikandi, *Slavery and the Culture of Taste*.

defining its rightful place in that order.'[39] And bodies, male and female, black and white, beautiful and ugly, were increasingly scrutinized for marks of difference, based in part on aesthetic criteria. But then how to place 'mulatto' bodies, and how to think about those white men who chose brown women as their 'housekeepers'?

In making his classifications, Long's primary focus was on skin colour: there were 'Whites' and 'Negroes'. How was he to deal with those in between? Not all whites were the same, and 'mulattos', 'Marons', as Long called them, freed Africans and enslaved people of many different African ethnicities were all present in Jamaica. A simple black/white, free/unfree binary was a fantasy. But he tried to hold it. He classified the different 'classes', as he named them: 'Creoles, or natives; Whites, Blacks, Indians, and their varieties; Europeans and other Whites; and imported or African Blacks'. This classification was supplemented with the recognition that the 'intermixture' of Whites, Blacks and Indians had generated different 'casts', given denomination by the Spanish who, he wrote, had created a 'kind of science'.[40] He may have hoped that he, in turn, was going to contribute to this new 'kind of science'. Jamaica, he recorded, did not follow the range of distinctions utilized by the Spanish to demarcate degrees of 'descent from the Negro Venter'. 'The laws' in the colony 'permit all, that are above three degrees removed in lineal descent from the Negro ancestor, to vote at elections, and enjoy all the privileges and immunities of his majesty's white subjects of the island.'[41] These were those individuals who could claim legal whiteness. All those of mixed heredity in Jamaica, he might have added, were called 'mulatto'.

Whites

Long's dream for Jamaica was of an ordered society with an exact scale of gradations from the lowest to the highest. In the divinely created world, he believed, we could 'perceive a regular order and gradation from inanimate to animated matter'.[42] His first 'class' were the 'native white men, or Creoles'. He had no illusions that all whites were the same. In Jamaica there were white inhabitants, recognized by their skin, to be counted as against enslaved and free blacks and mulattoes, but whites included indented servants, officers, seamen, transients, unsettled whites, able white men, resident white men, soldiers, white children and white women. Whites were divided by class, gender and ethnicity: there were 'the lower order' to be concerned about, as

---

[39] Schiebinger, *Nature's Body*, xii.
[40] Long, *History*, II. 260.
[41] Ibid., II. 261.
[42] Ibid., II. 337.

well as women, the Scots and the Irish.[43] Nevertheless, he opined, the special character of a slave society was that 'the whites are nearly on a level: and the lowest can find the way of bringing the highest to public justice for any injury or oppression'.[44] The creole colonists, those born on the island, were his first concern, for they should stand at the peak of the hierarchy. 'Although descended from British ancestors', he noted, 'they are stamped with these characteristic deviations.' The sockets of their eyes were deeper, to provide protection from the sun, their joints were supple and they possessed 'surprising agility', making them excellent dancers (unlike the English). Since the humoral body was understood as porous, climate could affect appearance. It had perhaps 'had some share in producing the variety of feature which we behold among the different societies of mankind, scattered over the globe', but, he quickly added, it could not be the cause of a change in skin complexion.[45] Long's account of 'Creoles who never have quitted the island' was generous: he needed to represent them as capable of directing the colony, though he had concerns as to the effects of creolization and the dangers it represented to the pure white English stock that he so valued. Their many excellent qualities included courage, good nature, love of freedom and sociability; they were tender fathers, indulgent masters, firm friends, and practised 'a noble and disinterested munificence'.[46] They had faults too: indolence in their affairs, bad management, an addiction to conspicuous consumption and to debt, while 'not always the most chaste and faithful of husbands'.[47] And, as he noted at many other points in the *History*, they lacked public spirit and a sense of patriotism. These were mild words in comparison with the diatribes that Long indulged in at other times, particularly about white men and their African mistresses. But it was essential to defend white creoles against the critique of the cruelty of the slave-owners made by 'Mr Sharpe' (*sic*). If excesses had happened, then it was the 'barbarians' amongst the 'British overseers' who were to blame, the 'wretches' that the mother country had 'disgorged' upon the unwitting colony.[48] White domestic servants were similarly lambasted; they were perhaps a necessary evil, but one to be avoided if possible, for 'Negroes', Long was convinced, provided much better service. A splitting between the 'lower orders' and planters was one way of dealing with the problem of unsavoury whites. Soldiers were discussed at some length. They were essential to the defence of the colony and their presence was vital if new colonists were to be

---

[43] Ibid., II. 287.
[44] Ibid., II. 431.
[45] Ibid., II. 261–2.
[46] Ibid., II. 262–3.
[47] Ibid., II. 265–6. Criticisms of the gluttony, drunkenness and sexual promiscuity of the white slave-owners became persistent in subsequent decades; Christer Petley, 'Gluttony, Excess, and the Fall of the Planter Class', *Atlantic Studies* 9.4 (2012), 85–106.
[48] Long, *History*, II. 269–70.

secured: 'Men must first believe their life and fortune tolerably secure', he wrote, 'before they will venture to settle.'[49] Soldiers should be properly housed, clothed and fed. Some might, he hoped, prove in time to be industrious residents of the new settlement he proposed.

Turning his attention to the white women, he noted that the climate encouraged an early maturity, but also an early decline. The sun resulted in a 'suffusion of red' on the faces of both men and women, but the 'genuine English breed ... untainted with heterogeneous mixtures' had white skin as pure and delicate as any in the mother country.[50] Physical distinctions from the mother country were few and the qualities of the ladies were many: they were handsome, lively, polite, affable, humane, faithful in friendship, chaste in conversation. He was hopeful that relations between the sexes were improving; there were signs of 'reformation' and 'polite intercourse'. 'In the genteeler families', conversation continued after dinner and there was greater 'temperance, urbanity and concord'.[51] With 'great reluctance', however, he had to acknowledge that the women inclined to 'listless indolence', yielding to the influence of the climate.[52] Their refusal to breastfeed their own children was particularly troubling to him, for the blood of the 'Negro' or 'Mulatto' wet nurse might be 'corrupted'.[53] And despite his strictures on the subject of white domestics, 'Negro domestics' should not be employed to look after white children. Their 'drawling, dissonant gibberish' infected the young both in language and in manners.[54] The lack of proper education for girls was shameful. He was particularly concerned about those growing up in the 'sequestered country parts' without access to urban sociability. One might see

> a very fine young woman awkwardly dangling her arms with the air of a Negro-servant, lolling almost the whole day upon beds or settees, her head muffled up with two or three handkerchiefs, her dress loose, and without stays. At noon, we find her employed in gobbling up pepper-pot, seated on the floor, with her sable hand-maids around her. In the afternoon, she takes her *siesta* as usual; while two of these damsels refresh her face with the gentle breathings of the fan; and a third provokes the drowsy powers of Morpheus by delicious scratching on the sole of either foot. When she rouzes from slumber, her speech is whining, languid, and childish.[55]

---

[49] Ibid., II. 310.
[50] Ibid., II. 274.
[51] Ibid., II. 281.
[52] Ibid., II. 280.
[53] Ibid., II. 276.
[54] Ibid., II. 278.
[55] Ibid., II. 279. In his revision of the manuscript, Long deleted this passage. BL Add MSS 12405.

Having reached maturity, the young woman would become aware of her ignorance and abscond in shame from 'the sight or conversation of every rational creature'. Her only talk would be of 'the business of the plantation, the tittle-tattle of the parish; the tricks, superstitions, diversions, and profligate discourses, of black servants, equally illiterate and unpolished'.[56] Steeped as Long was in a belief in the importance of polite conversation between the sexes as an index of civilization, the neglect, by both the parents and the legislature, of the importance of the education of white children, both boys and girls, was, as we have seen, a serious matter for him. Without proper training these girls could not grow up to be responsible wives and mothers, capable of drawing their menfolk away from the seductions of 'mulatto' beauties.

White creoles, both men and women, raised problems and unfortunately merited criticism which he tried to minimize. For Knight, too, creolization had provoked concerns about degeneracy, that notion that what had once been pure had become degraded. What had happened to Englishness? Could these creole men really rule a colony? Where was their public spirit? When would they learn to control their passions? Planter society was dangerously lacking in moral fibre, too addicted to pleasure. For Jamaica to be the place he wanted it to be, important changes were necessary. What was more, the white population must increase. Until men married and had white children who could be educated to take a proper place in an established racial hierarchy, the island would not be a stable place.

When it came to the Scots and the Irish, Long thought that, as migrants, they did better than the English. They often had patrons and family connections who helped them on their way. The north Britons who came in search of fortune were prudent and clever, and made 'their way through every obstacle'. The English, unfortunately, tended to resemble 'the blind goddess Fortune', scattering their favours to all in their way.[57] The only distinctions that ought to operate on the island, he opined, were between good and bad citizens, an identity only open to white men. When it came to 'the lower order of white people', the artisans and servants, he had praise once more for the north Britons but contempt for many others, whether bricklayers who scarcely knew a brick or bookkeepers who could neither read nor write.[58] Improvement was sorely needed.

The Jewish presence on the island, centred in Spanish Town and Kingston, concerned him. Members of a 'nation' in his opinion, they had settled in the very early days, attracted both by trade and by the relative lenience of the government on matters of religion. He had to admit that 'these people have

---

[56] Long, *History*, II. 279.
[57] Ibid., II. 287.
[58] Ibid., II. 287–9.

shewn themselves very good and useful subjects upon many occasions'.[59] They were allowed to practise their religion and own property, and were required to bear arms in the militia in the expectation that they would protect white power against internal and external enemies. All of this gave them a permanent stake in the colony. The 'chief men' he deemed 'very worthy persons' who should not be blamed for the 'vices and villainies of the lower rabble'. It was 'the rabble' who fuelled his antisemitic comments. They were 'selfish and tricking, fraudulent in their trade and rigid in their transactions', known for their 'rascally tricks' and for having avoided militia service in 1760 on spurious religious grounds.[60] Class figured significantly for Long: his notion of an exact scale of gradations encompassed a ladder with many rungs, very few of which were occupied satisfactorily in his estimation. His judgement as to whether these gradations could be fixed or altered was unstable.

Free Blacks and 'Mulattos'

Varieties of whiteness represented a problem, but in a colony in which white meant freedom and black signified subjection, how were free blacks and 'mulattos' to be boundaried and contained? What threats did they represent? How serious was the presence of propertied people of colour? How deep a cause of concern was the weakness of marriage and the scale of concubinage? For Long, sitting in Chichester writing his *History*, how could he represent the sexual economy of this tropical colony, such a different kind of place from England? How could he describe the motley population in a way that would represent it as providing a basis for a successful society, one that should be defended and protected by the mother country?

His commentary on 'Freed Blacks' was extremely limited. He identified three 'classes'. There were those who had been manumitted but were still subject to the slave courts, 'for they were not supposed to have acquired any sense of morality by the mere act of manumission', nor could they vote in elections.[61] Morality, he believed, resided in the white body: freedom would not give black men a moral sense. Those who were free-born were allowed some limited rights in the courts, while those few who had been granted legal whiteness possessed significant privileges. None of these groups, however, was numerically significant enough for him to consider writing about them at length. Francis Williams, however, an 'uppity' and English-educated free black man, represented a serious antagonist whose presence in Spanish Town must have been a severe provocation for him. He devoted an entire chapter to an attempted demolition of him.

[59] Ibid., II. 294.
[60] Ibid., II. 18, 293, 459.
[61] Ibid., II. 320.

The 'mulattos', as we have seen, evoked deep ambivalence. Long was repulsed by miscegenation, by the mixing of blood and the 'tainting', as he understood it, of white purity. Such practices were intolerable in England where the idea of a 'numerous race of walnut-coloured beings, by way of foil to the complexion of her genuine breed', was horrific to him.[62] Jamaica, however was a different matter, since potentially they could provide not only a middle stratum between the colonists and the enslaved, but also, if armed, a counterweight to the Maroons, 'whose insolence, during formidable insurrections has been most insufferable'.[63] The growing population of those described as 'mulatto', the Spanish term which was widely utilized in eighteenth-century Jamaica, was troubling. Persons of colour were increasing fast. Between the 1730s and 1770s their numbers had nearly quadrupled and people of African descent were nearly one-third of the free population.[64] In 1764 Long estimated that there were 3,408 such persons across the three counties. By 1774 he thought the figure might have risen to 3,700.[65] A large majority were in Kingston and Spanish Town, where their presence would have been familiar to him. He paid little attention to the free women of colour, black or 'mulatto', the schoolmistresses, midwives and widows living alongside the hoteliers and brothel-keepers with their thriving urban businesses. They did not fit neatly into his classifications; free women who were economically active in the market were disturbing to his masculinist assumptions. A proportion of the enslaved on Lucky Valley would certainly have been 'mulatto', some probably serving as 'House Negroes'. The increase in the population of colour (including free and freed blacks and 'mulattos') made an uncomfortable contrast with the failure of the white population to reproduce itself. Eighty per cent of the children of white fathers and enslaved mothers inherited their servitude from their mothers. Only a minority were freed by their fathers, while an even smaller number were fully recognized.[66] But those who were free might have to be reckoned with.

A 'mulatto', Long explained to his readers, utilizing their 'proper denomination, invented by the Spanish', was the child of a White man and a Negro woman. The child of a White man and a Mulatta was a Terceron, the child of a White man and a Terceron was a Quateron, the child of a White man and a Quateron was a Quinteron, and the child of a Quinteron with a White Man was deemed to be White.[67] Following a challenge in 1733 from a prominent

---

[62] Ibid., III. 936 Appendix.
[63] Ibid., II. 334.
[64] Walker, *Jamaica Ladies*, 288.
[65] Long, *History*, II. 337. The white population in 1774 is estimated at 15,300 and the free people of mixed race at 4,093, while there were 192,787 enslaved persons; Livesay, *Children of Uncertain Fortune*, 24, table.
[66] Livesay, *Children of Uncertain Fortune*, 3.
[67] Long, *History*, II. 260.

free planter of colour, John Golding, as to his right to vote, it had been determined that 'anyone with less than one-eighth African ancestry was no longer mulatto'.[68] It was possible to become white in the eyes of the law if the line of descent was sufficiently elongated. 'Genealogical definitions of whiteness which defined white status through the absence or gradual diminution of African or Indian blood', as Brooke Newman explains, 'allowed for the possibility of white racial regeneration, a gradual whitening of the population through mixture over several successive generations.'[69] The Jamaican law permitted, as Long put it, in a slight deviation from the Spanish system, all 'that are above three degrees removed in lineal descent from the Negro ancestor, to vote at elections, and enjoy all the privileges and immunities of his majesty's white subjects of the island.' 'Corrupted blood' could be sufficiently diluted to whiten those three degrees removed from 'the Negroe Venter'.[70]

This mixed-race population – an inevitability given the sexual economy of colonial Jamaica with its marked preponderance of white men with power – produced deeply ambivalent responses from the eighteenth-century colonial state.[71] Anxieties about demographic imbalance motivated experiments in empowering mixed-race elites in the period after 1733. It was possible for individuals to submit 'privilege petitions', as we have seen, and claim legal whiteness given sufficient wealth and what were seen as appropriate civilizational standards. This permitted whitening was designed to facilitate alliances between elite men and women of mixed race and white colonists, providing a class bulwark for white domination against 'intestine' enemies. At times of political tension and crisis, however, the colonists attempted to harden racial boundaries as they did in 1761 in the wake of the rebellion.[72] The two strategies could be simultaneous, fuelled as they were by contradictory needs. Long shared this ambivalence: anxieties as to the failure of the white population to reproduce itself or grow sufficiently through migration underpinned the decision to allow legal whitening. But the spectacle of the growth of the free population of colour, which might eventually outnumber the whites, was deeply alarming. Long was both horrified by the ever-growing evidence of miscegenation, convinced that 'corrupted blood' could never be fully washed out, while at the same time hoping that 'freed blacks' and 'mulattos' could eventually form a useful population and act as a buffer between black and

---

[68] Livesay, *Children of Uncertain Fortune*, 38.
[69] Newman, *A Dark Inheritance*, 16.
[70] Long, *History*, II. 260-1.
[71] On the contested legal position of free black persons, see Ogborn, *Freedom of Speech*.
[72] Livesay, *Children of Uncertain Fortune*; Newman, *A Dark Inheritance*; Newman, 'Gender, Sexuality and the Formation of Racial Identities'; Gad Heuman's *Between Black and White. Race, Politics and the Free Coloreds in Jamaica, 1792-1865* (Westport, CT, 1981) is the text which originally studied the population of colour in Jamaica.

white. The scale of miscegenation, however, was 'a potent symbol of white Jamaica's lack of control': he would do what he could to counter it.[73]

Long's discussion of 'mulattos' in the *History* was not concerned with those illegitimate children of well-do-do men who were brought to the metropole and provided for. Alderman Beckford, for example, at the time of his marriage in 1756, had at least eight such children, birthed by three different mothers, who were cared for and accepted by his wife.[74] Long's idea of what was acceptable was very different. Nor did he concern himself with the successful businesswomen, retailers, hoteliers and brothel-keepers who were an important presence in the towns.[75] He began his account with the Act of 1761 which attempted to limit the inheritance of illegitimate mixed-race descendants. This legislation was a response to the events of 1760, as we have seen, for colonists were convinced the rebellion was facilitated by the instability of clear lines of power and racial demarcation. Having entered the assembly in November 1761, Long was involved in the debates. The proposed legislation was initially challenged in the metropole, for it threatened to undermine the sacred rights of men to freely dispose of their property. Long responded vigorously: a slave-holding society required different laws from those of England. He strenuously defended the need for special laws of inheritance on the island to prevent real estate passing into what he described as 'such hands'.[76] Jamaica was not like England: it required more circumscribed laws of inheritance than England, the home of 'rational freedom'.[77] His tone was that of the horrified moralist, the responsible family man who had no truck with the unbounded passions and loose morals of too many colonists, those men who chose bachelorhood with its many possibilities of illicit intimacies. Lady Nugent famously remarked in relation to Simon Taylor, that he had 'a numerous family, some almost on every one of his estates'.[78]

Long was unusual in his denunciations of the practices of his fellow colonists. He preferred to keep at a distance the exercises of power of men such as

---

[73] Daniel Livesay, 'The Decline of Jamaica's Interracial Households and the Fall of the Planter Class, 1733–1823', *Atlantic Studies* 9.1 (2012), 108.
[74] Gauci, *William Beckford*.
[75] See, for example, Linda L. Sturtz, 'Mary Rose: "White" African Jamaican Woman? Race and Gender in Eighteenth Century Jamaica', in Judith A. Byfield, LaRay Denzer and Anthea Morrison (eds.), *Gendering the African Diaspora. Women, Culture, and Historical Change in the Caribbean and Nigerian Hinterland* (Bloomington, IN, 2010), 59–87; Walker, *Jamaica Ladies*.
[76] Long, *History*, II. 323.
[77] Ibid., II. 401.
[78] Philip Wright (ed.), *Lady Nugent's Journal of her Residence in Jamaica from 1801–1805* (Kingston, Jamaica, 2002), 68; Christer Petley, '"Home" and "This Country": Britishness and Creole Identity in the Letters of a Transatlantic Slaveholder', *Atlantic Studies* 6.1 (2009), 43–61.

Thomas Thistlewood, the rapes and 'acts of sexual terror'.[79] He never acknowledged, as we have seen, his brother Robert's illegitimate daughter. Rather than facing the everyday realities of interracial sex with its roots in violence, he moved swiftly to questions of blame. Thistlewood simply recorded, apparently devoid of moral sense; Long, as Toni Morrison notes, was engaged in justification.[80] The problem was the men's lack of self-control, he maintained, alongside a widespread acceptance of concubinage, the ubiquitous 'housekeepers' of white colonists. It was their fault too, and he denounced them as 'common prostitutes'.[81] Denigrating them in this way was another strategy for avoiding thinking of the violence at the heart of these relations. He appreciated the clause in the *Code Noir* which condemned illegitimacy and stipulated that free men who had illegitimate children with enslaved concubines should be fined. Furthermore, if the man was not married and he then married the slave, both the woman and child should be free. This, Long noted, meant that in the French colonies, 'the institution of marriage is wisely promoted; and the chastity of female slaves, in some measure, guarded against that violence and constraint which may be supposed to follow the absolute power and authority of their masters'.[82] This was a rare moment of recognition from him of what that 'absolute power and authority' meant for enslaved women. The institution of marriage was the bedrock of a good society in Long's view, one of its 'main links' and supports. In England, he maintained, it was understood that 'promiscuous intercourse' and 'uncertain parentage' would soon 'dissolve the frame of the constitution, from the infinity of claims and contested rights of succession'.[83] To have an illegitimate child was therefore seen as a punishable violation. He was clearly not entirely convinced, however, that a proper moral sense was adequately embraced in England and expressed his concerns in his *Sentimental Exhibition*, a very different text from the *History*, intended entirely for a domestic audience.

When it came to Jamaica's unfortunate illicit practices, all were to blame. The men claimed that it was 'the heavy and intolerable expenses' that it would incur that prevented them from marrying. As a result, they engaged in 'disorderly connexions', with resulting miseries. They became 'infatuated' with 'black women'. They lost, Long implied, their proper sense of themselves and were unmanned by their passion for a black woman, becoming 'the abject, passive slave to all her insults, thefts and infidelities'. And slavery of this order was a wretchedly unEnglish condition, something that disgusted Long. Not

---

[79] Douglas Hall notes that Thistlewood's conduct appears to be typical; *In Miserable Slavery*, xvii; Burnard, *Mastery, Tyranny, and Desire*; Vermeulen, 'Thomas Thistlewood's Libidinal Linnean Project', 29.
[80] Morrison, *The Origin*.
[81] Long, *History*, II. 327.
[82] Ibid., III. 924 Appendix.
[83] Ibid., II. 325.

only did such irresponsible men, blind to their social and political duties, 'lavish their fortune with unbounded liberality' on those Long defined as common prostitutes; what was more, these unthinking men might 'disperse' their estates between their paramour 'and her brats' when there was not even a guarantee that they were the father.[84] 'The offspring of promiscuous conjunctions has no father,' Long insisted in a footnote; 'Marriage ascertains the father.'[85] This absence of the father provided a justification for the 'old civil rule ... of "partus sequitur ventrem"', since enslaved women were unmarried: her master must take on that responsibility.[86] In rhetorical mode he posed an enraged question, 'whether ... it would be more for the interest of Britain, that Jamaica should be possessed and peopled by white inhabitants, or by Negroes and Mulattos?' His answer spoke to his visceral fears of blood-mixing:

> Let any man turn his eyes to the Spanish American dominions, and behold what a vicious, brutal, and degenerate breed of mongrels has been there produced, between Spaniards, Blacks, Indians, and their mixed progeny; he must be of opinion, that it might be much better for Britain, and Jamaica too, if the white men in that colony would abate of their infatuated attachments to black women, and instead of being 'grac'd with a *yellow offspring not their own*' perform the duty incumbent on every good citizen, by raising in honourable wedlock a race of unadulterated beings.[87]

His reference to '*yellow offspring not their own*' was to Virgil's *Aeneid*, a claim for classical legitimation for his racialized slur.[88] The effect of such conduct was 'a vast addition of spurious offsprings of different complexions'. The absence of restraint on the passions which characterized tropical Jamaica seduced European men, loosening their manners and encouraging them to 'every kind of sensual delight'. They looked for 'some black or yellow *quasheba* ... by whom a tawny breed is produced ... a tarnished train of beings'. Resorting to animalizing metaphors in his outpouring of venom, Long maintained that many men would 'much rather riot in these goatish embraces, than share the pure and lawful bliss derived from matrimonial, mutual love'. Modesty, he concluded regretfully, 'has but very little footing here' and those on the island who disapproved of fornication were seen as simpletons.[89] His sense of revulsion at this 'yellow brood' was given full flow in his description of the fathers who sent their mixed-race children to England to be educated for

---

[84] Ibid., II. 327.
[85] Ibid., II. 326 fn.
[86] Ibid., III. 925.
[87] Ibid., II. 327.
[88] Ibid., II. 327 fn.
[89] Ibid., II. 328; Trevor Burnard, '"Rioting in Goatish Embraces": Marriage and Improvement in Early British Jamaica', *History of the Family* 11.4 (2006), 185–98.

a civilized society, only to have such offspring faint on their return to Jamaica at the sight of their blood relations. Miss Fulvia recoiled in horror when her father told her that 'black *Quasheba* is her own mother'.[90]

The best way of luring men away from such connections, he thought, would be to improve the education of white women, making them more attractive and agreeable, better companions, trustier and more faithful than any African woman would be. White men's desire could be blamed on the women. Long's depiction of the African or 'mulatta' mistress was vicious. White colonists were weak, open to seduction. Black women were full of wiles, positively evil. Her kin, and indeed her other lovers, he opined, fastened on her white 'keeper like so many leeches'. They bled him dry, almost to madness. She revelled in her deception of him, her pretended admiration for his beauty, her jealous love for him. She enacted paroxysms of 'outrageous sorrow' at his death, while at the same time 'she had rummaged his pockets ... concealed his watch, rings and money in the feather-bed upon which the poor wretch had just breathed his last'. 'Such is the mirror', Long believed, 'of almost all these conjunctions of white and black! Two tinctures which nature has dissociated, like oil and vinegar.'[91]

Nevertheless, no sooner had he pronounced this damning verdict on any 'conjunction' between white and black than he was impelled to backtrack. There were political reasons to think that 'such alliances' might be useful. 'No freed or unfreed mulatto ever wished to relapse into the Negro': their yellow skin marked their status. The 'pride of amended blood is universal', Long noted; to call anyone 'by a degree inferior to what they really are' was 'the highest affront'.[92] What was more, he himself believed that corrupted blood would remain corrupted. A moral sense was born in white men; it went with their blood and their skin. 'Mulattos' would be so anxious to keep their distance from those blacker than themselves that it was unclear whether a 'middle class' could increase stability. The most prosperous withdrew to England; those in the middling rank 'are not much liked by the Negroes', who hated the idea of being slaves to the descendants of slaves, and those of the lowest rank were in no way superior to the Africans. However, the 'lower class' of these mixtures were 'a hardy race'. In his imagination they could form, he opined, 'the centre of connexion between the two extremes, producing a regular establishment of three ranks of men, dependent on each other, and rising in a proper climax of subordination, in which the Whites would hold the highest place'.[93] Here was his vision of a harmonious society, one of gradation

---

[90] Long, *History*, II. 328–9. Livesay's *Children of Uncertain Fortune* follows the changing fortunes of these mixed-race children sent to England and Scotland as attitudes hardened in the later eighteenth and early nineteenth century.
[91] Long, *History*, II. 332.
[92] Ibid.
[93] Ibid., II. 333.

and order, as designed by divine providence; the picture of a society 'drenched in violence', in which rape was an integral part, was totally disavowed.[94] The best strategy for the future would be to bind these children to their white betters. He could see 'no mischief' in enfranchising 'every Mulatto child'. Long understood that the law could only control certain aspects of sexual behaviour. Since men would continue to gratify their passions, it would make sense to 'turn unavoidable evils to the benefit of society'; this would be 'the best reparation that can be made for this breach of its moral and political institutions'.[95] The colonial state should accept its responsibilities and educate the boys in Christian morals, apprentice them to tradespeople and artisans, train them to be 'orderly subjects and defenders of the country'. Colonists could be encouraged to invest in this way by payments from the legislature. The child could be schooled at the expense of the colony, apprenticed for four years and be paid to engage in public works, or serve in the militia, on the same rates as the Maroons. They would provide 'a corps of active men', better able to operate in the woods and mountains in search of runaways and rebels than were the regular soldiers, a most useful counterweight to the Maroons.[96]

Since, in Long's eyes, 'Mulattos ... partake more of the white than the black', they had good qualities, being lively, sensible and capable of kindness, though simultaneously, he judged, lascivious, vain and irascible. In his opinion, when they intermarried, their 'matches' were generally 'defective and barren': 'They seem in this respect to be actually of the mule-kind, and not so capable of producing from one another as from a commerce with a distinct White or Black.'[97] Here he was registering his disagreement with Buffon, who, he claimed, saw nothing strange in two individuals being unable to propagate, for there could be 'some slight opposition in their temperaments' or defects in genital organs. 'If the negro and the white could not reproduce together', Buffon had written, 'if even their offspring remained infertile, if the mulatto were truly a mule, there would be then two well distinct species: the Negro would be to man what the donkey is to a horse; or rather, if the white was a man, the Negro would no longer be a man; he would be a distinct animal, like the ape.' Then, Buffon continued, 'we would be entitled to think *that the white and the Negro would not have a common origin*' (my emphasis). This was Long's proposition, precisely what he thought, on the basis of his Jamaican experience: the White and the 'Negro' did *not* have a common origin. 'But even this supposition is given lie to by fact,' Buffon elaborated, 'and since all men can communicate and

---

[94] Patterson, 'Life and Scholarship', xix.
[95] Long, *History*, II. 333.
[96] Ibid., II. 334.
[97] Ibid., II. 407, 335.

reproduce together, all men come from the same stock and are of the same family.'[98]

Long's insistence that the unions of two 'mulattos' were either barren or the children failed to grow to maturity provided evidence for him that Buffon was wrong. It is hard to understand how he manged to maintain this fiction and deny the realities all around him. The psychic energy involved must have been profound. 'The White and the Negro', he insisted, 'had not one common origin.' Indeed, he was convinced,

> there are extremely potent reasons for believing, that the White and the Negroe are two distinct species . . . It is certain, that this idea enables us to account for those diversities of feature, skin, and intellect, observable among mankind; which cannot be accounted for in any other way, without running into a thousand absurdities.[99]

Long, beset with anxieties about the failure of both the white and the enslaved populations to reproduce themselves and horrified at the exponential growth of the population of colour, tried to persuade himself that 'mulattos' could not 'breed' and that White and 'Negroe' were 'distinct species', while looking to those same children as potential loyal and industrious subjects of the colony. He knew that sheep needed to crossbreed, for 'otherwise they degenerate'.[100] But he chose not to apply this thinking to people: were humans different from animals? He could not square the circle of his thinking.

'Marons'

If Maroons, or 'Marons', a fourth and very significant group of free Blacks, were at times 'insufferable' on account of their 'insolence', they were also essential to the security of the island, as 1760 had conclusively demonstrated. Long was as ambivalent towards the Maroons as he was to 'mulattos', their 'in-betweenness' was, for him, a terrible provocation. There is no evidence that he had any direct knowledge of them, though at one point he claimed to have met Cudjoe. He had no eyewitness authority and had to rely on the words of others. Their origins on the island went back to the days of the English conquest when Africans attached to the Spanish, some free and others enslaved, had escaped into the mountains, venturing out from their hideouts to harass the English soldiers. Major-General Sedgewick's prophecy that 'these Blacks would prove thorns in our sides' proved all too correct.[101] In 1693, their numbers increased and they commenced more open hostilities. By 1730 they were 'so formidable'

---

[98] Leclerc, comte de Buffon, *Histoire naturelle*, IV. 388–9. Thanks to Silvia Sebastiani for this citation.
[99] Long, *History*, II. 335–6.
[100] Ibid., III. 865.
[101] Ibid., II. 338.

that two regiments of regular troops were brought in to defeat them. The enemy's 'dastardly method of conducting the war', however, meant that they avoided 'pitched battle', murdered under cover of darkness and concealed themselves in the many 'secret avenues' that they knew made them invincible.[102] The assembly resolved to build a series of fortified barracks, with strong garrisons, near enemy strongholds, and this, plus a force of Mosquito Indians, was a somewhat more successful strategy.

By 1739 both sides were weary of conflict and a treaty was concluded. For Knight, living in the shadow of this war, they were always 'Rebellious Negroes', an 'intestine Enemy, who threatened no less than the extirpation of the White Inhabitants',[103] a danger from which the island was only saved by the treaty. Their leaders, including Cudjoe, secured the Maroons in possession of land and the right to cultivate it, and they were confirmed in 'that full enjoyment of freedom for which they had so long and obstinately contended'.[104] The treaty, marking 'the first successful revolt of the enslaved in history' in Orlando Patterson's view, was a major concession.[105] The Maroons carried the status of black British subjects and owned land and the right to cultivate it, with limitations. Their notion of land-ownership, however, was very different from that of the colonists: land was not an economic asset to be bought and sold; rather, it was their place of belonging, the source of their subsistence. The British thought the Maroons comfortably contained and pacified. The Maroons saw it differently: they had won partial sovereignty. This free black population formed two separate communities in different parts of the island, 'leeward' and 'windward', and 'provided a constant reminder for all that to be black and to be enslaved were not synonymous'.[106] In return they would assist the colonial authorities in the suppression of rebels or foreign enemies and would be paid for bringing in runaways. If injured by a white person, they should seek redress from a magistrate. Their leaders dealt with crime within their own communities and were expected to 'wait on the governor once a year if required' to demonstrate their continued loyalty. They were not permitted to purchase 'slaves' or grow sugar. Two white men were to 'constantly reside with Cudjoe and his successors, to keep up friendly correspondence'.[107]

Long's judgement of the Maroons was laced with a combination of patronage and repressed fear. 'They have been very serviceable,' particularly those in the leewards, 'in suppressing several insurrections' and such 'service', he believed, was easily repaid. The governors would present them with some

---

[102] Ibid., II. 341.
[103] Knight, *History*, II. 510. His hope was that they would not remain separate; rather they would in time become 'one People'.
[104] Long, *History*, I. 124.
[105] Patterson, 'Life and Scholarship', xliv. Patterson was devastated by their later betrayal, particularly in 1865.
[106] Ogborn, *Freedom of Speech*, 25.
[107] Long, *History*, II. 345.

'trifling douceur' when they met, 'an old laced coat or waistcoat', hat or sword, which appeared, he thought, to win their hearts and strengthen 'their dutiful attachment'.[108] The bond would be increased, he believed, if they were to receive some moral instruction, for there was always the question, could they be trusted? Would they be capable of moral instruction? They were, after all, Africans. The effects of the treaty, however, had been good: lands had been opened up, bringing opportunities for new settlers, and the island was 'increasing in plantations and opulence'. Long could not resolve his ambivalence, however, as witnessed in his description of their 'singular ... manner of engaging with an enemy'.[109] Governor Lyttelton's tour of St James in 1764 had occasioned a ceremonial encounter with the Trelawny Maroons, who arrived in force with their women and children. This was the only point at which Long recognized the existence of Maroon peoples as living in communities, for the existence of these established settlements in the midst of a plantation society was disturbing. He confined his attention to the fighting men, the 'wild Negroes' as they were called in the early days. In so far as he acknowledged any womanly presence, it would have corroborated his view that they were treated as 'drudges', doing the work that the men would not do.[110] The Maroons used the occasion of the governor's tour to demonstrate their martial and masculine skills: an affirmation of firepower accompanied by 'hideous yells', 'war-hoops', 'wild and warlike capers', looks of 'savage fury'. This was combined with a declaration of loyalty to King George from Captain Cudjoe, and a laying of their weapons at the feet of the governor. Long tried to banish his fear of them with his animalizing depiction of their skipping about 'like so many monkies', flourishing their 'rusty blades' and being dismissed 'perfectly well satisfied' after a dinner ordered for them and 'a present of three cows'.[111] 'Maroon performances of difference', Kathleen Wilson writes, 'crystallized and destabilized the strategies of class, caste, and race in the Jamaican plantation complex, bringing together playful forms of violence and deadly serious forms of play that could cast the assumptions of planter society into question.'[112] Maroons were essential to the island's security, but a potential threat to white power.

Long wanted to believe in the stability of the treaty. In his account of the uprising in St Mary in 1765, he attempted to dispel the anxiety, raised by some of those under interrogation and torture, that Maroons, 'disgusted at the little respect shewn them', were involved in the conspiracy.[113] The plan, it was alleged, was to divide the country between them and the Coromantees. The

---

[108] Ibid., II. 347.
[109] Ibid., II. 348.
[110] For a discussion of women and marronage, see Morgan, *Reckoning with Slavery*, 228–37.
[111] Long, *History*, II. 348–9.
[112] Wilson, 'The Performance of Freedom', 49.
[113] Leigh and Sorrell, 'How to Control the History of a Slave Rebellion'.

Maroons would have the 'woody and uncultivated parts, as being most convenient for their hog-hunting'. The 'white people' would give no credit to such a notion, thought Long. The Maroons had always been the allies of the colonists. They had been properly encouraged; they would not risk their lives and liberty in collaboration with such a 'dangerous set of confederates' who would greatly outnumber them.[114] Possibly, he surmised, if there was any truth to this story, the Maroons might have had their own plot, thinking that they could benefit from such a rebellion by supporting the authorities as they had done in 1760. It was too alarming for Long to consider that they might have seriously thought of abandoning their treaty obligations which secured the stability of the island. Unfortunately, Maroons were necessary. They were a special category, different from 'Negroes', their black skin overlooked in the interests of their skills in 'bush-fighting'. But there was always a lurking suspicion. Splitting the subjected and privileging some was a key strategy for empire builders, but it could go wrong. Long had left the island by the time of the next Maroon war in the early 1790s, and no record of his reaction to what he would have seen as their 'betrayal' has survived.

'Negroes'

Long placed his discussion of 'Negroes', which included his engagement with the Enlightenment debates, as a new book, with separate sections devoted to the classifications he sought to secure.

'Guiney Africans'

While recognizing distinctions between Africans in Africa and those of African descent on the island, Long frequently slipped back into insisting on their uniformity, demonstrated, he thought, by their bodies and minds. In addition to the 'free Blacks' and 'Marons', there were 'Guiney Africans' and two categories of 'Negroes', the term he utilized for the enslaved, namely 'the native, or Creole blacks, and the imported, or Africans', a distinction that was crucial for his account of a future for Jamaica.[115] By naming those born on the island 'Creole', he was distancing them in his mind from Africa and pointing attention to the changes that resulted from the place of their birth. First, however, he introduced his readers to 'Negroes in general, found on that part of the African continent, called Guiney, or Negro-land'. He utilized comparative analysis to explicate what he saw as their key characteristics, their physical and cognitive specificities, marking them as different from Europeans. The point in which 'they differ *most essentially* from the Whites' (my italics) was 'in respect to their bodies, viz. the dark membrane which

---

[114] Long, *History*, II. 469.
[115] Ibid., II. 351.

communicates that black colour to their skins, which does not alter by transportation into other climates, and which they never lose'.[116] It was bodies, and most of all, black skin and the membrane beneath it, which came first. A fascination with the colour of skin dated from the seventeenth century: Robert Boyle, for example, had examined 'The nature of Whiteness and Blackness'.[117] As the European slavery business gathered pace in the eighteenth century, the 'prodigious enigma' of blackness was preoccupying essayists, theologians, natural historians and anatomists.[118] Whiteness provided the norm. What caused blackness? And what did it signify? When and why had 'degeneration' begun? In 1741 the Bordeaux Academy of Sciences had chosen for their annual prize essay topic, 'What is the physical cause of the Negro's color, the quality of [the Negro's] hair, and the degeneration of both [Negro hair and skin]?'[119] They had received sixteen essays in response, from theologians, natural historians and anatomists. Skin colour was particularly fascinating, exercising the skills of artists in their efforts to represent it and anatomists in their efforts to locate its sources inside the body. It was 'anatomy', argues Andrew Curran, that 'produced the most authoritative statements regarding the particularities of the black African body' and located blackness on the *inside* rather than the *outside*.[120] Explanations based on the surface of the skin were associated with climate and environment; anatomists, on the other hand, claimed their explanations were rooted in the blood and bile of the black body.[121] Long cited Winslow, who believed that it was dissection that revealed the truth of the layering of skin, and Pierre Barrère, a French doctor who had spent three years in Cayenne serving as the king's botanist and performing anatomies on the bodies of enslaved Africans.[122] 'Their bile is always as black as ink ... their blood is blackish red,' he had written in an essay published in 1741; 'the epidermis on the outer skin of the Negro derives its black color distinctly from its own tissue'.[123] This was music to Long's ears, for it confirmed his conviction that the Ethiopian could not change his skin and that their 'corrupted' blood legitimated enslavement. It was essential to challenge those who followed Montesquieu in seeing climate and environment as key to

---

[116] Ibid., II. 351–2.
[117] Esther Chadwick, '"This deepe and perfect glosse of Blacknesse": Colour, Colonialism and *The Paston Treasure's* Period Eye', in Andrew Moore, Nathan Flis and Francesca Vanke (eds.), *The Paston Treasure. Microcosm of the Known World* (London, 2018), 102–9.
[118] The phrase is that of the anatomist Barrère quoted in Gates and Curran, *Who's Black and Why?*, 190.
[119] Ibid., 1.
[120] Mechthild Fend, *Fleshing out Surfaces. Skin in French Art and Medicine* (Manchester, 2017); Curran, *Anatomy of Blackness*, 4.
[121] Curran, *Anatomy of Blackness*.
[122] Long, *History*, II. 351 fn.
[123] Gates and Curran, *Who's Black and Why?*, 190.

skin colour, and the most influential voice was that of Buffon, the natural historian whom Long hoped to undermine in his *History*. 'This black colour of Negroes', Buffon maintained, 'if they were translated into a cold climate, would gradually wear off and disappear in the course of ten or twelve generations.' Long disputed this. Europeans living in the hottest parts of the West Indies were not becoming black and Ethiopians were not blacker now than in the days of Solomon. 'Let us be content', he wrote, 'with acknowledging, that it was just as easy for Omnipotence to create black-skinned, as white-skinned men.'[124] Difference was rooted in the internal substances of the body as well as being located on the surface of the skin: it was doubly inscribed. 'Negroes', he insisted, 'or their posterity, do not change colour, though they continue ever so long in a cold climate.' Yet his assertion was not quite as secure in his mind as it might seem. Indeed, he had noted the change in the eye sockets of white creoles as a result of living in the tropics, while quickly assuring himself that no 'change of complexion' would occur. If Englishmen were to live in Guiney, there would be no exchange of 'hair for wool, or a white cuticle for a black'.[125] He wanted to be sure as to the permanence of skin colour and that what was external carried the internal traits, but the visible effects of miscegenation disturbed any such certainty. The growing number of 'bronzed' persons in London were a troubling fact.

In his account of 'Guiney Africans', Long drew on a range of intensely hostile travellers' tales and allowed his racism full play, with stereotyped caricatures of cannibalism and bestiality. His 'fabrication of an Africanist persona' allowed him to situate savagery 'out there' and not in the coercive power of the slave-owners.[126] To depict African 'savagery' was necessary, for it enabled him to counterpose it to the 'civilization' that he wanted to associate with the plantation. Despite the vast continent of Africa, he was sure that there was a 'general uniformity' across regions and peoples.[127] Africans shared black skin, together with '[a] covering of wool, like the bestial fleece, instead of hair'. He remarked on their 'round eyes', 'tumid nostrils, flat noses, invariable thick lips', and the large size of 'female nipples'. Large black lice infested their bodies. They all had a 'bestial or fetid smell' to a greater or lesser extent. As to the 'faculties of their minds', they had remained 'in the same rude situation' for at least two thousand years. They were incapable of progress in 'civility or science', possessed no system of morality, no taste 'but for women', gluttony, drink and idleness, were barbarous to their children, 'their nature below even that of brutes'. 'They are everywhere degenerated into a brutish ... and superstitious people.' Their houses were miserable, their country

---

[124] Long, *History*, II. 351–2 fn.
[125] Ibid., II. 262.
[126] Morrison, *Playing in the Dark*, 18.
[127] Long, *History*, II. 353.

a wilderness. 'They are represented', he wrote', 'by all authors as the vilest of the human kind, to which they have little more pretension or resemblance than what arises from their exterior form.'[128] Long created a chain of equivalences linking skin colour, hair, facial features, mind and lack of civilization: any one of these could 'become the signifier for the other'.[129] He pooh-poohed any idea of former glories, for Greek and Roman authors had despised them as 'odious, despicable, savage'. He wished that such ugly descriptions were exaggerated, but the 'consistent testimony' of so many men who had visited the coast corroborated the accounts.

Furthermore, Long claimed, these representations 'tally exactly with the character of the Africans who are brought into our plantations'. When first imported into the island they were 'wild and savage to an extreme ... intractable and ferocious', requiring 'a rod of iron'. It was not clear, he pondered, 'why this race of men were so degraded'. Perhaps it was because the early English settlers were following the established practices of the 'Portugueze and other nations'. But '[P]erhaps', on the other hand, it was because

> the *depravity of their nature, much more than their colour* gave rise to a belief of their inferiority of intellect; and it became an established principle to treat those as brute beasts, who had so little pretensions to claim kindred with the human race, except in the shape of their bodies, and their walking upon two legs instead of four.[130]

Here was his dilemma: was it nature, or history, or the body, or the mind which condemned Africans to subjection? Or was it all of them? His repetition of 'brute' and 'brutish' evoked a particular connotation. Animals were brutes. 'Brute' facts were those which could be 'observed in the world, they were exterior to the human', associated with nature; '"Brute"', argues Amitav Ghosh, 'evolved into a trans-species term.'[131] Both Hobbes and Locke used the term 'brute' to refer to humans in a state of nature, the '*wild men*' associated by Indians, as Long wrote, with the orangutan.[132] The 'Yahoos' of Swift's construction in *Gulliver's Travels*, the awful, ugly, greedy, disgusting, filthy creatures that Gulliver encountered, were certainly brutes. 'My horror and astonishment are not to be described, when I observed in this abominable animal a perfect human form.'[133] Yet they were terrifyingly close in form to

---

[128] Ibid., II. 352–3.
[129] Wheeler, *The Complexion of Race*, 213; Hall, *Fateful Triangle*, argues that it is the chain of equivalences between nature and culture that enables race to function discursively as a system of representation; 57.
[130] Long, *History*, II. 497; my italics.
[131] Amitav Ghosh, *The Nutmeg's Curse. Parables for a Planet in Crisis* (London, 2022), 187.
[132] Long, *History*, II. 363.
[133] Swift, *Gulliver's Travels*, 273; Laura Brown, 'Reading Race and Gender: Jonathan Swift', *Eighteenth Century Studies* 23.4 (1990), 425–43.

Gulliver himself. Were they human? When the female Yahoo evinced passionate desire for him, Gulliver had to recognize with dismay that he was indeed a Yahoo. So what kind of degeneration was this? If Gulliver was a Yahoo, what was Long's connection to blackness? He was not like that; White and Black were quite different. But what if they were not? In positing the connection between the African and the orangutan, Long was marking a boundary with himself. Surely *they* were a different species?[134] Those Africans who were young when they arrived might become less brutish as they learned 'a regular discipline of life', but 'many are never reclaimed', sharing 'the same bestial manners, stupidity, and vices' which distinguished Africans from the rest of humankind.[135] Despite their acquaintance with Europeans for hundreds of years, they showed no progress in 'mechanic arts, or manufacture'. They were stuck in time, incapable of progress. The Chinese, Mexicans or northern Indians, in contrast, exhibited 'amiable endowments', 'ingenious' qualities and 'nothing of the barbarian'.[136]

Long's account of 'the African' led him to conclude that, 'When we reflect on the nature of these men, and their dissimilarity to the rest of mankind, must we not conclude, that they are a different species of the same *genus*?'[137] In writing his response to Mansfield's judgment, Long had relied on the established legality of the 'Negro' as property and commodity. But his opening reference in his pamphlet to the impossibility of the Ethiopian changing his skin was an indication of his conviction as to the significance of bodily differences: 'White' and 'Negro' connoted freedom and subjection and his black labour force was enslaved. His reading of his fellow West Indian Samuel Estwick's first edition of his attack on Mansfield had focused on questions of commerce, law and property, just as Long had in his *Candid Reflections*. Estwick refused to use the term 'slavery', considering it an 'odious word', and preferred to refer exclusively to 'property'. 'Negroes are the fortune of those who possess them,' he wrote. It was the law that determined the relation between the enslaved and his master: 'as *Negroe* and *Owner*: he is made matter of trade; he is said to be property; he is goods, chattels and effects, vestable and vested in his owner'.[138] If Somerset was property, then he could not claim *habeas corpus*. By the time Estwick published a second, much enlarged edition, Somerset had successfully claimed personhood in law. Granville Sharp's challenge to the planters – 'to prove, that a Negro slave is neither man, woman, nor child ... if they are not able to do this, how can they presume to consider such a person as a mere *chose in action*' – needed a riposte.[139] Estwick's was to elaborate his view on the

---

[134] As Cora Kaplan pointed out to me, Spivak shows in 'Three Women's Texts' how the description of Bertha in *Jane Eyre* breaches the divide between animal and human.
[135] Long, *History*, II. 354.
[136] Ibid., II. 355.
[137] Ibid., II. 356.
[138] [Estwick], *Considerations*, 10, 30, 35.
[139] Sharp, *A Representation*, 15.

nature of the African. 'What was the cause of that remarkable difference in complexion' which had puzzled so many? he asked. 'What signifies the black skin and the flat nose?' Montesquieu had asked; 'what could have given rise to this degradation and debasement of human nature?'[140] Human nature was universally assumed to be the same, Estwick reflected, but this had not been proved. The 'science of man' was little studied; 'Man only, who examines all Nature else, stands unexamined by himself.' It was widely recognized that there were many kinds of animal, 'each kind having its proper species subordinate thereto'. Yet was 'man' *'universally the same?'* Might it not make more sense to recognize that 'human nature is a class, comprehending an order of beings, of which man is the genus, divided into distinct and separate species of men?'[141] It was 'the great Mr Locke' who had said that it was reason that distinguished between man and beasts. But what distinguished between man and man? The 'learned Doctor Hutchinson' had established the importance of man's *moral sense*, but as Locke had pointed out it was the power of exercising that faculty that was critical. Did 'Negroes' possess that faculty?[142] They have no histories, Estwick asserted, whereas polished nations, as Hume had noted, had preserved pasts. He utilized the authority of Hume, citing his footnote claiming that 'Negroes' were inferior to whites. Nature, Hume believed, had made an 'original distinction' between breeds of men. And he referred to the case of 'one negroe' in Jamaica, 'a man of parts and learning: but it is likely he is admired for very slender accomplishments, like a parrot, who speaks a few words plainly'.[143]

Hume had written in 1753 of four or five different *kinds* of men, but Estwick's conclusion, based on his experience as a planter, was 'that there is but *one genus* or *kind* of man (under the term *mankind*) subordinate to which there are several *sorts* or *species* of men, differing from each other upon the principle that I have assigned'.[144] This 'principle' was the possession of a *moral sense*. It was this which distinguished man from man. Negroes were 'incapable of moral sensations', he claimed, and could only perceive them, as 'beasts do ... as simple ideas'.[145] All authors on 'the African', he maintained, insisted on their barbarity combined with an absence of morality. Ethiopians could not change their skin, nor leopards their spots. Negroes differed 'from other men, not in *kind*, but in *species*'. And he cited 'that unerring truth of Mr Pope',

---

[140] [Estwick], *Considerations*, 84–5.
[141] Ibid., 71–3.
[142] Ibid., 74.
[143] Hume, 'Of National Characters', 252. Hume argued in a later text that 'there is no universal difference discernible in the human species'. Aaron Garrett and Silvia Sebastiani, 'David Hume on Race', in Naomi Zack (ed.), *The Oxford Handbook of Philosophy and Race*, online edn (Oxford, 2017).
[144] [Estwick], *Considerations*, 78 fn.
[145] Ibid., 79 fn.

> Order is heaven's first law; and this confest,
> Some are, and must be, greater than the rest.[146]

The legislature had perceived 'the *corporeal* as well as intellectual differences of Negroes from other people' and supposed 'they were an inferior race of people', so named them 'articles of its trade and commerce'.[147] The emphasis on perception pointed to the significance of seeing: blackness was in the line of vision, it represented an inner blackness, an absence of moral sense. Estwick ended his diatribe with a warning as to the increasing numbers of Africans in England. It was vital to 'preserve the race of Britons from stain and contamination'.[148]

Estwick's thinking provided Long with a way of putting together the fruits of his experience in Jamaica, his certainty that cane, and the wealth that flowed from it, could only be produced by enslaved Africans, with selected arguments from the Enlightenment debates on the human. It was imperative for him to show his familiarity with these texts, to position himself as a man of science, who could claim to be 'impartial'.[149] As a planter he claimed to have observed the limited capacities of the enslaved, disavowing his knowledge of their multiple skills on which Lucky Valley depended.[150] He adopted the language and persona of 'the philosopher', a name he chose for himself, and engaged with a range of well-known figures – anatomists, natural historians and travellers – claiming a place in their ranks and writing in a quite different idiom from that of the literary man or the political arithmetician.[151] One *genus*, different *species*: this was conceptualized as an explanation of the differences between Africans and 'the rest of mankind'. It was well known that animals were of many *kinds*, with subordinate *species*, wrote Long. The Divine Being had inaugurated a 'general system of the world', built on gradation and difference.

> In this system we perceive a regular order and gradation from inanimate to animated matter; and certain links, which connect the several *genera* one with another; and, underneath these *genera*, we find another gradation of species, comprehending a vast variety, and, in some classes, widely differing from each other in certain qualities.[152]

---

[146] Ibid., 82.
[147] Ibid., 83.
[148] Ibid., 95.
[149] Long, *History*, I. 2.
[150] 'Long was a historian whose archive authorized his ability to discern which theory is correct'; James Vernon, personal communication.
[151] Long was prone to describing himself as 'the Philosopher' in his letters to his daughter Elizabeth; Howard, *Records and Letters*, II. 327.
[152] Long, *History*, II. 356.

The Supreme Being had made use of one model, that of man/Adam, in his creation, but he had varied it in every possible way so that 'man might equally admire the simplicity of the plan, and the magnificence of the execution'.[153]

Long had already remarked, as we have seen, in his account of 'Mulattos', that 'the White and the Negroe had not one common origin'. This, he wrote, was 'an opinion, which several have entertained'. 'For my own part', he had continued, 'there are extremely potent reasons for believing, that the White and the Negroe are two distinct species.' This provided an explanation for the 'diversities of feature, skin, and intellect' amongst humankind.[154] He had written this in response to Buffon's conviction that 'Mulattoes' could reproduce with each other, a view which Long disputed. Now, having adopted Estwick's distinction between *genus* and *species* as a way of demarcating Africans from 'the rest of mankind', and offering that as a theory of human difference, he expatiated on the many varieties of dogs, horses and monkeys, coming to the '*oran-outang*' species, which had 'the strongest similitude to mankind, in countenance, figure, stature, organs, erect posture, actions or movements, food, temper, and manner of living'.[155] Here he paused, to document his major disagreement with Buffon. The boundary between human and other was established by Buffon as between the Hottentot and the orangutan. Long aimed to blur that distinction.[156]

The figure of the orangutan or chimpanzee was central to debates on the science of man from the 1630s to the 1770s. What, if anything, distinguished the ape from the human? Most natural historians agreed that though apes had human characteristics, they were not human. Much attention was devoted to questions as to whether they could think, speak, walk erect or create culture.[157] Comparison between animals and humans, or different groups of human, was a major epistemological tool for these thinkers, and the chimpanzee, arriving in Europe often as part of the same commercial network as the enslaved, occupied a particular place in these comparisons.[158] Madame Chimpanzee, as she was named, was exhibited in London in 1738. The spectacle of her polite table manners and tea drinking provoked much public comment, her civility offering a counterpoint to imagined African 'savagery'. Orangutans it was

---

[153] Ibid., II. 358. In making this claim, as Suman Seth observes, Long was basing his argument on natural history while acknowledging the significance of divine intervention: his argument was about the racial present, not the biblical past. Seth, *Difference and Disease*, 255.
[154] Long, *History*, II. 336.
[155] Ibid., II. 358.
[156] See Ogborn, *Freedom of Speech*, 6–15, for an excellent analysis of Long's attempt to theorize racial difference.
[157] Schiebinger, *Nature's Body*.
[158] Silvia Sebastiani, 'Challenging Boundaries: Apes and Savages in Enlightenment', in Wulf D. Hund, Charles W. Mills and Silvia Sebastiani (eds.), *Simianization. Apes, Gender, Class, and Race* (Zurich, 2015), 105–38.

believed had human feelings, a capacity to express sensibility, grief and compassion. The work of comparative anatomists such as Edward Tyson, who had dissected a chimpanzee in London in 1698 and compared it point-by-point with the human body, provided important evidence. Tyson had concluded that, despite the many physical similarities, the divide between humans and apes was unbridgeable, depending as it did on mind and soul, not just the body. Long drew on a range of texts, from Tyson to Linnaeus, to link the orangutan with the 'wild man' as 'Indians' had done. In his intended revisions for a second edition, he called upon classical authors Herodotus, Aristotle and Philostratus, who 'mix the negroes and these Wild men in the same class of Brutality, allowing them the semblance of Men, without the intellectual qualifications essential to the perfect dignity and rank of the human character'.[159] His aim was to challenge Buffon's 'rather too precipitate conclusions' that the orangutan, despite organs of speech and of brain, '*does not speak*' and '*does not think*', since it was not 'animated with a *superior principle*.'[160] For Buffon the orangutan was very close to humans and should be placed in the 'second class of animal beings'. But, Long insisted, Buffon had no 'decisive proofs' of this.[161] And 'how can we be sure of this?', he wrote in a later note.[162] Orangutans had 'social feeling', passions, traces of reason, they were 'nearest to brutes'.[163] Linking the orangutan sexually to the African, he wrote, 'Ludicrous as the opinion may seem, I do not think that an oran-outang husband would be any dishonour to an Hottentot female.' For, he asked rhetorically, 'what are these Hottentots?' They were stupid and brutal, 'more like beasts than men . . . one of the meanest nations on the face of the earth'.[164] 'Has the Hottentot a more manly figure than the oran-outang? . . . That the oran-outang and some races of black men are very nearly allied, is, I think, more than probable.'[165] This was the crux of Long's claim. 'The animalization of the "savage"', as Silvia Sebastiani suggests, was 'construed through the humanization of the ape': when the human/animal divide narrowed, the divide between 'savage' and 'civilized' people 'increased and crystallized', facilitating the establishment of a racial hierarchy.[166]

---

[159] BL Add MSS 12405, f. 291r.
[160] Long, *History*, II. 363.
[161] Ibid., II. 365.
[162] BL Add MS 12405, f. 294.
[163] Long, *History*, II. 364, 371.
[164] Ibid., II. 364–5.
[165] Ibid., II. 365
[166] Silvia Sebastiani, '"A Monster with Human Visage": the Orangutan, Savagery and the Borders of Humanity in the Global Enlightenment', *History of the Human Sciences* 32.4 (2019), 80–99; Sebastiani, 'Enlightenment Humanization and Dehumanization, and the Orangutan', in Maria Kronfeldner (ed.), *The Routledge Handbook of Dehumanization* (London, 2021), 64–82.

Having stated his claim, Long turned to new authorities, the French natural historian Le Pluche and Lord Monboddo, the Scottish judge and philosopher, to buttress his challenge to Buffon. Le Pluche had pronounced 'the preeminence of man over brutes'. The tokens of superiority were many: the erect position of his head and body, his upright walk, the *'noble position of his body'*, all making him *'master of all'*. His muscles, legs and arms, all demonstrated a dignity 'denied to his *slaves*, the *inferior animals*'. It was his arm and hand, above all, that carried his 'effectual sovereignty'. 'Since man has an arm, I say, he is master of everything on earth,' wrote Long. Combined with a stomach that could digest all that was wholesome and nourishing, his teeth and his capacity for speech, all in all man's dignity 'arises from the *right use* to which his *reason* enables him to apply his corporeal powers and senses'.[167] Speech had long been understood as central to the definition of the human and Buffon maintained that the orangutan 'has eyes, but sees not; ears has he, but hears not; he has a tongue and the human organs of speech, but *speaks not*; he has the human brain, but does not think; forms no comparisons, draws no conclusions'.[168] But, asked Long, how can we know the measure of their intellect, 'human organs were not given him for nothing', and he compared the sounds they made with 'the gabbling of turkies, like that of the Hottentots'. 'For my own part', he wrote, stating his claim to be one of the experimental scientists, 'this race may have some language by which their meaning is communicated.'[169] Orangutans, he maintained, were not 'at all inferior in the intellectual faculties to many of the Negroe race'. 'An ingenious modern author', Lord Monboddo, had argued for the humanity of the orangutan and claimed that the faculty of speech was learned, not given – that 'the want of articulation, or expressing idea by speech, does not afford a positive indication of a want of intellect'.[170] The orangutan, Long concluded, 'has in form a much nearer resemblance to the Negroe race, than the latter bear to white men'. It might have been the pleasure of the Deity to 'diversify his works', infuse *'superior principles'* into the 'different classes and races of human creatures' in such a way as to 'form the same gradual climax towards perfection in this human system, which is so evidently designed in every other'.[171] Citing 'our immortal Shakespeare' on the differences in men, he argued, 'The species of every other *genus* have their certain mark and distinction, their varieties, and subordinate classes', why not 'the race of mankind'?[172]

Long backed up his conviction with an account of the many differences, both physical and intellectual, amongst African nations, from Moors and

---

[167] Long, *History*, II. 367–8.
[168] Ibid., II. 369.
[169] Ibid., II. 370. He may have had Swift's Houyhnhnms in his mind.
[170] Ibid., II. 370, 370–1 fn.
[171] Ibid., II. 371.
[172] Ibid., II. 372.

Arabs to Giagas and Angolans, those whom he had previously described as being all the same. The greater the distance from 'Negro-land', the lighter the skin, until perfection was reached in the 'pure white'.[173] 'The measure of the several orders and varieties of these Blacks', he maintained, 'may be as compleat as that of any other race of mortals; filling up that space, or degree, beyond which they are not destined to pass; and discriminating them from the rest of men, not in *kind* but in species.' 'It is not a variety of climate that produces various complexions,' he insisted.[174] Hume's observation that Africans 'were inferior to the rest of the species' provided him with philosophical authority, and Mr Beattie's attempt to disprove this had, in his opinion, offered no evidence. He returned finally to his conviction that Africans could not combine ideas or reason, had no literature, arts or sciences, and only foolish laws when laws were justly regarded as 'the master piece of human genius'.[175] They worshipped innumerable gods and made snakes into deities, the women bore children with no labour, they were botanists by instinct, their cannibalism had been proved by many travellers, and their passions were uncontrolled. They could not claim personhood.

Having in his own mind despatched Africans as a lesser breed based on both body and culture, Long turned to 'Guiney Slaves' and the trade. His conviction, as we have seen, was that no blame was to be attached to the slave trade since it was a contract and in Africa 'slaves' were considered 'actual *staple products*, as much as wool and corn are to Great Britain'.[176] 'The colony man is only the buyer,' as he put it in his later notes, so carried no responsibility as to how the people he had bought were acquired.[177] The Africans, he maintained, were already 'slaves' and had only 'exchanged their owner and laws'. They gained, he asserted, 'life, for death; clemency, for barbarity; comfort and convenience, for torture and misery; food for famine'.[178]

Of the Creole Slaves and African Negroes in Jamaica

In representing Africans living in Jamaica, Long's aim was now to persuade his metropolitan readers that the crossing of the Atlantic and the plantation had civilized the enslaved and resulted in the production of new subjects, 'Creoles'. No longer claiming to be a philosopher, he returned to the mode of planter and eyewitness, natural historian, close observer of the distinctive features of African life. The distinction he sought to make between those born on the island and 'Imported Africans' was essential, as we have seen, to his hopes for a settled colony. Yet he continually undermined such a distinction in his

---

[173] Ibid., II. 375.
[174] Ibid., II. 375, 374–5 fn.
[175] Ibid., II. 378.
[176] Ibid., II. 390.
[177] BL Add MS 12405, insert f. 318.
[178] Long, *History*, II. 403.

writing. The conscious intent of his depiction of 'Creoles', based on his experience of Lucky Valley and his own household, was to demonstrate that they could become reliable servants of both planters and empire. The old proverb 'Like master like man', he maintained, provided the key to the '*general character*' of creoles. All depended on how they were 'worked upon', since they were undoubtedly prone to idleness rather than a 'life of labour'. Yet a 'regular course of discipline', learned from infancy, could be very effective.[179] If the owners of plantations, especially absentees, would only take seriously their responsibilities and not rely on overseers who might have 'callous hearts ... impenetrable to the feelings of human nature', then the problem of what Long was anxious to define as 'occasional cruelty' would be addressed. It was indeed, as he emphasized throughout his writing, in the 'planter's best interest to be humane'.[180] (He did not consider his own choice to become an absentee and rely on a paid attorney to manage his estate.) His initial *general* characterization of 'Creoles' described them as capable of *being made* (my emphasis) 'diligent ... moderately faithful'. He subsequently named them 'irascible, conceited, proud, indolent, lascivious, credulous, artful ... excellent dissemblers and skilful flatterers'. They were good natured but ungrateful and prone to hold grudges. Treacherous, cowardly and 'a blind anger, and brutal rage, with them stand frequently in place of manly valour'.[181] To look for 'manly valour' in face of the brutal punishments to which the enslaved were subjected seems particularly redolent of disavowal. But Long was quick to acknowledge that though they did not like to fight out in the open, they were excellent at tracking, knowing each other's haunts much better than whites could ever know. (This, of course, made those who were 'loyal' invaluable to their masters.) Unlike the white creole planters he had described with such pride, Long represented African 'Creoles' as very limited in their ideas: they lived in the moment, their only preoccupations were 'the common occurrences of life, food, love, and dress: these are frequent themes for their dance, conversation, and musical compositions'.[182] He avoided what he feared and could not understand of 'Creole' life by tying his account of funeral rites and obeah to the Coromantees, those he wished to evacuate from the island. Violence, in his mind, did not lie with the planters: he projected it on to those Africans he feared, ensuring that all those other, creolized Africans could remain the sinews of the plantation system.

His assertions of the distinctions between the 'savage African' and the 'civilized creole' were constantly undercut by his assumptions of a difference which could not be eradicated. 'Guinea Slaves', he maintained in one breath,

---

[179] Ibid., II. 404.
[180] Ibid., II. 405–7.
[181] Ibid., II. 407.
[182] Ibid., II. 408–9.

were quite different from 'Creoles'. Yet he frequently admitted that, given the scale of intermixture with the native Africans, 'Creoles' 'differ but little in many articles'.[183] They were, after all, all Africans. But then again, they differed much, 'not only in manners, but in beauty of shape, feature and complexion'.[184] No sooner was beauty mentioned than it was offset with 'Creole' proneness 'to debauch and venereal excess'. The soles of their feet were described as acquiring 'the firmness of a hoof', evoking cattle, since they walked without shoes, and their dread of rain put down to the fact that 'their woolly fleece', as with sheep, 'would absorb it in large quantities'.[185] 'Like other animals', Long wrote, 'they are fond of caterwauling all night, and dozing all the day.'[186] But his use of animalizing language never slipped into thinking that 'Negroes' were not human. It was their human characteristics that the planters depended on.

'Imported Africans' he dismissed as 'addicted to the most bestial vices', particularly drunkenness and theft. Anything they saw they immediately wanted to possess. This meant that they were extremely quarrelsome: their master should play the role of umpire. 'Creoles', on the other hand, were 'more exempt from ebriety' and were, in his view, contemptuous of the 'salt-water slaves'. Their plantation life had civilized them in body as well as in behaviour. It was 'mild and humane usage' that was the key. 'Keen and well timed rebukes' combined with a 'very moderate instruction in the Christian rules' would make the whip quite unnecessary, he claimed, with his eye on the reports of the abolitionists.[187] Just as in his depiction of the plantation he had judged himself to be the master of all, the head that determined the conduct of the whole, so in his account of the 'Creoles' he imagined that their masters could determine who they were: a fantasy which inevitably fell apart when faced with rebellion and which he tried to deal with through his depiction of the Coromantees.

When it came to the habits of the 'Creoles', he slipped between a representation of them as 'improved' and an underlying anxiety that this was a surface phenomenon. He had observed both the labour and lives of the enslaved closely, but his prejudices constantly interrupted and shaped his depictions. In the mornings, he reported, they were slow in their labour but as it became hotter they were more alert. The openness of their pores meant that they sweated a great deal and gave 'a free transpiration to bad humours'. They could have enjoyed 'robust health' if 'they were less prone to debauch, and venereal excess'.[188] He was perfectly aware of the scale of mortality on the plantations, the presence of illness and hunger, but disavowed that knowledge.

[183] Ibid., II. 407.
[184] Ibid., II. 410.
[185] Ibid., II. 412.
[186] Ibid., II. 413.
[187] Ibid., II. 411.
[188] Ibid., II. 412.

Rather, he blamed any problems on their immorality. Their ability to carry heavy burdens on their heads, resting the load on a *cotta* made from plaited dried plantain leaf, reminded him of London porters. And that *cotta* had another use: the voluntary divorce of husband and wife could be effected by cutting the *cotta* in half, each party taking half. A fortunate practice, Long might have observed, since they were not allowed legal marriage. What he described as 'Creole' 'marriage customs' often involved several partners, some of whom might be on another estate, allowing them to build family connections across the island. This ensured their knowledge of 'all affairs of the white inhabitants, public and private', an alarming thought for the slave-owners given the revolts large and small which took place in the 1760s and an interesting counterpoint to the network of marriage alliance which the white elite had constructed.[189] They exercised authority over their children, he noted, paying no attention to *his* claim to 'ownership' of those children, and seemed to hold 'filial obedience in much higher estimation than conjugal fidelity'. They usually prioritized one husband or wife: the rest, although called 'wives', were only 'a sort of occasional concubines, or drudges' whom the husband might claim to work on his land or sell his goods.[190] Long's language made it clear that here it was the men whose habits he was mainly concerned with and whose doings he observed. They laughed at the idea of an indissoluble marriage between two people: their notion of love, Long thought, 'is free and transitory'.[191] Given the relatively small numbers of planters who were married, to Long's dismay, and the ubiquity of 'housekeepers', 'concubines' and expectations as to the sexual availability of enslaved women, Long might have reflected that their laughter was hardly surprising. 'Creoles' liked to imagine an ancestry, he opined, and it was 'the greatest affront' that could be offered to a 'Creole' man to 'curse his father, mother, or any of his progenitors'.[192] In his understanding, this was because they liked to mimic their masters: his failure to grasp the struggles of the enslaved to re-make the networks of kin that had been taken from them is breath-taking.[193]

When it came to cleanliness, their houses and bodies were well kept, their diet pulses and vegetables, and they were especially fond of salt fish, with the more stink the better in their view. Their cooks were careful to wash before preparing food, but Long clarified this point by distinguishing between 'Creoles' and the 'better sort of the Africans', while the rest 'feed with all the

---

[189] Ibid., II. 414.
[190] Ibid.
[191] Ibid., II. 415.
[192] Ibid., II. 410.
[193] Sarah Pearsall's exploration of polygamy in North America, *Polygamy. An Early American History* (London, 2019), argues that traditions like polygamy in enslaved communities were more than a subversion of European norms; they indicated 'the profound dynamics of Atlantic transformation'; 116.

bestiality peculiar to the genuine breed of Guiney'.[194] He lingered over his description of one of their favourite delicacies, a roasted and stuffed cane rat, which 'with their goggle eyes and whiskers, is enough to turn an European stomach'.[195] It suited him to tell of what he considered disgusting habits and to avoid thinking about the hunger and malnutrition which stalked the plantations.[196]

Knight, like Long, spent time observing 'his Negroes'. In general they have 'a Natural gloomy Countenance,' he remarked, not pausing to consider why this might be, 'and seldom look cheerful or pleased'. It was 'difficult for a Person who is unacquainted with Their language or Custom' to know when they sang and played 'on Their Musick, whether it proceeds from Mirth or Sorrow; unless they Cry at the same time, which They often do, when They are very much grieved'. They would play 'when They are under any affliction or trouble, to dissipate Melancholy thoughts, as well as to amuse and divert Themselves upon other Occasions'. Their tunes were in general, he thought, 'extremely Melancholly'. Like Long, however, he chose not to reflect on that 'melancholly', only noting that 'Nature has implanted in Them, as well as the rest of mankind, Pride, Ambition, Dissimulation and all other passions and Vices; though They have not the same Opportunity of exerting Them'. But, he continued, 'They are particularly Remarkable for the Art of Concealing Their passions' – an odd comment to make after recognizing their grief.[197] Long admitted 'their good ear for music', but immediately undercut this by his judgement of their songs as lacking in poetry. Sometimes there was a melody, but the tone was often 'flat and melancholy'.[198] Like Knight he chose not to consider what the source of that melancholy might be. He recognized the poignancy of their satire, often at the expense of the overseer, particularly if he should happen to be nearby. The *merry-wang* was a favourite instrument, as was the *goombah*.[199] Long had clearly watched and admired their pleasure in dancing. The 'female dancer', he recorded, in a rare moment of appreciation which cut across his desire to 'evacuate Africans from the order

---

[194] Long, *History*, II. 414.
[195] Ibid.
[196] Trevor Burnard, 'A Brutal System: Managing Slaves and Slave Welfare in Jamaica, 1763–1891', in Burnard, *Jamaica in the Age of Revolution*, 70–102.
[197] Knight, *History*, II. 486–7.
[198] Long, *History*, II. 422.
[199] There is considerable interest in a collection of pages inserted into the Long Papers and including notations and words of songs. Devin Leigh 'The Jamaica Airs: an Introduction to Unpublished Pieces of Musical Notation from Enslaved People in the Eighteenth Century', *Atlantic Studies* 17.4 (2020), 462–84. The unknown author intended to write an ethnographic history of Jamaica and sent his manuscript to Long, an indication of how Long's position made him 'a magnet for informal scholarship on the island'; 470. Long, following Sloane in his interest in musical notation, intended to use the work in his revised second edition.

of culture' and insist that they were without aesthetic sense, 'is all languishing and easy in her motions', while the man was 'all action, fire and gesture',[200] keeping exact time with the music, 'corresponding in their movements with a great correctness of ear, and propriety of attitude', all of which, he had to admit despite himself, 'has a very pleasing effect'.[201] This led him to the Christmas holiday and the masquerades, recording the forms of mimicry associated with *John Connu*. These had their origins in West Africa, he realized, and he noted that in 1769 'several new masks appeared' amongst Eboes and Papaws.[202] Most white spectators did not enjoy 'these exercises ... on account of the ill smell', a 'complication of stinks' which were so 'rank and powerful, as totally to overcome those who have any delicacy in the frame of their nostrils'. This 'rancid exhalation', he argued, had no obvious cause in uncleanliness or diet. Rather, as he told the tale, it was the essence of their beings and any attempt to wash it off was as hopeless as was the attempt to wash a 'Black-a-moor white'.[203]

With this he returned to his attack, this time on the minds of 'the Negroes'. They were only capable of 'technical memory', did not understand the calendar, spoke in 'bad English, larded with the Guiney dialect'.[204] The 'better sort' tried to improve their language by listening carefully to 'Whites', but he was contemptuous of their efforts since they misheard and misapplied the words. It gave them 'knowledge and importance in the eyes of their brethren', however, which 'tickled their vanity' and 'made them more assiduous in stocking themselves with this unintelligible jargon'. They confounded moods, tenses and conjugations, producing a 'form of gibberish', and threatening to infect 'many of the white Creoles' who they cared for as children, which, as we have seen, disturbed Long greatly.[205] He concluded his account by arguing that instruction in Christianity, something which critics of the plantocracy were beginning to propose, would answer no purpose, given 'Negro' addiction to their 'favourite superstitions and sensual delights'. 'The mere ceremony of baptism', he maintained, 'would no more make Christians of the Negroes ... than a sound drubbing would convert an illiterate faggot-maker into a regular physician.'[206] 'Their barbarous stupidity', combined with their 'ignorance of the English language, which render them incapable of understanding or reasoning upon what is said to them', would, he was convinced, 'foil the

---

[200] Long, *History*, II. 424; Gikandi, *Slavery and the Culture of Taste*, 267–8.
[201] Long, *History*, II. 424.
[202] Ibid.; Barbero Martinez-Ruiz, 'Sketches of Memory: Visual Encounters with Africa in Jamaican Culture', in Barringer et al. (eds.), *Art and Emancipation*, 103–20.
[203] Long, *History*, II. 426.
[204] Ibid.
[205] Ibid., II. 428–9.
[206] Ibid., II. 428.

most zealous endeavours'.[207] The French might have better hopes in converting their 'Negroes' to Catholicism, he believed, since they were used to a despotic system of government which reduced the masters to a 'state of servility' not unlike that of their 'Negroes', while the church depended heavily on 'subordination... and awful ceremonies'.[208] The contrast with 'our islands' could not be greater, thought Long, since here 'the word *liberty* is in every one's mouth' and 'the assemblies resound with the clamour of "liberty and property"' which was echoed back 'by all ranks and degrees'; even the 'Negroes' grew 'familiar with the term'.[209] All this carried dangers. As Montesquieu had understood, colonies with moderate governments should be very careful as to the numbers of their 'Negroes'. 'Nothing more assimilates a man to a beast', he had written, 'than living among freemen; himself a slave. Such people as these are the natural enemies of the society; and their numbers must be dangerous.'[210]

This was his stark warning.

Some years later Long instructed his eldest son, a schoolboy at Harrow, of what he would need to understand to fulfil his inheritance – his ownership of Lucky Valley and his position as the next head of the family. At first sight, he wrote, the world might seem a puzzling place given 'the disparity of bulk, strength, dispositions, manners, intellect', but his son should observe the 'general harmony + order in the universe. All things are held within their allotted bounds by settled invariable laws.' 'Nothing is more apt to strike the attention', he continued, 'than the inequality of Genius, + of Condition, which marks the different individuals belonging to any society.' Why did some 'so far surpass others in perfection of the intellectual faculty, or in corporal endowments? Why that variety in creatures of the same species? Why that vast dissimilitude of minds as well as features?' 'Residential circumstances' mattered, but there was 'a certain inborn discrimination'. 'Members of the largest civilied [sic] community seems as it were destined to act some respective part on this great theatre,' and were 'qualified' in pursuing their own interests to promote that of others. 'Every one therefore, in his several sphere, has abilities to be exerted and functions to be exercised, which perpetually are cooperating' to produce order and harmony. It was only when individuals did not fulfil their allotted tasks that 'disorder [would] arise, + anarchy prevail'.[211]

---

[207] Ibid., II. 428–9.
[208] Ibid., II. 430.
[209] Ibid., II. 431.
[210] Ibid.
[211] Long to his eldest son, Edward Beeston Long, then at Harrow, n.d., Cumbria Archives.

All should know their place and keep to it. Long lived under what Adam Smith characterized as 'the mysterious veil of self-delusion', covering from his view the 'deformities of his own conduct' and the inconsistencies of his own thinking.[212]

---

[212] Adam Smith, 'Of the Sense of Duty', in *Theory of Moral Sentiments*, Part 3, 221.

Epilogue

The only interest in history is that it is not yet finally wrapped up. Another history is always possible, another turning is waiting to happen.

Stuart Hall

'History People' and Politics

'History people' was the name that Audene Brooks from the Jamaica Heritage Trust used to describe the group of us searching for Lucky Valley. We had no modern map to guide us. The only way to find the site of the plantation was to ask passers-by for directions ... turn left at the rum shop, right at the Pentecostal church, keep the river on your left ... somebody would know. We would eventually find it, catching sight of the sign for 'The Church of God in Jamaica, Lucky Valley, Clarendon. Established 1920'. This was the only building now in the vicinity. We hailed Mr Ivan Calabalerro, who came down on his donkey from his home on the top of a nearby hill and greeted us, reminding us that these cane fields now devoid of life had once been a workplace and home for hundreds of enslaved people. After pausing a while to pick ackees off a laden tree to take back with us to Kingston, we began to explore the site, picking up fragments of pottery and investigating what was left of the water wheel – the ghostly traces of plantation life. (See Figures E.1–E.2.)

Edward Long and I are both 'history people' in the sense that we write history and we hope that it will have an effect, that the writing might shift what Long, following Hume, would have called *opinion*. Governmental authority, Hume believed, rested on opinion. And Long certainly hoped to influence it. He was convinced that the major political intervention he could make in support of the whole slavery business was by writing his *History*, 'that most civilized of documents', redolent with all 'the tropes and devices of Enlightenment natural history and social theory'.[1] In Jamaica he had seen his work in the assembly as necessary and important. Once in England he chose to focus first on finishing his *History* and subsequently worked hard with

---

[1] Thanks to Kathleen Wilson for this formulation; personal communication, January 2023.

Figure E.1 Pottery fragments found at Lucky Valley estate, including tableware ceramics and glassware imported from Britain and elsewhere between the eighteenth and nineteenth centuries. Image courtesy of Zachary J. M. Beier.

Figure E.2 Following the trail of Edward Long into contemporary Jamaica. Image courtesy of Zachary J. M. Beier.

his West Indian associates lobbying government and MPs and providing testimony in support of the slave trade and slavery. He collected many materials and revised some of his text for a second edition, but this task was never completed. He never chose to seek a place in the House of Commons, as numbers of the absentees did. His writing did influence 'opinion', though not always in the ways that he intended. His words were repeated, his racialized assumptions reformulated and reused. His fears of white Englishness being polluted by 'bronzing' are still potent.

In the time after empire, some erstwhile colonial subjects have found a diasporic identity a place from where it is possible to think, to see the past unravelling and possibilities of a different future emerging. The dysfunctions, 'everything that refuses to fit neatly into a narrative', are placed at the forefront by the displacements: new ways of telling and speaking emerge.[2] The similarities and differences between 'here' and 'there' gain salience, allowing a rethinking of the power relations of the past, dreams of other mappings of the world, other forms of agency. Living in a very different time, Edward Long, slave-owner and colonizer, found no such thing. His return to England solidified his commitment to being a West Indian; he campaigned for slavery into the early 1790s and aimed to ensured his legacy in his *History*. At the very same time he reaffirmed his commitment to Englishness. His capacity to split was firmly embedded, any displacement vigorously denied. England was his place of belonging, it was 'home'. But it was changing in ways that were not always to his liking. He had left it at twenty-three, made a goodly fortune and was thirty-five on his return to England, still a relatively young man with energy and ambition. His daughter Elizabeth was born to Mary before they left Jamaica in 1759; their twins, Robert Ballard and Charles Beckford, were born in Chichester in 1771. He could provide comfortably for his family of six children. Jamaica and slavery were the source of his income and occupied a quite separate space in his mind, the place he knew so well, but did not call 'home'. Jamaica, he wanted to insist, *was* English. The sugar islands, he reflected, should be considered as though 'they were a parcel of the Kingdom itself – or rather as a detached County, producing a peculiar commodity, useful to us for home consumption, or for Export; such as no other County in the realm is capable of furnishing; cultivated and manufactured by our own people; and received from their hands in exchange for the products of our other Counties'.[3] Planters were not distant colonists but free-born Englishmen, separated only by geography. Long's *History* was designed to tell that story, notwithstanding contrary evidence, whether of violence, excessive gluttony or sexual

---

[2] Hall, *Familiar Stranger*, 171; Avtar Brah, *Cartographies of Diaspora. Contesting Identities* (London, 1996).
[3] BL Add MS 12407, f. 14.

promiscuity. Jamaica was becoming *more* English, he hoped, more polite, more familial, more restrained and regulated.

Only four years after publishing the *History*, Long produced a quite different text. The American War of Independence had begun and Adam Smith's earlier denunciation of slave-owners as lacking in sympathy was now complemented by his *Wealth of Nations* critiquing colonialism and mercantilism. North American colonists were being identified as enemies, their slave-holding an aspect of their distinctive identities, making them *not-British*. These were troubling times for the West Indians, as their profits were badly affected by the war and their political position weakened by the break with the Americans.[4] Long may have felt that it was time to assert his proudly English credentials. *English Humanity no Paradox: or, an Attempt to Prove, that the English are Not a Nation of Savages* appeared in 1778. It was published anonymously, as the *History* had been, by T. Lowndes of Fleet Street, who was responsible not only for Long's volumes but for many other pro-slavery offerings. The opening 'Advertisement to the Reader' noted that, 'It may seem not a little extraordinary, that one who is defending the humanity of his countrymen, should himself have committed a species of cruelty, for which some folks may think he deserves to be called to an account.' This, he claimed, referred to his dreadful cruelty in dismembering and disembowelling syllables. Even the 'charming word Liberty' might become 'L—y'.[5] Readers who guessed the author might have interpreted this somewhat heavy-handed literary disavowal differently, suspecting a denial of the accusations of slave-owners' cruelty. The text opened with the assertion that 'It is the wish of every good Englishman to acquire a praiseworthy character, and preserve it when acquired.'[6] Almost ninety pages were then devoted to demonstrating that 'we' (he unproblematically identified himself as English) have 'well-founded pretensions to the reputation of being *an humane people*', endowed with qualities of '*valour*' and a '*good humour* ... wholly irreconcilable with cruelty'.[7] In his familial context Long imagined himself as possessed of 'a natural felicity of Temper', averse to denying others, preferring 'Compliance'.[8] It is hard to put this together with his lack of compassion for the sufferings of those left to die hanging in cages in the Kingston sun.

Long's 'passionate *love* of *our Country*' was rooted in '*that free* and *admirable Constitution* transmitted to us by our forefathers'. It was that which meant that 'we have a right to wear those distinctions, which exalt every man who is

---

[4] On the economic effects, see Selwyn H. H. Carrington, *The British West Indies during the American Revolution* (Dordrecht, 1988); on the political, O'Shaughnessy, *An Empire Divided*; Ryden, *West Indian Slavery*.
[5] [Long], *English Humanity*, iv.
[6] Ibid., 1.
[7] Ibid., 2.
[8] Howard, *Records and Letters*, I. 272.

master of himself', not only 'above the grovelling brute species', but also 'above such of the human as have been metamorphosed by oppression into passive beasts of burden'.⁹ The contradictions were glaring, the splitting transparent. No wonder critics accused slave-owners of hypocrisy. As Dr Johnson had noted in his commentary on the American colonists, 'How is it that we hear the loudest yelps for liberty from the drivers of negroes?'¹⁰ Long's exaltation of those who are masters of themselves emphasized their proud posture, the 'noble' position of the body, which, he was convinced, demonstrated a dignity 'denied to his slaves, the inferior animals'.¹¹ His use of the passive voice in 'have been metamorphosed' neatly avoided any question of whose oppression, who made captive, who enslaved. He had 'always perceived' himself, he asserted, 'a partner in the obvious distresses of my fellow-creatures'. Englishmen were not savages; it was the 'Negroes of *Afric*, and the Indians of *America*' (with their almost entirely vegetable diet, unlike the good beef of England) who were capable of actions of 'unequivocal, genuine *cruelty*'.¹² He would have been much happier, he continued, if the British had not had to rely in the American War on '*negroe servants* to butcher their masters' or '*Cannibal Indians* to scalp, tomahawk, and torture' their enemies.¹³ Long's racial fears, it was clear, continued unabated. Those who were not 'fellow-creatures' must be expelled, white butchery projected into them.

One astute foreigner, he observed, had remarked that 'of all places in the world, *England* was the country to *think* in'. Yet Long appeared incapable of putting the split parts of himself together. Some foreigners condemned the use of the birch in English schools, and Long sympathized with this view. Schools could be a 'pretty exact model of a Despotic Form' in a 'free State' and hearts steeled 'against the compunctions of pity' might take pleasure in flogging. Such punishment produced 'an indelible hatred to tyrannic Rule'. But the 'tyrannic Rule' he particularly hated was that of colonial governors. Despite the thirty years which had elapsed since his 'freedom from Bondage' (in school), he himself, he recorded, still had nightmares of being whipped by '*Dr Tickletail*'. He would 'supplicate his clemency with tears or try to mollify his rage with Entreaties'. But his tormentor was 'Deaf and insensible to the voice of woe, his bloody, boisterous threats, now thunder in my ear; my very soul is agonized with terror'. It was all too much: nature 'reprieves me from the lash; I wake; and

---

⁹ [Long], *English Humanity*, 2, 9–11.
¹⁰ Samuel Johnson, 'Taxation no Tyranny. An answer to the resolutions and address of the American colonists', in *The Works of Samuel Johnson* (14 vols., New York, 1913), XIV. 144. But as Christopher Leslie Brown notes in *Moral Capital*, 134, 151, Johnson did not choose to address equivalent West Indian/English hypocrisies; his focus was his opposition to the claims of the American colonists.
¹¹ Long, *History*, II. 367–8.
¹² [Long], *English Humanity*, 21, 32.
¹³ Ibid., 81.

rejoice to find, *it is but a Dream!*' He wished that every 'Advocate for Tyranny' might be haunted 'with these nocturnal visions, till he recants his error, and vows eternal enmity against all power unduly and rancorously exercised'. He trusted that 'the spirit of English Youths, if not wholly broken and debased by this early process of slavery', would survive 'with redoubled vigor, in support of that manly character and love of just freedom'.[14] The naming of these boyhood experiences as 'slavery', and the disconnect between his own fear of the birch by the tyrannical master and the everyday use of the whip on the plantation, seems almost unbelievable. How could he maintain it?

Long had no capacity for sympathy with the 'other' and, indeed, a powerful compulsion to block any such sentiment.[15] His love for his family and friends, his fears of languishing and pining in the absence of those he cared for, occupied a different compartment of his mind from those named as 'Negroes'. 'Afric', in his fevered imagination, was the 'parent of everything that is monstrous in nature'.[16] The White man he invented in his *History* could only exist in contrast to that 'brute species', those 'passive beasts of burden', those terrifying Coromantins whom he also wrote into existence. 'Not only must the black man be black', as Fanon understood, 'he must be black in relation to the white man.'[17] Not only must the White man be White, Long might have written, he must be White in relation to the Black man. Long's racialized vision of the world depended on the construction of that binary. Without the 'Negro' he could not exercise his full mastery of himself. That meant those others must be expelled: there could be no sympathy.

Ignatius Sancho, the African shopkeeper, actor, composer, celebrated letter writer and servant to the Duchess of Montagu, had engaged in correspondence with Lawrence Sterne. Those letters were widely available by the mid-1770s. 'Of all my favourite authors', wrote Sancho in 1766, 'not one has drawn a tear in favour of my miserable black brethren – excepting yourself, and the humane author of Sir George Ellison. – I think you will forgive me; – I am sure you will applaud me for beseeching you to give one half hour's attention to slavery, as it is this day practiced in our West Indies.' Sancho wanted a human response to the practice of the slave trade and enslavement. Surely, he thought, this 'horrid wickedness' would 'produce remorse in every enlightened and candid reader'. Sterne replied, ''tis no uncommon thing, my good Sancho, for one half of the world to use the other half of it like brutes, then endeavour to make 'em so'.[18]

---

[14] Ibid., 36–7.
[15] Heather Andrea Williams, *Help Me to Find My People. The African American Search for Family Lost in Slavery* (Chapel Hill, NC, 2012), notes the seemingly purposeful blocking of sympathy amongst nineteenth-century white slave-holders.
[16] Long, *History*, II. 383.
[17] Fanon, *Black Skin, White Mask*, 77.
[18] Vincent Carretta (ed.), *Letters of the Late Ignatius Sancho, an African* (London, 2015), 128, 165, 312.

The story that Sterne subsequently wrote in *Tristram Shandy* told of the poor 'Negro' girl of whom the Corporal asked, 'is a black wench to be used worse than a white one? ... 'tis the fortune of war that has put the whip in our hands *now* – where it may be after, heaven knows.'[19] Sancho shared Long's passion for Thomson's *The Seasons*. But Long was incapable, unlike Sancho and Sterne, of extending human sympathy to those unlike himself. Both he and his wife were subscribers to the *Letters of the Late Ignatius Sancho, an African* published in 1782. We have no record of his response to it.

Long would not be drawing a tear in favour of Sancho's 'miserable black brethren'. His identification was with the West India lobby. A loose group of colonists protecting West Indian interests had been in existence for some decades, led by Beckford in the 1750s and 1760s. It was gathering strength in the 1770s. The author of the new *History of Jamaica* was clearly an excellent recruit, given his knowledge of the island, his political experience and his unquestioning support for slavery. Meetings were being held by the agents (appointed to represent the islands), London merchants and absentees to hear reports and discuss strategy in the face of growing threats. Increasingly vocal abolitionists made for trouble. But so did the rising taxes that resulted from the treasury's recognition of colonial trade as a source of valuable revenue, particularly in light of the huge increase in the national debt in the wake of the Seven Years War, widely blamed on the defence of the American colonies. Some slave-owners were unenthusiastic about the identity of 'West Indian', disliking their brashness and vulgarity. 'My greatest pride', wrote John Pinney in 1778, 'is to be considered as a private country gentleman'; he hoped to avoid 'the name of a West Indian', for they were a 'dissipated, unthinking race'.[20] Others, however, were keen to protect their financial position as best they could. The merchants were the first group to formalize their organization. Their interests did not always coincide with those of the planters, who relied heavily on their credit and were persecuted by debt, but by the 1770s they were increasingly ready to cooperate. The outbreak of the American War in 1775 posed dangers to all concerned with the trade: delegations and petitions requested armed convoys and more protection for the islands. Despite sympathy with the American colonists in their claim for autonomy, the West Indians were never inclined to join them. As Bryan Edwards understood very well, 'It is to Great Britain alone that our West India planters consider themselves as belonging ... even such of them as have resided in the West Indies from their birth, look on the islands as their temporary abode only.' England was 'home' and 'the fond notion of being able to go home (as they emphatically term a visit to England) year after year animates their industry

---

[19] Sterne, *Tristram Shandy*, 811.
[20] Pares, *A West India Fortune*, 141.

and alleviates their misfortune'.[21] The colonists wanted autonomy and self-government, as had been made very clear during the Privileges Controversy, but knew that they were dependent on the economic and military protection of the metropole. Faced with war, for all his patriotism about Jamaica and the 'rights of freeborn Englishmen', Long's attacks on prerogative government necessarily weakened. In the end, the colony must bow to the interests of the mother country.

By the 1780s the Society of West India Merchants, chaired by Edward's Uncle Beeston, was meeting in the London Tavern, next to his lavish residence on Bishopsgate Street, and focusing particularly on questions of commerce. After the American War the Society of West India Merchants and Planters (the Society), with explicitly political aims, united the two groups and held both formal and informal meetings, dealing with all aspects of policy relating to sugar.[22] Samuel Long, Uncle Beeston's oldest son, was the treasurer, and his brother Beeston Junior took over from his father as chair of the West India Merchants. An annual dinner club, of which Edward was a member, was just one of their activities, mixing business with the pleasures of pepper-pot and political, neighbourly and familial gossip. Long found himself part of a strong network of West Indians, many of them intermarried, utilizing their connections and access to government to lobby, petition and propagandize in defence of their privileged position and in the face of unsympathetic government policies. In 1781 North's government had raised sugar duties and in 1783 an Order in Council had enforced the Navigation Acts, making it increasingly difficult for the planters to access lumber and provisions. Long penned a pamphlet in response, but with further restrictions on trade with the USA in the post-war period, West Indian interests were no longer comfortably aligned with Britain: 'the system that for so long had enriched the West Indians was by the 1780s being turned against them'.[23] Long understood that it was the protection the West Indians enjoyed in the domestic market that was responsible for their prosperity: they must do all they could to preserve the monopoly. 'We are all equally the citizens', he wrote, 'of one and the same great

---

[21] Bryan Edwards, *Thoughts on the Late Proceedings of Government Respecting the Trade of the West India Islands with the United States of North America* (2nd edn, London, 1784), 39.

[22] Andrew Jackson O'Shaughnessy, 'The Formation of a Commercial Lobby: the West India Interest, British Colonial Policy and the American Revolution', *HJ* 40.1 (1997), 71–95; O'Shaughnessy, *An Empire Divided*; Ryden, *West Indian Slavery*; Ryden, 'Sugar, Spirits and Fodder'.

[23] [Long], *A Free and Candid Review of a Tract Entitled 'Observations on the Commerce of the American States' Shewing the Pernicious Consequences, Both to Great Britain, and to the British Sugar Islands of the Systems Recommended in that Tract* (London, 1784); Julian Hoppit, 'Introduction', to M. W. McCahill (ed.), *The Correspondence of Stephen Fuller, 1788–1795. Jamaica, the West India Interest at Westminster and the Campaign to Preserve the Slave Trade* (Chichester, 2014), 7.

metropolis.'[24] Yet it seemed that their loyalty was not being rewarded, and intense lobbying was bringing few rewards. Jane Catherine Long reported to her brother in 1785 that he should not expect to hear from their father, since he was 'obliged every day either to attend Mr Pitt or a West India Committee'.[25] She also told him some of the London gossip. 'Do you recollect anything of Alpress a West Indian?', she inquired, continuing,

> her youngest daughter, a child of about 13 years and a ½ old, has lately taken a trip to Gretna Green, with Mr Bulkely – an Irish fortune hunter, upwards of 30 years old, and who was scarcely acquainted with her. Conceive her Impudence. She told him that she was determined upon running away, and that if he objected to being her companion in her flight she would look out for someone else. She had a very good fortune, of course he was not fool enough to object to her proposal, and she absolutely got into a Hackney Coach and *pulled* him in after her. Heiresses, I know, ought to do this, but I think a girl of her age must have had an amazing stock of assurance to bring herself to it.

'The Mother swears she will never forgive her,' she concluded, but she was not surprised herself that the girl wanted to leave her, and she utilized the racialized stereotype, naming her 'a terrible Quashiba'.[26] These were just the horrors that Long associated with miscegenation: girls without modesty or decency, ashamed of their mothers, running off to Gretna Green with adventurers. His daughter clearly had some respect for 'the amazing stock of assurance' the girl possessed. It would have been fascinating to hear a discussion of this over the Longs' dinner table.

West Indian pressure, however, had limited success. As Eric Williams argued, the American Revolution dealt a deathblow to the slave-owners: 'The rise and fall of mercantilism', he wrote, 'is the rise and fall of slavery.'[27] From a different perspective, Chris Brown argues that it was the American Revolution which shifted the terms of debate over slavery, ensuring that it became a political as well as a moral issue and marking the distinctions between what was British and what was American. The colonists' love of freedom, as Burke

---

[24] [Long], *A Free and Candid Review*, 4.
[25] Howard, *Records and Letters*, I. 178.
[26] Ibid., I. 177–8. Quasheba is a West African (Akan-Twi) day-name for a woman born on Sunday. The set of fourteen day-names came over to the New World with the enslaved, and creolized versions of them are very common in estate inventories listing enslaved people. They are by far the most widespread names of African origin found in those listings. Long was the earliest to identify their origin as day-names; *History*, II. 247: 'Many of the plantation Blacks call their children by the African name for the day of the week on which they are born.' Thanks to Margaret Williamson, personal communication, 26 November 2022. Jane Catherine Long was clearly using the name pejoratively.
[27] Williams, *Capitalism and Slavery*, 136.

argued, arose from the multitudes of the enslaved.[28] The debates over the war opened up new and uncomfortable questions as to the meanings of 'liberty' and its relation to Britain and 'slavery'.

Long had taken a lease at 46 Wimpole Street in 1781, near other absentees who liked to gather in the smart new neighbourhood of Marylebone. He attended many meetings in the 1780s and early 1790s.[29] His London residence was combined with a series of rented country properties, all within easy reach of Westminster. Stephen Fuller, the agent for Jamaica, was a man of whom Long approved as unusually devoted to 'the public good'.[30] Fuller was a West Indian merchant, factor and planter, part of the Sussex gentry/colonial family, married into other slave-owning families and with close connections to the Longs. He was the principal strategist and organizer for the West Indians. Numerous grievances were articulated, from taxation and trade regulations to the demand for more military and naval protection and concerns over the mobilization of free and enslaved 'Negroes' in the face of war. Once it was clear that Prime Minister Pitt took Wilberforce's interest in the abolition of the slave trade seriously, the Society, which had been slow to recognize the scale of the danger, launched into action. Fuller established subcommittees to draft petitions, serve on deputations and act as witnesses. By dint of aligning with Ultra Tories, the House of Lords and the royal family and stressing the connections between slave rebellion and the Jacobins, in the wake of the revolution in Saint-Domingue and the French Revolution, he was critical to holding off the abolition of the slave trade for more than a decade.[31] There were bursts of activity at times of danger, and Long's *History* meant that he was called upon as an authority. In February 1788 Thomas Steele, Long's nephew by marriage, was acting as secretary to Pitt and keeping his uncle informed as to likely developments on abolition. He had found Pitt reading the *History* and his 'admiration of the performance' enabled Steele to propose a meeting. 'He hungers and thirsts after knowledge', he reported 'and you are more likely than any other person I know to satisfy his voracious appetite.'[32] Pitt, aware of the need for evidence, had convened a Privy Council Committee on Trade and Plantations with Lord Hawkesbury in the chair. Long was in correspondence with Hawkesbury, who declared himself 'certainly impatient to know your opinion on these subjects, with which you are so widely acquainted ... I am so much disposed to place confidence in that opinion.'[33]

---

[28] Brown, *Moral Capital*, 143.
[29] Ryden estimates that he attended forty-six meetings of the Society, his cousin Samuel seventy-nine and cousin Beeston Junior a hundred; *West Indian Slavery*, 57.
[30] Long, *History*, I. 122.
[31] On Fuller, see Hoppit, 'Introduction'.
[32] Howard, *Records and Letters*, I. 254.
[33] Ibid.

A subcommittee was set up in 1788 to prepare evidence for the Privy Council for defence on 'the subject of Negroes'. New abolitionist thinking had been building in the wake of the Mansfield decision. Phillis Wheatley, 'the extraordinary Poetical Genius', had visited London in 1773 and her *Poems on Various Subjects, Religious and Moral* were widely reviewed and acclaimed. Treated in London as an exotic visitor despite her youth and enslaved status, she met many well-known people including Benjamin Franklin, while Granville Sharp served as her main tour guide.[34] Her authorship, certain to be challenged, was confirmed by a testimonial from eighteen of Boston's most respected gentlemen who had examined her. Was this young woman capable of writing such poetry? Representing herself as an Ethiopian, Wheatley adopted a position of moral authority derived from her experience. A child, as she named herself in her most famous poem, 'brought from AFRICA to AMERICA', it was physical slavery that had enabled her spiritual freedom.[35] Even Voltaire, no friend to Africans, was convinced that Hume's dictum that Africans could only mimic was disproved by 'her very fine English verse'.[36] A decade later it was the publication of James Ramsay's *An Essay on the Treatment and Conversion of African Slaves in the British Sugar Colonies* (1784) that created a more widespread debate as to British responsibility for slavery. As an Anglican clergyman and slave-owner on St Kitts for twenty years, Ramsay had extensive knowledge of both the trade and the plantations. His eyewitness account was a powerful antidote to that of Long. The assertions of 'the ingenious author of a late History of Jamaica' were directly contradicted by Ramsay, as were the comments of Hume, derided as unworthy of the status of 'observations'. 'That there is any essential difference between the European and African mental powers', wrote Ramsay, 'as far as my experience has gone, I positively deny.'[37] Neither skin colour, hair nor anatomy provided any basis for assumptions as to inequality: God was a 'God of universal nature'.[38] A number of cases of named individuals, including an enslaved 'poor negress', Babay, provided testimony of African capacity for generosity, loyalty and goodness of heart. Ramsay addressed himself to 'the man of feeling', aware, unlike Long, of the need to evoke sympathy in his attempt to win support for

---

[34] Carretta, *Phillis Wheatley*, 138.
[35] Wheatley's poetry has had a mixed reception from African-Americans over generations. Henry Louis Gates Jr, *The Trials of Phillis Wheatley. America's First Black Poet and her Encounters with the Founding Fathers* (New York, 2003).
[36] Carretta, *Phillis Wheatley*, 165. On Voltaire, see Curran, *Anatomy of Blackness*, 148; Gianamar Giovannetti-Singh, 'Racial Capitalism in Voltaire's Enlightenment', *HWJ* 94 (2022), 22–41.
[37] James Ramsay, *An Essay on the Treatment and Conversion of African Slaves in the British Sugar Colonies* (London, 1784), 231, 203.
[38] Ibid., 207.

'civilizing' and Christianizing Africans.[39] Like Sharp he was directly critical of the slave-owners with their commitment to the 'Kingdom of I'.[40] The levels of cruelty and excess, rather than being the product of individual 'bad apples', as Long claimed, were a consequence, Ramsay insisted, of the unnatural relationship of master and slave. And this was a matter of legality, requiring intervention. Quaker activism had revived in 1785 and Thomas Clarkson's *Essay* followed in 1786, with its details of the horrors of the slave trade.[41] By 1787 the Society for Effecting the Abolition of the Slave Trade had been established in London and was actively producing pamphlets and petitions. The iconic image of the kneeling enslaved man asking for help on Wedgwood's anti-slavery medallion spoke to an emergent common sense: black men *were* brothers, albeit in need of white agency. Meanwhile, the views of white clerics like Ramsay as to the capacities of Africans were being vindicated at home by the growing public presence and example of men such as Olaudah Equiano or Gustavus Vassa. Equiano was writing letters to the press and book reviews, explicitly taking on two of the pro-slavery authors who had violently attacked Ramsay. He offered testimony to the Privy Council inquiry (which was not accepted), wrote an open letter to MPs and attended debates in the House of Commons, making his black presence visible.[42] Simon Taylor, still living in Jamaica, had nothing but contempt for the black activists whom he described as 'vagabond negroes': their existence enraged him.[43]

The West Indians knew they must defend their position. Long and Uncle Beeston, alongside Henry Dawkins and Chaloner Arcedeckne, Jamaican absentees and associates of Drake and Long, worked closely with Fuller preparing evidence for their committee.[44] The Jamaicans dominated the lobby, something that was not always appreciated by the other islanders. Fuller and William Chisholm (another substantial Clarendon planter), together with Long, presented testimony which could have been taken directly from the *History*. It was designed to demonstrate that 'Negroes' were well treated but profligate, always in need of discipline. 'Upon the whole', they maintained, 'we believe them to be far better clothed, lodged, and fed in Jamaica than the Peasantry of Europe in general.'[45] This was an argument

---

[39] Ibid., 259.
[40] Brown, *Moral Capital*, 249.
[41] Thomas Clarkson, *An Essay on the Slavery and Commerce of the Human Species* (London, 1786).
[42] Vincent Carretta, *Equiano, the African. Biography of a Self-made Man* (London, 2006).
[43] Petley, *White Fury*, 157.
[44] McCahill, *The Correspondence of Stephen Fuller*, 73; Ryden, *West Indian Slavery*, 44.
[45] *Report of the Lords of Committee of Council appointed for the consideration of all matters relating to Trade and Foreign Plantations; the evidence and information they have collected in consequence of His Majesty's Order in Council, dated the 11th of February 1788, concerning the present state of the trade to Africa, and particularly the trade in slaves;*

that was to be repeated for decades. On 'well-regulated estates' 'Negroes' had 'unbounded Liberty' in their provision grounds, but most were 'improvident and negligent'. They were equipped with clothes, food and 'perfectly convenient' houses, a hothouse, doctors for the sick, and care for the aged and disabled. Questioned as to mortality and birth rates on the plantations, they responded that 'Prudent' planters encouraged 'Connexions' on their own estates 'as a Means of preventing them from rambling every Night to other Estates in the Neighbourhood, and of reducing them to a temperate and orderly Habit of Life'. Unfortunately, 'great Dissoluteness and Inordinancy of manners and Habits', together with the 'vicious and irregular Practices' of 'the Negroes', resulted in high levels of mortality and the failure of 'natural Increase'. They claimed that special care was provided for pregnant, lying-in and breastfeeding women and that young children were properly tended: precisely the recommendations that Long had been making in the notes for his revised edition of the *History*. The testimony was designed to demonstrate that accusations of cruelty were mistaken and improvements were being made. But the plantations could not function, they insisted, without slavery. Europeans would die in the sun, while free 'Negroes' would not do agricultural labour and 'have all the Vices of Slaves ... no Planter could controul them'. A great deal of attention was devoted to the 'deluded Negroes', prey to superstition, who believed in the 'supernatural Power' of obeah men. Not only had obeah played a critical part in the 'formidable Insurrection' of 1760, but the fetishistic practices associated with it, many of which had come from Africa, were evidence of essential 'difference'.[46] All this added up, they hoped, to a watertight case for the continuation of the trade.

A Select Committee of the House of Commons, a delaying tactic of the pro-slavers, heard evidence from 1790 to 1791. Long and his friend Chisholm attended the hearings daily, and as Fuller reported, the West Indians were 'very politely treated by the late and present Speaker ... indulged with seats under the Gallery, instead of being crowded in heaps behind the clock, or waiting with our Footmen in the Lobby'.[47] Wilberforce too was regularly in attendance. His first motion for abolition was, however, defeated.[48] When it came to the debate in April 1792, the West Indians knew that 'We have Mr Pitt, Mr Fox & Mr Burke the great Orators against us, but we flatter ourselves that Common Sense is with us.'[49] 'Common Sense', they hoped, linked as it was to profit, would win through. Fuller knew that they had lost the moral argument. As Bryan Edwards had noted, 'the term *Slave-holder*' now conveyed to their critics

and concerning the Effects and Consequences of this Trade, as well in Africa and the West Indies, as to the general Commerce of this Kingdom (London, 1789), Section 1, Part 3, n.p.
[46] Ibid., passim.
[47] McCahill, *The Correspondence of Stephen Fuller*, 125–6, 136–7.
[48] Roger Anstey, *The Atlantic Slave Trade and British Abolition, 1760–1810* (London, 1975).
[49] McCahill, *The Correspondence of Stephen Fuller*, 121–2.

'an idea of everything that is oppressive, rapacious, remorseless, and bloody-minded'.[50] But Fuller was convinced that if the case for Britain's national interest was mobilized, they would stave off defeat. Long would have been horrified to hear the evidence he had collected for his *History* utilized by these 'great Orators'.[51] Wilberforce cited Long's authority three times in his extensive speech arguing for abolition of the trade: the historian 'had argued at great length on the danger of importing such numbers of Africans' and had himself proposed a 'temporary prohibition of the importation of African slaves' in an effort to stop slave-owners getting into so much debt. Furthermore, he had recognized that the scale of absenteeism was undesirable and that the majority of insurrections had occurred on the properties of those who were not resident. Dundas also appealed to 'the Author of the History of Jamaica, I mean Mr Long'; he continued, 'and I ask whether there is any man who does not agree in the plain account given by that historian, *that the great danger in the West Indies arises in reality from the importation of the African Slaves into the Islands?*' Fox too noted, 'Even Mr Long's history of Jamaica points out the probable benefits of such a prohibition.'[52] Long's pride in the influence of his work must have been tempered by his recognition that he could not control the ways in which his writings were used. Some gains were made by the abolitionists in 1792, but these were delayed by the friends of the pro-slavers in the House of Lords. Faced with these challenges, both Long and Beeston served on a further subcommittee to orchestrate a more aggressive public campaign, with pamphlets and press coverage. The events in Saint-Domingue and in France and the fears associated with revolutionary politics put paid, however, to any further abolitionist efforts and reduced the immediate need for the West Indians to defend themselves.

In January 1793 Long received a report from the assembly on the state of the sugar and slave trade, naming their 'heavy grievances'. Their 'principal staple' had been 'limited in a mode most unprecedented and unjustifiable' and they had been granted 'insufficient military protection'. 'Every species of calumny continues to be sanctioned by some of his majesty's principal ministers of state,' they continued, and these words were heavily underlined by Long, 'to render his majesty's loyal subjects in the West-Indies odious in the eyes of their fellow-subjects in Great Britain'. They feared that 'the British Parliament'

---

[50] Bryan Edwards, *A Speech Delivered at a Free Conference between the Honourable the Council and Assembly of Jamaica, 19 Nov. 1789, on the subject of Mr Wilberforce's propositions in the House of Commons concerning the slave-trade* (Kingston, Jamaica, 1789), 7.

[51] The use of 'common sense' here is somewhat ironic since the Scottish School of Common Sense included James Beattie and other critics of Hume. Personal communication, Silvia Sebastiani.

[52] *Debate on a Motion for the Abolition of the Slave Trade in the House of Commons on Monday 2nd April 1792, reported in detail* (London, 1792), 7, 10, 13, 106–7, 128.

would pass an Act stopping the trade, when 'it is undoubtedly the duty of administration to protect the rights of the colonists'. The report was signed by Simon Taylor and others, and their covering note to Fuller asked him to consult with Bryan Edwards, Long and George Hibbert (who was emerging as a key supporter in the House of Commons and was soon to become the agent for Jamaica) to ensure that the report was circulated.[53] In March Long was asked by 'our friends in Jam' (sic) to convene a group to discuss 'a business' of immense 'Difficulty and Delicacy'.[54] This concerned a petition from free people of colour on the island, emboldened by similar claims in Saint-Domingue, for greater civil rights. Long would have had no sympathy for such a petition, but may have been aware it was more difficult to ignore such demands in the context of Saint-Domingue and the dangerously vulnerable position of small numbers of white colonists. Once the House of Lords had blocked the abolition bill, Long perhaps felt able to withdraw: he chose to retire into family life.[55]

He continued to read extensively in the early 1790s, collecting his thoughts and notes for a possible second edition of the *History*, something that never materialized. On his return from Jamaica he had been able to adopt unproblematically the identity of 'eye-witness'. He could no longer claim to be that. As a planter in the 1760s he had been part of a 'ruling class at the peak of its powers': the 1760 rebellion had been crushed, free people of colour firmly put in their place, Britain dominated the Caribbean and profits were soaring.[56] But the combination of the American War, abolitionism, the French Revolution and Saint-Domingue had changed the landscape. He may have experienced the classic diasporic problem of being both 'out of place' and 'out of time': as an absentee he no longer belonged in Jamaica, but England was changing too.[57] But while postcolonial writers have been able to find new voices, he could find no place to be, no new identity. Writing during and after the American War, he continued to insist on the primacy of colonial interests and the right of the assembly to legislate on internal matters. Judiciously chosen passages from Locke on the need for the consent of the governed were reiterated. The problem with the Jamaican constitution, he recognized, was that it was not 'truly English'.[58] The colonists were 'like Bees', he opined, who had flown 'their hive to labour apart from their Countrymen, but for the common benefit of the whole'. They were 'entitled to the full enjoyment of English franchises, and more particularly, as by their sequestred industry, they become in time the

---

[53] BL Add Mss 12432, Report of Committee of the Jamaican House of Assembly on the Slave Trade, November 1792, 2. On Hibbert's role, see Donington, *The Bonds of Family*.
[54] McCahill, *The Correspondence of Stephen Fuller*, 209.
[55] He had bouts of ill health at this time, necessitating time in Bath; ibid., 158.
[56] Burnard, 'Harvest Years?', 548.
[57] Edward Said, *Out of Place. A Memoir* (London, 1999).
[58] BL Add MSS 12402, f. 48.

most solid props of the liberty, property, and happiness enjoyed by their Coutrymen at home'.[59] Yet White colonists were *not* quite English; the assembly was *not* the House of Commons, nor was the Council the House of Lords.[60] The colonial assemblies had won the right to raise revenue and, since the assembly stood in place of parliament with respect to internal affairs, colonists could not be taxed by parliament: 'two co-ordinate powers cannot subsist at one time in any government'.[61] The North Americans had gone to war to establish this, but the Jamaicans had paid the tax on sugar and retreated from the threats they made at various points as to secession. They had not joined the Americans and had accepted their dependence on the 'mother country'. They were in danger, he wrote at one point and without any hint of awareness of the ironies of his terminology, of being reduced to 'splendid English Slaves', tyrannized by the imperial parliament.[62] His friend and successor Bryan Edwards had lived between England and Jamaica over some years, and was active in both the Society and the assembly.[63] His *History*, published in 1793, owed much to Long but adopted a somewhat more conciliatory tone. He claimed that he was 'no friend to slavery in any shape' and understood by 1797 that the slave trade would be abolished and that the best that could be hoped for was that the colonial assemblies should do this themselves, rather than having their powers usurped.[64] Perhaps Edwards had taken on the mantle of his mentor who could now withdraw. Long had been compelled to recognize that slave-owners must adapt, that the slave trade would be abolished, that forms of amelioration would have to be accepted, 'some degree of liberty' might have to be granted, enslaved women should be encouraged to reproduce.[65] But he never penned a repudiation of slavery.

Long continued to puzzle over 'the very different races of Man': what defined the difference between the human and the animal, and between different varieties of humans?[66] He argued with Buffon, read Goldsmith, pondered over the polygenist Pinkerton, reflected on Jefferson's *Notes on Virginia*. The unresolved question was: what caused these differences? Was it external, was it internal, was it fixed? Was it the air or 'a particular natural or indelible effect of some other cause'?[67] Was it the capacity to improve, or was it

---

[59] BL Add MSS 12404, f. 1.
[60] Long wrote extensively on the inadequacies of the constitutional position of the council which had no independence. See particularly Add Mss 12402, ff. 32–8.
[61] BL Add MSS 12403, f. 157.
[62] BL Add MSS 12402, n.p.
[63] Olwyn M. Blouet, 'Bryan Edwards FRS, 1743–1800', *Notes and Records of the Royal Society of London* 54.2 (2000), 215–22.
[64] Edwards, *Speech*, 80. In 1797 he supported this proposal from Charles Ellis which divided the pro-slavers.
[65] BL Add MSS 12405, f. 430.
[66] BL Add MSS 12438, 'On the Different Races of Mankind', f. 1r.
[67] BL Add MSS 12438, f. 11r.

the soul, or the power of speech, or judgement or curiosity? But monkeys, he had to admit, were curious. He wanted to believe, along with Aristotle, that some men were *naturally* slaves: 'some men there are says he who are born to be slaves, that is seem adapted & intended by Nature for servitude'.[68] Varieties of dogs occupied him along with the horse, the orangutan and humans of many different shapes and colours. The natural historians, philosophers and theologians debated, and disagreed: he continued to read and note. Whereas in the *History* he had had no trouble in articulating his contradictory convictions, that 'Negroes' were *essentially* different, fixed in their bodies, and that 'Creoles' could improve, he could no longer find a clear position from which to write. The materials to be consulted were ever expanding – new anatomical findings, new theories. But he had no new evidence to bring. '[H]ow is it possible', he asked himself, 'to reconcile these facts which are incontestable?'[69] His *History*, with its celebration of the wealth Jamaica produced for Britain and its claims for the rights of free-born Englishmen, belonged to a particular moment, one which had passed. His moment as a 'history man' had passed too. He had been unable to control the world through his text.

The longer he was in England the more English in some respects he became, more embedded in familial life and conscious of the dangers of enemies at home. He had been deeply shocked by the Gordon Riots in 1780 and the making of London into a 'Garrison City' defended by the military. It was one thing for Jamaica to rely on the military, another matter for England. He trusted that the destruction was the work of a 'confused rabble' rather than a 'political mob'.[70] The riots may have taken him back to his memories of London in 1745, barricaded against the Jacobites. England could be endangered, not just by the French but by its own internal enemies, a deeply disturbing thought. It should be protected by its constitution and embedded beliefs in liberty and property. But the French Revolution, Tom Paine and the Rights of Man cast a worrying shadow over the England he wanted to protect. Enemies could become allies in this context, Fox praised for his denunciation of the tyranny 'exercised by the majority over the minority'.[71] His last published work was *The Antigallican*, a horrified reflection on the dangers of 'the *Levelling System* of France' infecting Britain. He reiterated his belief in inequality and subordination: 'Black will not become white' because the Convention decrees it, he insisted. Disaster occurred when 'people' take command: then 'manners, order, virtue' disappear, 'Wives, children, slaves, will shake off all subjection'. His class prejudice was in full flow, condemning the 'lower ranks of

---

[68] BL Add MSS 12405, f. 354.
[69] BL Add MSS 12438, f. 5v.
[70] Howard, *Records and Letters*, I. 142.
[71] Long, *The Antigallican; or strictures on the present form of government established in France* (London, 1793), 13.

people', Burke's 'swinish multitude', who were 'not in the habit of reasoning'.[72] 'We are formed with unequal capacities of body and mind'; 'subordination is very necessary for society'. The idea of all being equal, of sharing property, was menacing: 'we should all degenerate into brutes' ... '*Our tails would grow.*'[73] Subordination was essential; the destruction of rank meant the demolition of property. He summoned up Defoe, who 'very properly made Robinson Crusoe to command, and Friday to obey'.[74] How pertinent that what should come into his mind, even when facing unrest 'at home', was that apocryphal account of the subordination of the 'native' to the colonizer.

Long had found over the years that his income was uncomfortably volatile. As early as 1771, when he was only recently settled in Chichester, his Uncle Charles had promised not to take any 'disagreeable measures' in the face of his incapacity to pay his dues on their contract. He was clear, however, that there would be no special familial dispensations: the arrears and interest must be paid the following year.[75] Sugar production at Lucky Valley rose in the 1770s but then declined as a result of hurricanes and crop failure and was badly hit by the war. Long's optimistic account of the wealth that Jamaica produced for Britain was no longer so convincing: the island was losing its pre-eminent position. A table documenting production at Lucky Valley between 1763 and 1787 showed the scale of the fluctuations, and particularly gloomy figures for 1786/7 when the yield was substantially down.[76] The situation was very precarious, Long reported to Edward Beeston: hurricanes had destroyed the crop and washed away the aqueduct; he feared he might have lost more than £2,500.[77] These were the years of terrible hunger for the enslaved and falling profits for the planters. He was receiving and responding to regular reports from Jamaica, both on his property and on the political affairs of the colony. The revolution in Saint-Domingue brought new opportunities for the British slavers in the wake of the collapse of the French trade and production recovered after 1791. Over-investment and speculation in low-quality sugars, however, then resulted in a glut of the sugar market, a problem magnified by the competition from the better-quality product that foreign rivals were delivering. Lucky Valley sugar production was significantly down once more by the early 1800s and continued to fall.[78] Long found himself in straitened circumstances and was particularly angry at the tax rise imposed by the

---

[72] Ibid., vi, 12, 29, 46.
[73] Ibid., 71–2.
[74] Ibid., 72–4.
[75] Howard, *Records and Letters*, I. 130.
[76] BL Add MSS 18961, f. 80v.
[77] Howard, *Records and Letters*, I. 252.
[78] Thanks to James Dawkins for his analysis of the Accounts Produce for Lucky Valley over this period. The Lucky Valley output was roughly in line with the island's sugar production during this time.

ministry in 1803, leaving the growers with a 'pittance' of profit.[79] The glory years of slave-owners' prosperity, at least in the 'old colonies', tied as Long knew to their protected position in the British market, were over. The trade was not to be abolished until 1807. By then the sugar glut and a catastrophic drop in land values left Long with a greatly diminished income.[80] His years of political agitation were over. His beloved wife, Mary, had died in 1797; his siblings, children and grandchildren occupied his mind. The monument constructed by his family after his death in 1813, close to the altar and above his tomb in St Mary's church, Slindon, featured Clio, the muse of history, cast in white marble. (See Figure E.3.) She is represented in classical pose, holding a scroll, the knowledge that will inform subsequent generations, and beside her are further scrolls, summoning up the volumes of the *History*. The memorial is suitably bland, emphasizing Long's genealogy, his *History*, law and property, and his 'long and unblemished life, beloved and lamented by his family, honoured and respected by all who knew him'.[81]

And what of his legacy? He did not live to see the abolition of slavery, only the demise of the trade in 1807. The abolition of slavery in 1833 did not end the forms of racialization that he had characterized so effectively in his *History*. They provided a reservoir of stereotypes that have been drawn from across generations.[82] Some of the slave-owners and their descendants who speedily abandoned their defence of chattel slavery in the wake of emancipation rewrote racial hierarchies for new times. Charles Kingsley, shattered by emancipation and what was to his mind the inadequacy of compensation, plus the loss of the family fortune in Barbados, was one of those who complicated the Black/White binary by introducing the figure of the indentured Indian 'coolie'. His brother Henry took his racialized thinking with him to the new colony of white settlement in Australia and told stories of 'bushmen' and their dangerous encounters with Aboriginal 'savages'.[83] Three of Long's great-nephews, the sons of Beeston Long Junior, travelled to Queensland in the hope of making fortunes in Australia's new sugar industry. One drowned, another returned to

---

[79] Howard, *Records and Letters*, II. 336–7.
[80] Ahmed Reid and David Beck Ryden, 'Sugar, Land Markets and the Williams Thesis: Evidence from Jamaica's Property Sales, 1750–1810', *S&A* 34.3 (2013), 401–24.
[81] Catherine Hall, 'Whose Memories? Edward Long and the Work of Re-remembering', in Katie Donington, Ryan Hanley and Jessica Moody (eds.), *Britain's History and Memory of Transatlantic Slavery. Local Nuances of a 'National Sin'* (Liverpool, 2016), 129–49. The parish council at Slindon, concerned by this bland memorial, has agreed new wording for an additional plaque that recognizes Long's racism.
[82] A research project could be built on exploring the influence of Long not only in the UK but in the USA and beyond.
[83] Hall, 'Reconfiguring Race'; Hall, 'Writing Histories, Making "Race": Slave-owners and their Stories', *Australian Historical Studies* 47.3 (2016), 365–80; see *Writing Slavery into Biography. Australian Legacies of British Slavery*, the special issue of *Australian Journal of Biography and History* 6 (2022).

Figure E.3 Edward Long's funerary monument within St Mary's church, Slindon, West Sussex. The monument was designed in 1813 by Sir Richard Westmacott, one of the most prominent sculptors of the period. Image courtesy of Liberty Paterson.

England, while the third, Edward Maitland Long, established a plantation at Habana, employing South Sea Islanders, another new source of racialized labour.[84] In the England of the late 1840s, when emancipation had lost its aura and the ending of the protection of British sugar in 1846 had left the planters in rage and despair, Thomas Carlyle drew on Long's repertoire of racist tropes.[85] It was white men who had made the Caribbean; the sugar islands in his imagination had been jungle and swamp when the colonists arrived, the 'cinamon, sugar, coffee, pepper black and gray lying all asleep, waiting the white enchanter who should say to them, Awake!' It was not 'Black Quashee' who had enriched the tropics; it had required 'European heroism'. Carlyle loathed what he saw as the refusal of Black people to work, their capacity to draw subsistence

---

[84] Emma Christopher, 'Dreams of a New Plantation Society in Queensland, Australia', LBS blog, 25 July 2018.
[85] Hall, *Civilising Subjects*.

from the fecundity of the land. 'He who shall not work shall not eat,' he thundered.[86]

Long's racial encoding of 'order, as whiteness, and disorder, as blackness' was to be reworked multiple times across the centuries. It was Black migration from the Caribbean to the metropole from the 1940s that 'functioned as the trigger', releasing and organizing new memories of empire and new configurations of race in the white population.[87] These revived memories of empire were 'less the product of the mind than of sensation and feeling, a knowledge of ethnic inheritance lodged deep in the body'.[88] This was an 'ethnic inheritance' that Long had proclaimed in the 1770s as indeed 'deep in the body'. Sections of the white population now saw themselves as under attack, their fears mobilized by Enoch Powell, their authority lost in the face of the 'invasion' of 'others'. Those peoples once colonized, kept safely at a distance, were now occupying the homeland, claiming 'We are here because you were there.' At the same time new forms of Black British domestic politics were emerging, with 'Black' as an inclusive identity and Blackness and Whiteness at its heart.[89] Young Black men learned that 'English society *is* racist – it *works through race.*'[90] That working through was structured by the changing forms of capitalist exploitation that characterized the British economy in the 1970s and 1980s. Black under-employment, combined with what low-paid work was available in the labour market, was experienced through race. White workers who resented the displacements and threats, as they saw it, to their status and rights, focused their grievances through race. The form of racial capitalism built primarily on enslaved colonial labour that had operated in the mid-eighteenth-century Atlantic sugar business had been reconfigured. In the heyday of industrial capitalism, enslaved labour in the USA and the indentured and bonded labour of colonized peoples had provided a massive external resource together with the extraction of raw materials from the empire, all securing a better standard of living for white workers 'at home'. Racial capitalism was reconfigured again from the mid-twentieth century as financialization and new forms of globalization took hold, bringing a new set of racialized

---

[86] Thomas Carlyle, 'Occasional Discourse on the Negro Question', *Fraser's Magazine* 40 (1849), 673–5.

[87] Bill Schwarz, *Memories of Empire, volume I: the White Man's World* (Oxford, 2011), 10–11; Camilla Schofield, *Enoch Powell and the Making of Postcolonial Britain* (Cambridge, 2013).

[88] Schwarz, *Memories of Empire*, 54.

[89] Kennetta Hammond Perry, *London is the Place for Me. Black Britons, Citizenship and the Politics of Race* (Oxford, 2015); Rob Waters, *Thinking Black. Britain, 1964–1985* (Berkeley, 2018).

[90] Stuart Hall, Chas Critcher, Tony Jefferson, John Clarke and Brian Roberts, *Policing the Crisis. Mugging, the State and Law and Order* (London, 1978), 347.

relations 'at home' alongside the continued outsourcing of much work.[91] Race became 'the modality in which class is lived ... the medium in which class relations are experienced ... Capital reproduces the class as a whole, structured by race. It dominates the divided class, in part, through those internal divisions which have "racism" as one of their effects.'[92]

Using the tools of postcolonial/decolonial thinking has facilitated the emergence of new forms of politics, new fictions and new forms of history writing. New generations of 'history people' are addressing gender, race and class as interconnected axes of power, all imbricated in the making of 'home' and 'away'. Confronting Edward Long and immersing myself in his life and work has meant focusing on this early iteration of White mastery and Black subjection. The aim was to undo his racialized, essentialized and naturalized hierarchies and situate them fully in their political, economic, intellectual and cultural contexts. How did race *work* in eighteenth-century Jamaica, providing a set of meanings that braided the structures into the lived experiences of colonizers and colonized? How did colonial governments create the distinctions between the free and the unfree? How did an economic system which depended on mercantile credit, capture, enslavement and coercion and brought wealth and power to some, bring devastation, hunger, hardship and high mortality rates to hundreds of thousands of others? How did the colonizing practices associated with a plantation economy deforest the island and erode the soil in the interests of an export crop, leaving the land diminished? These structures were lived through characterizations of White men as born to master and Black people to serve. Skin colour was lived internally: 'colour-based racialization is not merely *under the skin*', writes Avtar Brah. 'The colour of our skin is exactly what "colours" us, our very being, across asymmetrical power relations.'[93]

'I want to set aside the Enlightenment figures of coherent and masterful subjectivity, the bearers of rights, holders of property in the self, legitimate sons with access to language and the power to represent, subjects endowed with inner coherence and rational clarity, the masters of theory, founders of states, and fathers of families,' wrote Donna Haraway in 1992. This was the very cohort that Long belonged to. What possibilities were there, Haraway asked, for figures of 'critical subjectivity, consciousness and humanity – not in the sacred image of the same, but in the self-critical practice of "difference", of the I and we that is/are never identical to itself, and so has hope of connection to

---

[91] For an analysis of racial capitalism in one sector of the late twentieth-century British economy, see James Vernon, 'Heathrow and the Making of Neoliberal Britain', *Past and Present* 252.1 (2021), 213–47.
[92] Hall et al., *Policing the Crisis*, 386–7.
[93] Avtar Brah, 'The Scent of Memory: Strangers, Our Own and Others', *Feminist Review* 61.1 (1999), 24.

others?'[94] Long's hierarchical mapping of his world meant such a connection was impossible for him. He *chose* to take on the mantle of an Enlightenment figure of masterful subjectivity, a bearer of the rights of a free-born Englishman, the holder of property in himself, 'his' land and other human beings, a legitimate son with access to language and the power to represent, a founder of a colonial state, a father of a family who denied those rights to others. He could have chosen differently. We can. We are still inhabiting a world that Long had a hand in making. Unpicking the catastrophe he represented as progress can play a part in the work of repair. What does it mean to be human, we might ask, if we cannot hope for a connection with others and welcome difference?

Francis Williams

Long's refusal of any notion of human connection with a Black man was spelt out in his vicious attack on Francis Williams. His attempted demolition of him, a 'personage' he 'introduced upon the stage', constituted the final scene for his account of racial difference, his attempted denouement. It was his test case, intended to be a conclusive performance of the 'inferiority of the Negroes to the race of white men'. Whilst claiming that he would practise 'the impartiality' that became him and do 'all possible justice', his sustained contempt for Williams was designed to confirm any doubts that either he himself or his readers might have as to the essential superiority of White men.[95] Williams had received a classical English education and had entered the Inns of Court, just like Long. Long's white skin meant that he was able to practise law and engage in government in Jamaica. Williams was barred on account of his blackness. But he was prepared to challenge his status, believing there was no shame in bearing 'a white body in black skin', a claim that was wholly at odds with Long's view of natural subordination.[96] The very existence of a man such as Francis Williams, trained in Latin, owning property in land and people, and claiming legal privileges, was a provocation to Long. His family owned the portrait of Francis Williams that has survived and it seems probable that he was looking closely at it when

---

[94] Donna Haraway, 'Ecce Homo, Ain't (Ar'n't) I a Woman, and Inappropriate/d Others: the Human in a Post-Humanist Landscape', in Judith Butler and Joan W. Scott (eds.), *Feminists Theorize the Political* (New York, 1992), 87.

[95] Long, *History*, II. 475.

[96] A translation of a self-reflective passage in Williams's Latin poem. Long misquoted it as 'a *white* man acting under a *black* skin'; ibid., II. 478.

he wrote his damning critique.[97] (Plate 11.) He may have chosen to read the portrait as a caricature, a possible interpretation of the oversized head, tye-wig, elongated arm, spindly legs, splayed feet and sword. He may perhaps have been comparing what he saw as the garish overdressed Black man with his own conventional family portraits: his grandfather Colonel Charles Long resplendent with flowing black locks, elaborately curled in the style of the Stuarts; his father, Samuel, with his striking eyebrows and sharp nose; his brother Robert as a young child in velvet.[98] But his preoccupation with Williams was on account of the threat that he posed as a Black man of learning, the fear that rather than being his brutish 'other', he was much like himself. Williams represented the 'constitutive outside whose very existence the identity of race depends on'. He had attempted to refuse an abjected and expelled position 'outside' and to 'trouble the dreams of those who were comfortable inside'.[99] It was imperative to 'cut him down to size', to reduce him if possible to a bad joke.

The portrait was the work of an unknown artist, possibly, the art historian David Bindman has suggested, Williams himself.[100] Such an oil painting was a sign of substance and gentility: it was also an assertion of personhood. Williams was pictured standing in his library in Spanish Town. The book on the elegant table in front of him is Newton's *Philosophiae Naturalis Principia Mathematica* (1687) and he appears to be instructing a pupil in the theory of gravity, the force that unites the movement of the planet with the physical ground beneath. One hand is pointing to an open copy of Newton, the other gesturing towards a celestial globe on the table paired with a terrestrial globe

---

[97] It was acquired by the Victoria and Albert Museum (V&A) in 1928 from Spink and Son Ltd., who gave it to the museum on the condition that Viscount Lord Bearsted paid Spink £150. The auction company had bought the portrait for £250 from Major H. Howard, the author of the Long family history. The museum's original interest was in the mahogany furniture featured in the portrait. V&A files.

[98] The portraits are reproduced in miniature form in Howard, *Records and Letters*, I.

[99] Hall, *Selected Writings on Race and Difference*, 362.

[100] I have been very fortunate in having conversations on Williams with David Bindman, Esther Chadwick and Fara Dabhoiwala. We are currently in discussion with the V&A about further work with the portrait. Paints were available in Spanish Town (James Robertson, personal communication, 1 July 2021) and published manuals for amateurs gave instructions on how, for example, to produce perspective. Bindman, 'Portraiture Amateur and Professional: Francis Williams and Philip Wickstead', unpublished paper; I am very grateful to the author for allowing me to see this. David Bindman, Helen Weston and Paul Kaplan, 'The City between Fantasy and Reality', in Bindman and Henry Louis Gates Jr (eds.), *The Image of the Black in Western Art, volume III: From the 'Age of Discovery' to the Age of Abolition. Part 2: The Eighteenth Century* (Cambridge, MA, 2011), 1–50; Bindman, 'Francis Williams', seminar paper, Hutchins Center, Harvard University, 23 March 2022.

440 EPILOGUE

on the floor near his feet.[101] Other titles such as those of Robert Boyle and Locke, marking his interest in the mind, and Milton's *Paradise Lost*, demonstrating his preoccupation with the divine as well as the physical and political world, can be glimpsed on the well-stocked shelves, indicators of the subject's learning. Scientific instruments provide evidence of his mathematical, geographical and astronomical skills. A quill pen reminds the viewer of his reputation as a poet. Elaborately carved furniture and genteel clothing, from the smart blue coat (a colour that some think was associated with scholars), with its yellow bindings and decorated buttons, to the blue satin waistcoat with its braid and tassels, all speak to a propertied man of substance. A landscape, possibly Spanish Town, is visible through the window, with tropical trees and buildings. Williams looks directly at the viewer, a black man proud of who he is.[102]

As a literary man with scientific credentials and a successful and well-to-do free black professional man in Spanish Town, Williams was troublesome for Long. He had become a relatively well-known figure in England, an African who had featured as a focus for debates on the nature and character of the Black man, a debate often focused on the capacity to write, since writing was seen as the visible sign of reason, a principal measure of African humanity.[103] Hume had referenced him negatively, noting that the speech of a supposedly educated 'Negro' reminded him of 'a parrot who speaks a few words plainly'.[104] The West Indian pro-slaver Samuel Estwick had repeated Hume's judgement, elaborating it with his conviction that Africans were incapable of 'moral sensations'.[105] Hume's verdict had been challenged by James Beattie, in a passage reprinted in the *Gentleman's Magazine* in 1771, together with an anonymous editorial comment reading,

> Blacks, if properly educated are capable of the same improvements as Whites. About forty years ago, Mr Williams, an African of fortune, who dressed like other Gentlemen in a tye-wig, sword etc. and who was honoured with the friendship of [the famous surgeon] Mr [William]

[101] Michele Valerie Ronnick suggests that one hand is pointing to an empty space on the bookshelves, an indication of new ideas and writings to come; 'Francis Williams: an Eighteenth Century Tertium Quid', *Negro History Bulletin* 61.2 (1998), 19–29.
[102] Vincent Carretta, 'Who was Francis Williams?', *Early American Literature* 38.2 (2003), 213–37. Some commentators have wondered if the portrait was intended as a caricature, for the body is somewhat out of proportion, the head large and the legs, in wrinkled stockings, extremely thin. Others have suggested that the portrait could be read as an unconscious exposure of the impossibility of Black colonial gentility. On the practice of refusal in Black photography, see Tina M. Campt, *Listening to Images. An Exercise in Counterintuition* (Durham, NC, 2017).
[103] Henry Louis Gates Jr, 'Writing "Race" and the Difference it Makes', *Critical Inquiry* 12.1 (1985), 1–20.
[104] Hume, 'Of National Characters', 252.
[105] [Estwick], *Considerations*, 78.

Cheselden, and other men of science, was admitted to the meetings of the Royal Society and, being proposed as a member, was rejected solely for a reason unworthy of that learned body, viz. on account of his complexion ... Mr Hume ... might have known, that souls are of no colour, and that no one can tell, on viewing a casket, what jewel it contains.[106]

In attacking Williams, Long was countering the critics of slavery who were, most regretfully to his mind, gathering force. He gave him a full first name and surname, unlike any other black man in the *History*, describing him as already a 'conspicuous figure' in England. He relied partially on heavy irony to do the work of destruction for him. A native of Jamaica and the son of 'free Negroes', as Long told it, Williams had been 'the subject of an experiment' by the Duke of Montagu, inspired by Locke, 'to discover, whether by proper cultivation, and a regular course of tuition at school and the university, a Negroe might not be found as capable of literature as a white person'. He was sent to England, educated at a grammar school and then at Cambridge, returned to Jamaica and set up a school in Spanish Town, teaching reading, writing, Latin and mathematics. He selected and trained 'a Negroe pupil' to be his successor, but the 'abstruse problems of mathematical institution turned his brain', demonstrating, in Long's opinion, 'that every African head is not adapted by nature to such profound contemplations'. The chief pride of the lad was to imitate his tutor with 'tye periwig, a sword, and ruffled shirt', hoping, perhaps, that these 'superficial marks' would give him the status of a 'great scholar' amongst 'Negroes' who knew no better. These forms of mimicry would remind readers of Hume's judgement, which Long repeated. Convinced, as he was, of the importance of reasoned speech to white superiority, such an accusation was grist to his mill. Williams's insistence on his right to speak was a particular provocation for Long.[107] He might not speak 'gibberish', but what was the depth of his understanding? Estwick's elaboration of Hume's case as to the absence of moral sense was then reiterated and underlined with a rhetorical question: 'whether all the species of the human kind have this instinctive sense in equal degree?'[108] The answer to this, in Long's view, was that indeed they did not. Long claimed that Williams was 'haughty, opinionated, looked down with sovereign contempt on his fellow Blacks', had an absurdly inflated sense of his own knowledge, was disdainful of his parents and severe 'bordering upon

---

[106] Beattie's text was from his *Essay on the Nature and Immutability of Truth*; Carretta, 'Who was Francis Williams?', 214–15. On Beattie and his challenge to Hume, see Sebastiani, *The Scottish Enlightenment*, 110–15. Ramsay continued the debate in 1784, arguing that 'we may say of his example, Francis Williams, the negroe poet and mathematician, that though his verses bear no great marks of genius, yet, there have been bred at the same university an hundred white masters of arts, and many doctors, who could not improve them'; *Essay*, 238.
[107] Ogborn, *Freedom of Speech*, 57–63.
[108] Long, *History*, II. 476–7.

cruelty' in his treatment of 'his children and his slaves'. He paid much attention to dress, sporting a 'huge wig' and adopting a 'grave cast' of countenance, an attempt to imply 'wisdom and learning'. 'The moral part of his character' could be deduced from all this: his vanity meant that 'he had not the modesty to be silent'.[109]

Williams was christened in 1697 in St Catherine and was in England by the 1710s. His father, John, was a wealthy merchant, exporting sugar and other tropical goods, importing provisions and clothing for the plantations, and lending money on a considerable scale. Initially enslaved, he had been freed by his owner, Colonel Bourden, who died in 1697.[110] By 1708 he possessed enough property and enslaved people to successfully claim the privilege both of trial by jury and of preventing his human property giving evidence in court against him. This right was then extended to his wife and three sons in 1716. Francis clearly had mathematical abilities, for in 1716 he was proposed as a fellow of the Royal Society but was not elected. He was entered at Lincoln's Inn in 1721, but was back in Jamaica by 1724 after his father's death. Having inherited substantial property from his father and more from his mother, he seems to have lived off his riches rather than engaging in agriculture or commercial activity. At some point he established a school.

Long was far from being Williams's only antagonist on the island. The Rev. John Lindsay knew him and penned an equally hostile account, describing him as 'Black Williams'. 'Mr Long's account … is true so far', Lindsay wrote, 'as the picture taken of him is in his best array, and when in his best days … when he was admitted to the Governor's levee – in his tie-wig and sword.' He knew Williams in his later years, when he had been 'reduced to keeping a Negroe school', and was renowned for keeping 'a favourite scholar … Brown – a fantastical blockhead, whose *chef d'oeuvre* was copying writings: and who made so honest and indiscreet use of his pen, as to be a few years ago transported as a vagabond, for giving run-away negroes, forged tickets of a master's leave of absence'.[111] Williams was embroiled in a conflict in 1724 with a former attorney general, Brodrick, over a series of insults that he was said to have made which would act as 'great encouragement to the negroes of the island' and were likely to have 'ill consequences' for the White people. Tensions over Maroon hostilities in the late 1720s made the white elite anxious about the claims of free Black people, and a bill was prepared aiming to render 'free negroes more serviceable to the island' and imposing new forms of discrimination.[112] Williams petitioned the metropole against this legislation.

---

[109] Ibid., II. 478.
[110] John Gilmore, 'Williams, Francis (*c.* 1690–1762), Writer in Jamaica', *ODNB*, 2004, https://doi.org/10.1093/ref:odnb/57050.
[111] Higman, *Proslavery Priest*, 232.
[112] Carretta, 'Who was Francis Williams?', 222–3.

He and his family would suffer, he argued, now that 'the enslaved men and women he saw as his property could testify in court against him'.[113] He won his case: the legal rights that he had secured on account of his property were seen in London as more significant than the colour of his skin. For Long, however, as for the colonists, skin colour was vital: Somerset had demonstrated that the law would not protect their enslaved property. They must ensure that the body mattered.

Williams had died in 1762, his riches by then dispersed; only some books and fifteen enslaved people remained. A decade later, however, Long was determined to demolish his claims to equality. He may have been particularly outraged by Williams's attempt to define himself as 'a *white* man acting under a *black* skin' and to insist that 'neither art, virtue, nor prudence respects the barriers of colour'. As Locksley Lindo argues, this was a 'revolutionary principle' in eighteenth-century Jamaica. Elsa Goveia agrees: 'It was just the sort of universalistic claim that spelt danger for the particularistic structure of the slave society.'[114] Furthermore, Williams maintained that 'a Negro was superior in quality to a Mulatto', since the 'heterogeneous mixture' of Black and White was inferior to the perfect specimens of each.[115] For Long the defence of the superior possibilities of 'Mulattos' given that they carried white blood was contrasted with his belief in the natural taint of the African. Offended by what he saw as the displaced vanity of the man in authoring a Latin ode and presenting it to Governor Haldane on his arrival in Jamaica, he published, translated and annotated a version of the poem.[116] Writing in Latin was suited to white gentlemen, not 'Negroes'. Proud of his own classical accomplishments and determined that his sons should possess these skills, he nevertheless noted to his eldest that if scholarship was to be 'of any real value, it must arise from the Honour of getting Rank'.[117] It was not the linguistic skill that mattered, it was the status it conferred. For a Black man, whose father had once been enslaved, to claim the governor's attention, to appear at the levées, to define himself as a 'Black Muse', aligned with the ancient muses of Greek mythology, was enraging. He disparaged the scholarly capacities of his opponent in the references and footnotes he provided and mocked his 'superlative panegyric, scarcely allowable even to a poet'. He scorned the exaltation of Haldane to the skies as Achilles, the Caesar of America, and Williams's self-adulation as 'erudite and modest', with a wise heart, immaculate morals, and abounding with patriotism.[118] It was important, as John Gilmore argues, for Long to

---

[113] Ogborn, *Freedom of Speech*, 61.
[114] Locksley Lindo, 'Francis Williams: a "Free" Negro in a Slave World', *Savacou* 1.1 (1970), 75–80; Introduction by Goveia.
[115] Long, *History*, II. 478.
[116] Long's published version is the only surviving copy.
[117] Howard, *Records and Letters*, I. 150.
[118] Long, *History*, II. 483–4.

belittle Williams since he was known for his Latin verse; indeed he was probably the first Black author whose name circulated in the empire, predating Phillis Wheatley, Ignatius Sancho and Equiano.[119] Long padded out his translation to make it fit his couplets, thus representing Williams as more ponderous and pompous than he was in the Latin.[120] Yet his contempt for the poem is misplaced. Williams's use of metre skilfully combined Ovidian forms (in which he would have been trained at school and university) with the freer style associated with Catullus. This was the form, argues Lindo, that he employed when expressing an idea that broke with convention.[121]

> Worth itself and understanding have no colour;
> There is no colour in an honest mind, or in art.

Such a proposition made it abundantly clear why Long would feel an urgent need to counter him.[122] As a free Black man owning enslaved persons and claiming civilized gentility, Williams aligned himself with aspects of colonial society. But his 'pretensions', as Long and others saw them, to be a political and intellectual equal with white people, were not to be tolerated. Feigning impartiality in his discussion of the merits of the poem, Long argued that it was vital to forget that the writer was a '*Negroe*' since 'If we regard it as an extraordinary production, merely because it came from a *Negroe*, we admit at once that *inequality* of genius which has been before supposed.'[123] Was the composition in any way superior to what might be expected from 'a middling scholar at the seminaries of Westminster or Eaton [sic]?' The Spanish have a proverbial saying, he noted, 'though we are Blacks, we are men'. 'The truth of which', he continued, no one will dispute. 'But if we allow the system of created beings to be perfect and consistent', he continued,

> and that this perfection arises from an exact scale of gradation, from the lowest to the highest, combining and connecting every part into a regular and beautiful harmony, reasoning them from the visible plan and operation of infinite wisdom in respect to the human race, as well as every other series in the scale, we must, I think, conclude, that,
> The general *order*, since the whole began,
> Is kept in *nature*, and is kept in *man*.
> *Order* is heaven's first law; and, this confest,
> *Some are*, and, *must be, greater* than the rest.[124]

---

[119] John Gilmore, 'The British Empire and the Neo-Latin Tradition: the Case of Francis Williams', in Barbara Goff (ed.), *Classics and Colonialism* (London, 2005), 92–106.
[120] John Gilmore, 'Latin in Black and White: John Alleyn, Francis Williams and Caribbean Poetry', unpublished paper (1998). Many thanks to the author for allowing me to see it.
[121] Lindo, 'Francis Williams', 77.
[122] Gilmore, 'Williams, Francis', *ODNB*.
[123] Long, *History*, II. 484.
[124] Ibid., II. 484–5.

In (mis)quoting the immortal Christian poet Pope, by connecting two separate couplets, he racialized the lines and hoped to secure his case.

'In the struggle to shape the future', Vincent Brown writes in his book on the centrality of death to the Atlantic world, 'the dead do not necessarily have the last word. But they always have a voice.'[125] Long and his *History* will stand as a monument to the claim for White power which has done and continues to do such damage. But Williams's ability to represent himself was his riposte to the planters. He might have been astonished to see that in the early twenty-first century – in the aftermath of new patterns of migration and globalization, of environmental disasters and ever-increasing inequalities, of George Floyd's killing, of police violence and Black Lives Matter – new histories are emerging that place the agency of Black, Brown and other men and women of colour at their centre. Other histories are indeed possible: new collective mentalities emerging which 'far from being paralysed by the disavowals of the past' can engage with it, recognize damage, and reach for forms of reparation.[126]

[125] Brown, *The Reaper's Garden*, 261.
[126] Hall, *Familiar Stranger*, 93.

BIBLIOGRAPHY

Abbreviations Used in Notes

AHR	American Historical Review
EconHR	Economic History Review
HJ	Historical Journal
HWJ	History Workshop Journal
JBS	Journal of British Studies
JICH	Journal of Imperial and Commonwealth History
S&A	Slavery and Abolition
TRHS	Transactions of the Royal Historical Society
WMQ	William and Mary Quarterly

Archives and Manuscripts

UK Archives

British Library Additional Manuscripts

BL Add MSS 12402–5; 12407; 12438; 18271; 18959–63; 30001. Papers of Edward Long.

BL Add MSS 12432. Report of Committee of the Jamaican House of Assembly on the Slave Trade, November 1792.

BL Long Add MSS 12435. Papers of Edward Long. Papers ... Relative to the Statistics of Jamaica.

BL Add MSS 22639. Original Papers Relating to the Company of the Mines Royal in Jamaica.

BL Add MSS 43379. Papers of Edward Long. Plans etc. of the Lucky Valley Estate.

Cumbrian Archives Centre

DHW/8/32. Long correspondence.

The National Archives, Kew

Records of the Prerogative Court of Canterbury ... including Wills. PROB 11.

Staffordshire Record Office, William Salt Library
Ricketts Family Papers.

Suffolk Record Office
HA/18/GD/1. Mr Long's Proposals for his Property at L. Valley, November 1777.

University of London, Senate House Library
West India Committee Papers. M915 [microfilm].

Jamaican Archives

Jamaica Archives (JA)
Accounts Produce, Liber 5, Liber 6.
Inventory of Charles Long, Liber 37, 1B/11/3/37.
Inventory of Samuel Long, Liber 37, 10/11/3/37.
St Catharine Parish, List of Freeholders, 1757–1840, 2/2/27
St Catharine's Vestry Book, 1771–4, 2/2/22

Papers in the Jamaica Island Record Office (IRO)
Book of Wills, vols. 3–5.
Indentures, correspondence, etc. Volumes 15, 156, 158, 173, 179, 192, 193, 199, 204, 209, 231, 252.

Journals of the Assembly of Jamaica (JAJ)
Vols. 5–6, 1756–67.

National Library of Jamaica (NLJ)
Anthony Robinson's Jamaica Birds, MS 178, Picture 26.
Minutes of the Council of Jamaica, MS 60. vol. 32. 1755–8.

Contemporary Published Sources

Books and Pamphlets by Edward Long

The Anti-Gallican; or, the History and Adventures of Harry Cobham, Esquire. Inscribed to Louis the XVth by the Author (London, 1757).
The Antigallican; or strictures on the present form of government established in France (London, 1793).
Candid Reflections upon the Judgement Lately Awarded by the Court of King's Bench in Westminster Hall on What is Commonly Called the Negroe Cause, by a Planter (London, 1772).
English Humanity No Paradox: or, an Attempt to Prove, that the English are Not a Nation of Savages (London, 1778).

A Free and Candid Review of a Tract entitled 'Observations on the Commerce of the American States' Shewing the Pernicious Consequences, Both to Great Britain, and to the British Sugar Islands of the Systems Recommended in that Tract (London, 1784).

The History of Jamaica: or, General Survey of the Ancient and Modern State of that Island, with Reflections on its Situation, Settlements. Inhabitants, Climate, Products, Commerce, Laws and Government (3 vols., London, 1774; facsimile edn, Cambridge, 2010).

The Prater by Nicholas Babble (London, 1756).

The Sentimental Exhibition; or, Portraits and Sketches of the Times (London, 1774).

The Trial of Farmer Carter's Dog Porter for Murder. Taken Down Verbatim *and* Literatim *in Short-hand. And now Published by Authority, from the Corrected Manuscript of COUNSELLOR CLEAR-POINT, Barrister at Law. NB. This is the only true and authentic Copy; and all others are spurious* (London, 1771).

Other Published Sources

Anon. [Edward Trelawny?], *An Essay concerning Slavery and the danger Jamaica is expos'd to from the too great number of Slaves and the too little Care that is taken to manage them. And a proposal to prevent the further importation of Negroes into that Island* (London, n.d.).

A Jamaica Proprietor, *Negro Emancipation No Philanthropy. A letter to the Duke of Wellington* (London, 1830).

Addison, Joseph, *The Spectator*, no. 69, 19 May 1711.

—— *The Works of Joseph Addison*, ed. George Washington Greene (6 vols., New York, 1854).

Ashton, T. S. (ed.), *Letters of a West Indian Trader. Edward Grace, 1767–70* (London, 1950).

Barbados Slave Code: Act of 1661. Extracts in *Slavery*, ed. Stanley Engerman, Seymour Drescher and Robert Paquette (Oxford, 2001), 105–13.

Beattie, James, *An Essay on the Nature and Immutability of Truth* (Edinburgh, 1770).

Beckford, William, *A Descriptive Account of the Island of Jamaica: with remarks upon the cultivation of the sugar-cane, throughout the different seasons of the year, and chiefly considered in a picturesque point of view; also observations and reflections upon what would probably be the consequences of an abolition of the slave trade, and of the emancipation of the slaves* (2 vols., London, 1790).

—— *Remarks upon the Situation of Negroes in Jamaica, impartially made from a local experience of nearly thirteen years in that Island* (2 vols., London, 1788).

Benezet, Anthony, *A Short Account of the Part of Africa Inhabited by the Negroes* (2nd edn, Philadelphia, 1762).

Bosman, Willem, *A New and Accurate Description of the Coast of Guinea, Divided Into the Gold, the Slave, and the Ivory Coasts* (London, 1705).
Bourke, Nicholas, *The Privileges of Jamaica Vindicated* [1766] (Jamaica, 1810).
Browne, MD, Patrick, *The Civil and Natural History of Jamaica (in 3 parts)* (London, 1756).
Burke, Edmund, *Reflections on the Revolution in France* (London, 1790).
Burke, William and Edmund Burke, *An Account of the European Settlements in America. In Six Parts* [1759] (5th edn with improvements, London, 1770).
Burnett, James, Lord Monboddo, *Of the Origin and Progress of Language* (6 vols., Edinburgh, 1773–94).
Carlyle, Thomas, 'Occasional Discourse on the Negro Question', *Fraser's Magazine*, 40 (December 1849).
Carretta, Vincent (ed.), *Letters of the Late Ignatius Sancho, an African* (London, 2015).
Clarkson, Thomas, *An Essay on the Slavery and Commerce of the Human Species* (London, 1786).
Cumberland, George, *Bromley-Hill. The Seat of the Rt Hon. Charles Long, MP* (London, 1816).
Debate on a Motion for the Abolition of the Slave Trade in the House of Commons on Monday 2nd April 1792, reported in detail (London, 1792).
Defoe, Daniel, *A Tour thro' the Whole Island of Great Britain, divided into circuits or journies* (3 vols., London, 1724–7).
Edwards, Bryan, *The History, Civil and Commercial, of the British Colonies in the West Indies* (3 vols., Dublin, 1793).
   The History, Civil and Commercial, of the British Colonies in the West Indies (2 vols., London, 1794).
   A Speech Delivered at a Free Conference between the Honourable the Council and Assembly of Jamaica, 19 Nov. 1789, on the subject of Mr Wilberforce's propositions in the House of Commons concerning the slave-trade (Kingston, Jamaica, 1789).
   Thoughts on the Late Proceedings of Government Respecting the Trade of the West India Islands with the United States of North America (2nd edn, London, 1784).
Equiano, Olaudah, *The Interesting Narrative and Other Writings*, ed. Vincent Carretta (London, 2003).
[Estwick, Samuel], A West Indian, *Considerations on the Negroe Cause, commonly so called, addressed to the Right Honourable Lord Mansfield, Lord Chief Justice of the Court of King's Bench* (London, 1772).
Feurtado, W. A., *Official and Other Personages of Jamaica, from 1655–1790* (Kingston, Jamaica, 1896).
Grainger, James, *Essay on the More Common West-India Diseases* [1764] (Edinburgh, 1802).
   On the Treatment and Management of the More Common West-India Diseases, ed. J. Edward Hutson [1764] (Kingston, Jamaica, 2005).

450 BIBLIOGRAPHY

The Sugar Cane, in John Gilmore, *The Poetics of Empire. A Study of James Grainger's* The Sugar Cane *(1764)* (London, 2000).
Hanway, Jonas, *Thoughts on the Plan of a Magdalen House for Repentant Prostitutes* (London, 1758).
Howard, R. Mowbray, *Record and Letters of the Family of the Longs of Longville, Jamaica, and Hampton Lodge, Surrey* (2 vols., London, 1925).
Hume, David, *The History of England, from the Invasion of Julius Caesar to the Revolution in 1688* (2 vols., London, 1754).
  'Of Commerce', 'Of National Characters' and 'Of the Jealousy of Trade' [1753], in volume III of *The Philosophical Works of David Hume*, ed. T. H. Green and T. H. Grose (4 vols., London, 1882).
  'Of Contiguity and Distance in Space and Time' [1739–40], in volume II of *The Philosophical Works of David Hume*, ed. T. H. Green and T. H. Grose (4 vols., London, 1882).
Johnson, Samuel, *A Dictionary of the English Language* (4th edn, London, 1773).
  Journey to the Western Islands of Scotland [1775] (Edinburgh, 1792).
  'Taxation no Tyranny. An answer to the resolutions and address of the American colonists', in volume XIV of *The Works of Samuel Johnson* (14 vols., New York, 1913).
Knight, James, *The Natural, Moral, and Political History of Jamaica and the Territories Thereon Depending, from the first discovery of the island by Christopher Columbus to the year 1746* [1746], ed. Jack P. Greene (2 vols., Charlottesville, VA, 2021).
Leclerc, Georges-Louis, comte de Buffon, *Histoire naturelle, générale et particulière, avec la description du Cabinet du Roi* (36 vols., Paris, 1749–1804).
Leslie, Charles, *A New and Exact Account of Jamaica ... With a particular account of the sacrifices, libations, etc. at this day, in use among the Negroes. The third edition. To which is added an appendix, containing an account of Admiral Vernon's success at Porto Bello and Chagre* (Edinburgh, 1740).
  A New History of Jamaica. In Thirteen Letters from a Gentleman to his Friend (Dublin, 1741).
Lesuire, Robert-Martin, *Les sauvages de l'Europe* (Paris, 1762).
Lewis, Rhodri (ed.), *William Petty on the Order of Nature. An Unpublished Manuscript Treatise* (Tempe, AZ, 2012).
Ligon, Richard, *A True and Exact History of the Island of Barbadoes* (London, 1657).
Lind, James, *An Essay on Diseases Incidental to Europeans in Hot Climates* [1768] (London, 1771).
Locke, John, *Two Treatises of Government* [1689] (London, 1821).
Macaulay, T. B., 'William Pitt. Earl of Chatham' [Jan. 1834], in *Literary and Historical Essays* (Oxford, 1913).
Martin, Samuel, Sr, *An Essay upon Plantership Inscribed to Governor George Thomas* (4th edn, London and Antigua, 1765).

Marx, Karl, *Capital* (3 vols., Moscow, 1961).
Millar, John, *The Origin of the Distinction of Ranks* [1771, rev. edn 1773], ed. Aaron Garrett (Indianapolis, 2012).
Moreton, J. B., *West India Customs and Manners: containing strictures on the soil, cultivation, produce, trade, officers, and inhabitants: with the method of establishing a sugar plantation. To which is added the practice of training new slaves* (London, 1793).
Morgan, Kenneth (ed.), *The Bright–Meyler Papers. A Bristol–West India Connection, 1732–1837* [2007] (Oxford, 2016).
Oldmixon, *The British Empire in America, Containing the History of the Discovery, Settlement, Progress and Present State of all the British Colonies on the Continent and Islands of America* (2 vols., London, 1708).
Ramsay, James, *An Essay on the Treatment and Conversion of African Slaves in the British Sugar Colonies* (London, 1784).
Report of the Lords of Committee of Council, Parliamentary Papers 1789, vol. 69.
Sharp, Granville, *A Representation of the Injustice and Dangerous Tendency of Tolerating Slavery in England. Or of admitting the least claim of private property in the persons of man in England* [1769] (Cambridge, 2014).
Sloane, Hans, *A Voyage to the Islands Madera, Barbados, Nieves, S. Christophers and Jamaica With the Natural History of the Herbs and Trees, Four-footed Beasts, Fishes, Birds, Insects, Reptiles, &c. Of the last of those Islands* (2 vols., London, 1707).
Smith, Adam, *Lectures on Jurisprudence*, in *The Glasgow Edition of the Works and Correspondence of Adam Smith, volume V*, ed. R. L. Meek, D. D. Raphael and P. G. Stein (Oxford, 1978).
The Theory of Moral Sentiments [1759] (London, 1767).
The Wealth of Nations [1776] (2 vols., London, 1910).
Smollett, Tobias, *The Adventures of Roderick Random* [1748] (London, n.d.).
Humphry Clinker [1771] (Harmondsworth, 2008).
Stephen, James, *The Crisis of the Sugar Colonies* (London, 1802).
Sterne, Lawrence, *The Life and Opinions of Tristram Shandy, Gentleman* [1759] (Oxford, 2020).
[Stewart, John], *An Account of Jamaica and its Inhabitants by a Gentleman Long Resident in the West Indies* (London, 1808).
Swift, Jonathan, *Gulliver's Travels, The Tale of Tub, Battle of the Books, etc.* [1726, 1704] (Oxford, 1949).
A Modest Proposal (1729).
Taylor, John. *Jamaica in 1687. The Taylor Manuscript at the National Library of Jamaica*, ed. David Buisseret (Kingston, Jamaica, 2008).
Trapham, Thomas, *Discourse of the State of Health in the Island of Jamaica* (London, 1679).
Voltaire, *Letters on England* (London, 1733).
Wesley, John, *Thoughts upon Slavery* (3rd edn, London, 1774).

Wood, Betty (ed.) with assistance of T. R Clayton and W. A. Speck, *The Letters of Simon Taylor of Jamaica to Chaloner Arcedekne, 1765–1775* (Cambridge, 2002).
Wright, Philip (ed.), *Lady Nugent's Journal of her Residence in Jamaica from 1801–1805* (Kingston, Jamaica, 2002).
Young, Arthur, *Political Essays Concerning the Present State of the British Empire: Particularly Respecting 1. Natural Advantages and Disadvantages* (London, 1772).

Published Secondary Sources

Amussen, Susan Dwyer, *Caribbean Exchange. Slavery and the Transformation of English Society* (Chapel Hill, NC, 2007).
Anderson, Jennifer L., *Mahogany. The Costs of Luxury in Early America* (Cambridge, MA, 2012).
Anstey, Roger, *The Atlantic Slave Trade and British Abolition, 1760–1810* (London, 1975).
Apter, Andrew, 'The Blood of Mothers: Women, Money and Markets in Yoruba–Atlantic Perspective', *Journal of African-American History*, 98 (1) (Winter 2013), 72–98.
  'History in the Dungeon: Atlantic Slavery and the Spirit of Capitalism in Cape Coast Castle, Ghana', *American Historical Review*, 122 (1) (2017), 23–53.
Atkinson, Lesley-Gail (ed.), *The Earliest Inhabitants. The Dynamics of the Jamaican Taino* (Kingston, Jamaica, 2006).
Atkinson, Richard, *Mr Atkinson's Rum Contract. The Story of a Tangled Inheritance* (London, 2020).
Barber, Karin, 'When People Cross Thresholds', *African Studies Review*, 20 (2) (2007), 111–23.
Barker, Anthony J., *The African Link. British Attitudes to the Negro in the Era of the Atlantic Slave Trade, 1550–1807* (London, 1978).
Barrell, John and Harriet Guest, 'On the Use of Contradictions: Economics and Morality in the Long Eighteenth-Century Poem', in *The New Eighteenth Century*, ed. Felicity Nussbaum and Laura Brown (London, 1987), 121–43.
Barrell, John, *English Literature in History, 1730–1780. An Equal, Wide Survey* (London, 1983).
Barringer, Tim, 'Picturesque Prospects and the Labor of the Enslaved', in *Art and Emancipation in Jamaica*, ed. Tim Barringer, Gillian Forrester and Barbaro Martinez-Ruiz (New Haven, CT, 2007), 41–64.
Bashford, Alison and Joyce C. Chaplin, *The New Worlds of Thomas Robert Malthus. Rereading the Principle of Population* (Princeton, 2016).
Baucom, Ian, *Specters of the Atlantic. Finance Capital, Slavery and the Philosophy of History* (Durham, NC, 2005).

Beckert, Sven, *Empire of Cotton. A New History of Global Capitalism* (London, 2014).
Beckles, Hilary M., *Natural Rebels. A Social History of Black Women in Barbados* (New Brunswick, 1989).
  'Perfect Property: Enslaved Black Women in the Caribbean', in *Confronting Power, Theorizing Gender. Interdisciplinary Perspectives in the Caribbean*, ed. Eudine Barriteau (Kingston, Jamaica, 2003), 142–58.
  'Sex and Gender in the Historiography of Caribbean Slavery', in *Engendering History. Caribbean Women in Historical Perspective*, ed. Verene Shepherd, Bridget Brereton and Barbara Bailey (Kingston, Jamaica, 1995), 125–40.
Beirne, Piers, 'A Note on the Facticity of Animal Trials in Early Modern Britain; or, the Curious Prosecution of Farmer Carter's Dog for Murder', *Crime, Law and Social Change*, 55 (2011), 359–74.
Bell, David, *The Cult of the Nation in France. Inventing Nationalism, 1680–1800* (Cambridge, MA, 2009).
Benjamin, Walter, 'On the Concept of History', in *Selected Writings, volume IV: 1938–1940*, ed. Howard Eiland and Michael W. Jennings (Cambridge, MA, 2003).
Benn, Denis, *The Caribbean. An Intellectual history, 1774–2003* (Kingston, Jamaica, 2004).
Benton, Lauren, *A Search for Sovereignty. Law and Geography in European Empires, 1400–1900* (Cambridge, 2002).
Berg, Maxine, *Luxury and Pleasure in Eighteenth-Century Britain* (Oxford, 2005).
  'Women's Property and the Industrial Revolution', *Journal of Interdisciplinary History*, 24 (2) (1993), 233–50.
Berg, Maxine and Pat Hudson, *Slavery and the Industrial Revolution* (Cambridge, 2023).
Bermingham, Ann, *Landscape and Ideology. The English Rustic Tradition, 1740–1860* (London, 1987).
Besson, Jean, *Martha Brae's Two Histories. European Expansion and Caribbean Culture-Building in Jamaica* (Chapel Hill, NC, 2002).
  Transformations of Freedom in the Land of the Maroons. Creolization in the Cockpits, Jamaica (London, 2015).
Best, Lloyd and Kari Polanyi Levitt, *The Theory of Plantation Economy. A Historical and Institutional Approach to Caribbean Economic Development* (Kingston, Jamaica, 2009).
Best, Lloyd and David Scott, 'The Vocation of a Caribbean Intellectual', *Small Axe*, 1 (1997), 119–40.
Bhandar, Brenna, *Colonial Lives of Property. Law, Land and Racial Regimes of Ownership* (London, 2018).
Bindman, David, *Ape to Apollo. Aesthetics and the Idea of Race in the Eighteenth Century* (London, 2002).
Bindman, David, Helen Weston and Paul Kaplan, 'The City between Fantasy and Reality', in *The Image of the Black in Western Art, volume III: From the 'Age*

of Discovery' to the Age of Abolition. Part 2: The Eighteenth Century, ed. David Bindman and Henry Louis Gates Jr (Cambridge, MA, 2011), 1–50.

Blackburn, Robin, *The Making of New World Slavery. From the Baroque to the Modern, 1492–1800* (London, 1997).

Blouet, Olwyn M., 'Bryan Edwards FRS, 1743–1800', *Notes and Records of the Royal Society of London*, 54 (2) (2000), 215–22.

Bohls, Elizabeth A., 'The Gentleman Planter and the Metropole: Long's *History of Jamaica* (1774)', in *The Country and the City Revisited. England and the Politics of Culture, 1550–1850*, ed. Gerald Maclean, Donna Landry and Joseph P. Ward (Cambridge, 1999), 180–96.

Slavery and the Politics of Place. Representing the Colonial Caribbean, 1770–1833 (Cambridge, 2014).

Brah, Avtar, *Cartographies of Diaspora. Contesting Identities* (London, 1996).

'The Scent of Memory: Strangers, Our Own and Others', *Feminist Review*, 61 (1) (1999), 4–26.

Brantlinger, Patrick, *Fictions of State. Culture and Credit in Britain, 1694–1994* (Ithaca, 1996).

Brathwaite, Edward, *The Development of Creole Society in Jamaica, 1770–1820* (Oxford, 1971).

Bressey, Caroline, 'Invisible Presence: the Whitening of the Black Community in the Historical Imagination of British Archives', *Archivaria*, 61 (2006), 47–61.

Brewer, Holly, 'Slavery, Sovereignty, and "Inheritable Blood": Reconsidering John Locke and the Origins of American Slavery', *American Historical Review*, 122 (4) (2017), 1038–78.

Brewer, John, *The Pleasures of the Imagination. English Culture in the Eighteenth Century* (London, 1997).

The Sinews of Power. War, Money and the English State, 1688–1783 (Cambridge, MA, 1990).

Brown, Christopher Leslie, *Moral Capital: Foundations of British Abolitionism* (Chapel Hill, NC, 2006).

Brown, Kathleen M., *Good Wives, Nasty Wenches, and Anxious Patriarchs. Gender, Race and Power in Colonial Virginia* (Chapel Hill, NC, 1996).

Brown, Laura, 'Reading Race and Gender: Jonathan Swift', *Eighteenth Century Studies*, 23 (4) (1990), 425–43.

Brown, Vincent, *The Reaper's Garden. Death and Power in the World of Atlantic Slavery* (Cambridge, MA, 2008).

'Social Death and Political Life in the Study of Slavery', *American Historical Review*, 114 (5) (2009), 1231–49.

'Spiritual Terror and Sacred Authority in Jamaican Slave Society', *Slavery and Abolition*, 24 (1) (2003), 24–53.

Tacky's Revolt. The Story of an Atlantic Slave War (Cambridge, MA, 2020).

Browne, Randy M., *Surviving Slavery in the British Caribbean* (Philadelphia, 2017).

Browne, Randy M. and John Wood Sweet, 'Florence Hall's "Memoirs": Finding African Women in the Transatlantic Slave Trade', *Slavery and Abolition*, 37 (1) (2016), 206–21.

Burnard, Trevor, 'The Atlantic Slave Trade and African Ethnicities in Seventeenth-Century Jamaica', in *Liverpool and Transatlantic Slavery*, ed. D. Richardson, S. Schwarz and A. Tibbles (Liverpool, 2007), 138–63.

'European Migration to Jamaica, 1655–1780', *William and Mary Quarterly*, 53 (4) (1996), 769–96.

'A Failed Settler Society: Marriage and Demographic Failure in Early Jamaica', *Journal of Social History*, 28 (1) (1994), 63–82.

'Family Continuity and Female Independence in Jamaica, 1655–1734', *Continuity and Change*, 7 (2) (1992), 181–98.

'"The Grand Mart of the Island": the Economic Function of Kingston, Jamaica in the mid-Eighteenth Century', in *Jamaica in Slavery and Freedom. History, Heritage and Culture*, ed. K. E. A Monteith and Glen Richards, (Mona, Jamaica, 2002), 225–41.

'Harvest Years? Reconfigurations of Empire in Jamaica, 1756–1807', *Journal of Imperial and Commonwealth History*, 40 (4) (2012), 533–55.

Jamaica in the Age of Revolution (Philadelphia, 2020).

Mastery, Tyranny, and Desire. Thomas Thistlewood and his Slaves in the Anglo-Jamaican World (Chapel Hill, NC, 2004).

Planters, Merchants and Slaves. Plantation Societies in British America, 1650–1820 (Chicago, 2015).

'"Rioting in Goatish Embraces": Marriage and Improvement in Early British Jamaica', *History of the Family*, 11 (4) (2006), 185–98.

Burnard, Trevor and John Garrigus, *The Plantation Machine. Wealth and Belonging in French St Domingue and British Jamaica, 1748–1788* (Oxford, 2016).

Burnard, Trevor and Aaron Graham, 'Security, Taxation and the Imperial System in Jamaica, 1721–1782', *Early American Studies: An Interdisciplinary Journal*, 18 (4) (2020), 461–89.

Burnard, Trevor and Emma Hart, 'Kingston, Jamaica and Charleston, South Carolina: a New Look at Comparative Urbanization in Plantation Colonial British America', *Journal of Urban History*, 39 (2) (2012), 214–34.

Burnard, Trevor and Kenneth Morgan, 'The Dynamics of the Slave Market and Slave Purchasing Patterns in Jamaica, 1655–1788', *William and Mary Quarterly*, 58 (1) (2001), 205–28.

Camp, Stephanie M. H., *Closer to Freedom. Enslaved Women and Everyday Resistance in the Plantation South* (Chapel Hill, NC, 2004).

Campt, Tina M., *Listening to Images. An Exercise in Counterintuition* (Durham, NC, 2017).

Carby, Hazel V., *Imperial Intimacies. A Tale of Two Islands* (London, 2019).

Carretta, Vincent, *Equiano, the African. Biography of a Self-Made Man* (London, 2006).

Phillis Wheatley. Biography of a Genius in Bondage (Athens, GA, 2011).
  'Who Was Francis Williams?', *Early American Literature*, 38 (2) (2003), 213–37.
Carrington, Selwyn H. H., *The British West Indies during the American Revolution* (Dordrecht, 1988).
Casid, Jill, *Sowing Empire. Landscape and Colonization* (Minneapolis, 2005).
Césaire, Aimé, *Discourse on Colonialism* [1955] (New York, 1972).
Chadwick, Esther, '"This deepe and perfect glosse of Blacknesse". Colour, Colonialism and the Paston Treasure's Period Eye', in *The Paston Treasure. Microcosm of the Known World*, ed. Andrew Moore, Nathan Flis and Francesca Vanke (London, 2018), 102–9.
Chakrabarti, Pratik, *Materials and Medicine. Trade, Conquest and Therapeutics in the Eighteenth Century* (Manchester, 2010).
Checkland, S. G., 'Finance for the West Indies, 1780–1815', *Economic History Review*, 10 (3) (1958), 461–9.
Christopher, Emma, *Slave Ship Sailors and their Captive Cargoes, 1730–1807* (Cambridge, 2006).
Clarke, Austin, *The Polished Hoe* (Toronto, 2003).
Clarke, Norma, *Brothers of the Quill. Oliver Goldsmith in Grub Street* (Cambridge, MA, 2016).
Cody, Lisa Forman, *Birthing the Nation. Sex, Science and the Conception of Eighteenth-Century Britons* (Oxford, 2005).
Colley, Linda, *Britons. Forging the Nation, 1707–1837* (London, 1992).
  Captives. Britain, Empire and the World, 1600–1750 (London, 2002).
Corrigan, Philip and Derek Sayer, *The Great Arch. English State Formation as Cultural Revolution* (Oxford, 1985).
Craton, Michael, *Empire, Enslavement and Freedom in the Caribbean* (London, 1997).
  'Jamaican Slave Mortality: Fresh Light from Worthy Park, Longville and the Tharp Estates', *Journal of Caribbean History*, 3 (1971), 1–27.
  'Property and Propriety: Land Tenure and Slave Property in the Creation of a British West Indian Plantocracy, 1612–1740', in *Early Modern Conceptions of Property*, ed. John Brewer and Susan Staves (London, 1996), 497–529.
Craton, Michael and Garry Greenland, *Searching for the Invisible Man. Slavery and Plantation Life in Jamaica* (Cambridge, MA, 1978).
Craton, Michael and James Walvin, *A Jamaican Plantation. The History of Worthy Park, 1670–1970* (London, 1970).
Crowley, John E., 'Picturing the Caribbean in the Global British Landscape', *Studies in Eighteenth Century Culture*, 32 (2003), 323–46.
Curran, Andrew S., *The Anatomy of Blackness. Science and Slavery in an Age of Enlightenment* (Baltimore, 2011).
Davidoff, Leonore, *Thicker than Water. Siblings and their Relations, 1780–1920* (Oxford, 2012).
Davidoff, Leonore and Catherine Hall, *Family Fortunes. Men and Women of the English Middle Class, 1780–1850* [1987] (3rd edn, London, 2018).

Davies, R. R., *The First English Empire. Power and Identities in the British Isles, 1093–1343* (Oxford, 2000).
Davis, David Brion, *The Problem of Slavery in the Age of Emancipation* (New York, 2014).
Dayan, Colin, *The Law is a White Dog. How Legal Rituals Make and Unmake Persons* (Princeton, 2011).
Delbourgo, James, *Collecting the World. The Life and Curiosity of Hans Sloane* (London, 2017).
Devine, T. M., 'An Eighteenth-Century Business Elite: Glasgow West India Merchants, c. 1750–1815', *Scottish Historical Review*, 57 (163) (Part 1) (1978), 40–67.
Dillman, Jefferson, *Colonizing Paradise. Landscape and Empire in the British West Indies* (Tuscaloosa, 2018).
Dillon, Elizabeth Maddock, 'Zombie Biopolitics', *American Quarterly*, 71 (3) (2019), 625–52.
Ditz, Toby L., 'Shipwrecked: or Masculinity Imperiled: Mercantile Representations of Failure and the Gendered Self in Eighteenth-Century Philadelphia', *Journal of American History*, 81 (1) (1994), 51–80.
Donington, Katie, *The Bonds of Family. Slavery, Commerce and Culture in the British Atlantic World* (Manchester, 2020).
Draper, Nicholas, *The Price of Emancipation. Slave-Ownership, Compensation and British Society at the End of Slavery* (Cambridge, 2010).
Drayton, Richard, *Nature's Government. Science, Imperial Britain and the 'Improvement' of the World* (London, 2000).
Du Bois, W. E. B., 'The Conservation of Races', in *W. E. B. Du Bois Speaks. Speeches and Addresses, 1890–1919*, ed. Philip S. Foner [1897] (New York, 1970).
'The Souls of White Folk' [1920], in Du Bois, *Darkwater. Voices from Within the Veil* (Oxford, 2007).
Dubois, Laurent, 'An Enslaved Enlightenment: Rethinking the Intellectual History of the French Atlantic', *Social History*, 31 (1) (2006), 1–14.
Dunn, Richard S., 'Dreadful Idlers in the Cane Field: the Slave Labor Pattern on a Jamaican Sugar Estate, 1762–1831', in *British Capitalism and Caribbean Slavery. The Legacy of Eric Williams*, ed. Barbara L. Solow and Stanley L. Engerman (Cambridge, 1985), 163–90.
Sugar and Slaves. The Rise of the Planter Class in the English West Indies (London, 1973).
A Tale of Two Plantations. Slave Life and Labor in Jamaica and Virginia (Cambridge, MA, 2014).
Ellis, Markman, '"The Cane-land Isles": Commerce and Empire in Late Eighteenth-Century Georgic and Pastoral Poetry', in *Islands in History and Representation*, ed. Rod Edmond and Vanessa Smith (London, 2003), 43–62.
The Coffee-House. A Cultural History (London, 2004).
'Poetry and Civic Urbanism in the Coffee-House Library in the mid-Eighteenth Century', in *Before the Public Library. Reading, Community and Identity in*

the Atlantic World, 1650–1850, ed. Mark Towsey and Kyle B. Roberts (Leiden, 2017), 52–72.
Endelman, Todd M., *The Jews of Britain, 1656 to 2000* (Berkeley, 2002).
Erickson, Amy Louise, 'Coverture and Capitalism', *History Workshop Journal*, 59 (2005), 1–16.
  Women and Property in Early Modern England (London, 1993).
Erickson, Peter, *Rewriting Shakespeare, Rewriting Ourselves* (Berkeley, 1991).
Fanon, Frantz, *Black Skin, White Masks* [1952] (London, 1986).
  The Wretched of the Earth (New York, 1966).
Fend, Mechthild, *Fleshing out Surfaces. Skin in French Art and Medicine* (Manchester, 2017).
Fergus, Claudius, '"Dread of Insurrection": Abolitionism, Security, and Labor in Britain's West Indian Colonies, 1760–1823', *William and Mary Quarterly*, 66 (4) (2009), 757–80.
Finch, Janet, Lynn Hayes, Jennifer Mason and Lorraine Wallis, *Wills, Inheritance and Families* (Oxford, 1996).
Finn, Margot, *The Character of Credit. Personal Debt in English Culture, 1740–1914* (Cambridge, 2013).
Finn, Margot and Kate Smith (eds.), *The East India Company at Home, 1757–1857* (London, 2018).
Fischer, Kirsten, *Suspect Relations. Sex, Race and Resistance in Colonial North Carolina* (Ithaca, 2002).
Fisher, David R., 'George Ellis', in *The History of Parliament. The House of Commons, 1790–1820*, ed. R. Thorne (London, 1986).
Freud, Sigmund, *An Outline of Psycho-analysis* (1940), in vol. XXIII of *The Standard Edition of the Complete Psychological Works of Sigmund Freud*, ed. James Strachey in collaboration with Anna Freud (24 vols., London, 1964).
Fryer, Peter, *Staying Power. The History of Black People in Britain* (London, 1984).
Garrett, Aaron and Silvia Sebastiani, 'David Hume on Race', in *The Oxford Handbook of Philosophy and Race*, ed. Naomi Zack, online edn (Oxford, 2017).
Gascoigne, John, *Joseph Banks and the English Enlightenment. Useful Knowledge and Polite Culture* (Cambridge, 1994).
Gates, Henry Louis, Jr, *The Trials of Phillis Wheatley. America's First Black Poet and her Encounters with the Founding Fathers* (New York, 2003).
  'Writing "Race" and the Difference it Makes', *Critical Inquiry*, 12 (1) (1985), 1–20.
Gates, Henry Louis, Jr and Andrew S. Curran (eds.), *Who's Black and Why? A Hidden Chapter from the Eighteenth-Century Invention of Race* (Cambridge, MA, 2022).
Gattrell, V. A. C., *The Hanging Tree. Execution and the English People, 1770–1868* (Oxford, 1994).
Gauci, Perry, 'The Attack of the Creolian Powers: West Indians at the Parliamentary Elections of mid-Georgian Britain, 1754–74', *Parliamentary History* 33 (1) (2014), 201–22.

Emporium of the World. The Merchants of London, 1660–1800 (London, 2007).
  William Beckford. First Prime Minister of the London Empire (London, 2013).
Gawthorpp, Humphrey, 'George Ellis of Ellis Caymanas: a Caribbean Link to Scott and the Bronte Sisters', *eBLJ* [*British Library eJournal*] (2005), www.bl.uk/eblj/2005articles/article3.html.
Gay, Peter, *Voltaire's Politics. The Poet as Realist* [1959] (London, 1988).
Gerrard, Christine, *The Patriot Opposition to Walpole. Politics, Poetry and National Myth, 1725–1742* (Oxford, 1994).
Ghachem, Malick W., 'Montesquieu in the Caribbean: the Colonial Enlightenment between *Code Noir* and *Code Civil*', *Historical Reflections/Réflexions historiques*, 25 (2) (1999), 183–210.
Ghosh, Amitav, *The Nutmeg's Curse. Parables for a Planet in Crisis* (London, 2022).
Gikandi, Simon, *Slavery and the Culture of Taste* (Princeton, 2011).
Gilmore, John, 'The British Empire and the neo-Latin Tradition: the Case of Francis Williams', in *Classics and Colonialism*, ed. Barbara Goff (London, 2005), 92–106.
  The Poetics of Empire. A Study of James Grainger's The Sugar Cane *(1764)* (London, 2000).
Gilroy, Paul, *The Tanner Lectures on Human Values* (New Haven, CT, 2014).
Ginzburg, Carlo, 'Killing a Chinese Mandarin: the Moral Implications of Distance', *Critical Inquiry*, 21 (1) (1994), 46–60.
Giovannetti-Singh, Gianamar, 'Racial Capitalism in Voltaire's Enlightenment', *History Workshop Journal*, 94 (2022), 22–41.
Goede, Marieka de, *Virtue, Fortune and Faith. A Genealogy of Finance* (Minneapolis, 2017).
Gould, Eliga H., *The Persistence of Empire. British Political Culture in the Age of the American Revolution* [1993] (Chapel Hill, NC, 2000).
  'Zones of Law, Zones of Violence: the Legal Geography of the British Atlantic, circa 1772', *William and Mary Quarterly*, 60 (3) (2003), 471–510.
Goveia, Elsa V., *A Study on the Historiography of the British West Indies to the End of the Nineteenth Century* (Mexico City, 1956).
  'The West Indian Slave Laws of the 18th Century', in *Chapters in Caribbean History, volume II*, ed. D. G. Hall, E. V. Goveia and F. R. Augier (Eagle Hall, Barbados, 1970), 7–53.
Grassby, Richard, *Kinship and Capitalism. Marriage, Family and Business in the English Speaking World, 1580–1740* (Cambridge, 2001).
Green, Toby, *Fistful of Shells. West Africa from the Rise of the Slave Trade to the Age of Revolution* (London, 2019).
Greene, Jack P., *Evaluating Empire and Confronting Colonialism in Eighteenth-Century Britain* (Cambridge, 2013).
  Exclusionary Empire. English Liberty Overseas, 1600–1900 (Cambridge, 2009).
  'The Jamaica Privilege Controversy, 1764–66: an Episode in the Process of Constitutional Definition in the Early Modern British Empire', in *Negotiated Authorities. Essays in Colonial Political and Constitutional History* (Charlottesville, VA, 1994), 350–93.

'Liberty, Slavery, and the Transformation of British Identity in the Eighteenth-Century West Indies', *Slavery and Abolition*, 21 (1) (2000), 1–31.

Peripheries and Center. Constitutional Development in the Extended Polities of the British Empire and the United States, 1607–1788 (London, 1986).

Settler Jamaica in the 1750s (Charlottesville, VA, 2016).

Groot, Joanna de, *Empire and History Writing in Britain, c. 1750–2012* (Manchester, 2013).

Grove, Richard H., *Green Imperialism. Colonial Expansion, Tropical Island Edens and the Origins of Environmentalism, 1600–1860* (Cambridge, 1995).

Guasco, Michael, *Slaves and Englishmen. Human Bondage in the Early Modern Atlantic World* (Philadelphia, 2014).

Guha, Ranajit, *Dominance without Hegemony. History and Power in Colonial India* (Cambridge, MA, 1997).

Gust, Onni, *Unhomely Empire. Whiteness and Belonging, c.1760–1830* (London, 2021).

Guyer, Jane I., *Marginal Gains. Monetary Transactions in Atlantic Africa* (Chicago, 2004).

Habakkuk, John, *Marriage, Debt and the Estates System. English Landownership, 1650–1950* (Oxford, 1994).

Hall, Catherine, *Civilising Subjects. Metropole and Colony in the English Imagination, 1830–1867* (Cambridge, 2002).

'Doing Reparatory History: Bringing "Race" and Slavery Back Home', *Race and Class*, 60 (1) 2018), 3–21.

'Gendering Property, Racing Capital', in *History after Hobsbawm. Writing the Past for the Twenty-First Century*, ed. J. H. Arnold, M. Hilton and J. Ruger (Oxford, 2018), 17–34.

Macaulay and Son. Architects of Imperial Britain (London, 2012).

'Racial Capitalism: What's in a Name?', *History Workshop Journal*, 95 (2022), 5–21.

'Reconfiguring Race: the Stories the Slave-Owners Told', in Catherine Hall, Nicholas Draper, Keith McClelland, Katie Donington and Rachel Lang, *Legacies of British Slave-Ownership. Colonial Slavery and the Formation of Victorian Britain* (Cambridge, 2014), 163–202.

'Whose Memories? Edward Long and the Work of Re-remembering', in *Britain's History and Memory of Transatlantic Slavery. Local Nuances of a 'National Sin'*, ed. Katie Donington, Ryan Hanley and Jessica Moody (Liverpool, 2016), 129–49.

'Writing Forward, Writing Back: Eric Williams and Edward Long' (forthcoming).

'Writing Histories, Making "Race": Slave-Owners and their Stories', *Australian Historical Studies*, 47 (3) (2016), 365–80.

Hall, Catherine and Daniel Pick, 'Thinking about Denial', *History Workshop Journal*, 84 (2017), 1–23.

Hall, Catherine, Nicholas Draper, Keith McClelland, Katie Donington and Rachel Lang, *Legacies of British Slave-Ownership. Colonial Slavery and the Formation of Victorian Britain* (Cambridge, 2014).

Hall, Douglas, 'Botanical and Horticultural Enterprise in Eighteenth-Century Jamaica', in *West Indies Accounts. Essays on the History of the British Caribbean and the Atlantic Economy in Honour of Richard Sheridan*, ed. Roderick A. McDonald (Kingston, Jamaica, 1996), 101-25.
  'Incalculability as a Feature of Sugar Production during the Eighteenth Century', *Social and Economic Studies*, 10 (3) (1961), 340-52.
  In Miserable Slavery. Thomas Thistlewood in Jamaica, 1750-1786 (Kingston, Jamaica, 1989).
Hall, Kim F., *Things of Darkness. Economies of Race and Gender in Early Modern England* (Ithaca, 1995).
Hall, Stuart, *The Fateful Triangle. Race, Ethnicity, Nation*, ed. Kobena Mercer (Cambridge, MA, 2017).
  'The Multicultural Question', in *Un/settled Multiculturalisms: Diasporas, Entanglements, Transruptions*, ed. Barnor Hesse (London, 2000), 209-41.
  Selected Writings on Marxism, ed. and with commentary by Gregor McLennan (London, 2021).
  Selected Writings on Race and Difference, ed. Paul Gilroy and Ruth Wilson Gilmore (London, 2021).
Hall, Stuart, with Bill Schwarz, *Familiar Stranger. A Life between Two Islands* (London, 2017).
Hall, Stuart, Chas Critcher, Tony Jefferson, John Clarke and Brian Roberts, *Policing the Crisis. Mugging, the State and Law and Order* (London, 1978).
Hallock, Thomas, 'Male Pleasure and the Gender of Eighteenth-Century Botanic Exchange: a Garden Tour', *William and Mary Quarterly*, 62 (4) (2005), 697-718.
Hancock, David, *Citizens of the World. London Merchants and the Integration of the British Atlantic Community, 1735-1785* (Cambridge, 1995).
  '"A World of Business to do": William Freeman and the Foundations of England's Commercial Empire, 1645-1707', *William and Mary Quarterly*, 57 (1) (2000), 3-34.
Handler, Jerome S., 'Custom and Law: the Status of Enslaved Africans in Seventeenth-Century Barbados', *Slavery and Abolition*, 37 (2) (2016), 233-55.
Haraway, Donna, 'Ecce Homo, Ain't (Ar'n't) I a Woman, and Inappropriate/d Others: the Human in a Post-Humanist Landscape', in *Feminists Theorize the Political*, ed. Judith Butler and Joan W. Scott (New York, 1992), 86-100.
Harris, Cheryl, 'Whiteness as Property', *Harvard Law Review*, 106 (8) (1993), 1707-91.
Harrison, Mark, *Medicine in an Age of Commerce and Empire. Britain and its Tropical Colonies, 1660-1830* (Oxford, 2010).
Hartman, Saidiya, *Scenes of Subjection. Terror, Slavery and Self-Making in Nineteenth-Century America* (New York, 1997).
Harvey, Karen, 'The History of Masculinity, circa 1650-1800', *Journal of British Studies*, 44 (2) (2005), 296-311.

The Little Republic. Masculinity and Domestic Authority in Eighteenth-Century Britain (Oxford, 2012).
Harvey, Mark, 'Slavery, Indenture and the Development of British Industrial Capitalism', *History Workshop Journal*, 88 (2019), 66–88.
Harvey, Mark and Norman Geras, *Inequality and Democratic Egalitarianism. 'Marx's Economy and Beyond' and other Essays* (Manchester, 2018).
Hay, Douglas and Paul Craven (eds.), *Masters, Servants and Magistrates in Britain and the Empire, 1562–1955* (London, 2004).
Heuman, Gad, *Between Black and White. Race, Politics and the Free Coloreds in Jamaica, 1792–1865* (Westport, CT, 1981).
Higman, B. W., *Jamaica Surveyed. Plantation Maps and Plans of the Eighteenth and Nineteenth Centuries* (Kingston, Jamaica, 2001).
  Montpelier, Jamaica. A Plantation Community in Slavery and Freedom, 1739–1912 (Kingston, Jamaica, 1998).
  Plantation Jamaica, 1750–1850. Capital and Control in a Colonial Economy (Kingston, Jamaica, 2005).
  Proslavery Priest. The Atlantic World of John Lindsay, 1729–1788 (Kingston, Jamaica, 2011).
  Slave Population and Economy in Jamaica (Cambridge, 1976).
  'The Sugar Revolution', *Economic History Review*, 53 (2) (2000), 213–36.
Hoock, Holger, *Empires of the Imagination. Politics, War and the Arts in the British World, 1750–1850* (London, 2010).
Hoppit, Julian, *Britain's Political Economies. Parliament and Economic Life, 1660–1800* (Cambridge, 2017).
  'Introduction' to *The Correspondence of Stephen Fuller, 1788–1795. Jamaica, the West India Interest at Westminster and the Campaign to Preserve the Slave Trade*, ed. M. W. McCahill (Chichester, 2014).
  'Political Power and British Economic Life, 1650–1870', in *The Cambridge Economic History of Modern Britain, volume I: 1700–1870*, ed. Roderick Floud, Jane Humphries and Paul Johnson (Cambridge, 2014), 344–67.
Hopwood, Nick, (2018), 'The Keywords "Generation" and "Reproduction"', in *Reproduction. Antiquity to the Present Day*, ed. N. Hopwood, R. Flemming and L. Kassell (Cambridge, 2018), 287–304.
Hudson, Nicholas, 'From "Nation" to "Race": the Origins of Racial Classification in Eighteenth-Century Thought', *Eighteenth Century Studies*, 29 (3) (1996), 247–64.
Hudson, Pat, 'Slavery, the Slave Trade and Economic Growth: a Contribution to the Debate', in *Emancipation and the Remaking of the British Imperial World*, ed. Catherine Hall, Nicholas Draper and Keith McClelland (Manchester, 2014), 36–59.
Hunter, David, 'Handel Manuscripts and the Profits of Slavery: the "Granville" Collection at the British Library and the First Performing Score of Messiah Reconsidered', *Notes*, 76 (1) (2019), 27–37.

Ingrassia, Catherine, *Authorship, Commerce and Gender in Early Eighteenth Century England* (Cambridge, 1998).
Jeppesen, Chris, 'Growing up in a Company Town: the East India Company Presence in South Hertfordshire', in *The East India Company at Home*, ed. Margot Finn and Kate Smith (London, 2018), 251-71.
Johnson, Walter, *The Broken Heart of America. St Louis and the Violent History of the United States* (New York, 2020).
  River of Dark Dreams. Slavery and Empire in the Cotton Kingdom (Cambridge, MA, 2013).
  Soul by Soul. Life inside the Antebellum Slave Market (Cambridge, MA, 1999).
  'Time and Revolution in African America: Temporality and the History of Atlantic Slavery', in *A New Imperial History. Culture, Identity and Modernity in Britain and the Empire, 1660-1840*, ed. Kathleen Wilson (Cambridge, 2004), 197-215.
Jones, Cecily, *Engendering Whiteness. White Women and Colonialism in Barbados and North Carolina, 1627-1865* (Manchester, 2007).
Jones-Rogers, Stephanie E., *They Were Her Property: White Women as Slave Owners in the American South* (New Haven, CT, 2019).
Jordan, Winthrop D., *White over Black: American Attitudes towards the Negro, 1550-1812* (London, 1969).
Kars, Marjoleine, *Blood on the River. A Chronicle of Mutiny and Freedom on the Wild Coast* (London, 2020).
Kaul, Suvir, *Poems of Nation, Anthems of Empire. English Verse in the Long Eighteenth Century* (London, 2008).
Klein, Lawrence E., 'Politeness and the Interpretation of the British Eighteenth Century', *Historical Journal*, 45 (4) (2002), 869-98.
Klein, Melanie, *Envy and Gratitude and Other Work* (London, 1988).
Kriz, Kay Dian, *Slavery, Sugar and the Culture of Refinement. Picturing the West Indies, 1700-1840* (London, 2008).
Kuper, Adam, *Incest and Influence. The Private Life of Bourgeois England* (Cambridge, MA, 2009).
Lambert, David, 'Master-Horse-Slave: Mobility, Race and Power in the British West Indies, c. 1780-1838', *Slavery and Abolition*, 36 (4) (2018), 618-41.
  Mastering the Niger. James MacQueen's African Geography and the Struggle over Atlantic Slavery (Chicago, 2013).
  White Creole Culture. Politics and Identity during the Age of Abolition (Cambridge, 2005).
Langford, Paul, *A Polite and Commercial People, 1727-1783* [1989] (Oxford, 1998).
  Public Life and the Propertied Englishman, 1689-1798 (Oxford, 1991).
Legassick, Martin and David Hemson, *Foreign Investment and the Reproduction of Racial Capitalism* (Cape Town, 1976).
Leigh, Devin, 'The Jamaica Airs: an Introduction to Unpublished Pieces of Musical Notation from Enslaved People in the Eighteenth Century', *Atlantic Studies*, 17 (4) (2020), 462-84.
  'The Origins of a Source: Edward Long, Coromantee Slave Revolts and *The History of Jamaica*', *Slavery and Abolition*, 40 (2) (2018), 295-320.

Leigh, Devin and Clifton E. Sorrel III, 'How to Control the History of a Slave Rebellion: a Case Study from the Sources of Blackwall's Revolt in St Mary's Parish, Jamaica, 1765', *Journal of Caribbean History*, 5 (1) (2021), 19–56.
Lemmings, David, *Gentlemen and Barristers. The Inns of Court and the English Bar, 1680–1730* (Oxford, 1990).
Lettow, Susanne, 'Population, Race and Gender: On the Genealogy of the Modern Politics of Reproduction', *Distincktion: Scandinavian Journal of Social Theory*, 16 (3) (2015), 267–82.
— (ed.), *Reproduction, Race and Gender in Philosophy and the Early Life Sciences* (New York, 2014).
Levenson, Thomas, *Money for Nothing. The South Sea Bubble and the Invention of Modern Capitalism* (London, 2020).
Lewis, Jeremy, *Tobias Smollett* (London, 2003).
Lindo, Locksley, 'Francis Williams: a "Free" Negro in a Slave World', *Savacou*, 1 (1) (1970), 75–80.
Linebaugh, Peter and Marcus Rediker, *The Many-Headed Hydra. Sailors, Slaves, Commoners and the Hidden History of the Revolutionary Atlantic* (London, 2000).
Livesay, Daniel, *Children of Uncertain Fortune. Mixed-Race Jamaicans in Britain and the Atlantic Family, 1733–1833* (Chapel Hill, NC, 2018).
— 'The Decline of Jamaica's Interracial Households and the Fall of the Planter Class, 1733–1823', *Atlantic Studies*, 9 (1) (2012), 107–23.
Lorimer, Douglas A., 'Black Slaves and English Liberty: a Re-examination of Racial Slavery in England', *Immigrants and Minorities: Historical Studies in Ethnicity, Migration and Diaspora*, 3 (2) (1984), 121–50.
Lovejoy, Paul, *Transformations in Slavery. A History of Slavery in Africa* (3rd edn, Cambridge, 2012).
McCahill, M. W. (ed.), *The Correspondence of Stephen Fuller, 1788–1795. Jamaica, the West India Interest at Westminster and the Campaign to Preserve the Slave Trade* (Chichester, 2014).
McCormick, Ted, *William Petty and the Ambitions of Political Arithmetic* (Oxford, 2009).
McKittrick, Katherine, *Demonic Grounds. Black Women and the Cartographies of Struggle* (Minneapolis, 2006).
— 'Plantation Futures', *Small Axe*, 42 (2013), 1–15
McNeill, J. R., *Mosquito Empires. Ecology and War in the Greater Caribbean, 1620–1914* (Cambridge, 2010).
Mair, Lucille Mathurin, *A Historical Study of Women in Jamaica, 1655–1844*, ed. and intro. Hilary M. Beckles and Verene A. Shepherd (Kingston, Jamaica, 2006).
— *Women Field Workers in Jamaica during Slavery. Elsa Goveia Memorial Lecture, 1986* (Mona, Jamaica, 1986).
Mamdani, Mahmood, *Neither Settler nor Native. The Making and Unmaking of Permanent Minorities* (Cambridge, MA, 2020).

Mancke, Elizabeth, 'Empire and State', in *The British Atlantic World, 1500-1800*, ed. D. Armitage and M. J. Braddick (London, 2002), 193-213.

Marshall, P. J., *The Making and Unmaking of Empires. Britain, India and America, c. 1750-1783* (Oxford, 2007).

'Parliament and Property Rights in the Late Eighteenth Century British Empire', in *Early Modern Conceptions of Property*, ed. John Brewer and Susan Staves (London, 1996), 530-44.

Martinez-Ruiz, Barbaro, 'Sketches of Memory: Visual Encounters with Africa in Jamaican Culture' in *Art and Emancipation in Jamaica*, ed. Tim Barringer, Gillian Forrester and Barbaro Martinez-Ruiz (New Haven, CT, 2007), 103-17.

Metcalf, George, *Royal Government and Political Conflict in Jamaica, 1729-1783* (London, 1965).

Miller, Joseph C., *Way of Death. Merchant Capitalism and the Angolan Slave Trade, 1730-1830* (London, 1988).

Miller, Kei, *Augustown* (London, 2016).

Mintz, Sidney W., 'The Jamaica Internal Marketing Pattern: Some Notes and Hypotheses', *Social and Economic Studies*, 4 (1) (1955), 95-103.

Sweetness and Power. The Place of Sugar in Modern History (New York, 1985).

Mintz, Sidney W. and Douglas Hall, *The Origins of the Jamaican Internal Marketing System* (New Haven, CT, 1960).

Mintz, Sidney W. and Richard Price, *An Anthropological Approach to the Afro-American Past. A Caribbean Perspective* (Philadelphia, 1976).

The Birth of African-American Culture. An Anthropological Perspective (Boston, 1976).

Mirzoeff, Nicholas, *The Right to Look. A Counter-History of Visuality* (Durham, NC, 2011).

Molineux, Catherine, *Faces of Perfect Ebony. Encountering Atlantic Slavery in Imperial Britain* (Cambridge, MA, 2012).

Montano, John Patrick, *The Roots of English Colonialism in Ireland* (Cambridge, 2011).

Morgan, Jennifer L., 'Archives and Histories of Racial Capitalism: an Afterword', *Social Text*, 33 (4) (2015), 153-61.

Laboring Women. Reproduction and Gender in New World Slavery (Philadelphia, 2004).

Reckoning with Slavery. Gender, Kinship and Capitalism in the Early Black Atlantic (Durham, NC, 2021).

Morgan, Kenneth, *Bristol and the Atlantic Trade in the Eighteenth Century* (Cambridge, 1993).

'Bristol West India Merchants in the Eighteenth Century', *Transactions of the Royal Historical Society*, 6 (3) (1993), 181-206.

'Slave Women and Reproduction in Jamaica, 1776-1834', *History*, 91 (302) (2006), 231-53.

Morgan, Philip D., 'The Black Experience in the British Empire, 1680–1810', in *Oxford History of the British Empire. The Eighteenth Century*, ed. P. J. Marshall (Oxford, 1998), 465–86.
  'Slavery in the British Caribbean', in *Cambridge World History of Slavery*, ed. David Eltis and Stanley L. Engerman (Cambridge, 2011), 378–406.
Morris, R. J., *Men, Women and Property in England, 1780–1870* (Cambridge, 2005).
Morrison, Toni, *Beloved* (New York, 1987).
  The Origin of Others (Cambridge, MA, 2017).
  Playing in the Dark. Whiteness and the Literary Imagination (New York, 1992).
Muller, Hannah Weiss, *Subject and Sovereign. Bonds of Belonging in the Eighteenth-Century British Empire* (Oxford, 2017).
Nelson, Louis P., *Architecture and Empire in Jamaica* (New Haven, CT, 2016).
Nelson, William Max, 'Making Men: Enlightenment Ideas of Racial Engineering', *American Historical Review*, 115 (5) (2010), 1364–94.
Newman, Brooke N., *A Dark Inheritance. Blood, Race, and Sex in Colonial Jamaica* (London, 2019).
  'Gender, Sexuality and the Formation of Racial Identities in the Eighteenth-Century Anglo-Caribbean World', *Gender and History*, 22 (3) (2010), 585–602.
Newman, Gerald, *The Rise of English Nationalism. A Cultural History, 1740–1830* (London, 1987).
Newman, Simon P., *Fortune Seekers. Escaping from Slavery in Restoration London* (London, 2022).
  A New World of Labor. The Development of Plantation Slavery in the British Atlantic (Philadelphia, 2013).
Newton, Melanie, 'Returns to a Native Land: Indigeneity and Creolization in the Anglophone Caribbean', *Small Axe*, 41 (2013), 108–22.
Nicholson, Bradley J., 'Legal Borrowing and the Origins of Slave Law in the British Colonies', *American Journal of Legal History*, 38 (1) (1994), 38–54.
Nussbaum, Felicity A., *The Limits of the Human. Fictions of Anomaly, Race and Gender in the Long Eighteenth Century* (Cambridge, 2003).
Nyquist, Mary, *Arbitrary Rule. Slavery, Tyranny, and the Power of Life and Death* (Chicago, 2013).
O'Brien, Karen, 'Imperial Georgic, 1660–1789', in *The Country and the City Revisited. England and the Politics of Culture, 1550–1850*, ed. Gerald Maclean, Donna Landry and Joseph P. Ward (Cambridge, 1999), 160–79.
  Narratives of Enlightenment. Cosmopolitan History from Voltaire to Gibbon (Cambridge, 1997).
O'Shaughnessy, Andrew Jackson, *An Empire Divided. The American Revolution and the British Caribbean* (Philadelphia, 2000).
  'The Formation of a Commercial Lobby: the West India Interest, British Colonial Policy and the American Revolution', *Historical Journal*, 40 (1) (1997), 71–95.

Ogborn, Miles, 'Discriminating Evidence: Closeness and Distance in Natural and Civil Histories of the Caribbean', *Modern Intellectual History*, 11 (3) (2014), 631–53.
The Freedom of Speech. Talk and Slavery in the Anglo-Caribbean World (Chicago, 2019).
Spaces of Modernity. London's Geographies, 1680–1780 (New York, 1998).
Ogborn, Miles and Charles W. J. Withers (eds.), *Georgian Geographies. Essays on Space, Place and Landscape in the Eighteenth Century* (Manchester, 2004).
Pares, Richard, 'A London West-India Merchant House, 1740–1769', in *Essays Presented to Sir Lewis Namier*, ed. Richard Pares and A. J. P. Taylor (London, 1956), 75–107.
Merchants and Planters, 4th supplement to *Economic History Review* (1960).
A West India Fortune (London, 1950).
Paton, Diana, *The Cultural Politics of Obeah. Religion, Colonialism and Modernity in the Caribbean World* (Cambridge, 2015).
'The Driveress and the Nurse: Childcare, Working Children and Other Work under Caribbean Slavery', *Past and Present*, 246, supplement 15 (2020), 27–53.
'Gender History, Global History, and Atlantic Slavery: On Racial Capitalism and Social Reproduction', *American Historical Review*, 127 (2) (2022), 726–54.
'Punishment, Crime, and the Bodies of Slaves in Eighteenth Century Jamaica' *Journal of Social History*, 34 (4) (2001), 923–54.
Patterson, Orlando, *Die the Long Day* (London, 1972).
'Life and Scholarship in the Shadow of Slavery', introduction to 2nd edn of *The Sociology of Slavery* (Cambridge, 2022).
Slavery and Social Death. A Comparative Study (Cambridge, MA, 1982).
'Slavery and Slave Revolts: a Sociohistorical Analysis of the First Maroon War, 1665–1740', in *Maroon Societies. Rebel Slave Communities in the Americas*, ed. Richard Price (2nd edn, Baltimore, 1996), 246–92.
The Sociology of Slavery. Black Society in Jamaica, 1655–1838 [1967] (2nd edn, Cambridge, 2022).
Paugh, Katherine, 'The Curious Case of Mary Hylas: Wives, Slaves and the Limits of British Abolitionism', *Slavery and Abolition* 35 (4) (2014), 629–51.
Pearsall, Sarah M. S., *Atlantic Families. Lives and Letters in the Later Eighteenth Century* (Oxford, 2008).
Polygamy. An Early American History (London, 2019).
Penson, Lilian M., *The Colonial Agents of the British West Indies. A Study in Colonial Administration Mainly in the Eighteenth Century* (London, 1924).
Perry, Kennetta Hammond, *London is the Place for Me. Black Britons, Citizenship and the Politics of Race* (Oxford, 2015).
Pestana, Carla Gardina, *The English Atlantic in an Age of Revolution, 1640–1661* (Cambridge, MA, 2004).
The English Conquest of Jamaica. Oliver Cromwell's Bid for Empire (Cambridge, MA, 2017).

'State Formation from the Vantage Point of Early English Jamaica: the Neglect of Edward Doyley', *Journal of British Studies*, 56 (2017), 483–505.

Petley, Christer, 'Gluttony, Excess, and the Fall of the Planter Class', *Atlantic Studies*, 9 (4) (2012), 85–106.

'"Home" and "This Country": Britishness and Creole Identity in the Letters of a Transatlantic Slaveholder', *Atlantic Studies*, 6 (1) (2009), 43–61.

'"Legitimacy" and Social Boundaries: Free People of Colour and the Social Order in Jamaican Slave Society' *Social History*, 30 (4) (2005), 481–98.

White Fury. A Jamaican Slaveholder and the Age of Revolution (Oxford, 2018).

Pettigrew, William A., *Freedom's Debt. The Royal African Company and the Politics of the Atlantic Slave Trade, 1672–1752* (Chapel Hill, NC, 2013).

Phillips, Mark Salber, 'Reconsiderations on History and Antiquarianism: Arnaldo Momigliano and the Historiography of Eighteenth-Century Britain', *Journal of the History of Ideas*, 57 (2) (1996), 297–316.

Phillipson, Nicholas, *Hume* (London, 1989).

Pincus, Steve, *1688. The First Modern Revolution* (London, 2009).

'Addison's Empire: Whig Conceptions of Empire in the Early Eighteenth Century', *Parliamentary History*, 3 (1) (2012), 99–117.

'Re-thinking Mercantilism: Political Economy, the British Empire and the Atlantic World in the Seventeenth and Eighteenth Centuries', *William and Mary Quarterly*, 69 (1) (2012), 3–34.

Plumb, J. H., *Sir Robert Walpole. The Making of a Statesman* (London, 1956).

Pocock, J. G. A., *The Machiavellian Moment. Florentine Political Thought and the Atlantic Republican Tradition* (Princeton, 1975).

'The Mobility of Property and the Rise of Eighteenth-Century Sociology', in *Virtue, Commerce, and History. Essays on Political Thought and History, Chiefly in the Eighteenth Century* (Cambridge, 1985), 103–24.

'The Varieties of Whiggism from Exclusion to Reform: a History of Ideology and Discourse', in *Virtue, Commerce, and History. Essays on Political Thought and History, Chiefly in the Eighteenth Century* (Cambridge, 1985), 215–310.

Pollard, Sidney, *The Genesis of Modern Management. A Study of the Industrial Revolution in Great Britain* (London, 1965).

Poovey, Mary, *A History of the Modern Fact. Problems of Knowledge in the Sciences of Wealth and Society* (Chicago, 1998).

Powers, Anne M., *A Parcel of Ribbons. The Letters of an Eighteenth Century Family in England and Jamaica* [2012] (n.p., 2022).

Pratt, Mary Louise, *Imperial Eyes. Travel Writing and Transculturation* (London, 1992).

Price, Jacob M., 'Credit in the Slave Trade and Plantation Economies', in *Slavery and the Rise of the Atlantic System*, ed. Barbara L. Solow (Cambridge, 1991), 293–339.

Quilley, Geoff, 'Pastoral Plantations', in *An Economy of Colour. Visual Culture and the Atlantic World, 1660–1830*, ed. Geoff Quilley and Kay Dian Kriz (Manchester, 2003), 106–28.

'Questions of Loyalty: the Representation of the British West Indian Colonies during the American Revolutionary War', in *Conflicting Visions. War and Visual Culture in Britain and France, c. 1700-1830*, ed. John Bonehill and Geoff Quilley (Aldershot, 2005), 114-35.

Quilley, Geoff and Kay Dian Kriz (eds.), *An Economy of Colour. Visual Culture and the Atlantic World, 1660-1830* (Manchester, 2003).

Rabin, Dana Y., *Britain and its Internal Others, 1750-1800. Under Rule of Law* (Manchester, 2017).

'"In a Country of Liberty?": Slavery, Villeinage and the Making of Whiteness in the Somerset Case', *History Workshop Journal*, 72 (2011), 5-29.

Radburn, Nicholas, 'Guinea Factors, Slave Sales and the Profits of the Transatlantic Slave Trade in Late Eighteenth-Century Jamaica: the Case of John Tailyour', *William and Mary Quarterly*, 72 (2) (2015), 243-86.

Rediker, Marcus, *The Slave Ship. A Human History* (London, 2008).

Reid, Ahmed and David Beck Ryden, 'Sugar, Land Markets and the Williams Thesis: Evidence from Jamaica's Property Sales, 1750-1810', *Slavery and Abolition*, 34 (3) (2013), 401-24.

Renton, Alex, *Blood Legacy. Reckoning with a Family's Story of Slavery* (Edinburgh, 2021).

Richardson, David, *Principles and Agents. The British Slave Trade and its Abolition* (New Haven, CT, 2022).

Roach, Catherine, '"The Higher Branches": Genre and Race on Display at the British Institution, London, 1806', *Art History*, 44 (2) (2021), 312-40.

Roach, Joseph, *Cities of the Dead. Circum-Atlantic Performance* (New York, 1996).

Roberts, Justin, *Slavery and the Enlightenment in the British Atlantic, 1750-1807* (Cambridge, 2013).

Robertson, James, 'Eighteenth Century Jamaica's Ambivalent Cosmopolitanism', *History*, 99 (337) (2014), 607-31.

'An Essay Concerning Slavery: a mid-Eighteenth-Century Analysis from Jamaica', *Slavery and Abolition*, 33 (1) (2012), 65-85.

Gone is the Ancient Glory. Spanish Town, Jamaica, 1534-2000 (Kingston, Jamaica, 2005).

Robinson, Cedric J., *Black Marxism. The Making of the Black Radical Tradition* (London, 1983).

Rodney, Walter, *West Africa and the Atlantic Slave Trade* (Nairobi, 1967).

Rogers, Nicholas, *Mayhem. Post-War Crime and Violence in Britain, 1748-1753* (London, 2012).

Rohl, Darrell J., 'The Chorographic Tradition and Seventeenth and Eighteenth Century Scottish Antiquaries', *Journal of Art Historiography*, 5 (2011), 1-18.

Ronnick, Michele Valerie, 'Francis Williams: an Eighteenth Century Tertium Quid', *Negro History Bulletin*, 61 (2) (1998), 19-29.

Root, Winifred T., 'The Lords of Trade and Plantations, 1675-1696', *American Historical Review*, 23 (1) (1917), 20-41.

Rosenthal, Caitlin, *Accounting for Slavery. Masters and Management* (Cambridge, MA, 2018).
Rothschild, Emma, *The Inner Life of Empires. An Eighteenth-Century History* (Princeton, 2011).
Rugemer, Edward B., 'The Development of Mastery and Race in the Comprehensive Slave Codes of the Greater Caribbean during the Seventeenth Century', *William and Mary Quarterly*, 70 (3) (2013), 429–58.
  Slave Law and the Politics of Resistance in the Early Atlantic World (Cambridge, MA, 2018).
Ryden, David Beck, 'Sugar, Spirits and Fodder: the London West India Interest and the Glut of 1807–15', *Atlantic Studies*, 9 (1) (2012), 41–64.
  West Indian Slavery and British Abolition, 1783–1807 (Cambridge, 2009).
Said, Edward, *Out of Place. A Memoir* (London, 1999).
Saunders-Wedd, Stephen, *The Governors-General. The English Army and the Definition of Empire, 1569–1681* (Chapel Hill, NC, 1979).
Schaub, Jean-Frédéric and Silvia Sebastiani, *Race et histoire dans les sociétés occidentales (XVe–XVIIIe siècle)* (Paris, 2021).
Schiebinger, Londa, *Nature's Body. Gender in the Making of Modern Science* [1993] (New Brunswick, 2004).
  Plants and Empire. Colonial Bioprospecting in the Atlantic World (Cambridge, MA, 2004).
Schofield, Camilla, *Enoch Powell and the Making of Postcolonial Britain* (Cambridge, 2013).
Schwarz, Bill, *Memories of Empire, volume I: the White Man's World* (Oxford, 2011).
Scott, David, *Conscripts of Modernity. The Tragedy of Colonial Enlightenment* (London, 2004).
  Irreparable Evil. An Essay in Moral and Reparatory History (New York, 2024).
  'The Paradox of Freedom: an Interview with Orlando Patterson', *Small Axe*, 40 (2013), 96–243.
  'The Permanence of Pluralism', in *Without Guarantees. In Honour of Stuart Hall*, ed. Paul Gilroy, Lawrence Grossberg and Angela McRobbie (London, 2000).
  'The Re-Enchantment of Humanism: an Interview with Sylvia Wynter', *Small Axe*, 8 (2000), 119–207.
Scott, Julius S., *The Common Wind. Afro-American Currents in the Age of the Haitian Revolution* (London, 2018).
Sebastiani, Silvia, 'Challenging Boundaries: Apes and Savages in Enlightenment', in *Simianization. Apes, Gender, Class, and Race*, ed. Wulf D. Hund, Charles W. Mills and Silvia Sebastiani (Zurich, 2015), 105–38.
  'Enlightenment Humanization and Dehumanization, and the Orangutan', in *The Routledge Handbook of Dehumanization*, ed. Maria Kronfeldner (London, 2021), 64–82.
  'Global Integration, Social Disintegration: Edward Long's History of Jamaica, 1774', in *Nations, Empires and Other World Products. Making Narratives across Borders*, ed. Jeremy Adelman and Andreas Eckert (forthcoming).

'"A Monster with Human Visage": the Orangutan, Savagery and the Borders of Humanity in the Global Enlightenment', *History of the Human Sciences*, 32 (4) (2019), 80–99.

'National Characters and Race: a Scottish Enlightenment Debate', in *Character, Self and Sociability in the Scottish Enlightenment*, ed. Thomas Ahnert and Susan Manning (London, 2011), 187–206.

The Scottish Enlightenment. Race, Gender, and the Limits of Progress (London, 2013).

Sen, Sudipta, 'Uncertain Dominance: the Colonial State and its Contradictions (with Notes on the History of Early British India)', *Nepantla: Views from South*, 3 (2) (2002), 391–406.

Senior, Emily, *The Caribbean and the Medical Imagination, 1764–1834. Slavery, Disease and Colonial Modernity* (Cambridge, 2018).

Seth, Suman, *Difference and Disease: Medicine, Race and the Eighteenth Century British Empire* (Cambridge, 2018).

Sharples, Jason T., *The World that Fear Made. Slave Revolts and Conspiracy Scares in Early America* (Philadelphia, 2020).

Sheller, Mimi, *Consuming the Caribbean. From Arawaks to Zombies* (London, 2003).

Shepard, Alexandra, 'Crediting Women in the Early Modern English Economy', *History Workshop Journal*, 79 (Spring 2015), 1–24.

Shepherd, Verene A., *Livestock, Sugar and Slavery. Contested Terrain in Colonial Jamaica* (Kingston, Jamaica, 2009).

Sheridan, Richard B., 'The Crisis of Slave Subsistence in the British West Indies during and after the American Revolution', *William and Mary Quarterly*, 33 (4) (1976), 615–41.

Sugar and Slavery. An Economic History of the British West Indies, 1623–1775 (Baltimore, 1973).

Shilliam, Robbie, 'Decolonizing the *Manifesto*: Communism and the Slave Analogy', in *The Cambridge Companion to the Communist Manifesto*, ed. Terrell Carver and James Farr (Cambridge, 2015), 195–213.

Shyllon, Folarin, *Edward Long's Libel of Africa. The Foundation of British Racism* (Newcastle upon Tyne, 2021).

Singh, Nikhil Pal, 'On Race, Violence and So-Called Primitive Accumulation', *Social Text*, 34 (3) (2016), 27–50.

Smail, John, 'Credit, Risk and Honour in Eighteenth-Century Commerce', *Journal of British Studies*, 44 (3) (2005), 439–56.

Smallwood, Stephanie E., 'The Politics of the Archive and History's Accountability to the Enslaved', *History of the Present*, 6 (2) (2016), 117–32.

Saltwater Slavery. A Middle Passage from Africa to American Diaspora (Cambridge, MA, 2007).

'What Slavery Tells us about Marx', *Boston Review*, 21 February 2018.

Smith, S. D., '*Planters and Merchants* Revisited', *Economic History Review*, 55 (3) (2002), 434–65.

Slavery, Family, and Gentry Capitalism in the British Atlantic. The World of the Lascelles, 1648–1834 (Cambridge, 2006).
Spivak, Gyatri Chakraborty, 'Three Women's Texts and a Critique of Imperialism', *Critical Inquiry*, 12 (1) (1985), 247–72.
Spurdle, Frederick G., *Early West Indian Government. Showing the Progress of Government in Barbados, Jamaica and the Leeward Islands, 1660–1783* (Palmerston, New Zealand, n.d.).
St Clair, William, *Lord Elgin and the Marbles* (Oxford, 1998).
Staves, Susan, *Married Women's Property in England* (Cambridge, MA, 1990).
Stern, Philip J. and Carl Wennerlind (eds.), *Mercantilism Reimagined. Political Economy in Early Modern Britain and its Empire* (Oxford, 2013).
Stock, Paul, '"Almost a Separate Race": Racial Thought and the Idea of Europe in British Encyclopaedias and Histories, 1771–1830', *Modern Intellectual History*, 8 (1) (2011), 3–29.
Stoler, Ann Laura, *Along the Archival Grain. Epistemic Anxieties and Colonial Commonsense* (Princeton, 2009).
Sturtz, Linda L., 'Mary Rose: "White" African Jamaican Woman? Race and Gender in Eighteenth Century Jamaica', in *Gendering the African Diaspora. Women, Culture, and Historical Change in the Caribbean and Nigerian Hinterland*, ed. Judith A. Byfield, LaRay Denzer and Anthea Morrison (Bloomington, IN, 2010), 59–87.
Swaminathan, Srividhya, 'Developing the West Indian Proslavery Position after the Somerset Decision', *Slavery and Abolition*, 24 (3) (2003), 40–60.
Sweet, Rosemary, *The Writing of Urban Histories in Eighteenth Century England* (Oxford, 1997).
Swingen, Abigail L., *Competing Visions of Empire. Labor, Slavery and the Origins of the British Atlantic Empire* (New Haven, CT, 2015).
Syrett, David, *Shipping and the American War. A Study of British Transport Organisation* (London, 1970).
Tadmor, Naomi, *Family and Friends in Eighteenth-Century England. Household, Kinship and Patronage* (Cambridge, 2001).
Taylor, Clare, 'Planter Comment upon Slave Revolts in Eighteenth Century Jamaica', *Slavery and Abolition*, 3 (3) (1982), 243–53.
Taylor, S. A. G., *A Short History of Clarendon* (Kingston, Jamaica, 1976).
  The Western Design. An Account of Cromwell's Expedition to the Caribbean (Kingston, Jamaica, 1965).
Thompson, E. P., *Customs in Common* (Harmondsworth, 1993).
  Whigs and Hunters. The Origin of the Black Act (London, 1975).
Thornton, A. P., *West-India Policy under the Restoration* (Oxford, 1956).
Thrush, Coll, *Indigenous London. Native Travellers at the Heart of Empire* (London, 2016).
Tise, Larry E., *Proslavery. A History of the Defense of Slavery in America, 1701–1840* (London, 1987).
Tobin, Beth Fowkes, *Colonizing Nature. The Tropics in British Arts and Letters, 1760–1820* (Philadelphia, 2005).

Trouillot, Michel-Rolph, *Silencing the Past. Power and the Production of History* (Boston, 1995).
Truxes, Thomas, 'Doing Business in the Wartime Caribbean: John Byrn, Irish Merchant of Kingston, Jamaica (September–October 1756)', in *Ireland, Slavery and the Caribbean. Interdisciplinary Perspectives*, ed. Finola O'Kane and Ciaran O'Neill (Manchester, 2023), 87–100.
Turner, Sasha, *Contested Bodies. Pregnancy, Childrearing, and Slavery in Jamaica* (Philadelphia, 2017).
— 'Home-Grown Slaves: Women, Reproduction and the Abolition of the Slave Trade, Jamaica, 1788–1807', *Journal of Women's History*, 23 (3) (2011), 39–62.
— 'The Nameless and the Forgotten: Maternal Grief, Sacred Protection and the Archive of Slavery', *Slavery and Abolition*, 38 (2) (2017), 232–50.
Unsworth, Barry, *Sacred Hunger* (London, 1992).
Vasconcellos, Colleen A., *Slavery, Childhood, and Abolition in Jamaica, 1788–1838* (London, 2015).
Vergès, Françoise, *The Wombs of Women. Race, Capital, Feminism* (London, 2020).
Vermeulen, Heather V., 'Thomas Thistlewood's Libidinal Linnean Project: Slavery, Ecology, and Knowledge Production', *Small Axe*, 55 (2018), 18–38.
Vernon, James, 'Heathrow and the Making of Neoliberal Britain', *Past and Present*, 252 (1) (2021), 213–47.
Walker, Christine, *Jamaica Ladies. Female Slaveholders and the Creation of Britain's Atlantic Empire* (Chapel Hill, NC, 2020).
Wallerstein, Immanuel, 'American Slavery and the Capitalist World Economy', *American Journal of Sociology*, 81 (5) (1976), 1199–213.
Ward, J. R., 'The Profitability of Sugar Planting in the British West Indies, 1650–1834', *Economic History Review*, 2nd ser. 31 (1978), 197–213.
Waters, Rob, *Thinking Black: Britain, 1964–1985* (Berkeley, 2018).
Watson, Tim, *Caribbean Culture and British Fiction in the Atlantic World, 1780–1870* (Cambridge, 2008).
Watts, Carol, *The Cultural Work of Empire. The Seven Years War and the Imagining of the Shandean State* (Edinburgh, 2007).
Wennerlind, Carl, *Casualties of Credit. The English Financial Revolution, 1620–1720* (Cambridge, MA, 2011).
Wheeler, Roxann, *The Complexion of Race. Categories of Difference in Eighteenth Century British Culture* (Philadelphia, 2000).
Whitson, Agnes M., *The Constitutional Development of Jamaica, 1660 to 1729* (Manchester, 1929).
Williams, Eric, *Capitalism and Slavery* (Chapel Hill, NC, 1944).
Williams, Heather Andrea, *Help Me to Find My People. The African American Search for Family Lost in Slavery* (Chapel Hill, NC, 2012).
Williams, Raymond, *The Country and the City* (London, 1973).
— *Keywords. A Vocabulary of Culture and Society* (London, 1976).

Williamson, Margaret, 'Africa or Old Rome? Jamaican Slave Naming Revisited', *Slavery and Abolition*, 38 (1) (2017), 117–34.

Wilson, Kathleen, *The Island Race. Englishness, Empire and Gender in the Eighteenth Century* (London, 2003).

'The Performance of Freedom: Maroons and the Colonial Order in Eighteenth Century Jamaica and the Atlantic Sound', *William and Mary Quarterly*, 66 (1) (2009), 45–86.

' Rethinking the Colonial State: Family, Gender, and Colonial Governmentality in Eighteenth-Century British Frontiers', *American Historical Review*, 116 (5) (2011), 1294–322.

The Sense of the People. Politics, Culture and Imperialism in England, 1715–1785 (Cambridge, 1998).

Strolling Players of Empire. Theater and Performances of Power in the British Imperial Provinces, 1656–1833 (Cambridge, 2022).

'Three Theses on Performance and History', *Eighteenth-Century Studies*, 48 (4) (2015), 375–90.

Wilson, Lee B., *The Bonds of Empire. The English Origins of Slave Law in South Carolina and British Plantation America, 1660–1783* (Cambridge, 2021).

Wood, Betty and T. R. Clayton, 'Slave Birth, Death and Disease on Golden Grove Plantation, Jamaica, 1765–1810', *Slavery and Abolition*, 6 (2) (1985), 99–121.

Wynter, Sylvia, 'Jonkonnu in Jamaica: Towards the Interpretation of the Folk Dance as a Cultural Process', *Jamaica Journal*, 4 (2) (1970), 34–48.

'Novel and History, Plot and Plantation', *Savacou*, 5 (1971), 95–102.

'Unsettling the Coloniality of Being/Power/Truth/Freedom: Towards the Human, after Man, its Overrepresentation – an Argument'. *CR: the New Centennial Review*, 3 (3) (2003), 257–337.

Young, Hannah L., 'Negotiating Female Property and Slave-Ownership in the Aristocratic World', *Historical Journal* 63 (3) (2020), 581–602.

Zahedieh, Nuala, '"A Frugal Prudential and Hopeful Trade": Privateering in Jamaica, 1655–89', *Journal of Imperial and Commonwealth History*, 18 (2) (1990), 145–68.

'Trade, Plunder, and Economic Development in Early English Jamaica, 1655–89', *Economic History Review*, 39 (2) (1986), 205–22.

Entries in the Oxford Dictionary of National Biography

All entries are in the online edition at www.oxforddnb.com

Austin, P. B., revised by Nuala Zahedieh, 'Beeston, Sir William (1636–1702), Merchant and Colonial Governor'.

Colvin, Howard, 'Long, Charles, Baron Farnborough (1760–1838), Politician and Connoisseur of the Arts'.

Gilmore, John, 'Williams, Francis (c. 1690–1762), Writer in Jamaica'.

Goodwin, George and Michael Erben, 'Long, Charles Edward (1796–1861), Genealogist and Antiquary'.

Handley, Stuart, 'Price, Sir Charles, First Baronet (1708-1772), Politician in Jamaica'.
Marshall, P. J., 'Lyttelton, William Henry, First Baron Lyttelton and First Baron Westcote (1724-1808), Colonial Governor and Diplomat'.
O'Shaughnessy, Andrew Jackson, 'Long, Samuel (1638-1683), Planter and Politician in the West Indies'.
Tiedemann, Joseph S., 'Moore, Sir Henry, First Baronet (1713-1769), Colonial Governor'.
Zahedieh, Nuala, 'Modyford, Sir Thomas, First Baronet (c. 1620-1679), Planter and Colonial Governor'.

Unpublished Secondary Sources: Theses

Dawkins, James, 'The Dawkins Family in England and Jamaica, 1664-1823' (PhD, University College London, 2018).
Day, Thomas R., 'Jamaican Revolts in British Press and Politics, 1760-1865' (MA, Virginia Commonwealth University, 2016).
Newman, Rachel, 'Conjuring Cane: the Art of William Berryman and Caribbean Sugar Plantations' (PhD, Stanford University, 2016).
Prykhodko, Yaroslav, 'Mind, Body, and the Moral Imagination in the Eighteenth-Century British Atlantic World' (PhD, University of Pennsylvania, 2011).
Sivapragasam, Michael, 'After the Treaties: a Social, Economic and Demographic History of Maroon Society in Jamaica, 1739-1842' (PhD, University of Southampton, 2018).
Young, Hannah L., 'Gender and Absentee Slave-Ownership in Late Eighteenth-Century and Early Nineteenth-Century Britain' (PhD, University College London, 2017).

Unpublished Secondary Sources: Other

Bindman, David, 'Francis Williams' (seminar paper, Hutchins Center, Harvard University, 23 March 2022).
    'Portraiture Amateur and Professional: Francis Williams and Philip Wickstead' (unpublished paper).
Cody, Lisa, 'Coverture and Consent in Eighteenth-Century English Marriage' (seminar paper, Institute of Historical Research, London, 28 November 2020).
Draper, Nick, 'The Role and Significance of Annuities in the British Caribbean Plantation Economy' (unpublished paper, 2019).
Gilmore, John, 'Latin in Black and White: John Alleyn, Francis Williams and Caribbean Poetry' (unpublished paper, 1998).
Harvey, Mark, 'Picketty, Property, Slavery' (unpublished paper, 2021).
Ogborn, Miles, 'Deliberative Power: Speech, Politics and Empire in Jamaica's late C17th Constitutional Crisis' (forthcoming).
Pincus, Steve, 'Thinking the British Empire Whole' (seminar presentation, King's College London, October 2020).

Shelford, April G., 'Before Breadfruit: Natural History and Sociability in Eighteenth-Century Jamaica' (unpublished paper, August 2016).

Websites

Centre for the Study of the Legacies of British Slavery, www.ucl.ac.uk/lbs/
Jamaican inventories, https://www.ucl.ac.uk/lbs/project/invdesc/.
Runaway Slaves in Britain, www.runaways.gla.ac.uk/
Slave Voyages, www.slavevoyages.org
Henry and Hannah Norbrook family tree, Ancestry, https://www.ancestry.co.uk/family-tree/person/tree/4416130/person/-1441477233/facts
Brown, Vincent, *Slave Revolt in Jamaica, 1760–1761. A Cartographic Narrative*, http://revolt.axismaps.com/.
Christopher, Emma, 'Dreams of a New Plantation Society: Legacies of British Slavery in Queensland, Australia'. Legacies of British Slavery blog, 25 July 2018, https://lbsatucl.wordpress.com/2018/07/25/dreams-of-a-new-plantation-society-legacies-of-british-slavery-in-queensland-australia/
Paugh, Katherine, 'The New History of Capitalism and the Political Economy of Reproduction', *Past and Present* blog, 10 December 2020, https://pastandpresent.org.uk/the-new-history-of-capitalism-and-the-political-economy-of-reproduction/

INDEX

Illustrations are indicated by page numbers in italics.
All references to family members are in relation to Edward Long (EL).

abolition and anti-slavery. *See also*
  Sharp, Granville
  arguments and strategies, 152, 173, 427
  growing support for, 135, 156, 174, 198, 376, 422, 426, 429, 430
  historical study of, xxvi
Addison, Joseph, 5, 63, 66, 70, 75, 76, 83, 192, 193, 194, 280, 281, 282
Africans
  racial identity and, 42, 187
  representations of, 22, 33, 135, 136, 139, 142, 146, 147, 149, 174, 175–7, 178, 339, 344, 348, 351, 353, 361, 370, 373, 376, 381, 382, 398–414
agrarian capitalism, 62, 108, 281
'amelioration', 334
American War of Independence, 37, 147, 189, 257, 289, 365
  effects on Jamaica of, 419, 422
  significance for slavery, 424, 430
  Stamp Act and, 367
Anti-Gallican, or, the History and Adventures of Harry Cobham, Esquire, 79–83, *80*, 148, 194, 313
Antigallican, The, or, strictures on the present form of government established in France, 432–33
Arcedeckne, Chaloner, 111, 113, 138, 144, 147, 185, 427
architecture, 274, 275, 277
artisans, 124, 126, 130, 144, 184

race and, 386
Asians, 22, 381

Back River, 102, 115
Bacon, Francis, 74
Bank of England, 179, 183, 191, 194
Barbados, 49, 50, 51, 58, 136, 293, 434
  Codrington College, 300
Barham, Henry, 13, 132, 137, 307
Barrère, Pierre, 399
Bath (Jamaica), 301, *302*, 332
Bayly, Zachary, 341
Beattie, James, 377, 440
Beckford, Thomas, 98
Beckford, William, 72, 75, 90, 93, 94, 100, 131, 144, 146, 147, 213, 314, 318–19, 350, 390, 422
Beckford, William, Jr, 127, 130, 132
Beckles, Hilary, 58, 142, 145
Beeston (née Hopegood), Anne (great-grandmother of), 204, 229, 230
Beeston, William (great-grandfather of), 11, 18, 34, 41, 47, 58, 165
  challenges to RAC's monopoly, 54
  death of, 56
  as founding figure of the family dynasty, 204, 207, 208, 224, 368
  imprisonment of, 54
  inheritance and, 227, 229
  as lieutenant-governor and governor, 56
  medical knowledge and, 292, 302

477

Beeston, William (cont.)
  as member of the assembly, 48, 53, 333
  as merchant and planter, 56, 178, 225
  political and social connections with Samuel Long, 55
Bernier, François, 382
Berryman, William, xxiii, 95, *96*, 116, *133*, 133, *149*
Best, Lloyd, 28, 166
Blackstone, William, 143, 321
Blair, James, 114, *117*
Board of Trade and Plantations, 94, 318
Bosman, Willem, 14, 17, 175
Boswell, James, 73, 320
Bourke, Nicholas, 365
  The Privileges of the Island of Jamaica Vindicated, 365-7, 368
Boyle, Robert, 399, 440
Bright, Henry, 92, 171, 189
Britain, xxii. *See also* Seven Years War
  anti-Catholicism and, 16, 54, 71, 313, 321
  colonization of Jamaica and, 12, 36, 39, 41, 43-6, 51, 157, 210, 265, 331
  conflicts with Spanish empire, 12, 41, 268, 270, 316, 363
  conflicts with the Dutch, 315, 316
  conflicts with the French, 270, 316
  as dominant global power, 316
  as fiscal-military state, 166, 179, 191, 199, 314-16, 317
  Irish colonization and, 53, 187, 330, 331, 366
  nationalism and, 21
  as protectorate, 44
  racial capitalism and, 26
  reactions to the 1760 slave insurrection, 345
  rights and, 16
  tensions between metropolitan and colonial interests, 27
  West India trade and, 87
British army
  1760 rebellion and, 36, 341
  early years of occupation in Jamaica, 43
  first direct encounter with Africans, 42
  officers and, 383
  parliament and, 317
  sickness and mortality in the Caribbean theatre, 292
  soldiers and, 383
British monarchy
  Charles I, 366
  Charles II, 11, 43, 47, 66, 315, 362, 368
  control of colonies and, 338
  George II, 82
  Henry VIII, 66
  James II, 43, 47, 48, 53, 169, 315
  slavery and, 378
  Stuarts, 59, 368
  William III, 315
British Museum, 241, 258
British navy
  1760 rebellion and, 36, 341
  parliament and, 317
  role in trade, 166, 315
  sickness and mortality in the Caribbean theatre, 292
British West Indies, 29
  prosperity of, 96
  sickness and disease, 293
  trade and, 15, 35, 87, 165, *172*
Brown, John, 83, 314
Brown, Vincent, 92, 137, 163, 323, 343, 361, 445
Browne, Patrick, 13, 307
Buffon, comte de (Georges-Louis Leclerc), 14, 149, 373, 431
  miscegenation and, 394
  theorizing race and, 400, 405, 406
Burke, Edmund, 99, 162, 428
Burke, John, 111
Burke, William, 98, 162
Burnard, Trevor, 89, 110, 213, 332, 361

Candid Reflections, 372, 377-80, 402
capitalism
  historical study of, 27
Caribbean
  British domination of, 430
  emergence of plantation slavery and, 49
  high mortality and, 56
  racial capitalism and, 26, 28, 166

Seven Years War and, 92, 270
  Spanish empire and, 42
  trade and, 48, 158
Carlisle, Earl of (Charles Howard), 53
Carlyle, Thomas, 435
Carter (née Long), Ann (aunt of), *260*
Carter, Philip (uncle by marriage of), 260
chattel slavery. *See* plantation slavery
Childe, Josiah, 13
Chisholm, William, 427, 428
Cicero, 7
Clarendon, xxii, 1, 46, 58, *101*, *114*, 271
  early settlement, 46
  geography and, 97
  landscape and, 282
  military and, 290, 357
  naming of, 270
  prosperity of, 97, 100, 131
  slave uprising in 1690, 337
Clarendon, Earl of (Edward Hyde) (historian), 13
Clark, Ann, 206, 222
Clarkson, Thomas, 427
class, 24, 87
  education and, 291
  influence on legal and political relations, 48
  military and, 289
  plantation slavery and, 93, 126, 212
  race and, 383
Cockpit, 97, 98, 239
  Maroons and, 337
cocoa, 101, 309
coffee, 101, 309
coffee houses, 69, 72
colonialism, 87. *See also* imperialism
  role of slavery and, 15
colonists (English)
  colonial patriotism, 18, 55
  conflicts with the crown and colonial government, 11, 36, 44, 100, 230–1
  delaying of abolition and, 37
  identity as free-born Englishman, xxix, 9, 16, 42, 43, 71, 331, 362–70, 418, 422, 432
  as lobbyists, 318, 372, 380, 382, 422, 425
  movement between England and Jamaica, 63, 318, 430
  RAC and, 316
  religious life and, 354
  sickness and health of, 36, 294, 300–3
commerce. *See also* rum; slave trade; sugar industry
  benefits of, 8
  bills of exchange and, 35, 168, 171, *172*, 182, 183, 190
  British ambivalence towards credit and, 191–6
  commission system and, 165, 173, 185
  connection to contemporary intellectual developments, 74
  dangers of, 70, 321
  economic botany and, 303, 309, 312
  imperialism and, 162, 179, 206
  luxury goods and, 163
  rise of commercialism, 58, 70–2
Company of Royal Adventurers, 47. *See also* Royal African Company (RAC)
Cooper, Hannah, 261
corn, 101
Cornwall (Jamaica), 270, 272
Coromantees, 21, 36, 144, 312
  associations with slave insurrections, 30, 112, 340, 346–7, 350, 360–1, 397, 409
  oaths and, 324
  obeah and, 354
Coromantins. *See* Coromantees
cotton, 309
couverture, 210, 212, 231, 259
Craskell, Thomas, *107*
creoles, black, 111, 275, 354–5. *See also* obeah
  representations of, 108, 136, 154, 174, 261, 354–5, 362, 382, 398, 408–14
creoles, white, 122, 208, 215, 218, 228, 301, 373, 383–4, 386, 400
Cromwell, Oliver, 12, 42, 268
  origins of English imperialism and, 41
Cuba, 270, 272

Davenant, Charles, 5, 13, 162, 179, 192, 193, 315
Dawkins, Henry, 119, 181, 184, 427
Dawkins (née Long), Jane Catherine (daughter of), 203, 245, 260, 424
Dawkins family, 100, 181
Dawkins' Wharf, *114*
Defoe, Daniel, 14, 16, 66, 192, 193, 433
  Moll Flanders, 69
Devon (née Long) Mary (granddaughter of), 223
Dickinson, Frances, 182
disavowal, 24, 141, 157, 175
  Africans' experiences of pain and, 139
  credit and, 190
  engravings and, 278
  enslaved persons' humanity and, 51, 328
  kinship rights of enslaved persons and, 140
  projection and, 32
  splitting and, 32, 368, 418, 420
  terminology and, 31
  violence and, 159, 161, 176, 177, 421
D'Oyley, Edward, 12, 42, 43, 338
Drake and Long, 35, 68, 119, 156, *180*, 181, 184, 186, 188, 200, 221
  founding of, 206, 225
  history of, 178
  lobbying and, 427
  slave trade and, 165
  transportation of military supplies and, 189
Drake, Roger (uncle by marriage of), 179, 221, 238
  inheritance and, 225
Draper, Nicholas, xxv, *167*
drivers, 123
  role of, 127, 128
Du Bois, W. E. B., 366
Dunwich, 60

East Anglia, 60
East India Company (EIC), 238
Edwards, Bryan, 102, 213, 422, 428, 430, 431

Elgin Marbles, 241
Elletson, Roger Hope, 367
Ellis, George (brother-in-law of), 90, 232, 258
Ellis, George Rose (nephew of), 233
Ellis, John, 233
Ellis (née Long), Susannah Charlotte (sister of), 68, 90, 208
  inheritance and, 232–3
Endelman, Todd, 74
English Humanity no Paradox: or, an attempt to prove, that the English are not a nation of savages, 419–21
engravings, 8, 275, 278, 285
Enlightenment, 4, 17
  Jamaica and, xxvii, 5, 15, 23, 303
  morality and, 108
  natural histories and, 36, 147, 303
  racial difference and, xxiii, xxvii, xxviii, 12, 27, 43, 136, 140, 187, 373, 381, 399, 402, 428, 443
enslaved children, 144
  infant mortality and, 147, 153
  labour and, 128
  as property of their master, 141
enslaved persons, 12
  Barbadoes, 110, 111
  birth rates and, 139
  Black Betty, 111
  Bob, 110
  Caffee, 348
  as captives, 168, 169, 170, 171
  Cato, 111
  Charles, 111
  clothing and, 134
  Congo Warwick, 111
  Coromante Warwick, 111
  Creole Celia, 111
  Cubah, 353
  Cuffee, 110, 111
  Cupid, 111
  Daphne, 111
  denial of kinship bonds, 26, 154, 204, 209
  Dunwick, 111
  everyday forms of resistance and, 349
  Fortune, 361
  Hampshire, 111
  housing and, 116, 133, 154

INDEX 481

Jacob, 111
Jamaica, 341
Jemmy, 348
Jubao Quashie, 111
Kate, 111
Kent, 111
Kingston, 361
labour outside working hours and, 88
London, 111
Lucky Valley and, 111
Lydia, 111
medical knowledge and, 300, 310–12
Mimba, 111
mortality of, 137
Mulatto James, 111
Mulatto Ned, 111
mutinies and, 113
Nanny, 111
Old Bess, 111
Old Prue, 111
productive labour and, 35, 88, 119, 123
provision grounds and, 131, 266
representation as chattels, 103, 210, *271*, 273
Robert, 111
as runaways, 72, 267, 272, 312, 349, 379
Sam, 111
Sambo, 111
Sarah, 111
sickness and disease, 153
Suffolk, 111
Sugar, 111
Tacky, 36, 341, 352–3, 381
Trinculo, 111
Wager (Apongo), 341
Yankee, 348
York, 111
enslaved women
1760 rebellion and, 353
abortion and, 146
as domestics, 131, 266
as field labourers, 130
as midwives, 147
as mothers, *152*
representations of, 393
reproductive labour and, 34, 35, 57, 88, 140, 142, 144, 203, 209

as supervisors for the grass gang, 131
as wetnurses and caregivers to white children, 148, *149*, 385
Equiano, Olaudah, 169, 170, 171, 427, 444
Erickson, Amy, 209, 210
Estwick, Samuel, 159, 380, 402–4, 440
ethnicity, 24
Africans and, 123, 349, 358, 383
ethnic inheritance, 436
whiteness and, 383
Europeans, 20, 22, 74, 168

family economy, white propertied, 202, 203, 206, 207
Fanon, Frantz, xxvii, 33, 421
Fearon, Thomas, 101, 282, 365
Fielding, Henry, 75, 79, 82, 280, 320
Foote, Sam, 83
Fort Charles, 290
Fox, Charles James, 428, 432
France, 13, 75, 326, 333, 432. *See also* French Revolution; Seven Years War
Franklin, Benjamin, 294, 303, 426
free blacks, 12, 273, 357, 381, 387
free people of colour, 27, 331, 358, 359, 388, 390
freedom. *See also* liberty
autonomy from Britain and, 362
conflict with commercialism, 71
dependence on black subjugation, 10, 41, 378, 380, 424
distinction from slavery, 51, 366
as English subjects, 363
free blacks and, 387
Maroons and, 339
political rights and, 324
property and, 369
white women as reproducers of, 203
French Revolution, 425, 429, 430
Freud, Sigmund, 31
Fuller, Rose, 90, 92, 94, 380
Fuller, Stephen, 344, 425, 427, 428

Garrick, David, 75
Gauci, Perry, 182, 212, 318

INDEX

gender, 24
  domesticity and, 77–8, 204, 209
  education and, 290, 305
  ideas about white English manhood, 34, 78, 79, 124, 182, 314
  ideas about white English womanhood, 69, 78, 148, 218, 379, 393
  influence on legal and political relations, 48
  organization of enslaved labour and, 34, 109, 130
  organization of property and, 35, 204–14, 231, 259
  political rights and, 203, 212, 215, 219, 324
  proper relations between the sexes, 204, 214, 215, 217, 351, 385, 390–3
  race and, 352, 383
  representations of credit and, 193, 194, 199, 200
  rights of property and freedom for whites, 87, 369
  'taste' and, 70–1
Gikandi, Simon, 73, 355
Gilpin, William, 286
Golding, John, 389
Goldsmith, Oliver, 7, 75, 431
Goveia, Elsa, 29, 48, 328, 443
governors, 53, 92, 324
Grainger, James
  benevolent depictions of slavey and, 129
  on commerce, 279
  on credit, 191
  Essay on the More Common West-India Diseases, 153
  on infant morality, 147
  on protecting enslaved persons' value, 108
  on sickness and disease, 296
  Sugar Cane, The, 104–6, 112, 127, 138, 281
Greene, Jack P., 14, 93, 368
Grenville, Anna Eliza, 228
grocers and retailers, 173, 184
Gronniosaw, Ukawsaw, 376
Grotius, Hugo, 30, 155

Habakkuk, John, 211
Haiti, 259
Haldane, George, 340, 351, 443
Hales, Stephen, 303–4, 309
Halifax, Earl of (George Montagu Dunk), 94
Hall, Florence, 169
Hall, Stuart, *xx*, xxii, 416
Halley, Edmond, 304
Hampton Lodge, xxiv
  inheritance and, 223
Hancock, David, 181, 183
Hanover (Jamaica), 144, 284
Hanway, Jonas, 69
Hawksmoor, Nicholas, 66
health, dress and diet, 265, 266, 292–303, 310–12
Heming (née Long), Amelia (sister of), 259
Heming (née Long), Mary Charlotte (niece of), 221, 223
Heming, Samuel Scudamore (nephew of), 259
Heywood, Peter, 59, 230
Hibbert, George, 430
Hibbert, Thomas and John, 112, 113
Hibbert House, 112
Hibberts and Jackson (Kingston factors), 188
Higman, Barry, 89, 123, 157
Hillary, William, 293, 294
Hispaniola, 41, 270
History of Jamaica
  abolitionists' use of, xxvii
  genres and, 7, 8, 270, 279
  long-term significance of, 6, 10, 13, 23, 163–4, 309, 434–7
  natural history and, 35, 265, 266, 303–12
  poetry and, 8, 268, 279, 280, 281, 286, 287–8
  proposed second edition, 153, 418, 430
  publication of, 1, 372
  scope of, 11–13
  significance for LBS, xxvi
Hobbes, Thomas, 401
Hogarth, William, 73, 75

INDEX

Homer, 4, 63, 287
Horace, 76
horses, 267–8
Howard, Charles. *See* Carlisle, Earl of (Charles Howard)
Howard (née Long), Elizabeth (daughter of), 203, 245, 418
Howard, Robert Mowbray (direct descendant of), 95
Howell (née Long), Lucy Anne (niece of), 221, 223
Hume, David, 4, 5, 7, 11, 12, 13, 15, 37, 193, 313, 316, 320, 416, 426
   theorizing race and, 21–2, 403, 408, 440
Hurt's Hall, 59, *224*, 224, 231, 232, 260
Hyde, Edward. *See* Clarendon (historian)

imperialism
   commerce and, 71, 206
   historical study of, xxiv
   promotion of colonization of Jamaica, 4, 8–9, 35, 103, 119, 162, 164, 265, 266, 270, 272, 288, 289, 292, 303, 312, 335
   science and, 303–12
   xenophobia and, 73
'improvement'
   agrarian capitalism and, 62, 104, 106, 316
   colonialism and, 312, 332–3
   contradiction with essentialism of racial difference, 374
   forest protection and, 309
   manners and, 70
indigo, 309, 333
inheritance between propertied white people, 35, 203, 229, 238, 368
   primogeniture and, 212–13, 219
   reinforcing racial difference and, 209
   transmission of wealth and, 209, 211, 212, 229–38
Ireland, 87, 160, 386

Jacobites, 16, 62, 73, 75, 313, 319, 320, 432
Jamaica
   agriculture and, 12

climate and, 101
culture and, 23
dependence on Britain, 362
development of roads and, 116, 267, 271, 279, 312, 335
emancipation and, 137
gender balance and, 143
as 'helpless colony', 9, 362
inadequacies of militia and, 358
legal and, 36, 196, 325–37
Magna Carta of 1729, 19, 325, 363, 368
map of, *3, 101*
Maroon war and, 95, 318, 337–9, 395–6, 397
military and, 12, 44, 46, 92, 101, 125, 199, 270, 289–90, 323, 325, 332, 336, 338, 340, 345, 349, 357, 363
natural history of, 11, 12, 13
notion of colony becoming more like England, 16, 215, 288–9, 335, 371
as profitable commercial colony based on slavery, xxix, 9, 23, 26, 44, 50, 52, 55, 87, 155, 157, 162, 163, 269, 270
racial imbalance of the population and, 87, 93, 157, 202, 215, 271, 325, 335, 388, 389
sickness and mortality, 206, 209, 292–303
slave trade and, 17, 136, 165, 271
slavery and servitude in the 1660s, 48
small numbers of white women and, 228
type of colony, 18
Jamaica, Council of 12, 44, 94, 331, 359
Jamaica Coffee House, 183, 184
Jamaica House of Assembly, 5, 36
   aftermath of 1760 rebellion and, 357–60, 363, 390
   attempts to assert autonomy from colonial government, 52–4, 325, 360, 362, 363–8
   laws and, 53, 383, 389
   origins of, 44, 48
   'privileges controversy' and, 332, 337, 362, 365, 368, 423
   role of, 324, 331, 364, 431
James, C. L. R., 29

Jenkinson, Charles (Lord Hawkesbury), 425
Jews, 12, 16, 73, 265, 313, 353, 357, 381
  whiteness and, 386
Johnson, Samuel, 18, 22, 104, 211, 280, 317, 420
Johnson, Walter, 29, 109, 204, 343

King's House, 274, *276*
Kingsley, Charles, 434
Kingsley, Henry, 434
Kingston, xxiii, 69, 90, 228, 270, 273, 277, *342*
  1760 rebellion and, 341
  as capital, 94, 318
  free blacks and, 273
  harbours and, *302*
  in the 1750s, 91
  military and, 290
  mulattoes and, 388
  public health and, 277, 297
  slave trade and, 112–13
Klein, Melanie, 32
Knight, James, 14, 54, 56, 93, 94, 95, 165, 315, 325
  1760 rebellion and, 346
  autonomy of colonists and, 362
  benevolent depiction of slavery and, 132, 133
  improvement and, 104
  on authority and responsibilities of planters, 104, 121
  on Maroon war, 337–8, 396
  on merchants, 179
  on purchasing slaves, 112, 135
  recognition of African medical knowledge, 311
  slavery's contributions to British wealth and, 160
  theorizing race and, 386, 412
Knowles, Charles, 93–4, 302, 318, 323, 351

landscape, 8, 265, 266, 268, 270, 282, 284–5, 287, 288, 312
Law, John, 191
Lawes, Nicholas, 58, 204, 217
laws and legal principles related to slavery, 26, 268
  'An Act for the Better Ordering and Governing of Negro Slaves', 50, 58
  Barbados code as model of, 49, 327
  black mobility and, 266, 357
  'chattel principle', 329
  classification of whiteness and, 383
  Code Noir, 326, 334, 391
  codification of racialization and, 51, 123
  credit and, 196, 199
  Debt Recovery Act of 1732, 196, 378
  deficiency laws and, 51, 215
  development of chattel slavery and, 50, 197
  distinctions between white servants and enslaved persons, 51
  emergence of racial slavery and, 72
  enslaved persons as real estate, 210
  essential for slavery as a continuing institution, 48
  establishment of chattel slavery as permanent and, 54, 328
  family law and slavery, 211, 213–14
  government regulation, 177
  influence of Roman law, 142
  jus sanguinis, 330
  lex loci, 50, 231, 359, 380
  Negro Code, 13
  race and, 150
  selling of slaves as personal property, 58
  Servant Act, 50, 51
  slave code of 1674, 142
  slave code of 1696, 266, 327
  slave code of 1751, 330
  Somerset trial, 3, 4, 10, 36, 273, 327, 334, 344, 362, 372, 377, 380, 426
  strict control to deal with unrest, disturbance and rebellion, 51, 267
  Yorke–Talbot opinion (1729), 2, 376
Legacies of British Slave-ownership project (LBS), xxv–xxvi, *101*, *207*, 228
Leslie, Charles, 14, 91, 95, 105, 122, 164, 272
Levitt, Kari, 28, 166
liberty. *See also* freedom
  chattel slavery and, 322

INDEX

dependence on slavery of, 425
as English subjects, 363
excess of, 333
property and, 321, 432
race and, 19
as relaxation of restraints, 19
Ligon, Richard, 14, 142
Lind, James, 294–5
Lindo, Locksley, 443
Lindsay, John, 308, 354
  attacks on Francis Williams, 442
Linnaeus, Carl, 22, 25, 148, 382, 406
livestock, 88, 97, 101, 102, 103, 116, 129
Livy, 63
Lloyd's, 183, 184
Locke, John, 19, 74, 319, 360, 369, 382, 401, 440
  consent of the governed and, 430
  theorizing race and, 403, 441
London, 65, 69
  as commercial centre of Europe, 91, 179
  Gordon Riots and, 432
  high society's passion for French culture, 74
  merchant houses and, 183
  new metropolitan life and, 70
  public hangings and, 320
  slave trade and, 165, 172
Long (née Hume), Amelia (first cousin by marriage of), 240, *241*
Long (née Lawes), Amy (grandmother of), 204, 208
Long (née Walpole), Catherine (daughter-in-law of), 223
Long (née Streete), Elizabeth (great-grandmother of), 204, 208, 236
Long (née Neave), Frances Louisa (first cousin by marriage of), 227
Long (née Tucker), Frances Monro (daughter-in-law of), 258
Long (née Maitland), Jane (first cousin by marriage of), 227
Long (née Beeston), Jane Modyford (grandmother of), 56, 58, 59, 178, 204, 208, 220, 224, 227
  inheritance and, 229, 231, 232, 234, 261

Long (née Cooke), Lucy, 222
Long (née North), Mary (aunt by marriage of), 232
Long (née Tate), Mary (mother of), 61, 89, 208, 215, 216, 221, 243
Long (née Devon), Mary (granddaughter of), 259
Long (née Beckford), Mary Ballard (wife of), xxiii, 1, 98, 208, 245, *246*, 258, 323, 336
  death of, 434
  inheritance from father, 98
Long (née Crop), Sarah (aunt by marriage of), 62, 178, 227
Long family, 34, 35
  disavowal and, 259–60, 262
  genteel lifestyle in the metropole and, 207
  inheritance and, 213, 220, 229, 234, 238, 239, 242
  naming patterns and, 217
  portrait of Francis Williams and, 438
  reproduction of social relations of production and, 209
  significance of *History of Jamaica* and, 242
  slavery as source of wealth, 26, 203, 204, 206, 207, 210, 219, 418
  three branches of, 204
Long, Beeston (first cousin of), 206, 227, 423, 434
Long, Beeston (William) (uncle of), 35, 62, 64, 70, 84, 99, 181, 189, 204, 215, 221, 225
  inheritance and, 227
  as lobbyist, 318, 324, 423, 427, 429
Long, Charles (brother of), 126, 155, 208, 217, 323
  career of, 89, 238–9
  death of, 83, 89, 94, 95
  as member of the assembly, 94
  property of, 97, 223
  wealth and, 242
Long, Charles (first cousin of), 223, 224, 228, 234, *241*, 258
  inheritance and, 232, 234, 239, 242
  as prominent art collector, 240, 241

Long, Charles (grandfather of), 178, 204, 208, 223, 227, 231, 439
  death of, 60, 220
  debts and, 60, 193
  first marriage to Amy Lawes, 58
  inheritance from father, 57, 220
  Jamaica Council of Twelve and, 58
  lawsuit against Anne Beeston, 230–1
  marriage to Jane (née Beeston) Modyford, 56, 229
  as member of the assembly, 58
  military career of, 336
  political loyalties to the Whigs, 59
  Royal Mines Company of Jamaica and, 60
  seat in the House of Commons, 60
Long, Charles (uncle of), 99, 110, 116, 144, 204, 208, 221, 224, 433
  inheritance and, 220, 231, 232, 234
Long, Charles Beckford (son of), 203, 245, 258, 418
Long, Charles Edward (grandson of), 258
Long, Dudley (first cousin of), 232
Long, Edward, xix, 148
  agricultural knowledge and, 102, 108, 128
  antisemitism and, 196, 198, 357, 387
  anxiety and, 63, 293, 295–6, 343, 349, 361, 373, 381, 389
  arrival in Jamaica, 89, 245
  attack on Francis Williams, 438–45
  attitudes towards the French, 79, 333
  birth of, 61
  boyhood of, xxvii, 4, 39, 63, 216
  colonial patriotism and, 6, 18, 268, 333, 334–7
  death of, 434, *435*
  defence of violence against enslaved persons, 127, 145, 320, 321, 322, 344–5, 349, 360, 369
  disavowal and, 107, 109, 118–19, 141, 189, 198, 200, 219, 265, 266, 268, 273, 280, 281, 282, 284, 292, 361, 368, 381, 394, 412
  double consciousness of, 15
  as 'father of English racism', xxvi
  as free-born Englishman, 318, 322, 362, 364, 368
  gender roles and, 67, 68, 69, 77, 78, 81, 82, 83, 147, 218
  as husband and father, 35, 140, 216, 217, 219, 243, 434
  illness and, 313
  as law student, 34
  as lawyer and judge, 5, 319, 324, 329, 376
  as lobbyist, 137, 174, 416–18, 422, 423, 427, 429
  marriage of, 34, 98, 208
  medical knowledge and, 294, 299
  as member of the assembly, 36, 124, 181, 324–6, 331–3, 336, 358, 360, 363, 416
  move to London as young man, 65, 179
  as natural historian, 25, 222, 303, 305, 307–12, 404
  as planter, 25, 30, 31, 32, 57, 83, 103, 106, 110, 112, 145, 208
  'privileges controversy' and, 365, 367
  racism and, 15, 16, 17, 118–19, 135, 139, 150–1, 215, 261, 311–12, 330, 373, 378, 379, 388, 393, 399, 400–8
  return to England and, 1, 3, 245, 253, 313, 344, 372
  signficance of 1760 rebellion and, 36, 289
  social classification and, 20, 358, 379, 387
  source of wealth and, 34
  theorizing race and, 36, 121, 326, 331, 369, 370, 372, 381–415, 431, 436, 443
  young manhood of, 39, 65–84
Long, Edward Beeston (son of), 7, 103, 116, 203, 208, 222, 223, 239, 245, 414
Long, Edward Maitland (great-nephew of), 435
Long, Elizabeth (aunt of), 58
Long, Elizabeth (great-aunt of), 57
Long, Frederick Beckford (grandson of), 223, 239

Long, Henrietta Maria (niece of), 206, 208, 214, 217
Long, Henry Lawes (grandson of), 217, 222, 223, 225
Long, Jane (first cousin of), 224, 234, 242
Long, Jane (great-aunt of), 225
Long, John (great-uncle of), 57
Long, Mary (great-aunt of), 57
Long, Robert (brother of), 13, 34, 61, 89, 110, 206, 208, 308, 391, 439
  inheritance from father and brother, 97, 220, 221, 223
Long, Robert Ballard (son of), 245, 418
  inheritance and, 239
  military career and, 259, 336
Long, Samuel (brother of), 61
Long, Samuel (father of)
  birth of, 58, 204
  death of, 83, 89, 95, 217
  debts and, 61, 95, 193, 243
  early life of, 61
  as free-born Englishman, 68
  as gentleman farmer, 62
  inheritance and, 231
  as judge, 320
  marriage and, 216
  as member of the assembly and council, 94, 181, 323
  military and, 239, 336
  as planter, 97, 140, 204, 208, 223
  portrait of, 439
  return to Jamaica, 208
Long, Samuel (first cousin of), 189, 206, 423
  inheritance and, 227
Long, Samuel (first cousin once removed), 242
Long, Samuel (great-uncle of), 57
Long, Samuel (great-grandfather of), xxvii, 9, 11, 18, 34, 36
  challenges to RAC's monopoly, 54
  death of, 56
  as early colonist and planter, 46, 362
  as founding figure of the family dynasty, 204, 207, 220, 223, 368
  imprisonment of, 54
  influence on EL, 41
  Jamaica Council of Twelve and, 53
  marriage to Elizabeth Streete, 57
  as member of the Jamaican Assembly, 48, 52, 323, 325, 333
  as planter, 45, 98
  political and social connections with William Beeston, 55
  politics of, 53
  Western Design and, 41, 336
Long, Vere (great-aunt of), 57
Long, William (first cousin of), 228, 234
  inheritance and, 242
Long, William (first cousin once removed of), 242
Longville, 34, 96, *101*, 220, 221
  improvements and, 116
  loss of, 222
  origins of, 46
  present-day, 95
  prosperity of, 95
  proximity to Lucky Valley, 100
  sharp decline in sugar production and, 63
  split between EL and Robert, 98
Longville Park, 220, 222, 223
  inheritance and, 223, 239
Longville Park Pen, 102, 126, 155
Lords of Trade and Plantations, 51, 53, 55, 359, 363
  establishment of, 52
  'privileges controversy' and, 365
Lowndes, T., 76, 419
Lucky Valley, xxii, 1, *101*, 220, *417*
  artwork of, 116–18
  bequest to Henry Lawes Long, 223
  cane calendar and, 127
  capital value of, 118, 120
  dilapidated state in 1701, 59
  dilapidated state in 1760, 99
  EL's purchase of, 99, 110, 222
  fluctuations of sugar production and, 433
  housing for enslaved persons and, 134
  improvements and, 100, 103, 113, 114, 115, 116, 123
  inheritance and, 223, 224, 232, 239, 259
  labour force and, 110, 112, 144
  mulattoes and, 388

Lucky Valley (cont.)
  overseer and, 124
  present-day, *118*, 416
  provision grounds and, 116, 131
  proximity to Longville, 100
  Samuel Long's purchase of, 34, 46
  sharp decline in sugar production and, 63
  social hierarchy and, 124–6
  survey of, 114–15, *117*
Lynch, Thomas, 56
Lyttelton, William Henry, 100, 360, 363–5, 367, 397

Macaulay, Thomas Babington, xxiv, xxv, 314
Macaulay, Zachary, xxiv, 31
McClelland, Keith, xxv
McKitrick, Kathleen, 132
Mair, John, 188, 215
Mair, Lucille Mathurin, 127, 143, 145, 211, 229
managers, 153, 154
Mansfield, Lord (William Murray), 3, 37, 378, 380
maps, 8, 15, 36, *107*, 265, 268, 269
Maroons, 11, 12, 88, 265, 268, 289, 442
  1760 rebellion and, 36, 341, 345, 351, 352
  Cudjoe, 339, 395, 396
  essential role in island's security, 395, 396, 398
  legal rights and, 339, 381, 396
  oaths and, 324
  origins of, 395
  representations of, 395–8
  role in early slave insurrections, 337
marriage between white people, 35, 203
  between cousins, 234
  protections for women and, 210, 211
  transmission of wealth and, 212, 219, 228–38
Martin, Samuel, 105, 106, 123
Marxism, 27, 202
Marylebone, 425
mercantilism
  connection to contemporary intellectual developments, 74
  slavery and, 424

state and, 35, 87, 140, 158, 165, 315, 325
  wars and, 316
merchants, 24, 35, 94, 179
  centrality to economic prosperity of, 157, 159, 160, 165, 167, 178, 198, 199–200, 202
  determining the price of sugar and, 119, 120, 173
  disavowal and, 188
  double-entry bookkeeping and, 186
  free trade and, 316
  inheritance and, 211, 225
  interest rates and, 196
  as lobbyists, 422, 423
  masculinity and, 182
  as politicians, 189
  providing credit and, 87, 165, 166, 168, 171, 172, 173, 174, 180, 190
  roles of, 183, 184
  shipping and, 189
Middlesex (Jamaica), 232, 270, 272
Millar, John, 376
Milton, John, 76, 280, 288, 306, 440
miscegenation, 27, 37, 388, 389, 391–5, 424
moderation, 83, 300–1
Modyford, James, 58
Modyford, Thomas, 45, 48, 52, 58
Monboddo, Lord (James Burnett), 14, 407
Montego Bay, 270, 277, 278, 279, 290
Montesquieu, 14, 217, 370, 399, 403, 414
Moore (née Long), Catherine Maria (sister of), 61, 90, 208, 351
Moore, Henry (brother-in-law of), 69, 90, 110, 113, 258, 340, 351, 360
Moore Hall, 239
Morant, Edward, 100
Moravians, 12, 265
Morgan, Jennifer, 58, 140, 187
Morgann, Maurice, 376
Morrison, Toni, xxviii, 391
mulattoes
  definition of, 388
  education and, 394
  inheritance and, 332

miscegenation and, 140, 382
  representations of, 12, 20, 27, 292, 335, 359, 370, 387–95
  restrictions on mobility of, 357
Murray, William, 376. *See* Mansfield, Lord (William Murray)

Nanny Town, 337
national histories, historical study of, xxiv
nationalism
  anti-French sentiment and, 75, 83, 313, 315
  essential difference and, 76
  gender and, 83
  literature and, 83
Navigation Acts, 27, 42, 43, 166, 315, 423
Needham, Henry, 69
Negro Trade, 157. *See* slave trade
'Negroes', xxvii, 21, 50. *See also* enslaved persons
Newman, Brooke, 330, 359, 389
Newman, Gerald, 74, 83
Newton, Isaac, 74, 192, 304, 439
Norbrook, xxiii, 220, 223, 224, 234, 261
Norbrook, Henry, 261
North American colonies
  relations with Britain, 361, 419
  South Carolina, 363
  trade and, 87, 157, 163, 166
  Virginia, 141, 142
North American Indians, 20, 381

oath taking, 33, 324
obeah, 33, 301, 325, 343, 347, 357, 409
  creoles and, 353–5
  criminalization of, 356–7
  role in 1760 rebellion, 352, 353–4, 428
Ogborn, Miles, 48, 49, 307, 324, 349
Old Harbour Bay, xxiii, 100, 101, 102, 126, 283
Oldmixon, John, 162, 316
Oliver (née Long), Jane Catherine Sarah (niece of), 221, 223
Oliver, Thomas Long (great-nephew of), 222

Orby, Charles, 230
overseers, 132, *152*, 155, 266, 267

Palmer, John, 90, 98, 258
Parker, John, 63, 67
parliament
  1791 inquiry into the mistreatment on Jamaican plantations and, 123
  House of Commons as model for Jamaica House of Assembly, 365
  Jewish Naturalization Bill and, 73
  military and, 317
  property and, 321
  resistance to abolition of slave trade and, 425, 428, 429
  slave trade and, 49, 378, 427
  West Indians election to the House of Commons, 72
Paterson, William, 191
Paton, Diana, 51, 143
patriarchy, 203, 204, 212, 214, 215, 217, 219, 351, 385, 390–3
Patterson, Orlando, xxiii, 24, 141, 169, 330, 337, 340, 396
Penn, William, 12, 336
Pennant, Thomas, 268
Pennington, W. C., 329
Petty, William, xxi, 186, 187, 192, 331
Pigott (née Long), Charlotte (granddaughter of), 223
Pindar's River, 102, 115
Pinney, John Frederick, 110, 182, 422
Pitt, William, 72, 75, 83, 93, 240, 287, 314, 318, 363, 424, 425, 428
plantation slavery
  acceptance of human bondage across the early modern world and, 49
  benevolent and benign depictions of, xxiii, 10, 102, 121, 122, 132, 134, 135, 136, 151–2, 155, 156, 174, 177, 198, 201, 262, 269, 282, 427
  'breeding' and, 147, 149
  centrality of violence and coercion, 31, 36, 51, 58, 88, 92, 119, 123, 124, 126, 136, 140, 145, 168, 188, 204, 266, 322–3, 330, 349, 360
  civilizing effects of, 20, 409
  connections to white freedom, 41

plantation slavery (cont.)
  defence of, 15, 146, 175, 259, 322, 334, 361, 372, 380
  dehumanization of enslaved persons, 87, 107–8, 118–19, 136, 145, 165, 220, 328, 378
  dependence of British wealth on, xxix, 12, 17, 156, 159, 160, 161, 190, 272, 344, 372, 429, 432
  distinctions between servants and slaves, 49
  divide and rule system, 123, 124
  as domestic marketing system, 88
  gang system and, 89, 127, 128–9, 130
  as hereditary and permanent, 58, 140, 141–3
  notion of enslaved women as 'increasers', 58
  as offshoot of timeless English institution, 372, 377, 378
  organization of skilled and unskilled labour, 124, 126, 128, 130
  statistical depictions of, 118–19, 136, 151, 159, 188, 200, 265, 269, 271
  terminology and, 49, 159
  time management and, 124
planters, 30, 34. *See also* slave-owners
  absentees, 114, 125, 131, 153, 166, 318, 335, 372, 418, 427
  centrality to economic prosperity of, 157, 159, 160, 167, 178, 198, 199–200, 202
  concubinage and, 145, 351, 387, 391, 411
  conflicts with the crown and, 52, 93
  credit and, 47, 87, 158, 166, 172, 182, 190, 197
  debt and, 156, 158, 172, 190, 199, 206
  dependence on skills of labour force, 107
  disavowal and, 189
  elite slave-owners' aspiration to become landed gentry, 208, 212
  identity and, xxix
  morality and, 118–19
  profit and, 87, 173, 174
  purchasing of slaves and, 110, 111
  sexual power and, 145, 389, 391
  tensions with other colonists, 94

Pluche, Noël-Antoine, 407
Pocock (née Long), Charlotte Mary (daughter of), 203, 245
Pocock, J. G. A., 192, 193
politeness, culture of, 77, 83, 148
Pope, Alexander, 76, 192, 280, 281, 305, 445
Port Antonio, 290, 334
Port Royal, 48, 56, 90, 228, 270, *272*, 273, 277, 297, *302*, 341, *342*
Portugal, 42, 169, 327
postcolonialism, xxv, xxviii, 437
Postlethwayt, Malachy, 162, 315
Poulet, Catherine, 67, 69
Poyning's system, 53
Prater, The, 69, 76–9, 106, 148, 194, 216, 281, 352
Prescott, George (first cousin by marriage of), 227, 236, 320
Prescott (née Long), Sarah (first cousin of), 227, 236
Price, Charles, 283–4, 286
Priestley, Joseph, 106, 303–4
property, 324, 368

Quakers, 12, 427
Queen's Square, 59, 231, 232

Rabin, Dana, 74, 380
race. *See also* enslaved children; enslaved persons; free blacks; free people of colour; white children; white women
  classifications of, 388
  definitions of, 21
  as hierarchy of power, 212
  influence on legal and political relations, 48
  interracial relations, 331
  legal rights and, 324
  political rights and, 389
  theorizing of, 373, 381–415
  vs. nation, 21–3
racial capitalism, 24
  centrality of sugar-based plantation slavery, 158
  dynasties and, 212
  property and marriage law and, 209

INDEX

system of, 87–9, 164, 174, 200
terminology and, 26, 28
understanding how race works and, 437
racial difference, 174
African women's bodies and, 142
binary of white and black, 381, 382, 421
defence of violence and, 177
early ideas about, 43, 187, 399
as essential and natural, xxiii, xxvii, xxviii, 27, 136, 140, 373, 381, 428
health and sickness, 300
permanence of skin colour and, 399, 402, 443
racialization, 24, 31, 36, 87, 109, 143, 158, 265, 266
racism, 24, 25, 94, 125
twenty-first-century Britain and, xxix
white attitudes towards enslaved labour and labourers, 106, 107, 121, 124
Ramsay, James, 426
reparations, xxvi
repair, xxviii, 438
reproduction
biological, 34, 35, 57, 88, 137, 139, 140, 142, 144, 148–51, 203, 209
concept of, 24
racial capitalism and, 26
social, 209
Richardson, Samuel, 69
Ricketts, Mary, 185, 200
Ricketts, William Henry, 68, 90, 112, 115, 155, 200, 308, 372
Rio Minho, 45, 97, *118*
Roberts, Justin, 123, 136
'statistical fantasies', 136
Robertson, James, 7, *101*
Robinson, Anthony, 13, 222, 308
Royal African Company (RAC), 45, 162
breakup of its monopoly, 59, 170
development of the slave trade and, 47, 169
formation of, 47
monopoly and, 54, 315, 316
regulation and, 177
Rugemer, Edward, 58, 328
rum, 88, 101, 119, 123, 130, 332

Saint-Domingue, 29, 270, 301, 425, 429, 430, 433
Sallust, 63
Sancho, Ignatius, 421, 444
Sargeant, John, 183
Schiebinger, Londa, 148, 308, 382
science
classification and, 303, 308, 381, 382–3, 405–7, 432
economic value of, 305, 307
hereditary transmission of racism and, 150, 330
ideas about health and medicine, 293
role of the Divine in, 303, 304, 306, 374, 404–5
Scotland, 73, 102, 126, 160, 173, 384, 386
Sebastiani, Silvia, 406
Sedgwick, Robert, 42, 338, 395
servants, 12, 291
black, 72
indentured, 49, 51, 55, 157, 173, 383, 436
rights and punishments of, 51
white, 125
whiteness and, 386
Seth, Suman, 154, 293
Seven Years War, 1, 34, 72, 75, 93, 270, 289, 313–15
aftermath of, 365, 422
significance for Jamaica, 92, 318, 323, 350
Sharp, Granville, xxviii, 3, 122, 149, 344, 376, 402
Phillis Wheatley and, 426
A Representation of the Injustice and Dangerous Tendency of Tolerating Slavery in England, 3
Shickle, John, 119
Shields, William, 114
ships' captains, 168, 170
John Newton, 170
Samuel Murdoch, 112
William Snelgrave, 17, 151, 177
Simpson, James, *107*
slave insurrections, 11
Berbice uprising, 343
perceived threat of, 337, 339, 343, 349, 350, 352, 382

slave insurrections (cont.)
  prior to 1760, 337
  rebellion of 1760, 13, 17, 24, 289, 332, 334, 337–62, 363
  rebellion of 1765, 332, 343, 360, 367
  rebellion of 1766, 344
slave ships, 170
slave trade, 112, 135, 278
  abolition of, 434
  debates about abolition of, 15, 122, 135, 156, 423–30
  factors and, 171, 172
  impact on African population, 139, 158
  Kingston and, 91
  language of accounting and, 171
  legalized system of, 176, 178, 201
  massive boost to, 157
  Montego Bay and, 277, 278
  racial capitalism and, 202
  system of, 160, 165–74, 188
  violence and terror of, 169, 170
slave traders
  African, 168, 169
  European, 168, 170
slave-owners, xxix, 30, 88, 267, 282, 303. *See also* planters
Sloane, Hans, 11, 13, 146, 292, 294, 306
smallpox, 297, 298
Smallwood, Stephanie, 163, 169
Smith, Adam, 156, 315, 321, 377, 415, 419
Smollett, Tobias, 4, 66, 72, 75, 280
  The Adventures of Roderick Random, 79, 90, 293
Society of West Indian Merchants and Planters, 423, 425
Somerset, James, 3, 4, 10, 36, 273, 327, 334, 344, 362, 372, 377, 380, 426
South Sea Company, 60, 192, 193, 204, 227
Spain, 12, 41, 42, 47, 157, 272, 383
Spanish Town, xxiii, 37, 57, 69, 228, 261, 269
  1760 rebellion and, 340–1
  as capital, 46, 274, 277, 318, 332
  Francis Williams and, 439
  free blacks and, 273
  as healthy place to live, 298
  military and, 270, 289
  mulattoes and, 388
  St Catherine, 283

St Catherine's church, 57, 58, 185
White Church Street property, 98, 113, 125, 323
Spectator, 63, 76, 82
St Ann, 131, 272, 284
  military and, 290
  slave uprising in 1673, 337
St Catherine, 97, 259, 273
  Francis Williams and, 442
  slave uprising in 1678, 337
St Elizabeth
  1760 rebellion and, 341
St Helena, 112
St Jago de la Vega, 273, *276*. *See also* Spanish Town
St James, 278
St John, 271
St Mary, 283
  1760 rebellion and, 340, 346, 349, 351, 352
  1765 rebellion and, 332, 343, 360, 367, 397
St Mary's church, Slindon, xxiv, 434, 435
St Thomas-in-the-East (Jamaica), 302
Steele, Richard, 70, 75, 280, 282
Steele, Thomas (nephew by marriage of), 425
Stephen, James, 128
Sterne, Laurence, 421
  The Life and Opinions of Tristram Shandy, Gentleman, 5
Stewart, John, 134
Strange, Susan, 191
Strong, Jonathan, 3
Stuart, James (The Old Pretender), 73, 81
Suffolk estates, 34, 59, *224*, 224, 227, 231, 232, 234
sugar
  from luxury to everday commodity, 26, 70, 71, 97, 157, 164, 168, 173
  as symbol of plantation slavery, 81
sugar industry
  centrality to global trade of, 99, 109–10, 116, 119, 123, 157, 180, 190, 315, 364
  production and refining, 46, 87, 97, 104, 115, 127–30, 160, 163, 168, 173, 281

risks and, 103, 120, 156, 183, 433
Summers, George, 114
Surrey (England), 181, 227, 253
Suttons, 119
Swift, Jonathan, 76, 192
  A Modest Proposal, xxi
  Gulliver's Travels, xix–xxii, 372, 376, 401

Tacitus, 63
Tailyour, John, 171
Taino peoples, 13, 357
  under Spanish regime, 42
'taste'
  as political discourse, 70–1, 73, 76, 83, 280
  tea parties and, 71, 79, 82
Tatler, 63, 76
Taylor, John, 55
Taylor, Simon, 110, 111, 113, 123, 130, 138, 144, 147, 185, 390, 427, 430
tea, 71, 79, 82, 173, 180
The Sentimental Exhibition, 391
The Trial of Farmer Carter's Dog Porter for Murder
  publication of, 372
  as satire of English legal system, 374–6
Thistlewood, Thomas, 122, 145, 147, 308, 361, 391
Thompson, E. P., 320, 321
Thomson, James, 71, 75, 76, 77, 108, 280, 286, 288
Thurloe, John, 13, 42
tobacco, 180
Tom's Coffee House, 70
Tories, 73
tradespeople. *See* artisans
Trapham, Thomas, 46
Tredudwel, xxiv, 102, 232
  improvements and, 61
trees, 309, 332
Trelawny (Jamaica), 288, 306
Trelawny, Edward, 93, 146, 332, 339
Tucker, Josiah, 73
Tull, Jethro, 106
Tyson, Edward, 406

Vassa, Gustavus, 427. *See* Equiano, Olaudah
Vaughan, John, 52
Venables, Robert, 12, 336
Vespucci, Amerigo, 20

Virgil, 63, 76, 105, 280, 281, 287, 288, 392
Voltaire, 14, 15, 74, 317, 382, 426

Walpole, Charles, 61
Walpole, Edward, 61
Walpole, Horace, 73
Walpole, Robert, 60, 61, 314, 318, 320
Wesley, John, 156
West Africa, 26, 112, 165, 169, 170, 175
Western Design, 41, 43, 315
Westmacott, Richard, 435
Westmoreland (Jamaica), 131, 290, 341, 349, 360
Wheatley, Phillis, 377, 426, 444
Whigs, 316
  EL's introduction to, 63, 319
  ideology and, 15, 36, 59, 71, 73, 321
white children, 290–1, 332, 335, 383
white women
  as heads of households, 91
  household management and, 183
  inheritance and, 219, 231
  race and, 385
  reproductive labour and, 35, 203, 209
  as slave-owners, 220, 228
  social labour and, 209
whiteness, 21, 25, 399
  classification of, 20, 74, 383–7, 389
  freedom and, 380
  Irish and, 42, 187, 331, 384
  political rights and, 324, 366
  shifting definitions of, 330, 359
  terminology and, xxvii
Wilberforce, William, 354, 425, 428
Williams, Eric, 29, 424
  Capitalism and Slavery, xix, xxv
Williams, Francis, 13, 37, 438–45
Williams, Raymond, 62, 106
Wilmot, Henry, 68
Wilson, Kathleen, 71, 314, 346, 397
Winde, Scudamore, 259
Windsor, Thomas, 44
Wood, William, 111, 145
Wren, Christopher, 66
Wynter, Sylvia, 132, 266

yellow fever, 292–3
Young, Arthur, 105, 106, 135
Young, Hannah, 228

Zahedieh, Nuala, 47